# the Unofficial Guide® to

## Hawaii

### 2nd Edition

Rick and Marcie Carroll
with Lance Tominaga

**Hungry Minds™**

Best-Selling Books • Digital Downloads • e-Books • Answer Networks • e-Newsletters
Branded Web Sites • e-Learning

*New York, NY • Indianapolis, IN • Cleveland, OH*

Please note that prices fluctuate in the course of time, and travel information changes under the impact of many factors that influence the travel industry. We therefore suggest that you write or call ahead for confirmation when making your travel plans. Every effort has been made to ensure the accuracy of information throughout this book, and the contents of this publication are believed correct at the time of printing. Nevertheless, the publishers cannot accept responsibility for errors or omissions or for changes in details given in this guide or for the consequences of any reliance on the information provided by the same. Assessments of attractions and so forth are based upon the author's own experience and, therefore, descriptions given in this guide necessarily contain an element of subjective opinion, which may not reflect the publisher's opinion or dictate a reader's own experience on another occasion. Readers are invited to write to the publisher with ideas, comments, and suggestions for future editions.

Your safety is important to us, so we encourage you to stay alert and be aware of your surroundings. Keep a close eye on cameras, purses, and wallets, all favorite targets of thieves and pickpockets.

**Published by Hungry Minds, Inc.**
909 Third Avenue
New York, NY 10022

Produced by Menasha Ridge Press
Cover design by Michael J. Freeland
Interior design by Michele Laseau

ISBN 0-7645-6570-2
ISSN 1521-494X

Manufactured in the United States of America

10 9 8 7 6 5 4 3 2 1

# Contents

# List of Maps

# About the Authors and Contributors

**RICK CARROLL**, author of many Hawai'i books, is the creator of the best-selling *Hawai'i's Best Spooky Tales* series. A former daily journalist at the *San Francisco Chronicle,* Carroll wrote award-winning travel and feature stories about Hawaii and the Pacific for the *Honolulu Advertiser* and United Press International. He is contributing editor to *Hawai'i Magazine.* His stories appear on the Internet at www.hawaii.rr.com.

**MARCIE RASMUSSEN CARROLL,** freelance travel writer and former communications director for the Hawai'i Convention and Visitors Bureau, earlier wrote political, environmental, and other news for the *San Francisco Chronicle, San Jose Mercury-News* and UPI in Atlanta. She was a Journalism Fellow in Asian studies at University of Hawai'i and in energy studies at Stanford University.

Together, the Carrolls, who moved to Windward O'ahu in 1983, collected and edited *Travelers Tales Hawai'i: True Stories of the Island Spirit,* which an anthology one reviewer praised as "the best collection of contemporary Hawai'i travel stories." They are the authors of this extensivley revised and rewritten second edition of the *Unofficial Guide to Hawaii.*

**LANCE TOMINAGA** is the former editor of *Aloha Magazine,* which for 21 years brought the best of Hawaii into homes and offices throughout the world. He gained an immeasurable appreciation for the beauty and uniqueness of Hawai'i. Lance authored of the first edition of this guide.

**BETTY SHIMABUKURO,** who updated the dining chapter for this edition, is the food editor at the Honolulu Star-Bulletin, a job that encompasses everything from good home cooking, to mom-and-pop ethnic restaurants, to the finest in Hawaii Regional Cuisine. After a long journalism career that has included a dozen different news beats, she considers this to be the best gig in town.

# Introduction

## Making the Most of Your Hawaiian Dream

Hawai'i. Hear the word, and you're swept away by dreams of a tropical Eden, sensual swaying hula dancers, and visions of an endless, empty beach.

Can this place *really* be as magical as it seems? Or is it just an illusion? The right answers to those questions, are yes and no respectively. The tropical Eden is for real, hula is the heartbeat of the Hawaiian culture, and empty beaches stretch for miles on all the smaller islands. And volcanoes are still making Big Island beaches even more magical. This is, in all ways, a very special destination, unlike any other.

But it's more than a pretty place; it's an experience that can change your life, and that has to do with the people and their way of living. The lighthearted island attitudes, the warmth of people who go out of their way for you, and the sense of extended family soon begin to melt even the most resolute holdouts. Your stakes are huge in making the most of your visit to the Islands. If you get Hawai'i right, the place will grab you by the heart and make you feel good. The best way to enjoy it is to loosen up and let Hawai'i happen to you.

Approach Hawai'i like you would another country, which it was not so long ago. Be prepared for exotic customs, serendipity, and unexpected disruptions of your plans. Be a good sport. Brief yourself by reading this book, prowling the Internet, and talking to friends. For those who come to the Islands with advance knowledge and plenty of patience, delightful encounters are bound to happen. Bring your children and elders. They'll have a good time, and the people of Hawai'i cherish *keiki* (kids) and *kupuna* (wise older folks).

In Waikiki, don't expect idyllic huts by the sea (although you can find them elsewhere on the Islands). Expect high-rise hotels in an urban city-scape. Expect hustling on the sidewalks, although quite tame by big-city standards (most Waikiki hustlers want to hand you an ad). Don't expect to be met with a lei of flowers at the airport unless you have already paid for the greeting service or are being met by a friend who lives in the Islands. Brace yourself for hugs and kisses on the cheek when you meet effusive strangers, if you're lucky. Hawai'i is one of the world's safer destinations, but don't be surprised if your wallet and camera are pilfered when you leave them on the seat of a rental car while you run to look at a mesmerizing view.

Strip away the veil of Hawai'i's natural beauty and you'll find many of the same problems that burden other American communities: economic struggles, drugs, increasing crime, and traffic congestion. But you'll also find people who still smile at strangers here and largely rely on kindness, respect, and humor when dealing with one another. You'll discover skies that are blue rather than brown, sea water that is clear and warm, air that is soft and fresh, and scenery that soothes the soul.

A visit to Hawai'i is too precious to waste. So we're here to help you pursue your particular dream and along the way find some memorable experiences you never expected. Our purpose is to present a realistic view of contemporary Hawai'i that helps you make the most of your Island holiday. We'll provide some of the details in advance, so that you'll be free to have fun.

In this guide you'll discover how to find the best deals on lodging, whether you want hotels, condominiums, or bed-and-breakfasts. You'll get an up-to-date review of the best adventures, attractions, beaches, hotels, clubs, and restaurants. And you'll gain insights into local customs and learn a few Hawaiian words and phrases to make you feel more like a *kama'aina* ("child of the land"—longtime or native-born Hawai'i resident).

Along the way, we'll answer frequently asked questions like these:

- When is the best time to go?
- Which islands should we visit?
- Where are the best beaches?
- What hiking trails are recommended for families?
- Who are Hawai'i's must-see entertainers?

You want to make the most of your time in the Islands. You want to be at the right place at the right time, enjoying the very best Hawai'i has to offer, especially if it is your first trip. This book will help you. For those of you who have been to the Aloha State many times before and are ready to dig deeper, this book will suggest new possibilities. You may find a new discovery. So mix up a mai tai, put on your favorite Hawaiian music, and start your Hawaiian adventure with *The Unofficial Guide to Hawai'i*. *E komo mai!* Welcome.

# About This Guide

## How Come "Unofficial"?

Just as Hawai'i inspires unconventional ideals and promotes individuality, so does the "Unofficial" series. Most "official" guides to Hawai'i tout the well-known sights, promote the local restaurants and hotels indiscriminately, and leave out the nitty-gritty. This one is different. We'll be up-front with you. Instead of nabbing you by the ankles in a tourist trap, we'll tell you if it's not worth the wait for the mediocre food served at a well-known restaurant. We'll complain loudly about overpriced hotel rooms that aren't convenient, and we'll guide you away from the crowds and congestion for a break now and then. If a museum is boring or a major attraction is overrated, we say so—and, in the process, make your visit exactly that: *your* visit. We got into the guidebook business because we were unhappy with the way travel guides make the reader work to get any usable information. Wouldn't it be nice, we thought, if we made guides that were easy to use?

## Other Guidebooks

Most guidebooks are compilations of lists. This is true regardless of whether the information is presented in list form or artfully distributed through pages of prose. There is insufficient detail in a list, and with prose the presentation can be tedious and contain large helpings of nonessential or marginally useful information. Not enough wheat, so to speak, for nourishment in one instance, and too much chaff in the other. Either way, other guides provide little more than departure points from which readers initiate their own quests.

Sure, many guides are readable and well researched, but they tend to be difficult to use. To select a hotel, for example, a reader must study several pages of descriptions with only the names of the hotels in bold type breaking up the text. Because each description essentially deals with the same variables, it is difficult to recall what was said concerning a particular hotel. Readers generally have no alternative but to work through all the write-ups before beginning to narrow their choices. The presentation of restaurants, clubs, and attractions is similar except that even more reading is usually required. To use such a guide is to undertake an exhaustive research process that requires examining nearly as many options and possibilities as starting from scratch. Recommendations, if any, lack depth and conviction. By failing to narrow travelers' choices down to a thoughtfully considered, well-distilled, and manageable few, these guides compound rather than solve problems.

## How Unofficial Guides Are Different

Some Hawai'i guidebooks are full of pretty pictures. Others present a tedious stream of words with little practical advice. Many Hawai'i guidebooks lead you only to a sugar-coated version of the Islands, but this book strives to be different.

Our goal at *Unofficial Guides* is to help you make informed decisions about topics like this: Anyone can find the Bishop Museum, but when is the best time to go? How much walking is involved? Is the museum really worth the price of admission?

Hawai'i offers more things to do and see than you could pack into a lifetime of vacations. If you have only a week or two and you really just want to relax on a palm-fringed gold sand beach, no problem. We'll suggest that perfect beach and provide the information you need to enjoy it in a concise, easy-to-read format.

*The Unofficial Guide to Hawai'i,* written for repeat and first-time visitors alike, addresses typical planning concerns: "Can I leave my coat and tie at home?" or "Should I visit the Polynesian Cultural Center?" You'll find the answers to those questions and more in these pages.

Our philosophy: If it matters to you, then it matters to us. From the beginning, the people behind *Unofficial Guides* have worked diligently to deliver honest, straight-up reviews of major destinations and U.S. cities. For this book, the authors are former San Francisco daily newspaper journalists who have lived in Hawai'i and written about the Islands for two decades. They combine island knowledge with the ability to evaluate experiences from the visitors' point of view.

## Special Features

This *Unofficial Guide* includes these special features:

- Insightful introductions to Hawai'i's six main islands, highlighting the special appeal and character of each.

- A brief look at Hawai'i's fascinating history, from its discovery by the first Polynesians, through the missionaries, to today's multicultural, mid-Pacific reality.

- Explanations of local customs and island styles.

- Candid opinions on the best and worst of Hawai'i, including accommodations, beaches, restaurants, attractions, shows, clubs, and shops.

- Practical information on driving distances and how to avoid crowds, dodge traffic jams, and park cheaply. Or, on O'ahu, how to get around without a car.

- Suggested itineraries for families, honeymooners, seniors, and disabled travelers.

- A guide to the state's best golf courses.

## Comments and Suggestions from Readers

We welcome your suggestions and comments about all our *Unofficial Guides*, including this book. Should you find any errors or omissions, we would appreciate hearing from you. Some of the best suggestions come from our readers.

### How to Write the Authors:

Rick and Marcie Carroll
*The Unofficial Guide to Hawaii*
P.O. Box 43673
Birmingham, AL 35243
UnofficialGuides@menasharidge.com

When you write be mail, be sure to put your return address on your letter as well as on the envelope. And remember, our work takes us on the road for long periods of time, so please forgive any delayed response.

## How Information Is Organized: By Subject and By Geographic Zones

To give you quick access to information about the best Hawai'i has to offer, we've organized material in several formats.

**Hotels** So many Islands hotels, condos, and bed-and-breakfasts seek your business that choosing the right one can be daunting. We offer easy-to-read charts, maps, and rating systems as well as pertinent information on room size, cleanliness, service, amenities, cost, and accessibility to the beach.

**Restaurants** A highlight of every Hawaiian vacation is sampling Islands cuisine. The menu is vast and tasty, ranging from simple local favorites like plate lunches to extravagant gourmet repasts and Hawai'i's own regional cuisine. We take you to Hawai'i's best restaurants.

**Entertainment and Nightlife** Most visitors to the Islands take in a couple of shows or nightspots during their stay. This is especially true of visitors to O'ahu, where Waikiki is home to ongoing live theatrical productions and plenty of hotspots. We've reviewed a few of the best live productions, where the standards are reliably high. We also check out the best nightclubs and lounges.

**Golf** Golf is a major draw for many visitors. We detail vital stats of the state's top courses to help you choose the right one.

**Geographic Zones** For added convenience, we've divided Hawai'i into geographic zones. Perhaps you're interested in staying somewhere in Kapalua Resort on the Island of Maui but aren't sure where it is. We'll note for you that Kapalua is in Zone 9, which covers West Maui, and all other Zone 9 resorts, hotels, attractions, and restaurants will be in that vicinity. Maps of each zone follow.

| | |
|---|---|
| Zone 1 | Waikiki |
| Zone 2 | Greater Honolulu |
| Zone 3 | Windward O'ahu |
| Zone 4 | The North Shore |
| Zone 5 | Leeward O'ahu |
| Zone 6 | Central O'ahu |
| Zone 7 | Central Maui |
| Zone 8 | South Maui |
| Zone 9 | West Maui |
| Zone 10 | Upcountry Maui and Beyond |
| Zone 11 | Kona |
| Zone 12 | Hilo and Volcano |
| Zone 13 | Kaua'i |
| Zone 14 | Moloka'i |
| Zone 15 | Lana'i |

Please note that the Islands of Ni'ihau and Kaho'olawe, while technically among the main southernmost islands in the Hawaiian Island chain, are not designated as zones, nor are the older Northwest Hawaiian Islands that stretch hundreds of miles into the North Pacific. Ni'ihau is a private, family-owned island and is, with few exceptions, inaccessible to visitors. For decades, Kaho'olawe, the red dirt island that seems to be bleeding across the ocean from South Maui, was a target for U.S. Navy bombing practice. Now it is being transformed into a Hawaiian cultural preserve. The uninhabited island is off-limits, except by special invitation. Only one of the Northwest Islands is a limited visitor destination—Midway Islands, the famed World War II battle site and naval base that is now a wildlife refuge.

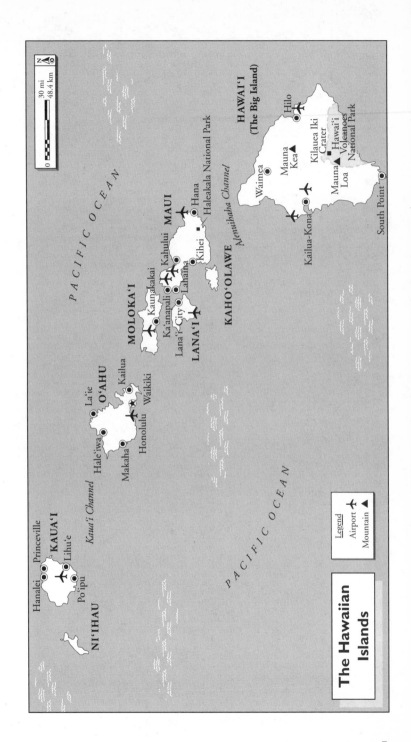

The Hawaiian Islands

Legend
Airport ✈
Mountain ▲

NI'IHAU

KAUA'I
Hanalei
Princeville
Lihu'e
Po'ipu
Kaua'i Channel

O'AHU
La'ie
Kailua
Hale'iwa
Waikiki
Makaha
Honolulu

MOLOKA'I
Kaunakakai
Ka'anapali
Lana'i City
LANA'I

MAUI
Kahului
Lahaina
Kihei
Hana
Haleakala National Park

KAHO'OLAWE
Mcnuiknha Channel

HAWAI'I
(The Big Island)
Waimea
Mauna Kea ▲
Hilo
Kilauea Iki Crater
Mauna Loa ▲
Hawai'i Volcanoes National Park
Kailua-Kona
South Point

PACIFIC OCEAN

PACIFIC OCEAN

N

0    30 mi
    48.4 km

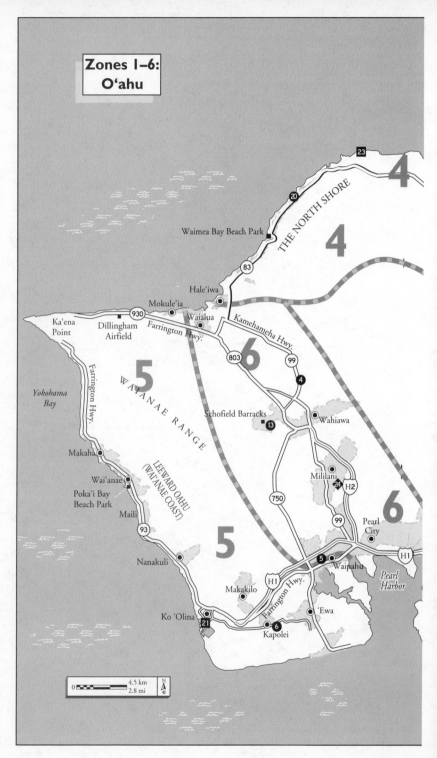

Zones 1–6:
O'ahu

THE NORTH SHORE

4

4

Waimea Bay Beach Park

83

Hale'iwa

Mokule'ia

Kamehameha Hwy.

930

Waialua

Ka'ena
Point

Dillingham
Airfield

Farrington Hwy.

803

6

99

4

Yokohama
Bay

Farrington Hwy.

WAIANAE RANGE

Schofield Barracks

13

Wahiawa

Makaha

Wai'anae

LEEWARD OAHU
(WAI'ANAE COAST)

Mililani

24

H2

Poka'i Bay
Beach Park

Maili

750

99

Pearl
City

H1

93

Nanakuli

5

5

H1

Waipahu

Pearl
Harbor

Makakilo

Farrington Hwy.

Ko 'Olina

21

6

Kapolei

'Ewa

0        4.5 km
         2.8 mi

N

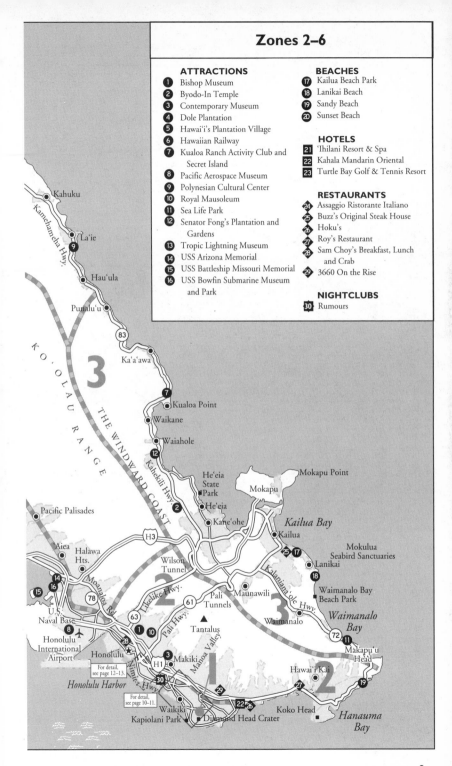

# Zones 2–6

## ATTRACTIONS
1. Bishop Museum
2. Byodo-In Temple
3. Contemporary Museum
4. Dole Plantation
5. Hawai'i's Plantation Village
6. Hawaiian Railway
7. Kualoa Ranch Activity Club and Secret Island
8. Pacific Aerospace Museum
9. Polynesian Cultural Center
10. Royal Mausoleum
11. Sea Life Park
12. Senator Fong's Plantation and Gardens
13. Tropic Lightning Museum
14. USS Arizona Memorial
15. USS Battleship Missouri Memorial
16. USS Bowfin Submarine Museum and Park

## BEACHES
17. Kailua Beach Park
18. Lanikai Beach
19. Sandy Beach
20. Sunset Beach

## HOTELS
21. 'Ihilani Resort & Spa
22. Kahala Mandarin Oriental
23. Turtle Bay Golf & Tennis Resort

## RESTAURANTS
24. Assaggio Ristorante Italiano
25. Buzz's Original Steak House
26. Hoku's
27. Roy's Restaurant
28. Sam Choy's Breakfast, Lunch and Crab
29. 3660 On the Rise

## NIGHTCLUBS
30. Rumours

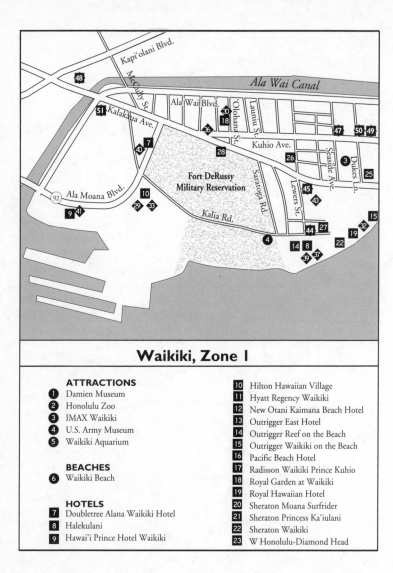

# Waikiki, Zone I

**ATTRACTIONS**
1. Damien Museum
2. Honolulu Zoo
3. IMAX Waikiki
4. U.S. Army Museum
5. Waikiki Aquarium

**BEACHES**
6. Waikiki Beach

**HOTELS**
7. Doubletree Alana Waikiki Hotel
8. Halekulani
9. Hawai'i Prince Hotel Waikiki

10. Hilton Hawaiian Village
11. Hyatt Regency Waikiki
12. New Otani Kaimana Beach Hotel
13. Outrigger East Hotel
14. Outrigger Reef on the Beach
15. Outrigger Waikiki on the Beach
16. Pacific Beach Hotel
17. Radisson Waikiki Prince Kuhio
18. Royal Garden at Waikiki
19. Royal Hawaiian Hotel
20. Sheraton Moana Surfrider
21. Sheraton Princess Ka'iulani
22. Sheraton Waikiki
23. W Honolulu-Diamond Head

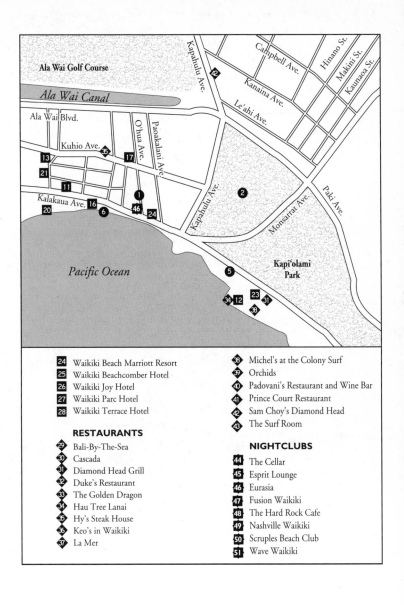

Ala Wai Golf Course

Ala Wai Canal

Ala Wai Blvd.

Kuhio Ave.

Kalakaua Ave.

Pacific Ocean

Kapahulu Ave.

O'hua Ave.

Paoakalani Ave.

Kapahulu Ave.

Campbell Ave.

Kanaina Ave.

Le'ahi Ave.

Hinano St.

Makini St.

Kaunaoa St.

Monsarrat Ave.

Paki Ave.

Kapi'olami Park

| | |
|---|---|
| 24 Waikiki Beach Marriott Resort | 38 Michel's at the Colony Surf |
| 25 Waikiki Beachcomber Hotel | 39 Orchids |
| 26 Waikiki Joy Hotel | 40 Padovani's Restaurant and Wine Bar |
| 27 Waikiki Parc Hotel | 41 Prince Court Restaurant |
| 28 Waikiki Terrace Hotel | 42 Sam Choy's Diamond Head |
| | 43 The Surf Room |

**RESTAURANTS**

29 Bali-By-The-Sea
30 Cascada
31 Diamond Head Grill
32 Duke's Restaurant
33 The Golden Dragon
34 Hau Tree Lanai
35 Hy's Steak House
36 Keo's in Waikiki
37 La Mer

**NIGHTCLUBS**

44 The Cellar
45 Esprit Lounge
46 Eurasia
47 Fusion Waikiki
48 The Hard Rock Cafe
49 Nashville Waikiki
50 Scruples Beach Club
51 Wave Waikiki

# Downtown Honolulu

**Punchbowl Crater**

Prospect St.

N. School St.

I'olani St.

Lunalilo Fwy.

Magellan Ave.

H-1

Pali Hwy.

Emma St.

Punchbowl St.

Vineyard Blvd.

Lusitania St.

**Pali Center** (Long's Drugs)

Queen St.

Queen's Medical Center

Beretania St.

S. Beretania St.

Maunakea St.

Nu'uanu St.

Fort St. Mall

S. Hotel St.

Alakea St.

State Capitol

Bishop St.

N. King St.

S. King St.

Kamehameha Statue

Kawaiaha'o Church

S. Alapa'i St.

Merchant St.

Bethel St.

Queen St.

Richards St.

Mililani St.

Emily St.

Keawe

PIER 13

PIER 12

PIER 11

Aloha Tower Marketplace

Nimitz Hwy.

Ala Moana Blvd.

Punchbowl St.

Halekauwila St.

PIER 10

PIER 9

PIER 8

PIER 7

PIER 6

PIER 5

PIER 4

Pohukaina St.

Restaurant Row

'Auahi St.

*Fort Armstrong Channel*

PIER 2C

*Sand Island*

# Honolulu, Zone 2

## ATTRACTIONS

1. Aloha Tower
2. Foster Botanical Garden
3. Hawai'i Children's Discovery Center
4. Hawai'i Maritime Center
5. Honolulu Academy of Arts
6. I'olani Palace
7. Mission Houses Museum
8. National Memorial Cemetery of the Pacific
9. Queen Emma Summer Palace

## BEACHES

10. Ala Moana Beach Park

## HOTELS

**11** Ala Moana Hotel

**12** Aston at the Executive Centre Hotel

## RESTAURANTS

**13** Alan Wong's Restaurant

**14** Chef Mavro Restaurant

**15** Don Ho's Island Grill

**16** Double Eight Chinese Restaurant

**17** Helena's Hawaiian Foods

**18** Indigo

**19** John Dominis

**20** L'uraku

**21** The Pineapple Room

**22** Sansei Seafood Restaurant and Sushi Bar

## NIGHTCLUBS

**23** Brew Moon

**24** Don Ho's Grill

**25** Kapono's

**26** Ocean Club

Zones 7–10:
Maui

0    2.5 mi
     4 km

N

Pailolo Channel

Honokohau
Bay

Pacific Ocean

Kahakuloa

Moke'ehia Island
(Seabird Sanctuary)

17
18

Kapalua

Napili

Kahana

Mahinahina

Kapalua–West Maui
Airport

Honokowai

Ka'anapali

WEST
MAUI

West Maui
Forest
Reserve

9

WEST

Kahekili Hwy.

Waihee

7

Kahului
Bay

Kanaha
Beach-Park

Ho'okipa
Beach Park

36

Spreckelsville

Pa'ia

340

See inset,
page 16

Ka'anapali
Beach

MAUI

Wailuku

330   340

3
5

'Iao Valley
State Park

MOUNTAINS

'Iao VALLEY

Kahului

Ka'ahumanu
Ave.

Kahului
Airport

23

18

Lahaina

See inset,
page 17

30

Honoapi'ilani

Waikapu

400

30

380

Pu'unene

350   36

Mokulele Hwy.

Haleakala Hwy.

37

7

Pu'unene Ave.

Olowalu

20

Hwy.

Ma'alaea

19
7

311

Kuihelani Hwy.

Pu'unene Ave.

8

30

Ma'alaea Beach

31

Maalaca Bay

Wailea

Maalaca Bay

25

Kihei

31

SOUTH
MAUI

Kilohana Dr.

31

Kihei Rd.

Piilani Hwy.

Kama'ole Beach Parks

See inset
at left

Maui
Meadows

Keokea

Okolani Dr.

Piilani Hwy.

Wailea

S. Kihei Rd.

Wailea Alanui Dr.

Kula Hwy.

16

Wailea Ike Rd.

'Ulua Beach

37

EUCALYPTUS

15

12

Makena

9

'Ulupalakua

8

FORESTS

10

11
24

Makena Alanui

Molokini
Crater

Pu'u 'Ola'i

14

Onela Beach (Big Beach)

Kaho'olawe

'Ahini-Kina'u
Natural Area Reserve

8

31

'Alalakeiki

14

# Zones 7, 8, 9 & 10: Maui

## ATTRACTIONS
1. Haleakala National Park
2. Hana Cultural Center
3. Hawai'i Nature Center
4. Hui No'eau Visual Arts Center
5. Kepaniwai Cultural Park
6. Kula Botanical Garden
7. Maui Ocean Center
8. Tedeschi Winery

## BEACHES
9. Makena
10. Wailea Resort Beaches

## HOTELS
11. Four Seasons Resort Maui
12. Grand Wailea Resort Hotel & Spa
13. Hotel Hana-Maui
14. Kea Lani Hotel, Suites & Villas
15. Outrigger Wailea Resort
16. Renaissance Wailea Beach Resort
17. Ritz-Carlton, Kapalua

## RESTAURANTS
18. Anuenue Room
19. A Saigon Café
20. Bamboo Bistro
21. Chez Paul's
22. Hali'imaile General Store
23. Mama's Fish House
24. Spago

## NIGHTCLUBS
25. Hapa's Brew Haus

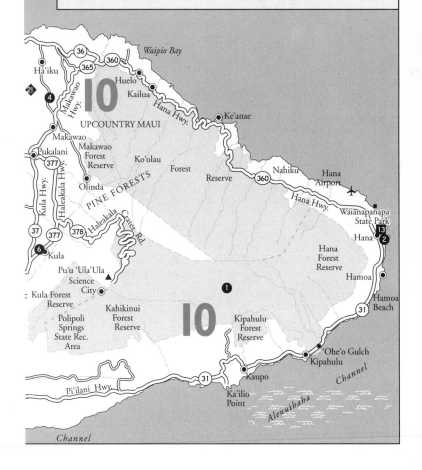

15

## Central Maui, Zone 7

### ATTRACTIONS

1. Alexander & Baldwin Sugar Museum
2. Bailey House Museum
3. Maui Tropical Plantation &
   Country Store

## West Maui, Zone 9

### ATTRACTIONS

1. Baldwin Home Museum
2. Brig Carthaginian
3. Hawai'i Experience Theater
4. Lahaina-Ka'anapali & Pacific Railroad
5. Whalers Village Museum
6. Wo Hing Temple Museum

### BEACHES

7. Ka'anapali Beach
8. Kapalua Beach

### HOTELS

9. Embassy Vacation Resort
10. Hyatt Regency Maui
11. Ka'anapali Beach Hotel
12. Kapalua Bay Hotel
13. Lahaina Inn
14. Maui Marriott Resort
15. Sheraton Maui
16. Westin Maui

### RESTAURANTS

17. The Bay Club Restaurant
18. David Paul's Lahaina Grill
19. Gerard's
20. Hula Grill
21. Kimo's
22. Longhi's
23. Roy's Kahana Bar & Grill
24. Roy's Nicolina
25. Pacific'O
26. Plantation House Restaurant
27. Sansei Seafood Restaurant and Sushi Bar

### NIGHTCLUBS

28. Maui Brews

# West Maui

Kapalua

Kahana

30

9

Honokowai

9

Ka'anapali
Beach Resort

7

15
20
11   5
16
14
10

## Lahaina

Front St.

4

Papalaua St.

30

28

Wahle Ln.

Lahainaluna Rd

21

19

6

18
13

21

3

Dickenson St.

2

Luakini St.

Waine'e St.

1

Front St.

30

Lahaina

30

See inset
at left

9

12
17
21

8

23
24

26

Zones 11 and 12:
The Big Island

The Kohala Coast

Hilo

Banyan Dr.

Hilo Bay

11

Kīlauea Ave

Kamehameha Ave

Mohouli St.

Ponahawai St.

19

200

Komohana St.

Kailua-Kona

11

19

Kuakini Hwy

Alii Dr.

190

Palani Rd.

19

132

Pahoa

137

130

130

THE PUNA REGION

Kahaualea
Natural Area Reserve

Mountain View

Chain of Craters Rd.

Volcano

40

Kīlauea Caldera

6

11

I2

Mauna Loa ▲

THE KA'U DESERT

Pahala

Punalu'u

Nā'ālehu

Waiōhinu

Ka Lae (South Point)

24

11

II

COAST

Keauhou

Kealakekua

Captain Cook

3

Napo'opo'o

Hawai'i Belt Rd.

11

17

22

Hoʻokena

Miloli'i

Keauhou
Bay

Kealakekua
Bay

Hōnaunau
Bay

37

51 2 21

57 52

33 1 7

55

20 30 31

14 57 42

10

19

# Zones 11 & 12: The Big Island

## ATTRACTIONS
1. Ahu'ena Heiau
2. Akatsuka Orchid Gardens
3. Amy B.H. Greenwell Ethnobotanical Garden
4. Astronaut Ellison S. Onizuka Space Center
5. Hawai'i Tropical Botanical Garden
6. Hawai'i Volcanoes National Park
7. Hulihe'e Palace
8. Kaloko-Honokohau National Historical Park
9. Kamuela Museum
10. Lyman Mission House and Museum
11. Mauna Loa Macadamia Nut Visitor Center
12. Nani Mau Gardens
13. Onizuka Center for International Astronomy and Mauna Kea Observatory
14. Pacific Tsunami Museum
15. Pana'ewa Rainforest Zoo
16. Parker Ranch Visitor Center and Historic Homes
17. Pu'uhonua O Honaunau National Historical Park
18. Pu'ukohola Heiau
19. Sadie Seymour Botanical Gardens
20. Suisan Fish Market and Auction
21. Volcano Winery
22. Wakefield Botanical Gardens

## BEACHES
23. Anaeho'omalu Beach
24. Green Sand Beach
25. Hapuna Beach State Recreation Area
26. Kauna'oa Beach
27. Pololu Beach

## HOTELS
28. Four Seasons Resort Hualalai
29. Hapuna Beach Prince Hotel
30. Hawai'i Naniloa Resort
31. Hilo Hawai'ian Hotel
32. Hilton Waikoloa Village
33. King Kamehameha's Kona Beach Hotel
34. Kona Village Resort
35. Mauna Kea Beach Hotel
36. Mauna Lani Bay Hotel & Bungalows
37. 'Ohana Keauhou Beach Resort
38. The Orchid at Mauna Lani
39. Outrigger Waikoloa Beach Hotel
40. Volcano House

## RESTAURANTS
41. Batik Restaurant
42. Café Pesto
43. Canoehouse
44. Coast Grille
45. Daniel Thiebaut Restaurant
46. Donatoni's
47. Edelweiss
48. The Grill and Lounge at the Orchid
49. Harrington's
50. Huggo's
51. Kilauea Lodge
52. Kona Ranch House
53. Merriman's
54. Oodles of Noodles
55. Pahu i'a at Four Seasons
56. Roy's at the King's Shops
57. Royal Siam
58. Sam Choy's Restaurant

# Zone 13: Kauai

## ATTRACTIONS
1. Grove Farm Homestead
2. Guava Kai Plantation
3. Kaua'i Museum
4. Kilauea Point National Wildlife Refuge
5. Kilohana Plantation
6. Koke'e National History Museum
7. Limahuli Garden
8. Moir Gardens
9. National Tropical Botanical Garden Lawai and Allerton Gardens
10. Wai'oli Mission House Museum

## BEACHES
11. Hanalei Bay
12. Kalapaki Beach
13. Ke'e Beach
14. Lumaha'i Beach
15. Po'ipu Beach Park
16. Polihale State Park (Barking Sands)
17. Secret Beach
18. Shipwreck Beach
19. Tunnels Beach

## HOTELS
20. Hanalei Bay Resort & Suites
21. Hyatt Regency Kaua'i Resort & Spa
22. Kaua'i Marriott Resort & Beach Club
23. Princeville Resort
24. Radisson Kaua'i Beach Resort
25. Sheraton Kaua'i Resort

## RESTAURANTS
26. The Beach House
27. Brennecke's Beach Broiler
28. Café Hanalei and Terrace
29. Casa Di Amici
30. Duke's Canoe Club
31. Hamura Saimin
32. Keoki's Paradise
33. Mema Thai Chinese Cuisine
34. Piatti
35. Postcards
36. Roy's Po'ipu Bar & Grill
37. Shells, at the Sheraton Kauai Hotel
38. Tidepools

Zone 13:
Kaua'i

N

9 km
5.6 mi

0

Po'ipu Resort

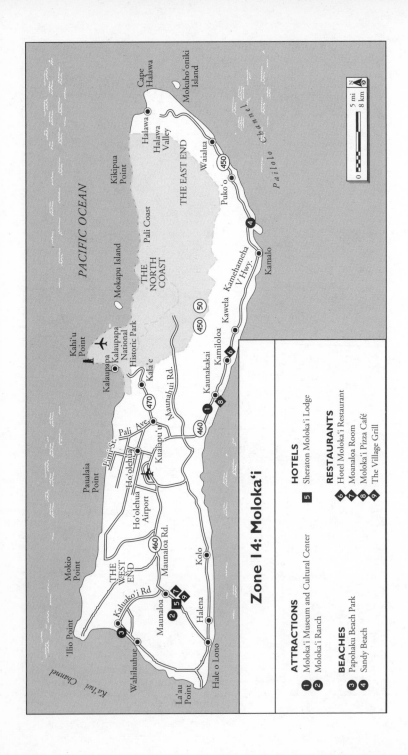

# Zone 14: Moloka'i

## ATTRACTIONS
1. Moloka'i Museum and Cultural Center
2. Moloka'i Ranch

## BEACHES
3. Papohaku Beach Park
4. Sandy Beach

## HOTELS
5. Sheraton Moloka'i Lodge

## RESTAURANTS
6. Hotel Moloka'i Restaurant
7. Moanaloa Room
8. Moloka'i Pizza Café
9. The Village Grill

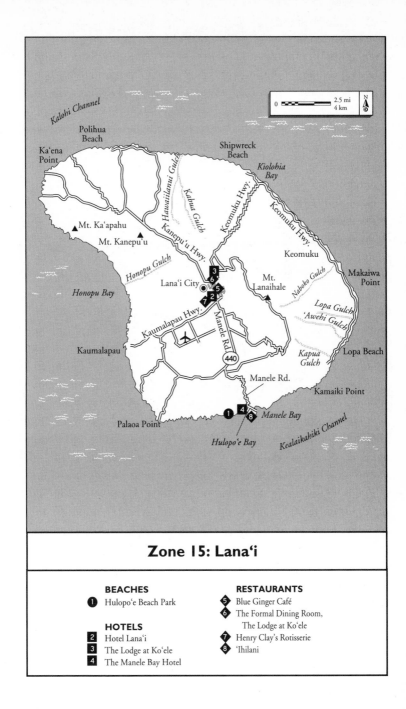

# Zone 15: Lana'i

**BEACHES**

1 Hulopo'e Beach Park

**HOTELS**

2 Hotel Lana'i
3 The Lodge at Ko'ele
4 The Manele Bay Hotel

**RESTAURANTS**

5 Blue Ginger Café
6 The Formal Dining Room,
   The Lodge at Ko'ele
7 Henry Clay's Rotisserie
8 'Ihilani

# Part One

# Getting Acquainted with Hawai'i

## About the Aloha State

The Hawaiian Islands, in the middle of the sea and far removed from any continent, are nonetheless an irresistible lure to anyone who's ever heard the word aloha. People from all over the world pay handsomely for the privilege of flying at least five hours to this jack's toss of islands in the tropical North Pacific. Hawai'i is the most isolated population center in the world, 2,390 miles from California, 3,850 miles from Japan, 4,900 miles from China, and 5,280 miles from the Philippines. Only seven of the 132 blips in the Hawaiian Islands archipelago are even inhabited, and one of those, Ni'ihau, is a private ranch.

Despite the remoteness of the destination, nearly seven million people found their way to Hawai'i last year to roam the sandy shores and volcanic peaks, enjoy the nearly perfect weather and easygoing lifestyle, gaze at the spectacular natural beauty, and dream of ways to drop out of sight and stay here forever.

Plenty of people have done just that. Since the Islands were discovered in about AD 650 by Polynesian seafarers, probably from the Marquesas, a wide range of folks have washed ashore—British and European explorers, field workers from all over Asia and some from Europe and the Caribbean, German planters, Scottish merchants, American missionaries and whalers, South Pacific and other Polynesian Islanders, Southeast Asian refugees, and rogues of all nations who jumped ship and were unwilling, or unable, to leave. Some early-twentieth-century wayfarers ran out of fuel, crash-landed their planes in the sea, and swam ashore. It's a colorful history that led to the racial rainbow of people and cultures that comprise modern Hawai'i. These Islands, America's only former royal kingdom complete with a fairy tale palace, have been a state since 1959. In their remarkable population, people of mixed blood outnumber other groups, no one is a majority, and the rarest soul of all is a pure Hawaiian.

In the beginning the Islands were empty slates, volcanic slopes in a beneficent climate rich with potential to sustain the good life. Creatures and plants blew in or were carried by the settlers, along with their heritage, customs, and languages. Imports mingled and thrived in the fecund tropical atmosphere, often at the expense of earlier arrivals. The riotous birds that wake the day and the fragrant flowers, lush plants, and towering trees that dress the landscape hail from India, the Americas, Asia, and still farther regions. Subtle native plants and shy native birds were crowded into small corners or vanished altogether. As a result, Hawai'i has the dubious reputation of being the endangered species capital of the world, with more than 75% of native birds extinct or threatened and more than 250 species on the endangered list.

Without the enemies of their homelands, exotic species have a very good life in the Islands. You don't often see the only native mammals, the hoary bat and the endangered monk seal, but men introduced hooved cattle, pigs, donkeys, deer, and sheep that went wild and flourished, to the detriment of the fragile landscape. Houseplants got loose to climb tree trunks, where they sprouted leaves as big as your face. The ficus trees pampered in pots in many a mainland living room are two-story giants with massive canopies in Hawai'i. The bright lantana blooming in the wild are said to have sprung from a single garden plant tossed into a garbage heap. Anything grows, larger than life, including the cityscape of Honolulu and the elaborate, world-famous beach resorts where each building component, investment dollar, computer, bed sheet, fork, vehicle, and tourist was shipped thousands of miles from another shore. Hawai'i is not only a special place; for better or worse, it's a marvel.

You can look forward to an unforgettable experience in Hawai'i, which is likely to call you back again. Hawai'i enjoys one of the highest repeat visitor rates of any destination.

Open your window shade on the plane and look out when the final descent begins, after miles of open sea, to see Mauna Kea and Mauna Loa looming through the clouds. Maui's Haleakala appears next, then the low red-dirt plains of Lana'i across from moody Moloka'i. As the plane approaches Honolulu, the water seems to get bluer. Then O'ahu appears, and the world's most remote and most unlikely city, sprawling along its southern shore. Excitement builds as you touch down and glide into Honolulu International Airport. You emerge in the open air, which smells of flowers, and feel the warm breeze on your skin. Welcome to Hawai'i.

# Choosing Your Island

Which island should you see first? It depends on what you want to do and who you're bringing along on this trip. Here's a thumbnail visitors' guide: The Big Island has active volcanoes, accessible cultural history, landscape diversity, and luxury golf resorts in the lava. Maui has wintering humpback whales, its own complement of big-time golf courses, and plenty of visitors to its sunny beach resorts, ranging from affordable condos to plush hotels. Moloka'i is the quietest and least oriented to tourism. Lana'i is a virtually private former pineapple plantation with two classy hotels and golf courses. O'ahu is the vibrant heart of the Islands—the cosmopolitan cities of Honolulu and Waikiki on one side and unspoiled country all around it. Kaua'i is the lush green movie set where nature pulls out all the beauty stops.

Want to simply kick back at a beach resort and get spritzed with Evian by the pool or have a butler fix your mai tais? Hawai'i offers at least two dozen upscale luxury choices, most of them clustered on South and West Maui and the Big Island's Kona-Kohala Coast, where you can be pampered in butlered bungalows for $5,000 a night.

Want to hike spectacular sea cliffs or green rain forests? You can't miss on Kaua'i, with pure wilderness on its Na Pali (The Cliffs) Coast, or the Big Island with its kipuka, oases of green forest amid black lava, and Hamakua Coast waterfall valleys. Equally spectacular are Maui's Upcountry cloud forests, O'ahu's sheer Ko'olau ridges, and Moloka'i's haunting fern-forested northeast coast.

Traveling with your family? Your kids will love Waikiki, especially the teenagers. Maui's Ka'anapali Resort is a top family destination, but kids love Po'ipu Beach on Kaua'i too. And what could be more educational than watching a Big Island volcano in action? You'll find kids are welcome, even cherished, all over the Islands.

Golf doesn't get much better than the spectacular courses of Maui, Lana'i, Kaua'i, and the Big Island. O'ahu adds its share, including the busiest and the most difficult courses in the nation.

You'd need more than a week to do justice to O'ahu, but the trick is to hit the road. Rent a car, ride the bus, but do get out of town and see the beauty of the Ko'olau Mountains, the Windward Coast, the North Shore, central plains filled with pineapple, and other destinations. Wear your swimsuit if you want to stop every now and then and go for a swim at a roadside beach. Spend a morning snorkeling at crowded Hanauma Bay, break for plate-lunch surfer chow, then go find your own choice of an empty near-shore reef to snorkel in the afternoon. Save another O'ahu day for learning how to surf at Waikiki; a day for hiking or riding in the

Windward hills or watching big waves on the North Shore; a day at the USS *Arizona* and USS *Missouri,* the Bishop Museum and Honolulu Academy of Art; a day browsing the designer boutiques; a day exploring Honolulu's natural history; a day kayaking or windsurfing at Kailua Beach; and a day to rest up after attending a Hawaiian music concert at Waikiki Shell and then boogying all night. Pretty soon it adds up to a real good time.

If you're Island-hopping, it's important to realize that many of Hawai'i's attractions and adventures—including a visit to the Polynesian Cultural Center on O'ahu, a Zodiac boat ride along Kaua'i's Na Pali Coast, coasting on a special bike from Maui's lofty summit of Haleakala down to the sea, a snorkel cruise to Lana'i, and a mule ride down Moloka'i's cliffs—take up most of a day or more. You need more than a day to fully explore the natural wonders of Hawai'i Volcanoes National Park, home of fire goddess Madame Pele and her ever-erupting Kilauea Volcano.

To get the most out of your Hawai'i visit, mix and match experiences: Combine the sparkle of Honolulu on O'ahu with the meditative beauty of Hanalei, Kaua'i or Hana, Maui. Supplement your big-game fishing adventure on the Big Island with a rugged trail ride on Moloka'i. Soak up the sun in Wailea's luxury resorts on Maui, then sail across the channel to Lana'i to cool off under the Upcountry pines at the affordable Hotel Lana'i or luxurious The Lodge at Ko'ele.

## The Weather Report

"Hawai'i has the weather California thinks it has."
—Earl der Biggers, Charlie Chan's *House Without a Key*

Blue skies, trade winds, and sunshine with almost 12 hours of daylight every day of the year: there's no better climate than Hawai'i. The reason is geographic. The Hawaiian Islands are located in the North Pacific, 1,700 miles north of the Equator, inside the Tropic of Cancer (stretching from 154 degrees 40 minutes to 179 degrees 25 minutes west latitude and 18 degrees 54 minutes to 28 degrees 15 minutes north latitude, to be precise).

While the Islands share latitudes with Havana, Hong Kong, Calcutta, and the Sahara Desert, they enjoy a key advantage over these hotspots. Hawai'i has natural air-conditioning. The islands are 2,781 miles south of Anchorage, Alaska, across open sea. The cold northeast winds, which historically propelled merchant's ships to Honolulu from the West Coast to earn the name "trade winds," still sweep down the Pacific, softening as the water warms. The tamed breezes arrive in Hawai'i as cooling trade winds, welcome whether gentle or blustery. Now and then, they die off in what is called Kona (meaning leeward) weather, hot and still and fretful.

Hawai'i's year-round average temperature of 77°F is judged the best in the United States. The difference between winter and summer, and between night and day, is about five to ten degrees on the shorelines, where most people live. Daytime highs are usually somewhere in the 80s, although they can be lower in winter, when storms hide the sun, or rise to the low 90s in steamy August and September. Nights are in the 70s in summer and 60s in winter, with rare dips into the 50s. Winter nights at the coldest record in decades got down to 55° in Honolulu, where summer highs are unlikely to be higher than 94°. The rest of the thermometer seems superfluous.

But it's not that easy. The Aloha State encompasses 21 of the 22 world climatic zones and features no fewer than 88 ecosystems, ranging from snowy mountaintops, rain forests, wetlands, and deserts to sea cliffs, beaches, and volcanoes.

Temperature zones vary with altitude, rather than with latitude. Around the coastlines all the islands are warm (highs in the 80s) and mostly sunny. As you gain altitude in the Upcountry, with 2,000–3,000-foot elevations, the weather cools off on all islands and is often wetter, too. On the mountaintops, the chill can be downright alpine, and the moisture turns to snow from time to time. Meterologists estimate the temperature drops 3.5° for every 1,000-foot rise above sea level. If the heat gets you down, go up and cool off. You may need a jacket or sweater and a blanket at Kula, Maui; Waimea on the Big Island; Nu'uanu on O'ahu; Koke'e State Park on Kaua'i; and Lana'i City, Lana'i.

All islands share another climactic trait: the weather is drier and hotter on the leeward sides; cooler, wetter, and windier on the windward sides. The line between is a northeast-southwest diagonal echoing the trade wind flow. Resorts tend to be located on the leeward coasts for the reliable sunshine: Waikiki and Ko'Olina on O'ahu; Makena, Wailea, Kihei, Lahaina, and Ka'anapali on Maui; Kailua-Kona and the Kona-Kohala coast on the Big Island; and the South Shore of Kaua'i around Po'ipu Beach.

Vacationers may not always agree, but rain is a good thing on islands too remote to import water. Hawaiians wrote chants about rain. And they created onomatopoetic words for water—*wai hu'ihu'i* (cool water), *wai kapipi* (sprinkling water), *wai konikoni* (tingling water), *wai noenoe* (misty water), and *wai kai* (brackish water). And more familiar, Waikiki (spouting water) was named not for the ocean but the fresh springs that gushed there. Rain creates rainbows, waterfalls, and plentiful fresh water. O'ahu's municipal water is adjudged some of the best in the world, and it tastes better than bottled designer water because it is filtered through lava for a half-century to reach the water table.

The average humidity level in the state ranges from 56% to 72%, but annual precipitation varies widely. Waikiki gets 25 inches of rain a year, but Manoa Valley, five miles inland, receives 158 inches.

Two of the wettest spots on Earth are found in Hawai'i:

■ Mount Wai'ale'ale on Kaua'i gets more than 400 inches of rainfall a year. Wai'ale'ale means "rippling or overflowing water," an apt title for the Kaua'i peak that one year received 950 inches of rain, nearly 80 feet.

■ Pu'u Kukui, the 5,871-foot-high summit of the West Maui Mountains, gets 350 inches a year. In 1982, it had a record rainfall of 654.83 inches, or 54.5 feet.

Hilo on the Big Island, meanwhile, has the soggy sobriquet of being the wettest city in the United States, averaging 128 inches of rain per year.

A word about rain showers: Don't get too excited about getting wet. It feels good. No one wears raincoats. Umbrellas are more often used to keep off the sun than the rain, and showers often come on winds that turn umbrellas inside out. If it rains while you're on the beach, get in the water or under a tree. If it rains during your al fresco brunch, put up the table umbrella and don't sit under the drip. The shower will probably be gone in a minute or two. With the ubiquitous Hawaiian "pineapple juice" showers that drift over while the sun shines brightly, everyone just gets wet one moment and dries off the next. Showers are considered blessings.

Weather can get extreme on these mid-Pacific pinpricks of land, but it's uncommon (see below).

## A Word about Directions

We try to orient you here somewhat with the familiar directions of north, east, south, and west. But these words won't be terribly helpful in Hawai'i. Local usage has little to do with the compass. The words you want to know are *mauka* (uphill, inland, toward the mountains) and *makai* (toward the sea). The other directions are known by a bewildering variety of local landmarks. In Honolulu, these are generally *'Ewa* (west, or where 'Ewa plantation used to be) and *Diamond Head* (that one's easy).

## Perils of "Paradise"

No place is perfect, even this one that seems heavenly enough that many call it "paradise." While nobody in Hawai'i likes to "talk stink" (say anything bad), each island has certain drawbacks.

O'ahu suffers hellish chronic traffic congestion—too many cars and not enough roads—which is worst at rush hour and lunchtime. Traffic is much lighter in summer when school is out. If you drive, be patient and polite. Let cars in front of you, as you'll see others do. Remember that it's bad manners to honk in Hawai'i unless you are signaling a friend, and rude gestures can get you in trouble. Parking is inexpensive in downtown Honolulu compared to most big cities, but it can mount up unless you get validated at offices, restaurants, or shops in the complex or use one of the municipal garages. Waikiki hotels charge for guest parking. Parking meters are generally 50 cents an hour on the streets. Mind the hours and tow-away zones.

Maui gets really windy most afternoons, when the breezes kick up white caps in the ocean, sling stinging sand in your face at the beach in Kihei, and make for bumpy landings at Kahului Airport. It's a natural phenomenon. Nearly constant trade winds accelerate when they pass through Maui's funnel-like isthmus.

Maui and Kaua'i both have traffic jams when big jets unload passengers around quitting time for the sugar mills or other businesses. On Maui, the jam is worst from Lahaina to Ka'anapali. On Kaua'i, it's worst between Lihu'e and Kapa'a. You'll also encounter crowds at rental car stands when DC 10s and 747s arrive. The best policy is to slow down and cool off. Allow more time. Strike up a conversation. Island pace just isn't as wiki-wiki (speedy) as the stressful life you're vacationing from, so you might as well get used to it. It's called "Hawaiian time."

Kaua'i is nicknamed the "Garden Island" because it is so green and lush and tropical. It thrives because it gets watered a lot, especially on the North Shore where short torrential downpours are common. The rickety wooden bridge over Hanalei River gets flooded out at least once a year, briefly cutting off the North Shore from the rest of the world (there's no more celebrated excuse for being late for work). Residents put up with it because the old bridge guards their beautiful home ground from major bus and truck traffic and full-scale development. Lots of Hawaiian songs celebrate Kaua'i's beauty, but it takes rain to make those triple rainbows and waterfalls, sometimes lots of it. That's even more true of Hilo and the Hamakua Coast on the Big Island, where the verdant waterfall valleys and profusion of orchids, anthuriums, fruit, nuts, and other crops are a live giveaway to the moist climate.

The Big Island of Hawai'i can thank its two active volcanoes, primarily Kilauea, for the hazy condition it often suffers, known as vog. That's short for "volcanic fog," which cloaks Kailua-Kona on many afternoons with a gray overcast that looks like doomsday. Sometimes a shift in the winds will carry the vog north to other islands. Vog can pose a discomfort to asthma victims and makes people drowsy or headachy. Something more acute, called laze, occurs close to active lava flows when volcano-produced sulfuric acid mixes with cool seawater and becomes hydrochloric acid, sometimes in a burst of steam. This is harmful to your health.

Moloka'i lacks many creature comforts. Its only resort is the Sheraton Moloka'i Lodge. The island receives milk and staples by once-a-week barge from Honolulu. If you shop the markets for food, you plan dinner around what there is to buy.

Clouds that delay takeoffs and landings often shroud the island of Lana'i. You may spend more time on Lana'i than you planned. Since the island is remote and there are only two resorts, everything is more costly, a fact of little concern to most of its high-budget visitors.

Besides the drawbacks above, real perils are few, but be forewarned:

Insects also love tropical Hawai'i—huge centipedes (and they bite, painfully); delicate, small scorpions (a bite like a bee sting, according to one victim); several species of big, scary-looking cockroaches that don't bite; huge, fast, hairy but harmless cane spiders; several sizes of ants; your average fly and superfly; and mosquitoes that seem to prefer tender flesh fresh from the mainland. You might even see a bold fruit rat traveling between houses on a power line.

Sunburn is a much bigger danger than bugs. Don't underestimate the power of tropical sun. It's strongest from 9 a.m. to 3 p.m. Do what you want when you want, but slather everyone with high-spf waterproof sunscreen and use sunglasses and hats as well. If you get scorched, slather up even more with aloe vera gel.

Shark attacks are rare in Hawai'i, but sharks are not. Those clear blue waters harbor a variety of the creatures, which, by Hawaiian legend, are more revered than feared as 'aumakua, or family guardian spirits.

The islands are subject to earthquakes, mostly small Big Island rumbles from Kilauea Volcano. Rogue waves can sweep you out to sea, and rip tides can carry you off toward Tahiti. You can slip off a cliff trail or fall into the volcano. All of these awful things have happened to people on a holiday in normally benign Hawai'i.

Hawai'i's most threatening perils are the occasional tsunami, high surf, and the temporary flash flooding that occurs when tropical cloud bursts, usually brief and intense, run off steep slopes. Sudden, heavy rains pose flash-flood danger, particularly in a downhill waterfall valley or on a road that briefly becomes a raging waterfall course. If you get caught by a squall while hiking by a stream, go immediately to high ground. If driving, park before you get to the deep water on a roadway and wait an hour or two. It will all be gone soon as the water flows out to sea.

# The Islands by Zone

## O'ahu: The Gathering Place

### O'AHU FACTS

**Flower** 'Ilima
**Color** Yellow
**State Capital, County Seat** Honolulu
**Area** 608 square miles
**Length** 44 miles
**Width** 30 miles
**Population** 876,156
**Highest Point** Ka'ala Peak (4,003 feet)
**Coastline** 112 miles

Of all the islands in the Pacific, only one boasts so much: two mountain ranges, great natural beauty, world-class shopping, lots of sandy beaches, accommodations ranging from surf shacks to five-star hotels, sleepy country villages, international sophistication, a modern city and urban resort with clean air and water, open space, high-rise towers, a multicultural population, nightlife, a major university, and considerable wealth, drawn by the quality of life.

Small wonder everyone sooner or later ends up on O'ahu, America's gateway to the Pacific and most-visited island in the chain. Ironically, an island famous for so much gets a bad rap from critics who complain of too many buildings and people. Perhaps they never left Honolulu. The truth is that the entire cityscape, the urban resort of Waikiki, and the lion's share of suburban housing are squeezed into a narrow 26-mile-long corridor between the Ko'olau Mountains and the Pacific. Leave that corridor and you have another O'ahu.

You need only cross over the mountains to the cool and scenic Windward Coast or head up the central valley between the Ko'olau and Wai'anae ranges to the North Shore to discover O'ahu's more natural side, or go west past the airport to be surrounded by sunny golf courses on old sugar lands.

### Zone 1: Waikiki

This century-old resort, where Hawaiian kings once played, changes luster like a pearl every few years. Now, after a costly facelift, Waikiki sports new gardens, walkways, pools, and street lighting, as well as a renewed emphasis on projecting Hawaiian culture to guests in the very un-Hawaiian environment of tall buildings and busy streets.

If you think of Waikiki as a lively urban resort where an incredible variety of people enjoy the most famous beach in the world, you'll love it, as public theater if nothing else. If you seek the good old days when cruise ship passengers were met by men and maidens who jumped in the sea and swam to the boats, then escorted passengers to a handful of hotels where they resided royally for months, having shipped their Rolls Royces over, then you will surely be disappointed. You won't find grass shacks to sleep in—sadly, the Uniform Building Code outlaws even thatched roofs in most instances. You can see hula, Hawaiian arts and crafts, and nostalgia, hear Hawaiian music, and watch surfers as long as you want.

Waikiki packs into a square mile of space about 33,000 visitor rooms in 175 hotel and condo properties, plus apartments that house some 50,000 residents, restaurants, boutiques, theaters, nightspots, fast-food joints, museums, beaches, boats, churches, and just across the Ala Wai Canal, a major convention center. The district is a narrow peninsula between **Waikiki Beach** and the canal paralleled by Kalakaua Avenue, the main one-way inbound boulevard; secondary thoroughfare Kuhio Avenue, a block back from the beach; the one-way outbound Ala Wai Boulevard; and the canal, which defines the district on two sides. Kapahulu Avenue more or less defines the Diamond Head end. One big chunk of Waikiki at the beginning of the man-made peninsula is **Fort DeRussy,** the only open spot along this end of the beach. This fortunately situated Army installation has a couple of high-rises for military visitors, plus low-rise buildings and lots of green. With even fewer buildings and more green, 170-acre **Queen Kapi'olani Park** at the other end, the foot of Diamond Head, is a similar beachfront respite from congestion. Thank King Kalakaua, who created the park in 1877 and named it for his queen. It is the home of the **Waikiki Shell,** an outdoor entertainment venue, and **Honolulu Zoo,** and like any urban park, it's a wonderful place for running, flying kites, having picnics, holding cultural festivals, and playing softball and tennis.

You could say Waikiki, in which an estimated 100,000 people sleep on any given night, is the antithesis of urban sprawl. The compaction puts everything within walking distance or a short bus ride. Waikiki is a city within a city, and while they might have done it better (no planners were used in the making of Waikiki), the resort accommodates, amazingly well, millions who seek sun and sand and a good time in a tropical urban setting.

Our suggestion is to visit Waikiki for at least two or three days, time enough to get your bearings, shake off jet lag, and press on, either elsewhere on O'ahu or to a neighbor island. While you're in Waikiki, go out early one morning, walk the beach when it's deserted and the sand is cool, and stop for an al fresco breakfast at one of the hotels you pass.

At night, the sidewalks of Kalakaua and Kuhio are constant parades of passersby, including visitors from every corner of the globe. Prostitution thrives in Waikiki after dark, despite periodic attempts to control it. One police officer noted that the most frequently asked question he receives from visitors is, "Is prostitution legal here?" It's not, but the world's oldest business goes on just the same.

Waikiki is a safe area. The Honolulu Police Department maintains a strong and reassuring presence there. In addition, a citizens group calling themselves the "Aloha Patrol" prowls the streets at night, assisting visitors and keeping an eye out for trouble.

After years of traffic congestion during Waikiki's facelift, residents from outside the tourist district rarely go there. To see what the local lifestyle is all about, you'll have to venture outside Waikiki and discover O'ahu.

## Zone 2: Greater Honolulu

Honolulu is the capital of Hawai'i and has been since 1850, when it was the heart of the kingdom. Today, its realms are financial, political, commercial, and cultural—during the daytime at least. Everyone goes home at night, and the lively downtown shuts down. Except for Chinatown and parts of the waterfront, the downtown restaurants and bars are open in daytime only, and so are the stores. But retail continues unabated into the evenings in the out-of-downtown shopping centers.

The main street of town is Bishop Street, a continuation of the Pali Highway that goes one-way makai all the way down to Honolulu Harbor. The companion mauka-bound thoroughfare is Alakea Street. The downtown area extends several blocks around them. Other boundaries are Ala Moana Boulevard, paralleling the harbor front, and Vineyard Boulevard on the uphill side, named for onetime wine vineyards planted long ago by a Spaniard, Don Marin. Through the middle, King and Beretania Streets, a pair of key one-way (through downtown) connectors, link neighborhoods for miles on either side of town. The downtown architecture is an interesting mix of historic buildings and new high-rises that speak of continued prosperity. Street trees and park areas, not to mention the mountain and ocean views at either end of the streets, make for a very attractive district. The government buildings and **Capitol District,** which includes **'Iolani Palace** and other historic structures, are just Diamond Head of downtown, within easy walking distance.

Just 'Ewa of downtown is the historic **Chinatown** district, now populated more by Vietnamese than Chinese. Twice in the past, Chinatown burned to the ground and was rebuilt. The latest assault was a matter of rising crime and drug use, but citizens have banded together to take Chinatown back. One key advance was the $30 million renovation of the 1,400-seat **Hawai'i Theatre,** a masterpiece in gilt and 1920s style.

## Zone 3: Windward O'ahu

For peace and scenic splendor without high-rise canyons, go over the mountains to the Windward beach town of **Kailua,** where hotels are banned but vacation rentals and bed-and-breakfasts offer affordable access to the excellent beaches; or **Hale'iwa,** former plantation town and home of big-wave surfers on the North Shore; or **Ko'Olina Resort,** the neighbor island-style luxury spread in west O'ahu.

No signs point the way to Kailua, but it's over the Pali Highway from downtown. There's no tourist booth and not many tourists. Kailua's great beaches were largely unknown to visitors until recently, but **Kailua Beach** and **Lanikai Beach** have been named two of America's best, and now the secret's out. A quaint beach town at the foot of the Ko'olau, Kailua is a bedroom community of about 50,000 and the bed-and-breakfast capital of O'ahu.

Bed-and-breakfasts in Hawai'i are most often rooms or suites in people's houses with breakfast or light kitchen facilities provided, rather than the quaint inns of the East Coast. Scores of B&Bs and other low-key places to stay, including vacation rentals on or near the beaches, can be found on the Internet. Many operate underground since the City and County of Honolulu, in a poor display of civic aloha, banned new bed-and-breakfasts years ago.

Windsurfing, kayaking, swimming, and snorkeling are the main water attractions here in the home of Robbie Naish, former world champion windsurfer who is now pioneering kitesurfing (See details, page 281). The scenic **Mokulua,** two photo-op islets off Lanikai, are the most popular kayak destinations. Rent all the gear you need right in Kailua Beach Park or at one of the shops in town.

Hikers scale 603-foot-high **Ka'iwa Ridge** for a panoramic view of the Windward side or hike other trails through the Ko'olau rain forests along the Windward Coast. Fearless hikers with sheer-cliff experience test their mettle on the spiky pinnacle of Olomana.

Kailua is the recommended choice on O'ahu for families with small kids, who can safely play in gentle waves lapping the shore. Opting for a vacation rental is one way to control expenses while maximizing exposure to local life—discovering unfamiliar foods in the supermarkets, for instance (or at the hour-long Thursday morning "People's Market" at 9 a.m. beside Kailua Middle School). Kailua is a favorite of many visitors seeking to live Hawaiian style rather than be a resort tourist. A rental car is necessary to make the most of it and to enjoy the surrounding Windward Coast. Farther up the reef-protected Windward shores, more than 50 miles of empty beaches (busier on weekends) are suitable for snoozing, swimming, shorefishing, spearfishing in the lagoon-like waters, or snorkeling.

Natural attractions include **Kaneʻohe Bay,** one of the most beautiful in the Pacific, with snorkel and dive trips departing from Heʻeia Pier; **Kualoa Ranch,** a 4,000-acre cattle ranch with 75 horses for trail rides and myriad other outdoor activities; and **Hoʻomaluhia Botanical Park,** a 400-acre municipal garden with Hawaiian ethnic plants at the foot of the cathedral-like Koʻolau.

## Zone 4: North Shore

Year-round, the sleepy North Shore sugar town of **Haleʻiwa** offers another alternative Oʻahu, with its modest plantation-style buildings that house surf shops, clothing stores, art galleries, and restaurants.

The pace quickens considerably when the surf rises in winter, drawing the world's best wave riders and a whole lot of people who simply have never seen a 25-foot wave before, much less someone surfing on it.

The North Shore has relatively few places to stay—a youth hostel; a few beach cottages, campgrounds, and private vacation rentals; plus the condo units and hotel rooms of the only area resort, Turtle Bay Resort Golf and Country Club. But it is a great day-trip destination that shows Oʻahu's country face.

To the west from Haleʻiwa is Mokuleʻia, relatively undeveloped stretches of wild beach fronting old sugar lands. The road ends shortly after **Dillingham Airfield,** where gliders, sky-diving, biplanes, and other aerial thrill rides are based. Oʻahu may have nearly a million residents, but it doesn't have a paved road that goes around the entire island. Kaʻena Point (see below) is a wilderness area for hiking and other pursuits. You can walk or bike around to the Waiʻanae Coast, but you can't drive there.

Agricultural landscapes still dominate the middle and upper central valley areas that culminate in the North Shore.

## Zone 5: Leeward Coast

The hot, dry **Waiʻanae Coast** is sheltered from view and separated from the rest of the island by the Waiʻanae Range. The beach area of **Makaha,** long a popular surf break, remains little explored and nearly unknown to visitors since the lone resort hotel closed several years ago. Some condos and timeshares exist—you can find affordable lodging in condos like the Hawaiian Princess and Makaha Beach Cabanas and in vacation rentals on the Internet.

Makaha means "gate" in Hawaiian, and it serves as the entry to Oʻahu's last true shoreline wilderness area, **Kaʻena Point Natural Area Reserve,** a world removed from Waikiki. On this remote shore at Oʻahu's western-most point, albatross nest in sand dunes, Hawaiian monk seals loll on empty beaches, and humpback whales cruise by in winter. Winter and spring bring the huge swells that draw surfers like magnets to this shore as well as to the North Shore communities around the point. But the paved road doesn't go through. You can drive to the end at **Yokohama Bay** (an old train used to stop here and drop off Japanese fishermen to fish the bay). Then it's a 90-minute walk down a dirt road to Ka'ena Point.

On the city end of the coast, the welcome mat will be out, and gilt-edged, at the nearest resort hotel, **'Ihilani Resort and Spa,** a luxurious retreat and elaborate spa with a man-made beach lagoon, beachfront suites, two fine-dining restaurants, and nearby, 18-hole **Ko Olina Golf Course.**

### Zone 6: Central O'ahu

The valley formed by Wai'anae Mountains on the west and Ko'olau Mountains on the east is a broad, scenic plain that from the sky resembles an avenue leading to **Pearl Harbor** and its war memorials. That's one path the Japanese warplanes took in 1941. On the way they bombed **Schofield Barracks Army installation,** halfway along the plain.

**Aloha Stadium,** the 50,000-seat facility that is home to annual NFL Pro Bowl games and other sports and entertainment events, neighbors **Pearl Harbor Naval Base.**

Today the Central Valley is still bucolic in the northern reaches, carpeted with gray-green rows of pineapple in the rich red dirt and wild cane where sugar plantations used to hold sway. You can stop at **Dole Pineapple Plantation** to learn about and taste the golden fruit, once a major Hawai'i crop. Toward the southern end are the newer suburbs of housing and shopping centers, including **Waikele Outlets.**

## Maui: The Valley Isle

**MAUI FACTS**

**Flower** Lokelani (rose)
**Color** Pink
**County Seat** Wailuku
**Area** 729 square miles
**Length** 48 miles
**Width** 26 miles
**Population** 128,094
**Highest Point** Haleakala (10,023 feet)
**Coastline** 120 miles

Maui's sunny resorts on its south and west coasts are mainly the reasons why just about everybody knows the name of this island, Hawai'i's second largest. Maui is composed of two volcanic masses joined by a valley with golden beaches and blue sea on either end. Then there's 10,000-foot

**Haleakala,** the dormant volcano whose sheer bulk forms more than half the island. But Maui seems to have more appeal than the sum of its parts. It combines a hint of the flash of Oʻahu with the genuine country attitudes of a rural plantation island and the sophisticated influence of its luxury spreads and the people who frequent them.

## Zone 7: Central Maui

Departing Kahului Airport, you may wonder why you came so far to see such familiar big-box landmarks (Costco, Wal-Mart, Barnes & Noble). Wander farther and you'll find more shopping centers, neighborhoods of this amorphous waterfront town, the port, and, on either side, beaches. Once you get beyond the retail center, you soon discover why everyone raves about Maui.

The famous windsurfing areas, **Kanaha and Hoʻokipa Beaches,** are just beyond the airport on the way to Hana. In the opposite direction, a small road wanders off toward Waiheʻe and eventually around the whole northwest shoulder of Maui to the western resort coast. This is one of Maui's most scenic and unspoiled drives along sea cliffs and through large ranches, although housing developments are threatening to overtake parts of it. The pavement narrows to one lane often as it winds around the base of the **West Maui Mountains,** so mind the road.

Up beyond Kahului is the county seat of **Wailuku,** historic and quaint, and the countryside immediately gets greener as you approach **ʻIao Valley State Park.**

The isthmus valley is a sea of waving green sugar cane fields, a vanishing sight in the Islands. Above it pokes the smokestack of still functional **Puʻunene Sugar Mill.**

From Kahului Airport the main roads lead to resort areas: Follow the signs to Kihei/Wailea/Makena in South Maui, Maʻalaea in the middle, and Lahaina, Kaʻanapali Beach Resort, and Kapalua Resort in West Maui. The Haleakala Highway leads up the flank of the mountain, and the Hana Highway along the North Shore leads around the back of Haleakala to the ranch village of Hana, hiding near the end of this windy road with its plentiful waterfalls.

## Zone 8: South Maui

A 20-minute ride through the cane brings you to the resort coast. **Wailea, Makena,** and **Kihei** are the resorts of choice to the south. Straight ahead is **Maʻalaea,** home of condos; the **Maui Ocean Center Aquarium;** and the harbor where the boats for many snorkel, whale-watching, and other cruise tours are sheltered.

If you're after sun on a budget, go to Kihei. When money's no object or the boss is paying or you're pining for spectacular golf, go to Kapalua or

Wailea. Got your sociable kids along? Go to **Ka'anapali,** where they can enjoy the action. Want more solitude and less bustle? Head for serene Makena at Maui's southern end. When time is no object, go to **Hana** and stay awhile in the quaint seaside village.

Thrifty travelers find affordable condos in Kihei, a beachside strip lined with shops and malls. Kihei is also the home of many people who work in the neighboring resorts, as well as the Air Force Super Computer complex nearby. The town fronts a ten-mile coast indented by black lava reefs that frame some excellent gold sand pocket beaches and broad strand beach parks. Most popular is **Kamaole Beach III,** in the heart of Kihei with a tree-shaded grass picnic area and park, views of Lana'i and Kaho'olawe, and free parking.

Hollywood celebrities, conference-goers, and honeymooners love Wailea Resort, a lush, groomed beauty spot where luxury and deluxe hotels share several great beaches with green space in between. The lower slope of Haleakala helps the mid-rise hotels hide from view. **Grand Wailea Resort Hotel & Spa, Four Seasons Maui, Outrigger Wailea Beach, Renaissance Wailea Beach,** and Arabian fantasy-styled **Fairmont Kea Lani** are interspersed with plushy waterfront condo homes and resorts. These temples of pleasure feature the renowned Grand Wailea spa and lesser spas; an elaborate water complex with mini-river canyons, slides, dives, waterfall caves, and a water-powered elevator so swimmers don't have to walk back up at Grand Wailea; gourmet restaurants; and suites costing up to about $10,000 a night.

Those who seek seclusion will find it beyond Wailea at Makena Resort, where the **Maui Prince Hotel** stands alone amid 1,800 acres of dryland keawe forest and several splendid beaches. South Maui is punctuated by Pu'uolai, a cinder-cone peninsula that juts into the sea. Makena is an old village where cattle from the upland 'Ulupalakua Ranch were once herded into the water to swim for the ships that would take them to market. The tiny community has a picturesque Hawaiian-language church by the water. Haleakala's last eruption spilled down to the sea south of Makena about 1790. It's now traversed by rough hiking trails. There the road ends.

Wailea Resort has three scenic golf courses, and Makena adds two more. Horseback riding, a sporting clay shooting range, hiking, a coastal trail, a competition tennis complex, new **Shops at Wailea** shopping village, and a shuttle bus to connect them are all part of the South Maui appeal.

### Zone 9: West Maui

Head to the right from Ma'alaea around the foot of the West Maui Mountains and you'll approach historic **Lahaina** town and **Ka'anapali Beach Resort,** prize-winning progenitor of the planned resort complex popular in Hawai'i and other destinations.

Lahaina, the old whaling capital, retains charm because of its quaint and preserved historic buildings. It's a happy, honky-tonk jumble of art galleries, coral jewelry and T-shirt boutiques, bars, restaurants ranging from David Paul's Lahaina Grill to waterfront Pacific 'O to Cheeseburger in Paradise, and 'Ulalena, the best theatrical show in all Hawai'i (see page 451 for details). You can elect to stay at the century-old **Pioneer Inn** for a real taste of history. It was once the hangout of lusty whalers on R&R, until the disapproving missionaries prevailed. Lahaina also has a variety of condo resorts, inns, vacation rentals, and bed-and-breakfast rooms. Like in Key West, in Lahaina many people stop what they're doing and gather to watch when the sun starts dropping like a fireball behind Lana'i and the boats in Lahaina harbor.

Ka'anapali is a three-mile hop north of Lahaina, but when the traffic is heavy, it can take more than half an hour. After nearly 40 years, park-like Ka'anapali continues to reinvent itself and remains a most popular destination. The 600-acre resort has two golf courses, mid-rise blocks of deluxe and luxury hotels and condos that line the four-mile beach and dot the hillside behind it, restaurants with a full range of open-air, ocean-view dining, and **Whalers Village Shopping Center.** The shops now include upscale European boutiques in an effort to attract Japanese shoppers. Ka'anapali also includes beachfront tennis, public accessways and beach parks, and a shuttle that connects to Kapalua/West Maui Airport (small aircraft).

Farther north, the luxury coast culminates in **Kapalua Resort,** part of a 23,000-acre pineapple plantation with rows of spiky plants that stretch for miles in hilly fields below Pu'u Kukui, second tallest peak on Maui. This is the most beautiful part of West Maui, its wide-open vistas framed by Moloka'i offshore and wild lands to the north. Two hotels, several luxury condo resorts, three notable golf courses, and, for contrast, the tidy, prim red plantation buildings share this setting. The roads are lined with signature Islands pines. Kapalua-bound guests can fly from Honolulu to West Maui Airport and avoid the congestion of Kahului. The hotel will send a limo to meet you.

If Kapalua is outside your budget, investigate the resorts and condos of **Napili Beach** right next door on the southern side of the resort. You can enjoy many of the same benefits.

### Zone 10: Upcountry Maui and Beyond

From central Kahului, a country road runs up Haleakala's lower slope and winds through the cool, pastoral community of **Kula,** where, at 3,000 feet, exotic protea, roses, carnations, and blue jacaranda trees bloom. Visitors can stay at **Kula Lodge** or in a variety of bed-and-breakfast bungalows. Kula is on the way to **Haleakala National Park.** It's an escape from tropical heat, featuring botanical gardens, flower farms, and the winery at 'Ulupalakua, **Tedeschi Vineyards.** They sell a lot of pineapple wine, but you can also taste other vintages and sparkling wine at the tasting room. A cool grassy setting under wild avocado trees is fine for picnics.

Maui's most famous road—the **Hana Highway**—takes you winding by magnificent sea views, waterfalls, and botanical gardens on a skinny road for 53 miles to the ultimate tropical retreat. Count on three hours each way for the drive to Hana, more if you stop to swim in waterfall pools. The small coastal village is populated by Hawaiians (and a few celebrities) who wisely resist change. The rich and famous fly to Hana in small planes, and you can too. There is a small airport served by planes from Kahului.

A stay on Maui promises sunny beaches, great golf on championship courses, winter whale watching, snorkeling and sailing, hikes, sunrise at Haleakala Crater, and a quiet nightlife outside of Kihei and Lahaina.

While the island caters to the wealthy and free-spending corporate incentive winners at many elegant hotels and resort condos, it also offers some affordable bargains for budget travelers. Hikers and campers like Maui for its natural attractions and parks.

Folks who live on Maui have the motto, "Maui No Ka Oi," which means Maui is the best. Satisfied readers of *Condé Nast Traveler* agree. For five years in a row, they've named Maui the "best island in the world."

## Hawai'i: The Big Island

**HAWAI'I FACTS**

**Flower**  Red lehua
**Color**  Red
**County Seat**  Hilo
**Area**  4,028 square miles
**Length**  93 miles
**Width**  76 miles
**Population**  148,677
**Highest Point**  Mauna Kea (13,796 feet)
**Coastline**  266 miles

Long before tourism became Hawai'i's livelihood, the pluckiest visitors were those who journeyed high above Hilo more than a century ago to see a live, erupting volcano. The volcano shows no sign of stopping. In its current phase, **Kilauea Volcano** has been erupting since January 1, 1983, adding ever more real estate to the already big Big Island of Hawai'i. **Mauna Loa,** the most voluminous structure on earth, is quiet but still active. It last erupted in 1984.

If you have but one day to spend on the Big Island, see Kilauea at **Hawai'i Volcanoes National Park.**

The Big Island not only has five volcanoes (Kilauea, **Mauna Kea,** Mauna Loa, **Hualalai,** and **Kohala**) but also a sixth one, a work in progress named **Lo'ihi,** now a seamount emerging from the ocean floor off the southeast coast. You can stargaze at the 9,000-foot-level Visitor Center of the 13,796-foot Mauna Kea, tallest mountain in the tropical Pacific, where the air is so clear and dark that scientists have set up a forest of high-tech telescopes to peer into deep space. If you are hardy, you can hike to the sub-Arctic summit of slightly shorter 13,680-foot-high Mauna Loa. Both mountains rise more than 30,000 feet from the ocean floor, making them technically the tallest mountains on the planet.

Some visitors head for **Ka Lae** or **South Point,** the windswept southernmost point in the United States, where carbon dating on fish hooks shows early Polynesians arrived around AD 650. Others go to **Holualoa,** an artists' village amid boutique backyard coffee farms on the hillside over Kailua. And lucky ones enjoy a sunny day in **Hilo,** gateway to the volcano park.

The Big Island is the only Hawaiian island big enough to take a road trip of more than an hour or two. Plan on three days to see natural attractions like **Akaka Falls, Waipio Valley,** Hawai'i Volcanoes National Park, the catch of the day at **Honokohau Harbor,** the coffee plantations of **Kona,** and **Pu'u Honua O Honaunau,** the ancient refuge where hapless victims and law breakers could find sanctuary and forgiveness.

The once drowsy Big Island appeals now to a wider variety of visitors than ever. Adventurers, vulcanologists, astronomers, hunters of trophy marlin, and other lovers of the great outdoors now are joined by golfers, international conferees, and the rich and famous.

## Zone 11: Kona

Kona is the word for "leeward" in Hawaiian, and it usually means warm and still. The Big Island's Kona Coast is the area where several hulking volcanoes act to block the ever-blowing northeast winds and calm the sea. Kailua-Kona is the fishing village-turned-junior-Waikiki that serves as headquarters for the Kona district. It's filled with affordable condos, hotel rooms, and suites (none of them terribly appealing) as well as shopping plazas, restaurants, and bars. Beaches are noticeably in short supply, although the King Kamehameha Kona Beach Hotel has one. Instead, this is primarily a rocky shoreline where the waters are so dependably docile that walkways, restaurants, and rooms hang right over the floodlit waves in several places.

To the south of Kailua-Kona is the somewhat tonier Keauhou Resort, with many deluxe condo resorts like the Kanaloa and a renovated hotel worth a try, the Aston Keauhou Beach Resort, which has historic features (King Kalakaua's summer cottage and small fish pond) on the handsome grounds, a spa, a tide pool under parts of it, and **Disappearing Sands Beach** next door.

To the north of the airport and Honokokau Harbor, where the world-famous Kona Coast marlin fishing fleet is moored, the lava spilled by Hualalai Volcano about 200 years ago lines the highway in endless, desolate reaches of black. The first time we saw it, we had decided to hold green Kaua'i for another visit and opted instead for the raw island of big hot volcanoes. Somewhere north of Kailua-Kona, our hearts sank. Then we cut across the lava to find palm-edged oases by the sea and discovered some of the world's great beach resorts.

The first is the area of **Ka'upulehu,** an ancient fishing village before it was overrun by lava and later metamorphosed into low-rise bungalow resorts. Honeymooners, CEOs, and families (except in September, when it is a kid-free zone) alike seek the Kona Village Resort, a low-key but expensive enclave of romantic, traditional private bungalows on the real ancient village site between the beach and surrounding protective lava. Kona Village has petroglyph fields, a famous lu'au, tennis, and many other pluses, but it is the only resort along this stretch of coast without a world-famous championship golf course. Next door is its new, opulent, and equally romantic modern neighbor, Four Seasons Resort Hualalai, which borders a golf course, exclusive condos and homes, and several swimming pools, including one made to look like a lava tide pool complete with tropical fish.

Up the highway at Waikoloa Beach Resort, the Hilton Waikoloa Village is a fantasy resort where you can swim with captive dolphins, ride a sleek silver tram to your tower, or take an Italian launch on a rail through a second-story waterway. The pools, falls, and water slide are so elaborate that you can forget there's no natural beach. But a postcard-perfect beach is next door at **'Anaeho'omalu Bay,** fronting the completely revamped deluxe Outrigger Waikoloa Beach Resort. Both hotels have spas, and the resort features two golf courses, the **Kings Village** shops, restaurants, and well-maintained historic features.

Next up the highway to the north is Mauna Lani Resort, with golf, tennis, walking trails, historic features, and the luxurious Mauna Lani Bay Hotel & Bungalows, where you'll find butlered hideouts beside the beach and **Orchid at Mauna Lani,** where you can bliss out with a massage in a tent by the sea at a "spa without walls."

Just north of Mauna Lani is **Mauna Kea Beach Resort,** home of the venerable **Mauna Kea Beach Hotel** and newer **Hapuna Beach Prince,** two golf courses, access to the two best beaches on the island, and all the bells and whistles wealth can summon. Hotels and golf courses on sites carved from beachfront lava can be traced to 1965, when Laurance Rockefeller opened the Mauna Kea Beach Hotel on a superlative beach that belonged to **Parker Ranch,** then the largest privately held cattle spread in the nation. The simple, elegant resort became a top choice of executives in search of a comfortable retreat, and their heirs kept up the tradition. ("Now I know where old Republicans go to die," once quipped Merv Griffin.) The art-filled hotel set the tone for all luxury Hawai'i beach resorts to come.

History is right on the surface throughout this coast—Kona Village, Waikoloa, and Mauna Lani Resorts all serve as stewards of petroglyph fields, lava beds covered with thousands of ancient primitive drawings. Mauna Lani and Waikoloa also boast well-kept ancient fishpond complexes with signage to tell you how they work. Federal and state parks preserve cultural monuments throughout this area.

Vacation rentals and bed-and-breakfasts are plentiful in Upcountry Holualoa, in the coffee country above Kailua-Kona, and in Waimea, Parker Ranch headquarters and a charming ranch town. Parker Ranch has a historic compound and rodeo grounds.

### Zone 12: Hilo and Volcano

Hilo tourism facilities were set up decades ago with great expectations for a tourism boom that didn't quite materialize. Some of the large hotels on Banyan Drive on **Hilo Bay** were transformed into residential dwellings. Reasonable rates predominate at the remaining ones, and some have been upgraded in recent years.

Hilo has a historic downtown district and a quiet charm. It gets plenty of rain and has the attributes of a wet, warm place—abundant flowers and tropical fruit (bananas hang in the lobbies of some hotels), huge shady trees, waterfalls and streams, and triple rainbows. Our recommendation is to stay a night or two at **Shipman House,** a restored Victorian bed-and-breakfast in a beautiful Hilo neighborhood, and to spend your days exploring Hawai'i Volcanoes National Park and the nearby lava-watch area at **Kalapana,** where hot lava may still be rolling into the sea when you are there. Both are less than an hour's drive away. Stroll through one of Hilo's famous gardens, such as the **Onomea Tropical Botanical Garden,** go for a swim in Hilo Bay, and enjoy the uncrowded pace. The **Lyman Mission House Museum** in downtown Hilo is an excellent small facility whose exhibits will give you a feel for life of early immigrants to the area.

Vacation rentals and bed-and-breakfasts make up the accommodations in upcountry Volcano, where you'll find charming lodging like Tom and Brenda Carson's 1925 tin-roofed **Volcano Cottage** and tasty dinners along with quaint rooms at **Kilauea Lodge** in the misty fern forests.

If your goal is to get back to nature, the Big Island is your choice; there is too much to see and do in the great outdoors in just a week, including skiing on the occasionally snowcapped cinders. But if you only have a week, spend two days at Hawai'i Volcanoes National Park, staying in Hilo or a nearby cottage, two days sightseeing or pursuing other activities, then splurge for three days at Kona Village, Four Seasons Hualalai, or Outrigger's Waikoloa Beach Resort, some personal favorites.

## Kaua'i: the Garden Isle

---

### KAUA'I FACTS

**Flower** Mokihana
**Color** Purple
**County Seat** Lihu'e
**Area** 549 square miles
**Length** 33 miles
**Width** 25 miles
**Population** 58,463
**Highest Point** Kawaikiki Peak (5,243 feet)
**Coastline** 90 miles

---

### *Zone 13: Kaua'i*

The island's a beauty all right, where roadside forests are a riot of flowering vines and mangos fall ripe to the ground. But it's not just another pretty place. It's tough and gritty and made for adventure. In modern times, it survived two monster hurricanes in a decade. In olden times, it was the only island to resist Kamehameha the Great's military attempt to unite the kingdom in the late 1700s, although its independent-minded chiefs gave up without a fight later when it seemed appropriate. While the young Big Island is still black with lava in many spots and raw with new life, Kaua'i is the oldest major island, and its jagged peaks, mantle of green over steep cliffs, and shoreline of fine beaches are all testimony to the scenic inevitability of erosion.

When you go you can hang out a fancy hotel in **Princeville** on the North Shore or **Po'ipu Beach** on the South Shore, or choose the so-called **Coconut Coast** in between, sipping Blue Hawai'i's by the pool, or you can get out and discover the island's true nature. Or both. The combination of rough nature and indulgent luxury is all the rage in Hawai'i.

Some hike into the 3,000-foot-deep **Waimea Canyon,** a multicolored chasm, or brave the cliff-side 11-mile Kalalau Trail that winds along the remote **Na Pali Coast.** Some go up to **Koke'e State Park** and venture into the cloud forests on the boardwalk trail into **Alaka'i Swamp,** last haunt of the Kaua'i 'O'o, a black bird with bright yellow thigh feathers. This 20-square-mile highland bog is home to rare plants, native birds, Hawai'i's only native land mammal, the Hoary Bat, and a mosquito-eating plant.

Others angle for big-game fish off nearby **Ni'ihau,** snorkel **Ke'e Beach's** fishy lagoon, and helicopter up to the 5,243-foot-high summit of **Mt. Wai'ale'ale,** a crater ribboned with waterfalls as befitting the wettest spot in the world. Twenty inches of rain in a single day is common.

All that water refreshes Kaua'i's seven rivers (you can kayak on the **Huleia, Hanalei,** and **Wailua**) and keeps the Garden Island the great green place it is.

Where to stay depends on the weather. Anyplace on Kaua'i can be sunny and hot, but showers are most likely to cool the moody green Hanalei (heavenly garland) area on the North Shore, a real-life version of movie land's Bali Hai (South Pacific was shot up here, a movie anyone over 50 might remember). Princeville Resort, a California-like development on a sea-cliff plateau with a spectacular view, has homes, condos, the Princeville Hotel with its over-the-top marble lobby, shopping, restaurants, a spa, and world-famous golf at Princeville Golf Course. Part of it overlooks **Hanalei Bay,** the taro patches of the **Hanalei River Valley,** a mile-long crescent beach, and the bowl of 4,000-foot cliffs creased by waterfalls that surrounds the valley. Seven miles beyond friendly, picturesque Hanalei town, the road ends at Ke'e Beach and an ancient footpath leads into the Na Pali wilderness. No roads cross the northwest section of the island, a series of dramatic deep valleys carved by ancient streams.

Midway between Hanalei and Po'ipu is the Coconut Coast, including a number of small communities from **Kapa'a** past the Wailua River to **Lihu'e,** the county seat and site of the airport. Affordable to deluxe beachfront condos and hotels share a golden beach. Water conditions can be rugged for all but surfers and body surfers. There is a sheltered swimming area at **Lydgate Park** by the river mouth. **Coconut Marketplace** offers most of the shopping and restaurants.

Lihu'e, mostly devoted to commerce and county government, has a museum worth a stop—the small coral-block **Kaua'i Museum** on Rice Street. Kaua'i Lagoons by the airport was once a pinnacle of the fantasy resort movement, but the 1992 hurricane rearranged its priorities. What's there now is the Kaua'i Marriott, part hotel and part timeshares, with an opulent lobby and ballroom/conference complex, seven-acre pool, extensive art collection, two well-regarded golf courses, and other amenities. Heading south, the highway passes a handsome historic manor on the right, known as **Kilohana.** It has been made into boutiques, where you'll see fine examples of Ni'ihau shell jewelry artistry, crafts and galleries, and a restaurant. It will give just a taste of how sweet life was for the onetime owners, the Wilcox family, on Kaua'i when sugar was king.

Sunseekers and families like Po'ipu Beach Resort, a coastal complex with a good swimming beach, golf courses, a tennis complex, several notable restaurants, a wide range of plentiful condo resorts, and a hotel row redefined by the 1992 hurricane. Hotels never get too old on Kaua'i. Presently Po'ipu features the Hyatt Regency Kaua'i Hotel, a fine example of Hawai'i-style art deco architecture, on the southern end and Sheraton Kaua'i Resort on the northern end.

Children and some adults get a kick out of **Spouting Horn,** a lava tube where surf sometimes shoots sea water 50 feet into the air. Inland from the resort area, **Koloa Town** is where the Hawaiian sugar industry was born more than 150 years ago. Now it's a collection of restaurants, bars, and surf-n-sun shops that you pass through to get from the highway to the beach.

Looking for flowers on the Garden Isle? Serious green thumbs go to **Lawai** to visit **National Tropical Botanical Garden,** a Congressionally chartered research facility whose 186 acres include an important collection of rare tropical plants, tropical experimental gardens, and, for contrast, the finely trimmed formal gardens of a former royal estate.

Honeymooners and couples seeking a romantic getaway will enjoy Kaua'i, as will those who come back with tiny shells in their pockets and red dirt on their hiking shoes.

## Moloka'i: the Friendly Isle

### MOLOKA'I FACTS

**Flower**  White kukui blossom
**Color**  Green
**County Seat**  Kaunakakai
**Area**  260 square miles
**Length**  38 miles
**Width**  10 miles
**Population**  6,717
**Highest Point**  Kamakou Peak (4,961 feet)
**Coastline**  88 miles

## Zone 14: Moloka'i

If you crave bright lights and busy nights, best avoid Moloka'i. The least-developed of Hawai'i's main islands, Moloka'i can be described by what it doesn't have: traffic lights, shopping malls, nightclubs. The lifestyle is slow and unpretentious, and people pride themselves on being a more traditional Hawaiian community.

For better or worse, Moloka'i has spurned, or been spared, "progress." Actually the island has sustained a number of economic hits over recent years—sugar and pineapple production ceased, residents decided against new hotels and tourism, and federal officials ordered all the cows killed to stamp out an obscure ailment that had been around for decades. Kalu-ako'i Resort, with its seaside golf course, blocks of unappealing hotel rooms in a park-like setting, and hotel services, closed down last year.

Islanders grow some prized produce, such as watermelons, sweet potatoes, boutique miniature veggies, honey, coffee, and macadamia nuts. Moloka'i folks are uncommonly friendly and down-home. And honest. Once we inadvertently left a return airplane coupon ticket at the rental car counter in Moloka'i's tiny airport. Three days later, it was still there—not far from the sign reminding passengers that airline rules prohibit carrying watermelons in the overhead racks.

If this is beginning to sound like your kind of place, read on.

The island is not a destination for everyone, especially those who like creature comforts, although there are some. The beaches are wild and lengthy but not usually safe or desirable for swimming. The greatest natural feature, the world's tallest sea cliffs on the jungled North Shore, is virtually inaccessible. The most famous, and poignant, attraction is an isolated but still inhabited former leprosy colony and the mule ride down a steep switchback trail to get there. **Kalaupapa National Park,** where Hansen's Disease victims were banished by royal edict in the 1860s, was the last home of famed Belgian priest Father Damien, who gave his own life treating the sick.

Why go to Moloka'i? Adventurers, families, those who love the great outdoors: This island's for you. There's plenty to do: mountain biking, horse back riding, snorkeling, diving, kayaking, fishing. The Nature Conservancy runs preserves and hike programs at **Mo'omomi Dunes,** where bones of flightless birds surface and at **Kamakou** in the high country, a cloud forest filled with rare native plants. Hikers have been known to trek through scenic **Halawa Valley** wilderness on the East End, although the ancient Hawaiian settlement was declared off-limits to visitors by the private owner. Check the status when you are on-island.

Sightseers find an odd assortment of natural and historic sites like ancient fishponds, the **Smith-Bronte Landing** (where the first airplane to Hawai'i crash-landed in 1927), **Mapalehu Mango Grove,** and **'Ili'ili'opae Heiau,** temple ruins of an ancient school of sacrificial rites.

The frontier-like town of **Kaunakakai** is a sleepy crossroads with a handful of stores and a beloved bakery. At Ho'olehua Post Office, you can address, stamp, and send a Moloka'i coconut home like a postcard.

Turn left out of town onto Kamehameha V Highway and you'll soon find the East End—lush, green, and tropical with ancient fishponds lining the coco-palm coast. Go right and you'll encounter the West End, arid and spiked with cactus. Condo resorts, bed-and-breakfasts, and vacation beach houses are available in either direction.

Go west to find Sheraton Molokai Lodge and Beach Village, with distinctive and recently built tourism facilities, including a stylish 22-room lodge, done in what might be called upscale paniolo (cowboy) decor recalling ranch history. The lodge has a fine-dining restaurant, capacious bar, and comfortable great room. A stay includes all the adventures you can sign up for, including mountain biking, kayaking, beach toys, and cultural hikes.

The rebuilt plantation town of **Maunaloa** encompasses the lodge and its Outfitters Center. The small community now offers movies, shops, eateries (including the island's first genuine fast-food joint, a Kentucky Fried Chicken outlet), and new, "affordable" plantation-style homes that start at $250,000. Some locals don't take well to change and are still seething.

However, the island has generally retained it's pastoral character. The **Moloka'i Ranch,** with 6,000 head of cattle, covers one third of Moloka'i, mostly with wide-open spaces. You're sure to get a good night's sleep overlooking quiet pastures and the sea. Just don't expect nightlife. After dark it's so quiet you can hear the cows dream.

## Lana'i: the Pineapple Island

---

### LANA'I FACTS

**Flower** Kaunaoa
**Color** Orange
**County Seat** Lana'i City
**Area** 141 square miles
**Length** 18 miles
**Width** 13 miles
**Population** 2,800
**Highest Point** Lana'ihale (3,366 feet)
**Coastline** 47 miles

---

## Zone 15: Lana'i

A short flight from Honolulu, Lana'i is a world removed. On this smallest of Hawai'i's six accessible islands, you can still see most of the island from its loftier spots.

Buildings are dwarfed by the rolling terrain of what was the world's biggest pineapple plantation until they gave it up in the 1980s and planted seeds for resorts and upscale tourism instead. The quaint plantation cottages of the ambitiously named village of **Lana'i City** are still there, in remarkable contrast to the elegant Lodge at Ko'ele, resembling a British hill station, and the lavish, Mediterranean-style Manele Bay Hotel, nestled on a coastal hillside.

When you land in the airport in Palawai Basin, where pineapple once grew as far as the eye could see, you discover an island of anomalies. It is rural yet sophisticated, with only three paved roads but a 100-mile network of red-dirt plantation lanes and a fleet of small SUVs to go four-wheeling on them. In former times, the days started with a plantation whistle at 5 a.m. Now, days in the sun begin with more discreet wakeup calls.

Lana'i is owned mostly by an American tycoon, who acquired it incidentally in a corporate purchase, and inhabited largely by Filipinos, who immigrated to work the pineapple fields and stayed to retrain as luxury hotel workers. Most plantation families still live there, sharing the streets of town with well-heeled world travelers and, increasingly, neighbors.

Golfers yearn to play either of the island's two magnificent 18-hole courses—the ocean-side **The Challenge at Manele** or the upland **The Experience at Koele,** possibly the most beautiful course anywhere. Yet while visitors are signing up for substantial fees, local golfers choose the little nine-hole upland course where fees are paid on the honor system, a few bucks in a tin can.

When it was a plantation, nobody went to Lana'i unless invited or fortunate enough to get one of the ten rooms in the 1920s-era Hotel Lana'i. Now the island appeals to those with means enough to enjoy peace and solitude. Pricey spreads are going up on the hillside so wealthy vacationers can stay longer under their own roofs.

Honeymooners, this is your island. Bill and Melissa Gates took over the island to get married here. Outdoors lovers like it, too. You can shoot clay pigeons at Lana'i Pine Shooting Clays or hunt real game like turkey, Mouflon sheep, and Axis deer. Lodge facilities include a riding stable and a couple of kinds of croquet on the lawns. Hiking trails lead off through the woods. Nightlife, however, is limited to whatever amusements the hotels have lined up.

Anyone who seeks peaceful surroundings with luxurious accommodations will want to visit Lana'i if only to explore a most atypical Pacific island. The island is a combination of hot, dry coastal cliffs and cool uplands with pine groves planted by a farsighted plantation manager long ago to trap clouds and bring water to the dry island. This is no tropical wonderland; its deep gorges and eroded plains speak of a hard agricultural life. But there's beauty to its hinterlands, headlands, and wide-open red dirt valley touched only by blue sky and puffy white clouds. While prowling the four-wheel roads, explorers can find historic sites like a crumbled sugar town and an ancient king's summer fishing residence.

On a clear day, from **Lana'ihale,** the 3,379-foot island summit, you can see five of the seven main Hawaiian islands in a single glance. Only distant Kaua'i and Ni'ihau remain over the horizon.

Overall, Lana'i is likely to appeal to anyone looking to get away from it all whatever the price. In addition to a half dozen bed-and-breakfasts, you have only two resort choices and the little lodge, all under the same ownership—you can go back and forth by shuttle van.

The lodge sits on a 1,700-foot-high hill at the head of a lane lined with tall pines and looks so important that you think a king might greet you instead of a uniformed hostess with a flower lei. It is cooler here, especially at night, which is why the lodge is a favorite with weekending Honolulu residents who love to dress up in sweaters and sit by a roaring fire. Downhill, beside the only safe swimming beach at **Hulopo'e Bay,** Manele Bay Hotel simmers around its pool, a lobby full of Asian art, and tropical gardens lining a man-made stream teeming with koi carp.

A drive into Lana'i City is like entering a time warp. Most of the island's residents live in tidy little tin-roofed plantation houses with a riot of flowers, fruits, and vegetables growing in their front yards. A few own their houses.

You can stop and "talk story" with the locals about the not-so-good old days when pineapple farming dominated life. And by all means, frequent the shops, restaurants, and art galleries in the tree-lined town square.

## A Brief History

Scientists believe the Hawaiian Islands were formed millions of years ago, each rising from a single "hot spot" on the floor of the Pacific Ocean and then moving north with shifting tectonic plates. The islands were barren until seeds carried by the wind or ocean currents took root and began to grow. Slowly but surely, birds and insects found their way to these islands, and humans too.

Historians believe seafaring Polynesian voyagers first discovered Hawai'i in the fourth century AD and took residence along the coasts and valleys where fresh water was plentiful. They introduced dogs, pigs, chickens, and plants, including taro, coconut, breadfruit, banana, sweet potato, and sugar cane. A second wave of Polynesian seafarers, this time from Tahiti, arrived some 500 years later.

The early Hawaiians embraced a simple lifestyle, living off the land and sea. Taro was a chief food source: Its root was pounded and mixed with water to make poi, the paste-like starch that remains a staple of Hawaiian diets and appears at every lu'au. Ahead of their time in understanding nature's ecosystem, early Hawaiians built and maintained large fishponds to ensure their chiefs an abundant supply of fish. Back then, a typical *hale* (house) was a wooden frame covered with pili grass; it looked like a haystack.

The Hawaiians lived under a strict caste system, and high-ranking *ali'i* (chiefs or rulers) wielded their power fully by imposing many *kapu* (laws or prohibitions). In some cases, even to cross the shadow of a powerful ali'i meant sure death. This was a system that brought much bickering among the people, adding to the hostilities among chiefs eager to gain more territory under their rule.

Still, the Hawaiians thrived. By the time Captain Cook arrived in the Islands in 1778, an estimated 400,000 Hawaiians were living on O'ahu, the Big Island of Hawai'i, Maui, Kaua'i, Moloka'i, Lana'i, Ni'ihau, and Kaho'olawe.

## Captain Cook's Arrival

On January 21, 1778, Captain James Cook, commander of Britain's *HMS Resolution* and *HMS Discovery*, became the first European to set foot on Hawaiian soil, landing at Waimea on the west coast of Kaua'i. Cook and his crew spent five days on Kaua'i before a short visit to Ni'ihau, where they traded salt and yams for goats, pigs, and water.

Cook's second contact with the Hawaiians occurred a year later, this time at Kealakekua on the Big Island. As fate would have it, his arrival coincided with the Hawaiians' annual *makahiki* celebration, a four-month festival honoring Lono, the god of peace, agriculture, and fertility. (Today, this event is echoed in the statewide Aloha Festivals.) Historians believe the Hawaiians, seeing these strange vessels heading for shore, thought it was Lono himself returning to the island. Cook and his men were treated to the greatest welcome in Hawai'i's history: Hawaiians greeted the ships by the thousands from the water, via surfboards and canoes, and from the shore. Cook wrote: "I have nowhere in this sea seen such a number of people assembled in one place; besides those in the canoes, all the shore of the bay was covered with people, and hundreds were swimming about the ship like shoals of fish."

After the makahiki ended and Lono-like Cook began to act more human, however, the Hawaiians were no longer quite so hospitable. A scuffle broke out and more than 200 warriors attacked Cook's landing party. Five British marines were killed, including Cook himself. His remains were buried in the deep blue water of Kealakekua Bay.

## The Kamehameha Dynasty

One Big Island warrior who took great interest in the foreigners was Kamehameha I. He had been wounded by a gun during the fight, and he realized that any chief who possessed such powerful weapons would have a decided advantage during battles.

Kamehameha set out to conquer all the Hawaiian Islands and bring them under his rule. He secured Maui and Lana'i in 1790, then conquered Maui again after losing it for a short time. He had his chief rival on the Big Island killed to claim sole leadership over the island. Then he conquered Moloka'i and O'ahu. Two attempts to invade Kaua'i failed. In 1810 Kaua'i's chief peacefully surrendered his island (and the neighboring island of Ni'ihau) to his persistent rival. The entire Hawaiian kingdom was finally unified under one ruler: King Kamehameha I.

Under Kamehameha's reign, trade with Europeans increased. Foreigners particularly valued Hawai'i's sandalwood, and the king allowed the exportation of the precious wood to China until the forests were cut to the ground and the supply exhausted.

Kamehameha succumbed to a lengthy illness in 1819 in the area now known as Kailua-Kona on the Big Island. His bones were hidden at a secret location "known only to the moon and the stars," believed to be somewhere on the Kona Coast. Historians estimate he was in his early 60s when he died.

His successor, his son Liholiho (Kamehameha II), had a short but eventful reign. Ka'ahumanu, the favorite of Kamehameha's numerous wives, made herself the joint ruler, or queen regent, of the Hawaiian kingdom and almost immediately abolished the despised *kapu* system of religious prohibitions. She did so by persuading Liholiho to sit down with her at a feast (it was kapu, or forbidden, for men and women to eat together). Seeing that the gods did not punish the guilty parties, Hawaiians' faith in their system crumbled. Ka'ahumanu and Liholiho declared that all idols and temples be destroyed.

Without their places of worship, the Hawaiians experienced a gaping spiritual vacuum. They were ripe for conversion when fate intervened. In 1820, 14 American missionaries from New England arrived aboard the brig *Thaddeus*. They preached in Honolulu and in Kona for what was supposed to be a one-year trial period. They never left. Those who came to do good did very well, as the saying goes, marrying Hawaiian royals and gaining land and power.

Liholiho and his queen, Kamamalu, died of the measles in 1924 in London, where they had journeyed in hopes of meeting King George IV. Liholiho's successor was his younger brother, Kauikeaouli (Kamehameha III). Ka'ahumanu, meanwhile, embraced Christianity and announced a new system of laws based on the missionaries' teachings.

The missionaries' impact on Hawai'i was to overwhelm the old culture. They built churches and schools throughout the Islands and condemned the people for their manner of dress. Hula, regarded by the missionaries as lewd, was banned. Christianity became the new religion in Hawai'i. The chiefs were converted first, and the commoners followed suit.

Kamehameha III took control of the kingdom in 1825. By then a new industry had replaced the exhausted sandalwood trade: whaling. From the mid-1820s through the 1850s, when whale blubber was replaced by oil as a source for light, the whaling industry was the kingdom's economic savior, and Lahaina became one of the most vital ports in the Pacific.

The king's 29-year reign was marked by several landmark events. The first came in 1843, when the Hawaiian kingdom fell to British control for a brief time. More significantly, in 1848 Kauikeaouli issued the Great Mahele, which divided Hawai'i's lands among the monarchy, government, and common people. For the first time, the working class could own land. Just two years later, foreigners were also allowed to own land, and 40 years after the Great Mahele was decreed, two-thirds of all government lands belonged to foreigners.

By this time, the introduction of foreign diseases, including syphilis and smallpox, to the defenseless Hawaiians, who had no immunity, was taking a terrible toll. By the end of Kamehameha III's reign, the Hawaiian population dropped to 70,000.

Sugar was fast emerging as the new lifeblood of the Islands economy, and Kauikeaouli knew he had to find more laborers to work in the plantations. With the population in steep decline, he turned to contract workers from foreign countries—the Chinese first, in 1852, when 293 laborers began working on the plantations for $3 a month. Then came the Japanese, Portuguese, Filipinos, Koreans, Puerto Ricans, Okinawans, Germans, Russians, and Spaniards. By the turn of the century, Polynesians were no longer the majority of Hawai'i's population.

Kauikeaouli died in 1854, and his nephew Alexander Liholiho ascended the throne as Kamehameha IV. He reigned for eight years before dying of an asthmatic attack at 29. His brother, Lot (Kamehameha V), served as king from 1863 to 1872, and upon his death, William Lunalilo was elected his successor. Lot's cousin, the Princess Bernice Pauahi, had been next in line to take the throne but adamantly refused. Lunalilo's reign was short-lived, however—he died after only a year as king.

## The Merrie Monarch

David Kalakaua was elected to succeed Lunalilo, and his tenure as Hawai'i's king proved to be as colorful as the man himself. Known as the "Merrie Monarch" for his passion for Hawaiian music and dance, Kalakaua began to restore traditional Hawaiian culture. He commissioned construction of 'Iolani Palace, an extravagant masterpiece. With a fondness for the good life, he took a trip around the world, hosted gala balls, and bet on local horse races.

Kalakaua was the first reigning king to visit Washington to meet with the president, Ulysses S. Grant, and Congress. The *New York Herald* reported, "[Kalakaua] is no common king, but one to whom we can give our allegiance with a clean conscience for we believe him to be a good man who has the happiness of his nation at heart." Kalakaua returned home with a desirable reciprocity treaty giving Hawai'i "favored nation" status and eliminating tariffs on sugar.

While recognizing the benefits of a strong relationship with America, Kalakaua fought to maintain Hawai'i's independence. The stronger the sugar industry grew, however, the more power shifted from the king to influential American businessmen. In 1887, an armed insurrection by this foreign political group forced Kalakaua to accept a new constitution that severely diminished his authority. The king's remaining years weren't happy ones, as he was relegated to a figurehead role in government. His health failing, he sought treatment in California in 1891. He died that year in San Francisco's Palace Hotel.

## End of the Monarchy

Kalakaua's successor, his sister Lili'uokalani, was determined to restore the Hawaiian monarchy to power. But, the queen was severely outmatched. In January 1893, pro-annexation forces struck. John B. Stevens, the U.S. Minister in Hawai'i, ordered American Marines from the visiting USS *Boston* to occupy Honolulu. It was a daring move that was not authorized by Washington, but it worked: The next day, a new government led by Sanford B. Dole was in place. Lili'uokalani was forced to abdicate her throne.

President Grover Cleveland was dismayed by the action, calling it "an act of war against a peaceful nation." His attempts at reinstating Lili'uokalani as Hawai'i's ruler, however, were resisted by Congress. In 1894, the new government, the Republic of Hawai'i, named Dole as its first president.

In January 1895, a group of royalists led by Robert Wilcox attempted a coup. The battle lasted for two weeks, with skirmishes erupting at Diamond Head Crater and in Manoa Valley, Punchbowl, and other sites on O'ahu. Ultimately, the revolt failed, and the government arrested the royalists and the queen, charging them with treason. She was imprisoned at 'Iolani Palace—her own home—for nearly a year.

In 1898, members of the republic got what they had wanted all along: Hawai'i was annexed to the United States. Two years later, it became a U.S. territory.

## World War II and Statehood

The next four decades brought the birth of Hawai'i's tourist industry as well as the sweet days of pineapple and sugar, backbone of the islands' economic system.

Then came December 7, 1941, when Japanese war planes bombed Pearl Harbor. The bombs sunk the USS *Arizona* and sent 1,200 sailors aboard the 608-foot battleship to a watery grave. The air raid on Hawai'i brought America to war with the battle cry: "Remember Pearl Harbor!"

Islands residents, devastated by the attack, enlisted and did what they could at home to support the American effort. In Waikiki hotels, were closed to visitors, then reopened to accommodate servicemen. The famed "Pink Palace," the Royal Hawaiian Hotel, was turned into an R&R center for military officers on leave. Barbed wire was strung all along the beach.

In the years following the war, Hawai'i pursued statehood and finally won it on August 21, 1959. The *Honolulu Advertiser* reported, "A phone call from Governor Quinn in Washington today is expected to set off the biggest winging in Island history to celebrate Statehood Day . . . the 52 air raid sirens on O'ahu will start screaming out the news . . . . Every church bell in town will begin pealing. Every ship in harbor will blow her whistle. Most folks will do a little shouting on their own, and, of course, there's nothing to stop you from hula-ing in the streets if you want to." And they did. President Dwight D. Eisenhower made it official, signing the proclamation welcoming Hawai'i as the 50th state in the union.

Not all Hawaiians favored statehood, but they were too few to stand in the way of history, and a once-proud Polyneisan nation became an American state.

# Hawai'i's Diverse Population

One of the outstanding features of Hawai'i is the diversity of its people. In the 50th state, no ethnic group comprises a majority of the state's population. The breakdown is as follows:

| | |
|---|---|
| Caucasian | 23.3% |
| Japanese | 20.0% |
| Filipino | 10.4% |
| Chinese | 4.6% |
| Black | 1.8% |
| Korean | 1.4% |
| Hawaiian | 0.8% |
| Samoan | 0.5% |
| Puerto Rican | 0.4% |
| Mixed race | 37.0% (about half are part-Hawaiian) |

Each ethnic group has made its mark on Hawaiian culture, contributing its foods, arts, music, and customs to Hawai'i's melting pot community. Many cultural groups hold annual festivals in Honolulu to celebrate their heritage—a great chance to sample the food, music, dance, national dress, and pride of the culture at hand. Several cultures share a passionate affinity for one form of noisy celebration: fireworks, which are more abundant in Hawai'i than anywhere else in the country. Fireworks are big for western New Year, Chinese New Year, Japanese New Year, Fourth of July, and, for good measure, every Friday night at the Hilton Hawaiian Village in Waikiki.

The Chinese were the islands' first immigrants. Nearly 300 workers from southeastern China came to the islands in 1852 after signing five-year contracts to work the sugar plantations for food, clothing, shelter, and a salary of $3 per month. Most of the Chinese lived near Honolulu Harbor on O'ahu and Lahaina on Maui. It was in Honolulu where Dr. Sun Yat-sen, regarded as the father of modern China, founded the Hsing Chung Hui, a revolutionary group instrumental in China's movement against foreign powers. The Chinese influence on the local community is visible today in the distinctively Hawaiian-style Chinese New Year celebrations, Chinese cuisine and arts, Chinese heritage of many prominent citizens, and a little Chinese blood in many local residents.

The first Japanese immigrants arrived in 1868 to work on the plantations. Although the conditions were often miserable, more Japanese made their way to what they referred to as Tenjiku, or "Heavenly Place." By the beginning of the twentieth century, more than 60,000 Japanese laborers and their families lived in Hawai'i. Like all immigrants, Japanese faced racial prejudices, but far more so after Japan's attack on Pearl Harbor. Many Japanese-Americans were taken away to internment camps on the mainland, and many more lost their family businesses, even though not a single case of Japanese-American treason or sabotage was ever documented. But, they rebounded strongly in Hawai'i after the war, gained prominence in politics and education, and integrated Japanese customs and design into everyday life. Today, Japanese-Americans are a major presence in Hawai'i, and most residents embrace at least some degree of Japanese custom, including removing shoes before entering a home. Sushi, sashimi, mochi, and miso soup are part of the Hawaiian table.

In 1903, the first Koreans arrived to work on the plantations. Ambitious and hardworking, Koreans today have the highest education and income level per capita of any ethnic group on the islands. Korean cuisine is extremely popular among Hawaiian residents, and you'll find Korean restaurants in every town. Try beef kal-bi (marinated beef) with rice and spicy kim chee (pickled vegetables).

A group of 15 Filipino laborers began working on Islands plantations in 1906; by mid-century, that number had swelled to 125,000. Every summer, the Filipina Fiesta festivals, held throughout the state, celebrate the colorful traditions and customs of the Filipino culture. Dishes such as chicken adobo and lumpia are favorites on any local menu.

Samoans are among the newer ethnic groups in Hawai'i, arriving from American Samoa shortly after the end of World War I. Most settled in the Mormon community in La'ie on O'ahu. Their many contributions to the islands include the celebrated fire-knife dance that highlights most Polynesian lu'au. Local Samoans have also made their mark in the world of football: In the 1990s, Jesse Sapolu (San Francisco 49ers), Mark Tuinei (Dallas Cowboys), and Ma'a Tanuvasa (Denver Broncos) all played significant roles in helping their teams win Super Bowl championships.

In multicultural Hawai'i, intermarriage is the norm rather than the exception, and a dizzying number of ethnic groups coexist at both the top and bottom of the economic scale. This tends to even things out. The ability to get along, born of necessity in plantation villages and perfected in the modern mix, may be Hawai'i's most valuable contribution, far more lasting than a suntan and an aloha shirt.

In order to get along, plantation people from around the world had to communicate, so they developed Hawaiian pidgin—a true creole language according to many scholars, one that borrows words and grammar from several languages. Pidgin endures today, despite efforts of many in and outside the education system to stamp it out, at least in school. Unofficially, it is lovingly cultivated as a kind of jive talk among kids, families, friends, and lovers. You'll see graffiti in pidgin. It's also still useful, since myriad ethnic immigrants continue to arrive. (See page 171 for a quick lesson in pidgin basics.)

Most people are proud of their diversity, but ethnic prejudices and stereotypes still occur. Caucasians can be the targets of slurs and jokes, along with everybody else. The word *haole* (foreigner) is widely used to refer to Caucasians, usually in a descriptive way. When using words to describe islanders, beware of a linguistic minefield. Don't call us

"Hawaiians" unless you mean Hawaiians, not just residents of the islands. Don't call anyone a "native" unless you're wearing your pith helmet, although "native Hawaiian" is still acceptable to distinguish the cultural group. Local is a somewhat more loaded word in Hawai'i than elsewhere, applying to the multicultural people with broader antecedents who were born here. It's more neutral when it means the opposite of "just visiting." *Kama'aina* (child of the land, as described earlier) and *malahini* (newcomer) refer to length of stay rather than race or culture. Now you see why the most popular pidgin phrase is "da kine" (as in "the kind"), a handy catch-all to refer to anything you can't or don't want to name specifically.

## Local Customs and Protocol

- When going to the *lua* (rest room) make sure you know the difference between *kane* (man) and *wahine* (woman), since many rest rooms are only identified in Hawaiian.

- Close your middle three fingers of either hand while keeping your thumb and pinky finger fully extended. Shake your hand a few times in the air. That's the *shaka* sign, a hand gesture expressing acknowledgment, goodwill, or appreciation. It's like *mahalo* (thank you).

- Every Friday is aloha Friday, when residents wear aloha shirts and *mu'umu'u* in celebration of Islands culture and lifestyle. Aloha wear is so in these days that it is worn any day. The first aloha shirt was sold in the mid-1930s in Honolulu. Boys during the time had been wearing similar shirts made from Japanese prints, and the idea caught on. The origin of the first *mu'umu'u* traces to missionary days when the missionary wives sewed "mother hubbard" nightgowns to clothe the half-dressed Hawaiian women.

- If you get lucky and are invited to a *kama'aina* home, remember that most follow the custom of removing shoes before entering the house. The forest of shoes in front of the door is your clue.

- Local people of all kinds profess a deep reverence for the *'aina* (land), although all that litter along Hawai'i's roads can't be from visitors alone. This is a beautiful place that deserves respect. Please don't trash it.

# Part Two

# Planning Your Visit to Hawai'i

## Best Time to Go

It's hard to think of a bad time to go to Hawai'i, but some times are better than others for you to visit, depending less on the weather than on your own plans. Seasonal changes are subtle, and the tourism industry is largely a 24/7/365 operation.

Hawai'i has winter, of a sort, when the daily highs lurk down around 80°F, sometimes even lower. It's the season of higher hotel and condo rates, when the weather where you live is more likely to be awful and more snowbirds flock to the tropics to escape. It's also the time to see migrating humpback whales, big surf, major golf events, squalls rolling across the horizon, and (perhaps) snow at nearly 14,000 feet atop Mauna Kea and occasionally down at 10,000 feet atop Haleakala. It's the rainier, slightly cooler, often less breezy time between late November and late March when bright amaryllis lilies spring up wild by the roadsides, the hills are particularly green, and at dusk you might need a windbreaker. Room rates peak from mid-December through March. In our first year on O'ahu, we were anxious to see what winter would bring. One late afternoon everyone got cold, rummaged around for a sweatshirt, and checked the thermometer: 74°. Everything's relative.

The land of perpetual good weather has a summer, too. It starts in June, the time of ripe mangoes, calmer seas on north shores, bigger surf on south shores, hurricanes and tropical storms marching west across the Pacific, somewhat warmer and drier weather, and an explosion of flowers (not that there weren't plenty in winter, too). The Southern Cross and Perseid metior showers appear in the skies in late summer. Rates for airfare and accommodations may or may not be lower, as summer is a busy time in Hawai'i since school is out and families head for fun in the sun. Once again, the weather where you live is more likely to be uncomfortable, only this time too hot.

Spring is glorious in Hawai'i, as everywhere, but it has the added advantage, like autumn, of lower rates and lesser crowds. If you're budget-conscious, time your trip between September and the December holidays or from mid-March to mid-June (excluding Easter), when hotel room rates dip. If you want to see the world's finest hula dancers, come the week after Easter for the annual Merrie Monarch Festival, to Hilo if you are lucky enough to get these rare tickets. Elsewhere, local television carries the colorful contest live.

If you just want to kick back under the tropical sun, watch the ads and the net and catch the next plane that suits your purse and schedule. The weather's not much of a deterrent any time of year.

# Gathering Information before You Leave

Know where you're going before you get there: get a map. The best Hawaiian islands maps are created by cartographer James A. Bier and published by the University of Hawai'i Press. Each topographic map includes island highways, roads, and trails as well as large-scale inset maps of population centers. The maps include points of natural, cultural, and historic interest; parks and beaches; sea channels; peaks and ridges (with altitudes); and Hawaiian words spelled with all their accent marks. These maps vary in price from $2.95 for Kaua'i to $3.95 for the Big Island of Hawai'i; printed on heavy paper, they fold and fit easily into a carry-on bag or backpack.

If your bookstore doesn't carry these maps, you can order them directly by writing the Marketing Department, University of Hawai'i Press, 2840 Kolowalu Street, Honolulu, HI 96822. Specify which island map you want. You can also request a free catalog of great books about Hawai'i and the Pacific. Call the University of Hawai'i Press at (808) 956-8255.

If you plan to camp at national parks and other popular spots, you may have to compete long before you arrive for reservations for rustic cabins and tent grounds. (See Camping, p. 296.)

## Read a Book

Every traveler to Hawai'i should read something about this complex destination before going there. Check your local bookstore or library (you can also visit Booklines, the biggest distributor of books in Hawai'i, on the Internet: www.booklines.com). Here are some suggested titles.

- *Hawaii Pono: An Ethnic and Political History,* by Lawrence H. Fuchs, published by Island Book Shelf, 1997. This book covers how ethnic groups made Hawai'i the "melting pot of the Pacific" and America's most cosmopolitan state.

- *Hawaiian Music and its Musicians: An Illustrated History,* by George S. Kanahele, published by University of Hawai'i Press, 1979. Hawai'i's music traces its roots from

ancient chants to slack key. This book contains biographical sketches, essays, anec-
dotes, and stories by a Hawai'i historian.

- *Shoal of Time: A History of the Hawaiian Islands,* by Gavan Daws, published by University of Hawai'i Press, 1994. This authoritative history book that reads like a novel.

- *Hawai'i True Stories of The Island Spirit,* edited by Rick and Marcie Carroll, published
  by Travelers Tales, San Francisco, 1999. This is an anthology of essays by 60 contributing authors, some famous, others unknown, but all insightful.

## Surf the Internet

Search the Internet for the word "Hawaii" and you're presented with a
virtual tsunami of matches. For a gaggle of islands in the middle of the
Pacific that's too much to surf. More Hawai'i websites appear every day.

Nothing comes close to actually being there, but the net does offer a
facsimile. You can:

- Watch the birth of Lo'ihi, the new volcano bubbling up slowly under the sea off
  the Big Island's south coast at www.soest.hawaii.edu/gg/hev/loihi.html.

- Check out a live shot of the Banzai Pipeline at www.surfline.com.

- Search for native birds on the Big Island at www.hawaii-forest.com.

Some other sites to check out are explained in more detail below.

**Hawaiian Spoken Here, Again**    For centuries, Hawaiians were master
chanters, orators, songwriters, and storytellers. In the 1800s, when missionaries put the sounds into letters and words and taught Hawaiians to
read them, the literacy rate in Hawai'i was higher than in any other part
of the world. The overthrow of the Hawaiian monarchy in 1893 brought
a ban on the Hawaiian language in public schools. Over the next century,
the language was nearly extinguished.

Now mellifluous Hawaiian is making a comeback, with attention to
proper pronunciation, spelling, and marking of its words. It is being res-
urrected in language courses, special language immersion schools designed
to teach young children in Hawaiian, on street signs, in the media, and on
the Internet. *'Oiwi: A Native Hawaiian Journal,* a contemporary online
anthology, features the work of Hawaiian writers and artists. The website
(**www.hawaii.edu/oiwi**) presents stories in both Hawaiian and English.
Surf over to **www.olelo.hawaii.edu** to find the University of Hawai'i
Hilo's Kualono page, which contains links to Hawaiian-language diction-
aries, books, computer fonts, and a radio program, "'Alana I kai Hikini,"
that broadcasts in Hawaiian online.

**Chinatown, Honolulu-style**    It's easy to solve the mysteries of Chinatown
by visiting its home page at **www.chinatownhi.com.** Tour the historic 17-
block district, visit open markets, drop in on Havana Cubana, pick up Alan
Lau's herbal remedy for the common cold at Tak Wah Tong in the Chinese
Cultural Center, and even read about the adventures of Charlie Chan.

**Visit Maui** The Maui Visitors Bureau home page (**www.visitmaui.com**) makes you want to go there now. It offers lots of solid information and useful links, including seven remote cameras with scenes of the island (one focuses on Ho'okipa windsurfers). Check out the surf report and daily temperatures, order a free vacation planner, book a B&B, and tour resorts.

**Mighty Mo, WW II Dreadnought** The battleship USS *Missouri,* upon whose deck Japan surrendered in Tokyo Bay to end World War II, is now anchored in Pearl Harbor next to the USS *Arizona* Memorial and also in cyberspace at **www.ussmissouri.com.**

"Mighty Mo" was saved from mothballs and towed across the Pacific to Hawai'i to commemorate peace. The relics are bookends to World War II—the attack on the *Arizona* during the surprise air raid on Pearl Harbor launched the American entry in the war; the surrender aboard the *Missouri* came 3 years, 9 months, and 25 days later.

For a virtual tour, surf to the URL listed above. The site is easy to navigate and filled with nostalgic detail. Click on the ship's wheel to take a tour, visit the Surrender Deck, see combat photos (the ship saw action in Korea and the Persian Gulf as well as World War II) and a video of Mighty Mo's nine 16-inch guns roaring. You may also take a 20-question quiz, order the ship's blueprints, join a chat room, and sign the ship's log.

**Surf Moloka'i** Going to Moloka'i is like "landing in rural Arkansas sometime back in the 1930s or 40s," novelist Fletcher Knebel once said. "I've had the feeling that if I turned on a radio, I'd hear Eddie Duchin on the piano, FDR in mid–fireside chat, or perhaps the Japanese bombing Pearl Harbor."

For such an atavistic island, Moloka'i has a big Internet presence: at least 54 home pages, from Moloka'i Ranch (**www.molokai-ranch.com**) to Monkey Pod Records (**www.monkeypod.com**), which promotes local musicians. One notable site details the somber history of the Kalaupapa Peninsula, where victims of leprosy were once banished. Now it's a national historic park reached by way of the Island's most famous attraction, the Moloka'i Mule Ride (**http://muleride.com**).

## Visitors and Convention Bureaus

In the early 1900s, several hoteliers in Hawai'i formed a tourist information bureau to attract those who had previously only dreamed of visiting the islands. Their earliest marketer went to San Francisco to foster those dreams and drew crowds with a stereo opticon lecture. The boosters later hired Mark Twain to extol the virtues of a Hawaiian vacation, mailed out enticing photos and postcards, and sent Hawaiian entertainers on the road to deliver aloha in person, a practice that continues today as the next best thing to being here. Today, the Hawai'i Visitors and Convention Bureau spends millions of dollars globally to promote Hawai'i as a top travel destination. Part of that job is to disperse information on islands, activities, accommodations, restaurants, and a calendar of festivals, cultural celebrations, sports events, and activities. Their website is filled with information and links, as are those of the individual islands.

### HAWAI'I'S VISITORS BUREAUS

Hawai'i Visitors and Convention Bureau
2270 Kalakaua Avenue, 8th Floor, Suite 801
Honolulu, HI 96815
(808) 923-1811 or (800) GO-HAWAII
www.gohawaii.com
Request a free copy of *The Islands of Aloha,* the bureau's vacation planner.

O'ahu Visitors Bureau
733 Bishop Street, Suite 1872
Honolulu, HI 96813
(808) 524-0722 or (877) 525-OAHU
www.visit-oahu.com, or link from www.gohawaii.com

Big Island Visitors Bureau (Hilo)
250 Keawe Street
Hilo, HI 96720-2823
(808) 961-5797 or (800) 648-2441
www.bigisland.org, or link from www.gohawaii.com

Big Island Visitors Bureau (Kona)
250 Waikoloa Beach, Suite B15
Waikoloa, HI 96738
(808) 886-1655 or (800) 648-2441
www.bigisland.org, or link from www.gohawaii.com

Maui Visitors Bureau
1727 Wili Pa Loop
Wailuku, HI 96793-1250
(808) 244-3530 or (800) 525-MAUI
www.visitmaui.com, www.gohawaii.com
Call or write for a free copy of *Maui, The Magic Isles,* a travel planner featuring the Maui County destinations of Maui, Moloka'i, and Lana'i.

Kaua'i Visitors Bureau
4334 Rice Street, Suite 101
Lihu'e, HI 96766-1801
(808) 245-3971 or (800) 262-1400
www.kauaivisitorsbureau.org, or link from www.gohawaii.com

Moloka'i Visitors Association
P.O. Box 960, 10 Kamenameha Highway
Kaunakakai, HI 96748
(808) 553-3876 or (800) 800-6367
www.molokai-hawaii.com, or link from www.gohawaii.com

---

**HAWAI'I'S VISITORS BUREAUS** *(continued)*

Destination Lana'i
P.O. Box 700, 730 Lana'i Avenue, Suite 102
Lana'i City, HI 96763
(808) 565-7600 or (800) 947-4774
www.visitlanai.net or link from www.gohawaii.com

**International Contacts**
*United Kingdom*
Hawai'i Visitors and Convention Bureau, United Kingdom
P.O. Box 208
Sunbury on Thames
Middlesex TW165RJ, England
44 (208) 941-4009
xcd16@dial.pipex.com

*Australia*
Hawai'i Visitors and Convention Bureau
c/o The Sales Team
Suite 2, Level 2
34 Burton Street
Milsons Point, NSW 2061, Australia
61 (2) 9955-2619
rlane@thesalesteam.com.au

*New Zealand*
Hawai'i Visitors and Convention Bureau
c/o Walshes World
18 Shortland Street, Level 6
Auckland, New Zealand
64 (9) 379-3708
darragh@walwor.co.nz

*Canada*
Comprehensive Travel Industry Services
1260 Hornby Street, Suite 104
Vancouver, BC V6Z1W2, Canada
(604) 669-6691
compre@intergate.bc.ca

---

## Recommended Magazines

Hawai'i is featured often in travel magazines like *Condé Nast Traveler,*
*National Geographic Traveler,* and *Travel and Leisure,* as well as airline in-
flight magazines, but only a few feature magazines devote coverage to the
islands.

- *Hawai'i Magazine*, a bimonthly journal featuring articles on Hawai'i's people, culture, arts, history, and travel is published by Fancy Publications in Irvine, California. It's available at major newsstands, or call (800) 365-4421 to subscribe.

- *Honolulu Magazine*, a monthly publication, has stories on politics, personalities, history, and arts in the city of Honolulu. It is published in Honolulu by Pacific Basin Communications. Call (808) 524-7400 to subscribe.

- *Maui No Ka 'Oi Magazine*, a quarterly celebrating the Valley Isle with profiles, coverage of local issues, restaurant reviews, and an events calendar, is published by Haynes Publishing Group on Maui. Call (808) 871-7765 or visit www.mauinokaoi.net to subscribe.

## Packing Wisely

Everyone brings too many of the wrong kinds clothes to Hawai'i. Californians, most of your wardrobe is too warm. East Coasters, think summer, no matter what the season is in Hawai'i. For packing purposes, it's always summer here.

If you're planning to ride horses, bring covered footwear and jeans and hang onto your hat. If you're going camping, you can bring or rent gear, according to your preference and the percentage of your trip you plan to camp. A night or two? Rent. A month? You might prefer your own stuff.

What men need: shorts, T-shirts and informal tops, favorite Hawaiian shirts, swim trunks, lightweight slacks, a light jacket or sweatshirt for going upcountry, and sandals, sports shoes, or loafers. Don't even bring a tie. If you're hanging out at stuffy fancy restaurants, bring a jacket or be forced to wear one of theirs for dinner.

What women need: sundresses, swimsuits, cover-ups, shorts, tops, light sweater or jacket, sandals, and maybe a mu'umu'u for the lu'au (it's best to buy one here). Lose the heels, hose, and other banes of your your wardrobe. Unless you're staying in butlered digs, minimize the high-maintenance wear of wrinkling silk and linen. Many hotel rooms come equipped with an iron and a board, if you insist.

Unless you're heading for Mauna Kea's 13,976-foot summit, you won't need any apparel heavier than a sweatshirt.

If you pack wisely for Hawai'i's tropical climate, you can put all your lightweight clothes in one case and bring an empty one for all the stuff and gifts you'll probably buy.

## Getting to Hawai'i

The flight to Honolulu International Airport is about five hours from the West Coast, eight from Dallas, nine from Atlanta, and eleven from New York. Most major U.S. and several international airlines serve Hawai'i, along with charters from other countries. Hawai'i-based Aloha Air Lines and Hawaiian Air Lines connect the islands with various West Coast cities, and Las Vegas (Hawai'i residents' favorite destination).

Honolulu International Airport (HNL) on O'ahu is one of the nation's busiest airports, with 1,400 daily operations, many of them to and from Asian and Pacific destinations, and more than 24 million passenger arrivals and departures annually.

Although the majority of flights from the U.S. mainland to Hawai'i touch down in Honolulu, some land on the Neighbor Islands. United has daily flights from Los Angeles and San Francisco to Keahole-Kona on the Big Island and Kahului on Maui, and from Los Angeles to Lihu'e on Kaua'i. Delta and American fly to Kahului from Los Angeles. Hawaiian Airlines offers flights between Seattle and Kahului.

All schedules are subject to change. Call the toll-free numbers below for updated information.

### AIRLINES

| | |
|---|---|
| Air Canada | (800) 776-3000 |
| Air New Zealand | (800) 262-1234 |
| Aloha Airlines | (800) 367-5350 |
| American Airlines | (800) 433-7300 |
| British Airways | (800) 247-9297 |
| Continental Airlines | (800) 523-3273 |
| Delta Airlines | (800) 221-1212 |
| Hawaiian Airlines | (800) 367-5320 |
| Northwest Airlines | (800) 225-2525 |
| TWA | (800) 221-2000 |
| United Airlines | (800) 241-6522 |

## Traveler Advisory

Honolulu's International Airport, is currently undergoing a $200 million improvement project to add an efficient security checkpoint, new people movers, and an information center. While renovations are underway, travelers may experience disruption, confusion, and construction noise. The project is scheduled to be completed by 2006.

Airports on the Neighbor Islands include Keahole Airport in Kona and Hilo Airport in Hilo on the Big Island; Kahului Airport, Hana Airport, and Kapalua Airport on Maui; Lihu'e Airport on Kaua'i; Moloka'i Airport on Moloka'i; and Lana'i Airport on Lana'i. You can't fly directly to all of these (see above), but all are used by island-hoppers (see Interisland Flights, page 70).

Booking your vacation through a travel agent may save you time and money, as the agent can plow through myriad fares and rates to find you the best airfares, lodgings, and car rentals and take advantage of specials offered only to agents.

If you make the arrangements on your own, here are some tips and advisories on finding a good deal on airfares.

■ To get the lowest possible fare, try to be flexible in your travel plans. The best deals are usually limited to travel on certain days of the week or hours of the day. Ask the reservations agent how you might save money by leaving a day earlier or later or by taking a different flight. Check carefully into fare restrictions and penalties if you change plans after purchase. Check various travel-related sites on the Internet to see if you can find cheaper fares. You can hold your telephone reservation on most airlines for a day or so before you commit to the ticket. In some cases you may have to call to cancel. In others you have to call to activate the reservation.

■ If your travel itinerary falls into a busy flight period, book early. Flights during holidays may sell out months ahead of time.

■ Many discount fares are nonrefundable and, in most cases, nontransferable (one exception is the coupon books offered at times by Hawai'i's airlines). If you want to change your discounted booking, you will pay more if that fare is not available on the new flight.

## How to Avoid Jet Lag

Start to combat jet lag before you depart. Jet lag, known in scientific terms as circadian desynchronization, occurs after flying across several time zones. It is not a state of mind; it is a condition with physical and mental ramifications, lasting anywhere from a few hours to a few days. You feel sleepy, disoriented, and a little out of synch.

Several books offer remedies to ease jet lag. One of the best is *Jet Smart* by Diana Fairechild, a veteran flight attendant whose 21 years of experience took her often to and from the Hawaiian islands.

Here are some practical tips.

■ Avoid coffee for a day or two before and after your flight and drink water, rather than coffee, sodas, or alcohol on the plane. Alcohol can sharply intensify jet lag. Drink lots of water to prevent dehydration—an eight-ounce glass for each hour of flight, according to our doctor.

■ During flight, remove your shoes to improve circulation. Flex your feet, ankles, and legs often. If possible, stroll through the cabin and stand for a while.

■ Adjust your watch to Hawai'i Standard Time (see the following section) as soon as you board the plane. This mentally prepares you as you adjust to Hawaiian time. Think of the time it is where you're going, not where you've been. On the ground, get acclimated to local time as soon as possible. Stay up until bedtime in the islands if you can, even though you may feel extremely tired.

■ Take a long soak in a bathtub or a warm pool or ocean. Not only will it replenish moisture lost during your flight; it also relaxes your nervous system. Don't attempt too much activity on the day or night of your arrival.

- Try to spend some time outside while it's sunny, as bright daylight helps the body adjust it's internal clock. Take care, however, to avoid overexposure; a sunburn is a miserable way to start your vacation.

## What Time Is It in Hawai'i?

On standard time, when it's noon in San Francisco, it's 10 a.m. in Honolulu. Hawai'i is two hours behind the West Coast and five hours behind the East Coast. Hawai'i doesn't change to Daylight Savings time, so when it's Daylight Savings Time on the mainland, April to October, then Hawaii is three hours behind the West Coast and six hours behind the East Coast.

With an average of 12 hours of sunshine daily, year-round, Hawai'i doesn't need to save daylight. Hawai'i's longest day, on June 21, is 13 hours and 26 minutes long. Its shortest day, on December 21, is 10 hours and 50 minutes. Hawai'i has its own time zone, known as Hawai'i Standard Time or HST.

## What *Not* to Bring

- Don't bring live animals or plants.
- Forget drugs, especially marijuana. Dogs are on duty at baggage claim and check in areas to sniff out illegal drugs, and the carriers are taken into custody on the spot.
- The Department of Agriculture bans most animals and plants from Hawai'i. Dogs and cats bound for Hawai'i end up in month-long, expensive quarantine. Snakes end up in the zoo or dead.
- Importation of unchecked flora and fauna can have a negative impact on Hawai'i's fragile ecosystem. The Department of Agriculture restricts shipping of fruit, plants, and other items from Hawai'i to the mainland to prevent the spread of fruit flies and other insects.

For inquiries, call the USDA Plant Quarantine Branch at (808) 586-0844 or the Animal Quarantine Branch at (808) 483-7171.

## Interisland Flights

The islands are linked by frequent, efficient jet service all day from sunrise to late evening by two Honolulu-based airlines, Aloha Airlines and Hawaiian Airlines, which share the interisland terminal at Honolulu Airport. Other airports served are Kona and Hilo on the Big Island; Kahului, Maui; Lihu'e, Kaua'i; and Moloka'i and Lana'i.

Island Air flies smaller twin-engine planes to smaller airports, including Kapalua and Hana on Maui and Kalaupapa on Moloka'i. Hawaiian has smaller craft as well.

Both Aloha and Hawaiian have small first-class seating areas, but the flights only take 25 to 45 minutes, so the chief advantage, besides bigger seats and personal service, is that you can board and deplane first. Check with the airlines for their carry-on baggage rules. Boogie boards, surf boards, full coolers, skateboards, and strollers are not allowed in the cabin.

When booking your interisland flight, ask about special promotions that may lower fares, such as coupon books. Or check Aloha's and Hawaiian's websites.

---

### HAWAI'I'S AIRLINES

**Aloha Airlines**
Toll-free: (800) 554-4833
O'ahu: (808) 484-1111
Maui: (808) 244-9071
Big Island: (808) 935-5771
Kaua'i: (808) 245-3691
www.alohaair.com

**Island Air**
Toll-free: (800) 652-6541
Moloka'i: (808) 567-6115
Lana'i: (808) 565-6744
www.islandair.com

**Hawaiian Airlines**
Toll-free: (800) 367-5320
O'ahu: (808) 838-1555
Maui: (808) 871-6132
Big Island: (808) 326-5615

Kaua'i: (808) 245-1813
Moloka'i: (808) 553-3644
Lana'i: (808) 565-7281
www.Hawaiianair.com

**Moloka'i Air Shuttle**
O'ahu: (808) 567-6847

**Pacific Wings**
Toll-free: (800) 575-4546
Maui: (808) 873-0877
www.pacificwings.com

**Paragon Air**
Toll-free: (800) 428-1231
Maui: (808) 244-3356
www.maui.net/wing/index.htm

**Trans Air**
Toll-free: (800) 836-8080

---

# Car Rentals

Once you've landed on an island, renting a car provides the greatest flexibility and mobility in Hawai'i. On O'ahu, a car can also put you right in the middle of the biggest traffic jam in the Pacific.

It's fun to cruise Hawai'i in a shiny convertible, but it's no fun to sit sweating in gridlock while heading back from the beach. So watch your timing to avoid rush-hour traffic, which runs early in the islands, a legacy from plantation days. Plan to leave later than 8:30 a.m. on weekday mornings and avoid the highways in the late afternoons, roughly 4–6 p.m. Listen to the radio for updates on particular problems. Summer driving is much easier because school's out.

Carry as little as possible in your rental car that might appeal to thieves. We usually leave ours empty and open; there's no sense in paying for a broken window. Whatever you do, don't leave your valuables in the car while you dash out to view the Windward Side from the Pali Lookout or the Blow Hole on the South Shore. These are favorite rip-off sites.

You can get by without a car on O'ahu, which has a highly praised municipal bus system, one of the best in the United States, as well as taxis, private transit, and (often) free shuttle vans. But it is a lot easier to explore the Windward Coast and North Shore and enjoy museums, botanical gardens, adventure areas, and vacant beaches with a car. One solution is to rent a car just for a day or two.

On Maui, Hawai'i, Kaua'i, and Moloka'i, where beaches and natural attractions are all over the islands, renting a car is a must unless you plan to hole up at your resort and commute on foot or by resort shuttle between your room and the beach or golf course. That's not a bad idea, but a limiting one.

On Lana'i, a resort shuttle will take you to most sites. But one of Lana'i's more popular activities is exploring the back roads in a rented four-wheel-drive vehicle, allowing you to discover backcountry and island history on your own.

Car rentals are available on all islands, and the cost is around $30 a day for an economy car. Rental car rates are lower in Hawai'i than in the rest of the nation as a whole. Shop for rates by telephone or the Internet, if making your own arrangements. Most major car rental firms offer special rates frequently and include car rentals in money-saving travel packages with airfare and accommodations. Check with your travel agent or call the car rental agencies for details before you go.

When making interisland flight reservations, ask the airlines for any special deals on rental cars. They often partner with car agencies in promotional fly/drive packages. All sorts of discounts will lower the rates as well. You may get a break of 5–15% for association memberships, credit cards, frequent-flier clubs, and coupons. Agency Internet sites (listed later) can offer up to 20% off regular rates.

All the major car rental agencies are located at or near the airports, and many have reservations desks at various resorts or stores. On Maui, besides Kahului Airport and the hotels, many car rental agencies operate at the Ka'anapali Transportation Center (30-1 Halawai Drive), a five-minute ride from the Kapalua Airport in West Maui (linked by free shuttle service).

Most car rental agencies have a large fleet of vehicles, ranging from economy cars and luxury sedans to four-wheel-drive Jeeps and shiny red roadsters. Luxury wheels like Ferraris and Vipers and Harley Davidson motorcycles are also available for rent.

As with car rentals in any destination, you can rent a car after you arrive, presuming one is available. Courtesy phones and free shuttles in airport terminals connect you to their nearby offices. However, you'd do better to reserve a car with the national agency before you go, usually a week or more ahead for the best rate. Rental rates are based on the number of cars available, so they constantly fluctuate. Because you don't have to pay up front, you can always recheck rates.

Expect to see that rental fee jump by the time you do pay, because several costs will be added on. Car rentals on all islands are subject to a $3/day state road tax and a nominal vehicle license tax (24–45 cents a day on O'ahu and 17–45 cents a day on the Neighbor Islands). In addition, transactions that take place at an airport are subject to an airport concession fee of 10% of the rental fee per day on O'ahu and 7.5% on the Neighbor Islands.

Optional insurance rates vary by car rental agency. It's a hard-sell situation when you're picking up the car, but remember that your own car insurance and often your major credit card provide insurance coverage when you're driving rental cars. Check before you leave.

Gas prices will look astronomical in Hawai'i compared to almost any mainland location, particular the East Coast. Fortunately, the rental cars today are rarely guzzlers, and the islands are small enough that you seldom rack up major mileage.

About island driving: Hawaiian islands (even O'ahu) don't have a lot of roads. Most roads are two lanes, and speed limits are lower than in other states. O'ahu has three short "interstate" highways that absorb much of the traffic. Mainland drivers will find the entry and exit setups otherworldly. But island driving manners are such that people will let you in if you landed in the wrong lane. Just take it slow, signal, look, smile a lot, and wave your thanks. Leave your aggressive driving habits at home. Hawai'i is a no-fault insurance state.

People talk of driving "around the island," but you can't really do that around the entire coastline of any of the islands. You can circle most but not all of the Big Island without backtracking, at least until the volcano rewrites the Chain of Craters Road map again.

## CAR-RENTAL AGENCIES

### Alamo Rent-A-Car

Toll-free reservations: (800) 327-9633

Website: www.goalamo.com

*O'ahu*

Honolulu Int'l Airport: (808) 833-4585

'Ilikai Hotel Nikko Waikiki: (808) 947-6112

*Maui*

Kahului Airport: (808) 871-6235

Ka'anapali Transportation Center: (808) 661-7181

*Big Island*

Keahole-Kona Int'l Airport: (808) 329-8896

Hilo Int'l Airport: (808) 961-3343

*Kaua'i*

Lihu'e Airport: (808) 246-0646

### Avis Rent-A-Car

Toll-free reservations: (800) 331-1212

Website: www.avis.com

*O'ahu*

Honolulu Int'l Airport: (808) 834-5536

Outrigger East Hotel: (808) 971-3700

*Maui*

Kahului Airport: (808) 871-7575

Ka'anapali: (808) 661-4588

Renaissance Wailea Beach Resort: (808) 879-7601

**Avis Rent-A-Car** *(continued)*
*Maui (continued)*
Ritz-Carlton Kapalua: (808) 669-6200
(for hotel guests only)
*Big Island*
Keahole-Kona Int'l Airport: (808) 327-3000
Hilo Int'l Airport: (808) 935-1290
*Kaua'i*
Lihu'e Airport: (808) 245-3512
Princeville Airport: (808) 826-9773
Hyatt Po'ipu Kaua'i: (808) 742-1627

**Budget Rent-A-Car**
Toll-free reservations: (800) 777-0169
Website: www.budgetrentacar.com
*O'ahu*
Honolulu Int'l Airport: (808) 836-1700
Hyatt Regency Waikiki: (808) 921-5808
*Maui*
Kahului Airport: (808) 871-8811
Ka'anapali: (808) 661-8721
*Big Island*
Keahole-Kona Int'l Airport: (808) 329-8511
Hilo Int'l Airport: (808) 935-6878
*Kaua'i*
Lihu'e Airport: (808) 245-1901
*Moloka'i*
Moloka'i Airport: (808) 567-6877

**Dollar Rent-A-Car**
Toll-free reservations: (800) 367-7006
Website: www.dollarcar.com
*O'ahu:*
Honolulu Int'l Airport: (808) 831-2330
Hawaiian Regent Hotel: (808) 952-4264
Hale Koa Hotel: (808) 952-4264
Waikiki: (808) 952-4242
*Maui*
Kahului Airport: (808) 877-2731
Hana: (808) 248-8237
Ka'anapali Transportation Center:
(808) 667-2651
*Big Island*
Keahole-Kona Int'l Airport: (808) 329-2744
Hilo Int'l Airport: (808) 961-6059

*Kaua'i*
Lihu'e Airport: (808) 245-3651
*Moloka'i*
Moloka'i Airport: (808) 567-6156
*Lana'i*
Lana'i Airport: (808) 565-7227

**Harper Car and Truck Rentals**
Toll-free reservations: (800) 852-9993
Website: www.harpershawaii.com
*Big Island*
Kauai: (808) 969-1478
Kona Int'l Airport: (808) 969-1478
Hilo: (808) 969-1478

**Hertz Rent-A-Car**
Toll-free reservations: (800) 654-3011
Website: www.hertz.com
*O'ahu*
Honolulu Int'l Airport: (808) 831-3500
Hyatt Regency Waikiki: (808) 971-3535
*Maui*
Kahului Airport: (808) 877-5167
2580 Keka'a Drive: (808) 661-7735
Westin Maui: (808) 667-5381
Maui Marriott: (808) 667-1966
*Big Island*
Keahole-Kona Airport: (808) 329-3566
Hilo Int'l Airport: (808) 935-2896
*Kaua'i:*
Lihu'e Airport: (808) 245-3356
Kaua'i Marriott Resort: (808) 246-0027

**National Car Rental**
Toll-free reservations: (800) CAR-RENT
Website: www.nationalcar.com
*O'ahu*
Honolulu Int'l Airport: (808) 831-3800
Kahala Mandarin Oriental: (808) 733-2309
*Maui*
Kahului Airport: (808) 871-8851
Ka'anapali Transportation Center:
(808) 667-9737
*Big Island*
Keahole-Kona Int'l Airport: (808) 329-1674
Hilo Int'l Airport: (808) 935-0891
*Kaua'i*
Lihu'e Airport: (808) 245-5636

# So Many Islands, So Little Time

Because Hawai'i has six major islands to see, two weeks still wouldn't be enough time to do and see it all. This is one factor that keeps visitors coming back again and again, to see their favorite sites and sample new ones.

We suggest that newcomers spend the first two or three days in Waikiki or elsewhere on O'ahu, slowing down enough to enjoy the pace of the islands. But that's just a suggestion. We have a friend who comes to Waikiki at least once a year and never goes anywhere else. Other visitors shun Waikiki completely.

All the ingredients of a grand tropical holiday can be found on O'ahu—sunny days, warm water, great beaches, stunning scenery, a wide range of accommodations (mostly hotels, from budget to upscale), museums and cultural events, stimulating atmosphere, cuisines of many cultures, excellent shopping, and great nightlife. If you want quiet, check into a B&B or vacation rental elsewhere on O'ahu, or pick another island and spend the rest of your time there.

Maui is the next most popular choice after O'ahu, followed by the Big Island of Hawai'i, Kaua'i, Moloka'i, and Lana'i.

## To Hop or Not to Hop?

First-time visitors may have ambitious visions of island-hopping from one end of the Hawaiian chain to the other. One word of advice: don't. You may think you can see all the Hawaiian Islands in a single week. You can *see* most of them in 20 minutes at 20,000 feet on the way in. But clearly, that's not enough. This is too fine a place to gloss over, so count on spending some time on one or two islands and coming back someday. If you do move between islands, the flights are only half an hour or so, but the airport transfers are time-consuming and plane tickets are expensive. Below are some factors to consider before island hopping.

- A round-trip interisland airline ticket is about $190 per person. Most interinterisland flights are to and from Honolulu. You may have to go to Honolulu just to connect to flights to other islands. *Tip:* Ask the airlines about discount coupons, where you can buy multiple flights' worth in advance for a cheaper rate.

- Expect to spend several hours commuting from place to place—to pack, check out, get to the airport, return your rental car if you have one or go early in a transit vehicle, check in for your flight and go through security, wait for the plane, board the plane, fly, deplane, get your luggage, get another rental car, drive to another hotel, register your room, and unpack.

- You can save money by staying longer on each island. Some major hotels offer a free night's stay when you book four to six consecutive nights.

We think a two-island stay is plenty for one vacation. But keeping the costs (in money and time) in mind, you can easily add a day trip for a specific activity, such as a round of golf or a look at the volcano.

The quickest way to see the islands is a scenic flight on a twin-engine airplane. Several companies offer low-altitude, half-day, and full-day scenic air tours over the main islands. One is Pacific Wings: call (808) 873-0877 or e-mail info@pacificwings.com.

Cruise lines offer voyages with port calls in Honolulu and on Maui, Kaua'i and the Big Island of Hawai'i. (See "Cruising Hawai'i," page 191.)

# Suggestions for Special Travelers

## Singles

**Best Island to Visit**  O'ahu

**Other Recommended Islands**  Maui and the Big Island

**Things to See and Do**  On O'ahu, join the crowd on Waikiki Beach, catch a ride on an outrigger canoe, and have a beer and listen to live Hawaiian music at Duke's Canoe Club at the Outrigger Waikiki. Check out the *pau hana* (after work) action at Aloha Tower Market Place, shop at Ala Moana Center. Discover local food—an instant picnic of inexpensive plate lunches or *mana pua* (stuffed Chinese steamed buns, otherwise known as *char siu bao)* from downtown lunch wagons. Explore Hawai'i's history at the Bishop Museum or Hawai'i Maritime Center. Climb Diamond Head Crater. Boogie in Waikiki nightclubs and indulge yourself the next day with a spa extravaganza at Hilton Hawaiian Village, the newest addition to the spa lineup.

On the Big Island, don't miss the volcano, and have a drink at the Volcano House, which overlooks a steaming live crater. Explore Waimea and Parker Ranch country. Share a fishing charter at Honokohau Harbor. Join a pickup golf group and play a round on a course you'll never forget.

If you choose Maui, ride with a bike tour down Haleakala or take a snorkel tour to Molokini or Lana'i. Drive to Makawao and Pa'ia and poke around the villages. Head further upcountry to Kula and taste Tedeschi wines at the winery at 'Ulupalakua Ranch. The places to party are Lahaina and Kihei.

**Comments**  O'ahu has the most things to do and places to see and will keep your itinerary filled. If you're hoping to meet new friends during your trip, O'ahu is the island with the most dance clubs and best nightlife.

## Couples

**Best Island to Visit**  Kaua'i

**Other Recommended Islands**  Lana'i, Maui, and the Big Island

**Things to See and Do**  Hang out in Hanalei, a naturally romantic setting you'll never want to leave; swim or body surf in Hanalei Bay; get to know some of the local citizenry at Tahiti Nui or neighboring spots. Go for a waterfall trail ride at Princeville Stables. Kayak down the Hanalei River to the bay and try to catch a wave on the way back. If the moon is full, go down to the beach to see if anyone is dancing hula in the moonlight, and join them. See for yourself what inspired Bob Nelson to write "Hanalei Moon," a well known song describing a tropical moonrise.

Stay at Princeville, which provides gorgeous views of Hanalei Bay and the surrounding mountains. Pick a new North Shore beach to discover every day, and don't forget your snorkel gear. If you're feeling schmaltzy, take the boat ride up Wailua River to Fern Grotto. If energetic, walk up the Kalalau Trail the first two miles to the unforgettable Hanakapi'ai Valley, and return. Go south to Po'ipu Beach for at least a day, ride horses by the beach near Hyatt Regency Kaua'i (a honeymoon hotel), and don't miss dinner at Tidepools.

On Lana'i, divide your time between the seaside Manele Bay, where you can wake up to spinner dolphins in the waters, and Lodge at Ko'ele, where evenings in the romantic environs are chilly enough for cuddling. Hike or drive out to the hinterlands, or ride a horse through the woods. Witness a green flash together, that magical prizm phenomenon that sometimes happens when the sun meets the sea at the horizon. On Maui, get up early to see the spectacular sunrise over Haleakala, then relax with massages for two in tents by the sea at Four Seasons Wailea and take a stroll on Wailea Beach. Then go to Hana to discover Maui's true cultural heart. On the Big Island, stay at Four Seasons Hualalai, but make time to drive over one afternoon and watch the lava flowing at sunset or hike the trails in Hawai'i Volcanoes National Park.

**Comments** Kaua'i is an obvious choice for Hawai'i's most romantic island, offering a blissful combination of postcard scenery and uncrowded settings.

## Hikers

**Best Island to Visit** Kaua'i

**Other Recommended Islands** Big Island, Maui

**Things to See and Do** Hike Kalalau Trail on Na Pali Coast (a difficult trek)—this is a round trip with a stopover of at least a night in the valley. Or hike one-way and arrange to catch a ride up the awesome coast on a Zodiac raft the other way.

Take the boardwalk on a sunny day through 'Alakai Swamp up at Koke'e State Park. Explore the trails of 4,000-acre Koke'e Wilderness Forest, or see how the goats hang onto the precipitous ledges in Waimea Canyon. Hike the ridge line above Kapa'a to the Sleeping Giant.

On the Big Island: Hike across simmering Kilauea Iki Crater and cool off by walking through Thurston Lava Tube. Hike the summit of Mauna Loa, but only if you're in shape for the high-altitude walking and are very experienced. On Maui: Hike the falls and forest at Kipahulu, beyond Hana.

**Comments** Hikes on Kaua'i are the most dramatic because of the natural landscape, from thin ledges along the seacoast to miles of trails in a cloud forest.

## Bikers

**Best Island to Visit** Big Island

**Other Recommended Islands** Maui, Kaua'i

**Things to See and Do** Maui invented the sport of coasting down a volcano, but you can bike down a lower slope of Mauna Kea as well. Touring the Big Island in three or four days on a bike remains a challenge. This is the only island where roads go all the way around, allowing you to circumnavigate without retracing your route. Pedal around Hawai'i, proceeding counterclockwise from Kona on the Upper Highway. Head south past the backyard coffee plantations, down across the lava wasteland of Ka'u Desert, then up through Hawai'i Volcanoes National Park to the village of Volcano. From there, you can coast downhill nearly 40 miles to Hilo. If you still have steam, pedal on to Waimea along the lush, green Hamakua Coast and cut across the wide, open lava fields of the Kohala Coast before reaching your starting point at Kona.

On Maui, you will always remember the thrill of coasting down 10,000-foot-high Haleakala 38 miles to the sea on a specially built bicycle on a guided cruise, the only sensible way to descend the mountain on two wheels. Mountain bikers should head for Kaua'i, Moloka'i, and O'ahu.

**Comments** Bike enthusiasts will want to test their stamina against the Big Island, the best all-around cycling island in the Pacific, because of its many challenging features: terrain that varies from lava desert to rain forest, steep inclines, and radically different temperatures from one area to the next.

## Nature Lovers

**Best Island to Visit** Kaua'i

**Other Recommended Islands** Big Island, Maui

**Things to See and Do** Snoop on boobies and goonies (Pacific sea birds) at Kilauea Point. See 600 species of palm trees and other tropicals at 300-acre National Tropical Botanical Garden. Wander in Waimea Canyon, the "grand canyon" of the Pacific. Spend the day in Limahuli Gardens, a botanical refuge for endangered native plants.

On the Big Island, explore Hawai'i Volcanoes National Park, hike Chain of Craters Road to witness red-hot lava flow into the Pacific, cool your heels in lush Onomea Botanical Garden near Hilo. Watch for rarely seen native Hawaiian forest birds. On Maui, look for rare silversword plants and the endangered Hawaiian nene geese at Haleakala National Park.

**Comments** Hawai'i's natural beauty is legendary; its wildlife (monk seals, nene geese, and native Hawaiian birds) may be endangered, but you will not be disappointed by the great outdoors, especially on Kaua'i, a botanical wonder all its own. The diverse nature of the Big Island with its lava rock coasts and highland rainforests is like nowhere else on Earth. Maui's fabled town of Hana is a prime destination for people who like to feel overwhelmed by the majesty of nature. If you're lucky you may win admission to the Pu'u Kukui nature preserve in the West Maui Mountains.

## Beachcombers

**Best Island to Visit** O'ahu

**Other Recommended Islands** Kaua'i and Maui

**Things to See and Do** With 50 miles of sandy shore, O'ahu has the most beaches in Hawai'i. People-watch at Waikiki Beaches. Windsurf Kailua Beach. Snorkel Hanauma Beach. Search for shells at Malaekahana Beach in spring and summer and at Pupukea Beach on the North Shore. Watch big winter waves at Waimea Beach. Explore empty Yokohama Beach. Hide out at Lanikai Beach. Have a picnic at Kualoa or Ka'a'awa or Hau'ula Beach Parks. Take a break from shopping at Ala Moana Beach, just across the street from the mall.

On Kaua'i, go body boarding at Poipu Beach, summer swimming at Hanalei Beach, snorkeling at Ke'e Beach and Tunnels Beach, or camping on 17-mile Polihale Beach, longest in Hawai'i. Maui's best beaches include golden Wailea Beach and scenic Kapalua Beach, as well as remote black-sand Hamoa Beach in Hana

**Comments** The best, safest and most dramatic beaches of Hawai'i are found on O'ahu where the abundance of choice suits almost everyone's style. Some beautiful beaches are found on Kaua'i and Maui, but O'ahu is the beach capital of Hawai'i.

## Families

**Best Island to Visit** O'ahu

**Other Recommended Island** Maui

**Things to See and Do** If you enjoy paid attractions, take the family to Sea Life Park, the Honolulu Zoo, Waikiki Aquarium, and Bishop Museum. See beneath the sea without getting wet with Atlantis Submarines. Enjoy some sun, surf, and sand at Waikiki Beach and Ala Moana Beach Park, two of the most swimmable beaches in Hawai'i.

Let the kids learn about the islands and make new friends at supervised children's programs at the many hotels (the one at the Hilton Hawaiian

Village is outstanding), while Mom and Dad get to enjoy some time on their own. Or, see if Hawai'i Nature Center programs coincide with your visit so the kids can discover what's in the forested hills behind Honolulu. A visit to the USS *Arizona* Memorial and the USS *Missouri* will help your family understand what World War II was about.

On Maui, don't miss the Maui Ocean Center, Hawai'i Nature Center, and Whalers Village Museum, all family-oriented attractions designed to educate as well as entertain.

**Comments** Maui's Ka'anapali Beach is the most popular family destination after Waikiki, but O'ahu offers more family-oriented attractions and activities than all other islands combined.

## Active Seniors

**Best Island to Visit** O'ahu

**Other Recommended Islands** Big Island, Kaua'i, Maui

**Things to See and Do** Visit O'ahu's historical attractions, including the Bishop Museum, 'Iolani Palace, Aloha Tower, Hawai'i Maritime Center, and the Mission Houses Museum. Hike up Diamond Head crater. Ride the open-air Waikiki Trolley. See Don Ho, still performing "Tiny Bubbles" and still a consummate entertainer who gives young singers and dancers a start. Learn Hawaiian crafts, like stringing lei, dancing a hula, or playing the 'ukulele. Swim in the comfort of the warm and salty Pacific, even if you're not comfortable in a bikini. Many couples renew their wedding vows on the beach at sunset.

Seniors will find excellent tours by Elder Hostel that probe the islands' interesting and educational facets at affordable rates. Contact Elder Hostel at www.elderhostel.org or (877) 426-8056.

On the Big Island, a functioning volcano is a prime draw for the awestruck of all ages. Don't miss this sight. If you love gardens, you will be intrigued by Honolulu's five municipal botanical gardens, including Foster Gardens downtown with its array of towering exotic trees. On Maui, the Maui Tropical Plantation gives a glimpse of sample fields of island crops, plus a great produce market. The only federally chartered research gardens, the National Tropical Botanical Garden, are definitely worth a visit on Kaua'i, at Lawa'i near Po'ipu Beach and Limahuli on the North Shore. On Maui, the 125-acre Kahanu garden of Pacific Island plants includes the state's largest archaeological site, Pi'ilanihale Heiau. Plenty of privately operated botanical gardens are sprinkled throughout the islands.

**Comments** Anyone with gray in their hair is viewed with respect in Hawai'i. You are considered a wise *kupuna* (elder), and doors are not closed to you. The healthy seniors who live in the islands surf, dance, play golf, swim daily, and do anything else they want. So can you. Many visitor attractions and some stores offer discounts for seniors..

## Visitors with Disabilities

**Best Island to Visit** Oʻahu

**Other Recommended Islands** Maui, Big Island

**Things to See and Do** Take in a concert, film, or dance performance at the historic Hawaiʻi Theatre in Honolulu, which provides special seating areas for the disabled.

Visit ʻIolani Palace, Sea Life Park, Polynesian Cultural Center, Honolulu Zoo, Hawaiʻi's Plantation Village, and Mission Houses Museum on Oʻahu; Haleakala National Park, Maui Tropical Plantation, and Maui Ocean Center on Maui; Hawaiʻi Volcanoes National Park, Panaʻewa Rainforest Zoo, Nani Mau Gardens, and Puʻuhonua O Honaunau on the Big Island; and the Kauaʻi Museum, Fern Grotto, and Kilauea Point National Wildlife Refuge on Kauaʻi—all of which accommodate disabled visitors.

On Oʻahu, curb-to-curb transportation service is provided by the City and County of Honolulu via the Handi-Van (call (808) 456-5555 for reservations, (808) 454-5050 for customer service). A sister company to TheBus, the Handi-Van transports some 2,000 passengers daily, operating from 5:30 a.m. to 11 p.m. Fares are $2 each way. City buses have elevator lifts for wheelchairs.

**Comments** *The Aloha Guide to Accessibility,* published by the State Disability and Communication Access Board, provides detailed information on accessibility features of island hotels, attractions, beaches, parks, theaters, shopping centers, transportation services, and medical and support services. Special transportation services are limited on the Neighbor Islands, but this free brochure covers that information as well. Write to the commission at 919 Ala Moana Blvd., Room 101, Honolulu, HI 96814, or call (808) 586-8121; you can also visit them online at www.hawaii.gov/health/dcab.

Hawaiʻi Centers for Independent Living has a website that provides useful information for the disabled at www.assistguide.com.

## Art Aficionados

**Best Island to Visit** Oʻahu

**Other Recommended Islands** Maui and the Big Island

**Things to See and Do** The Honolulu Academy of Arts and the Contemporary Museum, both in Honolulu, are the state's two best art museums. Maui has a thriving art community, with galleries in Lahaina, the Maui Arts and Cultural Center, and Hui Noʻeau Visual Arts Center. When you visit the Big Island, don't miss Volcano Art Center, housed in a historic building by the entrance of Hawai'i Volcanoes National Park.

**Comments** You can see and buy some local handicrafts by Hawaiian artisans at various crafts fairs held throughout the islands almost year-round, especially in November and December.

## Hawaiian Culture Seekers

**Best Island to Visit**  O'ahu

**Other Recommended Islands**  Maui, Kaua'i, the Big Island

**Things to See and Do**  Hawaiian culture is on display year-round but is especially in the spotlight during the Aloha Festivals, the biggest annual cultural celebration in the state. Colorful parades and pageantry, demonstrations of arts and crafts, and performances of music and dance are among the features. Aloha Festivals take place September through October, and each island has its own nine- or ten-day program. The Aloha Festivals committee sets festival dates years in advance; call (808) 545-1771 for a schedule.

The multiplicity of ethnic groups that contributed to the Hawai'i of today have heritage events throughout the year, on all islands but particularly on O'ahu. The University of Hawai'i often features its own cultural series of indoor and outdoor performances—showcasing contemporary Hawaiian music and dance, Chinese opera, and Japanese noh theater, among others. The Bishop Museum, repository of more than 20 million Pacific Islands cultural artifacts, is the best place to explore Hawai'i's rich past. The museum's new Waikiki annex at Hilton Hawaii Village offers a preview. A must-visit spot for art lovers is the new $3.5 million Luce Pavilion at Honolulu Academy of Arts, where guests can see ink sketches by John Webber (who sailed with Captain Cook), Maui landscapes by Georgia O'Keefe, and fiery canvases of Volcano School artists Jules Tavernier, Charles Furneaux, and D. Howard Hitchcock, who painted Madam Pele's volcanoes.

**Comments** Look for *hula halau* (school) fundraisers, slack key festivals, talk story events, and quilt shows; all offer a glimpse into the Hawaiian culture. You can also turn on the radio to an all-Hawaiian music station and get in the groove.

## Gourmets

**Best Island to Visit**  O'ahu

**Other Recommended Islands**  Maui, Big Island, and Lana'i

**Things to See and Do**  Superb fine-dining establishments can be found on every island. The best concentration of great restaurants, however, is in Honolulu on O'ahu. Many of Hawai'i's top regional cuisine chefs—

including Roy Yamaguchi, Alan Wong, Sam Choy, Phillipe Padovani, and George Mavrothalassatis—have restaurants on Oʻahu. In addition, Honolulu enjoys fine fusion versions of Japanese, Chinese, Thai, Vietnamese, Swiss, Korean, French, Italian, American, and other favorite cuisines.

The enthusiasm for creative chefs spreads to other islands, too, fed by the notable kitchens of luxury hotels that gather talented staffs and excellent fresh local foods.

**Comments** Be sure to treat your palate to a dinner of Hawaiʻi regional cuisine at Roy's, Alan Wong's, or Chef Mavro's, featuring fresh ingredients produced or grown in the islands. (See Part 9, "Dining in Hawaiʻi.")

## History Buffs

**Best Island to Visit** Oʻahu

**Other Recommended Islands** Big Island, Maui, Lanaʻi

**Things to See and Do** The greatest concentration of historical attractions is in a two-block area of downtown Honolulu, where the ʻIolani Palace, the State Capitol, the Governor's Mansion, Mission Houses Museum, Kawaiahaʻo Church, and the Hawaiʻi State Library are within easy walking distance of each other.

But in the tropics, where history vanishes quickly in the hot sun, salt air, and bug-laden environment, heritage sites are not always buildings. Rock platforms are all that's left of most *heiau*, or temple ruins, all over the islands. They are still sacred to many, however.

On the Big Island, clues to the somewhat mysterious past are everywhere if you care enough to search. The Kona-Kohala Coast resorts feature fields of ancient carvings and examples of early Hawaiian aquaculture techniques still in use today in fishponds. Out in the nearby lava, the C-shaped rock shelters built by early soldiers are still visible. In many places, including Waikoloa, you can make out the pathway through the lava made by bare human feet of royal messengers centuries ago. Ambitious plans are proceeding to raise some $30 million to unearth a particularly prized cultural treasure—Mokuʻula, the royal palace of King Kamehameha III, which lies buried beneath a county ball park but will one day be revealed by the restoration project.

The Piʻilanihale Heiau dig near Hana will appeal to archaeology buffs.

On Lanaʻi, you can drive and hike up to petroglyph rocks on a hill over Palawai Basin, or pilot a vehicle over rough roads to Kaunolu, King Kamehameha I's summer fishing camp.

**Comments** Spend a day in the Bishop Museum, the best place to get a handle on Hawaiʻi's history; it's in Kalihi at the Likelike Highway exit from H-1, a 20-minute drive from Waikiki.

## Sports Fans

**Best Island to Visit**  Maui

**Other Recommended Islands**  O'ahu, Big Island

**Things to See and Do**  Football fans have something to cheer about on O'ahu, scene of the NFL Pro Bowl every year and a Christmas Day doubleheader featuring two NCAA postseason bowl games. In December, the University of Hawai'i hosts the prestigious Rainbow Classic, an eight-team collegiate basketball tournament. Other major O'ahu sporting events include the Honolulu Marathon and Sony Open Golf Tournament, the Triple Crown of Surfing, the Kenwood Cup, the Trans-Pacific and other sailing races, annual lifeguard competitions, and a full schedule of outrigger canoe paddling contests.

Maui hosts the annual Hula Bowl (the college football all-star game), Maui Invitational (a nationally televised college basketball tournament), Kapalua's annual Mercedes Open (a golf tournament), windsurfing competitions, and the Maui Marathon.

The Big Island is home to the world's most famous triathlon, the annual Ironman Triathlon—which includes a 2.4 mile ocean swim, a rugged 112-mile bike ride, and a hot 26.2-mile run—and its one-up cousin, the Ultraman, which raises the bar to a 6.2-mile swim, 251.4-mile bike ride, and 52.3-mile run.

**Comments**  Sports teams may not be able to swing a regular Hawai'i playing schedule, but pros and collegiate all-star champions alike wouldn't miss their reward trip to Hawai'i to end a stellar season with the Hula Bowl and Pro Bowl games. For Hula Bowl tickets, see www.idatasports.com/hulabowl/tickets.html or call (808) 871-4141. For Pro Bowl tickets and special packages, you can find lots of options on the Internet, including official National Football League offerings at www.nfl.com/probowl/2002/tickets.html. Or contact the Aloha Stadium box office, (808) 486-9300.

## Business Travelers

Situated in the middle of the Pacific Ocean, the Aloha State is the only place in the world where you can conduct business live with major financial centers in New York, Japan, China, and Hawai'i all on the same day. The islands are becoming known as a good place to do business, especially when transactions involve linking U.S. concerns with Asia and the Pacific Rim. There's a sparkling new convention facility in Honolulu as well.

The islands are a great place for corporate groups to meet for fun and profit, rewarding top performers, top customers, and top prospects. The extensive choice of luxury resorts, outdoor sports and team-building events, al fresco parties, and other only-in-Hawai'i features draw groups back year after year. Hawai'i's remote setting, high degree of international air service, controlled access (nearly everyone flies in or out), and relatively safe and secure environment make it a favored choice for diplomats, scientists, political and economic leaders, and other international group gatherings. Hotels increasingly cater to business needs with office and fitness centers, in-room dataports, competent staff, and a hip-to-technology attitude. The fiber-optic system linking the islands to the West Coast is one of the best in the world, thanks to the presence of an Air Force supercomputer on Maui.

## The Hawai'i Convention Center

Located on the edge of Waikiki, the Hawai'i Convention Center combines high-tech wizardry with a Hawaiian sense of place. Designed by Hawai'i's own architectural firm of Wimberly Allison Tong and Goo, the airy four-story center opened to wide acclaim in the summer of 1998. The center has 100,000 square feet of meeting space, 200,000 square feet of exhibit space, a 36,000-square-foot ballroom, a 35,000-square-foot registration/lobby area, and an 800-space parking garage.

The ground floor houses the lobby area and exhibit hall, which is large enough to accommodate a reception for some 28,000 attendees. The second floor is reserved for parking; the third level features meeting rooms; and the fourth (top) floor houses the grand ballroom and rooftop garden terrace. A two-story glass wall enhances the lobby, where palms and tropical plants grow inside and out.

High-tech features include fiber-optic cables providing speedy, state-of-the-art communication; a press room with global links to any nation in the world; a built-in, six-station simultaneous translation room, allowing translators to view the speakers through a video monitor; a meeting room capable of hosting 400 computers working simultaneously; and an auditorium with built-in projection room and concert-quality sound system.

More than 30,000 hotel rooms and condominium units are within a one-mile radius of the center. The nearest, Ala Moana Hotel, is directly across the street. Plenty of restaurants are an easy walk away. Nearby Ala Moana Center offers dozens of restaurants and a food court. The older area around the convention center is still something of a motherlode of girly bars, strip clubs, Korean bars, and just plain bars, despite some efforts to banish them.

For more information, call the Hawai'i Visitors and Convention Bureau at (808) 923-1811 or surf over to www.hvcb.org/hconv.

# Tying the Knot

Hawai'i is one of America's favorite places to get married and go on a honeymoon. Lovers can get married on the beach (check out www.beachweddingshawaii.com for information), by waterfalls, under water amid tropical fish, in churches old and new, on sailboats, on off-shore islets, and up in the air while sky diving.

In old Hawai'i marriage ceremonies were reserved only for high-ranking citizens, *ali'i*. The first Christian marriage took place in 1822, two years after the arrival of American missionaries. For a time, it was illegal for non-Christian marriages to be held in the islands. Today, more than 10,000 out-of-state couples are wed here every year. For a time, legal same-sex marriages drew couples to Hawai'i. However, voters amended the state constitution in 1998 to classify marriage as pertaining to male-female relationships, and the state's supreme court upheld that in 1999. The long tradition in Polynesian culture of tolerance to the "third sex," or *mahu*, still means gay-oriented travel companies and commitment ceremonies are commonly accepted on the islands.

## How To Get Married

To get married in Hawai'i, you'll need a valid marriage license. You can obtain one at the State Department of Health, Marriage License Office, 1250 Punchbowl Street, Honolulu, HI 96813. The office is open from Monday to Friday, 8 a.m. to 4 p.m. (closed on holidays). Both bride and groom must be present when the license is issued. The license is valid statewide for 30 days. The fee is $50 in cash.

On the Neighbor Islands, you can get a license from a marriage license agent (ask your hotel concierge or wedding coordinator to direct you to the nearest agent).

Both the bride and the groom must be at least 18 years of age to be married without parental consent. If either partner has been married before, he or she is required to provide the date, county, and state (or country) in which the divorce was finalized for each previous marriage. The names of each person's parents and place of birth must also be provided.

A free "Getting Married" pamphlet is available from Hawai'i's Marriage License Office. Write to the address above or call them at (808) 586-4544. In addition, the Hawai'i Visitors and Convention Bureau has a list of wedding planners on all islands at www.gohawaii.com.

## Seven Romantic Places to Get Married in Hawai'i

### O'ahu

Kawaiaha'o Church, downtown Honolulu. This landmark coral block church, designed by New England missionary Hiram Bingham and dedicated in 1842, is one of O'ahu's most popular and stately venues for couples seeking a formal church wedding. Contact Kawaiaha'o Church at (808) 522-1333

### Waikiki Beach

Just walk out on the gold sand at sunset, adorned in flowers with your intended mate and your officiator, and say "I do" before lots of witnesses, who may join you in singing the "Hawaiian Wedding Song" as you dance across the *lana'i* (patio) at the House Without a Key. Don't forget to hire a photographer to capture the moment. Meanwhile, the Moët Chandon is chilling up in your Halekulani honeymoon suite. Contact Halekulani at (808) 923-2311 or www.halekulani.com.

### Maui

Waterfall Garden, Westin Maui Prince: At the waterfall pool in the open-air atrium where golden Japanese carp splash in black lava tide pools, many couples get married every weekend on Maui. It's been a popular wedding site in South Maui since the Hotel opened more than a decade ago. Contact Westin Maui Prince Hotel at Makena, (808) 874-1111.

### Big Island of Hawai'i

On a beach framed by coconut palms and serene ancient fishponds, one of Hawai'i's most romantic locations appeals to many wedding couples as the place to recite vows. Contact Outrigger Waikoloa Beach Hotel, (808) 886-6789.

### Kaua'i

On Kaua'i's North Shore, the Princeville Hotel overlooks the Bali Hai image you dream about: Hanalei Bay with jagged, waterfall-creased volcanic peaks in the background. *'Akamai* (with-it) couples wait for the golden hour around sunset when the blue sky is streaked with red and gold rays. Contact Princeville Resort, (808) 826-9644.

### Moloka'i

High noon or sundown, a wedding way out west on the Moloka'i Ranch is the way to go if the two of you love horses. You can choose a hilltop, a cliffside, or a beach for the main event before moseying back to the 22-room Sheraton Moloka'i for a reception overlooking the pastures and the sea. Call (808) 552-2791.

### Lana'i

At the Conservatory on Lana'i, exchange vows amid thousands of exotic orchids in the misty, glass-paned conservatory, then dance your wedding waltz in The Lodge at Ko'ele, a very romantic setting for weddings and honeymoons. Contact the Lodge at Ko'ele, (808) 565-7300.

# Part Three

# Lodging

## Where to Stay

In Hawai'i, you can choose the hotel that's just right for you from among more than 70,000 rooms, suites, condo units, apartments, and bungalows—from budget surfer digs to first-rate palaces, with prices to match—on the six main islands. Most are on or near a beach.

You'll find the familiar names of international hotel management firms—such as Westin, Hilton, Hyatt, Marriott, Prince, Sheraton, Ritz-Carlton, Four Seasons, Mandarin, and Fairmont—as well as locally owned Aston and Outrigger hotels and family-operated independents.

Views range from outstanding to average. In Waikiki, "ocean" views can be a peek of blue between high rises or a mesmerizing wall-to-wall panorama of the beach framed by Diamond Head or the city and sunset behind the Wai'anae Mountains in the distance. If you're off the beach, you may have a mountain view that reveals the haunting beauty of the Ko'olau Range, the twinkling neighborhood lights halfway up the slopes at night, and the busy paddlers on the Ala Wai Canal below. Garden rooms usually deliver tropical garden views.

Most rooms have sliding glass doors that open to outdoor lana'i for those of us who prefer Hawai'i's own balmy air to air conditioning.

The chief factors we used to rate hotels are: location (on the beach or nearby), views, service, amenities, character, price, and value. When you choose your lodging—whether through a travel agent or on your own—ask whether construction or other noisy endeavors are going to be happening nearby, whether your room was recently renovated, whether it has a balcony or patio, what extras are included in the rate (such as in-room coffeemaker, daily paper, movies, dataports, mini-bar, beach gear, Continental breakfast), and whether airport transfers are available. Most deluxe and luxury rooms come equipped with hair dryers, irons and boards, and safes; some also come with CD players. If these extras are important to you, ask about them.

If you're going upscale, inquire about the club floors. Rooms on these floors have keyed elevator access, a lounge with free drinks, Continental breakfast, light buffet lunch, evening *pupu* (appetizers), and sinful fresh-baked cookies, plus a concierge to call their own. The rates are higher, of course, but the buffets take care of breakfast, lunch, snacks, and cocktails, which are all costly at resorts. You can get your morning coffee and the children's breakfasts quickly and easily.

You don't have to go first class to get great service. Usually service at Hawai'i hotels is friendly and courteous at every level, from maids to general managers. Staff members exhibit lots of "aloha spirit" and wear flowers and tropical uniforms. They may not all speak your language, but they will find someone who does, and they are anxious to please you.

Waikiki gets the lion's share of visitors from around the world, but it's not for everyone. When you seek a quieter getaway on O'ahu, plan to stay at 'Ihilani Resort and Spa on the Leeward side, Kahala Mandarin Oriental Hotel in suburban Kahala southeast of Waikiki, Turtle Bay Golf & Country Club on the North Shore, or a B&B or vacation rental on the Windward side.

On Maui, Ka'anapali Beach Resort, like Waikiki, handles the greatest number of people very well, but the quieter resorts of Wailea, Kapalua, and Makena top our recommended list. Our favorite Big Island hotels are on the Kona-Kohala Coast. On Kaua'i, Po'ipu, and Princeville resorts are our favorites. Lana'i has two fine hotels and a small lodge; Moloka'i has an excellent 22-room lodge.

All lodging is subject to an 11% state tax (7% room tax plus 4% excise tax, charged at 4.17%).

## Great Places to Stay

Some of the world's greatest beach resort hotels and resorts are found in Hawai'i. They range from traditional favorites, like the century-old Sheraton Moana Surfrider Hotel on Waikiki Beach to newer stars, like the Four Seasons Hualalai Resort on the Big Island, that seem to define the Hawaiian experience for visitors of different eras. Some, like the Four Seasons Wailea Resort and Kapalua Bay Hotel, are elegant retreats; others are fantasies come true, like Grand Wailea Resort and Hyatt Regency Maui, Hilton Waikoloa Village on the Big Island and Kaua'i Marriott. A precious few evoke the memory of old Polynesia, such as Kona Village Resort. Here's our list of favorites by category:

### *Hopelessly Romantic*

**Halekulani, O'ahu**   No finer hotel exists in Waikiki for lovers or for anybody who can handle the five-star tab. You can watch the sun set from the House Without a Key as a hula dancer sways gracefully to old songs, or, if you prefer, watch the sunset reflect on Diamond Head from your in-room tub. Then settle into a private booth at La Mer for French champagne and haute cuisine. The rest is up to you. Phone (800) 367-2343 or visit www.halekulani.com.

**Ritz-Carlton Kapalua, Maui**   Hawai'i's only Ritz commands the last outpost of resort life in West Maui, which ensures unmatched views up the wild northwest coast and out to sea. Its caring management and celebrations of Hawaiian culture and art add to its romantic setting on an old pineapple plantation at the foot of the West Maui Mountains. You can get married in the historic little church on the grounds. An oasis of calm with old-fashioned Hawaiian hospitality, this Ritz is your pleasure. Phone (800) 262-8448 or visit www.ritzcarlton.com.

**Kona Village Resort, Big Island**   Sleep under thatch in a private island hale at Kona Village, created in the mid-1960s before there was road access. Guests flew or sailed into this retreat. Now you can drive from the airport in a few minutes across the lava field, but the sense of seclusion continues. The ultimate escape, this exclusive beach retreat is a collection of coastal huts in various Pacific Islands styles of architecture. It's ideal for kids and families, except during September when it's couples only. When you seek genuine peace and quiet, stay here. When you want privacy, put your coconut by the door. This is one of the few island resorts that features rates including three meals a day. Phone (800) 367-5290 or visit www.konavillage.com.

**Hotel Hana-Maui, Maui**   In misty green tropical Hana, this inn by the sea offers private Sea Ranch cottages for two with a bubbly hot tub and thick Turkish towels. Explore the neighborhood on foot or horseback—this sleepy area is all part of a large ranch. Phone (800) 321-HANA or visit www.hotelhanamaui.com.

**Hyatt Regency Kaua'i Resort & Spa**   On one of Kaua'i's wild beaches, this nostalgic hotel echoes island architecture of the 1920s to create a romantic setting with gardens, pools, and intimate restaurants often frequented by hand-holding couples, not all of them honeymooners. Phone (800) 55-HYATT or visit www.kauai-hyatt.com.

**Island Retreat, Kilauea, Kaua'i**   A private lakeside estate for lovers seeking total escape, Steve Hunt's Island Retreat has been featured by several bridal magazines. With its own 20-acre lake, beach, tropical gardens, boats, kayaks, boat dock, and putting green, the Kilauea estate is a honeymoon hideaway at $750 a night. Phone (310) 379-7842 or visit www.kauai.honeymoon.com.

## Great for Families

**Hilton Hawaiian Village**   Flamingos, peacocks, penguins, a secluded lagoon, three pools, and 3,000 rooms on 20 acres on Waikiki Beach: What more could a kid want? This tropical wonderland will appeal to your kids and the kid in you. A busy children's program full of daily surprises keeps everyone happy here. Plenty of grown-up entertainment is available as well, plus restaurants and a whole village full of shops. Kalia Tower opened in fall 2001, offering Waikiki's newest guest rooms, a full-scale spa, and a wellness center. Phone (800) 949-4321 or visit www.hawaiianvillage.hilton.com.

**Westin Maui at Ka'anapali Beach Resort**   This open, airy beachfront hotel looks like a Disney fantasy jungle—tropical foliage, waterfalls, and parrots everywhere inside the open atrium and Ka'anapali outside. Kids love the aquatic playground with a 128-foot slide, the easy-breezy feeling, and year-round summer camp–like fun. It's a big hit with big kids, too. Phone (800) WESTIN-1 or visit www.westinmaui.com.

**Fairmont Kea Lani, Wailea, Maui**   The shockingly white, smoothed, round towers and turrets, like something out of *Arabian Nights,* the luxurious Fairmont Kea Lani hotel delivers more than just fantasy. All the rooms are well equipped suites with high-tech stereos and kitchens, except for the great private villas with private plunge pools. Great beach, great restaurants. Kids are so welcome that there's a separate family pool and one for adults only. The south end of Wailea Resort is only walking distance on the coastal trail to neighboring shops and restaurants. Phone (800) 659-4100 or visit www.kealani.com.

## Great Historic Traditions

**Sheraton Moana Surfrider Hotel**   Enter this century-old hotel, and ghosts of old Waikiki past surround you. That could be Queen Liliu'okalani's carriage at the porte-cochere. You can almost hear Webley Edwards broadcasting "Hawai'i Calls" from the Banyan Court. The graceful grande dame of the beach has been revived with a painstaking historic renovation. Now entering its second century, Waikiki's first hotel is on the National Register of Historic Places. If only the walls could talk. Phone (800) 325-3535 or visit www.moana-surfrider.com.

**Royal Hawaiian Hotel**   They called it the "pink palace," and so it remains, from pink carpet to pink beach umbrellas. A hot flamingo pink landmark by the blue sea, the Royal Hawaiian is the bright spot in Waikiki's bland concrete jungle. Inspired by a Rudolph Valentino movie and built by Matson Steamship Lines in 1927 during Waikiki's golden age, this beach hotel endures as a monument to pleasure. Phone (800) 325-3535 or visit www.sheraton.com.

**Pioneer Inn, Lahaina, Maui**   Overlooking Lahaina Harbor, the Pioneer Inn turned 100 years old in 2001, holding on after a $5 million face-lift. This once-rowdy sailor's haunt is now a charming relic fit for all who "collect" old hotels and prefer tradition over trend. Phone (800) 457-5457.

**Westin Mauna Kea Beach Hotel, Big Island**   Nelson Rockefeller started a whole new trend in 1965 when he arranged for this gracious hotel and its world-famous golf course to stand beside a beautiful beach and invited the captains of industry to come take their rest (now their grandchildren carry on the tradition in many a family). He filled it full of Asian and Pacific art and triggered a renaissance in Hawaiian quilting arts by commissioning handmade quilts for wall hangings. A path was blasted through the lava to reach the hotel. The soaring indoor/outdoor architecture befits the climate, and the beach is still wonderful. There's no question about it—it's a classic, and you always feel at home here. Phone (800) 882-6060 or visit www.maunakeabeachhotel.com.

**Waimea Plantation Cottages, Waimea, Kaua'i**   This is a resort composed of restored tin-roof sugar shacks situated in a palm grove by the sea. History buffs will be delighted. Cottages are named for families who lived in them. Dating from the 1880s to 1930s, the cottages are updated with modern kitchens and bath and furnished with period wicker and rattan. Some are on the beach. The setting, near the Waimea River in West Kaua'i, is off the beaten track, but Captain Cook stepped ashore nearby more than 200 years ago and "discovered" Hawai'i in the process. Phone (800) 92-ASTON or visit www.astonhotels.com.

### Great for High Rollers

**The Lodge at Ko'ele, Lana'i**   Live like a grand poobah, if only for a few days, in this highland inn on a nearly private, red-dirt island of abandoned pineapple fields. It's deliciously decadent, outrageously expensive, and captivating. You won't ever want to leave. It begins to feel like a friend's country estate. Phone (800) 321-4666 or visit www.lanai-resorts.com.

**Four Seasons Resort Hualalai, Big Island**   Under dormant Hualalai volcano, this is Hawai'i's only new resort that didn't come out a high rise— instead, it is a series of clusters of handsome private bungalows arranged around pools by the beach, with outdoor shower gardens, tasteful decor, and oceanfront restaurants a step off the sand. From the thatched roofs over its outdoor whirlpool tubs to the natural amphitheater in a lava formation, Four Seasons Hualalai is wonderfully different and expensive, with rates up to $6,000 a night for bungalows by the sea. The resort is surrounded by golf greens, ranks of swanky condos, and private home lots. If you want a second home here, a lot with ocean view goes for $1 million, house extra. Phone (888) 340-KONA or visit www.fourseasons.com.

**Mauna Lani Beach Hotel and Bungalows, Big Island** Fish ponds, lava caves, petroglyphs—the physical evidence of early habitation is abundant on this shore. But it's doubtful they lived as well as current guests do, even though this was once a retreat for Hawaiian royalty. The Mauna Lani is the namesake hotel of Mauna Lani Resort, a 3,200-acre Kohala Coast retreat favored by Hollywood royalty who like the $4,750 per night bungalows with butlers by the shore. The Orchid Hotel at Mauna Lani, two spectacular golf courses, plushy condos, and private homes also share the enclave, which is protected by a lava wasteland. Phone (800) 327-8585 or visit www.maunalani.com.

**Westin Hapuna Beach Prince Hotel, Big Island** Built by a Tokyo tycoon, the Hapuna Beach Prince is a paean to the big ocean view from a cliff beside Hapuna Beach. The beauty is in the materials—burnished wood and slate with little other interior decor. Critics call it stark, but think of the Hapuna Beach public and private rooms as mere frames for the marine-scene painting beyond. The huge pool awaits those reluctant to take on the golden sands and nearly secret fishy cove below. A $6,500 per night, three-bedroom villa awaits your VIPs. The golf course, like the hotel, is a spare intrusion on the natural setting, a links-style natural course with native plants and par-busting views. Phone (800) 882-6060 or visit www.hapunabeachprincehotel.com.

### Great Bargains

**New Otani Kaimana Beach, Oʻahu** Under Diamond Head, this small hotel with a big attitude has a slightly removed view of Waikiki. Its beachfront location, gentle hospitality, famed Hau Tree Lanaʻi (where Robert Louis Stevenson read poems to Princess Kaʻiulani) and decent rates, make New Otani an old and valued favorite of repeat guests. Choose a corner suite and ask for the corner you want—ocean or Kapiʻolani Park view with Diamond Head or city/sunset exposure. On a budget, get a regular room (they're small) and enjoy your peaceful perch surrounded by the park instead of the traffic and crowds of central Waikiki. Phone (800) 356-8265 or visit www.kaimana.com.

**Outrigger Waikoloa Beach Resort, Big Island** In this ritzy neighborhood of high-end beach hotels, the newly remodeled, deluxe Outrigger Waikoloa, with the same great location, is the best value on the Kohala Coast. New features include a beach-view restaurant, a spa, and many upgrades. The hotel commands a site by a huge fish pond complex and palm-fringed ʻAnaehoʻomalu Beach, one of the Big Island's best. Phone (800) 922-5533 or visit www.outrigger.com.

**Garden Island Inn, Kauaʻi** Kalapaki Beach and Nawiliwili Harbor (where freight ships and cruise ships call), plus shops and restaurants are all across the street from your spacious, $125 per night suite with kitchen, wet bar, and private lana'i, with free, tree-ripe papayas daily. Phone (800) 648-0154 or visit www.gardenislandinn.com.

**The Napili Bay, Maui**    On a gold sand beach, the 33-unit condo hotel is close to golf and shopping in West Maui. Units are studios with full kitchen, queen bed, television, lana'i, and ceiling fans for $75 per night. Phone (888) 661-7200 or visit www.mauibeachfront.com.

**Malihini Hotel, O'ahu**    This small, no-frills, two-story, 28-unit hotel is a half block from Waikiki Beach, across from Fort DeRussy and costs just $45 a night. That's no typo, just the best deal for a clean, well-lighted place near the beach. Phone (808) 923-9644.

# Getting a Good Deal on a Room

Now that you've had a preview of some of Hawai'i's great places to stay, here's how to get the best deal.

- Book early.

- Go in fall and spring months (September–November, April, May, and early June).

- Educate yourself on what you want and where and when you want it before you go to a travel agent. They may have suggestions that alter your plan, but they'll surely do a better job for you if you narrow the search for them. More agents are charging customers a fee for their services these days, as well as collecting a percentage of the booking as their commission. In Hawai'i, hotel and condo commissions are usually 10%. Ask about your agent's fee policies in advance.

- Ask a travel agent to research package rates and other specials that combine your room with sports, spa, rental car, and other features. They have access to information you won't find as a consumer.

- Call the hotel to see what rate you can negotiate. Ask for the best rate they can offer, not the published rack rate. Check the Internet, too—sometimes rates and fares are cheaper if you book there.

- Pursue discounts for corporate travel, seniors, kids staying free in your room, military personnel, travel clubs, and other special status travel. See what frequent flier mileage you may gain from your hotel stay.

Several factors determine a hotel's room rate: demand, location, season, availability, view, grade of room, and proximity to beach, shopping centers, and entertainment.

Hawai'i room rates are highest from late December through late March, when everyone wants to escape winter. The average hotel room rate then is $146–$151. In the spring and fall, average room rates fall to $130–$144.

Hawai'i's visitor industry provides a quarter of the state's gross state product, a quarter of the state's tax revenue, and a third of the jobs.

Hawai'i's dependency on tourism is unlikely to fade. That means competitive rates and good deals for you.

## Where the Deals Are

### Newspaper Travel Sections

Check travel sections of major U.S. newspapers for good room deals and combinations with airfare, hotel or condo rental, and car rental.

### Surf the Internet

If the search is part of your journey, surf the web. You can preview islands, beaches, golf courses, hotels, condos, and vacation rentals. The Internet and this guide book, which highlights websites, will make your search easy. Also try your luck with Internet brokers, such as priceline. com, hoteldiscount.com, travelocity.com, and others dedicated to travel bargains.

### Other Money-Saving Suggestions

Many hotels offer their own periodic package deals with value-added amenities like a free rental car, food and beverage credits, rounds of golf, spa treatments, extra-special treatment for honeymooners (chocolates and champagne) and for families, and perhaps free or cheaper second rooms when you book the first room. Some hotels offer a free extra night if you book a room for a certain number of nights (usually four to seven). Hotels off the beach are cheaper, so are mountain- or garden-view rooms. Ask if kids can stay in your room free.

### Travel Packages

Travel packages save money, provide value, and eliminate the time-consuming search for separate deals for airfare, hotel rooms, and car rentals. By purchasing these components in bulk, the companies that offer travel packages save money. They can pass the savings on to consumers, who, in a sense, buy in bulk from them: flights, rooms, rental cars, and so on all at once. Packages have a single inclusive rate, but they differ from tour travel. On a tour, you are escorted by a guide who handles everything on the trip for you. Travel packages are for more independent travelers. However, the components of a package will clearly impact your itinerary, so it's wise to develop basic plans before booking.

In recent years, packages have become very flexible and include a wide range of rates and places to stay. Be a good shopper by knowing what your cost would be for each component of the package, and be sure the package total is cheaper and hopefully includes extras. However, be wary of packages that include extras you weren't planning to purchase in order to ratchet up the price. A package should include only travel components you intend to use.

## If You Make Your Own Reservation

If you hunt your own bargains, call the hotel directly instead of the chain's toll-free number. The clerk at a central site may not know about special local rates. The quoted, or "rack," room rates—the ones printed once a year for brochures to be placed in a rack—are nothing if not flexible. Virtually no one pays the full rack rate, except perhaps at peak travel times or for last minute bookings. Don't be shy about inquiring about lower rates, especially during the low season, when your bargaining position is improved. Ask for the lowest and best rates available to you, and inquire about any other special deals. Hotels would rather fill rooms at discounted prices than leave them empty. Do your bargaining, however, when you reserve a room, not after your arrival.

## Corporate Rates

Many hotels provide corporate rates (up to 20% off regular rack rates). Ask your hotel about them. Generally, you do not need to work for a large company or have a special relationship with a hotel to obtain corporate rates. Some hotels require a written request on company letterhead or some other verification of your employment status, but others will guarantee the rate over the phone.

## Travel Clubs

Travel clubs offer discounts of up to half off participating hotels' rack rates, but with restrictions. They generally apply on a space-available basis and are not available in blackout periods (usually during peak travel times). Some may apply only on certain days of the week. Not all hotels offer a true 50% discount. Some base their discount on an exaggerated rack rate. Before joining a discount program, compare the rates offered to members with those available elsewhere.

Most travel clubs or half-price programs charge an annual fee, up to $125 or more. When you join, you receive a membership card and directory of participating hotels, including on average about 100 in Hawai'i. It may be wise to evaluate your long-term travel plans when considering membership in a travel club, as you may not recoup the membership fee in a single trip. Clubs work best for frequent travelers and travelers with flexible schedules.

The following travel club programs offer lodging in Hawai'i:

- Encore, (800) 638-0930
- Entertainment Publications, (800) 285-5525

- International Travel Card, (800) 342-0558

- Quest, (800) 638-9819

## *Wholesalers*

Wholesalers annually purchase blocks of hotel rooms at a low, negotiated rate. They resell rooms during the coming year to travel agents, tour operators, and the public. Wholesalers can generally return unsold rooms to a hotel, but they are disinclined to do so because their ability to negotiate rates with the hotel is predicated upon the large volume of rooms they purchase. Wholesalers sometimes offer rooms at bargain prices to avoid returning them unsold. They prefer that you reserve packages through your travel agent but also deal directly with the public, frequently representing themselves as "reservation services." When you call, you can ask for a room at a particular hotel or at any hotel in a given area. If you have a price ceiling in mind, say so. Some wholesalers require you to pay them, by credit card, when making a reservation. Others allow you to pay at the hotel upon check out. More than 100 tour wholesalers offer Hawai'i travel packages, including these:

- All About Tours, (800) 274-8687

- Classic Custom Vacations, (800) 221-3949

- Creative Leisure International, (800) 426-6367

- Globetrotters/MTI Vacations, (800) 635-1333

- Pleasant Holidays, (800) 2-HAWAII

## *Travel Advisory*

The following advice applies to each of the money-saving methods of booking a room described above.

- Be wary of deals that seem too good to be true.

- Don't be pressured into accepting a deal on the spot. A good offer today should be a good offer tomorrow. Do not send money by messenger or overnight mail. Question any requests for you to send money immediately. Do not provide your credit card number or bank information over the phone unless you know the company.

- Ask questions. Find out what's covered in the total cost. Ask if there are additional charges. Ask about cancellation policies and refunds.

- Get all the information in writing before you agree to purchase a tour or travel package, and read it.

# Other Ways to Stay

## Condominiums

Condo units can be the perfect solution for family trips, two couples traveling together, or one couple seeking more space, privacy, convenience, and value than a hotel room might offer.

Hawai'i condo resorts are not your bare-bones ski units. They range from standard to first-rate with all the comforts home may not have. They come in small clusters or large buildings, by the beach or not, often with lobbies, front desks, maid service, and other hotel services. Frequently, they are located in major resort areas with the full menu of extras available to hotel guests, including golf, tennis, pools, restaurants, and shuttle service. The difference between some resort condos and hotels is hard to discern as a guest, other than the larger units and homelike facilities of condos. The units are individually owned, but the rentals are managed in a group. Units in one complex may be managed by several different companies, some of them hotel firms—just to confuse it further—and individual owners may rent out their own units, too.

Units range from 700–800 square feet for a one-bedroom unit to 2,000 square feet or more for a two-bedroom unit. Three-bedroom units and villas are larger still. With kitchens, you have the option of cooking meals or just putting together breakfast or lunch homestyle, then having dinner in restaurants. This gives you the chance to indulge in fresh tropical fruit, Kona coffee, and other Hawaiian specialties, and it virtually erases problems with fussy eaters, allowing everyone to have a better time. Condo unit prices can range from as low as $45 per night to more than $300 per night, depending on the type of accommodation, location, and dates of stay.

One choice is to book your condo through one of the dozens of central condo reservations agencies around the islands and the nation (some are listed below) to find Hawaiian units that suit your needs. State your preferences on location, unit size, price range, amenities, ambience, and the number in your party, and you'll receive a list of properties from which to choose. Some condo representatives offer extra services, like car rentals and lei greetings, and some handle private resort home rentals as well.

Kapalua Resort on Maui is one of several luxury resorts that has an on-site management operation handling some 200 luxury units and homes in several areas of the resort. Destination Resorts Hawai'i at Wailea Resort is another, handling a wide variety of condo units at Wailea.

If you go travel shopping on your own, you'll find plenty of condo travel packages are available in the same way that hotel packages are offered. Watch the ads, use the Internet, ask your friends, and keep on top of special offers. Also, individual owners may rent their units through the Internet and ads in magazines or newspapers.

Terms and policies differ. A deposit is usually required, payable by a major credit card. It's wise to book at least three months in advance, although late reservations are entirely possible. Again, holidays and other high-demand periods will mean more competition for the unit you want.

## RECOMMENDED CONDO RESERVATIONS AGENTS

**Statewide**
Hawaiian Condo Resorts
(800) 487-4505, (808) 949-4505
www.hawaiicondo.com

Aston Hotels and Resorts
(800) 92-ASTON
www.aston-hotels.com

Outrigger Hotels and Resorts
(800) 688-7444
www.outrigger.com

**Big Island**
Keauhou Property Management
(deluxe, Keauhou Resort)
(800) 745-KONA, (808) 326-9075

South Kohala Management (luxury units and homes, Kohala Coast)
(800) 822-4252, (808) 883-8500

Kona Hawaii Vacation Rentals
(affordable, Kailua-Kona)

(800) 553-5035, (808) 329-9393
www.konahawaii.com

**Maui**
Destination Resorts Hawai'i (Wailea Resort)
(800) 367-5246, (808) 879-1595
www.maui.net/~dhr

Kihei Maui Vacations (affordable; homes, too)
(800) 541-6284, (808) 879-7581
www.maui.net/~kmv

**Kaua'i**
Kaua'i Vacation Rentals (homes, too)
(800) 367-5025, (808) 245-8841

**O'ahu**
Aloha Waikiki Vacation Condos (Waikiki)
(800) 655-6055, (808) 923-4402
www.waikiki-condos.com

Here are our favorite condos, selected for their location, value, facilities, and the good time we had there.

**O'ahu: Waikiki Shore**   The only beachfront condo on Waikiki Beach, this is a true find beside the open Fort DeRussy beachfront. Beach, ocean, city, and mountain views in studios, one-bedroom, and two-bedroom units priced from $154 per night for two people. For a fee, guests can use services of neighboring Outrigger Reef on the Beach Hotel—offering pool, club floor, fitness center, lounge, massage facility, and signing privileges. Write 2161 Kalia Rd., Honolulu, HI 96815; call (800) 655-6055, (808) 923-4402; or visit www.waikiki-condos.com/shore.html.

**Maui: The Kapalua Villas**   Luxurious, spacious villas in low-rise clusters with views and proximity to beach and golf course. One bedroom to three bedrooms are available. Bring the whole clan and celebrate. Write

500 Office Rd., Kapalua, HI 96761; call (800) 545-0018, (808) 669-8088; or visit www.kapaluavillas.com.

**Kaua'i: Hanalei Colony Resort** These condos boast an incredibly beautiful and remote location. Take seven one-lane bridges past Princeville on the North Shore to find this low-rise hideaway of 48 two-bedroom units. Get groceries at Hanalei on the way, because commerce comes to a halt when you arrive, leaving only the breathtaking beachfront setting. Step off your lana'i onto sand. There's a restaurant next door, movie star homes just beyond that, and then the road ends at Na Pali Coast. Write P.O. Box 206, Hanalei, HI 96714; call (800) 628-3004, (808) 826-6235; or visit www.hcr.com.

**Big Island of Hawai'i: Kanaloa at Keauhou** Palatial bathrooms are a key feature of these one-, two-, and three-bedroom units that are large, comfortable, and well furnished. The low-rise units sprawl over a rocky headland at Keauhou, south of Kailua-Kona, with a restaurant, tennis, three pools, and lots of lazy lana'i ambience. Some are on the waterfront. They're great for families. Write 78-261 Manukai St., Kailua-Kona, HI 96740; call (800) 688-7444, (808) 322-9625; or visit www.kanaloa-kona.com.

**Moloka'i: Paniolo Hale** Wrapped in greens of the Kaluako'i Golf Course beside golden Kepuhi Beach, this is an architecturally appealing ranch-style retreat and the most interesting of several small low-rise condo complexes next to Kaluako'i Resort at Moloka'i's west end. The resort and golf course are currently closed, but not Paniolo Hale, which operates independently. Normally, one bonus of this complex is to be golf cart–driving or walking distance from the tees. But it's also close to the beach, moderately priced, and probably the best way to stay on Moloka'i. You can shop for food and find movies up the hill at Maunaloa. Write P.O. Box 190, Maunaloa, HI 96770; call (800) 367-2984, (808) 552-2731; or visit www.paniolohaleresort.com

## Bed-and-Breakfasts

A Hawai'i-style bed-and-breakfast can offer a satisfying personal island experience, like staying at a friend's home. It can also potentially be a disaster with no privacy and a surly or invasive host. With more than 700 B&B operations in Hawai'i, you should definitely do some investigating on the Internet before you book.

On the mainland, a "bed-and-breakfast" usually means a refurbished mansion or historic house. In Hawai'i, it's usually a cottage, studio, or guest room in a private home. Most prevalent are studios with kitchenettes or full kitchens. There are exceptions, such as Shipman House

Bed & Breakfast, a traditional inn in Hilo (131 Ka'iulani St., Hilo, HI 96720; (808) 934-8002 or (800) 627-8447; www.hilo-hawaii.com).

You probably won't get home-cooked breakfast at most of the in-house B&Bs, thanks to restrictive laws. But you can expect a basket of tropical fruit, breads, and Kona coffee.

Most operators require a minimum three-night stay. Ask whether units have private baths and entries.

Search the Internet to preview and reserve a B&B. Beach properties rent quickly and are usually booked year-round, often by returning guests. Plan to make reservations two or three months in advance, longer for holiday periods.

Prices range from $65 to $300 a night. A room in a private home averages between $55 and $75 a night for two people with Continental breakfast. A studio with private entrance, bath, and kitchenette ranges from $75 to $95 a night. A cottage averages $80 to $150 per night for two people. Call the hosts directly or use a reservation service, such as the following.

All Islands Bed & Breakfast
(800) 542-0344, (808) 263-2342
www.hawaii.rr.com/allislands

Bed & Breakfast Honolulu
(800) 288-4666, (808) 595-7533
www.aloha-bnb.com

Bed & Breakfast Hawai'i
(800) 733-1632, (808) 822-7771
www.bandb-hawaii.com

Hawai'i's Best Bed & Breakfasts
(800) 262-9912, (808) 885-4550
www.bestbnb.com

Terms and policies vary, but at most bed-and-breakfast agencies, a 20% deposit, plus 4.17 % excise tax on the deposit, is required to hold a reservation. A portion of the deposit is retained by the agency as a fee. Otherwise, deposits are generally refundable if you cancel your reservation at least two weeks in advance, but ask what the policy is before you commit yourself. Personal checks and credit cards are accepted for deposits The balance is usually paid in cash to the host family, though some agencies require payment in full before you arrive. You will receive a confirmation letter shortly after your deposit is received, followed by a welcome letter, map, and brochure.

Following are a few of our favorite B&Bs, cottages, and other rentals.

---

### RECOMMENDED HAWAI'I B&BS

**O'ahu**
Hawaiian Islands Bed & Breakfast/
Lanikai Bed & Breakfast
1277 Mokulua Dr.
Kailua, HI 96734
(808) 261-1059, (800) 258-7895
www.lanikaibb.com

Ke 'Iki Hale
59-579 Ke 'Iki Rd.
Hale'iwa, HI 96712
(808) 638-8229

Pat's Kailua Beach Properties
204 S. Kalaheo St.
Kailua, HI 96734
(808) 261-1653
www.10kvacationrentals.com/pats

**Maui**

Blue Horizons B&B
3894 Mahinahina St.
Lahaina, HI 96761
(808) 669-1965, (800) 669-1948
www.bluehorizonsmaui.com

Silver Cloud Ranch
RR II, Box 201
Kula, HI 96790
(808) 878-6101, (800) 532-1111
www.maui.net/~slvrcld

**Kaua'i**

Aloha Country Inn
505 Kamalu Rd.
Kapa'a, HI 96746
(808) 947-6019, (800) 634-5115
www.aloha.net/~wery

Po'ipu Bed & Breakfast Inn
2720 Ho'onani Rd.
Po'ipu, HI 96756
(808) 742-1146, (800) 227-6478
www.poipu.net

**Big Island (Hilo/Volcano)**

Carson's Volcano Cottage
P.O. Box 503
Volcano, HI 96785

(808) 967-7683 or (800) 845-5282
www.carsonscottage.com

Wild Ginger Inn
100 Pu'ueo St.
Hilo, HI 96720
(808) 935-5556, (800) 882-1887
www.wildgingerinn.com

Volcano Bed & Breakfast
P.O. Box 998
Volcano, HI 96785
(808) 967-7779, (800) 937-7786
www.volcano-hawaii.com

**Big Island (South Kona Coast)**

Dragonfly Ranch Tropical Fantasy
Lodging
P.O. Box 675
Honaunau-Kona, HI 96726
(808) 328-9570, (800) 487-2159
www.dragonflyranch.com

**Lana'i**

Dreams Come True
547 12th Street
Lana'i City, HI 96763
(808) 565-6961, (800) 566-6961
www.go-native.com/Inns

**Moloka'i**

Kamalo Plantation B&B
HC01, Box 300
Kaunakakai, HI 96748
(808) 558-8236
www.molokai.com/kamalo

# Hotels Rated and Ranked

We've ranked more than 60 hotels in Hawai'i, based on room quality (cleanliness, spaciousness, views, amenities, visual appeal), value, service, and location. These factors are combined into an overall rating, which is expressed on a five-star scale. These are our ratings, independent of any travel organization or club. The evaluations are Hawaii-specific, that is to say relative to properties on the islands. For details on a specific property, see the hotel profiles later in this section. These descriptions will help you understand the reasoning behind a hotel's rank.

## WHAT THE RATINGS MEAN

| | |
|---|---|
| ★★★★★ | Best of the best |
| ★★★★½ | Excellent |
| ★★★★ | Very good |
| ★★★½ | Good |
| ★★★ | Average |
| ★★½ | Below average |
| ★★ | Poor |

As the term implies, the overall rating takes into consideration all facets of a hotel. A property with a prime location, excellent restaurants, or a gorgeous lobby might rank highly despite mediocre rooms. Conversely, a property with elaborate rooms and little else may rank lower overall. Hence the one-to-five-star room quality ratings, which are specific to accommodations. Obviously, a room's size, the quality of its furnishings, and its level of cleanliness are prime factors in room quality. However, *Unofficial Guide* researchers also take careful note of the things most guests only notice when something is awry: noise levels, lighting, temperature control, ventilation, and security.

The value ratings, also given on a five-star scale, are a combination of the overall and room quality ratings, divided by the cost of an average guest room. They indicated a general idea of value for money. If getting a good deal means the most to you, choose a property by looking at the value rating. Otherwise, room and overall ratings are better indicators of a satisfying experience. If a wonderful property is fairly priced, it may only get an average or ★★★ value rating, but you still might prefer the experience to an average property with a ★★★★★ value rating.

## COST INDICATORS

| | |
|---|---|
| $$$$$ | Above $350 |
| $$$$ | $250–$350 |
| $$$ | $150–$250 |
| $$ | $100–$150 |
| $ | Below $100 |

The chart above indicates the symbols used in the subsequent table and profiles to correlate with various hotel prices. The rates used here are based on the rack rate for a standard ocean-view room (or suitable equivalent) during the tourism high season, which runs from December through March. Don't be intimidated by the cost indicators. Lower and higher prices (depending on the room category) are available at each hotel.

## HOW THE HOTELS COMPARE IN HAWAI'I

| Hotel | Overall Rating | Room Rating | Value Rating | Cost | Zone |
|---|---|---|---|---|---|
| **O'ahu** | | | | | |
| Halekulani | ★★★★★ | ★★★★★ | ★★★ | $$$$$ | 1 |
| 'Ihilani Resort & Spa | ★★★★★ | ★★★★★ | ★★★ | $$$$$ | 5 |
| Hyatt Regency Waikiki | ★★★★½ | ★★★★½ | ★★★ | $$$$$ | 1 |
| Hawai'i Prince Hotel Waikiki | ★★★★½ | ★★★★ | ★★½ | $$$$$ | 1 |
| Hilton Hawaiian Village | ★★★★½ | ★★★★ | ★★★ | $$$$ | 1 |
| Kahala Mandarin Oriental | ★★★★½ | ★★★★ | ★★ | $$$$$ | 2 |
| Royal Hawaiian Hotel | ★★★★½ | ★★★★ | ★★½ | $$$$$ | 1 |
| Sheraton Moana Surfrider | ★★★★½ | ★★★★ | ★★½ | $$$$$ | 1 |
| Sheraton Princess Ka'iulani | ★★★★ | ★★★★ | ★★ | $$$$ | 1 |
| Sheraton Waikiki | ★★★★ | ★★★★ | ★★ | $$$$$ | 1 |
| W Honolulu Diamond Head | ★★★★ | ★★★★ | ★★ | $$$$ | 1 |
| Waikiki Beach Marriott Resort | ★★★★ | ★★★★ | ★★ | $$$$ | 1 |
| Waikiki Parc Hotel | ★★★★ | ★★★★ | ★★★½ | $$$$ | 1 |
| Ala Moana Hotel | ★★★★ | ★★★½ | ★★★½ | $$$ | 2 |
| Aston at the Executive Centre Hotel | ★★★★ | ★★★½ | ★★ | $$$ | 2 |
| New Otani Kaimana Beach Hotel | ★★★★ | ★★★½ | ★★½ | $$$ | 1 |
| Royal Garden at Waikiki | ★★★★ | ★★★½ | ★★★ | $$$ | 1 |
| Turtle Bay Golf & Tennis Resort | ★★★★ | ★★★½ | ★★★ | $$$ | 4 |
| Waikiki Joy Hotel | ★★★★ | ★★★½ | ★★★ | $$$ | 1 |
| Waikiki Beachcomber Hotel | ★★★★ | ★★★ | ★★½ | $$$ | 1 |
| Doubletree Alana Waikiki Hotel | ★★★½ | ★★★½ | ★★ | $$$$ | 1 |
| Outrigger East Hotel | ★★★½ | ★★★½ | ★★ | $$$ | 1 |
| Outrigger Reef on the Beach | ★★★½ | ★★★½ | ★★ | $$$$ | 1 |
| Outrigger Waikiki on the Beach | ★★★½ | ★★★½ | ★★★ | $$$$ | 1 |
| Radisson Waikiki Prince Kuhio | ★★★½ | ★★★½ | ★★ | $$$ | 1 |
| Waikiki Terrace Hotel | ★★★½ | ★★★½ | ★★ | $$$ | 1 |
| Pacific Beach Hotel | ★★★½ | ★★★ | ★★ | $$$ | 1 |
| **Maui** | | | | | |
| Four Seasons Resort Maui | ★★★★★ | ★★★★★ | ★★★ | $$$$$ | 8 |
| Ritz-Carlton Kapalua | ★★★★★ | ★★★★★ | ★★★½ | $$$$$ | 9 |
| Grand Wailea Resort Hotel & Spa | ★★★★½ | ★★★★½ | ★★½ | $$$$$ | 8 |
| Embassy Vacation Resort | ★★★★½ | ★★★★ | ★★½ | $$$$$ | 9 |
| Fairmont Kea Lani Hotel, Suites & Villas | ★★★★½ | ★★★★ | ★★★ | $$$$$ | 8 |
| Hotel Hana-Maui | ★★★★ | ★★★★ | ★★ | $$$$$ | 10 |
| Hyatt Regency Maui | ★★★★ | ★★★★ | ★★½ | $$$$$ | 9 |
| Kapalua Bay Hotel | ★★★★ | ★★★★ | ★★ | $$$$$ | 9 |
| Maui Marriott Resort | ★★★★ | ★★★★ | ★★ | $$$$ | 9 |
| Outrigger Wailea Resort | ★★★★ | ★★★★ | ★★★ | $$$$$ | 8 |
| Renaissance Wailea Beach Resort | ★★★★ | ★★★★ | ★★ | $$$$ | 8 |

## HOW THE HOTELS COMPARE IN HAWAI'I *(continued)*

| Hotel | Overall Rating | Room Rating | Value Rating | Cost | Zone |
|---|---|---|---|---|---|
| **Maui** *(continued)* | | | | | |
| Sheraton Maui | ★★★★ | ★★★★ | ★★ | $$$$$ | 9 |
| Westin Maui | ★★★★ | ★★★★ | ★★½ | $$$$$ | 9 |
| Ka'anapali Beach Hotel | ★★★★ | ★★★½ | ★★★ | $$$$ | 9 |
| Maui Prince Hotel | ★★★★ | ★★★½ | ★★ | $$$$ | 8 |
| Lahaina Inn | ★★★★ | ★★★ | ★★★½ | $$ | 9 |
| **The Big Island** | | | | | |
| Four Seasons Resort Hualalai | ★★★★★ | ★★★★★ | ★★½ | $$$$$ | 11 |
| Mauna Lani Bay Hotel & Bungalows | ★★★★½ | ★★★★½ | ★★½ | $$$$$ | 11 |
| Hapuna Beach Prince Hotel | ★★★★½ | ★★★★ | ★★ | $$$$$ | 11 |
| Hilton Waikoloa Village | ★★★★½ | ★★★★ | ★★ | $$$$$ | 11 |
| Kona Village Resort | ★★★★½ | ★★★★ | ★★ | $$$$$ | 11 |
| Mauna Kea Beach Hotel | ★★★★½ | ★★★★ | ★★ | $$$$$ | 11 |
| The Orchid at Mauna Lani | ★★★★½ | ★★★★ | ★★ | $$$$$ | 11 |
| Hawai'i Naniloa Resort | ★★★★ | ★★★½ | ★★★ | $$ | 12 |
| 'Ohana Keauhou Beach Resort | ★★★★ | ★★★½ | ★★½ | $$$ | 11 |
| Outrigger Waikoloa Beach Hotel | ★★★★ | ★★★½ | ★★★ | $$$ | 11 |
| Hilo Hawaiian Hotel | ★★★½ | ★★★½ | ★★½ | $$ | 12 |
| King Kamehameha's Kona Beach Hotel | ★★★½ | ★★★ | ★★★½ | $$$ | 11 |
| Volcano House | ★★★½ | ★★★ | ★★ | $$ | 12 |
| **Kaua'i** | | | | | |
| Hyatt Regency Kaua'i Resort & Spa | ★★★★½ | ★★★★½ | ★★½ | $$$$$ | 13 |
| Princeville Resort | ★★★★½ | ★★★★ | ★★ | $$$$$ | 13 |
| Hanalei Bay Resort & Suites | ★★★★ | ★★★★ | ★★½ | $$$ | 13 |
| Kaua'i Marriott Resort & Beach Club | ★★★★ | ★★★★ | ★★ | $$$$$ | 13 |
| Sheraton Kaua'i Resort | ★★★★ | ★★★★ | ★★ | $$$$$ | 13 |
| Radisson Kaua'i Beach Resort | ★★★★ | ★★★½ | ★★ | $$$ | 13 |
| **Moloka'i** | | | | | |
| Sheraton Moloka'i Lodge & Beach Village | ★★★★½ | ★★★★ | ★★★ | $$$$$ | 14 |
| **Lana'i** | | | | | |
| The Lodge at Ko'ele | ★★★★½ | ★★★★ | ★★½ | $$$$$ | 15 |
| The Manele Bay Hotel | ★★★★½ | ★★★★ | ★★½ | $$$$$ | 15 |
| Hotel Lana'i | ★★★½ | ★★★ | ★★★ | $ | 15 |

## HAWAI'I HOTELS BY ZONE

### Zone 1: Waikiki
Doubletree Alana Waikiki Hotel
Halekulani
Hawai'i Prince Hotel Waikiki
Hilton Hawaiian Village
Hyatt Regency Waikiki
New Otani Kaimana Beach Hotel
Outrigger East Hotel
Outrigger Reef on the Beach
Outrigger Waikiki on the Beach
Pacific Beach Hotel
Radisson Waikiki Prince Kuhio
Royal Garden at Waikiki
Royal Hawaiian Hotel
Sheraton Moana Surfrider
Sheraton Princess Ka'iulani
Sheraton Waikiki
W Honolulu-Diamond Head
Waikiki Beach Marriott Resort
Waikiki Beachcomber Hotel
Waikiki Joy Hotel
Waikiki Parc Hotel
Waikiki Terrace Hotel

### Zone 2: Greater Honolulu
Ala Moana Hotel
Aston at the Executive Centre Hotel
Kahala Mandarin Oriental

### Zone 4: The North Shore
Turtle Bay Golf & Tennis Resort

### Zone 5: Leeward O'ahu
'Ihilani Resort & Spa

### Zone 8: South Maui
Fairmont Kea Lani Hotel, Suites & Villas
Four Seasons Resort Maui
Grand Wailea Resort Hotel & Spa
Maui Prince Hotel
Outrigger Wailea Resort
Renaissance Wailea Beach Resort

### Zone 9: West Maui
Embassy Vacation Resort
Hyatt Regency Maui

Ka'anapali Beach Hotel
Kapalua Bay Hotel
Lahaina Inn
Maui Marriott Resort
Ritz-Carlton Kapalua
Sheraton Maui
Westin Maui

### Zone 10: Upcountry Maui and Beyond
Hotel Hana-Maui

### Zone 11: Kona
Four Seasons Resort Hualalai
Hapuna Beach Prince Hotel
Hilton Waikoloa Village
King Kamehameha's Kona Beach Hotel
Kona Village Resort
Mauna Kea Beach Hotel
Mauna Lani Bay Hotel & Bungalows
'Ohana Keauhou Beach Resort
The Orchid at Mauna Lani
Outrigger Waikoloa Beach Hotel

### Zone 12: Hilo and Volcano
Hawai'i Naniloa Resort
Hilo Hawaiian Hotel
Volcano House

### Zone 13: Kaua'i
Hanalei Bay Resort & Suites
Hyatt Regency Kaua'i Resort & Spa
Kaua'i Marriott Resort & Beach Club
Princeville Resort
Radisson Kaua'i Beach Resort
Sheraton Kaua'i Resort

### Zone 14: Moloka'i
Sheraton Moloka'i Lodge & Beach Village

### Zone 15: Lana'i
Hotel Lana'i
The Lodge at Ko'ele
The Manele Bay Hotel

# Hotel Profiles

Details on hotels, resorts in alphabetical order by island follow.

## O'ahu

### ALA MOANA HOTEL                                                    $$$

OVERALL ★★★★  |  QUALITY ★★★½  |  VALUE ★★★½  |  ZONE 2

410 Atkinson Dr., Honolulu, HI 96814; (888) 367-4811 or (808) 955-4811; fax: (808) 944-6839; amhiresv@get.net; www.alamoanahotel.com

It doesn't front Waikiki Beach, but it does have a great central location, close to the everything. A sky bridge leads you to Ala Moana Center; the Hawai'i Convention Center is across the street; and it's a five-minute walk to Ala Moana Beach Park. Traffic in this area is always busy, views are disappointing but everything is handy.

#### SETTING & FACILITIES

**Location** On the fringe of Waikiki. **Dining** Aaron's is the signature restaurant here, offering fine Continental cuisine. Other dining options include Royal Garden (Chinese) and Tsukasa (Japanese). The Plantation Cafe serves a variety of international cuisine for breakfast, lunch, and dinner. **Amenities & Services** Room service, laundry facilities (coin-operated), ice and soda machines, ATM machine, business center, sundry shop, shopping arcade, concierge, self-parking ($9/day), valet parking ($12), swimming pool.

#### ACCOMMODATIONS

**Rooms** 1,152. Includes 67 suites; 28 rooms equipped for the disabled; 800 non-smoking rooms. **All Rooms** A/C, color TV, pay movies, clock radio, mini-fridge, in-room safe, 2 double beds, direct-dial phone system, dataport, in-room coffee, hair dryer, voice mail. **Some Rooms** King and 2 doubles, concierge services, in-room steam and Jacuzzi unit, iron and board, yukata robes. IBM PC–compatible systems available for additional $15/night. **Comfort & Decor** Very clean and well maintained. Rooms small to medium, decorated with light colors and Hawaiian-accented artwork, airy and bright ambience.

#### PAYMENT, RESERVATIONS, & RESTRICTIONS

**Family Plan** Children age 18 and under stay free in room with parents if using existing bedding. Each additional adult $25/night. Maximum of 4 people/room (maximum of 2/room in Kona Tower). Rollaway bed, $25/night; cribs free. **Deposit** To guarantee reservation, a deposit of 1 night's room rate is required within 10 days of confirmation. Cancellation notice must be given at least 72 hours prior to scheduled arrival for refund. **Credit Cards** All major credit cards accepted. **Check-In/Out** 3 p.m./noon. Early check-in possible if the room is available.

## ASTON AT THE EXECUTIVE CENTRE HOTEL                   $$$$

OVERALL ★★★★ | QUALITY ★★★½ | VALUE ★★ | ZONE 2

1088 Bishop St., Honolulu, HI 96813; (800) 321-2558 or (808) 539-3000; fax:
(808) 523-1088; res.exc@aston-hotels.com; www.aston-hotels.com

Stylish, all-suite hotel for the business traveler who must be on Honolulu's Bishop Street. The service staff is friendly and professional, and the
swimming pool and fitness center are welcome amenities. Don't expect a
resort atmosphere. Though downtown Honolulu is populated by an
intriguing mix of people by day, the streets are nearly deserted at night. If
you're here on business, this downtown hotel is the best choice.

### SETTING & FACILITIES
**Location** In the heart of the downtown business district. **Dining** Bronson
Restaurant serves a full menu of local-style favorites. It is closed on weekends.
**Amenities & Services** Swimming pool, fitness center, parking facilities ($8/day),
laundry and dry cleaning service.

### ACCOMMODATIONS
**Rooms** 116. All suites. **All Rooms** A/C, color TV, partial kitchen. **Some Rooms**
Full kitchen, washer and dryer, fax machines. **Comfort & Decor** Well-appointed,
spacious suites. Some rooms have fax machines (be sure to request a room with
one if you need it). The decor is elegant but subdued. Floor-to-ceiling windows
provide superb views of downtown Honolulu.

### PAYMENT, RESERVATIONS, & RESTRICTIONS
**Family Plan** Children age 18 and under stay free with parents. **Deposit** $400
(cash or credit card) refundable damage deposit. Cancellation notice must be
given at least 72 hours prior to scheduled arrival for refund. **Credit Cards** All
major credit cards accepted. **Check-In/Out** 3 p.m./noon. Early check-in and late
check out available on request (no guarantees).

## DOUBLETREE ALANA WAIKIKI HOTEL                        $$$

OVERALL ★★★½ | QUALITY ★★★½ | VALUE ★★ | ZONE 1

1956 Ala Moana Blvd., Honolulu, HI 96815; (800) 367-6070 or (808) 941-7275;
fax: (808) 949-0996; www.alana-doubletree.com

The hotel's Website claims that the property is just "steps" away from the
beach and Ala Moana Shopping Center, but it doesn't tell you how many.
The truth is, it's about a 15-minute walk either way. What this boutique
hotel lacks in location, it makes up for in hospitality. Service is friendly
and efficient, and there's a level of charm and comfort here that you won't
find in larger hotels. Padovani's, one of Hawai'i's favorite restaurants,
offers fine dining. Room views are so-so, because most of Diamond Head
is obscured by other hotel properties. Decorator suites are exceptional,
especially one with an outdoor lana'i that wraps much of the building.

## SETTING & FACILITIES

**Location** On the fringe of Waikiki, 15-minute walk to beach. **Dining** Breakfast, lunch, and dinner at Padovani's Bistro & Wine Bar, one of O'ahu's top fine-dining establishments, which serves superb classic southern French cuisine. **Amenities & Services** Room service, valet parking ($10/day), dry cleaning and laundry service, 24-hour business center, fitness center, swimming pool.

## ACCOMMODATIONS

**Rooms** 313. Includes 25 suites and a penthouse suite. Nonsmoking rooms available. **All Rooms** A/C, private lana'i, TV, mini-cooler, in-room safe, coffeemaker, hair dryer, iron and board. **Some Rooms** Living room with sofa-bed. **Comfort & Decor** Very spacious, tastefully appointed with plush sofas and chairs. Hawaiian-themed artwork adorns the walls.

## PAYMENT, RESERVATIONS, & RESTRICTIONS

**Deposit** Credit card guarantee with 1-night deposit. **Credit Cards** All major credit cards accepted. **Check-In/Out** 3 p.m./noon. Early check-in and late check out available by request.

## HALEKULANI                                                    $$$$$

OVERALL ★★★★★ | QUALITY ★★★★★ | VALUE ★★★ | ZONE 1

2199 Kalia Rd., Honolulu, HI 96815; (800) 367-2343 or (808) 923-2311; fax: (808) 926-8004; www.halekulani.com

The Halekulani is the best hotel in Waikiki, the best on O'ahu, and the only hotel in Hawai'i to win the prestigious AAA Five Diamond Award for both hotel and restaurant categories. It lives up to its reputation.

Amid the hustle and bustle of Kalakaua Avenue, the Halekulani remains a peaceful, elegant oasis with a postcard view of Waikiki Beach and Diamond Head.

No experience exemplifies this more than sunset cocktails at the House Without a Key, where a former Miss Hawai'i dances the hula to soothing Hawaiian music as the sun sinks in the Pacific.

Service is impeccable, and the rooms are spacious and well appointed, all with an ocean view. The two restaurants, La Mer and Orchids, are open-air and face the sea, the cuisine is outstanding, and the service almost fawning. A weekly manager's reception serves complimentary heavy hors d'oeuvres.

Geared more toward well-to-do couples than large families, the hotel has gained a loyal following; many come back every year.

## SETTING & FACILITIES

**Location** On Waikiki Beach. **Dining** The Halekulani has several notable fine dining establishments, including the AAA Five Diamond Award–winning La Mer, which serves neoclassic French cuisine. Orchids serves breakfast, lunch, and dinner. **Amenities & Services** Fresh fruit bowl and chocolates on arrival, complimentary morning newspaper, valet parking, self-parking ($10/day), fitness center, business center, heated swimming pool.

## ACCOMMODATIONS

**Rooms** 456. Includes 44 suites, 16 rooms for the disabled. Nonsmoking rooms available. **All Rooms** A/C, lana'i, 3 phones, cable TV, mini-fridge, clock radio. **Some Rooms** 2 bedrooms. **Comfort & Decor** Spacious, stylishly appointed decor with light colors and tasteful furnishings, high ceilings, plenty of drawer space. Large balconies include table, 2 chairs, and an adjustable folding chair.

## PAYMENT, RESERVATIONS, & RESTRICTIONS

**Family Plan** Children age 17 and under stay free in room with parents if using existing bedding; extra bed, $40/night. **Deposit** Credit card guarantees reservation with 1-night deposit within 14 days of confirmation. Cancellation notice must be given at least 72 hours prior to scheduled arrival for refund. **Credit Cards** All major credit cards accepted. **Check-In/Out** 3 p.m./noon. Hospitality room available for early arrivals and late departures. Early check-ins and late check outs based on availability.

## HAWAI'I PRINCE HOTEL WAIKIKI                    $$$$$

OVERALL ★★★★½  |  QUALITY ★★★★  |  VALUE ★★½  |  ZONE 1

100 Holomoana St., Honolulu, HI 96815; (800) 321-6248 or (808) 956-1111; fax: (808) 946-0811; reservationsHPHW@hiprince.com; www.princehawaii.com

An upscale pink marble monument overlooking Ala Wai Yacht Harbor, the Hawai'i Prince offers exceptional service and proximity to Ala Moana Center, Ala Moana Beach Park, and the Hawai'i Convention Center, all within easy walking distance. The hotel's business facilities and services are excellent. All 521 hotel rooms provide yacht harbor and ocean views. The expansive Italian marble lobby features a tuxedo-clad piano player. The fifth floor is often windy, but is still favorite hangout, with a swimming pool, sun deck, and terraces for sunset cocktails. If you're looking for a tee time, the Hawai'i Prince Golf Club isn't anywhere near the hotel (it's a 40-minute drive away on the 'Ewa side of O'ahu), but this is the only Waikiki hotel with a golf course to call its own. Guests of this hotel receive preferred tee times and shuttle service.

## SETTING & FACILITIES

**Location** On the outskirts of Waikiki at Ala Wai Yacht Harbor, 15-minute walk to Ala Moana Beach. **Dining** Two restaurants of note are the Prince Court, which features Hawaiian regional cuisine, and Hakone, specializing in exquisite Japanese fare. **Amenities & Services** Hot towels on check-in, valet parking, business facilities, fitness center, in-room safes, babysitting services, daily newspaper.

## ACCOMMODATIONS

**Rooms** 521. Includes 57 suites; 10 rooms for the disabled. Nonsmoking rooms available. **All Rooms** A/C, cable TV with pay movies, mini-fridge, in-room safe, hair dryer, robes. **Some Rooms** Extra bedroom and bath. **Comfort & Decor** Very spacious, with lavish decor and floor-to-ceiling windows that partially open, but no lanaʻi. Floral-theme artworks adorn walls in well-lit room with bright, warm colors.

## PAYMENT, RESERVATIONS, & RESTRICTIONS

**Family Plan** Children age 17 and under stay free in room with parents if using existing bedding. Maximum occupancy is 3 adults or 2 adults and 2 children/room; extra adult, $40/night. **Deposit** 1-night deposit due 14 days within booking. Cancellation notice must be given 72 hours prior to scheduled arrival for refund. **Credit Cards** Visa, MC, AmEx, DC. **Check-In/Out** 2 p.m./noon. Early check-in and late check out available on request.

## HILTON HAWAIIAN VILLAGE                                      $$$$

OVERALL ★★★★½  |  QUALITY ★★★★  |  VALUE ★★★  |  ZONE 1

2005 Kalia Rd., Honolulu, HI 96815; (800) 445-8667 or (808) 949-4321; fax: (808) 951-5458; www.hawaiianvillage.hilton.com

Hawaiʻi's largest hotel, this beachfront village epitomizes the term *self-contained resort*. You really don't have to leave. Expect crowds here, because the Hilton is top choice for tour groups. The hotel rooms are currently housed in four separate towers: Tapa, Rainbow, Diamond Head, and upscale Aliʻi. The new 453-room, 25-story Kalia Tower opened May 2001 at the hotel entry, where Buckminster Fuller's geodesic dome once stood. The tower includes a health and wellness spa, Hawaiian cultural center, and four floors of retail shops. Yet another new tower is planned.

The HHV also has five bars (with nightly entertainment provided), more than 100 shops and services, and activities ranging from undersea submarine rides to wildlife tours. This hotel is terrific for young families, as it offers one of Hawaiʻi's best year-round children's programs (including excursions to nearby attractions such as the Honolulu Zoo and Waikiki Aquarium). Lei making, hula, and ʻukulele lessons are daily activities. Every Friday, the King's Jubilee and Fireworks show features a precision rifle drill team, Hawaiian music, and fireworks.

## SETTING & FACILITIES

**Location** Fronting Duke Kahanamoku Beach (part of Waikiki Beach) near gateway to Waikiki. **Dining** Of the 7 restaurants located here, 2 stand out as among the finest on Oʻahu: Bali-by-the-Sea, an oceanfront restaurant serving innovative cuisine with an island accent, and Golden Dragon, serving Cantonese and Szechuan specialties. **Amenities & Services** 3 outdoor swimming pools, valet parking, parking garage, travel services, laundry and dry cleaning, wedding chapel, physicians on call, beauty and barber shops, post office and express mail pickup and delivery, meeting and banquet space, business services, children's program, florist.

## ACCOMMODATIONS

**Rooms** 2,998. Includes 363 suites; 526 nonsmoking rooms; 75 rooms for the disabled. **All Rooms** A/C, cable TV with pay movies, in-room safe, refreshment center. **Some Rooms** Evening pupu, concierge service, robes, sparkling water, in-room fax, upgraded bathroom amenities, valet laundry service. **Comfort & Decor** Moderate space, well-lit with airy, attractive Hawaiian decor, that includes wicker furnishings and floral-theme bedspreads.

### PAYMENT, RESERVATIONS, & RESTRICTIONS

**Family Plan** Children age 17 and under stay free in room with parents if using existing bedding. **Deposit** A 1-night deposit due within 10 days after confirmation. Cancellation notice must be given at least 72 hours prior to scheduled arrival for refund. **Credit Cards** All major credit cards accepted. **Check-In/Out** 2 p.m./11 a.m. Early check-in and late check out available (confirmed on arrival).

## HYATT REGENCY WAIKIKI                                             $$$$$

OVERALL ★★★★½ | QUALITY ★★★★½ | VALUE ★★★ | ZONE 1

2424 Kalakaua Ave., Honolulu, HI 96815; (800) 233-1234 or (808) 923-1234; fax: (808) 923-7839; info@hyattwaikiki.com; www.hyattwaikiki.com

Everything, including the beach, is just a short walk away. The Hyatt is composed of twin 40-story towers connected by the open-air Great Hall. The impressive lobby features a 10-story atrium with a man-made waterfall. The hotel has three floors of shops offering jewelry, apparel, and gifts. Free entertainment is provided in the lobby next to Harry's Bar. The Hyatt also has a new full-service spa and a wonderful children's program, Camp Hyatt, which provides kids ages 3–12 with fun and educational activities with an emphasis on Hawai'i's history and culture. The neighborhood is noisy at night.

### SETTING & FACILITIES

**Location** Across the street from Waikiki Beach. **Dining** Several restaurants here, including the Texas Rock 'n' Roll Sushi Bar (country-style food with a wide range of sushi creations) and Ciao Mein (Italian and Chinese food). **Amenities & Services** Room service, valet parking ($12) and self-parking ($10), children's program.

### ACCOMMODATIONS

**Rooms** 1,230. Includes 18 suites; 193 nonsmoking rooms; 24 rooms for the disabled. **All Rooms** A/C, TV, lana'i, refrigerator, mini-bar, hair dryer, iron and board, in-room safe, coffeemaker. **Some Rooms** Connecting parlor. **Comfort & Decor** Spacious, well maintained. Decor is sparse, but gracious, with rattan furnishings and subdued colors.

### PAYMENT, RESERVATIONS, & RESTRICTIONS

**Family Plan** Children age 17 and under stay free in room with parents if using existing bedding. **Deposit** 1-night deposit required within 10 days of confirmation. Cancellation notice must be given at least 72 hours prior to scheduled arrival for refund. **Credit Cards** All major credit cards accepted. **Check-In/Out** 3 p.m./noon. Early check-in and late check out available on request.

## 'IHILANI RESORT & SPA                                    $$$$$

OVERALL ★★★★★ | QUALITY ★★★★★ | VALUE ★★★ | ZONE 5

92-1001 'Olani St., Kapolei, HI 96707; (800) 626-4446 or (808) 679-0079; fax: (808) 679-0080; reservations@ihilani.com; www.ihilani.com

The 'Ihilani, which translates to "heavenly splendor," was built by the Japanese for Tokyo moguls on holiday, and today it's a favorite of O'ahu visitors seeking an alternative to Waikiki, which is only an hour but seemingly a world away.

Situated on the first of four man-made lagoons, 'Ihilani overlooks a gold-sand beach. The resort's full-service spa is regarded as one of the finest in the world.

Six state-of-the-art tennis courts, an acclaimed spa using seawater therapies, and nearby Ko 'Olina Golf Club make this a favorite for sports-minded visitors. Sports celebrity alert: During NFL Pro Bowl week (usually the first week in February), 'Ihilani hosts players and their families. Practices are often held on a nearby field.

### SETTING & FACILITIES

**Location** At the Ko 'Olina Resort in Kapolei, on the Leeward side of the island. **Dining** Azul is 'Ihilani's signature restaurant, serving an extensive menu blending the flavors of the Mediterranean and Hawai'i. **Amenities & Services** Twice-daily maid service, turndown service, daily ice delivery, 24-hour room service, full-service health spa, tennis club, beauty salon, year-round children's program.

### ACCOMMODATIONS

**Rooms** 387. Includes 36 luxury suites; 120 nonsmoking rooms; 14 rooms equipped for the disabled. **All Rooms** A/C, ceiling fan, color TV, in-house movie library, in-room safe, AM/FM radio with CD player, mini-bar, 3 phones, private lana'i, hair dryer, robes. **Some Rooms** Whirlpool spas, walk-in closets, large-screen TVs, 2 bathrooms. **Comfort & Decor** Very spacious (the smallest room is 640 square feet) and clean, rooms are decorated with local art and teak furnishings. One amenity here is that you can turn lights on and off, adjust the room temperature (in 1° increments), and even find out the current time anywhere in the world—right from your phone, which has instructions in six languages.

### PAYMENT, RESERVATIONS, & RESTRICTIONS

**Family Plan** Children age 17 and under stay free in room with parents if using existing bedding. Rollaway bed, $35. **Deposit** To guarantee reservation, a 1-night deposit is required within 14 days of booking. Cancellation notice must be received at least 72 hours prior to scheduled arrival for refund. **Credit Cards** All major credit cards accepted except Discover. **Check-In/Out** 3 p.m./noon. Early check-in available by request.

## KAHALA MANDARIN ORIENTAL                                  $$$$$

OVERALL ★★★★½  |  QUALITY ★★★★  |  VALUE ★★  |  ZONE 2

5000 Kahala Ave., Honolulu, HI 96816; (800) 526-6566 or (808) 739-8888; fax: (808) 739-8800; sales@mohg.com; www.mandarin-oriental.com

Old-timers recall this grand old beach hotel as the Kahala Hilton. The Mandarin is a good choice if you are a security-conscious golfer. This hotel sits between a private golf course and the ocean, so presidents and kings, who do stay and tee off here, sleep well.

Complimentary shuttle service transports you to and from major shopping destinations: Kahala Mall, Ala Moana Shopping Center, and Royal Hawaiian Shopping Center. The Mandarin has its own reef-protected beach, exotic gardens, waterfall, turtle ponds, dolphin lagoon, and beachfront lawn.

### SETTING & FACILITIES

**Location** In the upscale Kahala neighborhood, about 15 minutes from Waikiki. **Dining** The oceanfront Hoku's is one of O'ahu's best restaurants, serving fine international cuisine with fresh local ingredients. **Amenities & Services** Room service, laundry service, valet parking, business facilities, fitness center, children's program, 24-hour medical services.

### ACCOMMODATIONS

**Rooms** 371. Includes 33 suites. Nonsmoking and ADA-approved rooms available. **All Rooms** A/C, cable TV, CD player, clock radio, video games, 3 phones, mini-bar, computer outlets, dataport, hair dryer, in-room safe, bathrobes. **Some Rooms** Upgraded amenities. **Comfort & Decor** Spacious, luxurious, and clean, rooms have a stylish turn-of-the-century motif, mahogany furnishings, and teak parquet floors, rendering them warm, relaxing, and comfortable.

### PAYMENT, RESERVATIONS, & RESTRICTIONS

**Family Plan** Children age 17 and under stay free in room with parents if using existing bedding. Rollaway bed, $40. **Deposit** All reservations guaranteed by credit card. Cancellation notice must be given at least 72 hours prior to scheduled arrival for refund. **Credit Cards** All major credit cards accepted. **Check-In/Out** 3 p.m./noon. Early check-in and late check out available on request.

## NEW OTANI KAIMANA BEACH HOTEL                              $$$

OVERALL ★★★★  |  QUALITY ★★★½  |  VALUE ★★½  |  ZONE 1

2863 Kalakaua Ave., Honolulu, HI 96815; (800) 421-8795 or (808) 923-1555; fax: (808) 922-9404; rooms@kaimana.com; www.kaimana.com

What we like best about the Kaimana is its location. It's in Waikiki, yet somehow removed from traffic and noise of the main drag. A low-key hotel with stylish touches from the Orient, the Kaimana fronts Sans Souci Beach with Kapiʻolani Park in its back yard. The small, well-situated hotel is popular with residents who often lunch on the Hau Tree Lanaʻi overlooking Sans Souci Beach. Robert Louis Stevenson noted over a century ago, "If anyone desires lovely scenery, pure air, clear sea water, good food, and heavenly sunsets, I recommend him cordially to Sans Souci." We second the motion. This is Oʻahu's best small hotel.

## SETTING & FACILITIES

**Location** On Sans Souci Beach, near Diamond Head, across from Kapiʻolani Park. **Dining** The oceanfront Hau Tree Lanaʻi has one of Hawaiʻi's most romantic settings and offers Continental cuisine. Miyako serves traditional Japanese fare. **Amenities & Services** Room service, laundry and dry cleaning service, valet parking ($11/day), fitness center, business facilities.

## ACCOMMODATIONS

**Rooms** 124. Includes 5 suites and 3 ADA-approved rooms. All rooms permit smoking. **All Rooms** A/C, TV, VCR, lanaʻi, refrigerator, in-room safe, hair dryer; coffeemaker available on request. **Some Rooms** Mini-bar. **Comfort & Decor** Rooms are smallish, but clean and well maintained, with light, soft pastels and contemporary island-theme decor.

## PAYMENT, RESERVATIONS, & RESTRICTIONS

**Family Plan** Children age 12 and under stay free. Rollaway bed, $25; crib, $10. **Deposit** Credit card guarantee or 1-night deposit required. Cancellation notice must be given at least 72 hours prior to scheduled arrival for refund. **Credit Cards** All major credit cards accepted. **Check-In/Out** 2 p.m./noon. Hospitality room available for early arrivals and late departures.

## *OUTRIGGER EAST HOTEL*                                              $$$

OVERALL ★★★½  |  QUALITY ★★★½  |  VALUE ★★  |  ZONE 1

150 Kaʻiulani Ave., Honolulu, HI 96815; (800) 688-7444 or (808) 922-5353; fax: (808) 926-4334; www.outrigger.com

One of Outrigger's more popular properties, the Outrigger East is a good choice if you don't require unobstructed ocean views, because it's in the center of Waikiki and the beach is just a few minutes away on foot. Situated near the International Market Place and next to Kaʻiulani Park. It has suites with kitchenettes for visitors on extended stays. Nothing exceptional, but nothing subpar, either.

## SETTING & FACILITIES

**Location** At Kuhio and Kaʻiulani Avenues, 2 blocks from beach. **Dining** A trio of restaurants, including Pepper's Waikiki Grill & Bar (American, Southwest, and Mexican cuisine) and Chuck's Cellar (prime rib and seafood specialties). **Amenities & Services** Room service (7 a.m.–9:30 p.m.), activities desk, parking ($9/day), coin-operated washer and dryer.

## ACCOMMODATIONS

**Rooms** 445. Includes 25 suites; 5 rooms for the disabled. Half the rooms are designated nonsmoking. **All Rooms** A/C, cable TV, refrigerator, in-room safe, coffeemaker. **Some Rooms** Lanaʻi, kitchenette. **Comfort & Decor** Rooms are small to medium sized, with island-accented art and furnishings. Rooms were recently renovated.

## PAYMENT, RESERVATIONS, & RESTRICTIONS

**Family Plan** Children age 17 and under stay free in room with parents if using existing bedding. **Deposit** Credit card guarantee or 1-night deposit required. Cancellation notice must be given at least 72 hours prior to scheduled arrival for refund. **Credit Cards** All major credit cards accepted. **Check-In/Out** 3 p.m./noon. Early check-in and late check out available on request.

# OUTRIGGER REEF ON THE BEACH                    $$$$

OVERALL ★★★½ | QUALITY ★★★½ | VALUE ★★ | ZONE 1

Contact: 2169 Kalia Rd., Honolulu, HI 96815; (800) 688-7444 or (808) 923-3111; fax: (808) 924-4957; www.outrigger.com

The Outrigger Reef provides all the island hospitality this kamaʻaina chain is known for, plus the added convenience of being right on Waikiki Beach. The atmosphere here is very informal and is great for young families (the hotel offers a children's activity program). The lobby area includes 15 specialty shops. The Outrigger Reef is the home of the Honolulu Marathon, which takes place each December, and during the week of the event you can expect to see a lot of international runners here.

## SETTING & FACILITIES

**Location** On Waikiki Beach near Ft. DeRussy. **Dining** A quartet of eateries, including Shorebird Beach Broiler, a lively night spot serving burgers and sandwiches. **Amenities & Services** Room service, activities desk, parking, valet parking ($11/day), coin-operated washer and dryer.

## ACCOMMODATIONS

**Rooms** 883. Includes 25 suites; 450 nonsmoking rooms; 10 rooms for the disabled. **All Rooms** A/C, cable TV, refrigerator, in-room safe, coffeemaker. **Some Rooms** Kitchenette. **Comfort & Decor** Medium-sized, well-lit rooms are clean and comfortable with cool colors, simple furnishings.

## PAYMENT, RESERVATIONS, & RESTRICTIONS

**Family Plan** Children age 17 and under stay free in room with parents if using existing bedding. **Deposit** 1-night deposit or credit card guarantee. Cancellation notice must be given 72 hours prior to scheduled arrival for refund. **Credit Cards** All major credit cards accepted. **Check-In/Out** 3 p.m./noon. Early check-in and late check out available on request.

## OUTRIGGER WAIKIKI ON THE BEACH $$$$

OVERALL ★★★½ | QUALITY ★★★½ | VALUE ★★★ | ZONE 1

2335 Kalakaua Ave., Honolulu, HI 96815; (800) 688-7444 or (808) 923-0711; fax:
(808) 921-9749; www.outrigger.com; beachfront@outrigger.com

This is considered Outrigger's flagship property, and we know why. A
short stroll around the second-floor lobby tells you right away you're in
Hawai'i, with soft Hawaiian music, floral-motif carpeting, island artworks, a seashell-shaped chandelier, and, most telling, the soothing
sounds of the beach. The location is fabulous, too. Not only is the Outrigger Waikiki right on the beach it is also next door to Waikiki's largest
shopping complex, the Royal Hawaiian Shopping Center. Duke's Canoe
Club, the hotel's best-known restaurant, is worth a visit just to peruse
the historic photographs and other memorabilia paying tribute to Duke
Kahanamoku, Hawai'i's surfing legend. The Outrigger Waikiki is also
the home of the popular *Society of Seven* show, one of Waikiki's longest-
running dinner shows (see page 450 for a description). The atmosphere
is informal, colorful, and friendly.

### SETTING & FACILITIES
**Location** On Waikiki Beach, next to the Royal Hawaiian Shopping Center. **Dining** Duke's Canoe Club is a Waikiki favorite, serving breakfast, lunch, and dinner.
**Amenities & Services** Room service, parking, valet parking ($11/day), activities
desk, coin-operated washer and dryer.

### ACCOMMODATIONS
**Rooms** 530. Includes 30 suites. Half of the rooms are designated nonsmoking.
Rooms for the disabled are available. **All Rooms** A/C, cable TV, refrigerator, in-
room safe, coffeemaker. **Some Rooms** Kitchenettes. **Comfort & Decor**
Medium-sized rooms with subdued colors and few adornments are clean and
well maintained.

### PAYMENT, RESERVATIONS, & RESTRICTIONS
**Family Plan** Children age 17 and under stay free in room with parents if using
existing bedding. **Deposit** 1-night deposit or credit card guarantee. Cancellation
notice must be given at least 72 hours prior to scheduled arrival for refund.
**Credit Cards** All major credit cards accepted. **Check-In/Out** 3 p.m./noon.
Early check-in and late check out available on request.

## PACIFIC BEACH HOTEL $$$

OVERALL ★★★½ | QUALITY ★★★ | VALUE ★★ | ZONE 1

2490 Kalakaua Ave., Honolulu, HI 96815; (800) 367-6060 or (808) 922-1233; fax:
(808) 923-2566; reservation@hthcorp.com; www.pacificbeachhotel.com

Every Waikiki hotel tries to distinguish itself from the others in some
form or fashion, and the Pacific Beach Hotel makes a big splash with its

three-story, 280,000-gallon oceanarium, featuring hundreds of marine plants and animals. The oceanarium is the centerpiece of the hotel's dining establishments. A busy hotel with friendly service and a prime location, it's next to the beach.

### SETTING & FACILITIES

**Location** Across the street from Waikiki Beach. **Dining** Oceanarium, whose star attraction is not the food but the fish in 280,000-gallon saltwater tank. Shogun is a popular Japanese restaurant, and Neptune's Garden serves seafood, steaks, and Continental fare. **Amenities & Services** Swimming pool and whirlpool, full spa, tennis, parking, laundry service, travel desk, 24-hour fitness center, business facilities, meeting rooms.

### ACCOMMODATIONS

**Rooms** 837. Includes 10 suites; 5 floors of nonsmoking rooms; 13 rooms for the disabled. **All Rooms** A/C, cable TV, balcony, lana'i, coffeemaker, in-room safe, minifridge, bath slippers. **Some Rooms** Bathrobes, iron and board, vanity kit. **Comfort & Decor** Rooms are small to medium in size. Soft, pastel colors help brighten the room. Lana'i are open to scenic mountain or ocean views.

### PAYMENT, RESERVATIONS, & RESTRICTIONS

**Family Plan** Children age 18 and under stay free in room with parents if using existing bedding. Maximum of 4 people/room. **Deposit** 1-night deposit required within 14 days of confirmation. Cancellation notice must be given at least 72 hours prior to scheduled arrival for refund. **Credit Cards** All major credit cards accepted. **Check-In/Out** 3 p.m./noon. Early check-in and late check out based on availability.

## RADISSON WAIKIKI PRINCE KUHIO                                    $$$

OVERALL ★★★½  |  QUALITY ★★★½  |  VALUE ★★  |  ZONE 1

2500 Kuhio Ave., Honolulu, HI 96815; (800) 688-7444 or (808) 922-0811; fax: (808) 923-0330

Centrally located Prince Kuhio is a short hike to Waikiki Beach. The Ala Wai Canal, Honolulu Zoo, and Kapi'olani Park are also nearby. Kuhio Avenue can be just as busy as Kalakaua Avenue, and the area tends to get noisy at night. The lobby area is attractive but rather dimly lit. The hotel recently added a new fitness room and renovated its swimming pool.

### SETTING & FACILITIES

**Location** On Kuhio Avenue in Waikiki, 2 blocks from beach. **Dining** Trellises serves nightly theme buffets and Sunday brunch. Shanghai Garden serves Chinese cuisine and seafood specialties. **Amenities & Services** Room service, activities desk, parking ($9/day), coin-operated washer and dryer, swimming pool.

### ACCOMMODATIONS

**Rooms** 623. Nonsmoking rooms and rooms for the disabled available. **All Rooms** A/C, cable TV, refrigerator, in-room safe, coffeemaker. **Some Rooms** Balcony, kitchenette. **Comfort & Decor** Rooms are small to medium, tastefully appointed, and very clean, with floor-to-ceiling windows, Hawaiian artwork, and comfortable furnishings. Rooms were recently renovated.

## PAYMENT, RESERVATIONS, & RESTRICTIONS

**Family Plan** Children age 17 and under stay free in room with parents if using existing bedding. **Deposit** 1-night deposit or credit card guarantee required. Cancellation notice must be given 72 hours prior to scheduled arrival for refund. **Credit Cards** All major credit cards accepted. **Check-In/Out** 3 p.m./noon. Early check-in and late check out available on request.

## *ROYAL GARDEN AT WAIKIKI*                                    $$$

OVERALL ★★★★  |  QUALITY ★★★½  |  VALUE ★★★  |  ZONE 1

440 Olohana St., Honolulu, HI 96815; (800) 367-5666 or (808) 943-0202; fax: (808) 945-7407; hotel-info@royalgardens.com; www.royalgardens.com

It's a decent walk to the beach from this property—about 20 minutes— but the boutique Royal Garden is still a great recommendation. Everything is first-class here, from the service to the amenities. The setting is one of quiet refinement, with interiors inspired by Hawai'i's natural beauty. Lush gardens surround two swimming pools. The new King Kalakaua Plaza nearby—with Niketown, All Star Cafe, and Banana Republic—makes shopping simple. Jogging along nearby Ala Wai Canal is pleasant.

## SETTING & FACILITIES

**Location** In Waikiki, near Ala Wai Canal, 20-minute walk to beach. **Dining** Cascada serves Mediterranean and Pacific Rim cuisine; Shizu offers Ginza-style teppanyaki and traditional Japanese delicacies. **Amenities & Services** Laundry facilities, business center, fitness center, sauna, Jacuzzi, swimming pool, soda machines, shuttle service. Hair dryer, iron and board, and crib available on request.

## ACCOMMODATIONS

**Rooms** 220. Includes 19 suites. Nonsmoking rooms and rooms for the disabled available. Inquire when placing reservation. **All Rooms** A/C, cable TV, private lana'i, refrigerator, coffeemaker, voice mail, wet bar, in-room safe. **Some Rooms** Separate shower and Jacuzzi. **Comfort & Decor** Luxurious, with marble bathrooms, extra closet space, and tropical plants.

## PAYMENT, RESERVATIONS, & RESTRICTIONS

**Family Plan** Children age 12 and under stay free in room with parents if using existing bedding. **Deposit** 1-night deposit required within 10 days of confirmation. Cancellation notice must be given at least 72 hours prior to scheduled arrival for refund. **Credit Cards** All major credit cards accepted. **Check-In/Out** 3 p.m./ noon. Early check-in and late check out available on request (no guarantees).

## ROYAL HAWAIIAN HOTEL                                    $$$$$

OVERALL ★★★★½  |  QUALITY ★★★★  |  VALUE ★★½  |  ZONE 1

2259 Kalakaua Ave., Honolulu, HI 96815; (800) 782-9488 or (808) 923-7311; fax: (808) 924-7098; www.royal-hawaiian.com

This is the famed "Pink Palace." Few hotels in Hawai'i have a history like that of this property, which opened in 1927, inspired by a Rudolf Valentino movie. The Royal Hawaiian has aged well and still offers a great old-Waikiki experience. The hotel's design reflects a strong Moorish influence, with mission overtones supplied by cupolas resembling bell towers, and the atmosphere is reminiscent of Waikiki's golden years. The lobby area is as cool and elegant as can be, decorated in various outrageous shades of pink. The initial views are of lush gardens and shady lawns, but then the back end opens up to a dreamlike beach setting with imported gold sand and azure waters. Take a short walk to the Royal Hawaiian Shopping Center, Waikiki's biggest shopping complex. The hotel holds a lavish lu'au every Monday evening ($60 for hotel guests, free for their children ages 12 and under; $81 for non-hotel guests, $48 for children ages 5–12). Over the years, the Royal has hosted numerous celebrities and dignitaries, from Franklin Roosevelt to the Beatles.

### SETTING & FACILITIES
**Location** On Waikiki Beach, behind Royal Hawaiian Shopping Center. **Dining** The Surf Room serves breakfast, lunch, and dinner, including Friday seafood buffet and Sunday brunch. **Amenities & Services** Fresh flower lei greeting, fresh-baked Hawaiian banana bread on arrival, nightly turndown service, concierge, 24-hour fax service, morning newspaper, laundry and dry cleaning service, valet parking ($13), self-parking ($9/day), nurse and physician service.

### ACCOMMODATIONS
**Rooms** 527. Includes 33 suites; 58 nonsmoking rooms; 6 rooms with roll-in showers for wheelchair users. **All Rooms** A/C, color TV, refrigerator, in-room safe, robes. **Some Rooms** Wet bar, Continental breakfast. **Comfort & Decor** Very spacious bedrooms have high ceilings, chandeliers, and classic decor with Old World charm. The bathrooms are a little cramped, however.

### PAYMENT, RESERVATIONS, & RESTRICTIONS
**Family Plan** Children age 17 and under stay free in room with parents if using existing bedding. Rollaway bed, $25/night. **Deposit** Credit card guarantee or 1-night deposit required within 10 days of booking to guarantee reservation. Cancellation notice must be given 72 hours prior to scheduled arrival for refund. **Credit Cards** All major credit cards accepted. **Check-In/Out** 3 p.m./noon. Hospitality suite available for early arrivals and late departures.

## SHERATON MOANA SURFRIDER                              $$$$$

OVERALL ★★★★½ | QUALITY ★★★★ | VALUE ★★½ | ZONE 1

2365 Kalakaua Ave., Honolulu, HI 96815; (800) 782-9488 or (808) 922-3111; fax:
(808) 923-0308; www.moana-surfrider.com

Opened in 1901, this is Waikiki's oldest hotel. Nicknamed the "First Lady
of Waikiki," the Moana has lost none of her charm. We like the second-
floor balcony overlooking Kalakaua Avenue where you can kick back in a
rocking chair and watch the world go by. Ocean and beach views are
excellent. The staff is efficient, courteous, and smartly dressed—complete
with bow ties and sashes. Visit the mini-museum on the second floor for a
look at the golden age of the Moana and Waikiki. Memorabilia include
historic photos, postcards, room keys, stock shares, sheet music, menus,
and old brochures. You'll also see a sofa that once belonged to King
Kalakaua, Hawai'i's "Merrie Monarch." A historic centerpiece is the
hotel's 75-foot-high, 150-foot-wide banyan tree, near where "Hawai'i
Calls" was broadcast for 40 years. The central portion of the Moana is
listed on the National Register of Historic Places. In the late 1980s, the
hotel underwent a $50 million architectural restoration, reopening in
March 1989 to hurrahs.

### SETTING & FACILITIES
**Location** On Waikiki Beach. **Dining** The Ship's Tavern serves contemporary cui-
sine; the Beachside Cafe offers breakfast, lunch, and dinner in a casual setting;
Banyan Veranda serves breakfast, afternoon tea, cocktails, and an evening buffet.
**Amenities & Services** 24-hour room service, maid service, valet service, self-
parking ($9/day), fitness center, concierge, children's program.

### ACCOMMODATIONS
**Rooms** 793. Includes 46 suites; 18 ADA-approved rooms. Nonsmoking rooms
available. **All Rooms** A/C, cable TV, in-room safe, hair dryer, slippers, bathrobe,
coffeemaker. **Some Rooms** Oceanfront lana'i, wet bar, refrigerator, pullout sofa.
**Comfort & Decor** Rooms are small to medium in size, with high ceilings, oversized windows, and great views. The design is an interesting mix of old and new,
with Old World furnishings and modern amenities, including a video message and
check out system.

### PAYMENT, RESERVATIONS, & RESTRICTIONS
**Family Plan** Children age 17 and under stay free in room with parents if using
existing bedding. Maximum of 4 people/room. **Deposit** 1-night deposit or credit
card guarantee within 10 days of placing reservation. Cancellation notice must be
given 72 hours prior to scheduled arrival for refund. **Credit Cards** All major
credit cards accepted. **Check-In/Out** 3 p.m./noon. Early check-in and late check
out available on request.

## SHERATON PRINCESS KA'IULANI $$$$

OVERALL ★★★★ | QUALITY ★★★★ | VALUE ★★ | ZONE 1

120 Ka'iulani Ave., Honolulu, HI 96815; (800) 782-9488 or (808) 922-5811; fax: (808) 931-4577; www.princess-kaiulani.com

Named after Hawai'i's beloved Princess Victoria Ka'iulani, last heir to the Hawaiian throne, this hotel is situated on the site of her garden estate, 'Ainahau, where the princess spent her childhood.

The Princess Ka'iulani has 1,150 rooms in three separate wings—Princess, Ka'iulani, and 'Ainahau—surrounded by lobby areas, specialty shops, and gardens. The lobby area is airy, bright, and busy during the day. Original artwork and mementos from the era of Princess Ka'iulani are displayed throughout the hotel. Arts and crafts demonstrations are done daily, and poolside entertainment is provided nightly. The hotel offers *Creation—A Polynesian Odyssey* dinner show in 'Ainahau Showroom (see page 448).

### SETTING & FACILITIES

**Location** In Waikiki, next to the International Market Place, across the street from Waikiki Beach. **Dining** Momoyama serves Japanese specialties in traditional setting, Lotus Moon features an extensive Chinese menu. **Amenities & Services** Room service, swimming pool, valet parking ($15), parking ($8/day), coin-operated laundry machines.

### ACCOMMODATIONS

**Rooms** 1,150. Includes 12 suites; 13 ADA-approved rooms and 6 rooms with roll-in showers. Smoking-designated areas are available. **All Rooms** A/C, cable TV, mini-fridge, in-room safe ($3.25/day), hair dryer. **Some Rooms** Lana'i. **Comfort & Decor** Spacious, very clean. Simple but pleasant island decor reflects island accents.

### PAYMENT, RESERVATIONS, & RESTRICTIONS

**Family Plan** Children age 17 and under stay free in room with parents if using existing bedding. Maximum of 4 people/room. **Deposit** 1-night deposit or credit card guarantee. Cancellation notice must be given by 6 p.m. on date of scheduled arrival for refund. **Credit Cards** All major credit cards accepted. **Check-In/Out** 3 p.m./noon. Early check-in and late check out available on request (no guarantees).

## SHERATON WAIKIKI $$$$$

OVERALL ★★★★ | QUALITY ★★★★ | VALUE ★★ | ZONE 1

2255 Kalakaua Ave., Honolulu, HI 96815; (800) 782-9488 or (808) 922-4422; fax: (808) 923-8785; www.sheraton-waikiki.com

With its entire second floor dedicated to meetings and featuring Waikiki's largest indoor ballroom (26,000 square feet), this busy beach hotel is the second largest in the state—a 30-story wall of rooms full of conventioneers. The main lobby's centerpiece is a striking collection of colorful, ocean-theme glass sculptures, from fish and sharks to sea turtles. It personifies the hotel as a whole: pleasant but not stuffy. Hawaiian entertainment is provided nightly. For club-goers, the Sheraton offers Esprit nightclub.

## SETTING & FACILITIES

**Location** On Waikiki Beach. **Dining** Up on the 30th floor, Hanohano is renowned for its incredible views (it has the highest vantage point on Waikiki Beach) and award-winning Continental menu. Other restaurants include Ciao, serving Italian cuisine, and Ocean Terrace, with buffets with various international themes. **Amenities & Services** Valet parking ($13), self-parking ($9/day), meeting facilities, secretarial business services, nightly poolside entertainment, fitness center, travel services, daily children's program.

## ACCOMMODATIONS

**Rooms** 1,852. Includes 127 suites; 10 rooms for the disabled. Most rooms are nonsmoking. **All Rooms** A/C, private lana'i, color TV with first-run movies, clock radio, mini-bar, refrigerator, in-room safe, safety deposit box, in-room video message and check out facilities, room service, coffeemakers. **Some Rooms** Full kitchen. **Comfort & Decor** Rooms feature high ceilings, spacious bathrooms, a complete line of amenities, and stylish furnishings with island-accented decor.

## PAYMENT, RESERVATIONS, & RESTRICTIONS

**Family Plan** Children age 17 and under stay free in room with parents if using existing bedding. **Deposit** Credit card guarantee or 1-night deposit required. Cancellation notice must be given before 6 p.m. on scheduled day of arrival for refund. **Credit Cards** All major credit cards accepted. **Check-In/Out** 3 p.m./noon. Hospitality suite available for early arrivals and late departures.

## TURTLE BAY GOLF & TENNIS RESORT                    $$$

OVERALL ★★★★  |  QUALITY ★★★½  |  VALUE ★★★  |  ZONE 4

57-091 Kamehameha Hwy., Kahuku, HI 96731; (800) 445-8667 or (808) 293-8811; fax: (808) 293-9147; www.turtlebayresort.hilton.com

Situated on O'ahu's North Shore, the Turtle Bay rests on a scenic peninsula that juts into the Pacific. It's a far remove from Waikiki but still has all the creature comforts.

A former Hilton, it was sold after a major face-lift and now the new owner may cinch up its laid-back service. Atmosphere is comfortable and relaxed. Hawaiian entertainment is provided at the Bay View Lounge, with dancing on weekends. A choice spot for golfers and tennis players; the resort also offers snorkeling and horseback riding.

## SETTING & FACILITIES

**Location** On O'ahu's North Shore, at the tip of Kuilima Point. The hotel is near the North Shore's best surfing spots and beaches, including the legendary Banzai

Pipeline. **Dining** The Palm Terrace serves breakfast, lunch, and dinner daily, including theme buffets. **Amenities & Services** Room service, laundry service, valet and self-parking, swimming pool and Jacuzzi, exercise room, activity desk, tennis, golf, horseback riding.

## ACCOMMODATIONS

**Rooms** 485. Includes 26 suites; 5 rooms for the disabled. Nonsmoking rooms available. **All Rooms** A/C, cable TV, refrigerator, in-room safe, coffeemaker, dataport. **Comfort & Decor** Very spacious, clean, and rooms feature well maintained, light tropic colors, Hawaiian artwork, and tropical plants.

## PAYMENT, RESERVATIONS, & RESTRICTIONS

**Family Plan** Children age 17 and under stay free in room with parents if using existing bedding. **Deposit** 1-night deposit or credit card guarantee required within 10 days of confirmation. Cancellation notice must be given 48 hours prior to scheduled arrival for refund. **Credit Cards** All major credit cards accepted. **Check-In/Out** 3 p.m./11 a.m. Early check-in and late check out available for fee ($25 for 2 p.m. check-in, $50 for 5 p.m. check out).

## W HONOLULU–DIAMOND HEAD                         $$$$

OVERALL ★★★★  |  QUALITY ★★★★  |  VALUE ★★  |  ZONE 2

2885 Kalakaua Ave., Honolulu, HI 96815; (888) 924-7873 or (808) 924-3111; fax: (808) 923-2249; www.whotels.com

Formerly known as the Colony Surf Hotel, this small hotel is a hidden gem nestled at the foot of Diamond Head. The setting here is not beachfront, but it is peaceful and calm—a far cry from the nonstop action in the center of Waikiki. The service is very personal and friendly, about what you would expect of a hotel of this size. The views here are eye-catching no matter what room you're in, and if you decide to stay here, spend at least one evening at Diamond Head Grill, one of O'ahu's best restaurants. Waikiki Aquarium and Honolulu Zoo are a block or two away.

## SETTING & FACILITIES

**Location** Diamond Head end of Waikiki, short walk to beach. **Dining** Diamond Head Grill serves new American cuisine. **Amenities & Services** Room service, laundry service, valet parking ($14/day).

## ACCOMMODATIONS

**Rooms** 48 **All Rooms** A/C, radio, TV, refrigerator, lana'i, mini-bar, coffeemaker, hair dryer. **Some Rooms** 2 bedrooms. **Comfort & Decor** Very spacious and clean, the rooms' understated Balinese-style decor reflects tropical ambience. Light, sunny colors add to the overall pleasant look of the interiors.

## PAYMENT, RESERVATIONS, & RESTRICTIONS

**Family Plan** Rollaway bed, $45. **Deposit** Credit card guarantees reservation. Cancellation notice must be given 72 hours prior to scheduled arrival for refund. **Credit Cards** All major credit cards accepted. **Check-In/Out** 3 p.m./noon. Early check-in and late check out okay if available.

## WAIKIKI BEACH MARRIOTT RESORT                                    $$$$

OVERALL ★★★★ | QUALITY ★★★★ | VALUE ★★ | ZONE 1

2552 Kalakaua Ave., Honolulu, HI 96815; (800) 367-5370 or (808) 922-6611; fax:
(808) 921-5222; www.marriott.com

One of Hawai'i's larger hotels, the former Hawaiian Regent is now the
Waikiki Beach Marriott Resort, with a fresh new look. All public areas
and rooms in the Kuhio Tower were redone in a tropical style with new
art and furnishings. Hospitality here is warm and friendly. Another defi-
nite plus is the hotel's family-friendly location: Kuhio Beach Park (part of
Waikiki Beach) is just a walk across the street (the ocean views from the
hotel are dazzling), the Damien Museum is next door, and Kapi'olani
Park and the Honolulu Zoo are also nearby. One of Waikiki's more popular nightspots, Eurasia, is on the first floor of the hotel's Kalakaua Tower.
You can enjoy Hawaiian entertainment nightly at the lobby bar.

### SETTING & FACILITIES
**Location** Across the street from Waikiki Beach, 1 block from Honolulu Zoo.
**Dining** Acqua, serves cuisinewhich combines Mediterranean and Pacific Rim flavors. **Amenities & Services** Room service, laundry, parking, business center, fitness center.

### ACCOMMODATIONS
**Rooms** 1,308. Includes 6 suites; 4 nonsmoking floors; 18 ADA-approved rooms.
**All Rooms** A/C, TV, in-room safe, refrigerator, lana'i; hair dryer and coffeemaker
available on request. **Some Rooms** More space, upgraded amenities. **Comfort
& Decor** Tastefully appointed, medium-sized rooms have island-accented furnish-
ings and decor.

### PAYMENT, RESERVATIONS, & RESTRICTIONS
**Family Plan** Children age 17 and under stay free in room with parents if using
existing bedding. **Deposit** Credit card guarantee or 1-night deposit within 10
days of booking to guarantee reservation. **Credit Cards** All major credit cards
accepted except Diner's Club. **Check-In/Out** 3 p.m./noon. Early check-in and
late check out available on request.

## WAIKIKI BEACHCOMBER HOTEL                                    $$$

OVERALL ★★★★ | QUALITY ★★★ | VALUE ★★½ | ZONE 1

2300 Kalakaua Ave., Honolulu, HI 96815; (800) 622-4646 or (808) 922-4646; fax:
(808) 926-9973; reservations@waikikibeachcomber.com;
www.waikikibeachcomber.com

Although not as well known as many of Waikiki's name-brand hotels, the
Beachcomber has a lot going for it. On one side of the hotel is the International Market Place, where you can find bargains on all kinds of souvenirs and gifts; on the other side is a trio of big-screen movie theaters;

and directly across the street is the Royal Hawaiian Shopping Center. The beach is also across the street, about a block away The small lobby area displays a large pair of saltwater aquariums as well as striking Hawaiian artworks, including paintings, portraits, and framed Hawaiian quilts. We like the second-floor pool deck overlooking Kalakaua Avenue. The Beachcomber is the home of the *Don Ho Show* and the *Magic of Polynesia* (see page 449).

## SETTING & FACILITIES

**Location** In the heart of Waikiki, across street from beach. **Dining** Hibiscus Cafe serves everything from burgers and pizzas to a wide selection of international specialties. **Amenities & Services** Maid service, parking ($9/day), washer and dryer, swimming pool, ice machine.

## ACCOMMODATIONS

**Rooms** 500. Includes 7 suites; 7 wheelchair-accessible rooms. Nonsmoking rooms available on request. **All Rooms** A/C, cable TV with in-room movies, lana'i, refrigerator, in-room safe, voice mail, coffeemaker. **Some Rooms** 2 TV sets, 2 balconies, king-size bed. **Comfort & Decor** Spacious and clean. Soft tropical colors lead to a soothing and relaxing atmosphere. Decor is simple but pleasant, with Hawaiian paintings adorning the walls.

## PAYMENT, RESERVATIONS, & RESTRICTIONS

**Family Plan** Children age 17 and under stay free in room with parents if using existing bedding. Rollaway bed, $25/night. Maximum of 4 people/room. **Deposit** 1-night deposit due no later than 10 days after confirmation. Cancellation notice must be given 72 hours prior to scheduled arrival for refund. **Credit Cards** All major credit cards accepted. **Check-In/Out** 3 p.m./noon. Additional charge for early check-in of 50% the 1-day rack rate (guarantees check-in at 10 a.m.).

## WAIKIKI JOY HOTEL $$$

OVERALL ★★★★ | QUALITY ★★★½ | VALUE ★★★ | ZONE 1

320 Lewers St., Honolulu, HI 96815; (800) 922-7866 or (808) 923-2300; fax: (808) 924-4010; res.joy@aston-hotels.com; www.aston-hotels.com

This is one of Waikiki's best boutique hotels. Its location puts you near the action in Waikiki, but the beach is a couple of blocks away. The Italian marble open-air lobby sets the tone, but what makes it special are lavish touches in the rooms, half of which are suites with kitchenette facilities. Music lovers will appreciate the impressive stereo system in guest rooms, and each room features its own Jacuzzi tub). Every guest receives a free hour at the property's G. S. Studio, a karaoke center with 15 private rooms and more than 4,000 songs to select.

## SETTING & FACILITIES

**Location** In the center of Waikiki, a block mauka of Kalakaua Avenue, 15-minute walk to beach. **Dining** Cappucinos Cafe serves lunch and dinner. **Amenities & Services** Laundry service, valet parking ($10).

## ACCOMMODATIONS

**Rooms** 94. Includes 47 suites; 2 wheelchair-accessible rooms and 1 room with roll-in shower. Nonsmoking rooms available on request. **All Rooms** A/C, stereo entertainment center, cable TV, Jacuzzi, mini-fridge, hair dryer, dataport, voice mail, 1 hour free karaoke. **Some Rooms** Full kitchen. **Comfort & Decor** Spacious, ultra-luxurious, and clean. Rooms have their own marble entries, a state-of-the-art entertainment system with Bose speakers, and private Jacuzzis

## PAYMENT, RESERVATIONS, & RESTRICTIONS

**Family Plan** Children age 18 and under stay free in room with parents if using existing bedding. **Deposit** $50 cash if no credit card provided; prepay entire stay at registration; or 1–2 nights' deposit with credit card, depending on length of stay. Cancellation notice must be given 72 hours prior to scheduled arrival for refund. **Credit Cards** All major credit cards accepted. **Check-In/Out** 3 p.m./noon. Early check-in and late check out available on request (no guarantees).

## WAIKIKI PARC HOTEL                                                  $$$

OVERALL ★★★★  |  QUALITY ★★★★  |  VALUE ★★★½  |  ZONE 1

2233 Helumoa Rd., Honolulu, HI 96815; (800) 422-0450 or (808) 921-7272; fax: (808) 931-6638; www.waikikiparc.com

The Halekulani's little sister, this hotel isn't visually appealing—it's crammed in among its neighboring properties—but it has some practical advantages, like being near the Royal Hawaiian Shopping Center. It's also about 100 yards from the beach. If you want tastefulness without an ocean view, the Waikiki Parc might be for you.

## SETTING & FACILITIES

**Location** In Waikiki, across from Halekulani, a short walk to beach. **Dining** The Parc Cafe's buffets are popular with visitors and residentss alike. Kacho serves traditional Japanese fare. **Amenities & Services** Room service, laundry service, parking, concierge desk, business facilities.

## ACCOMMODATIONS

**Rooms** 298. Includes 3 floors of nonsmoking rooms; 1 room equipped for the disabled. **All Rooms** A/C, cable TV, 2 phones, mini-fridge, in-room safe, hair dryer; hot pots available on request. **Some Rooms** Lana'i. **Comfort & Decor** Spacious and well maintained rooms have ceramic tile floors with plush inlaid carpeting, shutters, tinted glass lana'i doors, and custom rattan furnishings. Color scheme is soft shades of white with accents of Pacific blue.

## PAYMENT, RESERVATIONS, & RESTRICTIONS

**Family Plan** Children age 14 and under stay free in room with parents if using existing bedding. Maximum of 3 people/room. **Deposit** Credit card guarantee or 1-night deposit due within 14 days of booking. Cancellation notice must be given 72 hours prior to scheduled arrival for refund. **Credit Cards** All major credit cards accepted. **Check-In/Out** 3 p.m./noon. Early check-in and late check out available on request (may be charged, depending on length).

## WAIKIKI TERRACE HOTEL                                    $$$$

OVERALL ★★★½ | QUALITY ★★★½ | VALUE ★★ | ZONE I

2045 Kalakaua Ave., Honolulu, HI 96815; (800) 367-5004 or (808) 955-6000; fax: (808) 943-8555; www.castle-group.com

Three blocks from the beach, this affordable hotel neighbors Fort DeRussy and the King Kalakaua Plaza shopping/restaurant complex. The Waikiki Terrace recently renovated all 242 of its guest rooms and suites. Service is friendly and enthusiastic, and the atmosphere is comfortable. Overall, a good value.

### SETTING & FACILITIES
**Location** At the gateway to Waikiki, next to Ft. DeRussy, 10-minute walk to beach. **Dining** The Eastern Garden serves breakfast, lunch, and dinner. **Amenities & Services** Room service, laundry and dry cleaning, swimming pool, Jacuzzi, business center, fitness center, parking ($8/day).

### ACCOMMODATIONS
**Rooms** 242. Includes 2 suites; 7 ADA-approved rooms. Nonsmoking rooms available. **All Rooms** A/C, cable TV, mini-fridge, lana'i, in-room safe, hot pot, hair dryer. **Some Rooms** Separate sleeping quarters, extra bathroom. **Comfort & Decor** Medium-sized rooms are clean and comfortable with soft colors and subtle island accents and decor.

### PAYMENT, RESERVATIONS, & RESTRICTIONS
**Family Plan** Children age 17 and under stay free with parents. **Deposit** Credit card guarantee or 1-night cash deposit due 14 days after booking. Prepay entire stay plus $50 deposit at registration. Cancellation notice must be given 72 hours prior to scheduled arrival for refund. **Credit Cards** All major credit cards accepted. **Check-In/Out** 3 p.m./noon. Early check-in and late check out available on request.

## Maui

## EMBASSY VACATION RESORT                                  $$$$$

OVERALL ★★★★½ | QUALITY ★★★★ | VALUE ★★½ | ZONE 9

104 Ka'anapali Shores Pl., Lahaina, HI 96761; (800) 669-3155 or (808) 661-2000; fax: (808) 667-5821; embassy@maui.net; www.embassy-maui.com

Opened in 1988, this was the first Hawai'i property to offer all-suite accommodations. Ninety percent of the suites provide ocean views (you can also see the neighboring islands of Moloka'i and Lana'i). A variety of island-flavored art adorns the resort's lobby. A popular feature here is the 42-foot water slide, which plops you straight into a 1-acre swimming pool. The young ones can participate in Beach Buddies, the resort's year-round children's program (for ages 5–12), which includes lei making, beachcombing, coconut weaving, and other activities. A challenging miniature golf course is also on the premises, although serious golfers may prefer taking on the championship courses located elsewhere at the Ka'anapali Resort.

### SETTING & FACILITIES

**Location** On Ka'anapali Beach. **Dining** The North Beach Grille serves steaks, seafood, chicken, and other American favorites. **Amenities & Services** Room service, laundry and housekeeping service, workout room, parking, children's day care.

### ACCOMMODATIONS

**Rooms** 413. All suites. 12 ADA-approved rooms. Most rooms are designated non-smoking. **All Rooms** A/C, cable TV, VCR, microwave, mini-fridge, in-room safe, hair dryer. **Comfort & Decor** Extremely spacious suites (over 800 square feet) have separate living rooms. An oversized soaking tub, separate shower, walk-in closets, dual marble vanities, and 35-inch-screen TV are among the luxuries. Decor has cool tropical appeal; cheerful and airy.

### PAYMENT, RESERVATIONS, & RESTRICTIONS

**Family Plan** Children age 17 and under stay free in room with parents if using existing bedding. **Deposit** 1-night deposit due within 10 days of booking. Cancellation notice must be given 72 hours prior to scheduled arrival for refund. **Credit Cards** All major credit cards accepted. **Check-In/Out** 4 p.m./11 a.m. Early check-in and late check out available on request. Hospitality suite available for early arrivals and late departures.

## FAIRMONT KEA LANI HOTEL, SUITES & VILLAS     $$$$$

OVERALL ★★★★½  |  QUALITY ★★★★  |  VALUE ★★★  |  ZONE 8

4100 Wailea Alanui Dr., Wailea, HI 96753; (800) 659-4100 or (808) 875-4100; fax: (808) 875-1200; info@kealani.com; www.kealani.com

This all-suite hotel features an extensive menu of in-room amenities, including a complete entertainment system. The hotel's open-air, stark white, Arabian-nights fantasy architecture is bold, but inside the resort evokes a quaint village feel. Children ages 5–12 can participate in Keiki Lani, the hotel's year-round children's program, which features hula and lei making lessons and swimming. The hotel has two marvelous swimming lagoons that are connected by a 140-foot water slide and swim-up beverage bar. One tasty feature on the property is the Organic Garden, which features more than 150 varieties of produce, including 18 varieties of rare exotic fruits. (The produce is used in the hotel's restaurants; inquire about a guided garden tour.) Readers of *Condé Nast Traveler* voted the Kea Lani one of the top five resorts in the Pacific region.

### SETTING & FACILITIES

**Location** On Polo Beach. **Dining** Nick's Fishmarket Maui is a popular seafood bistro, with fine-dining under the stars on its terrace. Caffe Ciao serves Italian cuisine in a garden setting. **Amenities & Services** Spa and fitness center, 3

swimming pools, tennis, golf, children's program, indoor and outdoor meeting/ conference space.

## ACCOMMODATIONS

**Rooms** 413. All suites. Includes 37 oceanfront villas; 201 nonsmoking suites; 11 suites for the disabled. **All Rooms** A/C, cable TV, stereo entertainment center (with CD player, VCR, and laser disc player), private lana'i. **Some Rooms** Private villas with pool, gourmet kitchen, sun deck, barbecue grill, extra bedrooms. **Comfort & Decor** Soft tropical colors provide cheerful ambience to very spacious suites, with separate living rooms. Exceptionally clean, suites feature luxurious furnishings with island-theme artworks and large European marble bathroom with soaking tub and twin pedestal sinks.

## PAYMENT, RESERVATIONS, & RESTRICTIONS

**Family Plan** Children age 18 and under stay free in room with parents if using existing bedding. Rollaway bed, $25. **Deposit** 2-night deposit due within 14 days after booking. Cancellation notice must be given 72 hours prior to scheduled arrival for refund. **Credit Cards** All major credit cards accepted. **Check-In/Out** 4 p.m./noon. Early check-in and late check out available on request.

## FOUR SEASONS RESORT MAUI                                  $$$$$

OVERALL ★★★★★ | QUALITY ★★★★★ | VALUE ★★★ | ZONE 8

3900 Wailea Alanui, Wailea, HI 96753; (800) 334-6284 or (808) 874-8000; fax: (808) 874-6449; resmaui@fourseasons.com; www.fourseasons.com

*Condé Nast Traveler* magazine named the Four Seasons the "Top Tropical Resort in the World" in 1993, and this luxurious resort continues to rate high among travel experts and patrons. (The resort garnered the AAA Five Diamond Award in 1999.) The breezy, open lobby is testament to the resort's island-accented architectural design, which includes commissioned reproductions of early Hawaiian furniture as well as Hawai'i-inspired paintings, sculptures, and other artwork. On-site features include a children's program, health club, game room, and salon. The service is professional and courteous. To top it all off, the Four Seasons is located at Wailea Resort, which offers three championship golf courses and the 11-court Wailea Tennis Center (known as "Wimbledon West"). Overall, the Four Seasons has to rate as one of the best resorts (if not the very best) on Maui.

## SETTING & FACILITIES

**Location** On Wailea Beach. **Dining** Spago showcases contemporary American cuisine with local produce and fresh seafood for dinner. **Amenities & Services** 24-hour room service, full laundry service, workout facilities, salon, business center, children's program, game room.

## ACCOMMODATIONS

**Rooms** 380. Includes 75 suites. ADA-approved and nonsmoking rooms available. **All Rooms** A/C, cable TV, VCR, lana'i, in-room safe, mini-bar, hair dryer, dataport, robes. **Some Rooms** Fax machines, extra bedroom. **Comfort & Decor** Very spacious, exceptionally comfortable, and well maintained. Soft white and gentle sunset hues, deep-cushioned rattan and wicker furnishings, large bathrooms with marble counters and dual vanities, and Island-themed artwork add to the warm atmosphere.

## PAYMENT, RESERVATIONS, & RESTRICTIONS

**Family Plan** Children age 17 and under stay free in room with parents if using existing bedding. **Deposit** 1-night deposit due within 7 days of booking. Cancellation notice must be given 14 hours prior to scheduled arrival for refund during January 3–April 30; 7 days prior during May 1–December 18. **Credit Cards** All major credit cards accepted. **Check-In/Out** 3 p.m./noon. Early check-in and late check out available on request.

## *GRAND WAILEA RESORT HOTEL & SPA*    $$$$$

OVERALL ★★★★½ | QUALITY ★★★★½ | VALUE ★★½ | ZONE 8

3850 Wailea Alanui Dr., Wailea, HI 96753; (800) 888-6100 or (808) 875-1234; fax: (808) 879-4077; info@gwrmail.com; www.grandwailea.com

Even if you don't stay here, this $600 million ultra-luxury resort is a worthy destination. Like most Hawaiian resorts, its stores, restaurants, lobby, and beach are open to the public. Stroll through the 40-acre property to see six major design themes—flowers, water, trees, sound, light, and art. There's more than $30 million in artwork in public areas, including an exceptional collection of huge lounging Bufano bronze sculptures in the lobby and an impressive collection of works by Hawai'i artists commissioned for the resort. Among the features here are Camp Grande, a 20,000-square-foot children's facility; the 50,000-square-foot Spa Grande; a breathtaking wedding chapel (complete with stained glass windows); and a 2,000-foot-long river pool that includes valleys, water slides, waterfalls, caves, grottos, whitewater rapids, a Jacuzzi, a sauna, and the world's only "water elevator," which lifts guests from the lower-level pool to the higher-level pool. Everything here is "grand"—some might say too grand. Though many will love this place, others might find it over the top. If you want opulence, this is it.

## SETTING & FACILITIES

**Location** On Wailea Beach. **Dining** Kincha serves Japanese cuisine in a traditional setting that includes rocks imported from Mt. Fuji. Bistro Molokini offers fine Italian fare, and the Humuhumunukunukuapua'a specializes in fresh seafood in a romantic open-air atmosphere. It is situated in a tidepool-like pond, with tropical fish and its own set of bronze sculptures commissioned by Hawaiian artists. **Amenities & Services** Room service, full-service spa and fitness center, wedding chapel, extensive conference facilities with a separate entrance, 3 championship golf courses, complimentary scuba lessons, squash/racquetball court, valet parking ($8), excellent children's program, high-tech water complex and Hawai'i's largest swimming pools (one with a manmade beach adjacent to the real beach). A $10/day resort fee is automatically charged to each room.

## ACCOMMODATIONS

**Rooms** 761. Includes 52 suites; 10 rooms for disabled. Nonsmoking rooms available. **All Rooms** A/C, cable TV, lana'i, in-room safe, honor bar, coffeemaker, hair dryer, robes, slippers. **Some Rooms** Larger accommodations, extra baths, 3-bedrooom suite. **Comfort & Decor** Very spacious, luxurious, with opulent furnishings and decor.

## PAYMENT, RESERVATIONS, & RESTRICTIONS

**Family Plan** Children age 18 and under stay free in room with parents if using existing bedding. Rollaway bed, $25. Maximum 4 people/room. **Deposit** 2-night deposit required within 14 days of booking (or reservation will be automatically canceled). Cancellation notice must be given 72 hours prior to scheduled arrival for refund (14 days for suites). **Credit Cards** All major credit cards accepted. **Check-In/Out** 3 p.m./noon. Early check-in and late check out available on request.

## *HOTEL HANA-MAUI*                                   $$$$$

OVERALL ★★★★  |  QUALITY ★★★★  |  VALUE ★★  |  ZONE 10

P.O. Box 9, Hana, HI 96713; (800) 321-4262 or (808) 248-8211; fax: (808) 248-7202; www.hotelhanamaui.com

What this cozy small hotel lacks (television and air conditioning), it makes up for in charm, location, and friendly, attentive service. Hana sits on 66 acres of landscaped gardens, and the ocean and mountain views are, like Hana, heavenly. Remote, quiet, romantic, this is the epitome of a honeymoon hotel. A weekly lu'au is held on the beach. Available outdoor activities include horseback riding, hiking, snorkeling, bike riding, and historical tours. A wellness center offers everything from massages to yoga. A favorite celebrity haunt, the Hotel Hana-Maui can only get better since it's been purchased by the owner of the Post Ranch in California's Big Sur.

## SETTING & FACILITIES

**Location** In Hana, east end of Maui, shuttle to Hamoa Beach. **Dining** The dining room serves Continental cuisine. **Amenities & Services** Room service (breakfast only), laundry service, parking, wellness center.

## ACCOMMODATIONS

**Rooms** 65. Includes 7 suites. Nonsmoking suite available. **All Rooms** Wet bar, lana'i, coffee- and tea-maker. **Some Rooms** Jacuzzis. **Comfort & Decor** Rooms are small to medium with comfortable atmosphere, bleached hardwood floors, wicker and bamboo furnishings, handmade quilts, and private patios.

## PAYMENT, RESERVATIONS, & RESTRICTIONS

**Family Plan** Children age 12 and under stay free in room with parents if using existing bedding. **Deposit** 1-night deposit required. Cancellation notice must be given 72 hours prior to scheduled arrival for refund. **Credit Cards** All major credit cards accepted. **Check-In/Out** 3 p.m./noon. Early check-in and late check out available on request.

## HYATT REGENCY MAUI                                             $$$$$

OVERALL ★★★★  |  QUALITY ★★★★  |  VALUE ★★½  |  ZONE 9

200 Nohea Dr., Lahaina, HI 96761; (800) 233-1234 or (808) 661-1234; fax: (808) 667-4497; www.hyatt.com

At first glance, it's easy to stamp the Hyatt Maui as a typical Hyatt hotel. By digging a little deeper, however, you'll uncover some features here that are unusual.

The hotel's nightly "Tour of the Stars" program gives guests a guided tour of the Hawaiian skies and allows them to peer through a state-of-the-art, computer-controlled 16-inch reflector telescope. A wildlife tour brings visitors face-to-face with the resorts menagerie of penguins, swans, parrots, macaws, flamingos, and koi. You can also tour the tropical gardens (it's about a two-mile walk) or browse the $2 million art collection. This hotel, one of the first fantasy-style hotels in the islands, offers something for travelers of all ages and interests, including a health spa. In 1996, the property underwent a $16 million renovation of all its guest rooms.

### SETTING & FACILITIES:

**Location** On Ka'anapali Beach. **Dining** Romantic Swan Court features Continental cuisine with Pacific Rim flair by a pool with stately swans swimming up for a handout, Spats Trattoria serves Italian food, and Cascades Grille and Sushi Bar offers fresh seafood and steak. **Amenities & Services** Fitness center, tennis, golf, outdoor dinner theater, activities desk, children's program, shops, meeting and convention facilities, rooftop astronomy program.

### ACCOMMODATIONS

**Rooms** 815. Includes 31 suites; 4 rooms for the disabled. Nonsmoking rooms available. **All Rooms** A/C, cable TV, honor bar, in-room safe, hair dryer, robes, coffeemaker. **Some Rooms** Living room, dining area, wet bar, refrigerator. **Comfort & Decor** Spacious and clean rooms have stylish earth and mauve Asian Pacific decor, comfortable furnishings, and attractive wall hangings.

### PAYMENT, RESERVATIONS, & RESTRICTIONS

**Family Plan** Children age 17 and under stay free in room with parents if using existing bedding. Maximum 4 people/room. **Deposit** 2-night deposit due within 14 days after booking. Cancellation notice must be given 72 hours prior to scheduled arrival for refund. **Credit Cards** All major credit cards accepted. **Check-In/Out** 3 p.m./noon. Early check-in and late check out based on availability.

## KA'ANAPALI BEACH HOTEL $$$$

OVERALL ★★★★ | QUALITY ★★★½ | VALUE ★★★ | ZONE 9

2525 Ka'anapali Pkwy.. Lahaina, HI 96761; (800) 262-8450 or (808) 661-0011; fax: (808) 667-5978; info@kbhmaui.com; www.kaanapalibeachhotel.com

Located on one of the widest stretches of Ka'anapali Beach, the Ka'anapali Beach Hotel is called Maui's "most Hawaiian" hotel. The management and staff here, schooled in Hawaiian hospitality, pride themselves on their aloha spirit, and the smiles and friendliness are downright contagious. Modern amenities aside, everything here is reminiscent of the islands' romantic plantation era. Four separate wings form a semicircle around a ten-acre courtyard. A variety of Hawaiian activities—including hula lessons, lei making, lau hala weaving, and ti leaf skirt making—are held daily, and employees provide Hawaiian entertainment three days a week. *Travel & Leisure* ranked this hotel tops for best value in Hawai'i. For visitors seeking a hotel that places a strong emphasis on Hawaiian hospitality, look no further.

### SETTING & FACILITIES

**Location** On Ka'anapali Beach. **Dining** The Tiki Terrace Restaurant serves Continental and island cuisine. *Black Illusion Dinner Show,* 5:30 p.m. Sunday–Thursday, is a Polynesian show with magician Jody Baran: $69, adults, $49, children/students ages 13–20, $29, children ages 6–12. **Amenities & Services** Laundry service, valet parking ($7), self-parking ($5/day), children's program.

### ACCOMMODATIONS

**Rooms** 430. Includes 14 suites. Nonsmoking rooms and rooms for the disabled available on request. **All Rooms** A/C, cable TV, in-room safe, refrigerator, coffeemaker. **Some Rooms** More space, upgraded amenities. **Comfort & Decor** Spacious, clean, and well maintained. Tropical green and golden sand hues accentuate the Hawaiian mood, along with Hawaiian quilt–style bedspreads, light tropical furniture, and local artwork.

### PAYMENT, RESERVATIONS, & RESTRICTIONS

**Family Plan** Children age 17 and under stay free in room with parents if using existing bedding. Rollaway bed, $15. **Deposit** 1- or 2-night deposit due 10 days after booking. Cancellation notice must be given 3–7 days prior to scheduled arrival for refund. **Credit Cards** All major credit cards accepted. **Check-In/Out** 3 p.m./noon. Early check-in and late check out available on request.

## KAPALUA BAY HOTEL                                        $$$$$

OVERALL ★★★★  |  QUALITY ★★★★  |  VALUE ★★  |  ZONE 9

One Bay Dr., Kapalua, HI 96761; (800) 367-8000 or (808) 669-5656; fax: (808) 669-4694; www.kapaluabayhotel.com

The Kapalua Bay Hotel doesn't have the pedigree of its neighbor, the Ritz-Carlton Kapalua, but it is in the same worldly class and has the added advantage of fronting one of Maui's finest beaches. The hotel, a gracious veteran recently redone, blends into its natural surroundings and lush tropical gardens. Piano and Hawaiian music are provided nightly at the Lehua Lounge, located below the lobby area. The Kapalua Shops, a mini-mall of some 20 boutiques shares the premises, and golf aficionados have a choice of three championship golf courses, one of which hosts the prestigious PGA Mercedes Open each January.

### SETTING & FACILITIES
**Location** On Kapalua Bay, adjoining a perfect beach cove. **Dining** The Bay Club serves seafood specialties for lunch and dinner. Gardenia Court offers international fare, including Friday night seafood buffet and Sunday brunch. **Amenities & Services** Room service, laundry service, valet parking ($10), self-parking ($6/day), tennis courts, children's program, shops.

### ACCOMMODATIONS
**Rooms** 194. Includes 12 suites; 1 floor designated for nonsmoking rooms; 6 rooms for the hearing impaired; 8 wheelchair-accessible rooms. **All Rooms** A/C, cable TV, in-room safe, mini-bar, lana'i, 3 phones, hair dryer. **Some Rooms** Washer and dryer, Jacuzzi, second bedroom. **Comfort & Decor** Oversized rooms have natural colors and marble accents and large private lana'i.

### PAYMENT, RESERVATIONS, & RESTRICTIONS
**Family Plan** Children age 17 and under stay free in room with parents if using existing bedding. **Deposit** 1-night credit card guarantee (5-night deposit during the Christmas holidays). Cancellation notice must be given 72 hours prior to scheduled arrival for refund. **Credit Cards** All major credit cards accepted except Discover. **Check-In/Out** 3 p.m./noon. Early check-in and late check out available on request.

## LAHAINA INN                                              $$

OVERALL ★★★★  |  QUALITY ★★★  |  VALUE ★★★½  |  ZONE 9

127 Lahainaluna Rd., Lahaina, HI 96761; (800) 669-3444 or (808) 661-0577; fax: (808) 667-9480; inntown@lahainainn.com; www.lahainainn.com

This hotel is proof that good things can come in small packages. Rick Ralston, founder and owner of the popular Crazy Shirts stores, is also a collector of fine antiques and other historic buildings in need of his special touch. Ralston restored the dozen rooms of this historic inn; pieces from his personal collection furnish each individually decorated room. Because of the value of the furnishings, children under age 15 are not allowed at this inn. A complimentary Continental breakfast is served at the end of the hall every morning. The inn's close proximity to Front Street is a "good news, bad news" situation: It's good to be close to the action (Lahaina is the island's most bustling town), but it also tends to get noisy. Also, keep in mind that there are no TV sets at the inn. Our guess is, the people who will most appreciate this type of setting are the type of folks who won't miss them for a second.

## SETTING & FACILITIES

**Location** In the heart of Lahaina, across from the waterfront, no beach. **Dining** David Paul's Lahaina Grill, one of Maui's best restaurants, serves New American cuisine. **Amenities & Services** Parking ($5/day), Continental breakfast.

## ACCOMMODATIONS

**Rooms** 12. Includes 3 suites. All are nonsmoking rooms (smoking permitted on lana'i). **All Rooms** A/C, ceiling fans. **Some Rooms** Lana'i, full bath and shower, king-size bed. **Comfort & Decor** Rooms are smallish and dimly lit, but well maintained and clean. Antique furnishings include restored brass and wood beds, period wall decorations, and wood armoires.

## PAYMENT, RESERVATIONS, & RESTRICTIONS

**Deposit** 1-night deposit required. Cancellation notice must be given 10 days prior to scheduled arrival for refund. **Credit Cards** All major credit cards accepted except Discover. **Check-In/Out** 3 p.m./11 a.m. Late check out (until noon) on request.

## *MAUI MARRIOTT RESORT* $$$$

OVERALL ★★★★ | QUALITY ★★★★ | VALUE ★★ | ZONE 9

100 Nohea Kai Dr., Lahaina, HI 96761; (800) 763-1333 or (808) 667-1200; fax: (808) 667-8300; www.marriott.com

This is a full-service resort with a casual, family-oriented atmosphere and friendly service. Waterfalls, koi ponds, and tall coconut palms adorn the attractive grounds. A year-round children's program is available, as are Hawaiian crafts lessons and a full menu of recreational sports and activities. The Marriott also has one of the island's best lu'au, held almost nightly on the beach. A mini-mall with 20 shops is on the premises.

## SETTING & FACILITIES

**Location** On Ka'anapali Beach. **Dining** VaBene serves Italian cuisine, three meals daily. **Amenities & Services** Room service (until 10 p.m.), valet parking and self-parking ($8/day), nightly lu'au (except Monday), 2 swimming pools, 2 Jacuzzis, fitness center, coin-operated laundry service, meetings and convention facilities.

## ACCOMMODATIONS

**Rooms** 606. Includes 16 suites; 14 rooms for the disabled. Nonsmoking rooms available. **All Rooms** A/C, cable TV, lanaʻi, refrigerator, in-room safe, coffeemaker. **Some Rooms** Sofa sleeper, larger lanaʻi, separate dressing area. **Comfort & Decor** Spacious rooms have tasteful furnishings and island artwork. Soft, pastel colors add to the overall pleasant ambience.

## PAYMENT, RESERVATIONS, & RESTRICTIONS

**Family Plan** Children age 17 and under stay free in room with parents if using existing bedding. Maximum of 2 adults and 2 children/room. **Deposit** Credit card guarantee. Cancellation notice must be given 72 hours prior to scheduled arrival for refund. **Credit Cards** All major credit cards accepted. **Check-In/Out** 3 p.m./noon. Early check-in and late check out available on request (no guarantees).

## MAUI PRINCE HOTEL                                    $$$$

OVERALL ★★★★ | QUALITY ★★★½ | VALUE ★★ | ZONE 8

5400 Makena Alanui, Kihei, HI 96753; (800) 321-6248 or (808) 874-1111; fax: (808) 879-8763; www.princehawaii.com

Situated on the shore below the cool slopes of Mount Haleakala and fronting lovely Maluaka Beach, this 1,800-acre resort is an isolated haven on the edge of wilderness. The picturesque grounds offer an interior courtyard with a koi pond and waterfall, which adds to the resort's tranquil, understated atmosphere. All rooms have views of the ocean as well as the neighboring islands of Molokaʻi, Lanaʻi, and Kahoʻolawe. The service here is impeccable. Snorkeling and scuba diving are among the outdoor activities available; there are six tennis courts nearby at the Makena Tennis Club, and two championship golf courses. A hula show is presented at the oceanfront Molokini Lounge. Resort shuttles run between the sports facilities, the hotel, and nearby Wailea Resort's shopping village.

## SETTING & FACILITIES

**Location** In Makena in south Maui, short walk to Makena Beach. **Dining** The Prince Court features Continental and island cuisine; Hakone offers traditional Japanese fare and a sushi bar. **Amenities & Services** Room service, welcome baskets on arrival, laundry service, fitness center, parking, children's program.

## ACCOMMODATIONS

**Rooms** 310. Includes 19 suites; 5–10 rooms for the disabled. Nonsmoking rooms available. **All Rooms** A/C, cable TV, lanaʻi, in-room safe, hair dryer, iron and board, bottled water, coffeemaker. **Some Rooms** Second bedroom. **Comfort & Decor** Spacious rooms have clean, simple decor with creamy pastel tones and island-theme artworks in a modern, casual setting.

## PAYMENT, RESERVATIONS, & RESTRICTIONS

**Family Plan** Children age 17 and under stay free in room with parents if using existing bedding. Extra adult, $40. **Deposit** 1-night deposit required. Cancellation notice must be given 72 hours prior to scheduled arrival for refund. **Credit Cards** All major credit cards accepted. **Check-In/Out** 3 p.m./noon. Early check-in and late check out available on request.

## OUTRIGGER WAILEA RESORT                                $$$$$

OVERALL ★★★★ | QUALITY ★★★★ | VALUE ★★★ | ZONE 8

3700 Wailea Alanui Dr., Wailea, HI 96753; (800) 688-7444 or (808) 879-1922; fax: (808) 874-8331; www.outrigger.com

Although it was opened as the Maui Inter-Continental Resort and formerly known as the Aston Wailea Resort, this oceanfront resort came under Outrigger management in early 1999 and underwent an extensive renovation after that. The resort's low-rise building design is a comfortable fit on 22 oceanfront acres. Lei-making classes and crafts demonstrations are offered regularly, and Hawaiian entertainment is provided nightly. Lu'au is staged four nights a week on the lawn. Arcade games, billiards, darts, and air hockey are among the diversions offered at Pa'ani, a game bar. A shuttle provides transportation to the Maui Ocean Center, half an hour away in Ma'alea. Overall, the Outrigger Wailea is a pleasant gem suitable for families and couples alike.

### SETTING & FACILITIES
**Location** At Wailea Resort, on the beach. **Dining** Kuma Bar & Grill specializes in steak and seafood, poolside Hula Moons features lighter fare and popular island favorites. **Amenities & Services** Laundry service, children's program, parking, business facilities, game room.

### ACCOMMODATIONS
**Rooms** 524. Includes 46 suites; 446 nonsmoking rooms; 10 rooms for the disabled. **All Rooms** A/C, cable TV, in-room safe, refrigerator, coffeemaker, hair dryer, iron and board. **Some Rooms** Robes. **Comfort & Decor** Very spacious, clean, well appointed rooms have sunny pastels, attractive tropical furnishings, artwork, and private lana'i.

### PAYMENT, RESERVATIONS, & RESTRICTIONS
**Family Plan** Children age 17 and under stay free in room with parents if using existing bedding. **Deposit** 1-night deposit required. Cancellation notice must be given 72 hours prior to scheduled arrival for refund. **Credit Cards** All major credit cards accepted. **Check-In/Out** 3 p.m./noon. Early check-in and late check out available on request.

## RENAISSANCE WAILEA BEACH RESORT              $$$$

OVERALL ★★★★ | QUALITY ★★★★ | VALUE ★★ | ZONE 8

3550 Wailea Alanui Dr., Wailea, HI 96753; (800) 992-4532 or (808) 879-4900; fax: (808) 874-5370; www.renaissancehotels.com

Another jewel property in Wailea. Opened in 1978 as the Stouffer Wailea Beach Resort, this 15-acre property received a dramatic face-lift in 1990. The main lobby is made of marble and limestone and features hand-blown Italian glass fixtures and a grand stairway. Outside, the landscape is dotted with waterfalls and tropical flora. Golfers choose from three championship courses in Wailea, and tennis action is available at the 11-court Wailea Tennis Center. The Renaissance also offers a recreational rarity among Hawai'i resorts: half-court basketball. For ambience and scenery, enjoy late-afternoon cocktails at the Sunset Terrace.

### SETTING & FACILITIES

**Location** At Wailea Resort, on the beach. **Dining** The Palm Court features Mediterranean cuisine and buffets for dinner. Hana Gion is an intimate Japanese eatery. Sunset lu'au held in oceanside garden setting. **Amenities & Services** Room service, laundry service, valet parking, self-parking ($5/day), fitness center.

### ACCOMMODATIONS

**Rooms** 345. Includes 12 suites. Rooms for the disabled and nonsmoking rooms available. **All Rooms** A/C, cable TV, VCR, private balcony, mini-fridge, hair dryer, coffeemaker. **Comfort & Decor** Spacious and clean, light colors and subtle tropical touches add to bright atmosphere. Island-theme furnishings and artworks.

### PAYMENT, RESERVATIONS, & RESTRICTIONS

**Family Plan** Children age 17 and under stay free in room with parents if using existing bedding. **Deposit** 1-night deposit due within 10 days of booking. Cancellation notice must be given 72 hours prior to scheduled arrival for refund. **Credit Cards** All major credit cards accepted. **Check-In/Out** 3 p.m./noon. Early check-in and late check out available on request.

## *RITZ-CARLTON, KAPALUA*                                      $$$$$

OVERALL ★★★★★  |  QUALITY ★★★★★  |  VALUE ★★★½  |  ZONE 9

One Ritz-Carlton Dr., Kapalua, HI 96761; (800) 241-3333 or (808) 669-6200; fax: (808) 669-2028; www.ritzcarlton.com

The Ritz is a perennial AAA Five Diamond Award recipient, and it's not hard to understand why. Everything here, from the service to guest rooms to dining, is perfect, with the exception of the weather, which can be surprisingly windy and cool. The atmosphere here is one of blissful luxury that isn't stuffy. Set on 50 acres, the Ritz features two six-story wings that step down the seaside slope, sheltering pools that step down with waterfalls in between. Public areas are enhanced by eighteenth- and nineteenth-century artwork as well as large murals, paintings, and ceramics created by local artists. Recently added to the property was a 19,200-square-foot special-function pavilion located adjacent to the hotel's entrance. The Ritz Kids program allows children (ages 5–12) to learn about Maui's culture, nature, art, and ecology. Evening entertainment is provided at the Terrace Restaurant and Lobby Lounge. Kapalua Resort has a trio of championship golf courses and ten tennis courts. The Ritz hosts several notable annual events, including the PGA Mercedes Championships (January), Celebration of the Arts (April), Kapalua Wine and Food Symposium (usually July), and the Earth Maui Nature Summit (September). The Ritz-Carlton Kapalua, is currently the world's only Audubon Heritage Cooperative Sanctuary Resort Hotel.

## SETTING & FACILITIES

**Location** At Kapalua Resort in West Maui, a short, but steep, walk to the beach. **Dining** The Anuenue Room, one of Maui's finest restaurants, features Hawaiian/ Provençal cuisine with fresh island flavors, and enjoys a superlative view. The Terrace Restaurant serves a popular buffet for breakfast and fresh local seafood for dinner. It also serves a Friday night seafood buffet and Sunday night Italian buffet. **Amenities & Services** 24-hour room service, twice-daily maid service, laundry service, fitness center, spa treatments, multilevel swimming pool, hydrotherapy pools, business facilities, children's program, golf, tennis, ocean activities.

## ACCOMMODATIONS

**Rooms** 548. Includes 58 suites. ADA-approved rooms and nonsmoking rooms available. **All Rooms** A/C, cable TV with pay movies, 3 phones, lana'i, in-room safe, honor bar, hair dryer, dataport, robes. **Some Rooms** Personal concierge service, complimentary food and beverages. **Comfort & Decor** Oversized rooms are well maintained with warm colors, opulent tropical-inspired furnishings, Hawaiian artworks, and large private lana'i (80% of rooms have ocean views).

## PAYMENT, RESERVATIONS, & RESTRICTIONS

**Deposit** Cancel reservations 7 days prior to scheduled arrival for refund. **Credit Cards** All major credit cards accepted. **Check-In/Out** 3 p.m./noon. Early check-in and late check out available on request (no guarantees).

## SHERATON MAUI $$$$$

OVERALL ★★★★ | QUALITY ★★★★ | VALUE ★★ | ZONE 9

2605 Ka'anapali Pkwy., Lahaina, HI 96761; (800) 782-9488 or (808) 661-0031; fax: (808) 661-0458; www.sheraton-maui.com

After extensive renovation, the Sheraton Maui is again a luxurious full-service resort. Its 23 acres comprise the premier real estate at Ka'anapali Beach Resort—front and center, incorporating the volcanic landmark Black Rock into its architectural design (some facilities were built atop the rock). Its elevated lobby opens to a wide panorama of the Pacific Ocean and a spectacular 147-foot-long oceanfront swimming lagoon. Children ages 5–12 can participate in the Keiki Aloha Club (available during the summer), which includes lei making and hula lessons, beach activities, and field trips to historic sites. Legendary Black Rock, a place where Hawaiians believed spirits of the dead departed this world, is considered one of the best snorkeling areas on Maui, and cliff divers used it for decades for spectacular sunset rituals.

## SETTING & FACILITIES

**Location** On Ka'anapali Beach. **Dining** The Coral Reef serves seafood specialties. Teppan Yaki Dan offers a noteworthy blend of European and Pacific cuisines (chefs prepare meals while you watch). **Amenities & Services** Swimming pool, room service, laundry facilities, valet parking ($13), self-parking ($5/day), fitness center, spa, children's program (summer). A $10/day resort fee is added to the room charge.

## ACCOMMODATIONS

**Rooms** 510. Includes 46 suites; 15 rooms for the disabled. Nonsmoking rooms available. **All Rooms** A/C, cable TV, in-room safe, mini-fridge, coffeemaker, iron and board, hair dryer. **Some Rooms** Microwave, second TV, parlor. **Comfort & Decor** Spacious and well maintained rooms have custom bedspreads, tropical furnishings, and large lana'i. Hawaiian artwork adorns the walls, and fine Hawaiian crafts are displayed throughout the public areas.

## PAYMENT, RESERVATIONS, & RESTRICTIONS

**Family Plan** Children age 17 and under stay free in room with parents if using existing bedding. **Deposit** 1-night deposit due 10 days after booking. Cancellation notice must be given 72 hours prior to scheduled arrival for refund. **Credit Cards** All major credit cards accepted. **Check-In/Out** 3 p.m./noon. Early check-in and late check out available on request.

## WESTIN MAUI                                              $$$$$

OVERALL ★★★★ | QUALITY ★★★★ | VALUE ★★½ | ZONE 9

2365 Ka'anapali Pkwy., Lahaina, HI 96761; (800) 937-8461 or (808) 667-2525; fax: (808) 661-5764; www.westin.com

A fantasy resort, the Westin has an elaborate water complex, sculpture and art displayed throughout, parrots and macaws stationed by the flagstone walkways, and a breezy casual atmosphere overall. The most notable physical feature here is the 87,000-square-foot aquatic playground. There are five pools, three joined together by a pair of water slides, and two divided by a swim-through grotto with twin waterfalls and a hidden Jacuzzi. One of the pools is designated for adults only and features a swim-up bar. The Westin Kids Club provides supervised fun and games for the *keiki*. Island-style entertainment is provided nightly. For night owls, a side benefit of staying in Ka'anapali is that it's just a five-minute drive away from Lahaina, where most of West Maui's afterdark action takes place.

## SETTING & FACILITIES

**Location** On Ka'anapali Beach. **Dining** Sen Ju features traditional Japanese delicacies. **Amenities & Services** Room service, laundry/valet service, parking, business center, health club, children's program.

## ACCOMMODATIONS

**Rooms** 741. Includes 28 suites; 14 rooms for the disabled. Nonsmoking rooms available. **All Rooms** A/C, cable TV, balcony, mini-bar, in-room safe, coffeemaker, iron and board, hair dryer. **Some Rooms** Sofa bed in living room, upgraded amenities. **Comfort & Decor** Spacious and clean rooms feature light colors and comfortable furnishings in a modern setting. The ambience is classy without being stuffy.

## PAYMENT, RESERVATIONS, & RESTRICTIONS

**Family Plan** Children age 17 and under stay free in room with parents if using existing bedding. Maximum of 4 people/room. **Deposit** 2-night deposit due within 15 days after booking. Cancellation notice must be given 72 hours prior to scheduled arrival for refund. **Credit Cards** All major credit cards accepted. **Check-In/Out** 3 p.m./noon. Early check-in and late check out if available.

# The Big Island of Hawai'i

## FOUR SEASONS RESORT HUALALAI                    $$$$$

OVERALL ★★★★★  |  QUALITY ★★★★★  |  VALUE ★★½  |  ZONE 11

P.O. Box 1269, Kailua-Kona, HI 96745; (888) 340-5662 or (808) 325-8000; fax: (800) 325-8200; www.fourseasons.com

Hawai'i's newest resort is less a hotel than an exclusive hideaway. Sitting on a dramatic landscape formed by eruptions from Hualalai volcano some 200 years ago, this AAA Five Diamond property features 36 low-rise, ocean-view bungalows strategically organized to ensure quiet and privacy. Hawaiian works of art—some dating back to the eighteenth century—are displayed throughout the resort. Located below the lobby is one of our favorite features at Hualalai: the Ka'upulehu Cultural Center, which presents Hawai'i's culture and history through artwork, exhibits, video and audio recordings, and hands-on educational programs. An additional special plus is the sports club/fitness center/spa facility, and yet another is the natural amphitheater formed by lava.

Enjoy swimming and snorkeling in the King's Pond, a large black lava pool inspired by the natural tidepools and brackish onshore lava ponds of this coast. You'll share it with some 3,500 colorful reef fish. The pond was sculpted from an ancient lava flow and is fed by natural artesian springs as well as water from the sea. It's one of several pools around which the bungalows are clustered. Ocean swimming here is limited by rough, shallow, rocky conditions.

## SETTING & FACILITIES

**Location** At Ka'upulehu on Kohala Coast, beach front. **Dining** Pahui'a serves international and local specialties from its spectacular setting on the beach **Amenities & Services** Valet and laundry service, self-serve washer and dryer, valet and self-parking, concierge service, Hawaiian Cultural Center, golf, tennis, 3 swimming pools, children's program.

## ACCOMMODATIONS

**Rooms** 243. Includes 31 suites; 14 rooms for the disabled. Most rooms are designated nonsmoking. **All Rooms** A/C, color TV, refrigerated private bar, lana'i, in-room safe, walk-in closets, fax line. **Some Rooms** Private, walled shower gardens afford the option of bathing indoors or out.. Bathroom windows look into the private garden. **Comfort & Decor** The suites are our favorite rooms of any luxury hotels, done up in beautiful woods, warm-colored slate, plantation shutters, and plenty of Indo-Pacific tropical chic. Large bathrooms have oversized tubs and separate showers.

## PAYMENT, RESERVATIONS, & RESTRICTIONS

**Family Plan** Children age 18 and under stay free in room with parents if using existing bedding. **Deposit** 1-night deposit due 7 days after booking. Cancellation notice must be given 14 days prior to scheduled arrival for refund Jan. 3–April 30, and 7 days prior to scheduled arrival May 1–Dec. 18. Greater deposit required effect during the Christmas holidays. **Credit Cards** All major credit cards accepted. **Check-In/Out** 3 p.m./noon. Early check-in and late check out available on request.

## HAPUNA BEACH PRINCE HOTEL                               $$$$$

OVERALL ★★★★½  |  QUALITY ★★★★  |  VALUE ★★  |  ZONE 11

62-100 Kauna'oa Dr., Kamuela, HI 96743; (800) 882-6060 or (808) 880-1111; fax: (808) 880-3142; www.hapunabeachprincehotel.com

Opened in 1994, the Hapuna Beach Prince Hotel is located next to its sister property, the Mauna Kea Beach Hotel. The layout of the property includes a large number of suites intermixed with guest rooms in buildings that ensure that every room has ocean views, a signature of Prince Hotels in Hawai'i. Built with a contemporary design, the hotel includes an open foyer and lobby that provide a stunning view of Hapuna Beach, regarded as one of the best beaches in Hawai'i. The fourth level of the hotel includes an indoor recreation area equipped with pool tables, table tennis, shuffleboard, foosball, board games, and a fully stocked bar (guests must be at least 21 years of age). There's a competition sized pool. Ocean activities include swimming, snorkeling, scuba diving, sailing, and whale-watching (in season).

## SETTING & FACILITIES

**Location** On the Big Island's Kohala Coast, overlooking Hapuna Beach. **Dining** Coast Grille specializes in fresh island seafood. Hakone serves traditional Japanese fare. The Ocean Terrace offers a wide menu of breakfast selections, including an extensive buffet. **Amenities & Services** Freshwater pool spa, Jacuzzi, welcome amenities, golf, water sports, beauty salon, game room, business services.

## ACCOMMODATIONS

**Rooms** 350. Includes 36 luxury suites; 2 floors designated for nonsmoking; 10 rooms for the disabled. One suite is a separate three-bedroom house. **All**

**Rooms** A/C, cable TV, lana'i, refrigerators, in-room safes **Some Rooms** Sitting rooms, upgraded amenities. **Comfort & Decor** Spacious and attractive, all rooms have ocean views, soft tropical colors, island-accented furnishings, and artwork.

## PAYMENT, RESERVATIONS, & RESTRICTIONS

**Family Plan** Children age 17 and under stay free in room with parents if using existing bedding. Maximum 2 adults and 2 children or 3 adults/room. **Deposit** 1-night deposit due 15 days after booking. Cancellation notice must be given 14 days prior to scheduled arrival for refund. **Credit Cards** All major credit cards accepted except Discover. **Check-In/Out** 3 p.m./noon. Early check-in and late check out available on request.

## HAWAI'I NANILOA RESORT                                        $$

OVERALL ★★★★  |  QUALITY ★★★½  |  VALUE ★★★  |  ZONE 12

93 Banyan Dr., Hilo, HI 96720; (800) 367-5360 or (808) 969-3333; fax: (808) 969-6622; hinon@aloha.net; www.naniloa.com

At first glance, this bayside hotel doesn't look like much. The exterior is rather drab and unattractive, although the bay is picturesque. The lobby, on the other hand, is airy and adorned in pleasant pastels. What we like best about the Naniloa is its attentive service and facilities, including the excellent fitness center and spa featuring exercise equipment, an ocean-front aerobics studio, whirlpool, sauna, and steam room (body massages are also available). The swimming pool is large and inviting. All in all, the Naniloa is a good-value hotel that rivals the neighboring Hilo Hawaiian Hotel as the premier Hilo resort. The hotel is also the head-quarters of the Merrie Monarch Festival, the world's most prestigious hula competition.

## SETTING & FACILITIES

**Location** Fronting Hilo Bay, no beach. **Dining** Continental fare is served at the Sandalwood Room, and Ting Hao Seafood Restaurant offers sumptuous Chinese cuisine. **Amenities & Services** Courtesy airport transfer service, laundry service, gift and sundry shop, ice machine, safety deposit box (at front desk).

## ACCOMMODATIONS

**Rooms** 325. Includes 20 suites; 3 floors with nonsmoking rooms; 1 floor for the disabled. **All Rooms** A/C, cable TV with pay movies. **Some Rooms** Kitchen. **Comfort & Decor** Rooms are small to medium, with attractive island decor and tasteful furnishings.

## PAYMENT, RESERVATIONS, & RESTRICTIONS

**Family Plan** Children age 17 and under stay free in room with parents if using existing bedding. **Deposit** 1-night deposit due within 10 days of confirmation. Cancellation notice must be given at least 72 hours prior to scheduled arrival for refund. **Credit Cards** All major credit cards accepted. **Check-In/Out** 3 p.m./noon. Early check-in and late check out available on request.

## HILO HAWAIIAN HOTEL $$

OVERALL ★★★½ | QUALITY ★★★½ | VALUE ★★½ | ZONE 12

71 Banyan Dr., Hilo, HI 96720; (800) 367-5004 or (808) 935-9361; fax: (808) 961-9642; www.castle-group.com

The Hilo Hawaiian doesn't qualify as a luxury resort, but it still rates as one of the best hotels in Hilo. Its sloping arc design blends well with its surroundings, including Hilo Bay. Built in 1974 and renovated in 1992, the hotel has attractive rooms, a friendly staff, and a popular seafood buffet (it's even a favorite among locals), but nothing stands out as extraordinary. This is a good choice for travelers who plan to spend most of their time exploring the island and want a comfortable, clean, and affordable place to stay.

### SETTING & FACILITIES

**Location** At Hilo Bay, no beach. **Dining** Queen's Court serves nightly seafood buffets. **Amenities & Services** Free parking, coin-operated laundry.

### ACCOMMODATIONS

**Rooms** 286. Includes 18 suites; 7 wheelchair-accessible rooms. Half the rooms are designated nonsmoking. **All Rooms** A/C, cable TV, refrigerator, hair dryers, and iron and board available on request. **Some Rooms** Lana'i, coffee, tea, miso soup. **Comfort & Decor** Spacious, mostly clean, and well maintained rooms have simple furnishings with a few island-inspired artworks but dim lighting.

### PAYMENT, RESERVATIONS, & RESTRICTIONS

**Family Plan** Children age 18 and under stay free in room with parents if using existing bedding. **Deposit** 1-night deposit or credit card guarantee within 10 days after booking. Cancellation notice must be given 72 hours prior to scheduled arrival for refund. **Credit Cards** All major credit cards accepted. **Check-In/Out** 3 p.m./noon. Early check-in and late check out available on request.

## HILTON WAIKOLOA VILLAGE $$$$$

OVERALL ★★★★½ | QUALITY ★★★★ | VALUE ★★ | ZONE 11

425 Waikoloa Beach Dr., Waikoloa, HI 96738; (800) 445-8667 or (808) 886-1234; fax: (808) 886-2900; waikoloa_rooms@hilton.com; www.hilton.com

Think of this 62-acre resort as an island-style Disneyland dedicated to vacation fun, complete with boat rides, lush tropical gardens, and encounters with some exotic but friendly creatures (ranging from parrots and mackaws to Atlantic bottlenose dolphins). The Hilton Waikoloa, the ultimate creation of Hawai'i's fantasy resort era of the late 1980s, consists of three separate towers surrounding a beautiful five-acre lagoon where the dolphins live and play. You can explore the hotel via canal boats or Swiss trams or by hoofing it on the mile-long museum walkway, which is adorned with a multimillion-dollar collection of Asian and Pacific replicated art. A daily lottery determines which lucky guests can get into the water and pet the dolphins and learn about these ocean mammals from a marine specialist. Another property that epitomizes the phrase "self-contained resort," the Hilton Waikoloa has something for everyone: restaurants, swimming and beachactivities at neighboring 'Anaeho'omalu Beach, shops, a health spa, children's programs, lu'au, entertainment, golf, and tennis. Families with children, in particular, will love this resort.

### SETTING & FACILITIES

**Location** In Waikoloa Beach Resort, oceanfront (no beach). **Dining** The Palm Terrace offers a wide range of international specialties. Donatoni's serves fine Italian cuisine. Imari features traditional Japanese fare. Kamuela Provision Company serves steak and seafood. **Amenities & Services** Room service, laundry service, valet parking ($8), business center, health spa, children's program, Dolphin Encounter program.

### ACCOMMODATIONS

**Rooms** 1,241. Includes 57 suites. Rooms for the disabled and nonsmoking rooms available. **All Rooms** A/C, cable TV, lana'i, honor bar, refrigerator, coffeemaker, in-room safe, hair dryer, iron and board. **Some Rooms** Second bedroom, upgraded amenities. **Comfort & Decor** Spacious rooms (standard rooms are 530 square feet) have bright atmosphere, lavish furnishings, and tasteful Hawaiian artwork.

### PAYMENT, RESERVATIONS, & RESTRICTIONS

**Family Plan** Children age 18 and under stay free in room with parents if using existing bedding. **Deposit** 1- or 2-night deposit due at least 10 days before arrival. Cancellation notice must be given 72 hours prior to scheduled arrival for refund. **Credit Cards** All major credit cards accepted. **Check-In/Out** 3 p.m./ noon. Early check-in and late check out available on request (no guarantees).

## KING KAMEHAMEHA'S KONA BEACH HOTEL          $$$

OVERALL ★★★½  |  QUALITY ★★★  |  VALUE ★★★½  |  ZONE 11

75-5660 Palani Rd., Kailua-Kona, HI 96740; (800) 367-6060 or (808) 329-2911; fax: (808) 923-2566; www.konabeachhotel.com

King Kamehameha's Kona Beach Hotel sits next to a historic grounds once home to royalty. In old Hawai'i, high-ranking ali'i used this site as a summer retreat. Kamehameha the Great himself made this his royal residence nearly two centuries ago. The focal point of this historic area is the Ahu'ena heiau, which dates back to the fifteenth century and was used for human sacrifices. One of the hotel's major pluses is its central location, within easy walking distance to restaurants, shops, and a small gold-sand beach. The hotel is also popular among kama'aina visiting from other islands.

## SETTING & FACILITIES

**Location** In the heart of Kailua-Kona, on the (only) beach. **Dining** The Kona Beach Restaurant serves breakfast and dinner buffets, plus Sunday champagne brunch. **Amenities & Services** Free parking, room service, laundry facilities, swimming pool, Jacuzzi, tennis.

## ACCOMMODATIONS

**Rooms** 457. Includes 12 suites; 10 rooms for the disabled. Nonsmoking rooms available. **All Rooms** A/C, cable TV, mini-fridge, in-room safe, coffeemaker, hair dryer, iron and board available on request. **Some Rooms** Refrigerator, pay movies. **Comfort & Decor** Medium-sized rooms with subdued colors, simple furnishings, and Hawaiian artworks.

## PAYMENT, RESERVATIONS, & RESTRICTIONS

**Family Plan** Children age 18 and under stay free in room with parents if using existing bedding. **Deposit** Credit card guarantee or 1-night deposit required. Cancellation notice must be given at least 72 hours prior to scheduled arrival for refund. **Credit Cards** All major credit cards accepted. **Check-In/Out** 3 p.m./ noon. Early check-in and late check out (up to 1 p.m.) available on request.

---

## KONA VILLAGE RESORT                                          $$$$$

OVERALL ★★★★½  |  QUALITY ★★★★  |  VALUE ★★  |  ZONE 11

P.O. Box 1299, Kailua-Kona, HI 96745; (800) 367-5290 or (808) 325-5555; fax: (808) 325-5124; kvr@aloha.net; www.konavillage.com

The ultimate retreat. Set between black lava fields and the blue Pacific, isolated, tranquil Kona Village offers the great tropical escape. No other place comes close, except maybe neighboring Four Seasons Hualalai, but there the ambiance is obviously upscale. Here, you'll pay handsomely too, for well appointed, but less fancy digs. This venerable resort, built in the mid-1960s when access was by boat or plane only, more closely echoes the old village on the same site where ancient fishermen once dwelt. Kona Village boasts a petroglyph field depicting symbols of life by the sea, including sailing and fishing, unique in the area. It has an ancient fishpond and ruins of houses among its clusters of guest quarters and enough specimen trees and Hawaiian medicinal plants to warrant a botanical tour. Lava fields on the mauka side keep the 21st century at a safe distance, but you can cross them in minutes via a gated road. This resort, casual and Hawaiian in spirit, has no airs. No one cares whether the guests are CEOs (many are), famous authors (some write novels there), movie producers, or just folks. Kona Village offers the kind of hang-loose peace and quiet that restores souls. Kids are cherished in this camp-like compound, except in September when it's adults only.

This collection of huts of different Pacific Island architectural styles strewn along the coast does without televisions, radios, phones, and air conditioning in the guest bungalows. (Phones are available by the office.) Each *hale,* or house, is a thatched-roof bungalow with king-sized beds, mini-fridge, lana'i, and other choice amenities. Some have a hot tub on the lana'i.

Upon arrival, you're greeted with a fresh flower lei and a glass of rum punch. Then you're set for an extraordinary holiday of total relaxation like you won't find anywhere else in the islands. Beach activities, snorkel sailing, spa, tennis, and a renowned Friday night lu'au are recreational options. Less is more here; you will know what we mean on the day you leave, reluctantly.

## SETTING & FACILITIES

**Location** In Ka'upulehu, 14 miles north of Kailua-Kona, fronting a beach cove. **Dining** Hale Moana serves a wide variety of international and American favorites for breakfast, al fresco lunch buffet, and dinner; the more formal Hale Samoa specializes in Pacific Rim cuisine. **Amenities & Services** Fitness center, beach facilities, tennis, complimentary programs for children ages 6–12, transportation to and from airport.

## ACCOMMODATIONS

**Rooms** 125 hale. 8 rooms for the disabled. Smoking permitted in all hale. **All Rooms** Ceiling fan, lana'i, mini-fridge, hair dryer, in-room safe, coffeemaker. No A/C, TV, or phone. **Some Rooms** Private whirlpool spa. **Comfort & Decor** Spacious, with high ceilings; furnishings are comfortable and simple, with a tropical motif in rich earth tones and tasteful island-themed art.

## PAYMENT, RESERVATIONS, & RESTRICTIONS

**Family Plan** Children age 3 and under stay free. However, note that during months of May and September, children pay the adult rates. **Deposit** 2-night deposit due within 14 days of booking. Cancellation notice must be given 14 days prior to scheduled arrival for refund (60 days for the Easter holiday, 90 days for the Christmas holiday). **Credit Cards** All major credit cards accepted except Discover. **Check-In/Out** 3 p.m./noon. Hospitality room available for early arrivals and late departures.

## MAUNA KEA BEACH HOTEL                        $$$$$

OVERALL ★★★★½ | QUALITY ★★★★ | VALUE ★★ | ZONE 11

62-100 Mauna Kea Beach Dr., Kamuela, HI 96743; (800) 882-6060 or (808) 882-7222; fax: (808) 882-5700; mkrres@maunakeabeachhotel.com; www.maunakeabeachhotel.com

The oldest Big Island resort—it opened in 1965—remains a favorite. The Mauna Kea keeps its loyal, graying clientele and adds their junior replacements with babes in arms. Three generations of guests have checked into this grand old lady of the Kohala Coast. The open-air architectural design, art-stuffed halls, perfect gold-sand crescent beach, and old-fashioned Hawaiian hospitality all contribute to the enduring success of this luxury inn. Longtime patrons were concerned when the hotel was renovated, but it reopened with all its old charm intact. Golfers have their choice of the Mauna Kea Golf Course or the Hapuna Golf Course; tennis players can serve and volley at the oceanside Tennis Park, which features 13 Plexi-pave courts. Mauna Kea Stables offers Parker Ranch trail rides. After dinner, it's customary to wander down to the floodlit platform by the water where manta rays come to have their evening meal, smaller fish attracted to the lights.

### SETTING & FACILITIES

**Location** On the Big Island's Kohala Coast, fronting Kauna 'Oa Beach, down a short incline from most rooms. **Dining** The Batik features classical Provence-inspired cuisine. The Pavilion offers Italian and Pacific Rim cuisine. The Terrace/Copper Bar serves steaks and fresh seafood. **Amenities & Services** Swimming pool, Jacuzzi, fitness center, maid service, golf, tennis, horseback riding, meeting facilities, beauty salon, children's program.

### ACCOMMODATIONS

**Rooms** 310. Includes 10 suites; 10 rooms for the disabled. No nonsmoking rooms designated. **All Rooms** A/C, private lana'i, clock radio, coffeemaker, TV (upon request). **Some Rooms** 2 full baths, sitting room, 2 TVs. **Comfort & Decor** Very spacious. Classy tropical adornments include rattan furnishings. Original watercolors are among the island-theme artworks.

### PAYMENT, RESERVATIONS, & RESTRICTIONS

**Family Plan** Children age 17 and under stay free in room with parents if using existing bedding. **Deposit** 1-night deposit due within 15 days after booking. Cancellation notice must be given 14 days prior to scheduled arrival for refund. **Credit Cards** All major credit cards accepted except Discover. **Check-In/Out** 3 p.m./noon. Early check-in and late check out available on request (no guarantees).

## MAUNA LANI BAY HOTEL & BUNGALOWS                    $$$$$

OVERALL ★★★★½ | QUALITY ★★★★½ | VALUE ★★½ | ZONE 11

68-1400 Mauna Lani Dr., Kohala Coast, HI 96743; (800) 367-2323 or (808) 885-6622; fax: (808) 885-1484; reservations@maunalani.com; www.maunalani.com

A perennial AAA Five Diamond Award winner, the Mauna Lani is one of our favorite resorts—especially the bungalows.

Service is friendly, island-style hospitality gracious, and the site ideal for a beach resort. And if you're fortunate, you can a stay at one of the resort's five world-class bungalows, only $4,900 a night. Each 4,000-square-foot bungalow has two bedrooms, a private swimming pool, and 24-hour butler service.

The hotel's main structure directly faces the ocean and has an atrium-style design with waterfalls, ponds, trees, and flora. Golf, tennis, and water sports are among the outdoor diversions available here, and kids ages 5–12 can participate in Camp Mauna Lani, which offers lei making, hula dancing, history tours, and other activities. The resort hosts the annual Cuisines of the Sun, a summer food festival spotlighting cuisines from around the world. Don't miss the Puako petroglyph field beside the resort or the self-guided history tour of the ancient dwelling caves and fish pond by the hotel. Mauna Lani Resort's coastal path makes a nice morning or late afternoon walk.

## SETTING & FACILITIES

**Location** On Big Island's Kohala Coast, fronting beach. **Dining** The Canoe House serves Pacific Rim cuisine. The poolside Ocean Grill features salads, gourmet pizza, fresh seafood. **Amenities & Services** 24-hour room service, twice-daily maid service, laundry and dry cleaning service, concierge service, meeting and banquet facilities, secretarial assistance, golf, tennis, spa, children's program.

## ACCOMMODATIONS

**Rooms** 350. Includes 5 exclusive bungalows, 10 suites, 28 villas; 12 rooms for the disabled. Nonsmoking rooms available. **All Rooms** A/C, cable TV, VCR, private lana'i, honor bar, in-room safe, refrigerator, clock radio, hair dryer, ceiling fan, flash-light, umbrella, robes, slippers. **Some Rooms** Bungalows have private swimming pool, 24-hour butler service, whirlpool spa. **Comfort & Decor** Very spacious and well kept, rooms reflect a tropical theme, with tasteful island decor and furnishings. Cool tones of white and beige, large private lana'i (more than 90% of the rooms have ocean views), atrium gardens, and pools lend a peaceful, tropical atmosphere.

## PAYMENT, RESERVATIONS, & RESTRICTIONS

**Family Plan** Children age 12 and under stay free in room with parents if using existing bedding. Maximum of 2 adults and 2 children or 3 adults/room. **Deposit** 2-night deposit required to guarantee reservation. Cancellation notice must be given at least 72 hours prior to scheduled arrival for refund (14 days for villas). **Credit Cards** All major credit cards accepted. **Check-In/Out** 3 p.m./noon. Early check-in and late check out available on request.

## 'OHANA KEAUHOU BEACH RESORT                    $$$

OVERALL ★★★★  |  QUALITY ★★★½  |  VALUE ★★½  |  ZONE 11

78-6740 Ali'i Dr., Kailua-Kona, HI 96740; (800) 922-7866 or (808) 322-3441; fax: (808) 322-3117; www.ohanahotels.com

This ten-acre oceanfront property reopened in March 1999 after an extensive $15 million renovation to its guest rooms and public areas. It remains a favorite for kama'aina visiting from other islands. The resort also features several prominent historic Hawaiian sites, including heiau and a replica of King Kalakaua's vacation hale. Children are welcome to explore several on-site tidal pools, and adults can enjoy snorkeling, scuba diving, or tennis on six courts.

## SETTING & FACILITIES

**Location** Oceanfront near Kahalu'u Bay in Kailua-Kona. **Dining** Kama'aina Terrace serves local favorites, pork, chicken and fish. **Amenities & Services** Daily maid service, fitness center, activities and travel desks, parking, swimming pool, sundry shop.

## ACCOMMODATIONS

**Rooms** 311. Includes 6 suites; 4 floors with nonsmoking rooms; 14 rooms for the disabled. **All Rooms** A/C, cable TV, private lana'i, clock radio, crib, hair dryer, iron and board, refrigerator available on request. **Some Rooms** Ceiling fans, bathtub. **Comfort & Decor** Spacious, with earthy tones, Hawaiian-style decor, and attractive wicker furnishings.

## PAYMENT, RESERVATIONS, & RESTRICTIONS

**Family Plan** Children age 18 and under stay free in room with parents if using existing bedding. **Deposit** 1-night deposit due 10 days after booking. Cancellation notice must be given at least 72 hours prior to scheduled arrival for refund. **Credit Cards** All major credit cards accepted. **Check-In/Out** 3 p.m./noon. Early check-in and late check out based on availability.

## THE ORCHID AT MAUNA LANI                                    $$$$$

OVERALL ★★★★½ | QUALITY ★★★★ | VALUE ★★ | ZONE 11

One N. Kaniku Dr., Kohala Coast, HI 96743; (800) 782-9488 or (808) 885-2000; fax: (808) 885-8886; www.orchid-maunalani.com

When Ritz-Carlton originally opened this property, they built a beautiful European hotel but forgot the Hawaiian touches. When people come to Hawai'i they want something that looks like Hawai'i. Now the Orchid delivers a Hawaiian "sense of place" and a first-class experience. Exquisite Hawaiian quilts and original artworks adorn the walls. Hawai'i's native koa wood is used prominently, from elevator walls to stairway banisters. Other physical features at this U-shaped hotel (divided into two six-story wings) include a 10,000-square-foot swimming pool, a gold-sand beach, and jogging and walking trail. Children ages 5–12 can make new friends at the Keiki Aloha Program, while adults relax at the Centre for Well-Being. The Orchid shares with Mauna Lani Resort access to two famous golf courses, a competition tennis complex, and the Puako petroglyph field and other historic features.

## SETTING & FACILITIES

**Location** On the Kohala Coast, a short walk to beach. **Dining** The Grill offers fresh seafood specialties, The Orchid Court serves California cuisine and American favorites. Brown's Beach House serves island fare with a "California twist." **Amenities & Services** Room service, twice-daily maid service, spa and fitness center, business facilities, concierge desk, swimming pool, golf, tennis, child care, daily newspaper. A daily resort fee of $12 is added to room charge.

## ACCOMMODATIONS

**Rooms** 539. Including 100 suites; 5 rooms and 1 suite for the disabled. Nonsmoking rooms available on designated floors. **All Rooms** A/C, cable TV, lana'i, 3 phones, honor bar, robes. **Some Rooms** Living room, extra bath, pullout sofa. **Comfort & Decor** Spacious and clean rooms have large Italian marble bathrooms, Hawaiian-accented decor with neutral tones and hand-crafted quilts, and private lana'i.

## PAYMENT, RESERVATIONS, & RESTRICTIONS

**Family Plan** Children age 18 and under stay free in room with parents if using existing bedding. **Deposit** Credit card guarantee only. Cancellation notice must be given 7 days prior to scheduled arrival for refund. **Credit Cards** All major credit cards accepted. **Check-In/Out** 3 p.m./noon. Early check-in and late check out (up to 2 p.m.) available on request.

## OUTRIGGER WAIKOLOA BEACH HOTEL                           $$$$

OVERALL ★★★★ | QUALITY ★★★½ | VALUE ★★★ | ZONE 11

69-275 Waikoloa Beach Dr., Waikoloa, HI 96738; (800) 688-7444 or (808) 886-6789; fax: (808) 886-7852; www.outrigger.com

Always the best bargain in a neighborhood of upscale beach hotels, the Outrigger Waikoloa Beach Hotel, is, after a $25 million renovation, now one of the best looking, too. It always had the best location, overlooking 'Anaeho'omalu Bay's fishponds and a picturesque gold-sand crescent beach framed by palm trees.

The reconstructed 15-acre property has a new open-air lobby, porte-cochere, restaurant, lounge, and meeting rooms. The lobby overlooks the resort's pool and gardens, and cultural sites, such as the extensive petroglyph field near the hotel front and large ancient Hawaiian fish pond, add a sense of relevance and history. The King's Shops, one of the better shopping spots in the area, is just across the road, and golfers can play one (or all) of three nearby courses in Waikoloa. In all, this is a good value hotel, and we expect even bigger and better things now that it's under Outrigger ownership.

## SETTING & FACILITIES

**Location** 'Anaeho'omalu Bay, on the Big Island's Kohala Coast. A short walk to the beach. **Dining** Hawai'i Calls serves breakfast, lunch, and dinner, and island favorites. **Amenities & Services** Room service, laundry service, swimming pool, business center, spa and fitness center, tennis, golf, children's program.

## ACCOMMODATIONS

**Rooms** 545. Includes 21 suites; 11 rooms for the disabled. Nonsmoking rooms available. **All Rooms** A/C, cable TV with pay movies, lana'i, in-room safe, coffeemaker, hair dryer, refrigerator, iron and board, robes. **Some Rooms** Oversized rooms, concierge service. **Comfort & Decor** Well-appointed, spacious, and clean. Rattan furnishings and island artwork add to tropical flavor.

**PAYMENT, RESERVATIONS, & RESTRICTIONS**

**Family Plan** Children age 17 and under stay free in room with parents if using existing bedding. **Deposit** 2-night deposit required. Cancellation notice must be given at least 72 hours prior to scheduled arrival for refund. **Credit Cards** All major credit cards accepted. **Check-In/Out** 3 p.m./noon. Early check-in and late check out available on request.

## VOLCANO HOUSE                                                                  $$

OVERALL ★★★½ | QUALITY ★★★ | VALUE ★★ | ZONE 12

P.O. Box 53, Hawai'i Volcanoes National Park, HI 96718; (808) 967-7321; fax: (808) 967-8429; www.funjet.com/koa/volc^^^/volc^^^.htm

On the edge of a volcano, inside Hawai'i Volcanoes National Park, this funky old lodge is a good place to stay if you plan to spend time at the park. The lobby features a warm fireplace (sometimes visited by Madame Pele herself) for those chilly nights, and the walls are covered with nostalgic photographs and paintings of Hawaiian royalty. The hotel's lone restaurant fills quickly with a bus load of tourists during lunch hour.

**SETTING & FACILITIES**

**Location** Inside Hawai'i Volcanoes National Park. **Dining** The Ka Ohelo Dining Room specializes in prime rib, and also features breakfast and lunch buffets. **Amenities & Services** Parking, snack shop.

**ACCOMMODATIONS**

**Rooms** 42. Includes 1 wheelchair-accessible room. All rooms permit smoking. **All Rooms** Portable heater, telephone. No TV. **Comfort & Decor** Spacious, with koa furnishings, Hawaiian comforters, and tasteful decor.

**PAYMENT, RESERVATIONS, & RESTRICTIONS**

**Family Plan** Children age 12 and under stay free in room with parents if using existing bedding. **Deposit** 1-night deposit due within 15 days of booking. Cancellation notice must be given at least 72 hours prior to scheduled arrival for refund. **Credit Cards** All major credit cards accepted. **Check-In/Out** 3 p.m./noon. Early check-in and late check out available on request.

### Kaua'i

## HANALEI BAY RESORT & SUITES                                                $$$$

OVERALL ★★★★ | QUALITY ★★★★ | VALUE ★★½ | ZONE 13

5380 Honoiki Rd., Princeville, HI 96722; (800) 827-4427 or (808) 826-6522; fax: (808) 826-6680; www.hanaleibaykauai.com

This 22-acre resort, with some hotel rooms but mostly vacation condo units ranging up to three bedrooms in size, has ocean views and a gold-sand beach down a steep cliff. Carved into a hillside and featuring lush tropical landscaping, the resort offers privacy and solitude, ideal for honeymooners. There are eight tennis courts on the premises, and a pair of world-class golf courses nearby.

### SETTING & FACILITIES

**Location** In the Princeville Resort area on North Shore. **Dining** The Bali Hai Restaurant serves Pacific Rim cuisine amid breathtaking views of Hanalei Bay below. **Amenities & Services** Free parking, coin-operated laundry facilities, dry cleaning service, 2 swimming pools, Jacuzzi, 8 tennis courts, children's programs (seasonally), babysitting.

### ACCOMMODATIONS

**Rooms** 250. Includes 50 suites; 2 rooms for disabled. Smoking permitted on lana'i. **All Rooms** A/C, cable TV, lana'i, refrigerator, in-room safe, coffeemaker. **Some Rooms** Full kitchens, washer and dryer, separate bedroom and bathroom. **Comfort & Decor** Spacious and tastefully appointed with island-theme art and furnishings and cool, tropical colors.

### PAYMENT, RESERVATIONS, & RESTRICTIONS

**Deposit** 1-night deposit or credit card guarantee due within 10 days after booking. Cancellation notice must be given at least 72 hours prior to scheduled arrival for refund. **Credit Cards** All major credit cards accepted. **Check-In/Out** 3 p.m./noon. No early check-ins granted. Hospitality room available.

## HYATT REGENCY KAUA'I RESORT & SPA                     $$$$$

OVERALL ★★★★½  |  QUALITY ★★★★½  |  VALUE ★★½  |  ZONE 13

1571 Po'ipu Rd., Koloa, HI 96756; (800) 554-9288 or (808) 742-1234; fax: (808) 742-1557; www.hyatt.com

Kaua'i's best beach resort, the Hyatt Regency Kaua'i is an architectural treat, recalling the 1920s nostalgia of Hawai'i's golden age. The open-air lobby is one of the most beautiful of a galaxy of luxurious ocean-view, gardened, waterfalled, opulent Hawaiian hotel offerings. View settings are dressed with art deco finishes, brilliant tropical flowers, koa wood furnishings, and handsome Italian marble. In terms of amenities and services, the Hyatt, last of the fantasy-oriented hotel boom, pulls out all the stops. One of the splashier centerpieces is a huge playground of saltwater lagoons and freshwater pools, complete with water slides. Among the highlights are a creative program of cultural and ecotourism activities, a children's program, a luxurious health spa, great dining, and nightly entertainment. Of course, it doesn't hurt that Po'ipu is a marvelous resort destination with a good-looking gold sand beach, but stick to the pools for safe swimming.

### SETTING & FACILITIES

**Location** Fronting Keoneloa Bay in Po'ipu, a short walk to beach. **Dining** Tidepools features Pacific Rim specialties; Dondero's serves northern Italian cuisine.

**Amenities & Services** Room service, parking, laundry service, business center, spa, beauty salon, children's program.

## ACCOMMODATIONS

**Rooms** 602. Includes 37 suites; 26 rooms for the disabled. Nonsmoking rooms available. **All Rooms** A/C, cable TV, lana'i, coffeemaker, iron and board, hair dryer. **Some Rooms** Kitchen, daily Continental breakfast and snacks. **Comfort & Decor** Very spacious (standard rooms are 600 square feet) and well maintained rooms have comfortable ambience with handsome wood furnishings and Hawaiian-themed art.

## PAYMENT, RESERVATIONS, & RESTRICTIONS

**Family Plan** Children age 18 and under stay free in room with parents if using existing bedding. **Deposit** 2-night deposit due within 14 days after booking. Cancellation notice must be given at least 72 hours prior to scheduled arrival for refund. **Credit Cards** All major credit cards accepted. **Check-In/Out** 3 p.m./ noon. Early check-in and late check out available on request.

## KAUA'I MARRIOTT RESORT & BEACH CLUB          $$$$$

OVERALL ★★★★ | QUALITY ★★★★ | VALUE ★★ | ZONE 13

Kalapaki Beach, Lihu'e, HI 96766; (800) 220-2925 or (808) 245-5050; fax: (808) 245-2993; www.marriotthotels.com/LIHHI

This well-sited resort (a mile from the airport on a sheltered beach by the harbor) has toned down its glitzy former self—it was one of the last fantasy resorts—but remains a world-class destination offering excellent service. The hotel, half of it now a time share operation, offers a seven-acre swimming pool for a focal point, lavish furnishings and art work, and a major ballroom and conference facility. Tranquil lagoons and inland waterways are traversed via mahogany launches, and horse-drawn carriages provide a leisurely exploration of the resort grounds. Kalapaki Beach is an excellent locale for swimming and promenading, making the Kaua'i Marriott a good choice for families. Golfers are advised to play at least a round at one of the resort's two championship Jack Nicklaus courses.

## SETTING & FACILITIES

**Location** On Kalapaki Beach. **Dining** Duke's Canoe Club serves steak, fish, and seafood specialties. The poolside Kukui's Restaurant & Bar features Pacific Rim cuisine. **Amenities & Services** Room service, coin-operated laundry facilities, free parking, maid service, valet service, business center, golf, tennis, free airport transportation, fitness spa.

## ACCOMMODATIONS

**Rooms** 356. Includes 11 suites; 10 rooms for the disabled. Nonsmoking rooms available. **All Rooms** A/C, cable TV, mini-bar, in-room safe, coffeemaker, hair dryer, iron and board. **Some Rooms** Kitchenette, microwave. **Comfort & Decor** Rooms are small to medium and pleasant, with subtle tropical decor and artwork.

**PAYMENT, RESERVATIONS, & RESTRICTIONS**

**Family Plan** Children age 17 and under stay free in room with parents if using existing bedding. **Deposit** 1-night deposit due within 10 days of booking. Cancellation notice must be given at least 72 hours prior to scheduled arrival for refund. **Credit Cards** All major credit cards accepted. **Check-In/Out** 4 p.m./noon. Early check-in (from 2 p.m.) and late check out (until 2 p.m.) available on request.

## PRINCEVILLE RESORT                                           $$$$$

OVERALL ★★★★½  |  QUALITY ★★★★  |  VALUE ★★  |  ZONE 13

5520 Ka Haku Rd., Princeville, HI 96722; (800) 826-4400 or (808) 826-9644; fax: (808) 826-1166; www.princeville.com

With the best view in the islands, Princeville is a Versailles by the sea, with a lobby full of black marble, glittering chandeliers, and Greek statues. You get the idea that it was planned for someplace other than red dirt Kaua'i, but the hotel overcomes its ostentation by setting a high standard of excellence, sufficient to win AAA's Five Diamond Award. Every effort is made to bring Hawaiian culture into the scene.

Everything's here: shopping, dining, a swimming pool, nightly Hawaiian entertainment, fine dining, a small gold-sand beach, and that incredible view of Hanalei Bay. Come here to be pampered in the world-class spa and play the Prince Course, considered the best golf experience in the islands.

**SETTING & FACILITIES**

**Location** At Princeville Resort on North Shore, rooms stepped down a sea cliff; a short walk to beach, with elevators handling most of the grade. **Dining** La Cascata serves Italian cuisine. Cafe Hanalei serves three meals a day with a to-die-for view of Hanalei Bay. **Amenities & Services** 24-hour room service, laundry service, concierge desk, valet service, health and fitness center, swimming pool, business center.

**ACCOMMODATIONS**

**Rooms** 252. Includes 51 suites; 7 rooms for the disabled. 7 of the resort's 11 floors are designated for nonsmoking rooms. **All Rooms** A/C, cable TV, honor bar, safe, oversized bathroom, hair dryer, iron and board, robes, most with no lana'i but with large windows that drink in the view. **Some Rooms** Lana'i, second TV, fax machine. **Comfort & Decor** Very spacious, with custom-designed furnishings and original artwork. Shower window provides wonderful scenic views of the ocean and surfers below (for you, not them; the liquid crystal glass goes opaque at the flip of a switch).

**PAYMENT, RESERVATIONS, & RESTRICTIONS**

**Family Plan** Children age 17 and under stay free in room with parents if using existing bedding. Cots, $60. **Deposit** 1-night deposit required. Cancellation notice must be given at least 72 hours prior to scheduled arrival for refund. **Credit Cards** All major credit cards accepted. **Check-In/Out** 3 p.m./noon. Early check-in and late check out available on request.

## RADISSON KAUA'I BEACH RESORT                    $$$

OVERALL ★★★★ | QUALITY ★★★½ | VALUE ★★ | ZONE 13

4331 Kaua'i Beach Dr., Lihu'e, HI 96766;  (808) 245-1955; fax: (808) 246-9085;
www.radisson.com

Just a few minutes away from Lihu'e Airport, this 25-acre former Outrigger property is now Radisson Kaua'i Beach Resort, providing everything you want in a great hotel with one notable exception: a great beach. Ocean conditions are considered unsafe here. There is a great swimming pool. The open-air design promotes a relaxing and refreshing atmosphere, and its central location makes the property a good starting point for adventure. The hotel offers four tennis courts; two are lighted for night play. Golfers tee off at adjacent Wailua Golf Course, Hawai'i's best municipal course.

### SETTING & FACILITIES
**Location** In Lihu'e, just minutes from the Lihu'e Airport. **Dining** The Naupaka Terrace steak house serves breakfast, lunch, and dinner, featuring American favorites. **Amenities & Services** Room service, free parking, business center, meeting facilities.

### ACCOMMODATIONS
**Rooms** 341. Includes 3 suites; 12 rooms for the disabled. One-third of the rooms are designated nonsmoking. **All Rooms** A/C, cable TV, lana'i, voice mail, mini-fridge, in-room safe, coffeemaker. **Some Rooms** Separate parlor, upgraded amenities. **Comfort & Decor** Small but attractive (recently renovated), with rattan furnishings, quilted bedspreads, and island artworks.

### PAYMENT, RESERVATIONS, & RESTRICTIONS
**Family Plan** Children age 17 and under stay free in room with parents if using existing bedding. **Deposit** 1-night deposit or credit card guarantee due within 10 days after booking. Cancellation notice must be given at least 72 hours prior to scheduled arrival for refund. **Credit Cards** All major credit cards accepted. **Check-In/Out** 3 p.m./noon.

## SHERATON KAUA'I RESORT                    $$$$$

OVERALL ★★★★ | QUALITY ★★★★ | VALUE ★★ | ZONE 13

2440 Ho'onani Rd., Koloa, HI 96756; (800) 782-9488 or (808) 742-1661; fax:
(808) 742-9777; www.sheraton-kauai.com

A $45 million renovation project created a Sheraton Kaua'i that blends with its beachfront surroundings. Half of the resort embraces Po'ipu Beach, and the other half seems to explode in a garden of ginger, anthurium, heliconia, and bamboo. No building is taller than a coconut tree, which adds to the sense of seclusion celebrated at this 20-acre resort.

The 413 rooms are housed in a trio of four-story buildings, each identified by major views (ocean, beach, and garden). All amenities are here, including a children's program, swimming pools, a fitness center, and beach activities.

## SETTING & FACILITIES

**Location** On Po'ipu Beach. **Dining** Shells Steak & Seafood serves a variety of international cuisine for breakfast, lunch, and dinner. Naniwa is a fine-dining Japanese restaurant. **Amenities & Services** Room service (breakfast and dinner only), parking, valet parking ($5), fitness center, laundry facilities, tennis, business facilities, children's program. An $11/day resort fee is added to the room charge.

## ACCOMMODATIONS

**Rooms** 413. Includes 14 suites; 12 rooms for the disabled. Smoking is permitted on lana'i only. **All Rooms** A/C, cable TV, radio, video games, refrigerator, in-room safe, hair dryer, iron and board, dataport, robes. **Some Rooms** Larger space, fresh flowers. **Comfort & Decor** Spacious and bright, rooms have warm earth tones and handsome wood furnishings.

## PAYMENT, RESERVATIONS, & RESTRICTIONS

**Family Plan** Children age 18 and under stay free in room with parents if using existing bedding. Children age 12 and under eat free in dining rooms when accompanied by an adult. **Deposit** 1-night deposit due within 10 days of booking. Cancellation notice must be given at least 72 hours prior to scheduled arrival for refund. **Credit Cards** All major credit cards accepted. **Check-In/Out** 3 p.m./noon. Early check-in and late check out available on request. Hospitality room available.

## Moloka'i

### SHERATON MOLOKA'I LODGE AND BEACH VILLAGE   $$$$$

OVERALL ★★★★½ | QUALITY ★★★★ | VALUE ★★★ | ZONE 14

Sheraton Moloka'i Lodge Reservations, P.O. Box 259, Maunaloa, HI 96770; (808) 660-2722; fax (808) 660-2724

Moloka'i's only upscale lodge sits on a 53,000-acre working cattle ranch with a long-distance view of the Pacific. The 22-room inn is decorated on a paniolo heritage theme with low-key, friendly service that isn't particularly wikiwiki. This is, after all, Moloka'i, and where else would the wait staff bring your dinners and then dance hula among the tables?

You can go to the beach, but it's a long, bumpy ride; you might prefer to splash in the infinity pool and hot tub.

Activities include horseback trail riding, mountain biking, kayaking, beachcombing, dude rodeo, archery, beach adventures, children's programs, clay shooting, cultural hikes, ocean expeditions (shoreline casting, throw netting, guided snorkeling/spearfishing), paniolo round-up, and spa treatments.

## SETTING & FACILITIES

**Location** Rare old Hawai'i ambience in a handsome new lodge, overlooking horse pastures and the blue Pacific. Located at the entrance to the historic (and rebuilt) plantation town of Maunaloa, it features wrap-around verandas for the panoramic views. **Dining** Breakfast and dinner are served in the Maunaloa Dining Room. Lunch, cocktails, and lighter fare are served in the Paniolo Lounge. **Amenities & Services** Great room with fireplace, meeting room, heated swimming pool, day spa and fitness center, in-room Internet access, complimentary local and toll-free calls, room service, activities desk, on-ranch transportation. A $10/day resort fee is added to room charge. Activity rates range from $25 to $125.

## ACCOMMODATIONS

**Rooms** 22. **All Rooms** Private lana'i, television with in-room cable, refrigerator, in-room safe, high-speed dataports. **Comfort & Decor** Each room, with a big ocean-facing view and outdoor lana'i, is furnished differently in tasteful rustic ranch style. Claw-foot tubs, *hikie'e* (large Hawaiian bedlike couch), and other spots offer space to curl up and read.

## PAYMENT, RESERVATIONS, & RESTRICTIONS

**Family Plan** Children 12 and under stay free with a paying adult. **Deposit** 1 night's deposit, refundable on cancellation within 72 hours of scheduled arrival. **Credit Cards** All major credit cards accepted. **Check-In/Out** 3 p.m./11 a.m.

# Lana'i

## HOTEL LANA'I                                                            $

OVERALL ★★★½ | QUALITY ★★★ | VALUE ★★★ | ZONE 15

P.O. Box 630520, Lana'i City, HI 96763; (800) 795-7211 or (808) 565-7211; fax: (808) 565-7377; hotelLanai@aloha.net; www.hotellanai.com

Opened in 1923 for visiting Dole Pineapple execs, the 11-room upcountry lodge known as Hotel Lana'i has always attracted a loyal following, even more so since Henry Clay Richardson opened his creole-inspired bistro in 1996. If you can't afford to stay at the Lodge at Ko'ele or Manele Bay Hotel, this is your alternative. Rooms are appealing and comfortable, service is friendly, and you'll probably meet some interesting local characters at pau hana time.

## SETTING & FACILITIES

**Location** In village of Lana'i City; beach is a 20-minute shuttle ride away. **Dining** Henry Clay's Rotisserie serves a hearty selection of spit-roasted meats, seafood, pasta, gourmet pizzas, and more. **Amenities & Services** Free parking. No room service or laundry service.

## ACCOMMODATIONS

**Rooms** 11. All are nonsmoking. **All Rooms** Ceiling fans. **Some Rooms** TV, bathtub. **Comfort & Decor** Medium-sized rooms with pine floors, ceiling fans, custom quilts, and original photographs depicting the island's plantation days.

## PAYMENT, RESERVATIONS, & RESTRICTIONS

**Family Plan** Children age 8 and under stay free in room with parents if using existing bedding. **Deposit** Pay deposit of half of total stay in advance on booking. Cancellation notice must be given 14 days prior to scheduled arrival for refund. Cancellations are charged a $10 processing fee. **Credit Cards** Visa, MC, AmEx. **Check-In/Out** 1 p.m./11 a.m. Early check-in and late check out available on request.

## THE LODGE AT KO'ELE                                          $$$$$

OVERALL ★★★★½  |  QUALITY ★★★★  |  VALUE ★★½  |  ZONE 15

P.O. Box 630310, Lana'i City, HI 96763; (800) 321-4666 or (808) 565-7300; fax: (808) 565-3868; reservations@Lanai-resorts.com; www.Lanai-resorts.com

Nestled on the island's central highlands, the Lodge at Ko'ele is reminiscent of an English hill station, complete with manicured lawns, cozy fireplaces, and afternoon tea. Paintings, sculptures, and artifacts adorn the resort's interiors. Paths meander through flower gardens, past an English conservatory, to an inviting swimming pool. The atmosphere is calm and relaxed, providing a welcome escape, but there is plenty to do: work out at the new fitness center; explore the rugged countryside astride a horse or a mountain bike, or on foot, or by four-wheeler; play tennis; or enjoy a round at one of Lana'i's two award-winning championship courses. Not much nightlife on this quiet island, but the lodge offers a weekly Visiting Artist Program, where guests meet and mingle with noted authors, chefs, and entertainers.

## SETTING & FACILITIES

**Location** Upcountry, on the island's central highlands; beach is a 25-minute shuttle ride away. **Dining** The award-winning Formal Dining Room showcases Pacific Rim cuisine with local ingredients. **Amenities & Services** Room service, concierge, laundry service, fitness center, swimming pool, golf, valet parking, children's programs, free shuttle service.

## ACCOMMODATIONS

**Rooms** 102. Includes 14 suites; 2 rooms for the disabled. The lodge is a nonsmoking facility. **All Rooms** Ceiling fans, cable TV, VCR, private lana'i, mini-bar, in-room safe, robes, slippers. **Some Rooms** Fireplaces, larger space, upgraded amenities, butler service. **Comfort & Decor** Very spacious and comfy with country-chic, chintz interiors a la Laura Ashley, hand-carved poster beds, quiet ceiling fans, and oil paintings by local artists.

**PAYMENT, RESERVATIONS, & RESTRICTIONS**

**Family Plan** Children age 14 and under stay free in room with parents if using existing bedding. Maximum of 4 guests/room (2 adults and 2 children). Extra person, $75. **Deposit** 2-night deposit due within 14 days of booking. Cancellation notice must be given 14 days prior to scheduled arrival for refund. **Credit Cards** All major credit cards accepted except Discover. **Check-In/Out** 3 p.m./noon. Hospitality rooms available.

## THE MANELE BAY HOTEL                    $$$$$

OVERALL ★★★★½ | QUALITY ★★★★ | VALUE ★★½ | ZONE 15

P.O. Box 310, Lana'i City, HI 96763; (800) 321-4666 or (808) 565-7700; fax: (808) 565-2483; reservations@lanai-resorts.com; www.lanai-resorts.com

Perched atop windswept sea cliffs, the Manele overlooks Lana'i's magnificent coastline and Hulopo'e Bay, a favorite playground of spinner dolphins. A blend of Mediterranean and Hawaiian designs, the Manele Bay Hotel is full of exotic artifacts and grand murals, some hand-painted by local residents. Lush tropical gardens add color to the resort's otherwise arid landscape, but still fall short of the spectacular ocean views. It's just a short stroll downhill to Hulopo'e Beach, one of the best beaches in Hawai'i, with excellent water clarity for snorkeling and scuba diving. Great golf awaits you at the Challenge at Manele. Like the Lodge at Ko'ele, Manele delivers a memorable experience.

**SETTING & FACILITIES**

**Location** At Hulopo'e Bay, short walk to beach. **Dining** The 'Ihilani Restaurant serves fine Hawai'i regional cuisine. **Amenities & Services** Room service, valet and self-parking, spa, golf, tennis, concierge service, children's program, babysitting.

**ACCOMMODATIONS**

**Rooms** 249. Includes 13 suites; 6 rooms for the disabled. Nonsmoking rooms available. **All Rooms** A/C, cable TV, VCR, radio, in-room safe, lana'i, mini-bar, hair dryer, sitting area, tub and shower. **Some Rooms** Butler service. **Comfort & Decor** Spacious, comfortable rooms have refined furnishings, floral-themed decor, and accessories collected from around the world.

**PAYMENT, RESERVATIONS, & RESTRICTIONS**

**Family Plan** Children age 15 and under stay free in room with parents if using existing bedding. Maximum of 4 people/room (2 adults and 2 children). Extra person, $75. **Deposit** 2-night deposit due within 14 days of booking. Cancellation notice must be given 14 days prior to scheduled arrival for refund. **Credit Cards** All major credit cards accepted except Discover. **Check-In/Out** 3 p.m./noon. Early check-in and late check out available on request (no guarantees).

Part Four

# Aloha! Welcome to Hawai'i

## When You Arrive

Honolulu International Airport, one of the busiest in the United States, is simple to navigate. Gates have numbers; just follow the signs. Baggage claim areas are designated by letters of the alphabet in the primary mainland arrival terminals, and by numbers in the interisland terminal. Note, however, that West Coast flights by the local carriers, Hawaiian Air Lines and Aloha Air Lines, use the interisland terminal for ticketing and baggage. Latest arrival and departure times appear on the usual video monitors. Upon your arrival, follow the clearly marked signs to baggage claim on the street level. The wait only seems longer because you're anxious to hit the beach.

Arriving in Hawai'i is a sensual experience. You smell flowers, hear 'ukulele and people singing Hawaiian music, and feel the tropical warmth and tradewinds. If you elect to walk to baggage claim outdoors rather than taking the Wikiwiki transit, look beyond the airport to the moody mountains ahead of you and the city and Diamond Head off to your right for your first big-picture view.

In baggage claim, you will find car rental agencies and courtesy phones. Outside, you will find taxis, buses, Waikiki shuttles, car rental shuttles, and private or hotel limousines.

If you arrive on an international flight, the first to wish you "aloha" in their fashion are U.S. Customs and Immigration agents. Honolulu is today a far better staffed and more efficient port of entry than it was in the past.

### Flying Interisland

We've noticed that interisland airlines and airports tend to be very efficient at handling the constant loads of passengers and bags—much more so than commuter connections on the mainland. For people who live on the islands, this process replaces public transit. Neighbor Island airports are smaller, less formal, and easier to navigate.

Of Maui's three airports, Kahului Airport, at the island's center, is the main terminal for interisland and mainland flights. Car rental desks and taxi service are available outside baggage claim. Most people take a shuttle to the car compound a few minutes away. Kapalua/West Maui Airport serves only interisland flights on smaller aircraft but is handy to area resorts and towns. Car rentals are available nearby, and resort shuttles serve the airport. Tiny Hana Airport serves small plane traffic.

The Big Island of Hawai'i has two major airports. Keahole-Kona International Airport is a full-service, open-air facility carved from the lava fields of the Kona Coast, eight miles from Kailua-Kona. Landing on this black landscape below a dormant volcano is a bit like landing in a barbecue pit. You get used to it, especially after you notice explosions of neon-colored bougainvillea and palm trees growing out of the cinders. Rental car desks are in an open building across the street from the terminal; you take a shuttle to get to most of the car compounds, located a few minutes away.

Hilo Airport at General Lyman Field serves the east side of the island. Hilo Airport is much larger than you might expect. It was designed and built a few decades ago when Hilo was expected to become a major port of entry into Hawai'i because it was closest to the U.S. mainland. Car rental agencies are on site.

The Lihu'e Airport is Kaua'i's main airport and is an upgraded, enclosed, and air-conditioned facility. Princeville Airport on the North Shore serves primarily general aviation and helicopters.

Moloka'i's airport is an older, island-style, open-air facility located mid-island near Kaunakakai. Lana'i's airport is a new, modern facility below Lana'i City. Arriving guests are met by resort staff and transported by resort bus.

## Ground Transportation

### O'ahu: Honolulu International Airport

**Rental Cars**   Five car rental agencies—Avis, Budget, Dollar, Hertz, and National—have customer service desks in most baggage claim areas at street level. Other car rental agencies are located in the vicinity of the airport and have courtesy phones inside the baggage claim area. See the preceding section on car rentals for more details.

**Airport-Waikiki Express**   From the baggage claim area, head outside and look for any ticket agent wearing a blue aloha shirt, he or she will direct you to the nearest pickup point. The cost is $8 per person one-way and $13 per person round-trip (cash only). The 18-seat, air-conditioned red, white, and blue shuttle—clearly marked Airport-Waikiki Express—arrives every half-hour around the clock. Call (808) 566-7340 for more information.

**Taxis**   Cabs are available just outside the baggage claim area. Look for a dispatcher wearing a mustard-colored shirt. The fare from the airport to Waikiki ranges from $20 to $27, not including tip.

**TheBus**   TheBus is the cheapest airport transfer, if you are traveling light. The fare is $1 per adult and 50 cents per child, exact change required. Luggage is limited to one bag measuring no more than 24" × 18" × 12" that must fit under your seat.

Look for the #19 and #20 buses marked Waikiki Beach & Hotels. Bus stops—two at the main terminal and one at the interisland terminal—are located on the second-floor (departures) level.

Buses arrive every 20 minutes during the day. In the evening, only the #19 bus serves the airport. Call (808) 848-5555 for more information. TheBus takes about 30 minutes to reach Waikiki, depending on traffic.

## Maui: Kahului Airport

**Rental Cars**   Alamo, Avis, Budget, Dollar, Hertz, and National are just outside the main terminal (turn right as you leave the baggage area). Thrifty, Regency, and Word of Mouth have a courtesy phones at the airport's information board inside the baggage claim area.

**Taxis**   Maui Airport Taxi has a dispatcher inside baggage claim. Or you can just walk directly across the street and hail a cab at the curb.

**Shuttles**   Use the courtesy phone mentioned above to contact the Airport Shuttle or Speedy Shuttle. The wait is usually less than 15 minutes; costs vary depending on the destination. The Airport Shuttle, for example, charges $22 for two passengers bound for Wailea and $32 to Ka'anapali. To reserve a shuttle in advance, call the Airport Shuttle at (808) 661-6667 or Speedy Shuttle at (808) 875-8070.

Roberts Hawaii also provides transportation to the Ka'anapali Beach Resort area from 9 a.m. to 4 p.m. daily, with an evening run between 6:30 and 7 p.m. Look for the customer service desk marked Airport Hotel Shuttle in the baggage claim area (directly across from carousel #4). Shuttles depart every half-hour. The cost is $13 per person.

## Maui: Kapalua Airport

**Rental Cars**   Use the courtesy phone at the baggage claim area for a free shuttle van to car rental offices. Taxis are curbside outside baggage claim area.

## *The Big Island of Hawai'i:*
## *Keahole-Kona International Airport*

**Car Rental**    The car rental counters for Avis, Alamo, Budget, Dollar, Hertz, National, and Thrifty are all located across the street from the main terminal (directly across from the Onizuka Space Center).

**Taxis**    Cabs are parked across the street from the baggage claim area.

**Public Transportation**    No public transportation service is available at the airport.

**Shuttles**    Various hotel shuttles will pick up arriving guests with advance notice. Be sure to let them know your arrival time. You can also call for a pickup at the information booth, just outside the baggage claim area.

### *The Big Island of Hawai'i: Hilo International Airport*

**Car Rental**    Car rental pickups for Alamo, Avis, Budget, Dollar, Hertz, and National are located directly across the street from the airport restaurant, near the main gates.

**Taxis**    Taxis are available curbside near the baggage claim area.

**Public Transportation**    No public transportation service is available at the airport.

**Shuttle**    The only shuttle that serves the airport is for guests of the Hawai'i Naniloa Resort in Hilo, and even this is based on availability. Visitors booked at the Naniloa should call (800) 442-5845 or check with a customer service agent at the visitors information desk near the baggage claim area.

### *Kaua'i: Lihu'e Airport*

**Car Rental**    Car rental pickups for Alamo, Avis, Budget, Dollar, Hertz, and National are conveniently located directly across the street from the airport restaurant, near the main gates.

**Taxis**    Taxis are lined up and available curbside near the baggage claim area, or use the dispatch phone by the visitors information desk to summon a cab.

**Public Transportation**    No public transportation service is available at the airport.

**Shuttle**    The neighboring Kaua'i Marriott has a free shuttle for guests. At the visitors information desk, phone the hotel and request a pickup.

### *Moloka'i: Moloka'i Airport*

**Car Rental**    Budget and Dollar are the only car rental agencies at the Moloka'i Airport. Their customer service desks are located by the baggage claim area.

**Taxis**   Two cab companies serve the airport: Kukui Tours (call (808) 336-0944 or (808) 553-4227 after 5 p.m.) and Moloka'i Off-Road (call (808) 553-3369). Neither has a courtesy phone. Look outside the baggage claim area to spot either taxi van. If none are around, call either for a pickup.

### Lana'i: Lana'i Airport

**Car Rental**   Dollar Rent-A-Car is the only car rental agency on Lana'i. Upon arrival, walk to the reception desk and use the red courtesy phone. A van will pick you up and transport you to Dollar's pickup location, about three miles away.

**Shuttle**   A convenient way to get around is Lana'i Resort's shuttles. The $10/person charge includes round-trip airport transportation and all shuttles between the island's two resorts, The Lodge at Ko'ele and the Manele Bay Hotel. The shuttle vans are located right outside the airport's baggage claim area.

# Things the Locals Already Know

## The Lei Tradition

A Hawaiian flower *lei* is one of the most extravagant presents in the world. Some lei take more than a thousand flowers and quite a bit of time and artistry to make. They fade and perish within hours or days of their creation. Often they are worn only once.

Lei giving is one of the most colorful traditions in Hawai'i. You'll see it first at the airport. But it isn't an embarrassing designation of a newly arrived tourist. Lei are a sign of honor, for a family member, friend, or special guest, of either gender.

Having a garland placed around your neck is a special welcome, farewell, or congratulations, usually followed by a hug or kiss on the cheek, especially if you know the donor. A lei greeting remains Hawai'i's most tangible expression of aloha. Local tradition is to drape loved ones up to their noses with lei at graduations; they are also given for anniversaries, birthdays, and other special celebrations. They're great ice breakers with local strangers, who want to admire the lei and congratulate you on your special occasion. It's also customary to share the lei around after you wear it for a while (take it off and give it to someone else to wear).

Hawaiian language advisory: The word, lei, is singular and plural; there is no "s" in the Hawaiian language.

The tradition of lei giving may have originated with Hawai'i's earliest settlers, who brought flowering plants to use for adornment. Early Hawaiians offered lei to their gods during religious ceremonies.

Today, long lei are also draped over the statues or images of important people in Hawaiian history, or over the bows of victorious racing canoes, or on anything worthy of commemoration. Each June, the King Kamehameha Day celebration kicks off with a colorful lei-draping ceremony at the King Kamehameha statue in downtown Honolulu.

Writer-poet Don Blanding initiated Lei Day, an annual May 1 celebration held since 1928. The biggest event is held at Kapi'olani Park in Waikiki, where floral creations by the state's top lei makers are displayed.

Fresh flower lei can be purchased throughout Hawai'i, at every major airport and many supermarkets, as well as florists. Home-style is to make your own, and many families still do. You'll find lei made of all kinds of flowers, including plumeria, gardenias, ginger, orchids, pakalana, roses, 'ilima, and carnations, as well as fragrant maile leaves, braids of ti leaves, kukui nuts, sea shells, flowers made of dollar bills, and, for the kids back home, even candy and gum .

Many high-quality, lower-priced lei stands are concentrated in Honolulu's Chinatown. Costs range from a few dollars for a simple crown flower or sweet-smelling tuberose lei to $40 for an intricately crafted rope lei. One of the most popular new lei is the cristina, an expertly sewn garland made of purple dendrobium orchids ($25–$30).

Often people try to keep a lei alive by refrigerating it. Here's another suggestion: Drape it over a doorknob or lampshade in your hotel room or some other place where it cheers you to see the flowers and smell the fragrance.

## A Tip about Tipping

Many service workers in Hawai'i depend on tips for their living. At the airport, tip a porter a dollar or two per bag. Taxi drivers receive a 15% tip of the total fare plus 25 cents per bag or parcel. At the hotel, tip the bellhop $5 for transporting your luggage to and from your room, and give the parking valet a couple of dollars. Tip your room housekeeper $1 for each day of your stay. For dining, tip 15% to 20% of the bill.

## State Holidays

In addition to all major U.S. holidays, Hawai'i celebrates three state holidays.

- Kuhio Day (March 26). This holiday honors Prince Jonah Kuhio Kalaniana'ole (1871–1922), a statesman and member of the royal family who served in the U.S. Congress in the early 1900s.

- King Kamehameha Day (June 11). Hawai'i's great king, Kamehameha I, united the islands into a kingdom under one rule. An imposing figure—some reported him as tall as eight feet—the Big Island–born monarch died in May 1819, when he was believed to be in his early sixties, and his bones were hidden at a secret location on the Kona Coast. Modern islanders celebrate the life of Kamehameha with colorful festivities, including lei-draping ceremonies, parades, and *ho'olaule'a* (public parties).

- Admission Day (third Friday in August). On August 21, 1959, U.S. President Dwight D. Eisenhower signed the proclamation welcoming Hawai'i as the 50th state, following a long, often emotional campaign for statehood that originated more than a century earlier. Many expected Hawai'i to be named the 49th state, but that distinction went to Alaska in 1958. Today, "Hawai'i—49th State" memorabilia, ranging from record labels to buttons, is highly prized by collectors.

## Saying It in Hawaiian

In Hawai'i, English and Hawaiian are both official languages.

The Hawaiian alphabet has only 12 letters—the vowels a, e, i, o, and u and the consonants h, k, l, m, n, p, and w. A diacritical mark called the *'okina,* pronounced as a glottal stop, is almost as vital as a letter, so that those vowels can do extra duty. The language takes practice and patience.

Here are some general rules of thumb for you to remember:

- Vowels are pronounced this way: *a* as "uh," as in "lava"; *e* as "ay," as in "hay"; *i* as "ee," as in "fee"; *o* as "oh," as in "low"; and *u* as "oo," as in "moon."

- All consonants are pronounced as in English except for *w*, which is usually pronounced as *v* when it follows an *i* or *e*. Example: 'Ewa Beach is pronounced as "Eva" Beach. When following an *u* or *o*, *w* is pronounced as *w*. When it is the first letter in the word or follows an *a*, there is no designated rule, so the pronunciation follows custom. Which means Hawai'i and Havai'i are both acceptable.

- Some vowels are slurred together in a diphthong, forming single sounds. Examples: ai as in "Waikiki," au as in "mauka," ei as in "lei," oi as in "poi," ou as an "kou," and ao as in "haole."

- Some are separated by a glottal stop, or 'okina, an upside-down and backward apostrophe that emphasizes a separate vowel sound, acting like another consonant, and keeps identically spelled words from being confused. For instance, pau means "finished," but pa'u is a skirt worn by women horseback riders. Pau is pronounced as "pow," and pa'u is pronounced as "pah-oo."

- A macron, or *kahako*, designates a long vowel. A macron is marked as a line directly over the vowel. Logically enough, long vowels last longer than regular vowels. The macron however, is used less frequently than the okina, in part because it isn't as often needed to distinguish between words. This book, like most English publications from Hawai'i, excludes macrons. However, don't be surprised if you see them over the i's in Waikiki. They indicate that the word is correctly sounded "why-kiki" rather than "why-kee-kee."

- Every Hawaiian syllable ends with a vowel. Thus, every Hawaiian word ends with a vowel. Which means the word "Hawaiian" isn't a Hawaiian word.

- If a word contains no macrons, the accent usually falls on the next-to-last syllable. Examples: a-LO-ha, ma-HA-lo, ma-li-HI-ni, and 'o-HA-na.

The most authoritative Hawaiian language book is the *Hawaiian Dictionary*, by Mary Kawena Pukui and Samuel H. Elbert

---

### COMMONLY USED HAWAIIAN WORDS AND PHRASES

| | |
|---|---|
| 'aina | Land, earth |
| aloha | Love, kindness, or goodwill; can be used as a greeting or farewell |
| 'E komo mai | Welcome! |
| hale | House |
| hana hou | Do again, repeat, or encore |
| haole | Formerly any foreigner, now primarily anyone of Caucasian ancestry |
| holoholo | To go out for a walk, ride, or other activity |
| ho'olaule'a | A big party or celebration |
| ho'oponopono | To correct or rectify a situation |
| ikaika | Strong, powerful |
| 'ilima | A native shrub bearing bright yellow or orange flowers; used for lei |
| kahuna | Priest, minister, expert |
| kala | Money |
| kama'aina | Native-born or longtime island resident |
| kanaka | Person, individual |
| kane | Male, husband, man |
| kapu | Taboo |
| keiki | Child |
| kohola | Humpback whale |
| kokua | Help, assistance, cooperation |
| kolohe | Mischievous, naughty; a rascal |
| kupuna | Grandparent |
| ku'uipo | My sweetheart |
| lana'i | Porch, verandah |
| lua | Toilet, bathroom |
| lu'au | A Hawaiian feast |
| luna | Foreman, boss, leader |
| mahalo | Thank you |
| makahiki | Ancient Hawaiian harvest festival with sports and religious activities |
| makai | Toward the ocean; used in directions |
| malihini | Newcomer |
| mana | Spiritual power |
| mauka | Inland direction, toward the mountain |
| Me ke aloha pumehana | With warm regards |
| mele | Song |

**COMMONLY USED HAWAIIAN WORDS AND PHRASES** *(continued)*

| | |
|---|---|
| Menehune | Legendary small people who worked at night, building fishponds, roads, and temples; according to legend, if the work was not completed in one night, it was left unfinished |
| mu'umu'u | Loose-fitting Hawaiian gown |
| 'ohana | Family |
| 'ono | Delicious |
| pau | Finished, done |
| pupu | Hors d'oeuvre, appetizer |
| tutu | Grandmother |
| wahine | Female, wife, woman |

## Pidgin

You may hear people talking in what sounds like abbreviated English, except that it's more colorful. Hawai'i-style pidgin, the local patois, is the third language of the islands. It combines words and syntax of several languages and was developed so that multicultural plantation people could communicate. Although it is a true creole language and not simply slang, it's definitely not an official tongue.

The pros and cons of pidgin have long been debated by local educators and cultural experts. Some say that the practice should not be encouraged because it is not an acceptable manner of speech, whereas others insist that pidgin is a treasured cultural asset that should not be looked down upon. In Hawai'i, it's not uncommon for a kama'aina to speak perfect English in an office setting, then pick up the phone and speak pidgin to a friend. Here are some commonly used pidgin words and phrases you might hear during your stay.

**COMMONLY USED PIGDIN WORDS AND PHRASES**

| | |
|---|---|
| an' den? | So? And then? |
| braddah | Brother or friend |
| brah | Short for "braddah" |
| bumbye | Do it later |
| bummahs! | That's unfortunate! |
| da kine | The kind of, that thing |
| fo' real? | Really? |
| garans | Guaranteed |
| geev' um! | Go for it! |
| go fo' broke | Give it your all (famous motto of the 442nd battalion in WW II) |

---

**COMMONLY USED PIGDIN WORDS AND PHRASES** *(continued)*

| | |
|---|---|
| **how you figgah?** | How do you think that happened? |
| **howzit!** | How are you? |
| **laytahs** | See you later |
| **li'dat** | Like that |
| **minahs** | Minor; no problem; don't worry about it |
| **mo' bettah** | Better |
| **no shame** | Don't be shy or embarrassed! |
| **'nuff already!** | That's enough! |
| **shaka** | Greetings; good job; thank you |
| **small keed time** | Childhood |
| **soah?** | Does it hurt? |
| **stink eye** | Disapproving glance, a dirty look |
| **talk story** | Converse, talk, or gossip |
| **t'anks, eh?** | Thank you |
| **whatevahs** | Whatever |
| **who dat?** | Who is that? |
| **yeah, no?** | That's right! |

## Important Phone Numbers

Here's a list of phone numbers that may come in handy during your stay. For interisland calls, use the area code (808) before the number. Be aware these calls generally are charged long-distance rates.

### All Islands
Police, fire, ambulance: 911
Directory assistance: 1411

### O'ahu
Weather forecast: 973-4380, 973-4381
Marine conditions: 973-4382
Time of day: 983-3211
Honolulu International Airport: 836-6413
Honolulu Physicians Exchange: 524-2575
Hawai'i Dental Association Hotline: 593-7956
Information and complaints: 523-4385
Office of Consumer Protection: 586-2630
Better Business Bureau: 536-6956

### Maui
(Note: Maui County also includes Moloka'i and Lana'i)
Weather forecast: 877-5111
Marine conditions: 877-3477
Time of day: 242-0212 (Maui), 553-9211 (Moloka'i), 565-9211 (Lana'i)
Kahului Airport: 872-3803, 872-3893

Kapalua Airport: 669-0623
Hana Airport: 248-8208
Moloka'i Airport: 567-6140
Kalaupapa Airport: 567-6331
Lana'i Airport: 565-6757
Office of Consumer Protection: 984-8244

**The Big Island of Hawai'i**
Weather forecast: 961-5582, 935-8555 (Hilo)
Marine conditions: 935-9883
Time of day: 961-0212
Volcano eruption information: 985-6000
Keahole-Kona International Airport: 329-3423
Hilo International Airport: 934-5801
Office of Consumer Protection: 974-6230

**Kaua'i**
Weather forecast: 245-6001
Marine conditions: 245-3564
Time of day: 245-0212
Lihu'e Airport: 246-1400

## Newspapers
Local daily newspapers include the *Honolulu Advertiser* and *Honolulu Star-Bulletin* on O'ahu; the *Hawai'i Tribute-Herald* and *West Hawai'i Today* on the Big Island of Hawai'i; the *Maui News* on Maui; and the *Garden Island* on Kaua'i.

A key source for entertainment news and listings is the *Honolulu Advertiser's* "TGIF" section, published each Friday.

## Safety Tips
You won't find state, city or tourism spokesmen bragging about this, but *Money Magazine* calls Honolulu the safest large city in the United States, according to an analysis of FBI crime statistics. Hawai'i is a peaceful state with few violent crimes. Much is invested in the safety of tourists, the state's biggest industry, but the state is not crime-free. We urge you to use the same common sense and self-protective measures you would at home.

- Carry only as much cash or travelers checks as you need for the day.
- Never leave your luggage unattended until you arrive at your hotel.
- Never display large amounts of cash during transactions, such as at automated teller machines.
- Beware of pickpockets, especially in crowds.
- Carry your purse close to your body.
- Carry your wallet in a front pocket rather than a rear pocket.

- Avoid waiting alone at a bus stop after dark.
- Never leave valuables in your rental car.
- If your vehicle is bumped from behind at night, do not stop; instead, proceed to the nearest public area and call 911 for assistance.
- Leave your hotel room key with the front desk when going out.

# Part Five

# Getting Around Hawai'i

## Transportation Considerations

It's easy to get around Hawai'i when you know how.

Only O'ahu is large and busy enough to pose a problem, and that's only during Honolulu's morning and evening commute hours, when traffic chokes freeways and city streets. Traffic in and out of Waikiki can get congested on weeknights and weekends. Hawaiian street names are difficult to read and recall, and gas is expensive. Fortunately O'ahu is also the island with an outstanding municipal bus system. It's called TheBus.

You can ride TheBus, take shuttle vans, or hail a taxi to get almost anywhere you want to go. An open-air, motorized Waikiki Trolley tour stops at visitor attractions and shopping.

What you won't find in the islands are trains or subway systems.

Before choosing your primary mode of transportation, weigh the factors of convenience, flexibility, time, and cost. For example, catching a taxi from Waikiki to the *Arizona* Memorial may be the fastest and most convenient option, but it will also set you back about $25. Catching TheBus is the cheapest way to go, but it will take longer and you won't have as much flexibility.

The only new highway, the Interstate H-3, links Pearl Harbor with Kaneohe Bay Marine Air Station on the Windward side of the island. This highway broke the bank (the most expensive in the nation at the time, topping $1 billion a mile) and triggered controversy because its route violated a sacred area and an ancient temple site. But the roadway today is underused and very scenic. It's worth a spin just for the views.

### Traffic Advisory

If you decide to explore O'ahu by car, remember that O'ahu reputedly has more cars per capita than any city in the United States. Avoid the freeways and major highways—H-1 in particular—during morning and evening weekday rush hours. It's worst on school days, particularly when classes start in August and September, and tends to jam up around downtown Honolulu at lunch time. Road work is as big a cause of traffic backup as anything. The truth is that even O'ahu's traffic looks tame next to many a big mainland city's problems. Drivers regularly exceed the posted speed limit here, but be aware that the Honolulu Police Department uses radar and cameras to nail offenders. Chief problem areas, says the HPD, are the H-1 Freeway, Pali Highway, and the Kalaniana'ole Highway, so be especially lawful on these roads.

## Getting around Neighbor Islands

You won't have to worry about major traffic jams on any of the Neighbor Islands, where the population is a small fraction of O'ahu's. Barring accidents, traffic backups are nonexistent on Moloka'i and Lana'i and the Big Island, the one island with well-designed roads, longer driving distances, and fewer cars. Maui and Kaua'i have developed their own commuter traffic, with the busiest times being 6:30–8:30 a.m. and 3:30–5:30 p.m. Road congestion intensifies on Maui and Kaua'i when jumbo jets and other planes land at once, and in Kapa'a on Kaua'i during lunch hour.

Hawai'i's road system is simple if somewhat arcane, with posted signs (white lettering against a dark green background) providing directions. Considering the number of vehicles, particularly on O'ahu where the number of registered vehicles doubled in the past two decades, Hawai'i's roadways and streets are in relatively good repair. You may hit rough spots along the H-1 (eastbound) near the 'Aiea exit and on Kamehameha Highway on Windward O'ahu and the island's North Shore.

## Drive Times

Here are some estimated drive times from popular resort areas to specific points of interest. The estimations are given for periods outside rush hour.

---

### DRIVE TIMES

**O'ahu**

| *From Central Waikiki to:* | *Time to Travel* |
| --- | --- |
| Ala Moana Shopping Center | 7 minutes |
| Aloha Tower Marketplace | 15 minutes |
| Arizona Memorial | 30 minutes |
| Bishop Museum | 20 minutes |
| Chinatown Honolulu | 15 minutes |
| Hale'iwa | 1 hour |
| Hanauma Bay | 30 minutes |
| Honolulu International Airport | 25 minutes |

**DRIVE TIMES** (continued)

### O'ahu

*From Central Waikiki to:*                    *Time to Travel*
Polynesian Cultural Center                    1 hour, 15 minutes
Sea Life Park                                 40 minutes
University of Hawai'i–Manoa                   15 minutes

### Maui

*From Kahului Airport to:*                    *Time to Travel*
Haleakala National Park                       1 hour, 45 minutes
Hana                                          2 hours, 30 minutes
Ka'anapali                                    50 minutes
Kapalua                                       1 hour
Kihei                                         25 minutes
Lahaina                                       45 minutes
Makena                                        40 minutes
Wailea                                        35 minutes
Wailuku                                       10 minutes

### Big Island

*From Kona to:*                               *Time to Travel*
Hilo                                          2 hours, 15 minutes
Volcano                                       2 hours, 30 minutes
Waimea (Kamuela)                              50 minutes

*From Hilo to:*                               *Time to Travel*
Volcano                                       45 minutes
Waimea (Kamuela)                              1 hour, 15 minutes

### Kaua'i

*From Lihu'e to:*                             *Time to Travel*
Kilauea                                       50 minutes
Koke'e                                        1 hour, 30 minutes
Po'ipu                                        30 minutes
Princeville                                   1 hour
Waimea Canyon                                 1 hour, 15 minutes

### Moloka'i

*From Moloka'i Airport to:*                   *Time to Travel*
Halawa Valley                                 2 hours
Kaunakakai                                    15 minutes
Kepuhi Beach                                  25 minutes
Mapulehu                                      35 minutes
Maunaloa                                      15 minutes
Papohaku Beach                                30 minutes

---

**DRIVE TIMES** *(continued)*

**Lana'i**
*From Lana'i Airport to:*                     *Time to Travel*
Garden of the Gods                           45 minutes
Hulopo'e and Manele Bays                     25 minutes
Lana'i City                                   5 minutes
Munro Trail                                  15 minutes
Shipwreck Beach                              35 minutes

---

## Parking

Finding a parking spot isn't a problem in most areas. Waikiki hotels and downtown Honolulu offices charge the highest parking rates in Hawai'i. Your hotel will charge you a daily rate of at least $10 a day to park your car. Some Neighbor Island resorts charge a daily fee if valets park your car long term, but they have free self-park lots as well.

Parking rates in private lots in Honolulu's main business district start at $3 per half hour, but banks, stores, restaurants, and most professional offices validate.

There are two city-operated affordable parking structures to keep in mind: the Ali'i Place lot at Alakea and Hotel Streets (enter off of Alakea) charges 50 cents per half hour for the first two hours and $1 per each following half hour. On weekends and evenings, the rate is only 25 cents per half hour, with a $2 maximum. The Chinatown Gateway Plaza lot at King and Bethel Streets (enter off of Bethel) also charges 50 cents per half hour for the first two hours and $1 per each additional half-hour.

In the downtown area near 'Iolani Palace, your best bet is finding a metered parking spot on the street, either Richards or Punchbowl Streets (the rate is $1 per hour, with a two-hour limit). There is no metered parking available on King Street.

You can also try to find a metered parking spot on Bethel, Merchant, and Nu'uanu Streets in Chinatown. The best times to find an empty space are mid-morning and mid-afternoon.

If you're catching a show at the Hawai'i Theatre downtown, we recommend parking at the Liberty House lot at King and Bethel (enter off Bethel Street). It's a flat rate of $3 any time after 4 p.m.

In Waikiki, the best option is to leave the car in your hotel parking garage and explore the area on foot. If you're driving into Waikiki, however, the best parking option is the multi-level IMAX garage located on Seaside Avenue (on the right immediately after turning left from Kalakaua Avenue). This parking garage is centrally located and has the most affordable rate (a flat fee of $6 for all-day parking). In the Honolulu

Zoo and Kapiʻolani Park area, street parking becomes much easier to find. Metered stalls there cost only 25 cents per hour, with a four-hour limit at Kapiʻolani Park and a three-hour limit near the zoo.

On Neighbor Islands, finding an available parking space is most difficult in Maui's congested Lahaina. The best option is to park at the Lahaina Center (enter from either Papalaua or Waineʻe Street). If you purchase anything from a shop—even a single postcard—they'll validate your parking, up to four hours.

Currently, no parking meters exist on the Neighbor Islands except near a few public office buildings. Downtown Hilo had meters, but they recently discontinued them.

All parking lots are fairly well lit, almost always filled to near capacity with frequent turnover (particularly in Waikiki), and considered safe for your person if not your valuables. Do not leave valuables in your car, even in the trunk.

# Public Transportation

## Using TheBus

TheBus is the inexpensive way to get from here to there on Oʻahu. It is safe, friendly, and efficient and has twice been recognized by the American Public Transit Association as the best in the nation. Each day, the fleet of buses collectively transports 260,000 passengers and travels 60,000 miles, equal to two and a half trips around the world.

The advantages of riding TheBus go beyond cost. This is an excellent opportunity to mingle with local residents, too (chances are you'll want to ask their help in figuring out which stop you want). Strike up a conversation and, hopefully, enjoy a sampling of Hawaiʻi's aloha spirit. Outside rush-hour traffic, the buses are usually uncrowded and the ride is pleasant. Tell the driver where you want to go, and he'll help make sure you get off at the right place.

The exact-change, one-way fare on TheBus is $1 for adults and 50 cents for students (ages six through high school). You can request a free transfer, which entitles you to board up to two other busses where routes intersect, at the time you pay your fare. Stopovers or picking up a bus again in a continuous direction are not permitted, and there is a time limit to the transfer. You can pay $1 per person and ride around the whole circle-island route, which takes about four hours.

If you plan on using TheBus frequently during your stay, we recommend purchasing a $10 visitor pass, which allows you unlimited rides for four days, or a $25 monthly pass ($12.50 for students). These passes are available at all ABC stores in Waikiki.

For bus route information, call (808) 848-5555 between 5:30 a.m. and 10 p.m. daily. Be sure you have a pencil and paper handy, and be ready to provide the following information: your current location, your desired destination, and the time of day you need to arrive at that destination. TheBus also has an informative website, www.thebus.org, with a complete schedule you can download.

Also, you can get recorded route information from Waikiki to some of the most popular visitor attractions by calling (808) 296-1818, entering code number 8287, and then following the directions. If you want to take TheBus to the Polynesian Cultural Center, for example, select option 13 and listen to the recording, which will instruct you to board any 'ewa-bound bus numbered 8, 19, 20, 47, or 58; ride to Ala Moana Shopping Center; then transfer to the #55 bus, which will take you to the cultural center. It's that simple.

For more information, call the customer service office at (808) 848-4500.

### ABBREVIATED LIST OF BUS NUMBERS AND THEIR DESTINATIONS

*Note: Routes and numbers are subject to change.*

| | |
|---|---|
| 3 | Kaimuki/Pearl Harbor |
| 4 | Nu'uanu/Punahou |
| 6 | Pauoa/Woodlawn (University of Hawai'i) |
| 8 | Waikiki/Ala Moana |
| 19 | Waikiki/Airport and Hickam |
| 20 | Airport/Halawa Gate |
| 47 | Waipahu |
| 52C | Wahiawa/Circle Island |
| 55C | Kane'ohe/Circle Island |
| 57 | Kailua/Waimanalo/Sea Life Park |
| 58 | Hawai'i Kai/Sea Life Park |
| 88A | North Shore Express |

## Riding the Waikiki Trolley

Take the Waikiki Trolley for a fun and pleasant way to get around Waikiki and Honolulu. You can choose the Red Line, Blue Line, or Yellow Line. You'll get a good look at O'ahu as you go.

The trolley's Red Line covers all of Waikiki and Honolulu, stopping at the Honolulu Zoo, Waikiki Aquarium, Bishop Museum, Chinatown, Aloha Tower, and 'Iolani Palace (26 stops in all).

The Blue Line traces O'ahu's scenic southern coast, including stops at Hanauma Bay and Sea Life Park (11 stops in all).

The Yellow Line takes passengers on a shopping and dining excursion, with dropoff/pickup points at Ala Moana Center, Ward Warehouse, Ward Centre, Duty Free Shoppers, and other locales (20 stops in all).

Four-day passes are available at the following rates: $30 per adult ($10 per child ages 4–11) for unlimited rides on either the Red and Yellow or Blue and Yellow routes, and $42 ($12 per child) for unlimited rides on all three routes. For a one-day pass, the cost is $18 per adult ($8 per child) for either the Red and Yellow or Blue and Yellow routes, and $30 ($10 per child) for all three routes. Passes may be purchased at all major hotel tour desks or from customer service representatives at selected stops.

The Waikiki Trolley, operated by 'E Noa Tours, runs daily from 8:30 a.m. to 11 p.m. Red Line trolleys arrive/depart at appointed stops every 20 minutes; Blue Line trolleys every 60 minutes; and Yellow Line trolleys every 10 to 30 minutes. All routes originate from the Royal Hawaiian Shopping Center depot in Waikiki on Royal Hawaiian Avenue.

'E Noa Tours also operates several tours via trolleys and air-conditioned vans to popular visitor attractions, such as the *Arizona* Memorial. Call (808) 596-2199 or (800) 824-8804 for more information.

## Taxis

A taxi is probably the best way to travel through Honolulu when you don't know your way around. Taxis are not cheap, but they will save you time and frustration. If you are staying in Waikiki for, say, only three days and have no plans to leave the beach resort, your best bet may be to take a taxi.

A fare from the Honolulu International Airport to Waikiki will be from $25 to $35, depending on which end of Waikiki your hotel is located. Typically, meters begin at $2, with 25 cents added for each eighth of a mile. A few taxi companies provide sight-seeing excursions at a fixed rate. At the airport, curbside attendants assign taxis to riders on a first-come, first-served basis outside baggage claim.

Of the 30 taxi cab companies on O'ahu, you may choose those with a flat rate, metered rate, or hire a limo for sight-seeing trips around the island.

If you need to call a cab from your hotel, we recommend Charley's Taxi and Tours, one of the oldest, locally owned companies, (808) 531-1333.

## Resort and Shopping Shuttles

Take a shuttle van, which is often free or inexpensive. Shuttles are air-conditioned vans or buses that go to and from a specific destination. Many hotels and resorts operate shuttles of their own, while private

---

## TAXI COMPANIES

### O'ahu

Aloha State Taxi: (808) 847-3566

Americabs: (808) 591-8830

Charley's Taxi and Tours: (808) 531-1333

City Taxi: (808) 524-2121

Royal Taxi and Tours: (808) 944-5513

SIDA Taxi: (808) 836-0011

TheCab: (808) 422-2222

### Maui

AB Taxi: (808) 667-7575

Ali'i Cab: (808) 661-3688

Caroline's Taxi: (808) 572-9915

Central Maui Taxi: (808) 244-7278

Classy Taxi: (808) 665+0003

Kahului Taxi Service: (808) 877-5681

Kihei Taxi: (808) 879-3000

La Bella Taxi: (808) 242-8011

Royal Sedan and Taxi Service: (808) 874-6900

Wailea Taxi and Tours: (808) 874-5000

### Big Island

A-1 Bob's Taxi: (808) 963-5470

Ace One Taxi: (808) 935-8303

Aloha Taxi: (808) 325-5448

Alpha Star Taxi: (808) 885-4771

C&C Taxi: (808) 329-0008

D&E Taxi: (808) 329-4279

Hilo Harry's Taxi: (808) 935-7091

Kona Airport Taxi: (808) 329-7779

Laura's Taxi: (808) 326-5466

Marina Taxi: (808) 329-2481

Paradise Taxi: (808) 329-1234

Percy's Taxi: (808) 969-7060

### Kaua'i

Ace Kaua'i Taxi: (808) 639-4310

Akiko's Taxi: (808) 822-7588

City Cab: (808) 245-3227

Po'ipu Taxi: (808) 639-2044

### Moloka'i

Moloka'i Off-Road Tours and Taxi: (808) 553-3369

Kukui Tours and Limousines: (808) 336-0944 or (808) 553-4227 after 5 p.m.

### Lana'i

No full-time taxi companies serve Lana'i. Dollar Rent-A-Car provides taxi service on a driver-available basis. Call (808) 565-7227.

---

operators, who pick up passengers by request or at multiple designated sites, tend to offer more elaborate routes. Ask your hotel concierge for any shuttles that serve your hotel. Some widely used shuttle services are the following.

## O'ahu

A trolley service between Waikiki and the Aloha Tower Marketplace is available daily from 9:15 a.m. (departing the Hilton Hawaiian Village) to 9 p.m. (departing the Marketplace). Pickup/dropoff points in Waikiki include the Hilton, Outrigger Islander Hotel, the Duke Kahanamoku Statue, Honolulu Zoo, Waikiki Aquarium, Outrigger Prince Kuhio, Outrigger West, Outrigger Waikiki Surf, and Waikiki Parkside. The one-way fare is $2 for adults and $1 for children. Call (808) 528-5700.

## Maui

Free shuttles offer visitor transportation within the island's Wailea Resort, with stops at the Renaissance Wailea Beach Resort, Grand Wailea Resort, Four Seasons Resort Wailea, Outrigger Wailea Resort, and the area's golf courses, and (on request) tennis facilities. The shuttle operates daily from 6:30 a.m., with the final dropoff at 8:30 p.m. Call (808) 879-2828.

In Ka'anapali, a shuttle transports guests between the Whalers Village Shopping Center and hotels within the resort area. The service is provided daily from 9 a.m. to 11 p.m. and costs $2 per person. Call (808) 669-3177.

Guests staying at Kapalua Resort can take advantage of a free shuttle that stops at the major hotels, golf courses, tennis facilities, and shops in the area. The daily service runs from 6 a.m. to 11 p.m. Call (808) 669-3177.

## Big Island of Hawai'i

In the Hilo area, the Hele-On Bus can get you to where you want to go. Fares can range from 75 cents to $6, depending on the length of the route. Several bus pass options are available. Call (808) 961-8744.

The daily shuttles of Roberts Hawai'i's Kona Coast Express System link resorts on the island's northeastern Kohala coast with shops along its southeastern Kona coast. All-day passes on one of three shuttles are $4, while a system-wide pass costs $13. Shuttles begin running between 6 and 8 a.m. and stop running between 10 and 11 p.m. A round trip averages two hours and ten minutes. For more information, including route stops, visit www.robertshawaii.com or call (800) 767-7551.

## Lana'i

Guests staying at either the Lodge at Ko'ele or Manele Bay Hotel on Lana'i enjoy shuttle service between the hotels and the airport. Other shuttles transport guests to the island's two championship golf courses: the Experience at Ko'ele and the Challenge at Manele. The charge of $10 per person covers rides during the entire length of your stay. Call (808) 565-7600.

## The Lahaina-Lana'i Ferry

Visitors to Maui and Lana'i can take advantage of Expeditions' Lahaina-Lana'i Passenger Shuttle, which makes five round trips daily between the two islands.

Departure times from Lahaina Harbor on Maui are 6:45 and 9:15 a.m. and 12:45, 3:15, and 5:45 p.m. Departure times from Lana'i are 8 and 10:30 a.m. and 2, 4:30, and 6:45 p.m. The fare is $25 each way for adults, $20 for children age 11 and under. Each trip takes between 45 and 55 minutes. If you're prone to motion sickness, take your Dramamine ahead of time, as the ride can get bumpy. Call (808) 661-3756.

# Part Six

# Excursions

## Adventures on Your Own

### Exploring Downtown Honolulu

Downtown Honolulu is small enough to conquer on your own, mostly on foot, with an abundance of historic buildings linked by gracious green public areas. In between, busy streets abound, so try to choose your timing around rush-hour traffic for a more relaxed experience.

Mission Houses Museum hosts a three-hour walking tour of downtown Honolulu on Thursdays at 9:30 a.m. You'll see the museum and pass by Kawaiaha'o Church, the gilded statue of King Kamehameha, 'Iolani Palace, Washington Place (the Governor's Mansion) and the State Capitol. Admission is $20 for adults, $19 for senior citizens and military, $6 for students, and free for children ages 6 and under. Reservations are recommended. Call (808) 531-0481.

But you can do the two- or three-block route yourself. Bring the kids, provided they are older than age 5 and able to handle the walk. You are bound to gain insights about Hawai'i that you never learned in school (especially if you take a tour of 'Iolani Palace) like the sad tale of how it came to be that Hawai'i's last queen, Lili'uokalani was imprisoned in her own palace while her kingdom was taken away. Call a day or two in advance to reserve space on palace tours, led by docents (see contact and schedule information following).

If you're in town on the third Wednesday in January, head for the State Capitol for the cultural and culinary extravaganza that traditionally marks opening day of the legislature. You'll never see the likes of it elsewhere. The nation's youngest legislature is in business through April in the volcano-shaped Capitol.

## Take TheBus

In Waikiki, catch the #2 or #13 bus on Kuhio Avenue and get off at Punchbowl Street. The drivers are friendly; ask them to let you know where to get off for the Capital District. You can drive into town and pay to park in lots under the Capitol or City Hall complexes or the inexpensive city lot in Aliʻi Plaza on Alakea (on the right just before Hotel Street).

## What to Wear and Bring

This downtown is tropical, so sundresses and aloha shirts are acceptable, shorts too. Wear shoes you can walk in, and sun protection. Carry a camera if you're so inclined.

## What It Will Cost

Bus fare is $1 per adult and 50 cents per child age 6–18. Admission to ʻIolani Palace is $150 for adults and $5 for children ages 5–12 (younger children not admitted to the palace). Mission Houses Museum admission is $10 for adults; $8 for seniors and military; $6 for high school and college students; and $4 for children ages 4–12.

## If You Get Hungry

Snacks and restaurants are a short walk away in the main business district along Bishop and Alakea Streets, a bonanza of ethnic eateries.

## Sights to See

**ʻIolani Palace, mauka (mountain) side of King Street**   The most unusual downtown sight you'll see outside of Europe is ʻIolani Palace. The Italianate architectural gem is the only royal palace on American soil and a far cry from the grass shacks of early Hawaiʻi residents. (The docent may tell you that the kings actually lived in a grass shack nearby and kept the palace for affairs of state.) Built in 1882, ʻIolani was the official residence of the kingdom's last two monarchs, King Kalakaua (who had it built for $360,000, which nearly bankrupted the kingdom) and Queen Liliʻuokalani. Liliʻuokalani surrendered the throne under hostile pressure from American businessmen in 1893 and later was imprisoned in her own rooms at the palace. Guided tours last about 45 minutes and are scheduled at 15-minute intervals. Pick up your tickets at ʻIolani Barracks, located on the palace grounds. The palace is open Tuesday–Saturday, 9 a.m.–2:15 p.m. Make advance reservations. Call (808) 522-0832.

**State Capitol Building**   Behind the palace, linked by a walkway through shady grounds, is the State Capitol, designed to reflect the islands' volcanic and oceanic origins. On the makai (seaward) side of the building is a bronze statue of Queen Liliʻuokalani. On the mauka side is a statue of Father Damien, the Belgian priest who dedicated his life to ministering to leprosy patients on Molokaʻi.

**Washington Place (Governor's Mansion)**   Across busy Beretania Street on the Richards Street or downtown end of the Capitol is the historic governor's residence, slated to become a museum when funds are raised. Banyan trees with giant roots shade the grounds.

**The Mission Houses Museum**   From the corner of Punchbowl and South King Streets, walk in the Diamond Head direction to the Mission Houses Museum, a complex of missionary-era buildings located on the makai side of King Street. This is where the first American missionaries established their headquarters in 1820. The structures are the oldest surviving Western-style buildings in the state. The first printed works in the North Pacific were produced in the Coral House. Guided tours of the complex are scheduled 9:30 a.m.–3 p.m. The museum is open Tuesday–Saturday, 9 a.m.–4 p.m. Call (808) 531-0481.

**Kawaiahaʻo Church**   From the museum, head ʻewa (west) to nearby Kawaiahaʻo Church. Dedicated in 1842, this historic church was a favorite place of worship for many Hawaiian monarchs. This handsome coral-block structure was the setting for Kamehameha IV's coronation and wedding. Listed on the State and National Registers of Historic Places, Kawaiahaʻo is one of the few churches left in Hawaiʻi that still offers services in the Hawaiian language.

**The King Kamehameha Statue**   Cross Punchbowl Street and walk on King Street until you reach the King Kamehameha statue, one of Hawaiʻi's most photographed. The king is shown holding a spear in his left hand, and his right arm is outstretched in a welcoming gesture.

**Hawaiʻi State Library**   Return to the palace and walk right, toward Diamond Head, passing by the State Archives building. The next big building is the Hawaiʻi State Library. Its Hawaiʻi and Pacific section houses the state's largest collection of Hawaiʻi-related books, periodicals, and documents. Library hours vary, but it usually opens at 9 a.m. on weekdays. Call (808) 586-3500.

**Honolulu Hale**   Across Punchbowl Street is Honolulu Hale, otherwise known as City Hall. This California-Spanish-style structure, built in 1927, is worth a visit with the kids at night during the Christmas season, when the grounds are a festive display of oversized cartoon characters and other holiday adornments.

From Honolulu Hale, cross South King Street and Punchbowl to the bus stop nearest the main intersection. Catch the #2 or #13 bus back to Waikiki.

## Dinner Cruises

For those who want to enjoy views from the sea, Hawai'i offers several nightly dinner cruises, daily sunset sails, and other short cruises. The scenery, especially at sunset, is mesmerizing, and most of the boats and crews provide state-of-the-art facilities and cheerful service. On O'ahu, Royal Hawaiian Cruises (call (808) 848-6360) operates the 141-foot *Navatek I,* a smooth-riding vessel that uses SWATH (Small Waterplane Area Twin Hull) technology to minimize motion sickness; the ship glides above the surface while twin submarine-like hulls ride below the waves. Rates are $70–$125 for adults and $50–$75 for children ages 2–11.

Also on O'ahu is Paradise Cruises (call (808) 983-7827), which operates the *Star of Honolulu,* a 232-foot, four-deck ship that offers daily and nightly cruises. The dinner cruises are $30–$199 per adult and $15–$60 per child age 3–11.

Both these ships sail from Honolulu Harbor and cruise waters off Honolulu and Waikiki.

Neighbor Islands cruise providers include the *Navatek II* (call (808) 873-3475) and Windjammer Cruises (call (808) 661-8600) on Maui; Captain Beans Cruises (call (808) 329-2955) and Body Glove Cruises (call (808) 326-7122) on the Big Island; and Captain Andy's (call (808) 335-6833) and Holoholo Charters (call (808) 246-4656) on Kaua'i. Call the operators for a schedule of available trips, which may range from morning excursions and whale-watching tours to sunset cruises.

Lunch and sunset meals are usually served buffet-style; evening dinners are typically sit-down affairs with a set beef/seafood menu.

At Wailua State Park on Kaua'i, you can putter up the Wailua River on a leisurely boat ride to the famous tourist stop of Fern Grotto. Smith's Tropical Paradise offers the 90-minute cruises daily. Call Smith's Tropical Paradise, (808) 821-6892.

## Helicopter Tours

Helicopter flight-seeing rides aren't for everyone, and they are not without risk, particularly in the weather conditions sometimes encountered. Helicopters are a good way to see the big picture, especially in roadless wilderness areas like Na Pali Coast, the rainy summit of Wai'ale'ale, or the active lava pool of Kilauea Volcano.

We've seen several adventurers return to terra firma and need a place to lie down. For those for whom motion sickness is not a problem, the best views of Hawai'i are from the air aboard a chopper.

Schedule flight-seeing tours early in your vacation; if the weather doesn't cooperate on the day of your tour, you'll have an opportunity to reschedule. Try to book a few days in advance—tours are often filled if you wait until the last minute, especially during high-season holidays. You can secure reservations with a major credit card.

Prices generally are $85 per person for a 20-minute flight, $130 for a 45-minute flight, and about $200 for a full-hour adventure. There are no age restrictions, but passengers weighing over 250 pounds are assessed an additional charge (usually 50%) because an extra seat will be blocked off for added comfort. Only a few operators offer ground transportation to and from hotels.

Passengers are weighed before the tour, and seats are assigned based on body weight to balance the helicopter. Generally, every other passenger is assigned a window seat. Most tours, however, use the new A-Star aircraft, which provides better viewing conditions than previous helicopters from interior seats. Accommodating up to six passengers, the A-Star is comfortable, air-conditioned, and fully enclosed.

Helicopter tours provide dramatic panoramas of such locales as Pearl Harbor, Punchbowl National Cemetery of the Pacific, and Diamond Head on O'ahu; Kilauea Volcano and the steep rainforest valleys of the Big Island; Haleakala and the West Maui Mountains on Maui; and the rugged Na Pali and Mt. Wai'ale'ale crater on Kaua'i. You'll get to see some spectacular hidden spots—waterfalls, black-sand beaches, lava fields, and cinder cones—that are otherwise inaccessible.

Each tour is fully narrated by the pilot, adding to the music humming in your specially equipped headset. Many pilots are certified tour guides, providing insights on history, geology, and nature and adding an educational facet to the tour.

The pilot also operates a multicamera system within the helicopter, capturing the scenery (and sometimes you!) on tape. You can buy the video at the end of your journey, usually for about $25.

About motion sickness: In addition to over-the-counter and prescription drugs that may help prevent motion sickness, you may want to try elastic wristbands that are designed to stimulate an acupuncture point on your wrist and counter air- or seasickness without drugs. Ginger is a favorite local remedy to prevent motion sickness; try drinking real ginger ale or snacking on ginger shortly before the flight.

## HELICOPTER OPERATORS

**O'ahu**
Magnum Helicopters (808) 833-1133
Makani Kai Helicopters (808) 834-5813

**Maui**
Alex Air Helicopters (808) 877-4354

**HELICOPTER OPERATORS** (continued)

**Maui** (continued)
Blue Hawaiian Helicopters (808) 871-8844
Hawai'i Helicopters (808) 877-3900
Sunshine Helicopters (808) 871-0722

**The Big Island**
Blue Hawaiian Helicopters (808) 961-5600
Safari Helicopters (808) 969-1259

**Kaua'i**
Air-1 Inter-Island Helicopters (808) 335-5009
Bali Helicopter Tours (808) 335-3166
Jack Harter Helicopters (808) 245-3774
Safari Helicopters (808) 246-0136

## Moloka'i Mule Ride

In today's era of high-tech attractions and showbiz wizardry, it's heart-warming to see that this rugged mule ride remains a favorite tourist activity. The Moloka'i Mule Ride to Kalaupapa stars sure-footed mules that carry their riders down a hair-raising, 26-switchback trail. The 90-minute excursion includes breathtaking views of Moloka'i's northern coast. Kalaupapa is the historic settlement where Father Damien de Veuster ministered to leprosy patients from 1873 to 1889. Offered daily except Sunday, the per-person tour includes a picnic lunch. Call (800) 567-7550 or check out the website at www.molokai-muleride.com.

## Submarine Rides

If you can't bring yourself to put your face in the water to snorkel, there is another way to admire the undersea beauty off Hawaiian shores. Atlantis Submarines offers narrated, air-conditioned tour rides on three islands in which you never get wet but can observe coral reefs teeming with yellow tangs, parrot fish, moray eels, and many other types of colorful sea life. On O'ahu, catch the sub ride at Hilton Hawaiian Village, where you board a shuttle boat and transfer to large (48–64 passenger) vessels. On Maui, shuttle boats depart from Lahaina and take you to a 48-passenger sub that explores the ocean channel between Maui and Lana'i. In Kailua-Kona on the Big Island, Atlantis's 48-passenger sub examines a large natural coral reef.

Rates are $89–$99 for adults and $40 for children. For more information, call (800) 548-6262.

# Cruising Hawai'i

If you haven't sailed among the Hawaiian Islands, you've missed one of the best experiences in the Pacific. A seven-day cruise delivers the true nature of the islands. You can lounge on the sun deck with a good book, but there's much to see: sunsets, rainbows, whales, and, when Kilauea Volcano is pumping, the eerie night spectacle of red-hot lava running like jelly into the sea. Shore excursions offer the chance to sample the sights, nature, and culture of the islands, not to mention golf and other outdoor sports.

Norwegian Cruise Lines has begun operating two luxury steamships in Hawai'i for week-long interisland voyages. *Norwegian Star,* a new, 2,200-passenger, $400 million "supership" reputed to be "the largest cruise ship ever to set sail in the Islands," launched weekly seven-day interisland cruises in late 2001. *Norwegian Wind* has cruised the high seas for almost a decade, but sports a remodeled deck and a new Hawaiian itinerary.

Rather like a floating resort, the *Norwegian Star* has 15 decks, 10 restaurants, and 14 cocktail lounges with a crew of 1,100 to attend up to 2,200 passengers. The 91-ton, 971-foot long vessel, powered by twin diesels, cruises at 25 knots under a Bahamas flag. It was built for Hawai'i service and is presently the only ship devoted exclusively to interisland cruises.

The ship embarks Sundays from Honolulu's Aloha Tower and Fridays from Lahaina Harbor on voyages with ports of call including Nawiliwili, Kauai; Hilo or Kailua-Kona, Hawai'i; and an exotic new destination way down in the Central Pacific: remote Fanning Island (Tabuaeran) in the Republic of Kiribati, part of the equatorial Line Islands.

One possible downside: The ship spends two full days at sea, cruising 2,000 miles south to Fanning Island and back. The side trip to remote Fanning, a tiny coral atoll, for a day-long foreign port of call, enables the cruise line to skirt the Jones Act which bans foreign-flagged vessels from sailing exclusively between U.S. ports. It also poses an interesting comparison for modern, American Hawai'i. Fanning is the Pacific paradise some dreamers expect to find in the wealthy, worldly islands to the north. On the other hand, Fanning's 1,300 residents are experiencing weekly visits by up to 2,200 cruising guests, which is bound to change the local culture more than any event since World War II.

The 754-foot, 50-ton *Norwegian Wind,* formerly the *Windward,* cruises at a top speed of 18 knots. She was built in 1993, refurbished and stretched with a new 130-foot midsection in 1998 and offers spacious surroundings and picture-window ocean views from most staterooms. With a capacity of 1,748 passengers and 689 crew, the *Norwegian Wind* is scheduled to make 10- and 11-day Hawaiian voyages, spending four days at sea en route to and from Fanning, with two days in Lahaina on the longer cruise and a sail-by view of Kilauea Volcano's fiery ribbons of lava, if they are flowing, on the shorter. The *Norwegian Wind* features 10 passenger decks, 5 restaurants, a dozen bars and lounges, and a casino, which won't feature gambling on Hawai'i cruises (Hawai'i is one of the few states where off-shore gambling is still against the law). This ship will cruise Australian and Alaskan waters before sailing to Hawai'i, where cruises are scheduled September through April.

Miami-based Norwegian Cruise Lines is offering some bargain fares to launch their service. Check out the fare and cruise schedule on the Internet or with a travel agent.

### Norwegian Cruise Line

(800) 327-7030; www. www.ncl.com/fleet/02/star.htm

**Type of Ship**  New and refurbished luxury oceanliners.

**Type of Cruise**  Destination, family oriented, casual and flexible.

**Comments**  New to Hawai'i, the *Norwegian Star* and *Norwegian Wind* fill the void caused by the demise of American Classic Voyages, parent of American Hawai'i Cruises, whose ships cruised the Islands for several decades, and United States Lines, whose new liner sailed only a year. The New Orleans–based cruise firm filed bankruptcy in the fall of 2001, and the ships were sold at auction. The new MS *Patriot,* a launched-and-left $114 million cruiser, remains moored in Honolulu Harbor, waiting for a new operator to start it up again.

The Norwegian Cruise Line ships, now sailing weekly, began service after our press deadline so we are unable to provide the usual rating and review comments.

## Cruising, Pro and Con

If you've never visited Hawai'i and want to see two or more islands, a cruise is a good solution. A slow boat between the islands is relaxing. You'll avoid changing hotels and save time and money, but there's a trade-off. Because a sea cruise usually allows only a day in each port, you'll only get of a hint of each island. Think of a cruise as a scouting expedition.

You can sign up for shore excursions offered by the cruise line or strike out on your own on foot, by taxi, or by rental car. If you have a place you simply must see, hire a rental car and go. You can reserve and rent a car while still on board ship.

Otherwise, check out the full roster of shore excursions offered by the cruise line. All cruise ships that call on Hawaiian ports offer shore excursions—a helicopter tour of Kaua'i, hikes and kayak tours, Kona deep-sea fishing, snorkeling, and dive trips—all easily booked on board.

With the exception of the Big Island and O'ahu, you can see a lot of island in a day in a rental car. If you sail from Honolulu, arrive a day or two early to see the island, or stay two or three days after the cruise.

All meals are included in the price, which means you will miss the best of the islands' regional cuisine. Food aboard is abundant, but it's not the same as regional cuisine at Alan Wong's Restaurant.

If you love the beach, you're out of luck except on Kaua'i, where Kalapaki Beach is a five-minute walk from Nawiliwili Harbor, the ship's anchorage.

## Other Touring Suggestions

### Around O'ahu

Hawai'i's most famous landmark, **Le'ahi Crater,** was renamed Diamond Head in the early 1800s by British sailors who claimed to see diamonds glittering on the crater. (The "diamonds" turned out to be merely sparkling calcite crystals.)

**Waikiki Beach** is actually a collection of small beaches, some with imported sand (from Moloka'i's empty beaches). The hotels block all ocean views from Kalakaua Avenue until Kuhio Beach, site of the Honolulu Police Department's Waikiki precinct house, surfboard racks, and the larger-than-life statue of Duke Kahanamoku, Hawai'i's legendary sports hero. He stands cast in bronze, back to the sea he loved, arms outstretched in perpetual greeting.

Duke Kahanamoku was a record-setting swimmer (he captured gold medals in the 1912 and 1920 Summer Olympics) who set the 100-meter freestyle world record in 1911. In later years, Kahanamoku traveled the world, staging surf exhibitions to popularize the sport. He died in 1968 at the age of 77.

In 1850, **Honolulu** became the capital of the kingdom. Today it is a 26-mile long urban strip, but the City and County of Honolulu not only encompasses all of O'ahu but also extends 1,400 miles northwest up the island chain to Kure Atoll.

In Hawai'i, folks call Honolulu "town," and everything else that lacks a building over three stories tall "country." Waikiki is Waikiki.

Drive up Ala Moana Boulevard to **Honolulu Harbor.** Until Pearl Harbor was made navigable in the early 1900s, Honolulu Harbor was the only protected body of water of its size in Hawai'i. In 1794, the English ship *Butterworth,* led by Captain William Brown, became the first foreign vessel to enter the harbor.

The centerpiece of the harbor remains the ten-story **Aloha Tower,** the tallest building in Honolulu when it opened in 1926. Its tenth-floor observation deck provides sweeping views of O'ahu's southern coastline.

From the 1930s to the 1950s, steamships carrying dreamy-eyed visitors radioed their arrival schedule to harbormasters at the tower. And as luxury liners such as Matson's *Lurline* and SS *Monterey* pulled into port, a festive celebration—"Boat Day"—took place, as residents welcomed *malihini* (visitors) with Hawaiian music, hula, and sweet-smelling flower lei. A modern version of Boat Day occurs when interisland steamships depart the harbor from the area of **Aloha Tower Marketplace,** a retail-restaurant complex with open-air waterfront restaurants that offer a seat on the busy harbor plied by tugboats and in- and out-bound ships.

From the harbor, take Alakea up to get on the Pali Highway and head to **Nu'uanu Valley,** gateway to the Ko'olau Mountains and O'ahu's Windward side.

At the top of the Pali in 1795, Kamehameha I and his army drove 300 O'ahu defenders over the cliff to their deaths. You can still see the squared outline of a gun rampart on top of the mountain from the highway, a reminder of the battle.

Today, the **Pali Lookout** is one of the island's most visited spots, as evidenced by the parking lot full of tour buses. Stop to be blown by the wind and admire the striking views of haunting Windward O'ahu.

*Travelers Advisory:* Pali Lookout is a prime area for *cockaroaches,* the pidgin term for car clout thieves who smash car windows and grab purses, cameras, or anything in sight. You can lock your car doors and trunk and still lose. It is best to take all items of value with you, or leave the car empty, open, and unlocked.

Up behind Waikiki is misty **Manoa Valley,** formed in part by the 2,013-foot **Mount Tantalus.** The rainbow-laced valley is home to **University of Hawai'i–Manoa,** with an enrollment of 20,000 students. The sprawling campus, shaded by specimen tropical tress, is a mix of disparate architecture, with Korean temples beside World War II–like barracks. The most graceful building is the East West Center, a think tank begun by President Lyndon B. Johnson with congressional funds to foster alliances in Asia and the Pacific.

Back in Waikiki, drive east on the H-1 to find the toney eastern neighborhood of **Kahala** and the Kahala Mandarin Oriental Hotel, surrounded by grandiose estates from the Japanese property-buying heyday of the 1980s, now passed. Continuing on Kalaniana'ole Highway, you enter suburban **Hawai'i Kai,** home to Roy's Restaurant, where foodies worship nightly at one of Hawai'i's first regional cuisine restaurants. **Koko Head Crater** looms over the suburban homes and marks the spot where O'ahu at last begins to reveal its raw, natural self along the Ka'iwi Coast with its rocky shoreline, sandy beaches, famous spouting **Halona Blowhole** (a geyser-like phenomenon caused when big waves hit a hole in the rocks) pocket beaches, and view of Molokaʻi 26 miles across the sea.

The main attraction here is not the crater (which you can climb on a steep trail) but **Hanauma Bay,** a coastal crater with a blown-out sea wall; the reef is a tropical fish preserve and the most popular snorkel spot in Hawaiʻi, attracting 3,000 visitors a day. Believe it or not, fish still out-number snorkelers.

## Windward Oʻahu

Continuing east from Koko Head crater affords you a scenic drive along Oʻahu's southeastern coastline. To your right you will spot **Makapuʻu Beach Park** and the crashing waves beyond. Note also a pair of offshore islands; the larger one (67 acres) is **Manana,** or Rabbit Island. In the late 1800s, its owner, John Cummins, used the island to raise European hares, and a small population of rabbits still resides there, although the island is mainly a seabird sanctuary.

Ahead is **Sea Life Park,** an old-fashioned marine attraction where captive creatures like dolphins jump through hoops. The park also serves as a rehab center for injured sea life rescued from Hawaiʻi waters.

Rising up 2,000 feet and more, the jagged spine of the majestic **Koʻolau Mountains** begins here, dramatic backdrop to the Windward towns of Waimanalo, Kailua, and Kaneʻohe. Geologists believe the sheer precipice of the Koʻolau may have been formed when a huge portion of the coast dropped off into the sea, leaving a vertical wall now cloaked in rainforest green.

In **Waimanalo,** a country settlement with a great bodysurfing beach, farmers grow abundant food and flower crops in the broad fertile plain below the cliffs. Nearby, the U.S. military has maintained a 1,500-acre seaside retreat beside an airfield known as Bellows. The first Japanese prisoner of war was captured on **Bellows Beach** shortly after the December 7, 1941, raid on Pearl Harbor, when his small submarine struck the reef in Waimanalo Bay and sank.

With nearly 60,000 residents, **Kailua** is the second largest town in the state. Kailua (it means "two seas") sits between the **Kawainui Marsh** and the Pacific Ocean. The marsh, the largest body of fresh water in Hawaiʻi, is slowly becoming a meadow. But Kailua is blessed with splendid beaches, a picturesque bay, natural vistas, and a strong sense of community. **Kailua Beach** is one of the state's best beaches, famous as a wind-surfing spot (onshore tradewinds blow nearly all the time). Nearby, **Lanikai Beach** is becoming a kind of Malibu of the Pacific, since plenty of celebrities either visit often or have homes here.

Neighboring Kaneʻohe, an undistinguished strip mall of a town, borders one of the world's most beautiful azure bays, **Kaneʻohe Bay,** dotted with islets and surrounded by steep cliffs.

Further up the Windward Shore, bound for the North Shore, you'll come to Kaʻaʻawa, home to **Kualoa Ranch,** a working cattle ranch that has turned to tourism to make ends meet and to share its magnificent setting. Activities offered here include horseback riding, helicopter tours, scuba diving, all-terrain-vehicle (ATV) riding, jet-skiing, shooting range, hiking, an ancient fish pond, and a hidden beach.

About 600 yards off **Kualoa Beach Park** stands one of Hawaiʻi's most photographed little islands: **Mokoliʻi,** known as Chinaman's Hat.

The best and safest way to take its photo is to leave the highway, either to enter the park or pull off along one of the beaches, to shoot it with Kaneʻohe Bay in the background.

## North Shore

Laʻie is where you'll find the **Polynesian Cultural Center,** one of the state's notable attractions.

Driving on around the northern point of the island, you approach the famous North Shore surfing beaches. Gone are the sweet-smelling scents of coconut oil and suntan lotion, replaced by the aroma of fresh salt air. Gone is the jungle of hotels and condominiums, replaced by surfer cottages and homes frequently threatened by massive winter surf. Gone are the friendly ocean waves of Waikiki, replaced by gigantic swells that have helped the North Shore gain worldwide notoriety as the undisputed capital of surfing.

Each winter, the world's top professional and amateur surfers make their annual pilgrimage to such renowned surf spots as **Sunset Beach, Aliʻi Beach,** and **ʻEhukai Beach** (and its famous Banzai Pipeline).

The heart of Oʻahu's North Shore is **Haleʻiwa,** a funky village of surf shops, art galleries, mom-and-pop shops, shaved ice stands, and small main-street bistros like Kua Aina Sandwiches and Café Haleʻiwa, where surfers stoke up when waves are flat. Jameson's by the Sea is an irresistible but crowded steak and seafood restaurant with an always-popular lanaʻi at sundown.

The best attraction is the **Haleʻiwa Surf Museum,** which traces the origins and history of the sport with photographs, artifacts, and memorabilia from Hollywood to Haleʻiwa.

## Leeward Oʻahu

Here on the **Waiʻanae Coast** in towns like Nanakuli and Makaha, pit bulls guard plantation houses with rusty pickups in the yard. This is one of the last enclaves of Hawaiians on Oʻahu. In general, the western side of Oʻahu turns its hot, dry back on tourists. Seldom (if ever) featured in travel magazines, this side of O'ahu has, however, some spectacular unspoiled places.

Once you get comfortable with the local scene, you'll begin to enjoy the reef-fringed 20-mile long stretch of coast that ends in exclamation at needle-nosed **Ka'ena Point,** Oahu's westernmost point and a popular fishing spot.

Though Ka'ena "points" toward Kaua'i, early Hawaiians believed the point was one place where human souls departed Earth—good souls to the right, less virtuous to the left.

Ka'ena means "heat" in Hawaiian. You'll understand why when you take the hike to the point that "throbs in the sun," according to a chant. Sunsets here are red hot. Bring plenty of water.

Heading back toward Honolulu, you'll arrive at **Makaha,** site of a popular longboard surf contest, emphasizing the surfing style favored in the 1950s and 1960s. The North Shore attracts worldwide attention, true surfing insiders know Makaha as one of Hawai'i's hottest surf spots. Here you'll find some of the finest surfers in the state, from young prodigies to legendary old-timers.

Beyond Makaha and Nanakuli is **Wai'anae,** a place often ignored by visitors. However, this may soon change. Recently, community leaders have talked about boosting Wai'anae's economic potential through cultural tourism, recognizing visitors' desire to learn about Hawai'i's culture. One realization of these discussions is the **Na Hana Lima Store,** a cooperative of a dozen Wai'anae-area artisans, located at Wai'anae Mall Shopping Center. The store includes Hawaiian jewelry, sculptures, woodwork, kapa, prints, pottery, and other items.

Nearby is **Ko 'Olina,** a lavish resort area featuring 'Ihilani Resort and Spa, a 387-room luxury retreat. The resort's eye-catching man-made lagoons are now open to all for swimming.

## Maui

On a map, Maui looks almost like a person. It's easy to make out a head, a neck, and a body. The **West Maui Mountains** form the head, the neck is the isthmus of the Valley Isle, and **Haleakala** is the body. Such diverse geographical anatomy makes it Hawai'i's second most popular island, attracting more than two million visitors a year.

Most arrive at the airport in Kahalui, the trafficky center of commerce, and head straight to one of the main resorts in Wailea, Kihei, Kapalua, or Ka'anapali. A lucky few avoid the crowds and fly from Honolulu directly to Kapalua/West Maui Airport or to the lush tropical retreat of Hana. Wherever you choose to stay on Maui, go for a ride at least once to get a glimpse of the rest of the island, outside the resort zone. Here are some day trips to consider.

At Maui's "chin" is **Ma'alaea,** a small waterfront community with a boat harbor, condos, surfing area, and a stop worth your attention, the **Maui Ocean Center.** It features a 600,000-gallon aquarium with hundreds of ocean creatures, including rays, sea turtles, reef fish, and sharks.

## South Maui

Driving south, you reach **Kihei,** a busy beach town with more than 100 small hotels and condos, shops, restaurants, and businesses. Kihei has nightlife, a rarity on the Neighbor Islands, in nightclubs, sports bars, and karaoke bars.

South of Kihei is the master-planned resort of **Wailea** ("water of Lea," goddess of canoes), a 1,500-acre oasis of luxury hotels and condos, set on five crescent beaches. After Wailea, the paved road ends at the isolated resort and old community of **Makena,** where the elegant Maui Prince Hotel sits amid 1,800 acres of mostly rugged, natural dryland slope and two championship golf courses. Beyond the Prince, the road continues past beachfront homes until it ends on an old lava flow.

Driving west from Ma'alaea, two-lane Highway 30 passes through a tunnel on the coastal route; there's a whale-watch lookout nearby at **McGregor Point,** as well as miles of open coastline and small tree-shaded beach parks, old graveyards, and views of Lana'i and Moloka'i.

## West Maui

Turn left into **Lahaina** (it means "the heat") to discover its historic buildings, harbor, and Front Street hangouts, popular day or night. The entire town is designated a National Historic Landmark, and Lahaina's storied past lives on in its restored relics that cluster around a mammoth banyan tree in the town square.

In the eighteenth century, Maui's ferocious high chief Kahekili, said to have built houses out of the skulls of defeated warriors to keep his enemies terrified, declared Lahaina his capital. He favored the area for its weather, lush thickets of banana and breadfruit trees, and defensible location between steep West Maui slopes and the sea, where it afforded a natural harbor. Kahekili, who gives his name to a nearby beach, survived all his foes and died in Waikiki in his eighties.

Lahaina was the focal point of the whaling industry in the mid-nineteenth century; at the height of the whaling era, more than 100 whaling ships dropped anchor at the town's harbor. Along with the ships came hundreds of pleasure-seeking sailors, the bane of the disapproving Christian missionaries. In 1825, a mob of British sailors threatened to kill missionary settler William Richards and set his house on fire unless a law forbidding prostitution and alcohol was repealed. Two years later, a cannon struck Richards's home from a visiting whaler. Wrote one missionary in 1837, "As a mass, the seamen are sunk in vice."

A short drive up from Lahaina is **Ka'anapali Beach Resort,** where Alexander and Baldwin converted sugarcane fields into the island's first master planned resort—a parklike setting on a four-mile gold-sand beach with two championship golf courses, hotels, condos and homes, and an open-air mall with shops and restaurants.

Beyond Ka'anapali other communities of condos and apartments dot the shoreline, but at the northwest end of the resort coast, **Kapalua Resort,** a picturesque resort with five exquisite bays, puts an end to human work and lets nature takes over. For hiking enthusiasts, the **Kapalua Nature Society** offers guests hikes in the West Maui Mountains. The road continues on to Kahului, paved now but still tortuous, skinny, and slow going. It's a great drive through a relatively unspoiled area of the island.

### North Shore

Heading toward Hana from Kahului on Highway 36 takes you to **Pa'ia,** a breezy former plantation town now famous for its **Ho'okipa Beach Park,** Hawai'i's top windsurfing spot. Ho'okipa's strong year-round winds and ideal wave conditions draw the world's top windsurfers, dubbed the Maui Air Force for their aerial antics. It is a sight to see these daredevils hit waves head-on, to gain "hang time" up in the air, before splashing down in the sea. Nearby, **Haiku** has inexpensive lodging in B&Bs and vacation rentals.

### Upcountry

From Pa'ia, you can head inland up through the open fields to the cooler heights of Maui called Upcountry. The drive up the foothills of Haleakala, a dormant volcano, takes you to **Makawao.** This *paniolo* (cowboy) town has avoided becoming a ghost town by becoming a kind of arts center. It's the scene of an unforgettable July 4 parade and rodeo.

Farther upcountry is **Kula,** a scenic community that clings to Haleakala's side at 3,000 feet, is known for its cool climate, its thriving flower farms (growing the strange South African flowers known as protea), its sweet onions, and '**Ulupalakua Ranch.** The 20,000-acre ranch, a nearly vertical spread where the volcano last erupted around 1790, raises cattle and elk and grows wine grapes.

Drop by the tasting room at **Tedeschi Vineyards** to sample the pineapple wine. Better yet, bring a picnic basket, pair it with a Maui vintage, and enjoy the afternoon in the cool uplands.

From Kula you can take the road up to **Haleakala National Park,** the island's greatest natural spectacle. According to Hawaiian legend, the demi-god Maui captured the sun with his magic lasso on Haleakala. He convinced the sun to slow down its travels, lengthening the days and giving his mother, Hina, more time to dry her tapa cloths.

Haleakala is one of only two places in the world—the Big Island is the other—where you may see the exotic silversword, an odd-looking plant with silvery leaves and tall spikes of yellow and violet florets from June through October.

## Hana

Taking a different route from Pa'ia starts you on the long drive to **Hana,** a three-hour trip, that crosses 56 one-lane bridges and takes 617 twists and turns (about 12 curves a mile). The rental car parade goes slowly so everyone can ogle Maui's natural beauty: crashing surf, steep green hills, waterfalls, and flowers.

Hana is a small community of about a thousand residents. The lifestyle here is slow and unpretentious. Highlights include the **Hana Cultural Center,** which retells area history, **Hana Coast Gallery, Hana Gardenland,** and **Hasegawa General Store.** A single resort hotel, Hotel Hana-Maui (now owned by the California folks who developed Big Sur's famed Post Ranch), a few condos, and B&Bs provide limited lodging.

Ten miles south of the town of Hana is **Kipahulu,** where Charles Lindbergh is buried in the back yard of a cliffside church. The famed American aviator—in 1927, he became the first person to fly solo across the Atlantic Ocean—first visited Kipahulu in the 1950s. "I love Maui so much, I would rather live one day in Maui than one month in New York," a cancer-stricken Lindbergh told his doctor. The "Lone Eagle" died on August 26, 1974 at age 72. Lindbergh's grave lies near **Palapala Ho'omau Congregational Church,** beneath *'ili'ili* stones and a block of Vermont granite.

## Big Island of Hawai'i

Youngest of the Hawaiian islands, the Big Island of Hawai'i, which lends its name to the entire archipelago, is by far the largest—twice the size of all other Hawaiian islands combined, with a grand total of 4,028 square miles. And of the 13 climatic regions on Earth, the Big Island has all but the two most extreme: Arctic and Saharan. Birthplace of Hawai'i's greatest king, Kamehameha I, the island is full of history, legend, and spirits.

The easiest way to plan your vacation itinerary here is to take a Big Island map and draw a vertical line right down the middle of the island. Locals refer to the left half of the island as the "Kona" side, and the right half is the "Hilo" side. Both sides are well worth a visit, necessitating a rental car.

### Kona Side

The hub of visitor activity is on the Kona side, particularly at the seaside village of **Kailua-Kona.** American humorist Mark Twain, who fell in love with the Hawaiian Islands during his visit in March 1866, once described Kailua-Kona as "the sleepiest, quietest, Sundayest-looking place you can imagine."

If Twain were alive today, perhaps he would put on his brightest aloha shirt and join the parade of people walking and driving along **Ali'i Drive.** His "Sundayest" place now is a Friday-night kind of place. Although a few landmarks from Twain's day remain, the town is now a busy jumble of hotels, condominiums, bars, restaurants, and shops.

Each August, Kailua-Kona hosts the **Hawaiian International Billfish Tournament,** a prestigious fishing event luring the world's top anglers. The largest fish caught during the event was a 1,166-pound marlin in 1993.

Five miles and 1,400 feet uphill from Kailua-Kona sits **Holualoa,** a village of coffee groves and artists' studios and galleries on the slopes of Hualalai.

South of Kailua-Kona and down the slope to the sea is mile-wide **Kealakekua Bay,** a state marine conservation district and favorite place to snorkel. A 27-foot white obelisk marks the spot of Captain Cook's death in 1779. The British sea captain and four of his men were killed in a skirmish with Hawaiians (4 Hawaiian chiefs and 13 commoners were also killed in the battle).

Farther south, 22 miles from Kailua-Kona, is **Pu'uhonua O Honaunau National Historical Park,** which in old Hawai'i was a sanctuary or place of refuge where anyone who violated *kapu* (religious taboo) could escape a death sentence, if he ran fast enough. The hapless could seek absolution and do penance, then be forgiven and allowed to return home safely.

Hawaiians of old strongly enforced their laws, believing that sins left unpunished would incur the wrath of their gods in the form of earthquakes, tidal waves, famines, and volcanic eruptions. They pursued violators relentlessly and killed them. Pu'uhonua O Honaunau is the best preserved of all Hawai'i's places of refuge. More than 400,000 visitors visit this 180-acre site each year. Each summer, the park hosts a cultural festival of Hawaiian arts and crafts, with *lau hala* weaving demonstrations, games, hula performances, and food.

Traveling all the way down the south coast is a full-day outing that ends at the southernmost part of the island, of any state in fact, **Ka Lae** (South Point).

### Kohala Coast

Go north from Kailua-Kona to find the sunny Kohala Coast and its luxury resorts, hiking trails, and gold-sand beaches. Historical points of interest are also prevalent here. The area has several ancient fishponds, where fish were raised for royalty. The fish would be wrapped in ti leaves and delivered by servants to their *ali'i* in Kailua-Kona. Parts of this "King's Trail" are still visible from the coast.

Inland from the Kohala Coast, in the foothills of Mauna Kea, is **Waimea** (also called Kamuela), the peaceful village where the *paniolo* (cowboy) lifestyle still thrives on rolling emerald hills and lush pastures that disappear in the often misty distance. This cool uplands is the home of the 225,000-acre **Parker Ranch,** one of the largest cattle ranches in the United States, and the site of a major rodeo held every July 4. The nearby **Parker Ranch Visitor Center and Museum** recites the history of the ranch as well as six generations of the Parker family.

North Kohala, the peninsula that forms the northernmost tip of the Big Island and ends in the village of Hawi, is the birthplace of Kamehameha I. His birthplace is near the giant **Mo'okini Luakini Heiau,** Hawai'i's first National Historic Landmark. The stones used for the construction of the *heiau* (temple) were supposedly passed hand to hand for nine miles from the coastline.

## Hamakua Coast

Heading east from Waimea, toward Hilo, is **Waipi'o Valley,** a deep gorge of 2,000-foot cliffs laced with waterfalls and carpeted with taro patches that run down to a black-sand beach. Once a thriving community and favorite retreat of Hawaiian royalty, the valley is accessible via a steep cliff, by shuttle tour, by four-wheel-drive vehicle, or on foot. It's easy going down, but a tough pull back up, so most take the shuttle.

**Hilo** is the island's county seat and largest town, with a population of 47,639. Yet it never outgrew its small-town feel. Most years, Hilo ranks as the wettest city in the United States, and the result is a profusion of tropical flowers, trees, and fruit. Orchids and anthuriums are everywhere.

Hilo was once the center of trade. The activity heightened with the arrival of Westerners, as Hilo Bay gave foreign vessels safe harbor. In August 1881, however, a lava flow from neighboring Mauna Loa cut a path straight toward Hilo, threatening to consume the growing town. On August 9, Princess Ruth Ke'elikolani—an imposing figure at six feet tall and 400-plus pounds—arrived from Honolulu and, standing at the edge of the lava flow, prayed and presented offerings of *'ohelo* berries, tobacco, flowers, red silk, and brandy to the goddess Pele. An observer later wrote: "Early the next morning, all of us went to the lava flow, and we couldn't believe our eyes. The flow had stopped right there."

Hilo was not as fortunate when it came to tidal waves. On April 1, 1946, the Hawaiian Islands were struck by devastating tidal waves, the result of an Alaskan earthquake. Hilo was the hardest hit, with nearly 100 deaths. In 1960, another tsunami struck Hilo, killing 61 residents.

When in Hilo, go downtown and walk around the restored historic buildings to find interesting shops and restaurants, and the twice-weekly Farmer's Market.

Other Hilo highlights include the 20-acre **Nani Mau Gardens,** the **Lyman Mission House and Museum,** and the new **Pacific Tsunami Museum,** which recalls the waves that almost wiped out Hilo.

It's nearly an hour's drive uphill from Hilo to **Volcano,** an Upcountry art community in a fern forest just outside **Volcanoes National Park,** the top visitor attraction in the state. Volcano viewing conditions depend on the weather and lava activity. Call (808) 985-6000 for recorded updates.

## Kaua'i

The northernmost major island and the oldest is also the most beautiful. Many believe that it was the first to be populated, rather than the Big Island. It is certainly the most independent, located as it is off on the remote end of the cluster of main islands, about 70 miles across the water from O'ahu. It's proven to be quite the movie star, serving as a setting for more than 50 films, including *South Pacific, Blue Hawaii, King Kong, Raiders of the Lost Ark,* and *Jurassic Park.*

The beauty runs deep. Kaua'i suffered and survived devastating damage from two major hurricanes in recent times, 'Iwa in 1982 and 'Iniki in 1992. But Kaua'i's 54,000 residents and abundant attributes have long since recovered.

### South Shore

You land in **Lihu'e,** a one-time plantation town with an airport surrounded by cane fields and sea on the southeastern part of the island. A drive along Rice Street takes you to the **Kaua'i Museum,** where the island's history is retold with artifacts, artworks, photographs, and other exhibit items. Also in Lihu'e is the island's major seaport, **Nawiliwili Harbor** and the **'Alekoko Fish Pond** (also known as the Menehune Fish Pond) further up the Hule'ia River. The Menehune, legendary elfin people, are credited with great feats of engineering overnight to create fishponds, roads, and temples. Just beyond Lihu'e are **Grove Farm Homestead,** a plantation-era home turned into a museum and, a few miles further, **Kilohana,** another plantation manor.

West just after the 520 turnoff toward Koloa and Po'ipu Beach Resort is Lawa'i, home of the **National Tropical Botanical Garden,** a 186-acre Eden that maintains the largest collection of tropical flora in the world.

### West Kaua'i

Farther leeward at the mouth of the Waimea River are the rocky remains of **Fort Elizabeth,** built in 1816 by Anton Schaeffer in an unsuccessful attempt to claim Kaua'i for the Russian crown.

In the town of **Waimea** stands a statue of Captain James Cook, who first set foot on Hawaiian soil at Waimea Bay on January 20, 1778.

Nearby is 3,567-foot **Waimea Canyon,** a 15-mile-long gorge with waterfalls, wild goats, and colorful striations that glow in fading light. Mark Twain dubbed it "the Grand Canyon of the Pacific." You can hike or ride horses in the canyon.

Just north of Waimea is the **Barking Sands Missile Range.** Check in at the gate and head to **Barking Sands Beach,** so named because of the "barking" sounds the sand makes as you hoof it on the beach. The beach is a safe distance from the still-active missile range.

Beyond lies 17-mile **Polihale Beach,** the longest beach in Hawaii, which ends on the island's northwest shore where Na Pali begins.

Driving uphill from Waimea, you'll come to **Koke'e State Park,** a favorite spot for camping and hiking, with 45 miles of trails into the **Alakai Swamp,** last stand of Kaua'i's endangered native birds. In old Hawai'i, Koke'e was revered as a sanctuary for the gods.

### Coconut Coast

The Wailua River and **Wailua State Park** mark an ancient historic area, with prominent heiau and birthing stones. High-ranking ancient women gave birth on such stones because they believed the children would grow up to be powerful chiefs. The baby's umbilical cord would be placed in a cloth and hidden in or under the navel stone (or *piko* stone), a practice continued very privately in some places today.

### North Shore

When you pass the busy town of Kapa'a , the crowds and buildings fall away and the road leads to the fabled North Shore. On the way, turn right at Kilauea and stop at the **Kilauea Point National Wildlife Refuge,** home to the largest seabird nesting areas and historic **Kilauea Lighthouse.** Spinner dolphins, humpback whales, sea turtles, monk seals, and albatross often can be seen here.

In another ten miles or so, you approach Princeville Resort on a high cliff marking one side of **Hanalei River Valley,** a green patchwork of taro ponds along the river surrounded by a bowl of mountains. It's worth stopping at the overlook. Then the road leads down to the valley floor, through Hanalei and on around the next mountain base, past seven one-lane bridges and several narrow valleys cut by streams. This is the scenery of your tropical dreams. Keep on until the road ends at the base of the magnificent **Na Pali Coast.** Na Pali ("the cliffs") is a dramatic 25-mile stretch of wind- and wave-worn precipices and hanging valleys cloaked in green. It is accessible only by foot on the ancient 11-mile Kalalau Trail, or by boat during summer months.

## Moloka'i

Moloka'i, was known as Moloka'i Pule O'o, or "Moloka'i of the Potent Prayers" in ancient times. It was an island of sorcerers, home to 1,381-foot high Mauna Loa on the west and 4,961-foot high Kamakou on the east. *Kahuna* (priests) there were so powerful that people believed they could "pray" someone to death—and their reputation spared Moloka'i from bloody battles waged by chiefs on other islands. Inhabitants of Moloka'i today use other powers to thwart development and lead a subsistence lifestyle enhanced by public assistance and a smattering of tourism.

You arrive at Ho'olehua Airport, the small, open-air lava rock terminal with rental cars and a lunch counter serving chili rice and Spam musubi. Which way you leave the airport depends on whether you like it hot and dry or lush and tropical. The 38-mile-long island divides at **Kaunakakai,** the funky main town, into two different climate zones, known locally as the West End and the East End. The West End looks like Mexico. The East End resembles Tahiti.

A sun-faded, three-block town with harbor and pier, Kaunakakai looks more like an old western movie than a tropical village. Moloka'i's chief settlement includes a bank, post office, drug and grocery store, medical center, and family-run businesses: Moloka'i Drive-Inn, Oviedo's Filipino Restaurant, and Kanemitsu Bakery, where 19 different types of bread are baked fresh daily. The brightest lights in town shine on **Mitchell Pau'ole Center,** site of softball games, "hulihuli" chicken roasts, and community events.

Above Kaunakakai, defunct **Kamakou Volcano,** the island's tallest mountain, is home to a virgin forest of native trees, including rare sandalwood. The Nature Conservancy runs the 2,774-acre **Kamakou Preserve,** home to native Hawaiian birds and 200 indigenous plants, which you can see on monthly tours given by the Nature Conservancy. Call (808) 553-5236 or fax (808) 553-9870. Or, e-mail, hike-molokai@popmailnc.org to take part in tours of this or other preserves on the island.

Most visitors head to the West End, where the **Moloka'i Ranch** dominates the red-dirt rolling hills covered by kiawe brush and cactus, above and below the road. The 53,00-acre spread is headquartered at **Maunaloa,** the restored plantation town where the ranch has branched into tourism with its Outfitters Center and stables—starting points for outdoor adventure. You can even learn traditional rodeo events like barrel racing. The ranch features the island's only upscale retreat, the 22-room Sheraton Moloka'i Lodge and Beach Village, an expensive lodge with fine dining and lots of ranchy ambience, as well as the 40-unit seaside Kaupoa Camp, an eco-tourism-oriented collection of tent cabins nestled by a beautiful, remote beach.

East of Kaunakakai, you'll find the top edge of the world's highest sea cliffs, which rise 3,250 feet from sea level and stretch 14 miles on the island's North Shore. On the way, you pass coffee plantations, the **Iron-wood Hills Golf Course,** and **Moloka'i Museum and Cultural Center** in a restored sugar mill.

For many years, most Moloka'i visitors stayed at Kaluako'i—the island's only resort area—but it closed last year and there was no word at press time about when it may reopen.

Nearby, on a plateau of Mauna Loa, is **Ka'ana,** a hill setting where tradition holds Laka, the goddess of the hula, created the native Hawaiian dance. Moloka'i celebrates the birth of the hula at the annual Moloka'i Ka Hula Piko, held each May at **Papohaku Beach Park,** a shady seaside grove on the island's West End. The day-long festival features hula performances, Hawaiian music, food, and local arts and crafts.

As you head to the East End, the island becomes lush, green, and tropical. Fishponds like 54-acre Keawanui Pond line the shore for 20 miles. Take a swim at **Waialua Beach at Mile Marker 19,** one of the island's best beaches, or **Mile Marker 20 Beach** for snorkeling.

At the **Mapulehu Mango Grove,** where 2,000 mango trees flourish by the sea, you can hitch a ride on the Moloka'i Horse and Wagon Ride to one of the spookiest places in Hawaii: **'Ili'ili'opae Heiau,** a school of sacrifice where kahuna taught final rites in the massive temple of doom that's three stories high and bigger than a football field. More than 700 years old, the heiau, legend has it, was built of car-sized boulders passed hand to hand from Moloka'i's opposite side in exchange for shrimp. (*'Ili'ili* means rock and *'opae* means shrimp in Hawaiian.)

On Kamehameha V Highway you'll discover affordable seaside condos, like Wavecrest Resort, and perfectly sited vacation rentals like Dunbar Beachfront Cottages and the Country Cottage at Pu'u O Hoku Ranch. The highway turns to hairpins on the very eastern end. After scenic vistas of pocket beaches, offshore islets, and dense jungles, it dead-ends at **Halawa Valley.**

Inundated by a tsunami in 1946, Halawa Valley, an ancient settlement, was abandoned. Now privately owned, the valley is closed, and the trail-head to 250-foot Moaula Falls is posted with no trespassing signs. Observe the kapu but enjoy **Halawa Beach County Park** and its black-sand beach with the island's only decent surf break.

People stricken with leprosy in 1860 were banished to **Kalaupapa Peninsula,** a lava shelf down below the famous sea cliffs. The victims were literally pushed from a boat into the waters off the peninsula and had to swim to shore. Father Damien de Veuster, a Belgian priest, arrived in 1873 and embraced the outcasts, cared for them, and sought medicine, food, shelter, and clothing for them. It was an exhausting labor of love, and Father Damien was mostly alone in his efforts. Any contributions by visiting doctors were left on a fencepost to avoid physical contact with patients. By the end of the 1870s, approximately 1,000 people had been exiled to Kalaupapa. On April 15, 1889, Damien himself died of leprosy at age 49. Some 60 patients, their disease controlled by modern medicine, still live at the settlement and serve as tour guides.

## Lana'i

Long ago Hawaiians believed Lana'i was haunted by spirits so wily and vicious that no human who went there could survive. Today, nearly everyone who goes there not only gets a good night's sleep but leaves reluctantly. Spirits still haunt the island, but they are thought to be benign.

In 1904, American businessman Charles Gay began purchasing various parcels on Lana'i; four years later he owned the entire island. Gay sold it in 1922 to James Dole, who quickly turned his $1.1 million investment into the pineapple capital of the world. For the next six decades, pineapple was king on Lana'i. Lana'i survives now by cultivating a few privileged visitors seeking peaceful surroundings, luxurious hotels, outstanding golf, and one of the best dive spots in the Pacific. The sweet and juicy pineapple once covered more than 19,000 acres of the island's red-dirt **Palawai Basin;** all that remains is a relic field so visitors can see what pineapple looks like.

In 1987, California tycoon David Murdock bought a controlling interest in Castle & Cooke, owners of Dole, and found that the deed to 98% of Lana'i came with the deal, along with plans for hotel development. He envisioned an island resort like no other, and in the early 1990s, the Lodge at Ko'ele and the Manele Bay Hotel opened. Visitors content with less palatial properties might enjoy the venerable 1920s-era Hotel Lanai, a 10-room highland lodge with a popular restaurant, Henry Clay's Rotisserie, a New Orleans–inspired Creole bistro many think is the island's best.

Golf is the sport of choice on Lana'i, at two 18-hole championship courses: **The Experience at Ko'ele,** designed by golf superstar Greg Norman and architect Ted Robinson, and **Challenge at Manele,** designed by Jack Nicklaus.

The chief landmark is 3,366-foot **Lana'ihale,** the highest point on the island.

A drive up **Munro Trail** to the summit on a clear day will afford a view of Maui, Moloka'i, Kaho'olawe, and the Big Island. Historians believe Lana'ihale served as a strategic vantage point so that chiefs could keep an eye on canoe traffic in the sea lanes.

Lana'i is regarded as a five-star locale among divers. *Skin Diver Magazine* rated **Cathedrals,** two large underwater caves near Hulopo'e Bay, as Hawai'i's top diving spot. On the opposite end of the island is **Shipwreck Beach,** where the rusted remains of the *Helena Pt. Townsend,* a World War II liberty ship, are still stuck on the reef.

The most significant historic site is **Kaunolu,** where once there was the summer retreat for King Kamehameha I, who tried his hand at fishing with the blessing of Kunihi, a three-foot stone fish god, filled with *mana* (power). The idol is believed to still exist somewhere on Lana'i. If you spot it, think twice before touching it. The last person to touch the idol is said to have died as a result.

## Ni'ihau: The "Forbidden" Island

You can not go easily to Ni'ihau, Hawai'i's other privately owned island, because ranch owners want to preserve the old ways in this last Hawaiian enclave where about 150–200 residents still speak Hawaiian and pay little heed to the world beyond.

Long off-limits to visitors without an invitation, the forbidden island can sometimes be seen by travelers like us whose curiosity gets the best of them. It takes written permission from the owners. You can go to beachcomb, fish, hunt wild pigs and goats, or just see a mostly raw island. You may not see any of the Hawaiians who live there. Interest in Ni'ihau, for most of us, began when we first read about this strange island bought for $10,000 in gold from a king more than 100 years ago and inhabited only by a "lost" tribe of 200 Hawaiians who are said to choose a pure and simple life over twenty-first-century trappings.

It all sounds wonderfully arcane, the stuff of Swiss Family Robinson: a 6- by 18-mile late-eighteenth-century island, 17 miles northwest of Kaua'i. It's actually owned now by a man named Robinson. Cattle ranching is Ni'ihau's primary business, along with helicopter tours, hunting safaris, and its precious shell jewelry.

To visit Ni'ihau, fax a written request to the Robinson family at (808) 338-1463 or sign up for a helicopter tour of its beaches.

## Kaho'olawe: The Target Island

From Maui or Lana'i, the island of Kaho'olawe appears forbidding and bleak, forgotten in time. Its huge red scars show where U.S. Navy pilots, who for nearly a half century practiced air-raid skills here, dropped tons of bombs.

The bombing was halted in 1990 by President George Bush, who was shocked to learn the U.S. Navy was still bombing one of the Hawaiian islands. The 45-square-mile island, about the size of San Francisco, was returned to native Hawaiians to become a cultural retreat someday, after the unexploded ordnance is all cleaned up. A $400 million Navy cleanup sweep then commenced.

Kahoʻolawe variously served in the past as penal colony in the monarchy period, as a cattle ranch during territorial days, and as the staging zone for World War II U.S. forces preparing for the invasion of Okinawa. In 1965, the U.S. Navy dropped a 500-ton TNT bomb on Kahoʻolawe to simulate an atomic explosion; the impact irreparably cracked a submarine water lens and turned the island's fresh water brackish.

## Tour Companies

Looking for more assistance in planning your Hawaiʻi trip? One option is to set up a tour through a local tour company. Each offers an extensive menu of sight-seeing excursions. The destination descriptions in this chapter and the profiles of specific attractions which follow allow you to determine what you most want to do with your time in Hawaiʻi. With that in mind, you can detemine if a guided tour suits your agenda. Tours operate according to set itineraries, so flexibility is clearly limited, however, they can also provide a very efficient day of sightseeing. Day tours range in price from $20 to $75, with extras such as luʻaus and meals ratcheting up the price further. Interisland day and overnight tours are pricier, but may well appeal to travelers bent on seeing another island despite time or budgetary constraints. Here are a few suggestions among the dozens of tour firms available in the Aloha State.

### TOUR COMPANIES

**Oʻahu**
ʻE Noa Tours
(808) 591-2561; (800) 824-8804
www.enoa.com

**Kauaʻi**
Hawaiʻi Movie Tours
(808) 822-1192; (800) 628-8432
www.hawaiimovietour. com

**Oʻahu, Maui, Big Island, Kauaʻi**
Polynesian Adventure Tours
(808) 833-3000 (Oʻahu); (808) 877-

4242 (Maui); (808) 329-8008 (Big Island); (808) 246-0122 (Kauaʻi); (800) 622-3011 (toll-free)
www.polyad.com

**Oʻahu, Maui, Big Island, Kauaʻi**
Roberts Hawaiʻi
(808) 523-7750 (Oʻahu); (808) 871-6226 (Maui); (808) 245-9101 (Kauaʻi); (800) 767-7751 (toll-free)
www.roberts-hawaii.com

*Part Seven*

# Hawai'i's Attractions

Choosing which attractions to visit during your Hawaiian vacation is daunting. So much to see and do and so little time! Most of Hawai'i's top visitor attractions, from museums and gardens to historic sites, have a nominal fee, but many are free. Reference the maps in the introduction to locate the attractions.

The following profiles provide basic information on the attractions, such as location, hours of operation, and cost. Each also features a rating for five age groups and a brief description. Given on a five-star scale, the ratings don't a guarantee that a certain segment of visitors will love or hate the attraction, but they do provide a reliable evaluation of each groups' typical reaction. For example, some teenagers want to visit historical sights, but more want to go to the beach. Together, the information, ratings, and descriptions will help you plan an itinerary pleasing to all members of your family or group.

## HAWAII ATTRACTIONS BY ISLAND

| Name | Type of Attraction | Rating | Zone |
|------|--------------------|--------|------|
| **O'ahu** | | | |
| Aloha Tower | Shopping/Restaurants | ★★★ | 2 |
| Bishop Museum | Museum | ★★★★½ | 2 |
| Byodo-In Temple | Temple/Gardens | ★★ | 3 |
| Contemporary Museum | Museum | ★★★ | 2 |
| Damien Museum | Museum | ★★½ | 1 |
| Dole Plantation | Historic Home/Gardens | ★★½ | 6 |
| Foster Botanical Garden | Gardens | ★★★ | 2 |
| Hawaiian Railway | Train Ride | ★★½ | 5 |
| Hawai'i Children's Discovery Center | Museum | ★★★★ | 2 |
| Hawai'i Maritime Center | Museum | ★★★ | 2 |
| Hawai'i's Plantation Village | Historic Home/Museum | ★★★ | 5 |

211

**HAWAII ATTRACTIONS BY ISLAND** (continued)

| Name | Type of Attraction | Rating | Zone |
|------|--------------------|--------|------|
| **O'ahu** (continued) | | | |
| Honolulu Academy of Arts | Museum | ★★★★ | 2 |
| Honolulu Zoo | Zoo | ★★★ | 1 |
| IMAX Waikiki | Theater | ★★★★ | 1 |
| Iolani Palace | Historic Home/Museum | ★★★★½ | 2 |
| Kualoa Ranch Activity Club and Secret Island | Outdoor Activities Complex | ★★★★ | 3 |
| Mission Houses Museum | Museum | ★★★ | 2 |
| National Memorial Cemetery of the Pacific | Historic Memorial | ★★★ | 2 |
| Pacific Aerospace Museum | Museum | ★★½ | 2 |
| Polynesian Cultural Center | Museum/Theater | ★★★★½ | 4 |
| Queen Emma Summer Palace | Historic Home | ★★★ | 2 |
| Royal Mausoleum | Historic Memorial | ★★½ | 2 |
| Sea Life Park | Aquarium | ★★★½ | 3 |
| Senator Fong's Plantation and Gardens | Historic Home/Gardens | ★★★ | 3 |
| Tropic Lightning Museum | Museum | ★★½ | 6 |
| U.S. Army Museum | Museum | ★★★½ | 1 |
| USS *Arizona* Memorial | Historic Memorial | ★★★★ | 6 |
| USS Battleship *Missouri* Memorial | Historic Memorial | ★★★★ | 6 |
| USS *Bowfin* Submarine Museum and Park | Museum | ★★★½ | 6 |
| Waikiki Aquarium | Aquarium | ★★★½ | 1 |
| **Maui** | | | |
| Alexander & Baldwin Sugar Museum | Museum | ★★★ | 7 |
| Bailey House Museum | Museum | ★★★ | 7 |
| Baldwin Home Museum | Museum | ★★★ | 9 |
| Brig Carthaginian | Museum | ★★★ | 9 |
| Haleakala National Park | National Park | ★★★★ | 10 |
| Hana Cultural Center | Museum | ★★★ | 10 |
| Hawai'i Experience Theater | Theater | ★★★½ | 9 |
| Hawai'i Nature Center | Museum | ★★★★ | 7 |
| Hui No'eau Visual Arts Center | Gallery | ★★★ | 10 |
| Kepaniwai Cultural Park | Gardens | ★★★ | 7 |
| Kula Botanical Garden | Gardens | ★★★ | 10 |
| Lahaina-Ka'anapali & Pacific Railroad | Hawaiian Railway | ★★★ | 9 |
| Maui Ocean Center | Aquarium | ★★★★ | 8 |
| Maui Tropical Plantation & Country Store | Historic Home/Gardens | ★★★ | 7 |
| Tedeschi Winery | Winery | ★★★ | 8 |

## HAWAII ATTRACTIONS BY ISLAND *(continued)*

| Name | Type of Attraction | Rating | Zone |
|------|-------------------|--------|------|
| **Maui** *(continued)* | | | |
| Whalers Village Museum | Museum | ★★½ | 9 |
| Wo Hing Temple Museum | Museum | ★★½ | 9 |
| **The Big Island** | | | |
| Ahu'ena Heiau | Temple | ★★½ | 11 |
| Akatsuka Orchid Gardens | Gardens | ★★★ | 12 |
| Amy B. H. Greenwell Ethnobotanical Garden | Gardens | ★★★ | 11 |
| Astronaut Ellison S. Onizuka Space Center | Museum | ★★★½ | 11 |
| Hawai'i Tropical Botanical Garden | Gardens | ★★★½ | 12 |
| Hawai'i Volcanoes National Park | National Park | ★★★★★ | 12 |
| Hulihe'e Palace | Historic Home/Museum | ★★★ | 11 |
| Kaloko-Honokohau National Historical Park | National Park | ★★★ | 11 |
| Kamuela Museum | Museum | ★★½ | 11 |
| Koke'e National History Museum | Museum | ★★★ | 13 |
| Lyman Mission House and Museum | Museum | ★★★ | 12 |
| Mauna Loa Macadamia Nut Visitor Center | Visitor Center/Gardens | ★★★½ | 12 |
| Nani Mau Gardens | Gardens | ★★ | 12 |
| Onizuka Center for Int'l Astronomy and Mauna Kea Observatory | Observatory | ★★★★½ | 12 |
| Pacific Tsunami Museum | Museum | ★★★ | 12 |
| Pana'ewa Rainforest Zoo | Zoo | ★★½ | 12 |
| Parker Ranch Visitor Center and Historic Homes | Visitor Center/ Historic Home | ★★★½ | 11 |
| Pu'uhonua O Honaunau National Historical Park | National Park | ★★★½ | 11 |
| Pu'ukohola Heiau | Temple | ★★★ | 11 |
| Sadie Seymour Botanical Gardens | Gardens | ★★★ | 11 |
| Suisan Fish Market and Auction | Market | ★★½ | 12 |
| Volcano Winery | Winery | ★★½ | 12 |
| Wakefield Botanical Gardens | Gardens | ★★½ | 11 |
| **Kaua'i** | | | |
| Grove Farm Homestead | Historic Home/Museum | ★★½ | 13 |
| Guava'i Kai Plantation | Historic Home/Gardens | ★★½ | 13 |
| Kaua'i Museum | Museum | ★★★½ | 13 |
| Kilauea Point National Wildlife Refuge | Wildlife Refuge | ★★½ | 13 |

## HAWAII ATTRACTIONS BY ISLAND *(continued)*

| Name | Type of Attraction | Rating | Zone |
|------|--------------------|--------|------|
| **Kaua'i** *(continued)* | | | |
| Kilohana Plantation | Historic Home/Gardens | ★★★ | 13 |
| Limahuli Garden | Gardens | ★★★★ | 13 |
| Moir Gardens | Gardens | ★★★ | 13 |
| National Tropical Botanical Gardens, Lawai and Allerton Gardens | Gardens | ★★½ | 13 |
| Wai'oli Mission House Museum | Museum | ★★½ | 13 |
| **Moloka'i** | | | |
| Moloka'i Museum and Cultural Center | Museum | ★★½ | 14 |
| Moloka'i Ranch | Outdoor Activities Complex | ★★★★★ | 14 |

## HAWAII ATTRACTIONS BY TYPE

| Name | Rating | Zone |
|------|--------|------|
| **Aquarium** | | |
| Maui Ocean Center | ★★★★ | 8 |
| Sea Life Park | ★★★½ | 3 |
| Waikiki Aquarium | ★★★½ | 1 |
| **Gallery** | | |
| Hui No'eau Visual Arts Center | ★★★ | 10 |
| **Gardens** | | |
| Akatsuka Orchid Gardens | ★★★ | 12 |
| Amy B. H. Greenwell Ethnobotanical Garden | ★★★ | 11 |
| Foster Botanical Garden | ★★★ | 2 |
| Hawai'i Tropical Botanical Garden | ★★★½ | 12 |
| Kepaniwai Cultural Park | ★★★ | 7 |
| Kula Botanical Garden | ★★★ | 10 |
| Limahuli Garden | ★★★★ | 13 |
| Moir Gardens | ★★★ | 13 |
| Nani Mau Gardens | ★★ | 12 |
| National Tropical Botanical Gardens Lawai and Allerton Gardens | ★★½ | 13 |
| Sadie Seymour Botanical Gardens | ★★★ | 11 |
| Wakefield Botanical Gardens | ★★½ | 11 |
| **Historic Home** | | |
| Queen Emma Summer Palace | ★★★ | 2 |

## HAWAII ATTRACTIONS BY TYPE *(continued)*

| Name | Rating | Zone |
|------|--------|------|
| **Historic Home/Gardens** | | |
| Dole Plantation | ★★½ | 6 |
| Guava Kai Plantation | ★★½ | 13 |
| Kilohana Plantation | ★★★ | 13 |
| Maui Tropical Plantation & Country Store | ★★★ | 7 |
| Senator Fong's Plantation and Gardens | ★★★ | 3 |
| **Historic Home/Museum** | | |
| Grove Farm Homestead | ★★½ | 13 |
| Hawai'i's Plantation Village | ★★★ | 5 |
| **Historic Home/Museum** *(continued)* | | |
| Hulihe'e Palace | ★★★ | 11 |
| Iolani Palace | ★★★★½ | 2 |
| **Historic Memorial** | | |
| National Memorial Cemetery of the Pacific | ★★★ | 2 |
| Royal Mausoleum | ★★½ | 2 |
| USS *Arizona* Memorial | ★★★★ | 6 |
| USS Battleship *Missouri* Memorial | ★★★★ | 6 |
| **Market** | | |
| Suisan Fish Market and Auction | ★★½ | 12 |
| **Museum** | | |
| Alexander & Baldwin Sugar Museum | ★★★ | 7 |
| Astronaut Ellison S. Onizuka Space Center | ★★★½ | 11 |
| Bailey House Museum | ★★★ | 7 |
| Baldwin Home Museum | ★★★ | 9 |
| Bishop Museum | ★★★★½ | 2 |
| Brig *Carthaginian* | ★★★ | 9 |
| Contemporary Museum | ★★★ | 2 |
| Damien Museum | ★★½ | 1 |
| Hana Cultural Center | ★★★ | 10 |
| Hawai'i Children's Discovery Center | ★★★★ | 2 |
| Hawai'i Maritime Center | ★★★ | 2 |
| Hawai'i Nature Center | ★★★★ | 7 |
| Honolulu Academy of Arts | ★★★★ | 2 |
| Kamuela Museum | ★★½ | 11 |
| Kaua'i Museum | ★★★½ | 13 |
| Koke'e National History Museum | ★★★ | 13 |
| Lyman Mission House and Museum | ★★★ | 12 |
| Mission Houses Museum | ★★★ | 2 |
| Moloka'i Museum and Cultural Center | ★★½ | 14 |
| Pacific Aerospace Museum | ★★½ | 2 |
| Pacific Tsunami Museum | ★★★ | 12 |
| Tropic Lightning Museum | ★★½ | 6 |
| U.S. Army Museum | ★★★½ | 1 |
| Hawai'i Volcanoes National Park | ★★★★★ | 12 |

## HAWAII ATTRACTIONS BY TYPE *(continued)*

| Name | Rating | Zone |
|------|--------|------|
| **Museum** (continued) | | |
| USS *Bowfin* Submarine Museum and Park | ★★★½ | 6 |
| Wai'oli Mission House Museum | ★★½ | 13 |
| Whalers Village Museum | ★★½ | 9 |
| Wo Hing Temple Museum | ★★½ | 9 |
| **Museum/Theater** | | |
| Polynesian Cultural Center | ★★★★½ | 4 |
| **National Park** | | |
| Haleakala National Park | ★★★★ | 10 |
| Kaloko-Honokohau National Historical Park | ★★★ | 11 |
| Pu'uhonua O Honaunau National Historical Park | ★★★½ | 11 |
| **Observatory** | | |
| Onizuka Center for Int'l Astronomy and Mauna Kea Observatory | ★★★★½ | 12 |
| **Outdoor Activities Complex** | | |
| Kualoa Ranch Activity Club and Secret Island | ★★★★ | 3 |
| Moloka'i Ranch | ★★★★★ | 14 |
| **Shopping/Restaurants** | | |
| Aloha Tower | ★★★ | 2 |
| **Temple** | | |
| Ahu'ena Heiau | ★★½ | 11 |
| Pu'ukohola Heiau | ★★★ | 11 |
| **Temple/Gardens** | | |
| Byodo-In Temple | ★★ | 3 |
| **Theater** | | |
| Hawai'i Experience Theater | ★★★½ | 9 |
| IMAX Waikiki | ★★★★ | 1 |
| **Train Ride** | | |
| Hawaiian Railway | ★★½ | 5 |
| Lahaina-Ka'anapali & Pacific Railroad | ★★★ | 9 |
| **Visitor Center/Gardens** | | |
| Mauna Loa Macadamia Nut Visitor Center | ★★★½ | 12 |
| **Visitor Center/Historic Home** | | |
| Parker Ranch Visitor Center and Historic Homes | ★★★½ | 11 |
| **Wildlife Refuge** | | |
| Kilauea Point National Wildlife Refuge | ★★½ | 13 |
| **Winery** | | |
| Tedeschi Winery | ★★★ | 8 |
| Volcano Winery | ★★½ | 12 |

---

### HAWAII ATTRACTIONS BY TYPE *(continued)*

| Name | Rating | Zone |
|------|--------|------|
| **Zoo** | | |
| Honolulu Zoo | ★★★ | 1 |
| Pana'ewa Rainforest Zoo | ★★½ | 12 |

---

## O'ahu

### *Aloha Tower*               *Zone 2 Waikiki*

**Location** Aloha Tower Marketplace, Pier 9 at Honolulu Harbor
**Phone** (808) 528-5700
**Website** www.alohatower.com/tower_index.htm
**Hours** Daily, 9 a.m.–sunset.
**Admission** Free
**When to Go** Any time
**How Much Time to Allow** 20 minutes
**Author's Rating** ★★★; Go to the top, look around, come down.
**Overall Appeal by Age Group**

| | | |
|---|---|---|
| Pre-school ★ | Grade School ★½ | Teens ★★★ |
| Young Adults ★★★ | Over 30 ★★★½ | Seniors ★★★½ |

**Description and Comments** Now dwarfed by high-rises in downtown Honolulu, Aloha Tower was once the tallest building in Hawai'i. The slender, square-shaped ten-story tower was erected in 1926 as a landmark welcoming passenger ships arriving at Honolulu Harbor. Now the centerpiece of the Aloha Tower Marketplace shopping/restaurant complex, the historic tower is perhaps the most recognized man-made structure in the islands, with its large clock with faces on each side, the huge letters A-L-O-H-A, and the 40-foot flagstaff. In 1997, the tower closed for two years, undergoing an extensive renovation (among the additions were handicapped-accessible restrooms, security cameras, and emergency exits). It reopened to visitors in April 1999. Take the elevator to the tenth floor and take in 360° views of Honolulu. You'll have sweeping views of the downtown area, Honolulu Harbor, and the leeward mountains.

**Touring Tips** Be sure to bring your camera or video camera.

**Other Things to Do Nearby** Aloha Tower Marketplace features shops, live entertainment, and restaurants. The tower is a short walk away from the Hawai'i Maritime Center.

### *Bishop Museum*              *Zone 2 Waikiki*

**Location** 1525 Bernice St.
**Phone** (808) 847-3511
**Website** www.bishopmuseum.org
**Hours** Daily (except Christmas), 9 a.m.–5 p.m.
**Admission** $14.95 for adults; $11.95 for children ages 4–12

**When to Go**  Any time
**How Much Time to Allow**  2½ hours
**Author's Rating**  ★★★★½; Don't miss the best natural history museum in Hawai'i and the Pacific.
**Overall Appeal by Age Group**

| | | |
|---|---|---|
| Pre-school ★★ | Grade School ★★★ | Teens ★★★½ |
| Young Adults ★★★★★ | Over 30 ★★★★★ | Seniors ★★★★★ |

**Description and Comments**  The Bernice Pauahi Bishop Museum boasts the world's largest collection of Hawaiian and Pacific artifacts. Literally thousands of cultural treasures are housed here, including ancient weaponry, feather cloaks, clothing, jewelry, koa bowls, photographs, illustrations, and even a re-created Hawaiian grass *hale* (house). At the entrance to the museum, you'll see the gift shop to the left (be sure to pay a visit before you leave, as the shop carries an impressive line of Hawaiian books, artwork, crafts, and souvenirs) and a small exhibit on Hawai'i's political and natural histories to your right. From the ticket office, proceed to Hawaiian Hall, the distinguished stone building that houses the bulk of the Hawaiian artifacts. Take your time and read the descriptions of each display—the galleries here provide probably the most powerful and effective way of discovering Hawai'i's rich past. The adjacent Castle Building houses visiting interactive exhibits. The planetarium educates visitors on how ancient Polynesian voyagers used the stars to navigate their arduous journeys throughout the Pacific.

Also, sports fan should take note that one of the newer attractions at the museum is the Hawai'i Sports Hall of Fame, located in the Paki Building. This insightful gallery pays tribute to Hawai'i's most storied athletes, coaches, promoters, and other contributors to local sports. Among them are famed surfer/swimmer Duke Kahanamoku, Alexander J. Cartwright (the father of baseball lived in Hawai'i for much of his life), sumo pioneer Jesse Kuhaulua, and legendary women's surfer Rell Sunn. Lei making and craft demonstrations at the museum are held regularly.

**Touring Tips**  Guided tours of the museum's Hawaiian Hall are scheduled daily at 10 a.m. and noon. Also, a garden tour is held at 12:30 p.m. The Journey by Starlight program at the planetarium is conducted daily at 11:30 a.m.

## Byodo-In Temple                    *Zone 3 Windward O'ahu*

**Location**  Valley of the Temples Memorial Park, 47-200 Kahekili Hwy.
**Phone**  (808) 239-8811
**Hours**  Daily, 8 a.m.–5 p.m.
**Admission**  $2 for adults; $1 for senior citizens and children ages 6–12
**When to Go**  Any time
**How Much Time to Allow**  45 minutes
**Author's Rating**  ★★; A peaceful spot to visit.
**Overall Appeal by Age Group**

| | | |
|---|---|---|
| Pre-school ★★ | Grade School ★★ | Teens ★★ |
| Young Adults ★★ | Over 30 ★★★ | Seniors ★★★½ |

**Description and Comments**  Nestled at the foot of the scenic Ko'olau Mountains, the Byodo-In Temple is a replica of the famous 900-year-old temple in Japan. A stroll of the temple grounds leads you to an immaculate Oriental garden, a colorful carp pool, a nine-foot Buddha statue, and a stately teahouse. Peacocks, swans, ducks, and shimmering waterfalls add to the scenery.

## Contemporary Museum                                   *Zone 2 Waikiki*

**Location**  2411 Makiki Heights Dr.
**Phone**  (808) 526-1322
**Website**  www.tcmhi.org
**Hours**  Tuesday–Saturday, 10 a.m.–4 p.m.; Sunday, noon–4 p.m.
**Admission**  $5 for adults; $3 for students and senior citizens; free for children under age 12
**When to Go**  The museum provides free admission to all comers on the 3rd Saturday of each month
**How Much Time to Allow**  75 minutes
**Author's Rating**  ★★★; If you love modern art, you'll enjoy this.
**Overall Appeal by Age Group**

| Pre-school ★★ | Grade School ★★½ | Teens ★★★½ |
| Young Adults ★★★½ | Over 30 ★★★½ | Seniors ★★★½ |

**Description and Comments**  Originally built in 1925 as a residence of a wealthy socialite, the Contemporary Museum opened its doors in 1988 as a modern art collection. The small museum features 1,300 works, dating from 1940 to the present, on rotating exhibits. A special highlight is a permanent walk-in multimedia exhibit by David Hockney, inspired by Maurice Ravel's opera *L'Enfant et les Sortiliges*. Works by local artists are also on display.

You'll probably spend as much time outside the museum as you will inside: The museum's 3.5-acre garden is dotted by a variety of bronze, ceramic, stainless steel, copper, and aluminum sculptures. The garden was originally created in the 1930s by a Honolulu reverend with a passion for landscape design, and it remains a blissful retreat. The Contemporary Cafe is a favorite spot for lunch, and shoppers will want to visit the museum's gift boutique.

**Other Things to Do Nearby**  Continue your drive up Mount Tantalus to see sweeping views of Honolulu.

## Damien Museum                                     *Zone 1 Greater Honolulu*

**Location**  130 'Ohua Ave.
**Phone**  (808) 923-2690
**Hours**  Monday–Friday, 9 a.m.–3 p.m.
**Admission**  Free
**When to Go**  Any time
**How Much Time to Allow**  30 minutes
**Author's Rating**  ★★½; Make a pilgrimage to this Damien shrine before you go to Moloka'i and Kalaupapa.
**Overall Appeal by Age Group**

| Pre-school ★ | Grade School ★ | Teens ★★½ |
| Young Adults ★★★ | Over 30 ★★★ | Seniors ★★★ |

**Description and Comments**   This mini-museum houses several artifacts belonging to Father Damien de Veuster (1840–1889), the Belgian priest who dedicated his life to caring for patients stricken with Hansen's disease (leprosy) at Kalaupapa settlement on Moloka'i. Among the displays here are some of Father Damien's possessions, including books, work tools, candlesticks, and personal letters. A 20-minute video highlights the minister's life and reflects on this sad chapter in Hawaiian history.

**Other Things to Do Nearby**   The Honolulu Zoo and Kapi'olani Park are a block away, and Waikiki Beach beckons just across Kalakaua Avenue, Waikiki's main thoroughfare.

## *Dole Plantation*                                    *Zone 6 Central O'ahu*

**Location**  64-1550 Kamehameha Hwy.
**Phone**  (808) 621-8408
**Hours**  Daily, 9 a.m.–5:30 p.m.
**Admission**  $5 for adults; $3.50 for military personnel; $3 for children ages 4–12
**When to Go**  Any time
**How Much Time to Allow**  90 minutes
**Author's Rating**  ★★½; The maze is more popular than the pineapple.
**Overall Appeal by Age Group**

| | | |
|---|---|---|
| Pre-school ★½ | Grade School ★★★★ | Teens ★★★★ |
| Young Adults ★★★ | Over 30 ★★★ | Seniors ★★★ |

**Description and Comments**   Situated just outside the town of Wahiawa, the Dole Plantation features outdoor displays of Hawai'i's pineapple history as well as the life of the plantation founder, Jim Dole. Sample some pineapple juice and stroll through the Pineapple Garden, which features 21 different varieties of the prickly fruit. Since its debut in 1998, the biggest attraction here (and the one the children most want to see) is the Pineapple Garden Maze, which covers nearly 2 acres and has a path length of 1.7 miles. The maze was built from 11,400 Hawaiian plants, including varieties of the official state flower, the hibiscus. The maze was recognized in 1998 by the *Guinness Book of World Records* as the world's largest maze.

## *Foster Botanical Garden*                                    *Zone 2 Waikiki*

**Location**  50 N. Vineyard Blvd.
**Phone**  (808) 522-7066
**Hours**  Daily, 9 a.m.–4 p.m.
**Admission**  $5 for adults; $1 for children ages 6–12
**When to Go**  In the morning, when it's coolest
**How Much Time to Allow**  1 hour
**Author's Rating**  ★★★; A thoroughly pleasant outing.
**Overall Appeal by Age Group**

| | | |
|---|---|---|
| Pre-school ★★ | Grade School ★★½ | Teens ★★★ |
| Young Adults ★★★ | Over 30 ★★★½ | Seniors ★★★½ |

**Description and Comments**   One of O'ahu's best-kept secrets, right on the edge of downtown Honolulu, is a beautiful 14-acre oasis. Foster Botanical Garden boasts one of the nation's largest collections of tropical plants (about 10,000 species), including many rare and endangered species. Among the highlights are an exquisite orchid garden, several rare and endangered trees (some of which are extinct in the wild), a herb garden, and an "economic" garden, which displays plants that are used for food, fabrics, dyes, and medicine. Foster Botanical Garden was placed on the Hawai'i Register of Historic Places in 1988 and was the setting for several Hollywood films and TV shows. It is the best known of Honolulu's five municipal botanical gardens.

**Touring Tips**   Guided tours are available weekdays at 1 p.m. Call for reservations.

## Hawai'i Children's Discovery Center          Zone 2 Waikiki

**Location**  111 'Ohe St.
**Phone**  (808) 524-5437
**Hours**  Tuesday–Friday, 9 a.m.–1 p.m.; Saturday and Sunday, 10 a.m.–3 p.m.
**Admission**  $8 for adults; $6.75 for children ages 2–17. No strollers permitted in the exhibit area
**When to Go**  Any time
**How Much Time to Allow**  2 hours
**Author's Rating**  ★★★★; Excellent children's museum; the kids will love it.
**Overall Appeal by Age Group**

| | | |
|---|---|---|
| Pre-school ★★★★ | Grade School ★★★★★ | Teens ★★★★ |
| Young Adults ★★★½ | Over 30 ★★★ | Seniors ★★★ |

**Description and Comments**   Originally opened in 1989 as the Hawai'i Children's Museum at Dole Cannery, the $10 million Children's Discovery Center reopened in 1998 at a larger, 37,000-square-foot location. Four separate galleries—Fantastic You, Our Town, Hawaiian Rainbows, and Your Rainbow World—are featured on three floors, each with a variety of hands-on, interactive galleries designed for children. Our favorites were Fantastic You, which helps children understand their bodies and organs, and Our Town, which features a working television station that lets children take on roles as news anchors and camera technicians. A gift shop sells a variety of educational toys, games, and books. The center stresses fun as much as education. The president of the center once explained its mission this way: "The museum isn't really to educate children. Instead, it's to motivate them, stimulate them, to arouse their curiosity about things, and to give them an excitement and joy about learning."

**Other Things to Do Nearby**   Kaka'ako Waterfront Park, directly across the street, provides a great picnic setting.

## Hawai'i Maritime Center          Zone 2 Waikiki

**Location**  Pier 7, Honolulu Harbor
**Phone**  (808) 536-6373
**Website**  http://holoholo.org/maritime
**Hours**  Daily, 8:30 a.m.–5 p.m.
**Admission**  $7.50 for adults; $4.50 for children ages 6–17
**When to Go**  Any time
**How Much Time to Allow**  75 minutes

**Author's Rating** ★★★; If you love ocean history and messing around with boats, see this shipshape museum.

**Overall Appeal by Age Group**

| | | |
|---|---|---|
| Pre-school ★★ | Grade School ★★★ | Teens ★★★ |
| Young Adults ★★★½ | Over 30 ★★★½ | Seniors ★★★½ |

**Description and Comments**  Hawai'i's colorful ocean history is the story line, from ancient Polynesian voyagers and rowdy whalers to the legendary Waikiki beach boys and the luxury liners of the 1920s and 1930s. Take an audio tour and browse through 50 displays, including a skeleton of a humpback whale (one of only two such displays in the world). Two major attractions here are the *Falls of Clyde* (built in 1817) and the well-traveled Polynesian voyaging canoe *Hokule'a*. You can board the *Falls of Clyde*, which is the last four-masted, full-rigged ship in the world and is a National Historic Landmark. The *Hokule'a* is a double-hulled sailing canoe in which modern Hawaiians retraced the voyages of ancient Polynesians in the 1970s and 1980s using only the stars and ocean currents to guide them.

**Other Things to Do Nearby**  The Aloha Tower Marketplace is next door.

## *Hawai'i's Plantation Village*                *Zone 4 The North Shore*

**Location**  94-695 Waipahu St.
**Phone**  (808) 677-0110
**Website**  http://openstudio.hawaii.edu/hpv/main.html
**Hours**  Monday–Friday, 9 a.m.–3 p.m.; Saturday, 10 a.m.–3 p.m. (guided tours begin at the top of every hour)
**Admission**  $7 for adults; $5 for military personnel; $4 for senior citizens; $3 for children ages 5–12
**When to Go**  Any time
**How Much Time to Allow**  90 minutes
**Author's Rating**  ★★★; Best place to learn about Hawai'i's plantation history.
**Overall Appeal by Age Group**

| | | |
|---|---|---|
| Pre-school ★ | Grade School ★★ | Teens ★★½ |
| Young Adults ★★★ | Over 30 ★★★ | Seniors ★★★ |

**Description and Comments**  Located in the former plantation town of Waipahu, this outdoor museum pays tribute to Hawai'i's plantation era. Included are artifacts, household items, photos, and documents representing the cultures and lifestyles of eight different ethnic groups that labored on the sugar plantations: Japanese, Chinese, Okinawans, Filipinos, Koreans, Puerto Ricans, Portuguese, and Hawaiians. Nearly 30 replicated dwellings dot the village's three acres, including a Chinese cookhouse, a plantation store, and a community bath. The different types of architecture illustrate the cultural differences of those workers and how they had to figure out how to get along while living together so closely. The park also features a display of medicinal plants.

## *Hawaiian Railway*                        *Zone 5 Leeward O'ahu*

**Location**  91-1001 Renton Rd.
**Phone**  (808) 681-5461

**Hours**  Sundays only, 12:30 and 2:30 p.m. (charter groups may schedule weekday rides)
**Admission**  $8 for adults; $5 for senior citizens and children ages 2–12
**When to Go**  Any time
**How Much Time to Allow**  2 hours
**Author's Rating**  ★★½; For train buffs.
**Overall Appeal by Age Group**

Pre-school ★★             Grade School ★★★          Teens ★★★
Young Adults ★★★          Over 30 ★★★               Seniors ★★★

**Description and Comments**  In the heyday of Hawai'i's plantation era, more than 40 sugar plantations utilized private railway systems to transport their crops. (Trains ran on every populated island except Ni'ihau.) Today, the Hawaiian Railway Society strives to preserve what's left of Hawai'i's railroad history with this 6.5-mile stretch of track. A trio of vintage diesel locomotives has been restored as well. The 90-minute ride begins at the 'Ewa station and travels at a leisurely pace of 15 miles per hour. Trained narrators tell of Hawai'i's railway history, explain how the trains were used by plantations, and point out sites along the way. The end of the line, literally, is scenic Kahe Point, and passengers can spend a few minutes enjoying views of the Pacific Ocean. Back at the 'Ewa station, you can browse the train yard, enjoy a picnic lunch, and visit the gift shop.

## Honolulu Academy of Arts                     Zone 2 Waikiki

**Location**  900 S. Beretania St.
**Phone**  (808) 532-8701
**Website**  www.honoluluacademy.org
**Hours**  Tuesday–Saturday, 10 a.m.–4:30 p.m.; Sunday, 1–5 p.m.
**Admission**  $7 for adults; $4 for students, senior citizens, and military personnel; free for children age 12 and under
**When to Go**  Any time
**How Much Time to Allow**  90 minutes
**Author's Rating**  ★★★★; The biggest and best Hawai'i art museum.
**Overall Appeal by Age Group**

Pre-school ★½            Grade School ★★½           Teens ★★★
Young Adults ★★★½        Over 30 ★★★★              Seniors ★★★★

**Description and Comments**  Founded by Anna Rice Cooke, Hawaiian-born daughter of New England missionaries, the Honolulu Academy of Arts opened in 1927 with 4,500 donated works of art. That number has grown to more than 34,000 pieces, ranging from paintings and textiles to sculptures and prints. The academy's collection is split evenly between Western and Asian art. The Western art collection includes Roman, Greek, and Egyptian works that date as far back as the third millennium BC to American and European works of the 1990s. The academy's collection of Asian works is among the most highly regarded in the country and includes paintings, sculptures, ceramics, lacquerware, and prints. Of special note is the sizable collection—more than 8,000 works in all—of Japanese wood block prints, most of which were donated by the famous American novelist James Michener. The collection represents the wood block printmaking masters of Japan in the 18th and 19th centuries. Also, the academy's collection of Chinese works includes more than 100 paintings, some of which date back to the Ming dynasty.

**Touring Tips** Guided tours are scheduled at 11 a.m. Tuesday–Saturday and 1:15 p.m. on Sunday. The museum is fairly large, and the tour will likely make your visit here more enjoyable.

**Other Things to Do Nearby** The Pavilion Cafe is Honolulu's newest (some say best) place for lunch. Across the street is Thomas Square Park, a leafy green space that often hosts local arts and craft fairs.

## Honolulu Zoo                                  *Zone 1 Greater Honolulu*

**Location** Kapi'olani Park; the entrance is on the makai side of the zoo
**Phone** (808) 971-7171
**Website** www.honoluluzoo.org
**Hours** Daily, 9 a.m.–4:30 p.m. (Special "Moonlight Walks" are offered from 6:30 to 8:30 p.m. once a month, before the full moon.)
**Admission** $6 for visitors age 13 and over; $1 for children ages 6–12; free for children under age 6
**When to Go** Any time
**How Much Time to Allow** 2 hours
**Author's Rating** ★★★; A zoo is a zoo, but why not if you've had enough sun?
**Overall Appeal by Age Group**

| Pre-school ★★★ | Grade School ★★★★ | Teens ★★★½ |
| Young Adults ★★★½ | Over 30 ★★★ | Seniors ★★★★ |

**Description and Comments** Set on 42 acres at Kapi'olani Park, the Honolulu Zoo is the largest zoo in the state—and the largest within a 2,300-mile radius. It is also big on history: The land for the zoo was donated in 1876 by King Kalakaua, Hawai'i's "Merrie Monarch." The zoo began exhibiting animals in 1914; A monkey, a bear, and a few lion cubs were among the first furry occupants. Today, the roster of wildlife has expanded to include more than 120 different species divided into four separate exhibits. The African savanna includes lions, hippos, gazelles, rhinoceros, giraffes, zebras, cheetahs, chimpanzees, crocodiles, warthogs, hyenas, flamingos, tortoises, pelicans, and more. The tropical rainforest features tigers, monkeys, sun bears, gibbons, alligators, black swans, Amazon parrots, king vultures, toucans, Burmese pythons, iguanas, and the zoo's biggest (literally) attractions: Mari and Vaigai, a pair of Indian elephants. A popular spot for the kids is the Children's Zoo, with a variety of donkeys, sheep, llamas, pot-bellied pigs, and common farm animals. The Islands of the Pacific exhibit spotlights a few indigenous bird and reptile species. The zoo has several spots for picnicking, and food stands and strollers are available. Also, the Zootique gift shop carries an impressive selection of wildlife-related merchandise that stresses education as well as fun.

**Touring Tips** The zoo holds moonlit tours each month from 6:30 to 8:30 p.m. These evening programs reveal some of the nocturnal habits of the zoo's residents and include some fascinating folk tales. Admission is $10 for adults and $7 for children under age 12 (not recommended for children under age 5). Purchase tickets in advance at the zoo's front desk.

**Other Things to Do Nearby** The zoo is located at Kapi'olani Park, a great place for picnicking. The Waikiki Aquarium is within easy walking distance, as is Waikiki Beach.

## IMAX Waikiki                         *Zone 1 Greater Honolulu*

**Location** 325 Seaside Ave.
**Phone** (808) 923-4629
**Website** www.imaxwaikiki.com
**Hours** Daily, 11:30 a.m.–9:30 p.m.
**Admission** $9.75 for adults, $8 for children ages 3–11
**When to Go** Any time
**How Much Time to Allow** 50 minutes
**Author's Rating** ★★★★; Simply good visual fun.

| | | |
|---|---|---|
| Pre-school ★★½ | Grade School ★★★★ | Teens ★★★★ |
| Young Adults ★★★★ | Over 30 ★★★★ | Seniors ★★★★ |

**Description and Comments** IMAX has a six-story $2 million theater with new screen and projector equipment capable of showing 3D films. A mix of 2D and 3D movies is shown daily. The 3D presentations require state-of-the-art, heavy-duty eyeglasses that are handed out before the show (unlike the light paper glasses with cellophane lenses that were used in the past, you can't take these glasses home). Altogether, this is a memorable visual and audio experience.

**Other Things to Do Nearby** Shopping opportunities abound at the nearby Royal Hawaiian Shopping Center and International Market Place.

## 'Iolani Palace                              *Zone 2 Waikiki*

**Location** King St. and Richards St.
**Phone** (808) 522-0832
**Website** www.iolanipalace.org
**Hours** Tuesday–Saturday, 9 a.m.–2:15 p.m.
**Admission** $15 for adults; $5 for children ages 5–12 (Children under age 5 are not allowed into the palace. Reservations are required.)
**When to Go** Any time
**How Much Time to Allow** 1 hour
**Author's Rating** ★★★★½; The only palace in America is the last vestige of the Monarchy Period and one of Hawai'i's architectural treasures.
**Overall Appeal by Age Group**

| | | |
|---|---|---|
| Pre-school — | Grade School ★★½ | Teens ★★★½ |
| Young Adults ★★★★½ | Over 30 ★★★★½ | Seniors ★★★★½ |

**Description and Comments** Built in 1882, 'Iolani Palace—the only royal palace standing on American soil—served as the royal residence of Hawai'i's last two monarchs, King Kalakaua and Queen Lili'uokalani. In its heyday, the palace was the scene of spectacular galas and events, including the fun-loving Kalakaua's extravagant 50th birthday jubilee. Sadly, it was also the site of political chaos, which led to the downfall of the kingdom in the late 1890s at the hands of American sugar planters. From then until 1969, when the State Capitol building was completed, the palace served as the capitol of the republic, territory, and finally state of Hawai'i. The palace was restored to museum-quality condition, and restoration efforts continue.

Now operated by the nonprofit Friends of 'Iolani Palace, this remarkable building is open five days a week for docent-guided public tours. The inside is striking, with a large koa wood staircase serving as a magnificent centerpiece. The Throne Room, adorned in maroon and gold, was the setting for royal audiences, receptions, and events of state. The Blue Room was the site of more informal gatherings and parties; the Dining Room is beautifully appointed with portraits of various world leaders of the past. The second floor includes the King's Suite, the Queen's Room, two guest rooms, and the Music Room.

A royal uproar of more recent vintage occurred in the summer of 1998, when the president of Friends of 'Iolani Palace actually sat on one of the palace's thrones for a photo session with a *Life* magazine photographer. Her faux pas caused some damage to the fabric. Bishop Museum officials later said that the throne's silk material was in such a deteriorated condition that any touch would have caused damage. The damage was repaired, but the president—a great-grandniece of King Kalakaua—was forced to resign.

**Touring Tips**   Guided tours are scheduled at 15-minute intervals, each lasting about 45 minutes. Pick up your tickets at 'Iolani Barracks, located on the palace grounds. The palace is wheelchair-accessible; call ahead about other special requirements.

**Other Things to Do Nearby**   The Mission Houses Museum, Kamehameha Statue, Hawai'i State Archives, Hawai'i State Library, and the State Capitol are all within easy walking distance from the palace.

## *Kualoa Ranch Activity Club and Secret Island*                 *Zone 3 Windward O'ahu*

**Location**  49-560 Kamehameha Hwy.
**Phone**  (808) 237-7321
**Website**  www.kualoa.com
**Hours**  Daily, 9 a.m.–5 p.m.
**Admission**  Rates for individual activities range from $18–$35
**When to Go**  Any time
**How Much Time to Allow**  2–6 hours
**Author's Rating** ★★★★; Offers myriad activities, with something for every age group, outdoors in one of the islands' most beautiful settings.
**Overall Appeal by Age Group**

| | | |
|---|---|---|
| Pre-school ★★½ | Grade School ★★★ | Teens ★★★★ |
| Young Adults ★★★★★ | Over 30 ★★★★ | Seniors ★★★ |

**Description and Comments**   One of O'ahu's best attractions, this 4,000-acre working cattle ranch offers more than 15 active outdoor activities. You could spend an entire day here enjoying one or more of the following: horseback riding, hiking, all-terrain vehicles, snorkel tours, jet-skis, target shooting, canoeing, volleyball, helicopter rides, tennis, a petting zoo, garden tour, badminton, kayak rides, and a ride around the ranch that includes a narrated ranch and movie set tour. Kualoa Ranch was the setting for several major Hollywood films, including *Windtalkers, Jurassic Park, Mighty Joe Young,* and *Godzilla.* In addition to its scenic mountainside headquarters and broad coastal valley, it includes an ancient fishpond, plant nursery, and aquaculture ponds. Our favorite activity here? Relaxing at Secret Island, a remote beach where you can nap in a hammock, play volleyball, go snorkeling, play table tennis, and more.

**Touring Tips**   Numerous tour packages are available, most including a buffet lunch and transportation to and from your hotel. You can also go directly to the ranch and sign up for whatever activities interest you.

## Mission Houses Museum          Zone 2 Greater Honolulu

**Location**  553 S. King St.
**Phone**  (808) 531-0481
**Website**  http://www.lava.net/~mhm
**Hours**  Tuesday–Saturday, 9 a.m.–4 p.m.
**Admission**  $10 for adults; $8 for senior citizens and military personnel; $6 for youths ages 13–18; $4 for children ages 4–12
**When to Go**  Any time
**How Much Time to Allow**  1 hour
**Author's Rating**  ★★★; A good bet for history buffs, but boring for kids.
**Overall Appeal by Age Group**
  Pre-school ★          Grade School ★½          Teens ★★
  Young Adults ★★★          Over 30 ★★★          Seniors ★★★

**Description and Comments**   This is where the first American Protestant missionaries established their headquarters in 1820. Built between 1821 and 1841, these structures—the oldest surviving Western-style buildings in all of Hawai'i—house such original artifacts as furniture, books, quilts, and other household items belonging to missionary families. Visit the white Frame House, which served as home to several of Hawai'i's most prominent missionaries; the Chamberlain House, which was used as a storehouse and separate home; and the Coral House, where the first-ever printing in the Pacific was done. (The first printed sheet was produced on January 7, 1922; Chief Ke'eaumoku had the honor of pulling the lever of a creaky wooden press. Through this printing press the missionaries brought literacy to the Hawaiian nation.) The missionaries also introduced the art of New England quilting to Hawaiian women, and this museum has a sizable collection of some early Hawaiian quilts.

**Touring Tips**   Guided tours are scheduled at 9:30, 10:30, and 11:30 a.m. and 1, 2, and 3 p.m.

**Other Things to Do Nearby**   The museum sits next to historic Kawaiaha'o Church and is near of the Hawai'i State Library, 'Iolani Palace, the State Capitol, the Kamehameha Statue, and State Archives.

## National Memorial Cemetery
## of the Pacific          Zone 2 Greater Honolulu

**Location**  2177 Pu'owaina Dr.
**Phone**  (808) 566-1430
**Hours**  Daily: March 2–September 29, 8 a.m.–6:30 p.m.; September 30–March 1, 8 a.m.–5:30 p.m.; Memorial Day, 7 a.m.–7 p.m.

**Admission** Free
**When to Go** Any time
**How Much Time to Allow** I hour
**Author's Rating** ★★★;A poignant experience for all.
**Overall Appeal by Age Group**

| | | |
|---|---|---|
| Pre-school ½ | Grade School ★ | Teens ★★ |
| Young Adults ★★½ | Over 30 ★★★½ | Seniors ★★★★ |

**Description and Comments** Also known as Punchbowl (the 112-acre site sits inside Punchbowl Crater), this national cemetery is the final resting place for more than 40,000 war veterans (and their family members) who served the United States in World War II, the Korean War, and the Vietnam War. It is a solemn sight, with rows of small, flat, white headstones stretching far across the crater floor. Among those buried here is famed war correspondent Ernest Taylor "Ernie" Pyle. (While serving as a correspondent with the 77th Infantry Division, Pyle was killed on April 18, 1945, by Japanese gunfire on the small Pacific islet of Ie Shima.) Panoramic views of Waikiki, Honolulu, and Pearl Harbor add to the experience here. Each Easter morning, the cemetery is visited by thousands of Hawai'i residents and visitors for the annual Easter Sunrise Service.

## *Pacific Aerospace Museum*　　*Zone 2 Greater Honolulu*

**Location** Central lobby, main terminal, Honolulu International Airport
**Phone** (808) 839-0777
**Hours** Daily, 8 a.m.–6 p.m.
**Admission** Free
**When to Go** Simply put, this is a good place to kill some time while waiting for your return flight home
**How Much Time to Allow** 40 minutes
**Author's Rating** ★★½; Fun for kids and adults alike.
**Overall Appeal by Age Group**

| | | |
|---|---|---|
| Pre-school ★★ | Grade School ★★★½ | Teens ★★★½ |
| Young Adults ★★★½ | Over 30 ★★★ | Seniors ★★★ |

**Description and Comments** A 27-minute multimedia presentation, *The Great Skyquest Theater,* highlights this $3.8 million, 6,500-square-foot mini-museum, which opened in December 1991. The presentation—staged in three adjoining theaters—traces the history of aviation in Hawai'i and the Pacific region and includes an account of the infamous Japanese attack on Pearl Harbor. Hands-on exhibits include a computerized globe that displays flight distances and lengths, a "learn to fly" lesson, a model of the moon, and (our favorite) a full-scale NASA space shuttle flight deck.

## *Polynesian Cultural Center*　　*Zone 4 The North Shore*

**Location** 55-370 Kamehameha Hwy.
**Phone** (808) 293-3333
**Website** www.polynesia.com
**Hours** Monday–Saturday, 12:30–9 p.m.; villages closes at 6 p.m.
**Admission** General admission is $27 for adults and $16 for children ages 5–11 and

includes admission to 7 Polynesian villages, canoe rides, the Pageant of Long Canoes, and a tram tour. Special deluxe packages featuring an IMAX film, a buffet, and the evening show *Horizons* are as follows: Ambassador Package, $99 for adults and $66 for children; Lu'au Package, $65 for adults and $44 for children; and Buffet Package, $49 for adults and $32 for children. Evening show with no dinner option is offered for $35 for adults and $20 for children.

**When to Go**  Any time. If you enjoy watching Samoan fire-knife dancers, however, be sure to come during the World Fire-Knife Dance Championships, which are held each year in April or May.

**How Much Time to Allow**  All day, including 2½ hours drive time to and from Waikiki

**Author's Rating**  ★★★★½; Most popular paid visitor attraction in Hawai'i.

**Overall Appeal by Age Group**

| | | |
|---|---|---|
| Pre-school ★★★ | Grade School ★★★★ | Teens ★★★★½ |
| Young Adults ★★★★½ | Over 30 ★★★★½ | Seniors ★★★★½ |

**Description and Comments**  Set on 42 acres in the Mormon university town of La'ie, home of Brigham Young University–Hawai'i, the Polynesian Cultural Center delivers a cultural experience that includes re-created villages representing the cultures of Samoa, Fiji, Tahiti, Tonga, New Zealand, Marquesas, and Hawai'i.

Friendly native Pacific Islanders, dressed in traditional attire, eagerly share their arts, crafts, songs, and dances. Most of them are students at the neighboring BYU-H campus. They work part time at PCC in exchange for tuition, room, board, and books. Hands-on demonstrations include coconut husking, wood carving, lau hala weaving, poi pounding, and tapa making. Waterways and lush gardens are the settings for canoe rides, a tram tour, and a colorful pageant of canoes. The seven-story-high IMAX theater adds to the experience with a film tracing the history of Polynesia.

A variety of buffet/show packages is available, culminating in an impressive evening show featuring a cast of more than 150 dancers and musicians. Alcohol is not part of the program at this Mormon institution.

## *Queen Emma Summer Palace*   *Zone 2 Greater Honolulu*

**Location**  2913 Pali Hwy.

**Phone**  (808) 595-3167

**Hours**  Daily, 9 a.m.–4 p.m.

**Admission**  $5 for adults; $1 for children under age 15

**When to Go**  Any time

**How Much Time to Allow**  1 hour

**Author's Rating**  ★★★; Worth a visit for Hawaiian history students.

**Overall Appeal by Age Group**

| | | |
|---|---|---|
| Pre-school ½ | Grade School ★★ | Teens ★★½ |
| Young Adults ★★★½ | Over 30 ★★★½ | Seniors ★★★½ |

**Description and Comments**  Maintained and operated by the nonprofit Daughters of Hawai'i, this charming white-frame house served as a summer retreat for Queen Emma, consort to Alexander Liholiho (King Kamehameha IV). Many of the queen's possessions are on display here, including an opulent gold necklace and various wedding and baby gifts presented to Emma by England's Queen Victoria. This was among the first Hawaiian properties to be listed on the National Register of Historic Places.

**Other Things to Do Nearby**   Behind the palace, off Pu'iwa Road, is Nu'uanu Valley Park, a serene hideaway favored for its shady trees.

## Royal Mausoleum                    Zone 2 Greater Honolulu

**Location**  2261 Nu'uanu Ave.
**Phone**  (808) 587-2590
**Hours**  Monday–Friday, 8 a.m.–4:30 p.m.
**Admission**  Free
**When to Go**  Any time
**How Much Time to Allow**  45 minutes
**Author's Rating**  ★★½; Not your typical visitor attraction.
**Overall Appeal by Age Group**

| | | |
|---|---|---|
| Pre-school ½ | Grade School ★½ | Teens ★★ |
| Young Adults ★★ | Over 30 ★★ | Seniors ★★★ |

**Description and Comments**   Considered the most sacred burial ground in the entire state, this three-acre site is the resting place for six of the eight Hawaiian monarchs: Kings Kamehameha II, III, IV, and V; King Kalakaua; and Queen Lili'uokalani. (The bones of Kamehameha I were hidden at a secret location on the Kona Coast of the Island of Hawai'i; William Lunalilo, or Kamehameha VI, per his wishes, was buried in a private tomb on the grounds of Kawaiaha'o Church.) This current site was prepared in 1865 by Kamehameha V to replace the original royal burial tomb on the grounds of 'Iolani Palace.

**Touring Tips**   Call ahead to arrange for guided tours.

## Sea Life Park                      Zone 3 Windward O'ahu

**Location**  41-202 Kalaniana'ole Hwy.
**Phone**  (808) 259-7933
**Website**  www.sealifeparkhawaii.com
**Hours**  Daily, 9:30 a.m.–5 p.m.
**Admission**  $25 for adults; $12.50 for children ages 4–12; free for children under age 4
**When to Go**  Any time
**How Much Time to Allow**  3–4 hours
**Author's Rating**  ★★★½; Even if you have similar attractions back home, this is a family fun spot.
**Overall Appeal by Age Group**

| | | |
|---|---|---|
| Pre-school ★★★★ | Grade School ★★★★★ | Teens ★★★★ |
| Young Adults ★★★★ | Over 30 ★★★★ | Seniors ★★★★ |

**Description and Comments**   The first feature you encounter on entering the park is the 300,000-gallon Hawaiian Reef Tank, filled with more than 2,000 species of reef fish, rays, hammerhead sharks, and other colorful marine life. From there, head to the Rocky Shores exhibit, which provides above- and below-water views of marine life in a tidal zone, and then the Sea Turtle Lagoon, where you'll get an up-close look at Hawai'i's protected green sea turtles. Children especially will want to drop by the Discovery Pool, where they can hold tiny sea critters, like sea cucumbers and spiny sea stars.

Other don't-miss exhibits include the Sea Lion Pool (you can purchase fish to feed the sea lions), Sea Bird Sanctuary, and Penguin Habitat (home to a successful breeding colony of Humboldt penguins). At Whaler's Cove, you can view the park's dolphins, whales, and Kekaimalu, the world's only known "wholphin" (half false killer whale, half dolphin). The park offers three live shows: The Hawai'i Ocean Theater, a 400-seat amphitheater, features performances by bottle-nosed dolphins, sea lions, and penguins. Whaler's Cove is the site of an entertaining show built around the amazing leaps and flips of the bottlenose dolphins. And the Kolohe Kai Sea Lion Show, in Makapu'u Meadow, spotlights a group of delightful sea lions and their trainers.

Also on the premises are two eateries: the Sea Lion Cafe and Rabbit Island Bar and Grill. Two gift shops—the Sea Life Park General Store and Little Treasures—offer a wide assortment of T-shirts, souvenirs, and park-related merchandise.

The special program Dosphin Adventures is offered three times daily. Dolphin Adventures lets you learn how the park's trainers use positive reinforcement to train the dolphins. Better yet, you'll have an opportunity to get in the water and interact with specially trained dolphins. The cost is $99 per person, and participants must be at least 13 years of age.

Splash University, meanwhile, also gives you an insider's look at how these friendly mammals are trained. You'll learn a few signals that dolphins respond to and participate in training sessions during shallow-water interaction. The cost is $79 for adults and $67 for children ages 4–12 (children under age 12 must be accompanied by an adult). Splash University is held four times daily

The Swim with the Sting Rays program offers participants an opportunity to swim with rays and learn their eating habits. The cost is $49 per person.

"Tuition" costs include general admission into Sea Life Park. Each program lasts approximately one hour. Be sure to bring swimwear and a towel. Call (808) 259-2500 for more information or to make a reservation.

**Touring Tips**   "The Hawaiian Reef Show" begins at 9:50 a.m.; "Hawai'i Ocean Theater" at 10 a.m.; "Kolohe Kai Sea Lion Show" at 11 a.m.; and "Whaler's Cove" at 11:15 a.m. The show rotation continues throughout the day, with the final set starting at 2:45 p.m.

**Other Things to Do Nearby**   Sandy Beach and Makapu'u Beach are just a few minutes away by car.

## Senator Fong's Plantation and Gardens                          Zone 3 Windward O'ahu

**Location**  47-285 Pulama Rd.
**Phone**  (808) 239-6775
**Website**  www.fonggarden.com/index.html
**Hours**  Daily, 9 a.m.–4 p.m.
**Admission**  $10 for adults; $8 for senior citizens; $6 for children ages 5–12
**When to Go**  Any time
**How Much Time to Allow**  90 minutes

**Author's Rating** ★★★; A Windward O'ahu outing featuring family-style aloha spirit.
**Overall Appeal by Age Group**

| | | |
|---|---|---|
| Pre-school ★★ | Grade School ★★½ | Teens ★★★ |
| Young Adults ★★★ | Over 30 ★★★★ | Seniors ★★★★ |

**Description and Comments** Hiram Fong was the first Asian American to serve in the U.S. Senate, retiring in 1977. Today, Fong and his family run this 725-acre private estate, with tropical flower gardens, more than 100 different fruits and nuts, and scenic views of Windward O'ahu. Hands-on activities here include lei making lessons using flowers picked from nearby gardens. A 50-minute tram tour takes visitors through valleys and tropical forests. A snack bar, fruit stand, and gift shop are on site.

**Touring Tips** Narrated tram tours are scheduled daily at 10:30 and 11:30 a.m. and 1, 2, and 3 p.m. Reservations are not needed.

## *Tropic Lightning Museum*          *Zone 6 Central O'ahu*

**Location** Schofield Barracks
**Phone** (808) 655-0438
**Hours** Tuesday–Saturday, 10 a.m.–4 p.m.
**Admission** Free
**When to Go** Any time
**How Much Time to Allow** 30 minutes
**Author's Rating** ★★½; Strictly for military buffs.
**Overall Appeal by Age Group**

| | | |
|---|---|---|
| Pre-school ★ | Grade School ★ | Teens ★★ |
| Young Adults ★★ | Over 30 ★★ | Seniors ★★★★ |

**Description and Comments** This cozy museum documents the history of Schofield Barracks and the famed "Tropic Lightning" 25th Infantry Division, which fought in World War II, the Korean War, and the Vietnam War.

## *U.S. Army Museum*          *Zone 1 Waikiki*

**Location** Battery Randolph, Ft. DeRussy, at the intersection of Kalia and Saratoga Rds., next to the Hale Koa Hotel; validated parking available in Ft. DeRussy's Saratoga parking lot
**Phone** (808) 438-2821
**Hours** Tuesday–Sunday, 10 a.m.–4:30 p.m.
**Admission** Donations accepted
**When to Go** Any time
**How Much Time to Allow** 1 hour
**Author's Rating** ★★★½; A wealth of war memorabilia, and you can't beat the price.
**Overall Appeal by Age Group**

| | | |
|---|---|---|
| Pre-school ★ | Grade School ★★★ | Teens ★★★ |
| Young Adults ★★★½ | Over 30 ★★★½ | Seniors ★★★★ |

**Description and Comments** Built in 1909, the Battery Randolph served as an imposing military fortress, ready to defend Waikiki from attacking battleships. (It was a part of the military's "Ring of Steel" that encircled O'ahu.) However, when it outlived its usefulness, officials faced a dilemma: The structure was nearly impossible to tear down. Its walls were 22 feet thick (solid concrete) and built to withstand a direct hit from a 2,000-ton artillery shell. Any attempt to bring it down with explosives would undoubtedly cause damage in the surrounding areas of Waikiki. In 1976, the battery was transformed into the 13,500-square-foot U.S. Army Museum, recalling the history of the American army in the Pacific.

Included here are more than 2,000 artifacts and 1,900 photographs tracing the U.S. military's presence in Hawai'i. The artifacts range from small (medals and tags) to huge (a Japanese battle tank). One popular exhibit pays tribute to the 100th/442nd Regimental Combat Team, a unit made up of local and mainland Japanese-American men who overcame prejudice to enlist in the U.S. Army during World War II. They became the most highly decorated unit in the war, living up to their battle cry of "Go for broke." A gift shop is available on the premises.

## USS Arizona Memorial                           Zone 6 Central O'ahu

---

**Location**  1 Arizona Memorial Pl.
**Phone**  (808) 422-0561
**Website**  www.arizonamemorial.org/memorial.html
**Hours**  Daily, 7:30 a.m.–5 p.m. Program runs 8 a.m.–3 p.m., weather permitting (shuttle boats to the memorial leave every 15 minutes between 8 a.m. and 3 p.m.)
**Admission**  Free
**When to Go**  Any time
**How Much Time to Allow**  Between 2 and 4 hours. Due to the popularity of this attraction, you are likely to wait in line for an hour or more. The program itself lasts about 75 minutes.
**Author's Rating**  ★★★★; A solemn, moving experience.
**Overall Appeal by Age Group**

| | | |
|---|---|---|
| Pre-school ★½ | Grade School ★★★ | Teens ★★★½ |
| Young Adults ★★★½ | Over 30 ★★★★½ | Seniors ★★★★★ |

**Description and Comments**  The museum exhibits numerous historic photos, news clippings, and touching memorabilia from December 7, 1941, the day Japanese war planes bombed Pearl Harbor. Visitors see a 23-minute film depicting the attack as well as events that led to it. Then you are transported to the memorial via shuttle boat. The memorial itself is a white structure that sits over the sunken *Arizona*, where 1,102 men went down with the ship and remain entombed. A marble wall pays tribute to the 1,177 sailors and marines who perished during the surprise attack. The memorial, designed by a Honolulu architect, was made possible after a benefit concert staged in Honolulu in 1961 by an ex-G.I. by the name of Elvis Presley.

**Touring Tips**  Tickets are issued on a first-come, first-served basis. Each guest must pick up his or her own ticket in person at the ticket office.

**Other Things to Do Nearby**  The USS Battleship *Missouri* and USS *Bowfin* Submarine and Park are both in the immediate vicinity.

## USS Battleship Missouri Memorial     Zone 6 Central O'ahu

**Location**  Ford Island, Pier Fox Trot 5
**Phone**  (808) 423-2263 or (877) MIGHTY-MO
**Website**  www.ussmissouri.com
**Hours**  Daily, 9 a.m.–5 p.m.
**Admission**  General admission: $14 for adults; $10 for military personnel; $7 for children ages 4–12; $5 for children of military personnel
**When to Go**  Any time
**How Much Time to Allow**  90 minutes–2 hours
**Author's Rating**  ★★★★; Forms an appropriate bookend to the USS *Arizona* Memorial.
**Overall Appeal by Age Group**

| | | |
|---|---|---|
| Pre-school ★½ | Grade School ★★★ | Teens ★★★½ |
| Young Adults ★★★½ | Over 30 ★★★★½ | Seniors ★★★★★ |

**Description and Comments**   One of America's most storied battleships now calls Pearl Harbor home as an interactive museum and memorial. The 45,000-ton "Mighty Mo," is the last of four Iowa-class battleships built during World War II. It was on the deck of the *Missouri* that Japan officially surrendered to the Allied Forces, marking the end of World War II in the Pacific theater. The *Missouri* earned three battle stars for missions in Iwo Jima, Okinawa, and Japan during that war, then five more while serving in the Korean War. More recently, the *Missouri* served during the Persian Gulf War. In 1986, it became the first battleship to circumnavigate the world.

Buses transport visitors to Ford Island, where the ship is anchored. Touring Mighty Mo, which is nearly three football fields long, you'll be able to view documents and photographs and hear a portion of a speech made by General Douglas MacArthur.

**Touring Tips**   A Chief's Guided Tour is available; it includes head-of-the-line privileges and a tour led by a crew member: $20 for adults; $16 for military personnel; $13 for children ages 4–12; $11 for children of military personnel. All tickets must be purchased before 4 p.m.

**Other Things to Do Nearby**   The USS *Arizona* Memorial and USS *Bowfin* Submarine Museum and Park.

## USS Bowfin Submarine
## Museum and Park                     Zone 6 Central O'ahu

**Location**  11 Arizona Memorial Dr.
**Phone**  (808) 423-1341
**Website**  www.bowfin.org
**Hours**  Daily, 8 a.m.–5 p.m.
**Admission**  Entry to both museum and submarine: $8 for adults; $6 for senior citizens and military personnel; $3 for children ages 3–13. Entry to museum only: $4 for adults; $2 for children ages 3–13
**When to Go**  Any time
**How Much Time to Allow**  1 hour to 90 minutes
**Author's Rating**  ★★★½; Excellent for military and history buffs.

**Overall Appeal by Age Group**

| | | |
|---|---|---|
| Pre-school ★½ | Grade School ★★★ | Teens ★★★½ |
| Young Adults ★★★½ | Over 30 ★★★★ | Seniors ★★★★½ |

**Description and Comments**   Nicknamed the "Pearl Harbor Avenger," the *Bowfin* is credited with 44 enemy ship sinkings on nine patrols. It is one of only 15 World War II U.S. submarines still in existence. Visitors can check out the interior of the vessel and examine defused torpedoes. The park houses a museum filled with submarine history, featuring outdoor exhibits and a mini-theater.

**Other Things to Do Nearby**   The USS *Arizona* Memorial and USS Battleship *Missouri* Memorial.

## Waikiki Aquarium                                    Zone 1 Waikiki

**Location**  2777 Kalakaua Ave.
**Phone**  (808) 923-9741
**Website**  www.mic.hawaii.edu/aquarium
**Hours**  Daily, 9 a.m.–5 p.m.
**Admission**  $7 for adults; $5 for senior citizens, military personnel, and college students; $3.50 for children ages 13–17 and people with disabilities; free for children age 12 and under
**When to Go**  Any time
**How Much Time to Allow**  1 hour
**Author's Rating**  ★★★½; Excellent small aquarium by the sea.
**Overall Appeal by Age Group**

| | | |
|---|---|---|
| Pre-school ★★★ | Grade School ★★★★ | Teens ★★★½ |
| Young Adults ★★★½ | Over 30 ★★★½ | Seniors ★★★½ |

**Description and Comments**   The Waikiki Aquarium's history is no mere fish story. Built in 1904, it is the third-oldest public aquarium in the United States and has distinguished itself as a living classroom for anyone interested in Hawai'i's ocean life. The aquarium is one of the first facilities in the world to successfully breed mahimahi (also known as dolphin fish) and the first in the United States to breed the chambered nautilus. Although not very large, the facility houses more than 2,000 ocean creatures representing some 350 different species. Here you can learn about endangered species, like the Hawaiian monk seal, and threatened species, like the Hawaiian green sea turtle. A gallery of aquariums display colorful reef fish, coral, a giant clam, jellyfish, and mahimahi. It's a great companion experience for your snorkeling adventures. In addition to the live exhibits, several educational classes focusing on Hawai'i's marine environment are available. Call for an updated schedule and class fees.

**Other Things to Do Nearby**   The Honolulu Zoo is within easy walking distance.

# Maui

## Alexander and Baldwin
## Sugar Museum                                 Zone 7 Central Maui

**Location**  3957 Hansen Rd.
**Phone**  (808) 871-8058

**Hours** Monday–Saturday, 9:30 a.m.–4:30 p.m.
**Admission** $5 for adults; $2 for children ages 6–17
**When to Go** Any time
**How Much Time to Allow** 45 minutes
**Author's Rating** ★★★; A look at Maui's sugar plantation history.
**Overall Appeal by Age Group**

| Pre-school ★½ | Grade School ★★ | Teens ★★½ |
| Young Adults ★★★ | Over 30 ★★★½ | Seniors ★★★½ |

**Description and Comments** Formerly the residence of a factory superintendent, this museum houses a number of artifacts, photographs, and a working scale model of sugar-processing machinery.

## Bailey House Museum                     Zone 7 Central Maui

**Location** 2375-A Main St.
**Phone** (808) 244-3326
**Website** www.mauimuseum.org
**Hours** Monday–Saturday, 10 a.m.–4 p.m.
**Admission** $5 for adults; $4 for senior citizens; $1 for children ages 7–12
**When to Go** Any time
**How Much Time to Allow** 1 hour
**Author's Rating** ★★★; Worth a stop for history buffs.
**Overall Appeal by Age Group**

| Pre-school ★½ | Grade School ★★ | Teens ★★½ |
| Young Adults ★★★ | Over 30 ★★★½ | Seniors ★★★½ |

**Description and Comments** The Bailey mission home, built in 1833 of lava rock and native woods, sits on land given to the missionaries by Hawaiian chiefs. Hawaiians attended reading and writing classes here, using Hawaiian language books printed on Maui. Today the Bailey House displays Hawaiian artifacts, including tapa, weaving, featherwork, and tools made out of stones, shells, and bones. A gallery of paintings—all from the late 1800s—portrays the beauty of the Valley Isle, and a stroll through the outside gardens reveals rare native plants, a koa wood canoe, and a surfboard once used by legendary surfer/swimmer Duke Kahanamoku. A gift shop offers crafts, apparel, Hawaiian music, and books.

**Other Things to Do Nearby** The Hawai'i Nature Center and Kepaniwai Park are a short drive away.

## Baldwin Home Museum                     Zone 9 West Maui

**Location** 120 Dickenson St.
**Phone** (808) 661-3262
**Hours** Daily, 10 a.m.–4 p.m.
**Admission** $5 for families; $3 for individuals; $2 for senior citizens
**When to Go** Any time
**How Much Time to Allow** 1 hour
**Author's Rating** ★★★; A peek into Hawai'i's missionary era.

## Overall Appeal by Age Group

Pre-school ★½          Grade School ★★          Teens ★★★
Young Adults ★★★       Over 30 ★★★½             Seniors ★★★½

**Description and Comments**  This two-story structure was the home of Reverend Dwight Baldwin, a Protestant medical missionary from 1838 to 1871. Today the home and its grounds, lovingly restored by the Lahaina Restoration Foundation, gives visitors a glimpse of what life was like for 19th-century missionary families in Lahaina. On display are various household items and furniture, photographs, and other historic artifacts. Ask for a free self-guided tour map of Lahaina's other restored treasures.

**Other Things to Do Nearby**  Located at Dickenson and Front Streets, the Baldwin Home is one of several historic sights in Lahaina. The Brig *Carthaginian* and Wo Hing Temple are among those within easy walking distance.

## Brig Carthaginian                          Zone 9 West Maui

**Location** Lahaina Harbor
**Phone** (808) 661-3262
**Hours** Daily, 10 a.m.–4 p.m.
**Admission** $5 for families (any size); $3 for individuals; $2 for senior citizens
**When to Go** Any time
**How Much Time to Allow** 75 minutes
**Author's Rating** ★★★; A cool way to learn about the whaling era of the mid-1800s.

## Overall Appeal by Age Group

Pre-school ★★          Grade School ★★½         Teens ★★★
Young Adults ★★★½      Over 30 ★★★½             Seniors ★★★½

**Description and Comments**  This 93-foot ship, a replica of a 19th-century brig, is a maritime museum featuring whale exhibits, audiovisual displays, and an original whale boat. The square-rigged ship is typical of the vessels that brought the first commerce to the Hawaiian islands. A video about humpback whales is shown.

**Other Things to Do Nearby**  The Wo Hing Temple and Baldwin Home Museum are a short walk away.

## Haleakala National Park             Zone 10 Upcountry Maui

**Location** The park extends from the 10,023-foot summit of Haleakala down the southeast flank of the mountain to the Kipahulu coastline near Hana. The summit area is accessible from Kahului via Rds. 37, 377, and 378. The park's Kipahulu area, at the east end of the island between Hana and Kaupo, can be reached via Hwy. 36. Driving time is about 3–4 hours each way.
**Phone** (808) 572-9306
**Website** www.haleakala.national-park.com
**Hours** Park Ranger Headquarters is open daily, 9 a.m.–4 p.m.; the Visitor Center is open daily, sunrise–3 p.m. (Overnight camping is permissible. The Hosmer Grove Campground in the summit area, located just inside the park's entrance, can be used without a permit; all other camping areas require permits.)
**Admission** $10/vehicle, good for 7 days

**When to Go**  Any time. Haleakala is renowned as a setting for dramatic sunrises and sunsets, although most people come for sunrise. Be sure to arrive at least 30 minutes before either event.

**How Much Time to Allow**  Half a day, depending on whether you plan to spend time hiking or taking part in one of the park's programs

**Author's Rating**  ★★★★; One of the great natural wonders of the world.

**Overall Appeal by Age Group**

Pre-school ★★               Grade School ★★★          Teens ★★★½
Young Adults ★★★★          Over 30 ★★★★               Seniors ★★★★

**Description and Comments**  Haleakala ("House of the Sun"), a dormant volcano that last spilled lava a bit more than 200 years ago, was designated as a national park in 1961. The park consists of nearly 29,000 acres, most of it wilderness. In the summit area, see the Park Ranger Headquarters and Haleakala Visitor Center, which houses a variety of cultural and natural history exhibits. Rangers are on duty and can be a tremendous help in making the most out of your visit. In the Kipahulu area, see the Kipahulu Ranger Station/Visitor Center. Each facility has a selection of books, maps, postcards, and other souvenirs for sale.

**Touring Tips**  Check the park's bulletin board for a schedule of daily programs and guided hikes. Obey all posted warning signs. It can be cold at the summit, so be prepared. Due to the high elevation and reduced oxygen at the park, anyone with heart or respiratory conditions is advised to check with their doctor before visiting.

## Hana Cultural Center                          Zone 10 Upcountry Maui

**Location**  4974 Uakea Rd.
**Phone**  (808) 248-8622
**Website**  www.planet-hawaii.com/hana
**Hours**  Daily, 10 a.m.–4 p.m.
**Admission**  Donations accepted
**When to Go**  Any time
**How Much Time to Allow**  1 hour
**Author's Rating**  ★★★; A reward after the long journey to Hana.
**Overall Appeal by Age Group**

Pre-school ★★               Grade School ★★½           Teens ★★½
Young Adults ★★★           Over 30 ★★★                 Seniors ★★★

**Description and Comments**  This cultural center is home to a quaint museum that features more than 500 artifacts, 600 books, 5,000 historic photographs of the Hana district, and, oddly enough, 680 Hawaiian bottles. Opened in 1983, the nonprofit museum houses Hawaiian quilts, poi boards, stones, kapa, ancient tools, fish hooks, gourd bowls, stone lamps, and a century-old fishing net. Also featured are tributes to some of Hana's most notable personalities. The cultural center also includes a series of old Hawaiian *hale* (houses), the historic Hana courthouse, and a jailhouse.

## Hawai'i Nature Center                         Zone 7 Central Maui

**Location**  875 'Iao Valley Rd.
**Phone**  (808) 244-6500

**Website** www.hawaiiweb.com/maui/html/sites/hawaii_nature_center.html
**Hours** Daily, 10 a.m.–4 p.m.
**Admission** $6 for adults; $4 for children ages 4–12
**When to Go** Any time
**How Much Time to Allow** 1 hour
**Author's Rating** ★★★★; Good hands-on learning experience.
**Overall Appeal by Age Group**

| Pre-school ★★★ | Grade School ★★★★ | Teens ★★★★ |
| Young Adults ★★★★ | Over 30 ★★★★ | Seniors ★★★★ |

**Description and Comments** The Nature Center's Interactive Science Arcade features more than 30 interactive exhibits celebrating Maui's natural environment. The main exhibit hall features an amazing 10-foot-high, 30-foot-long, three-dimensional replication of four streams that feed into the 'Iao Stream. Aquariums, rainforest explorations, arcade games, telescopes, and live insect and animal exhibits are among the other highlights. The gift shop features an extensive selection of nature-themed merchandise. All proceeds go to environmental education programs for Maui elementary school children.

**Touring Tips** Guided nature walks are offered daily. Call for reservations (required).

**Other Things to Do Nearby** Visit Kepaniwai Cultural Park and the Bailey House Museum.

## Hawai'i Experience Theater                    Zone 9 West Maui

**Location** 824 Front St.
**Phone** (808) 661-8314
**Hours** Daily, 10 a.m.–10 p.m. Tickets go on sale at 9:30 a.m.
**Admission** $6.95 for adults; $3.95 for children ages 4–12 (younger children free). If you purchase $25 worth of merchandise at the gift shop, you receive a free ticket to the show.
**When to Go** Any time
**How Much Time to Allow** 50 minutes
**Author's Rating** ★★★½; A diversion in the heart of Lahaina.
**Overall Appeal by Age Group**

| Pre-school ★★★ | Grade School ★★★½ | Teens ★★★½ |
| Young Adults ★★★½ | Over 30 ★★★½ | Seniors ★★★½ |

**Description and Comments** A planetarium-like theater with a 60-foot-tall domed screen, this attraction features a spectacular 40-minute film, "Hawai'i: Islands of the Gods" shown every hour.

**Other Things to Do Nearby** Historical attractions, including the Wo Hing Temple and Baldwin Home Museum, are within easy walking distance.

## Hui No'eau Visual Arts Center          Zone 10 Upcountry Maui

**Location** 2841 Baldwin Ave.
**Phone** (808) 572-6560
**Website** www.maui.net/~hui

**Hours** Monday–Friday, 8 a.m.–4 p.m. Gallery hours are Saturday, 10 a.m.–4 p.m.
**Admission** Donations accepted
**When to Go** Any time
**How Much Time to Allow** 1 hour
**Author's Rating** ★★★; A haven for art lovers.
**Overall Appeal by Age Group**

| | | |
|---|---|---|
| Pre-school ★★ | Grade School ★★½ | Teens ★★★ |
| Young Adults ★★★ | Over 30 ★★★½ | Seniors ★★★½ |

**Description and Comments** Occupying a beautiful nine-acre estate in Makawao, this nonprofit art center features works by both local and international artists. The estate itself is a historic landmark (built in 1917 for Harry and Ethel Baldwin) dotted with pine and camphor trees and adorned with an immaculate formal garden and reflecting pool. The arts center features classes and workshops for aspiring artisans, and exhibits are open to the public on Saturdays. The gift shop offers a selection of original artworks, note cards, books, and other gift items.

## *Kepaniwai Cultural Park*          *Zone 7 Central Maui*

**Location** 'Iao Valley Rd.
**Phone** (808) 243-7389
**Hours** Daily, 7 a.m.–7 p.m.
**Admission** Free
**When to Go** Any time
**How Much Time to Allow** 1 hour
**Author's Rating** ★★★; A pleasant stop if you're in the area.
**Overall Appeal by Age Group**

| | | |
|---|---|---|
| Pre-school ★★ | Grade School ★★½ | Teens ★★★ |
| Young Adults ★★★ | Over 30 ★★★½ | Seniors ★★★½ |

**Description and Comments** Picturesque gardens and architectural pavilions representing Hawai'i's different ethnic groups.

**Other Things to Do Nearby** The Hawai'i Nature Center and Bailey House Museum.

## *Lahaina-Ka'anapali and Pacific Railroad*  *Zone 9 West Maui*

**Location** 975 Limahana Pl., Suite 203
**Phone** (808) 661-0089 or (808) 661-0080
**Hours** 12 rides scheduled daily, beginning at 9:45 a.m.
**Admission** $15 for adults; $8.50 for children ages 3–12 (round-trip)
**When to Go** Any time
**How Much Time to Allow** 90 minutes
**Author's Rating** ★★★; A short train ride offering views of the West Maui coastline.
**Overall Appeal by Age Group**

| | | |
|---|---|---|
| Pre-school ★★½ | Grade School ★★★ | Teens ★★ |
| Young Adults ★★ | Over 30 ★★ | Seniors ★★½ |

**Description and Comments** The "Sugar Cane Train," with its 1890s locomotive and distinctive whistle, was used by the Pioneer Mill to transport sugar crops until the early 1950s. Today, the train shuttles visitors between Lahaina and the resort area of

Ka'anapali. The six-mile route through a cane field lasts about 40 minutes each way. A friendly conductor shares the history of Maui's sugar industry.

## Kula Botanical Garden                Zone 10 Upcountry Maui

**Location** RR 4, Box 288
**Phone** (808) 878-1715
**Hours** Daily, 9 a.m.–4 p.m.
**Admission** $5 for adults; $1 for children ages 6–12
**When to Go** Any time
**How Much Time to Allow** 90 minutes
**Author's Rating** ★★★; A botanist's dream come true.
**Overall Appeal by Age Group**

| Pre-school ★★ | Grade School ★★½ | Teens ★★½ |
| Young Adults ★★½ | Over 30 ★★★ | Seniors ★★★½ |

**Description and Comments**  Kula, blessed with a mild, cool climate and fertile soil, is the home of this five-acre wonderland originally owned by Princess Kekaulike. Opened in 1969, the garden today features more than 1,700 tropical plants, including exotic flora such as proteas, heliconias, orchids, anthurium, and gingers.

## Maui Tropical Plantation
## and Country Store                Zone 7 Central Maui

**Location** 1670 Honoapi'ilani Hwy.
**Phone** (808) 244-7643
**Hours** Daily, 9 a.m.–5 p.m.; tour hours, 10 a.m.–4 p.m.
**Admission** Free; tram tours cost $9.50 for adults and $3.50 for children ages 5–12
**When to Go** Any time
**How Much Time to Allow** 75 minutes
**Author's Rating** ★★★; When you want to know more about tropical crops, this the place. Pick up fresh fruits at the country store.
**Overall Appeal by Age Group**

| Pre-school ★★ | Grade School ★★½ | Teens ★★★ |
| Young Adults ★★★½ | Over 30 ★★★★ | Seniors ★★★★ |

**Description and Comments**  From the Visitor Center, head out to the plantation's 50-acre garden, which is filled with tropical plants, including pineapple, sugarcane, papaya, guava, star fruit, anthuriums, and protea. A restaurant and plant nursery are also available.

**Touring Tips**  Narrated tram tours of the garden are available. The rates are $8.50 for adults (plus tax) and $3.50 for children ages 5–12. The tour lasts about 40 minutes.

## Maui Ocean Center                Zone 8 South Maui

**Location** Ma'alaea Harbor Village, 192 Ma'alaea Rd.
**Phone** (808) 270-7000
**Website** www.mauioceancenter.com
**Hours** Daily, 9 a.m.–5 p.m.
**Admission** $18 for adults; $12.50 for children ages 3–12; senior citizens and military

personnel receive 10% discount

**When to Go** Any time

**How Much Time to Allow** 2 hours

**Author's Rating** ★★★★; A must for understanding island marine life.

**Overall Appeal by Age Group**

| | | |
|---|---|---|
| Pre-school ★★★★½ | Grade School ★★★★★ | Teens ★★★★★ |
| Young Adults ★★★★★ | Over 30 ★★★★★ | Seniors ★★★★½ |

**Description and Comments** The star attraction is the 600,000-gallon ocean aquarium tank with a walk-through acrylic tunnel so that you can get a good view of the inhabitants, including a six-foot tiger shark and other sharks, spotted eagle rays, mahimahi, triggerfish, sea turtles, eels, and a dazzling array of colorful reef fish. Other exhibits include a supervised touch pool for kids, allowing them to hold sea critters; interactive displays about the humpback whale; and smaller aquariums affording a close look at eels, shrimp, coral, and other sea life. The Reef Cafe and Seascape Cafe and Bar provide food and drinks, and the large gift shop carries logo and ocean-themed goods.

**Other Things to Do Nearby** The center overlooks busy Ma'alaea Harbor, where tour cruise boats come and go. Try combining a trip to the aquarium with a snorkeling tour to look at the sea creatures in the wilds.

## Tedeschi Winery                    Zone 8 South Maui

**Location** 'Ulupalakua Ranch, about 10 miles past the junction of Hwys. 377 and 37 in Kula

**Phone** (808) 878-6058

**Website** www.alternative-hawaii.com/profiles/trade/tedeschi.htm

**Hours** Daily, 9 a.m.–5 p.m.; guided tours are held from 10:30 a.m. to 1:30 p.m.

**Admission** Free

**When to Go** Any time

**How Much Time to Allow** 1 hour

**Author's Rating** ★★★; Worth a taste for wine lovers.

**Overall Appeal by Age Group**

| | | |
|---|---|---|
| Pre-school ★½ | Grade School ★★ | Teens ★★½ |
| Young Adults ★★★ | Over 30 ★★★ | Seniors ★★★ |

**Description and Comments** Tedeschi Vineyards is known for its island-style wine, including Maui Blanc pineapple wine. Wines are available for tasting and purchase at the tasting room in the King's Cottage, once used as a retreat by King Kalakaua. Hawai'i-made specialty goods, books, and gifts are also on sale.

**Touring Tips** The tour explains how the wines are processed and bottled. But it's not necessary to take a tour to enjoy sampling the wines and walking through the shady lawns and gardens.

## Whalers Village Museum              Zone 9 West Maui

**Location** Whalers Village (3rd floor), 2435 Ka'anapali Pkwy.

**Phone** (808) 661-5992

**Website** www.mauimapp.com/museums/whalersvillagemuseum.htm

**Hours** Daily, 9:30 a.m.–10 p.m.

**Admission** Free
**When to Go** Any time
**How Much Time to Allow** 1 hour
**Author's Rating** ★★½; Displays and historic artifacts about whaling will entertain the family if they get restless shopping.
**Overall Appeal by Age Group**

| | | |
|---|---|---|
| Pre-school ★★ | Grade School ★★½ | Teens ★★½ |
| Young Adults ★★½ | Over 30 ★★½ | Seniors ★★½ |

**Description and Comments**   This museum traces the history of Lahaina's colorful whaling era, roughly from 1825 to 1860. Among more than 100 items on exhibit are a six-foot model of a whaling ship, harpoons, maps, logbooks, and an extensive collection of scrimshaw.

### Wo Hing Temple Museum                    Zone 9 West Maui

**Location** Front Street
**Phone** (808) 661-3262
**Hours** Daily, 10 a.m.–4 p.m.
**Admission** Donations accepted
**When to Go** Any time
**How Much Time to Allow** 30 minutes
**Author's Rating** ★★½; Good for historians; young kids will be bored.
**Overall Appeal by Age Group**

| | | |
|---|---|---|
| Pre-school ★ | Grade School ★★ | Teens ★★ |
| Young Adults ★★½ | Over 30 ★★½ | Seniors ★★★ |

**Description and Comments**   A Buddhist shrine is the centerpiece of this restored Chinese temple, which provides a revealing look at how early Chinese settlers lived in Lahaina. Old photographs and artifacts are also on exhibit. A cookhouse (built separately from the main building to reduce the risk of a house fire) sits just to the right of the building. Two Hawai'i films shot in 1898 and 1906 by Thomas Edison are among the highlights. The temple is affiliated with Chee Kung Tong, a Chinese fraternal society with branches throughout the world.

**Other Things to Do Nearby**   The Baldwin Home Museum and Brig *Carthaginian* are nearby.

## The Big Island of Hawai'i

### Ahu'ena Heiau                    Zone 11 Kona

**Location** Next to Kamakahonu Beach, fronting the King Kamehameha's Kona Beach Hotel
**Phone** (808) 329-2911
**Hours** Always open
**Admission** Free
**When to Go** Any time
**How Much Time to Allow** Up to 1 hour
**Author's Rating** ★★½; One of Hawai'i's most treasured heiau

**Overall Appeal by Age Group**

| | | |
|---|---|---|
| Pre-school ★ | Grade School ★★ | Teens ★★ |
| Young Adults ★★½ | Over 30 ★★★ | Seniors ★★★ |

**Description and Comments**    Rebuilt by King Kamehameha I, this historic heiau—a temple of peace dedicated to Lono, the god of fertility—is part of a free walking tour offered at the King Kamehameha's Kona Beach Hotel. The heiau was used by ancient Hawaiians to pray for bountiful harvests, healthy children, and good weather. The tallest structure is the *anu'u* (oracle tower), where the *kahuna* (priest) received messages from the gods. Kamehameha spent the last seven years of his life in this area. Many Hawaiians still believe the heiau is a site of great spiritual significance, so access to the temple's platform is strictly forbidden. The grounds surrounding the platform are open to the public.

**Touring Tips**    Guided tours held Monday–Friday at 1:30 p.m. For self-guided tours, stop by the hotel's guest services desk to pick up a free brochure detailing the history of the heiau.

**Other Things to Do Nearby**    Hulihe'e Palace is just minutes away by car.

## Akatsuka Orchid Gardens            Zone 12 Hilo and Volcano

**Location**    Off Hwy. 11, just north of Volcano Village (on the way to Hawai'i Volcanoes National Park)
**Phone**    (808) 967-8234
**Hours**    Daily, 8:30 a.m.–5 p.m.
**Admission**    Free (self-guided tours)
**When to Go**    Any time
**How Much Time to Allow**    45 minutes
**Author's Rating**    ★★★; The variety of orchids is astounding.
**Overall Appeal by Age Group**

| | | |
|---|---|---|
| Pre-school ★ | Grade School ★★½ | Teens ★★½ |
| Young Adults ★★★ | Over 30 ★★★ | Seniors ★★★½ |

**Description and Comments**    This six-acre garden is recognized as a world leader in the hybridization of orchids, nurturing more than 400,000 plants. Many of the latest varieties were developed by noted horticulturist Mori Akatsuka. A gift shop offers orchids that can be shipped home.

**Other Things to Do Nearby**    Hawai'i Volcanoes National Park is minutes away by car.

## Amy B. H. Greenwell
## Ethnobotanical Garden            Zone 11 Hilo and Volcano

**Location**    82-6188 Mamalahoa Hwy., off Hwy. 11 in Captain Cook
**Phone**    (808) 323-3318
**Website**    www.bishopmuseum.org/greenwell
**Hours**    Monday–Friday, 8:30 a.m.–5 p.m.
**Admission**    A $5 donation is requested
**When to Go**    Any time
**How Much Time to Allow**    1 hour

**Author's Rating** ★★★; A first-class garden with lots of photo ops.
**Overall Appeal by Age Group**

Pre-school ★★      Grade School ★★      Teens ★★½

Young Adults ★★★      Over 30 ★★★      Seniors ★★★★

**Description and Comments** Owned by the Bishop Museum, this 12-acre ethnobotanical garden features more than 250 varieties of plants, including 10 native varieties that are on the endangered species list. These plants were used by ancient Hawaiians for food, medicine, and other daily necessities. Some of the crops on display include banana, breadfruit, sugarcane, and taro.

**Touring Tips** A guided tour is offered at 10 a.m. on the second Saturday of every month. Helpful information for self-guided tours is provided.

### Astronaut Ellison S. Onizuka Space Center     Zone 11 Kona

**Location** Keahole-Kona International Airport
**Phone** (808) 329-3441
**Website** www.planet-hawaii.com/astronautonizuka
**Hours** Daily, 8:30 a.m.–4:30 p.m.
**Admission** $3 for adults; $1 for children under age 12
**When to Go** While waiting for your flight out of Kona (arrive a half-hour early at the airport)
**How Much Time to Allow** 30 minutes
**Author's Rating** ★★★½; A hands-on attraction with equal parts fun and education.
**Overall Appeal by Age Group**

Pre-school ★★      Grade School ★★★★      Teens ★★★½

Young Adults ★★★      Over 30 ★★★      Seniors ★★★

**Description and Comments** This space museum features ten interactive exhibits and more than a dozen audiovisual displays, including an authentic *Apollo 13* space suit and a Space Theater showing NASA videos. You can launch a miniature space shuttle, log in to the space shuttle's computer program to learn about the system's components, and even attempt a "rendezvous" with an object in outer space. Proceeds from the gift shop help maintain the center, which is named in honor of Hawai'i's first astronaut, Ellison S. Onizuka. Born and raised in the Kona area, Onizuka was among the shuttle crew members who perished in the *Challenger* explosion as it launched into space on January 28, 1986.

### Hawai'i Tropical Botanical Garden     Zone 12 Hilo and Volcano

**Location** Onemea, RR 143A, 7 miles north of Hilo. Watch for a sign that says Scenic Route 4 Miles Long, turn right, then drive to the garden's headquarters and registration area.
**Phone** (808) 964-5233
**Website** www.htbg.com
**Hours** Daily, 8:30 a.m.–4 p.m.
**Admission** $15 for adults; $5 for children ages 6–16
**When to Go** Any time

**How Much Time to Allow** 1 hour to 90 minutes
**Author's Rating** ★★★½; One of the most beautiful spots in the state.
**Overall Appeal by Age Group**

| | | |
|---|---|---|
| Pre-school ★★ | Grade School ★★½ | Teens ★★½ |
| Young Adults ★★★ | Over 30 ★★★½ | Seniors ★★★★ |

**Description and Comments** This 45-acre nature preserve, opened to the public in 1984, offers a unique tropical rainforest experience. Visitors are provided with trail maps for self-guided tours. At the entrance, you're greeted by helpful volunteers who will answer any questions and even supply you with mosquito repellent or an umbrella in the event of rain. A 500-foot-long boardwalk leads you through a steep ravine filled with banana, bamboo, ferns, and other tropical plants. From there, other trails bring you to waterfalls, a lily pond, streams, an aviary, and more than 2,000 plant species, including palms, ferns, orchids, bromeliads, heliconia, ginger, and fruit trees collected from around the world. Upon your return, drop by the gift shop to browse through local arts and crafts, books, and other items. Proceeds go toward the preservation of the garden.

## Hawai'i Volcanoes National Park   Zone 12 Hilo and Volcano

**Location** About 30 miles from Hilo, traveling down Hwy. 11 (follow the road signs and turn left into the park entrance)
**Phone** (808) 985-6000
**Website** www.hawaii.volcanoes.national-park.com or www.nps.gov/havo
**Hours** The park itself is open 24 hours a day year-round; the Visitor Center is open daily, 7:45 a.m.–5 p.m.
**Admission** $10/vehicle. Admission is good for 7 days.
**When to Go** Any time; the best time of day to view eruption activity is after sunset
**How Much Time to Allow** At least half a day.
**Author's Rating** ★★★★★; Hawai'i's premier attraction. Don't expect up-close views of fountaining lava, however.
**Overall Appeal by Age Group**

| | | |
|---|---|---|
| Pre-school ★ | Grade School ★★★½ | Teens ★★★★ |
| Young Adults ★★★★½ | Over 30 ★★★★½ | Seniors ★★★½ |

**Description and Comments** The 377-acre Hawai'i Volcanoes National Park, established in 1916 by the National Park Service, is certainly one of the world's top wonders. Kilauea Volcano has been spewing lava continuously since 1983. Begin at the Visitor Center, which houses a gallery of volcano exhibits and a 200-seat mini-theater showing a terrific 23-minute film about the history of Hawai'i's volcanoes and their significance to the Hawaiian culture. Park rangers are on hand to answer any questions and offer suggested itineraries at the park.

Next door, the Volcano Art Center offers a wide range of works by some of Hawai'i's top artists. Drive on into the park to find the Thomas A. Jaggar Museum, which features exhibits spotlighting Hawai'i's volcanic history, current seismic activity, land formations, and a profile of Madame Pele, Hawai'i's goddess of fire, whose home is Halema'uma'u Crater and whose handiwork is evident in the eruptions of Kilauea.

From the museum, you can drive to any and all public trails in the park. Be respectful of the surroundings, which native Hawaiians regard as sacred to their culture.

**Other Things to Do Nearby**   The tranquil village of Volcano is just a mile from the park.

## Hulihe'e Palace                                                  Zone 11 Hilo

**Location**  75-5718 Ali'i Dr.
**Phone**  (808) 329-1877
**Hours**  Monday–Friday, 9 a.m.–4 p.m.; Saturday and Sunday, 10 a.m.–4 p.m.
**Admission**  $5 for adults; $4 for senior citizens; $1 for children under age 18
**When to Go**  Any time
**How Much Time to Allow**  45 minutes
**Author's Rating**  ★★★; A historic treasure in the heart of Kailua-Kona.
**Overall Appeal by Age Group**

| | | |
|---|---|---|
| Pre-school ★★ | Grade School ★★½ | Teens ★★★ |
| Young Adults ★★★½ | Over 30 ★★★★ | Seniors ★★★★ |

**Description and Comments**   Operated by the Daughters of Hawai'i, this hand-some Victorian structure was built in 1838 out of lava rock, coral, koa, and 'ohi'a wood for Governor John Kuakini. It later served as a vacation retreat for Hawaiian royalty. Among the treasures here are *kahili* (feathered staffs), stone tools, tapa, jewelry, and a collection of javelins that once belonged to Kamehameha I. *Note:* Photography and videotaping are not allowed inside the palace.

**Touring Tips**   Tours are offered throughout the day.

**Other Things to Do Nearby**   Ahu'ena Heiau and the Kailua Candy Company are among the other notable stops located in Kailua-Kona. A ten-minute drive from Kailua-Kona leads you to Holualoa, a town of artists studios.

## Kaloko-Honokohau National Historical Park   Zone 11 Hilo

**Location**  Situated at the base of Hualalai Volcano, 3 miles north of Kailua-Kona and 3 miles south of the Keahole-Kona International Airport (along Hwy. 11)
**Phone**  (808) 329-6881
**Hours**  8 a.m.–3:30 p.m.
**Admission**  Free
**When to Go**  Any time
**How Much Time to Allow**  1 hour
**Author's Rating**  ★★★; Worthwhile stop for anyone interested in Hawaiian history.
**Overall Appeal by Age Group**

| | | |
|---|---|---|
| Pre-school ★★ | Grade School ★★½ | Teens ★★½ |
| Young Adults ★★★ | Over 30 ★★★ | Seniors ★★★½ |

**Description and Comments**   This 1,300-acre park features more than 200 archaeological sites, including heiau, petroglyphs, fishing shrines, *holua* (stone slides), and fishponds. Several species of endangered animals and plants live here. Picnicking, fishing, snorkeling, swimming, bird-watching, and hiking are among the activities you can enjoy here. Overnight camping is not permitted.

## Kamuela Museum                                    Zone 11 Hilo

**Location** Waimea, at the intersection of Hwys. 25 and 19
**Phone** (808) 885-4724
**Hours** Daily, 8 a.m.–5 p.m.
**Admission** $5 for adults; $2 for children under age 12
**When to Go** Any time
**How Much Time to Allow** 1 hour
**Author's Rating** ★★½; Not worth going out of your way to see, but it has several intriguing exhibits.
**Overall Appeal by Age Group**

| | | |
|---|---|---|
| Pre-school ★½ | Grade School ★★½ | Teens ★★½ |
| Young Adults ★★★ | Over 30 ★★★ | Seniors ★★★ |

**Description and Comments** This cozy museum features an eclectic collection of island artifacts. Among the historical prizes are antique American furniture and Chinese porcelain.

## Lyman Mission House and
## Museum                                Zone 12 Hilo and Volcano

**Location** Hilo, 276 Haili St., a few blocks up from Hilo Bay
**Phone** (808) 935-5021
**Hours** Monday–Saturday, 9 a.m.–4:30 p.m.
**Admission** $7 for adults; $5 for senior citizens; $3 for children ages 17 and under
**When to Go** Any time
**How Much Time to Allow** 1 hour
**Author's Rating** ★★★; Good small museum about Hawai'i's missionary and plantation life.
**Overall Appeal by Age Group**

| | | |
|---|---|---|
| Pre-school ★ | Grade School ★★ | Teens ★★½ |
| Young Adults ★★★ | Over 30 ★★★ | Seniors ★★★★ |

**Description and Comments** The mission house was built in 1839 for David and Sarah Lyman, the first Christian missionaries to Hilo. This well-preserved New England–style home is the oldest standing wooden frame structure on the island and houses missionary-era furnishings, clothing, photographs, and other artifacts. Guides provide detailed information throughout the 25-minute tour. The adjacent two-story museum, built in 1973, showcases Hawai'i's natural and cultural histories. Exhibits here include mineral and shell collections, original documents, historic photographs, and period pieces reflecting the many people who immigrated to the islands. A gift shop is located on the ground floor.

**Other Things to Do Nearby** The Pacific Tsunami Museum is a few minutes away on Kamehameha Avenue.

## Mauna Loa Macadamia Nut
## Visitor Center                          Zone 12 Hilo and Volcano

**Location** On Hwy. 11, 5 miles south of Hilo. Turn onto Macadamia Road and drive to the road's end (you'll pass through Mauna Loa's 2,500-acre orchard)

**Phone** (808) 966-8612
**Website** www.maunaloa.com
**Hours** Daily, 8:30 a.m.–5:30 p.m.
**Admission** Free
**When to Go** Any time
**How Much Time to Allow** 1 hour
**Author's Rating** ★★★½; Life story of everyone's favorite nut, complete with free samples.
**Overall Appeal by Age Group**

| | | |
|---|---|---|
| Pre-school ★★ | Grade School ★★★½ | Teens ★★★½ |
| Young Adults ★★★½ | Over 30 ★★★½ | Seniors ★★★½ |

**Description and Comments**   Head to the Visitor Center first and enjoy a free sampling of Mauna Loa's macadamia nut products, then head outside and watch a brief video presentation about Mauna Loa and the macadamia nut industry. A mini-factory shows how macadamia nut chocolates are made. Adjacent to the Visitor Center is the company's nut-processing plant, where you can watch the proceedings through large viewing windows (helpful signs explain the process). Also on the premises is a pleasant nature walk through tropical foliage and a snack shop serving macadamia nut ice cream, soft drinks, Kona coffee, and other treats.

**Other Things to Do Nearby**   Both Nani Mau Gardens and Pana'ewa Rainforest Zoo are just minutes away by car.

## Nani Mau Gardens                    Zone 12 Hilo and Volcano

**Location**  421 Makalika St. From Hilo, drive about 3 miles south on Hwy. 11. Look for the Nani Mau Gardens sign and turn left onto Makalika St.
**Phone** (808) 959-3500
**Website** www.nanimau.com
**Hours** Daily, 8:30 a.m.–5 p.m.
**Admission** $10 for adults; $5 for children ages 6–18
**When to Go** Any time
**How Much Time to Allow** 1 hour to 90 minutes
**Author's Rating** ★★; The price is a little steep for our tastes, but Nani Mau certainly lives up to its name, which means "forever beautiful."
**Overall Appeal by Age Group**

| | | |
|---|---|---|
| Pre-school ★½ | Grade School ★★ | Teens ★★★ |
| Young Adults ★★★ | Over 30 ★★★½ | Seniors ★★★½ |

**Description and Comments**   This botanical garden, established in 1970, grows more than a hundred varieties of tropical fruit trees and some 2,000 varieties of tropical flowers, including anthuriums, orchids, and bromeliads. A handy map is provided on entry into the garden. Highlights include the Orchid Walkway, Hibiscus Garden, Bromeliad Garden, Lily Pond, Polynesian Garden, European Garden, Fruit Orchard, and Annual Garden. Everything here is immaculately maintained, with the exception of the Japanese Garden, which is somewhat disappointing. A restaurant and gift shop are also on the premises.

**Touring Tips**   A 35-minute tram tour is available for an additional $6.

**Other Things to Do Nearby** Attractions in the vicinity of Nani Mau Gardens include the Mauna Loa Macadamia Nut Visitor Center and Pana'ewa Rainforest Zoo.

## Onizuka Center for International Astronomy and Mauna Kea Observatory    *Zone 12 Hilo and Volcano*

**Location** Take Hwy. 200 to the Visitor Information Station, at the 9,300-foot elevation level on Mauna Kea
**Phone** (808) 961-2180
**Website** www.ifa.hawaii.edu/info/vis
**Hours** Visitor Information Station: Monday–Thursday, 5:30–10 p.m.; Friday, 9 a.m.–noon, 1–4:30 p.m., and 6–10 p.m.; Saturday and Sunday, 9 a.m.–10 p.m.
**Admission** Free
**When to Go** Any time; nights for stargazing, weekends for summit visits
**How Much Time to Allow** Half a day, or night
**Author's Rating** ★★★½; An "out-of-this-world" experience, especially for visitors who are able to ascend to Mauna Kea's summit.
**Overall Appeal by Age Group**

| | | |
|---|---|---|
| Pre-school ★ | Grade School ★★ | Teens ★★★★½ |
| Young Adults ★★★★½ | Over 30 ★★★★½ | Seniors ★★★½ |

**Description and Comments** The Onizuka Center offers several fascinating displays covering the observatory's history, programs, and accomplishments. The Visitor Information Station offers free tours to the 13,796-foot summit of Mauna Kea every Saturday and Sunday from 1 to 5 p.m. (weather permitting). Visitors should arrive promptly by 1 p.m., as participants are required to spend an hour of acclimation time here before ascending to higher elevations (see other warnings listed below in Touring Tips). At 2 p.m., participants return to their four-wheel-drive vehicles (regular cars cannot do this trek; check with your car rental agency about a four-wheel-drive vehicle) and are led to the summit, perhaps the finest spot on earth for stargazing. The clear, dark skies allow astronomers in observatories from 11 countries to peer into deep space.

Every night, the Visitor Information Station holds a stargazing program from 6 to 10 p.m. The program begins with an astronomy video, followed by a discussion of astronomy and Mauna Kea, then moves outside to observe celestial delights through two large telescopes: star clusters, double stars, white dwarfs, planetary nebulas, star-forming nebulas, supernova remnants, supernovas, planets, galaxies, and all of the constellations visible in Hawai'i. Even at 9,300 feet, the Visitor Information Station enjoys clear, dark skies at a higher elevation than most of the other major telescopes on the planet. Bring binoculars and flashlights with red filters. Most important, dress warmly—temperatures up there drop to 40–55° on summer nights and 26–50° on winter nights.

*Important note:* Be sure that you have a full tank of gas before driving up Mauna Kea. The steep grade, combined with the lower oxygen level, makes engines run inefficiently. Fuel is not available for purchase on Mauna Kea.

**Touring Tips** Children under age 16, pregnant women, and those with respiratory, heart, and severe obesity conditions are not allowed to travel to the summit. Be aware that the weather conditions at Mauna Kea can be quite severe, including freezing temperatures, snow, and high winds. Also, scuba divers must wait at least 24 hours after their last dive before being ascending to the summit. The drive up to the summit *requires* a four-wheel-drive vehicle; consult your rental car agency before planning a visit to Mauna Kea.

## Pacific Tsunami Museum — *Zone 12 Hilo and Volcano*

**Location** 103 Kamehameha Ave. in downtown Hilo
**Phone** (808) 935-0926
**Website** www.tsunami.org
**Hours** Wednesday–Saturday, 10 a.m.–4 p.m.
**Admission** Donations accepted
**When to Go** Any time
**How Much Time to Allow** 1 hour
**Author's Rating** ★★★; Sad but riveting reminder of the power of tidal waves and an important chapter in Hilo's history. Will make you look twice at that calm bay
**Overall Appeal by Age Group**

| Pre-school ★★ | Grade School ★★★ | Teens ★★★★ |
| Young Adults ★★★★ | Over 30 ★★★★½ | Seniors ★★★½ |

**Description and Comments** The Pacific Tsunami Museum pays tribute to the hundreds of Hilo residents who perished during the horrific tsunamis that struck the city in 1946 and 1960. It also educates today's residents about what to do when the next tsunami hits. Exhibits include informative video presentations and startling photographs.

**Other Things to Do Nearby** The Lyman Mission House and Museum is a few blocks away.

## Pana'ewa Rainforest Zoo — *Zone 12 Hilo and Volcano*

**Location** Mamaki St., off Hwy. 11 south of Hilo
**Phone** (808) 959-7224
**Hours** Daily, 9 a.m.–4 p.m.
**Admission** Free
**When to Go** Any time
**How Much Time to Allow** 1 hour
**Author's Rating** ★★½; The kids will love it.
**Overall Appeal by Age Group**

| Pre-school ★★★ | Grade School ★★★½ | Teens ★★★ |
| Young Adults ★★★ | Over 30 ★★½ | Seniors ★★½ |

**Description and Comments** This 12-acre zoo in the Pana'ewa Rainforest Reserve is the only tropical rainforest zoo in the United States. It spotlights the world's rainforest animals, reptiles, and birds, including a Bengal tiger, water buffalo, pygmy hippos, spider monkeys, deer, iguanas, feral goats, tapirs, and vultures—most of which can't be seen in the islands—as well as some native birds, including the nene goose, Hawai'i's state bird. Picnic tables and rain shelters are provided for rest and relaxation.

**Touring Tips** The tiger feeding is at 3:30 p.m. every day.

**Other Things to Do Nearby** The Mauna Loa Macadamia Nut Visitor Center and Nani Mau Gardens are minutes away by car.

## Parker Ranch Visitor Center
## and Historic Homes                                    *Zone 11 Kona*

**Location**  Parker Ranch Shopping Center, 67-1185 Mamalahoa Hwy.
**Phone**  (808) 885-7655
**Hours**  Daily, 9 a.m.–5 p.m.
**Admission**  Visitor center: $5 for adults, $3.75 for children ages 4–11; historic home: $8.50 for adults, $6 for children ages 4–11; both attractions: $12 for adults, $9.50 for children
**When to Go**  Any time
**How Much Time to Allow**  2 hours
**Author's Rating**  ★★★½; a good look at the Hawaiian paniolo way of life.
**Overall Appeal by Age Group**

| | | |
|---|---|---|
| Pre-school ★★½ | Grade School ★★★½ | Teens ★★★½ |
| Young Adults ★★★½ | Over 30 ★★★½ | Seniors ★★★½ |

**Description and Comments**  One of the largest privately owned ranches in the United States, the 225,000-acre Parker Ranch owns the town of Waimea (also known as Kamuela), in the heart of Big Island "paniolo country." The Parker Ranch Visitor Center traces the storied history of the Parker family through a variety of displays, photographs, artifacts, and a 20-minute video. In 1809, a sailor from Massachusetts named John Palmer Parker arrived in the islands, befriended King Kamehameha I, and married a Hawaiian princess. At the king's behest, Parker began domesticating the wild horses and cattle that roamed free and were harming the fertile slopes of Mauna Kea, and he was given a two-acre land grant in thanks. In the 1850s, Parker began purchasing more land in the area, laying the foundation for Parker Ranch. Today, guided or self-tours reveal Pu'u'opelu, a handsome ranch home with a fine art collection, and a replica of Mana Hale, the Parker family homes compound located about three-fourths of a mile from the Visitor Center. The Parker Ranch Store carries an assortment of paniolo apparel, hats, boots, buckles, music, artworks, greeting cards, and books.

**Touring Tips**  Wagon rides are now available. They last about 45 minutes to an hour and cost $8.50 for adults and $6 for children ages 4–11.

## Pu'uhonua O Honaunau National
## Historical Park                                       *Zone 11 Kona*

**Location**  Approximately 22 miles south of Kailua-Kona. From Hwy. 11, turn onto Hwy. 160 at the Honaunau Post Office near Mile Marker 103. Follow the road for about 3.5 miles to the park's entrance.
**Phone**  (808) 328-2326
**Hours**  Visitor Center: daily, 8 a.m.–4:30 p.m. Picnic area: Monday–Thursday, 6 a.m.–8 p.m.; Friday–Sunday, 6 a.m.–11 p.m.
**Admission**  $5 for one car, or $3 for adults; free for children under age 16
**When to Go**  Any time. If you visit during the weekend closest to July 1, you can take part in the park's annual cultural festival, featuring Hawaiian games, hula performances, and arts and crafts demonstrations
**How Much Time to Allow**  1–2 hours

**Author's Rating** ★★½; One of Hawai'i's most sacred cultural history attractions.

**Overall Appeal by Age Group**

| | | |
|---|---|---|
| Pre-school ★ | Grade School ★★ | Teens ★★½ |
| Young Adults ★★½ | Over 30 ★★★ | Seniors ★★★★ |

**Description and Comments**   In ancient Hawai'i, this area, flanked by huge lava rock walls, served as a place of refuge or sanctuary where minor offenders and refugees of war could seek safety and redemption. You'll find self-guided tour brochures and maps at the park's Visitor Center. You can listen to an audio message along the center's mural wall or sit in on an orientation discussion in the amphitheater. Then explore Hale O Keawe Heiau, built in 1650, as well as wooden *ki'i* images, canoe sheds, and other ancient artifacts and structures. Stop and observe cultural demonstrators working at their crafts; they are friendly and eager to share their knowledge of Hawaiiana. Hikers can follow a mile-long trail that hugs the Kona coastline and is dotted with several archaeological sites, including heiau.

**Touring Tips**   Orientation talks at the Visitor Center are scheduled at 10, 10:30, and 11 a.m. and 2:30, 3, and 3:30 p.m.

**Other Things to Do Nearby**   Kealakekua Bay, where Capt. Cook landed and met his death, is a five-minute drive north.

## *Pu'ukohola Heiau* *Zone 11 Kona*

**Location**   On the north end of the Kohala Coast near Kawaiahae Harbor. From the intersection of Rt. 270 and Hwy. 19, drive a quarter-mile north of Rt. 270 to the park's access road

**Phone**   (808) 882-7218

**Hours**   Daily, 7:30 a.m.–4 p.m.

**Admission**   Free

**When to Go**   Any time. In mid-August, the park stages a cultural festival featuring Hawaiian food and games, hula performances, a royal court procession, and arts and crafts demonstrations

**How Much Time to Allow**   1 hour

**Author's Rating**   ★★★; Important site for Islands cultural history.

**Overall Appeal by Age Group**

| | | |
|---|---|---|
| Pre-school ★ | Grade School ★★ | Teens ★★½ |
| Young Adults ★★½ | Over 30 ★★★ | Seniors ★★★★ |

**Description and Comments**   Two historic heiau—Pu'ukohola and Mailekini—are within a short walk of the Visitor Center. Pu'ukohola, with its huge stone walls facing the sea, looks like the war temple it was. The site was originally constructed in 1550 and rebuilt by Kamehameha I in 1790 when he launched his efforts to unite the islands into a kingdom. (There is, in fact, a third heiau, Hale O Kapuni, which rests underwater and is not visible.) Hiking and tours of the park (both guided and self-guided) are among the activities available here.

**Other Things to Do Nearby**   Spencer Beach County Park is within walking distance.

## Sadie Seymour Botanical Gardens      *Zone 11 Kona*

**Location** 76-6280 Kuakini Hwy.
**Phone** (808) 329-7286
**Hours** Daily, 24 hours
**Admission** Donations accepted
**When to Go** Any time
**How Much Time to Allow** 1 hour
**Author's Rating** ★★★; A beautifully kept Eden for nature lovers.
**Overall Appeal by Age Group**

| | | |
|---|---|---|
| Pre-school ★★ | Grade School ★★½ | Teens ★★½ |
| Young Adults ★★★ | Over 30 ★★★½ | Seniors ★★★★ |

**Description and Comments** Maintained and operated by the Kona Outdoor Circle, this international garden features beautiful landscapes and exotic flora representing areas from throughout the globe, including Hawai'i, the Pacific region, Asia, Central America, South America, and Africa. Brochures for self-guided tours are available.

## Suisan Fish Market and Auction     *Zone 12 Hilo and Volcano*

**Location** Hilo, 85 Lihiwai St., at the corner of Banyan Dr. and Lihiwai St.
**Phone** (808) 935-9349
**Hours** Monday–Saturday, opens at 7 a.m.
**Admission** Free
**When to Go** Any time
**How Much Time to Allow** 30 minutes
**Author's Rating** ★★½; For early risers with an appreciation of "fishy" business.
**Overall Appeal by Age Group**

| | | |
|---|---|---|
| Pre-school ★ | Grade School ★★★ | Teens ★★★ |
| Young Adults ★★★½ | Over 30 ★★★ | Seniors ★★★ |

**Description and Comments** The public is invited each morning to watch brokers representing restaurants and markets from around the state bid on the day's freshest catches, including 'ahi (tuna), mahimahi, snappers, marlin, swordfish, and squid. Consumers may purchase fresh fish at the market next door.

**Other Things to Do Nearby** Visit downtown Hilo.

## Volcano Winery      *Zone 12 Hilo and Volcano*

**Location** Off Hwy. 11, 30 miles south of Hilo. Turn onto Pi'i Mauna Dr. and follow the road (also called Golf Course Rd. on some maps)
**Phone** (808) 967-7479
**Website** www.volcanowinery.com
**Hours** Daily, 10 a.m.–5:30 p.m.
**Admission** Free
**When to Go** Any time
**How Much Time to Allow** 1 hour
**Author's Rating** ★★½; A great stop for sweet wine lovers on the way to (or from) Hawai'i Volcanoes National Park.

**Overall Appeal by Age Group**

| | | |
|---|---|---|
| Pre-school ★ | Grade School ★★ | Teens ★★ |
| Young Adults ★★½ | Over 30 ★★★ | Seniors ★★★ |

**Description and Comments**   The southernmost winery in the United States, this 18-acre vineyard, at the 4,000-foot elevation mark, produces 100% tropical honey and tropical fruit blend (half-grape, half-fruit) wines. Visit the tasting room and sample unique flavors including Macadamia Nut Honey Wine, Lehua Blossom Honey Wine, Guava Chablis, Passion Chablis, and Volcano Blush.

**Other Things to Do Nearby**   Winery borders Hawai'i Volcanoes National Park.

## *Wakefield Botanical Gardens*                     *Zone 11 Kona*

**Location**  City of Refuge Rd.
**Phone**  (808) 328-9930
**Hours**  Monday–Friday, 11 a.m.–3:30 p.m.; Saturday and Sunday, 8 a.m.–4 p.m.
**Admission**  Free
**When to Go**  Any time
**How Much Time to Allow**  1 hour
**Author's Rating**  ★★½; For botany lovers.
**Overall Appeal by Age Group**

| | | |
|---|---|---|
| Pre-school ★★ | Grade School ★★½ | Teens ★★½ |
| Young Adults ★★★ | Over 30 ★★★ | Seniors ★★★½ |

**Description and Comments**   More than a thousand varieties of plants and coexist in this small (five-acre) botanical garden and macadamia nut orchard.

# Kaua'i

## *Grove Farm Homestead*                     *Zone 13 Kaua'i*

**Location**  Just off Nawiliwili Rd. outside Lihu'e.
**Phone**  (808) 245-3202
**Hours**  Monday, Wednesday, and Thursday, guided tours at 10 a.m. and 1 p.m.; reservations required
**Admission**  Donations of $5 for adults and $2 for children ages 12 and under are requested
**When to Go**  Any time
**How Much Time to Allow**  90 minutes
**Author's Rating**  ★★½; A good visit if you're interested in the island's plantation history.
**Overall Appeal by Age Group**

| | | |
|---|---|---|
| Pre-school ★½ | Grade School ★★ | Teens ★★½ |
| Young Adults ★★★ | Over 30 ★★★ | Seniors ★★★½ |

**Description and Comments**   This peaceful 80-acre homestead, owned by a prominent plantation family, provides a revealing glimpse of plantation life during the 19th century. The complex encompasses a museum, washhouse, teahouse, and other plantation buildings

**Other Things to Do Nearby**   Kaua'i Museum is a short drive away on Rice Street in Lihu'e.

## Guava Kai Plantation                           Zone 13 Kaua'i

**Location**   At the end of Ku'awa Rd., off Hwy. 53 in Kilauea
**Phone**   (808) 828-6121
**Hours**   Daily, 9 a.m.–5 p.m.
**Admission**   Free
**When to Go**   Any time
**How Much Time to Allow**   45 minutes
**Author's Rating**   ★★½; A pleasant stop near Kaua'i's scenic north shore.
**Overall Appeal by Age Group**

| | | |
|---|---|---|
| Pre-school ★½ | Grade School ★★½ | Teens ★★½ |
| Young Adults ★★★ | Over 30 ★★★ | Seniors ★★★ |

**Description and Comments**   Visit the plantation's Visitor Center and enjoy free samples of guava juice. Here you can learn how the fruit is grown and processed. Take a stroll through the plantation's gardens.

**Other Things to Do Nearby**   The Kilauea Point National Wildlife Refuge is just a few minutes away by car.

## Kaua'i Museum                                  Zone 13 Kaua'i

**Location**   4428 Rice St.
**Phone**   (808) 245-6931
**Hours**   Monday–Friday, 9 a.m.–4 p.m.; Saturday, 10 a.m.–4 p.m. (guided tours are scheduled each Tuesday at 10 a.m.)
**Admission**   $5 for adults; $4 for senior citizens; $3 for children ages 14–17; $1 for children ages 6–12
**When to Go**   Any time
**How Much Time to Allow**   75 minutes
**Author's Rating**   ★★★½; History museum with a slightly different take on the past.
**Overall Appeal by Age Group**

| | | |
|---|---|---|
| Pre-school ★★ | Grade School ★★★ | Teens ★★★ |
| Young Adults ★★★ | Over 30 ★★★½ | Seniors ★★★★ |

**Description and Comments**   This compact little museum in a coral-block building in downtown Lihu'e says as much as most school children or people on vacation can absorb about Hawai'i's mysterious history at one time. Some of its exhibits of treasured artifacts and written legends are presented along a curving ramp like a timeline. It dates the earliest migrations of Polynesian voyagers from about AD 200, a few centuries earlier than the commonly accepted theory. Kaua'i, always the independent kingdom, is said to have been the home of ancient Tahitian ali'i who settled along the Wailua River and left behind many signs of their residence—including temples, birthing stones, and house sites. Kaua'i was never conquered by Kamehameha I like the other islands, but joined the kingdom voluntarily. Later, the Hawaiian sugar industry was born in Koloa. This particular history of the Garden Isle, within the overall history of Hawai'i, comes to life through the extensive collection of displays and artifacts.

## Kilauea Point National Wildlife Refuge    Zone 13 Kaua'i

**Location**  Turn off Hwy. 56 near Mile Marker 23, then take Kolo Rd. down to
Kilauea Rd.
**Phone**  (808) 828-1413
**Hours**  Daily, 10 a.m.–4 p.m.
**Admission**  $2 for adults; free for children age 16 and under
**When to Go**  Any time
**How Much Time to Allow**  75 minutes
**Author's Rating**  ★★½; The views from Kilauea Point are breathtaking.
**Overall Appeal by Age Group**

| Pre-school ★★ | Grade School ★★★ | Teens ★★★½ |
| Young Adults ★★★½ | Over 30 ★★★★ | Seniors ★★★★ |

**Description and Comments**  A variety of wildlife can be viewed from Kilauea
Point, including more than a dozen species of seabirds, spinner dolphins, Hawaiian green
sea turtles, Hawaiian monk seals, and, during the winter months, humpback whales. A
52-foot-high lighthouse, built in 1913, once boasted the largest lens of its kind in the
world. It was deactivated in 1976 and is now listed on the National Register of Historic
Places.

**Other Things to Do Nearby**  The Guava Kai Plantation is minutes away by car.

## Kilohana Plantation    Zone 13 Kaua'i

**Location**  Puhi, 3-2087 Kaumuali'i Hwy.
**Phone**  (808) 245-5608; carriage information (808) 246-9529
**Hours**  Daily, 9:30 a.m.–9:30 p.m. A 20-minute carriage ride is available (no reserva-
tions required), and a 1-hour horse-drawn wagon tour of the cane fields is offered 11
a.m. and 2 p.m. Monday–Thursday.
**Admission**  Free. The carriage ride costs $10 for adults and $5 for children under age
12. The wagon tour costs $24 for adults and $12 for children.
**When to Go**  Any time
**How Much Time to Allow**  1–2 hours
**Author's Rating**  ★★★; Shoppers will like the boutiques and galleries; kids will enjoy
the carriage ride.
**Overall Appeal by Age Group**

| Pre-school ★★½ | Grade School ★★★ | Teens ★★★ |
| Young Adults ★★★½ | Over 30 ★★★★ | Seniors ★★★★ |

**Description and Comments**  This 35-acre estate, owned by the kama'aina Wilcox
sugar plantation family, was built in 1935 and today features a wealth of agricultural displays, antiques, and other treasures from Kaua'i's plantation era. Shops, galleries, and a
restaurant are available.

## Koke'e Natural History Museum    Zone 13 Kaua'i

**Location**  Koke'e State Park
**Phone**  (808) 335-9975
**Website**  www.aloha.net/~kokee
**Hours**  Daily, 10 a.m.–4 p.m.

**Admission** $5 donation requested
**When to Go** Any time
**How Much Time to Allow** 1 hour
**Author's Rating** ★★★; A surprisingly good museum worth a visit if you're in the area.
**Overall Appeal by Age Group**

| | | |
|---|---|---|
| Pre-school ★½ | Grade School ★★½ | Teens ★★½ |
| Young Adults ★★★ | Over 30 ★★★½ | Seniors ★★★★ |

**Description and Comments** This is an intimate museum focusing on the island's ecology, geology, and climatology. Featured are stone artifacts, shells, samples of native Hawaiian woods, and an informative display about weather systems in the Pacific region (including information on Hurricane 'Iniki, which devastated Kaua'i in September 1992). The museum's gift shop has an impressive selection of Hawaiian books, maps, and hiking guides.

## Limahuli Garden                                         Zone 13 Kaua'i

**Location** In Ha'ena, near Ha'ena State Park, North Shore
**Phone** (808) 826-1053
**Website** www.ntbg.org
**Hours** Tuesday–Friday and Sunday, 9:30 a.m.–4 p.m.
**Admission** Guided tours are $15 for adults (reservations required); self-guided tours are $10 (no reservations needed); children under age 12 are admitted free
**When to Go** Any time
**How Much Time to Allow** 2 hours
**Author's Rating** ★★★★; Photographers, gardeners, and those who just want to walk in the rainforest will find few more appealing places than this.
**Overall Appeal by Age Group**

| | | |
|---|---|---|
| Pre-school ★ | Grade School ★½ | Teens ★★ |
| Young Adults ★★½ | Over 30 ★★★ | Seniors ★★★ |

**Description and Comments** This award-winning 17-acre garden and 990-acre forest preserve—it was named America's Natural Botanical Garden of the Year in 1997 by the American Horticultural Society—features terraced taro patches, gardens, and a lush rainforest walk. Three distinct ecological zones are found within the garden.

## Moir Gardens                                           Zone 13 Kaua'i

**Location** Kiahuna Plantation, 2253 Po'ipu Rd.
**Phone** (808) 742-6411
**Hours** Daily, 24 hours
**Admission** Free
**When to Go** Any time
**How Much Time to Allow** 1 hour
**Author's Rating** ★★★; A living symbol of why Kaua'i is the Garden Isle.
**Overall Appeal by Age Group**

| | | |
|---|---|---|
| Pre-school ★★ | Grade School ★★½ | Teens ★★½ |
| Young Adults ★★★ | Over 30 ★★★½ | Seniors ★★★½ |

**Description and Comments** Nearly 4,000 varieties of plant life are featured in this garden, which surrounds the former home of Koloa Plantation Company's last plantation manager. Lagoons, lily ponds, trees, and flowers provide photo opportunities. A highlight here is one of the finest cactus gardens in the world.

**Touring Tips**  Free guided tours are held Thursday at 10 a.m.

**Other Things to Do Nearby**  Lawai and Allerton Gardens are a short drive away in Lawai.

## National Tropical Botanical Garden
## Lawai and Allerton Gardens                    Zone 13 Kaua'i

**Location**  Near the end of Lawai Rd. in Lawai
**Phone**  (808) 332-7361 for tour information; (808) 742-2623 for reservations
**Website**  www.ntbg.org
**Hours**  The Visitor Center is open daily, 8:30 a.m.–5 p.m.
**Admission**  For guided tours: $25 for adults; $15 for children ages 13–18; $10 for children ages 6–12 (not recommended for toddlers)
**When to Go**  Any time
**How Much Time to Allow**  About 2½ hours for guided tours
**Author's Rating**  ★★½; The experience here is so serene, it borders on therapeutic.
**Overall Appeal by Age Group**

| | | |
|---|---|---|
| Pre-school ★ | Grade School ★½ | Teens ★★ |
| Young Adults ★★½ | Over 30 ★★★ | Seniors ★★★ |

**Description and Comments**  The National Tropical Botanical Garden in Lawai is a 186-acre Eden that boasts one of the world's largest collections of rare and endangered tropical flora, including palms, heliconia, orchids, and other plants that have been collected from tropical regions throughout the world. Neighboring Allerton Garden, meanwhile, features a large collection of flora and beautiful waterfalls, gazebos, and a bamboo jungle. A gift shop offers a charming collection of Island gift items.

**Touring Tips**  Lawai Garden has guided tours every Monday at 9 a.m. and 1 p.m. Allerton Garden offers guided tours Tuesday–Saturday at 9 and 10 a.m. and 1 and 2 p.m. Reservations are required.

## Wai'oli Mission House Museum                    Zone 13 Kaua'i

**Location**  Grove Farm Homestead
**Phone**  (808) 245-3202
**Hours**  Tuesday, Thursday, and Saturday, 9 a.m.–3 p.m. Guided tours are available
**Admission**  Donations of $5 for adults and $2 for children age 12 and under are requested
**When to Go**  Any time
**How Much Time to Allow**  1 hour
**Author's Rating**  ★★½; Recommended for anyone interested in Hawai'i's missionary era.
**Overall Appeal by Age Group**

| | | |
|---|---|---|
| Pre-school ★½ | Grade School ★★ | Teens ★★½ |
| Young Adults ★★½ | Over 30 ★★★ | Seniors ★★★½ |

**Description and Comments**  Built in 1837, this structure was the home of missionaries Lucy and Abner Wilcox. The New England–style Wai'oli Mission Hall and

Wai'oli Hui'ia Church are located on adjoining grounds. What brings it to life are docents in period dress who act the part.

# Moloka'i

## Moloka'i Museum and Cultural Center     Zone 14 Moloka'i

**Location**  On Kalae Hwy., just west of Kaunakakai
**Phone**  (808) 567-6436
**Hours**  Monday–Saturday, 10 a.m.–2 p.m.
**Admission**  $2.50 for adults; $1 for students ages 5–18
**When to Go**  Any time
**How Much Time to Allow**  1 hour
**Author's Rating**  ★★½; Not terribly exciting, but filled with history.
**Overall Appeal by Age Group**

| | | |
|---|---|---|
| Pre-school ★½ | Grade School ★★ | Teens ★★½ |
| Young Adults ★★★ | Over 30 ★★★ | Seniors ★★★½ |

**Description and Comments**  The museum is a converted sugar mill established in 1878 by Rudolph Wilhelm Meyer, an engineer and surveyor who arrived on Moloka'i in 1851 and married a Hawaiian princess. Now listed on the National Register of Historic Places, the mill houses original machinery and other artifacts from the island's sugar plantation days. Guided tours and Hawaiian cultural programs are offered.

## Moloka'i Ranch                          Zone 14 Moloka'i

**Location**  100 Maunaloa Hwy.
**Phone**  (808) 552-2791
**Website**  www.molokai-ranch.com
**Hours**  Monday–Saturday, 7:30 a.m.–4:30 p.m.
**Admission**  Prices for activities range from $35–50 for target archery and $45–65 for outrigger canoe paddling to $80–105 for a paniolo roundup (rodeo); half- and full-day children's activities range from $30–75
**When to Go**  Any time
**How Much Time to Allow**  Half a day
**Author's Rating**  ★★★★★; Moloka'i's biggest attraction has something for the entire family.
**Overall Appeal by Age Group**

| | | |
|---|---|---|
| Pre-school ★★½ | Grade School ★★★★ | Teens ★★★★½ |
| Young Adults ★★★★½ | Over 30 ★★★★ | Seniors ★★★½ |

**Description and Comments**  Encompassing more than 53,000 acres (a third of the island), Moloka'i Ranch is the place to find many great outdoor activities. At the ranch's Outfitters Center, you can sign up for a horseback ride or learn basic cowboy skills—you can even compete in the Malihini Rodeo. Fancy camping is one of the ranch's newer offerings, at a seaside cluster of well appointed solar tent cabins by remote Kaupoa Beach, with a full schedule of activities, meals, and transportation included. The activities include mountain biking, snorkeling, hiking, kayaking, outrigger canoe paddling, archery, a ropes challenge course, and winter whale-watching.

*Part Eight*

# Great Outdoors

Outdoor Hawai'i is what the islands are all about, so get out there and enjoy it! The weather seldom intrudes, the scenery lures you, no snakes or toxic plants block your path, and you have abundant choices, from lolling on hundreds of beaches to climbing Diamond Head Crater, plunging in waterfall pools to learning to surf. Golf is so popular that we devoted a lengthy section to various courses (see pae 312). Many activities and guided tours can be arranged by a concierge or hotel activity desk. You can do many on your own.

## Hawai'i by Sea: Get Wet

### The Beach Experience

A hotel swimming pool may look inviting, but we suggest you head for the beach first. The Hawaiian islands boast some of the world's finest beaches on 180 collective miles of sandy shoreline—243 beaches, all open to the public. Sands come not only in traditional gold but, on some beaches, also in black, green, or red. Beaches have appeal because of their natural splendor (such as Hanalei or Lanikai) or for their resort action (like Waikiki or Ka'anapali), but we're confident you will find beaches in Hawai'i that meet your every need: strolling, water sports, or just lying around.

Hawai'i's beaches often top the "Best Beach in America" list compiled by geologist Stephen Leatherman ("Dr. Beach") of Florida International University, who rates beaches on environmental quality, aesthetics, water safety, and amenities (visit www.topbeaches.com to learn more). We'll share our favorites, but encourage you to make your own list.

Beaches are not living things, they are not forever unchanging either, especially in Hawai'i, and may not be exactly the same from visit to visit. Beaches that are big in winter can be small in summer; the reverse is also true. Kilauea Volcano is still building beaches on the southeast shoreline of the Big Island, which is the youngest and least eroded in the chain and consequently has the fewest beaches. Kaua'i, oldest of the major islands, is ringed with scenic strands of sand of all shapes and sizes. Storms rage in every decade or so to remodel island sands, and human-caused coastal erosion is as much a problem in the Aloha State as it is anywhere else. Some beaches vanish overnight under high tides, like Kahalu'u Beach, known as Disappearing Sands Beach, on the Kona coast.

Lucky beachcombers can find treasures like shells and glass fishing floats on certain beaches, including those on north and east shores of Kaua'i and O'ahu. We have also found shells on Kihei beaches. People-watchers are endlessly entertained at crowded beaches, such as Waikiki. Seekers of solitude can leave resort beaches and easily find remote strands, where the only footprints are their own. But the resorts are located on certain beaches because the sands are superlative, so plenty of residents take advantage of public accesses to use them, and so can you.

Many resorts have public trails to walk or jog while you're checking out the beach action and perhaps looking for whales, like Wailea and Ka'anapali resorts on Maui or Mauna Lani and Mauna Kea on the Big Island. Hawaiian resorts on all islands have public beach access, parking, restrooms, and shower facilities in addition to their private guest amenities. Several also maintain publicly accessible historic sites. The public is welcome in hotel restaurants, spas, stores, and bars.

Though the beaches are grand, the water is even better. Even the most devoted sun-seeking beachgoers and teenyboppers who don't want to get their hair wet can't resist a refreshing dip in the ocean. The sea water is clear, ideal in temperature, and salty enough to make you quite buoyant. To swim easily in the ocean is a joyous experience and one of the most special aspects of Hawai'i, which is one of the best places to do it.

The same mid-Pacific location that keeps Hawaiian waters clean and warm demands great respect for the sea. Like any other natural environment, Hawaiian seas are not entirely hazard-free. The biggest dangers are seasonal surf and currents, posted on most park beaches. Heed lifeguards and warning signs and never turn your back on the ocean. Many Hawaiian beaches are sheltered by reefs, but those that are not get pounded, usually in winter, by relentless waves that slap the shore with such force that they can knock the unwary off their feet and send them out to sea. Folks on Kaua'i refer to part of Lumaha'i Beach as "Tourist Beach" because of the number of newlyweds and others swept away while posing for photos at the shoreline with their backs to big waves.

You can see and hear rising surf; it's an awesome phenomenon, best observed safely from shore. When the surf comes up, village stores may even shut down while local surfers head out to catch some waves. But novices are wise to consider big-wave surfing strictly a spectator sport. Swimming is out of the question. By the same token, most bodysurfers have heard of fabled Sandy Beach on O'ahu's south shore, a pinnacle challenge for that sport. But when the water is rampaging, the wicked shore break can break necks, too. It's Hawai'i's most dangerous beach.

Currents are insidious, because you can't always tell when and where they are. The major Hawaiian islands are sunken mountains with deep, steep sides and resulting strong currents. Kealaikahiki Channel, off the south coast of Lana'i, is famous for a powerful current that leads straight to Tahiti, 1,500 miles away. (That's what "Kealaikahiki" means—"the way to Tahiti.") Should you get carried out by a rip current, don't panic. Figure out which direction is perpendicular to the current and also leads toward shore, and swim across the current toward safety.

Shark attacks are rare in Hawaiian waters, but sharks themselves are not. Don't swim or surf alone at sunset when the predators feed. Most hazardous are invasions of jellyfish—box jellyfish, which appear often at Waikiki and Ala Moana beaches nine or ten days after the full moon, and are nasty enough that lifeguards issue warnings and supply soothing vinegar to treat the stings.

You might also encounter the milder, Hawaiian version of Portuguese man-o-war, known as blue bottles, which float in from time to time. Your first clue to their presence might be stepping on a small, blue balloon that pops along the debris line onshore. On the water's surface, this jellyfish appears as an innocent floating bubble, but the unseen trailing blue tendril leaves a burn that stings like a knife blade that may take a while to go away. Our hint for a quick antidote is the blue-colored aloe vera gel widely sold in Hawai'i as a sunburn soother. Be sure to keep a bottle in your beach bag. A dab on a blue-bottle sting will extinguish the fire for most victims. More extreme allergic reactions may require quick, expert medical care.

Swimmers and snorkelers sometimes run into coral heads and find later they got cut or scraped in the process. Coral cuts tend to infect quickly, and the antidote in this case is hydrogen peroxide, the WD-40 of tropical living. Put that in your beach bag, too.

Obviously, a foremost beach bag item should be sunscreen. No paleskin wants to return home from the islands without a golden, Hawaiian tan. But go easy—this tropical sun is strong, the ocean air is clear, and burns happen very quickly, particularly on children. Don't go out without sunscreen in Hawai'i—it's that simple. Apply it before you go outside; reapply it after swimming, snorkeling, or sweating a lot; and try to avoid midday exposure. You can get a great tan at 9 a.m. or after 3 or 4 in the afternoon, even with SPF 15 sunscreen. If skin cancer doesn't scare you, maybe wrinkles will (take a good look at the skin on senior surfers).

One other precaution about your beach bag. Leave your most valuable belongings in your room or in a safe when you head for the beach. If you carry a good camera or money, don't leave it unattended. You wouldn't tempt fate at home; don't do it in Hawai'i, either.

The best resource book about island beaches is *Hawai'i's Best Beaches,* by John R. K. Clark, a 150-page book published by the University of Hawai'i Press.

# Hawai'i's Top Beaches

---

### OUR PICKS: HAWAI'I'S BEST BEACHES

O'ahu: Lanikai Beach
Maui: Wailea Resorts Beaches
Big Island: Kauna'oa Beach (Mauna Kea Beach Resort)
Kaua'i: Hanalei Bay Beach
Moloka'i: Papohaku Beach
Lana'i: Hulopo'e Beach

---

## O'ahu

### *Ala Moana Beach Park*      *Zone 2 Greater Honolulu*

**Location** On Ala Moana Blvd., directly across from Ala Moana Center
**Activities** Swimming, surfing, bodyboarding, scuba diving, fishing
**Special Appeal** Safe swimming, good for kids, nearness to Waikiki and Ala Moana Center, park facilities, shade
**Comments** This shoreline oasis, stretching for more than a mile between Waikiki and Honolulu, is one of America's best urban beach parks and the most popular with local families. The beach is a narrow half-mile stretch of white sand with a deep swimming channel. Thanks to light surf, it's considered one of the most swimmable beaches in Hawai'i and one of the best for children.

Lifeguards are on duty daily. Magic Island, a 30-acre man-made extension at the eastern end of the park, is a popular spot for picnicking and jogging. Facilities include softball fields, tennis courts, a lawn bowling area, food concessions, showers, restrooms, the McCoy Pavilion, and more than 100 acres of picnic areas. Parking is limited, on the road between the park and beach and in a lot near Magic Island.

### *Kailua Beach Park*      *Zone 3 Windward O'ahu*

**Location** 450 Kawailoa Rd., Kailua
**Activities** Swimming, surfing, windsurfing, bodyboarding, bodysurfing, canoeing, kayaking, beachcombing, sailing, boating
**Special Appeal** Good walking, gentle waves, scenery, occasional brisk trades, shade, dunes, picnic areas

**Comments** "Best Beach in America" winner. The crescent-shaped, golden-sand beach is more than two miles long. The waters are ideal for swimming, surfing, and sailing. This is one of Hawai'i's best-known windsurfing and kayaking areas. Inexperienced surfers, bodyboarders, and bodysurfers will find waves they can handle. Facilities include restrooms, showers, a snack stand, equipment rentals, and picnic areas. Lifeguards are on duty daily.

## Lanikai Beach                                    Zone 3 Windward O'ahu

**Location** Fronting Mokulua Dr., Lanikai

**Activities** Swimming, kayaking, canoe paddling, snorkeling, windsurfing, surfing, sailing, fishing

**Special Appeal** Beauty, some shade, safe for small kids and swimmers, uncrowded on weekdays

**Comments** One of O'ahu's best family beaches. This scenic, mile-long stretch of golden beach with a vivid aqua and green lagoon bordered by photogenic islets is Hawai'i's best for swimming. Waves are docile, thanks to the sheltering reef, and thus offer safe swimming for children, the handicapped, and the elderly. It's a favorite spot for paddlers and for kayakers who head out to the Mokulua, two islets about three-fourths of a mile offshore. Both are state seabird sanctuaries, but the larger, more accessible Moku Nui, is a popular target for boaters and swimmers. Human access is restricted to its beaches. The Mokulua, particularly at sunrise, frame a breathtaking scene often used in ads and TV commercials, so it may look familiar to you. This neighborhood beach lacks public facilities or lifeguards. The beach is widest at the middle and northern ends. The southern end has been experiencing severe erosion. Public access is marked with signs on Mokulua Drive.

(For a terrific view of the Windward Coast and passing whales in winter, hike up Ka 'Iwa Ridge behind the community. As you drive into the one-way Lanikai loop, take the first right on Ka'elepulu, park near the cul de sac, and go uphill next to the fence. This is not for people afraid of narrow-ridge heights, but it's an easy climb to the concrete World War II bunkers and back.)

## Sandy Beach                                    Zone 2 Greater Honolulu

**Location** 8800 Kalaniana'ole Hwy., Hawai'i Kai, south shore

**Activities** Bodyboarding, bodysurfing, skimboarding, fishing

**Special Appeal** Daredevil body surfing

**Comments** Great local atmosphere. The 1,000-foot-long beach at the base of Koko Crater is known for its challenging shore break and feats of daring performed by local experts in wave riding. Some of O'ahu's best bodysurfers, skimboarders, and body-boarders strut their stuff here, and it's worth a visit to see them in action. Because the beach is subject to treacherous surf throughout the year, you should swim only when the waves are flat. Lifeguards are on duty daily. Restrooms, showers, and picnic areas are available.

## Sunset Beach                                    Zone 4 North Shore

**Location** 59-100 Kamehameha Hwy., Sunset Beach

**Activities** Surfing, bodysurfing, bodyboarding, summer swimming

**Special Appeal** Big-wave surfing, scenic beauty

**Comments** Some of the biggest winter waves in the world pound ashore along the coast from here to Hale'iwa. This is the fabled North Shore, nirvana for surfers. This mile-long beach and its neighbors draw expert surfers from all parts of the world. In summer, the golden sands stretch to a strand of more than 200 feet in width, popular with swimmers and body-surfers. But the beach narrows in winter, when waves rise ten feet or more and the pounding surf sometimes forces evacuations. The annual Triple Crown of Surfing professional events are held here. Lifeguards are on duty daily. Portable restrooms are available.

Neighboring North Shore beaches include 'Ehukai Beach, home of the world-renowned Banzai Pipeline, a curling wave that skilled surfers ride through, and Waimea Bay Beach, whose most famous wave is the 30-foot signature monster wave that introduced the television show *Hawai'i 5-0*, still in reruns.

## Waikiki Beach                                    Zone 1 Waikiki

**Location** Fronting Waikiki resort area
**Activities** Swimming, surfing, bodyboarding, snorkeling, outrigger-canoe riding, sailing, kayaking, fishing
**Special Appeal** Beachgoers of all ages, from the old-timers who play chess and cards in the sidewalk pavilions to the bikinied multitudes bronzing in the sand and the surfers offshore
**Comments** The world's most famous beach is a two-mile stretch of golden sand, from Hilton Hawaiian Village on one end to the cluster of high-rises at the base of Diamond Head at the other. Great for strolling the new beachside walkway, swimming, sunbathing, water sports, and people-watching. The average water temperature ranges 77° to 82°, depending on the season. Beachgoers are most concentrated in front of four neighboring hotels—Sheraton Waikiki, Royal Hawaiian, Outrigger Waikiki Beach, and Sheraton Moana Surfrider—and least crowded in the Kapi'olani Park beach areas, such as Queen's Surf Beach (by the aquarium) and Sans Souci Beach (by the New Otani Kaimana Beach Hotel).

Waikiki Beach is an amalgam of several beaches (in order from 'Ewa to Diamond Head): Duke Kahanamoku Beach, Ft. DeRussy Beach, Gray's Beach, Kuhio Beach, Queen's Surf Beach, and Sans Souci Beach. Sans Souci is our favorite—it's low-key and safe for swimming. Public facilities and services throughout Waikiki include restrooms, showers, equipment rentals, snacks, and surfing lessons. You can sign up for outrigger canoe and catamaran rides from the beach. Lifeguards are on duty daily. Free parking is limited to the streets of Kapi'olani Park.

# Maui

## Ka'anapali Beach                                Zone 9 West Maui

**Location** Honoapi'ilani Hwy., fronting Ka'anapali Beach Resort
**Activities** Swimming, bodysurfing, bodyboarding, snorkeling, scuba diving, windsurfing, kayaking, sailing, fishing
**Special Appeal** Places to hang for teens and young people, coastal walkway, boats that cruise from beach landings
**Comments** This is a popular resort beach. Swimming conditions are good when the surf is flat; this is subject, however, to strong currents and surf. The base of Black Rock, a volcanic cinder cone jutting up at the center of the four-mile beach, is a great spot for

snorkeling and diving. A lifeguard is on duty at the Lahaina end. Beach concessions and outdoor showers are available at various points along the walkway that links Ka'ana-pali's neighboring hotels and condos.

## Kapalua Beach                                    Zone 9 West Maui

**Location**  Lower Honoapi'ilani Hwy., Kapalua Resort
**Activities**  Swimming, snorkeling, scuba diving, sailing, kayaking
**Special Appeal**  Quiet atmosphere, good swimming, safe for kids, great scenery
**Comments**  This secluded strand in front of Kapalua Bay Hotel is one of Maui's best-looking and best swimming beaches. Lava promontories protect both sides of the beach from rough water. Public facilities are available, but no lifeguards are on duty. The sunset is often spectacular, spotlighting Moloka'i across the channel.

## Makena State Park                               Zone 8 South Maui

**Location**  Makena Alanui, Makena
**Activities**  Swimming, surfing, snorkeling, bodysurfing, bodyboarding, fishing
**Special Appeal**  Scenic beauty, undeveloped nature, walking (Big Beach)
**Comments**  Makena State Park at Maui's southern end has two scenic golden-sand beaches: Big Beach and Little Beach. Big Beach, 3,300 feet long, is Maui's longest beach and a favorite spot for experienced bodyboarders and bodysurfers. Little Beach, meanwhile, is a small cove with gentler ocean conditions, a good prospect for novice wave riders. No lifeguards are on duty, nor are there public restrooms or showers. Secluded Little Beach is one of Hawai'i's most popular "unofficial" nude beaches, even though public nudity is prohibited by law.

## Wailea Resort Beaches                           Zone 8 South Maui

**Location**  On Wailea Alanui, Wailea
**Activities**  Swimming, bodysurfing, bodyboarding, snorkeling, scuba diving, windsurfing, kayaking, sailing, fishing
**Special Appeal**  Scenic beauty, resort surroundings, public access facilities
**Comments**  Wailea Resort has five golden-sand beaches: Polo, Wailea, 'Ulua, Mokapu, and Keawakapu. Wailea Beach, shared by the Four Seasons Maui, Grand Wailea, and the public, is an appealing golden crescent about 1,000 feet long and a "Best Beach in America" winner. It's easy to see why. The waters are clear, with gentle waves to ride and a singular view dotted with neighboring islands. Snorkeling is rewarding along the rocky promontory that defines one side of the beach, and green sea turtles frequent the waters. Humpback whales pass by during the winter.

'Ulua is the centermost beach, 1,000 feet long and 200 feet wide, between the Renaissance Wailea and Outrigger Wailea Beach. Locals regard the offshore reef here as one of Maui's best snorkeling spots. A deeper reef, excellent for scuba diving, is about 100 yards out from shore.

Wailea Resort's 1.5-mile coastal trail links public accessways to all the beaches and private hotel and condo properties. The southern end of the trail, between the Four Seasons and Kea Lani, features a showcase Hawaiian native plant garden and historic house.

Public facilities include restrooms and showers. Beach concessions offer surf board rentals and instruction. No lifeguards are on duty.

# Big Island of Hawai'i

## 'Anaeho'omalu Beach
Zone 11 Kona

**Location** Queen Ka'ahumanu Hwy., Waikoloa Beach Resort, south shore of 'Anaeho'omalu Bay, by historic fish ponds and Outrigger Waikoloa Beach Hotel
**Activities** Swimming, surfing, snorkeling, scuba diving, windsurfing, kayaking
**Special Appeal** Scenic setting, historic features
**Comments** This beach is a picture-perfect finger of golden sand with palms for shade, on a bay where ancient kings played. Suitable for a wide range of ocean activities, this beach is favored for windsurfing. Novices can frolic in the calmer waters near shore, which they may share with sea turtles. Expert riders enjoy the more challenging wave conditions farther offshore. Public restrooms and showers are available. No lifeguards are on duty.

## Green Sand Beach
Zone 11 Kona

**Location** Mamalahoa Hwy. near Na'alehu at the southern tip of the island; turn off on South Point Rd. to Ka Lae (South Cape). The paved road ends at Kaulana Boat Ramp. This beach is about 2.5 miles east via a dirt road. You can park at the ramp and hike in or use a four-wheel-drive vehicle.
**Activities** Beachcombing, fishing
**Special Appeal** Green sand
**Comments** An off-the-beaten-path beach for active adventurers, but perhaps a bit rugged for little kids. The sand is green, fragments of olivene rock. High surf throughout the year can pose danger. No lifeguards are on duty. Beachcombers can hunt for gemstone-sized lumps of pale green olivine, a volcanic phenomenon.

This is the most famous green-sand beach, but if your kids are pining to see green sand, try searching the shore from the public beach park at Ka'upulehu between Kona Village Resort and Four Seasons Hualalei. We have found green mixed with white coral and black lava sands there.

## Hapuna Beach State Recreation Area
Zone 11 Kona

**Location** Queen Ka'ahumanu Hwy., Kohala Coast; look for a highway sign for the entrance to the park
**Activities** Swimming, surfing, bodyboarding, bodysurfing, snorkeling, camping
**Special Appeal** Biggest Big Island strand, the only one with camp cabins
**Comments** Hapuna Beach is a gold-sand jewel stretching more than half a mile and more than 200 feet across. It is very popular with bodyboarders and bodysurfers and can get crowded on weekends and holidays. Public restrooms, showers, camping shelters, and picnic pavilions are available. Lifeguards are on duty daily and can inform you of current ocean conditions, which are often rough during the winter. Walk up the coastal path in front of the Westin Hapuna Beach Prince a short distance and you'll discover a hidden snorkeling cove teeming with fish.

## Kauna'oa Beach
Zone 11 Kona

**Location** Queen Ka'ahumanu Hwy., fronting the Westin Mauna Kea Beach Hotel within Mauna Kea Resort, Kohala Coast

**Activities**  Swimming, surfing, bodyboarding, bodysurfing, snorkeling
**Special Appeal**  Great protected swimming, friendly waves, scenic setting
**Comments**  There's no finer way to begin your day than with a morning swim on this beach, the Big Island's best. The water is clear, calm enough to swim across from one side of the 2,500-foot strand to the other, and sends waves that roll you lazily to shore. The neighboring hotel is one of the oldest and most venerated, and this beach is one good reason why. The water is inviting to ocean enthusiasts of all types, from snorkelers to bodysurfers. No lifeguards are on duty, but hotel beach attendants know current ocean conditions. Public facilities are available. If you stay after dark, stroll along the coastal walk to a floodlit platform to watch the manta rays, that come to shore to feed on smaller creatures drawn to the light.

## Pololu Beach                                         Zone 11 Kona

**Location**  Highway 270, North Kohala; park at the end of the road and take the 15-minute hike down an ancient switchback trail from the Pololu Lookout
**Activities**  Beachcombing, surfing, bodyboarding, fishing
**Special Appeal**  Scenic beauty, hike, beachcombing
**Comments**  A scenic black-sand beach with plenty of photo ops. No lifeguards or public facilities are provided. Because this remote beach is exposed to treacherous surf throughout the year, do not swim here unless the ocean is flat. This is a favored site for beachcombers, who scour the shoreline for treasures blown in by storms or high surf.

# Kaua'i

## Hanalei Bay                                         Zone 13 Kaua'i

**Location**  Weke Rd., Hanalei Pavilion Beach Park, behind the village of Hanalei on Kaua'i's north shore
**Activities**  Swimming, surfing, bodyboarding, bodysurfing, snorkeling, windsurfing, sailing, fishing, canoeing
**Special Appeal**  Spectacular scenic setting, seasonally gentle bodysurfing waves, walking, winter surfing
**Comments**  Hanalei Bay is a dream come true. The golden sands extend about two miles around the scenic bay. On one side, the clear waters stretch out toward Japan; on the other is a bowl of lush, green mountains ribboned with waterfalls and capped with jagged volcanic peaks. The bay shore is bordered by private homes with public access via walkways and a trio of beach parks—Black Pot Beach Park, Wai'oli Beach Park, and Hanalei Pavilion Beach Park, in the center. Restrooms and showers are available at each. In summer, visiting yachts moor in the calm waters. In winter, the boats head for safer shelter because the surf can exceed ten feet, making Hanalei popular with the best surfers. Lifeguards are stationed at Black Pot Beach Park by the pier at the mouth of Hanalei River.

## Kalapaki Beach                                       Zone 13 Kaua'i

**Location**  Fronting Kaua'i Marriott Resort on Nawiliwili Bay in Lihu'e
**Activities**  Swimming, surfing, bodyboarding, bodysurfing, snorkeling, windsurfing, sailing, fishing

**Special Appeal**  Walking, safe swimming for kids, passing ships, restaurants and bars close by

**Comments**  One of Kaua'i's busiest beaches, this strand is protected by cliffs and a sea wall. The inlet between the cliffs leads to Nawiliwili's natural harbor and the Huleia River and Menehune Fish Pond behind it. While picnicking or playing on the beach, you may see large ships cruise by on their way into the harbor. Kalapaki is a safe playground for young children and a training ground for novice surfers. Showers and restrooms are provided for the public courtesy of the Kaua'i Marriott. Picnic facilities are available at Nawiliwili Park, adjacent to Kalapaki. No lifeguards are on duty.

## Ke'e Beach                                      Zone 13 Kaua'i

**Location**  End of Kuhio Hwy., Ha'ena State Park, North Shore; park along the road or in the small lot

**Activities**  Swimming, snorkeling, fishing

**Special Appeal**  Movie-set beauty *(Thornbirds)*, views of Na Pali Coast, near-shore snorkeling

**Comments**  The reef surrounding Ke'e Beach breaks the waves, except for the giants of winter, and provides excellent snorkeling conditions. The shallow, protected lagoon is home to several species of rainbow-colored fish and offers safe swimming. No lifeguards are on duty, but public restrooms, outdoor showers and some parking are provided. This area is the staging point for hikers bound for the Kalalau Trail, 12 miles along the precipitous Na Pali wilderness coast to Kalalau State Park beach, a true hiking commitment. Less devoted hikers will enjoy the scenic first two miles of the (often muddy) trail to Hanakapi'ai Valley, where a stream littered with boulders runs from a scenic inland waterfall to the sea. The surf is rough there, so save the swim for your return to Ke'e Beach.

## Lumaha'i Beach                                  Zone 13 Kaua'i

**Location**  Kuhio Hwy., at the foot of Lumaha'i Valley, North Shore; on the Hanalei end, park along the highway, then follow the trail down to the beach; on the far end, park in a grove of ironwood trees

**Activities**  Surfing, bodyboarding, bodysurfing, snorkeling, windsurfing, sailing, fishing

**Special Appeal**  Scenic splendor, walking

**Comments**  Some 4,000 feet long, this beautiful strip of shoreline was made famous in the movie *South Pacific*. It remains one of the most photographed beaches in the state. This beach is great for appreciating wild beauty from shore, but with no protective reef, swimming or even wading can be very risky. No lifeguards are on duty.

## Po'ipu Beach Park                               Zone 13 Kaua'i

**Location**  Ho'owili Rd., just off of Po'ipu Beach Rd., Po'ipu Beach Resort, South Shore

**Activities**  Swimming, bodysurfing, bodyboarding

**Special Appeal**  Kids' tidepool, resort beach

**Comments**  More than 1,000 feet long, Po'ipu Beach is a popular playground shared by public parks and accessways and private hotels, restaurants, and condo resorts. Portions are sheltered enough for safe swimming by young children. Restrooms, showers, and picnic tables are available; lifeguards are on duty daily. Wave riders should avoid the area past Brennecke's, a rocky and hazardous point.

### Polihale State Park (Barking Sands)          Zone 13 Kaua'i

**Location**  Kaumuali'i Hwy., Kekaha, end of the road on the west shore
**Activities**  Surfing, bodyboarding, windsurfing, summer swimming, camping
**Special Appeal**  Wide expanses of wild beauty at the foot of Na Pali
**Comments**  Polihale, 17 miles long and 300 feet wide, is Hawai'i's biggest beach. The "Barking Sands" are dunes that squeak and bark under your feet when walked on, special effects thanks to the composition of the coral sands. Hawaiians named such sites *ke one kani* (musical sands). In summer, the reef protects a plunge known as Queen's Pond. Facilities include restrooms, showers, parking, and a pavilion. No lifeguards are on duty.

### Secret Beach                                 Zone 13 Kaua'i

**Location**  Kuhio Hwy., near Kalihiwai Rd., Kilauea, between Kilauea Point and Kalihiwai Bay; public access via a dirt road
**Activities**  Swimming, surfing, bodyboarding, bodysurfing, snorkeling, windsurfing, sailing, fishing
**Special Appeal**  The Island's best known nude beach
**Comments**  This 3,000-foot-long golden beach is "secret" because it's not visible from any roads, not just because it is a favorite nude beach. From land, it can be seen only from the Kilauea Point National Wildlife Refuge. A haven for hippies in the early 1970s, Secret Beach is now a popular summer swimming spot. Winter surf, however, poses danger for swimmers. There are no public facilities or lifeguards here. *A reminder:* Nude sunbathing is technically against the law in Hawai'i, but certain beaches are so remote that no one seems to mind.

### Shipwreck Beach                              Zone 13 Kaua'i

**Location**  Fronting the Hyatt Regency Kaua'i in Po'ipu Beach Resort, South Shore
**Activities**  Surfing, bodyboarding, bodysurfing, windsurfing, fishing
**Special Appeal**  Coastal trail, dunes walk
**Comments**  Shipwreck Beach got its name from an unidentified wooden boat that lay crashed onshore for years until Hurricane 'Iwa washed it away in 1982. Low-lying rocks keep this golden-sand beach from being good for swimming, but bodysurfers and bodyboarders love it, especially in summer. The beach's most interesting sunbathers are often endangered Hawaiian monk seals or green sea turtles, who surf the waves between the Hyatt and nearby Embassy Vacation Resort. Public restrooms and showers are available. A coastal walkway about a mile long along the cliffs leads to sand dunes that once served as a Hawaiian burial site. No lifeguards are on duty, but ocean conditions are posted.

### Tunnels Beach                                Zone 13 Kaua'i

**Location**  Kuhio Hwy., about 0.5 mile beyond Ha'ena Beach Park, North Shore
**Activities**  Surfing, bodyboarding, snorkeling, scuba diving, windsurfing, beachcombing, fishing

**Special Appeal** Scenic splendor, seasonal shells, shade, near-shore reef tunnels
**Comments** Tunnels is a grainy, gold-sand beach with good summer snorkeling around reefs and coral heads close to shore. Its name refers to the reef "tunnels" that are found in the lagoon inside of Makua Reef, a popular scuba-diving spot. When the surf's up, Tunnels is one of Kaua'i's best surfing spots for expert wave riders. Restrooms and showers are available at the public beach park. No lifeguards are on duty.

# Moloka'i

## *Papohaku Beach*       *Zone 14 Moloka'i*

**Location** Kaluako'i Rd., just beyond Kaluako'i Resort
**Activities** Surfing, bodyboarding, bodysurfing, snorkeling
**Special Appeal** Broad strand, wild beauty, shady picnics, great sunset views of O'ahu
**Comments** Two miles long and 400 feet wide, Papohaku Beach is the biggest beach on Moloka'i and one of the only sandy Moloka'i beaches that is easily accessible for families. This isn't a swimming beach, but board riders favor it. It has a wilderness atmosphere but with good paved road access and public beach park facilities: restrooms, showers, parking, and camping sites sheltered in the shoreline keawe forest. Dangerous swimming conditions exist because the beach is fully exposed to the force of the sea and surf. High surf conditions can occur any time of year. No lifeguards are on duty.

## *Sandy Beach*       *Zone 14 Moloka'i*

**Location** Kamehameha V Hwy., 7 miles past the Wave Crest Resort, Kaunakakai, at Mile Marker 21, East End
**Activities** Swimming, bodysurfing
**Special Appeal** Good swimming, views of Maui
**Comments** It's not easy to find a swimming beach on Moloka'i, which has rough open seas, sheer cliffs, and muddy fish ponds. This small, reef-sheltered pocket beach is a rare exception. Soft, golden sands and gentle waters make it great for kids. Don't stub your toes on the rocky bottom while admiring the West Maui Mountains across the channel. Restrooms are available, but no lifeguards are on duty. Good swimming conditions also prevail at nearby Waialua Beach, just before Mile Marker 19.

# Lana'i

## *Hulopo'e Beach Park*       *Zone 15 Lana'i*

**Location** Manele Rd., near Manele Bay Hotel, 8 miles from Lana'i City
**Activities** Swimming, surfing, bodyboarding, bodysurfing, snorkeling, fishing, picnicking, camping
**Special Appeal** Kids' tidepool, shade, scenic features
**Comments** This is the only beach park on Lana'i, a former pineapple plantation transformed into a luxury resort enclave. But it's a fine one, another Hawai'i strand recognized as a "Best Beach in America." It features a large tidepool carved into a lava cliff with all-season swimming for children. Palms offer shade along the golden beach, which is 1,500 feet long and 200 feet wide. Swimming is subject to wave action, but it's usually calm enough inshore. Snorkeling is rewarding along the sheltering lava headland, a place to explore on shore, too. Public restrooms, showers, picnic areas, and campsites are

provided by the private owner. Camping at the three sites, limited to six people each, costs $5 per person per night for up to a week and requires a $5 permit from Lana'i Company. Write Attn: Camping Permits, P.O. Box 310, Lana'i City, HI 96763, or call (808) 565-8206. Facilities include restrooms, showers, picnic tables, grills, and drinking water.

# Kayaking: Different Strokes

Since the first voyagers landed in Hawai'i from the South Pacific, paddling the seas has been a way of life. Outrigger canoe paddling is a fiercely competitive local sport. You'll often see paddlers practicing offshore. Today's Hawaiian kayaks are made of fiberglass and come in a variety of shapes and sizes.

The biggest kayak contest, the annual World Championship Kayak Race, takes off from Kepuhi Beach on Moloka'i each May with solo paddlers who run across the dunes and beach carrying their kayaks, jump in when they hit water, and paddle to O'ahu 32 miles away.

For expert ocean kayakers, we recommend a summertime trip along Kaua'i's picturesque Na Pali Coast, when the sea is calm. In summer, the eastern Moloka'i shore from Halawa to Kalaupapa also offers wilderness kayaking and beach camping. (Read *Paddle Your Own Canoe,* by solo kayaker Audrey Sutherland.)

Novices can rent a kayak in Kailua and head out for the Mokulua islets off O'ahu's Lanikai Beach. On Kaua'i, paddle down the peaceful Hule'ia, Wailua, and Hanalei Rivers. Maui kayakers may find themselves whalewatching closer than most in winter, when the humpbacks loll around quiet inshore waters. On the Big Island, tranquil Hilo Bay is perfect for kayaking. Try riding gentle waves to shore for a thrill, or maybe a splash, in Kaua'i's Hanalei Bay, O'ahu's Mamala Bay, or Maui's Wailea Bay.

Rentals for single-person kayaks are $30–$35 for a full day; for tandem kayaks, about $42–$50 per day. A short lesson is usually included in the price, and all kayaking equipment can be transported to the beach for you. Any of the following outfitters can rent you equipment and teach you how to use it. Kayak Kaua'i Outbound in Hanalei and Outfitters Kaua'i in Po'ipu Beach have rental equipment and guides for Na Pali Coast outings. The listed firms offer paddles on the Hule'ia, Wailua, and Hanalei Rivers.

---

**KAYAK RENTALS**

**O'ahu**
Twogood Kayaks, Kailua, (808) 262-5656
Go Banana Kayaks, Kapahulu, (808) 737-9514
Kailua Sailboards and Kayaks, Kailua, (808) 262-2555

---

**KAYAK RENTALS** *(continued)*

**Maui**
Maui Ocean Activities, Ka'anapali Beach, (808) 667-1964
South Pacific Kayaks, Kihei, (808) 875-4848
Tradewind Kayaks, Kihei, (808) 879-2247

**Big Island**
Hawai'i Pack and Paddle, Captain Cook, (808) 328-8911
A. Banyan Bicyle, Kayak and Scuba Adventure, Hilo, (808) 933-1228
Ocean Safari's Kayak Tours and Rentals, Kailua-Kona, (808) 326-4699

**Kaua'i**
Kayak Kaua'i Outbound, Hanalei, (800) 437-3507
Outfitters Kaua'i, Po'ipu Beach, (888) 742-9887
Kayak Wailua, Kapa'a, (808) 822-3388

---

# Scuba: Dive, Dive, Dive

A growing segment of diving enthusiasts have discovered Hawai'i's particular underwater treasures—lava caverns, reefs full of fish, humpbacks, and other sea life.

Most dive excursions require participants to be certified by a scuba training organization, such as the Professional Association of Diving Instructors (PADI), National Association of Underwater Instructors (NAUI), National Association of Scuba Diving Schools (NASDS), or World Association of Scuba Instructors (WASI). Specialized dives—including explorations of wrecks and caves and night diving—require more advanced training.

Most divers arrive certified, but certification courses are offered at dive shops throughout the islands. Rates range from $75 for a beachside lesson to $300 or more for full open-water instruction and certification. You pay an additional $10–20 for a scuba certification card. Equipment is provided.

Would-be divers can see how it feels by way of introductory dives, usually conducted in a pool. No experience is required. Participants receive basic instruction, get fitted for scuba gear, and dive with the instructors. The entire experience lasts two to four hours, with rates ranging from $100 to $150.

Dive tour rates range from $75 to $250, depending on the size of the boat, equipment, and number of dives included on the trip. Booking deposits are usually required, refundable if you cancel in advance. Expect to spend at least half a day for a guided scuba adventure. The actual time you spend in the water will vary—the deeper water you're in, the faster you use your air supply—but usually it's between 90 minutes to 2 hours. The diver-to-guide ratio has a legal maximum of six to one.

A few tips:

- In choosing a dive operator, ask about their experience in the business, safety expertise, type of boat, type of dive destination, and so on to make sure they meet your expectations and needs.

- Be careful where you put your hands and feet underwater. Some marine life—such as eels, jellyfish, and scorpionfish—can bite or sting. Do not touch any animal you don't recognize. Try to avoid touching or crushing coral, leaving a permanent dent in the underwater environment.

- Never dive alone.

- If you're attempting underwater photography for the first time, shoot from within four feet. For best results, use an underwater camera with a 15mm or 20mm lens.

A fun alternative in the sea is snuba tours, where snorkelers can go underwater tethered by a breathing tube to an air-supply float on the surface. Snuba of O'ahu (call (808) 396-6163) offers shallow-water diving for people age eight and older on three bays; Snuba Big Island (call (808) 326-7446) guides snuba dives in Kailua-Kona. Wet-N-Wonderful (call (888) 945-DIVE) offers snuba on Kaua'i.

Hawai'i has more than 250 diving sites, with depths ranging from 20 to 150 feet. The most popular and one of the best is Molokini, a crescent-shaped sunken cinder cone about three miles off the coast of South Maui, near Kaho'olawe. Molokini, a Marine Life Conservation District, has high visibility and thriving ocean life, including reef fish, sea turtles, and manta rays. But it gets swamped with snorkelers and tour boats as the day goes on. One solution is to book one of the boats that leave early directly from the nearest Maui beach, at Makena or Wailea, rather than those that depart from Ma'alaea Harbor.

A favorite South Maui site is La Perouse Pinnacle, in the middle of picturesque La Perouse Bay beyond Makena. The pinnacle rises 60 feet from the sea floor to about 10 feet below the ocean's surface and is exceptional for snorkeling as well as shallow dives. Look for brilliant damselfish, triggerfish, puffers, and wrasses.

Divers of all skill levels probe Five Caves in Makena. Lava ridges and small pinnacles provide food and shelter for angler fish, sea turtles, eels, and white-tipped sharks. The waters here are around 30–40 feet deep and can be accessed from shore as well as boat.

Lana'i's deep, clear waters (there is little runoff on this dry island) draw divers from around the world. At Cathedrals, off the south shore, a stained-glass effect occurs when sunlight pours through the holes in twin underwater caves. This dive is for experienced divers only.

If diving with giant wintering whales is your dream, sign up with Captain Ed Robinson on Maui, who knows how to find them. Nautilus Dive Center in Hilo offers divers a chance to see the underwater lava flow from Kilauea Volcano. Kona Aggressor II offers week-long luxury diving excursions aboard a yacht (call (800) 344-kona). Lucky Boy Charters in Kilauea, Kaua'i, offers trips to dive and fish off the private island of Ni'ihau and uninhabited islet of Nihoa.

Here are some dive company recommendations.

---

### SCUBA-DIVING OUTFITTERS

**O'ahu**
Aaron's Dive Shops, Kailua, (808) 262-2333
Aloha Dive Shop, Hawai'i Kai, (808) 395-5922
Clark's Diving Tours, Honolulu, (808) 923-5595

**Maui**
Ed Robinson's Diving Adventures, (808) 879-3584
Lahaina Divers, (808) 667-7496
Maui Dive Shop, five offices, (800) 542-3483
Mike Severns Diving, Kihei, (808) 879-6596

**The Big Island of Hawai'i**
Jack's Diving Locker, Kailua-Kona, (808) 329-7585
Natuilus Dive Center, Hilo, (808) 935-6939
Kohala Divers, Kawaiahae, (808) 882-7444

**Kaua'i**
Dive Kaua'i Scuba Center, Kapa'a, (808) 822-0452
Fathom Five Divers, Po'ipu Beach, (808) 742-6991
Seasport Divers, Po'ipu Beach, (808) 742-9303

---

# Snorkeling: Exploring the Undersea World

Although not as "deep" an experience as scuba diving, snorkeling is an underwater adventure anyone can do. Just wade in backward in your flippers, look through your face mask, and breathe through your J-tube.

Some practical snorkeling tips:

- Know how to swim. Although some snorkeling spots are shallow, being able to swim is the best way to ensure your own safety in the water.
- Novices should practice in shallow water.
- Always snorkel with a buddy or in groups.
- Don't stray too far from shore or the boat.
- Check your snorkel gear carefully before entering the water. Popular wisdom

requires you to spit on your mask and rub it around the lens before dunking it in salt water and then putting it on. Make sure it fits, airtight, to your face.

The most famous snorkeling spot is O'ahu's Hanauma Bay, the best place for novice snorkelers. Huge schools of friendly reef fish populate this picturesque bay, which often seems overpopulated by snorkelers.

Here are some excellent snorkeling beaches.

### Hanauma Bay Nature Preserve　　　Zone I Waikiki

**Location** Kalaniana'ole Hwy., at Koko Head Regional Park (7455 Kalaniana'ole Hwy), Hawai'i Kai, South Shore. Head east on the H-1 Fwy., which turns into Kalaniana'ole Hwy., and go up the hill just beyond Hawai'i Kai.

**Activities** Snorkeling, scuba diving

**Comments** Just wade in and look down: You are surrounded by glamorous tropical fish that teem in this too-tame bay where fish somehow still outnumber snorkelers about a thousand to one.

This U-shaped bay aquarium in a broken crater, a third of a mile point to point, has near-shore reefs ideal for novice snorkelers and more challenging reefs further out. Lifeguards are on duty daily. Facilities include restrooms, showers, picnic areas, a snack bar, and snorkel rentals. Ask at the beach desk about free educational tours of the bay. The parking fee is $1 per vehicle, and admission is $3 for all nonresidents over the age of 12. Hanauma Bay is open six days a week (closed on Tuesday) from 6 a.m. to 7 p.m. Smoking is prohibited. Feeding reef fish—once a favorite pastime—is now kapu. Go early, before 8 a.m. if possible, as incoming vehicles are turned away when the parking lot is full.

### Ahihi-Kinau Preserve　　　Zone 8 South Maui

**Location** On remote south shore of Maui, beyond Makena, at end of a dirt road

**Activities** Snorkeling

**Comments** Black, barren lava reefs reach into aquamarine pools full of tropical fish. The best snorkeling on Maui is in this scenic 2,000-acre nature preserve on the rugged south coast, where Haleakala last spilled red-hot lava into the sea in 1790. It's difficult to reach but easy to enjoy. No facilities.

### Kealakekua Bay　　　Zone 11 Kona

**Location** On Kona coast of the Big Island, south of Kailua-Kona and downhill from Captain Cook

**Activities** Snorkeling, scuba

**Comments** An octopus's garden shared by free-swimming moray eels, parrotfish, and, once in a while, a pod of spinner dolphins in this deep blue, mile-wide bay that's the Big Island's best snorkeling spot. Coral heads, lava tubes, and underwater caves provide an excellent habitat for Hawai'i's tropical fish, and the warm, clear water is a natural attraction for snorkelers. Snack bar, bathroom, and showers are available.

### Ke'e Beach　　　Zone 13 Kaua'i

**Location** End of Kuhio Hwy., Ha'ena State Park, North Shore;. park along the road or in small lot

**Activities**  Swimming, snorkeling, fishing

**Comments**  Here you can float like a leaf on a pond, sucking air through a snorkel and watching little yellow fish dart here and there in crystal-clear water. You can float face up, staring at green-velvet cathedral cliffs, under a blue sky with long-tailed tropical birds riding tradewinds. Palms rustle, a wave breaks. If this isn't perfection, what is? Bathrooms, showers, and parking are available.

## Kaupoa Beach                              Zone 14 Moloka'i

**Location**  West End, on Moloka'i Ranch property (limited to ranch guests, unless you can navigate a boat there)

**Activities**  Summer snorkeling, swimming, beachcombing, sunbathing

**Comments**  Head for Kaupoa Beach by ranch bus or on horseback, swap boots for flippers, and take a plunge in the warm salt water, soothing after a morning in the saddle on Moloka'i Ranch. Horses graze under coco palms. You snorkel with triggerfish. The trail boss grills rib-eye steak. Way, way out west on Moloka'i, this is what surf and turf is all about. Facilities include beachside bar and dining pavilion, showers, and bathroom.

## Five Needles                              Zone 15 Lana'i

**Location**  Off remote south shore of Lana'i

**Activities**  Snorkeling, swimming

**Comments**  Spiky sea stacks dominate an almost secret snorkel spot on Lana'i's rugged, seldom-seen south side. Go there only by kayak, sailboat, or launch, mostly by tours departing from Maui. Take *Navatek II* or *Trilogy* from Maui's Maalea Harbor for this unforgettable outing (see information on guided tours below). Clarity of water and abundant sea life make this snorkel site excellent. No facilities.

## Guided Tours

Guided snorkeling adventures are available on every island, priced from $35. In addition, many shops rent snorkeling equipment, including fins, masks, snorkels, and gear bags. Most snorkel and dive shops accept major credit cards. Guided snorkel tours take about half a day. Instruction for beginners is available. Snorkel outings are weather dependent.

**Snorkel Bob's,** one of the most popular outfits, has locations on O'ahu (phone (808) 735-7944); Maui (call (808) 879-7449, (808) 669-9603, or (808) 661-4421); the Big Island (call (808) 329-0770); and Kaua'i, (call (808) 823-9433 and (808) 742-2206).

Here are our favorite guided snorkel tours.

### O'ahu

Avoid the hassle—go to Hanauma Bay with **B. T. Snorkel** on a three-hour van and snorkel tour that includes all gear and transportation from Waikiki hotels to the bay and back for under $15. It's the best deal. Call (808) 396-8144.

## Maui

*Navatek II,* an 82-foot, 149-passenger SWATH vessel (it's a smooth cruiser), sails from Maalaea Harbor to Lana'i's remote south shore on the "Voyage of Discovery," the best family snorkel adventure because of its high-tech boat. It's stable to calm queasy stomachs, easy to get on and off in deep water, and the crew grills hamburgers to order for lunch. *Navatek II* and several other snorkel sail cruises are operated by Royal Hawaiian Cruises. Call (800) 852-4183, or visit www.royalhawaiiancruises.com.

*Trilogy,* a 64-foot cutter-rigged sailing catamaran operated by brothers Jim and Rand Coon and their families, takes blue-water sailors on six-hour snorkel excursions to Lana'i, Molokini, or Ka'anapali. Trilogy Excursions is the veteran operator for Maui-to-Lana'i sails with a well deserved reputation for delivering a superior experience. Call (888) MAUI-800, or visit www.sailtrilogy.com.

## The Big Island of Hawai'i

*Fair Wind II,* a 60-foot catamaran run by Puhi and Mendy Dant since 1971, delivers 100 snorkelers to Kealakekua Bay every morning for four-and-a-half-hour snorkel dive. The big, safe boat is a solid favorite of families. Call (800) 677-9461, or visit www.fair-wind.com.

## Kaua'i

Hold on for a wet ride to Kaua'i's remote beaches, sea caves, and waterfalls with a picnic and snorkeling stop. Capt. Zodiac (aka Clancy Greff) pioneered rides on 15-passenger, 20-foot fortified rubber rafts down Na Pali Coast in the 1970s and is still going strong. Call (800) 422-7824.

## Moloka'i

Walter Naki of **Moloka'i Action Adventures** takes four snorkelers on four- or six-hour dives in seldom-explored territory aboard his 21-foot Boston whaler. Call (808) 558-8184.

# Surfing: Catch a Wave

Hawai'i's own kings perfected surfing, and no place does it better. Hawai'i offers the most consistent surf, biggest waves, and deepest tubes. The best big-wave surfers test their skills here in the winter when O'ahu's North Shore turns into the world's surfing capital and the setting for annual professional competitions.

No one knows exactly when surfing originated, but many historians believe Polynesians were already well versed in the sport when they migrated to the Hawaiian Islands nearly 2,000 years ago. Big Island petroglyphs depict board-riding figures. Ancient Hawaiians called surfing *he'e nalu* (wave sliding). Only the high chiefs enjoyed access to the best surf spots. King Kamehameha I was said to be an avid surfer.

Today, waves are shared according to skill. Beginning surfers can get quick lessons from Waikiki beach boys or sign up for more formal training with an expert instructor, such as Hans Hedemann, a veteran pro and former surfing champion. **Hans Hedemann Surf School** (call (808) 924-7778) offers lessons on the beach at Waikiki. Equipment is provided.

Lessons for one or two students or groups up to five per instructor are conducted in areas where the waves are small and the beach relatively crowd-free. Students learn the basics on the beach, including ocean safety and how to paddle a surfboard, how to get up and stand on the board, proper foot placement, and where to shift body weight. Then they get in the water to do it again, and then catch a real wave and ride it. Once you get the hang of it, you'll learn other basic maneuvers, such as turning your board to move in a certain direction.

Surfers come in all shapes, sizes, and ages. You should know how to swim and expect to do a lot of paddling and kicking in the water. Most schools have a minimum age of five to seven years for surfing lessons. "If you think you can do it, you probably can," said one instructor. Hedemann said almost everyone is "up and riding" on their first lesson. Then you may be hooked for life, because the feeling of being one with the sea, flying in on a cresting wave, is a thrill like no other.

Other recommended surfing schools include **Hawaiian Rush** (call (808) 596-0580) and **Hawaiian Watersports** (call (808) 255-4352) on O'ahu, and **Buzzy Kerbox Surf School** (call (808) 573-5728 or kerbox@aol.com) and the **Nancy Emerson School of Surfing** (call (808) 244-7873) on Maui. Surfing instruction is available year-round.

Group rates are generally about $60 for one-hour lessons to $225–$250 for all-day lessons. Private lessons are about $85–$125 for one-hour lessons and $425–$450 for all-day lessons. Multiday and week-long rates are also available. Book at least a day in advance, although most surf schools will try to accommodate last-minute students.

For experienced surfers able to deal with surfing etiquette and crowds, O'ahu is the place to be, with the widest choice of quality surf spots in the state. Surf conditions are good somewhere on the island nearly year-round, and plenty of surf breaks are just right for less-than-expert surfers. Weather forecasters routinely report surf conditions on radio and television. Maui has some great surf spots near Lahaina and just past Pa'ia. Kaua'i has excellent surf spots at Hanalei, Princeville, and elsewhere on its north shore and at Po'ipu and south shore locales. Big Island has a few good surfing areas, like 'Anaeho'omalu at Waikoloa Resort, although many are inaccessible by car. A helpful book on the best surf spots is the *Surfers Guide to Hawai'i* by Greg Ambrose (published by Bess Press), which includes tips, descriptions, and maps.

Keep in mind the following safety and etiquette tips before heading out to ride Hawaiian waves.

- Check with lifeguards first. They can point out the hazardous rip currents, jagged reefs, and tricky waves to avoid. Obey posted warnings.

- Never surf alone, and make sure someone on shore knows where you are.

- Be considerate of other surfers. Don't drop in on someone else's wave.

- Don't surf after dark.

- Use leg ropes to control your board, for your safety and the safety of fellow surfers.

- If you get in trouble, don't panic. Signal for help by raising one arm vertically.

## Windsurfing: Ride the Wind

A whole different sport seeks to challenge the wind as well as the waves—the combination of sailing and surfing known as windsurfing or board sailing. A day of brisk tradewinds prompts a hatch-out of colorful, butterfly-like sails as windsurfers zip here and there across the water, enjoying the pure sensation of natural speed. In Hawai'i, where water sports are a way of life, many ocean devotees surf when the waves are right, windsurf when the winds are right, and kayak when it's calm.

Expert windsurfers will want to try their hands or just watch the pros at **Kanaha Beach** and **Ho'okipa Beach** on Maui's North Shore, known as "the Aspen of windsurfing," where the world's top wave riders gather to take advantage of strong winds and optimum waves.

**Diamond Head Beach Park** near Waikiki is favored for wave-jumping, quite a spectacle to watch. Windsurfers fly up the face of a wave and soar, sometimes doing somersaults and other feats before returning to water.

To learn to windsurf on O'ahu, cross the Ko'olau to **Kailua** and **Lanikai** beaches on Windward O'ahu for scenic rides and gentle seas, although periodic blustery tradewinds will sideline the beginners and bring out the experts. Robbie Naisch was one of the early stars of windsurfing, and **Naisch Windsurfing Hawai'i** in Kailua (call (808) 261-6067), is the oldest windsurf shop in the state. There you can buy or rent gear and accessories and sign up for lessons at all skill levels. Private lessons are $55; lessons for two are $75, including equipment rental. Naisch also pioneered the new spin-off sport of kitesurfing—windsurfing with the extra speedy lift of a hang-gliding kite attached, popular on Kailua Bay.

**Ocean Sports Waikoloa** provides windsurfing services at **'Anaeho-'omalu Bay** at Waikoloa Beach Resort on the Big Island. Call (888) SAIL-234. On Kaua'i, **'Anini Beach** on the North Shore near Princeville is a good place to learn the sport. Sailboard rentals are $25–$40 for a full day. **Alan Cadiz's HST** (call (808) 871-5423) on Maui offers two-and-a-half-hour lessons for $69.

# Charter Sportfishing: Reely Big Ones

If you've ever dreamed of hooking a 1,000-pound "grander" Pacific blue marlin, go to the Kona Coast, the best place to land the fish of a lifetime.

The giants, lesser marlin, and desirable food fish roam the seas off all islands, but the best chance of hooking a trophy fish is off Kona, considered the big-game fishing capital of the world because of its history of record catches. Kona has an optimal fishing environment, thanks to the seas that plunge to great depths right outside the mouth of Honokohau Harbor and to the hulking volcanoes that tend to block onshore winds and high seas. A charter boat may chase a fish on a line for many miles and hours (or days), but it rarely has to go farther than five or six miles out to sea to hook one.

About 100 charter boats operate out of Honokohau Harbor. We recommend that you contact one of the charter boat associations to choose yours. They handle plenty of boats and customers and can connect you with people who want to share a charter, put you on a tag-and-release boat if you choose, or connect you with a crew that will give you a share of your edible catch. Most captains have commercial fishing licenses and keep the food fish caught on their boat to sell, sharing proceeds with the crew. Marlin over 50 pounds are not considered good to eat, particularly after they have been dragged all over the sea. **Kona Charter Skippers Association** (see contact info on following page) also offers fishing trip packages and group bookings.

We suggest browsing the Internet, asking other fishermen, and checking activity guides to familiarize yourself with your fishing options. Experience and frequency of trips, plus electronic gear, help your captain know where the fish are biting.

Most charters offer half-, three-quarter-, and full-day fishing adventures that last four, six, and eight hours. Departures are usually 7 a.m., with half-day charters returning by noon and full-day charters returning by 4 p.m. Prices vary according to the size and amenities of the boat, among other factors.

To maximize your chances of landing a big-game fish, book a full-day charter. It can take an hour or more to catch live bait—usually an aku, a skipjack tuna of up to 20 pounds—and when you add the time required to handle lines and tackle for both small bait and big game, you won't have much time left for fishing on a half-day excursion. Half-day charters often use lures as a result, and big marlin seem to prefer live bait.

Walk-up bookings are available, but it's better to make your reservations in advance so that you can get the type of boat you want and, if you choose, share a charter with someone. A deposit is usually required (up to half the charter cost) and is refundable up to 48 hours prior to the fishing date. Most charters accept major credit cards and personal checks.

Most boats are licensed to hold six passengers, plus the captain and two deckhands, but four passengers is a more comfortable crowd. The crew provides instruction and equipment. You don't need a fishing license for offshore fishing. Bring your own food and drinks (liquor is allowed) for the ice chest, and sun and seasickness protection. Shorts, swimsuits and T-shirts are appropriate wear, plus a sweatshirt or light jacket as needed.

Charter boats range in size from 25 to 58 feet, with the average being 33 to 35 feet. If you're new to sportfishing (most Kona fishermen are, other than participants in the frequent jackpot money tournaments) you may want to splurge on a midsized or larger boat so that you enjoy the experience of luxuriating on the water, even if the fish aren't biting that day. But remember—the size of the boat doesn't guarantee the catch. The fish don't care how much you spent or how big your boat is.

Three types of marlin roam Hawaiian waters: black, blue, and striped. Though the chances are good that a marlin will strike your bait, the odds of actually landing one of the tenacious fighters are about one in three. With luck, you might catch one of the "granders"—a trophy marlin of 1,000 pounds or more. You can see what one looks like on the wall of the King Kamehameha Beach Hotel in Kailua-Kona.

You won't need the strength of an Olympian to land a giant marlin. If you're using up to 130-pound test line, the drag is about 40 or 50 pounds, meaning the most you have to worry about pulling in is between 40 and 50 pounds. If you can pull 20 pounds around for a while, you can reel in a marlin, says one captain, adding, "Anyone can do it. No one's going to catch a fish by brute force, because a 200-pound person versus a 200-pound marlin is going to lose every time if it comes to strength. They're going to use the techniques we teach them." What you may need is staying power. Some big-game fish fight for hours before exhausting themselves.

Besides marlin, there are plenty of other fish in the sea. Some you might want to meet are 'ahi (yellowfin tuna) and other tuna species, ono (wahoo), mahimahi (dolphin fish), and other billfish and spearfish. Some

Kona boats go after snappers, onaga, and ʻopakapaka, and other bottom fish using a rigorous Asian fishing method called jigging. The *Sea Strike* is one (call (800) 264-4595, or visit www.kona-fishing.com).

Mahimahi, ono, and marlin are present throughout the year, except for striped marlin, which is a winter fish. Spearfish are also more abundant in the winter months, and ʻahi are more numerous in summer.

For a different fish tale, you might want to try some inland bass fishing on Kauaʻi's South Shore freshwater reservoirs. **JJ's Big Bass Tours** (call (808) 332-9219) and **Cast & Catch Freshwater Bass Guides** (call (808) 332-9707) will take you there.

### HAWAIʻI OCEAN SPORTFISHING CHARTERS

| Operator | Phone |
| --- | --- |
| **Statewide** | |
| Sportsfish Hawaiʻi | (877) 388-1376 |
| | www.sportsfishhawaii.com |
| **Big Island** | |
| Kona Charter Skippers Association | (800) 7-MARLIN |
| | www.konabiggamefishing.com |
| Capt. Bob's Kona Coast Sportsfishing Charters | (808) 895-7000 |
| | www.konacharters.com |
| Kona Activities Center | (800) 367-5288 |
| | www.41web.com/charterfishing |
| **Oʻahu** | |
| Inter-island Sportsfishing | (808) 591-8888 |
| | www.maggiejoe.com |
| Island Charters | (808) 593-9455 |
| **Maui** | |
| Fish Maui | (808) 879-3789 |
| | www.fishmaui.com |
| **Kauaʻi** | |
| Anini Fishing Charters | (808) 828-1285 |
| | www.kauaifishing@hawaiian.net |
| Kai Bear Sportfishing | (808) 826-4556 |
| | www.kaibearsportfishing.com |
| Lahela Ocean Adventures | (808) 635-4020 |
| | www.sport-fishing-kauai.com |
| Sport Fishing Kauaʻi | (808) 742-7013 |
| | www.fishing-kauai-hawaii.com |
| **Molokaʻi** | |
| Alyce C Sportfishing | (808) 558-8377 |
| | www.worldwidefishing.com |

# Whale-Watching

Two-thirds of the Pacific humpback whale population migrate to warm Hawaiian waters each winter to breed and bear and nurse their young. Right behind them come the whale-watchers. Few sights match the spectacle of a whale leaping out of the sea.

Whales cruise so close to shore, you can often see them from coastal roads and hotel lanaʻi. For a closer look, take a whale-watching cruise if you are in Hawaiʻi between mid-December and mid-April. Whale-watching excursions are offered throughout Hawaiʻi, but are concentrated off the south and west coasts of Maui, the heart of the whale migration.

Luck plays a big role in observing interesting actions by large, live creatures on the move, but some tours offer substantial expertise and special equipment, such as state-of-the-art hydrophones that let you hear whale songs, and support marine conservation nonprofits like Pacific Whale Foundation and Whales Alive.

Experience makes a big difference between whale-watching and whale "glimpsing," as federal law requires boats to stay at least 100 yards away from the whales. Some cruises guarantee sightings by giving you a rain check if you don't actually see a whale.

Whale-watching boats come in all sizes, from rubber rafts that bounce through the surf to large, motorized catamarans and sleek sailing sloops, and offer a wide range of comforts, such as shaded decks, beverages, and marine heads.

Daily humpback whale–watching cruises cost $20–$60 for adults and $12–$30 for children age 11 and under. Book your tour several days in advance during holiday periods. Most tours last two to three hours and provide snacks and juice. Some tours offer hotel transportation. Wear swimsuits or casual attire, and bring binoculars and cameras.

*Tip:* To see whales best from shore, get to an elevated viewing post that gives you a better perspective. Look for whale spouts, geysers of sea spray that shine in the sun and seem to disappear into thin air. Look for large black bodies poking their noses above water as they "spy-hop," possibly to get a better look at you.

If you're in the resort area of Wailea, Maui, check the telescope in front of the Outrigger Wailea Beach. The first person to report a whale sighting to the cafe each day gets a free breakfast.

Though humpbacks visit the islands only in winter, Hawaiʻi has five other whale species that can be viewed throughout the year—sperm whales, pilot whales, melon-headed whales, false killer whales, and beaked whales. Big Island boat captain Dan McSweeney, based in Kailua-Kona, is one of the few operators who offers year-round whale-watching adventures spotlighting these lesser-known marine mammals, with tours out of Honokohau Harbor three times a week.

Informative websites on humpback whales include www.pacificwhale.
org and www.ilovewhales.com. The following is a list of some whale-
watching tours.

**WHALE-WATCHING CRUISE OPERATORS**

| Operator | Phone |
|---|---|
| **Maui** | |
| Maui Princess | (808) 667-6165 |
| | www.mauiprincess.com |
| Whale Mist Charters | (808) 667-2133 |
| Pacific Whale Foundation | (808) 879-8860 |
| | www.pacificwhale.org |
| **Big Island of Hawai'i** | |
| Dan McSweeney's Year-Round Whale Watch | (808) 322-0028 |
| | www.ilovewhales.com |
| Hawai'i Sailing Co. (luxury yacht) | (808) 776-1505 |
| **O'ahu** | |
| Hawaiian Sailing Co. | (808) 239-3900 |
| | www.honsail.com |
| Royal Hawaiian Cruises | (808) 848-6360 |
| | www.atlantisadventures.com |
| **Kaua'i** | |
| Capt. Zodiac Raft Expeditions | (808) 826-7197 |
| | http://planet-hawaii.com/zodiac |
| Capt. Andy's Sailing Adventures | (808) 335-6833 |
| | www.sailing-hawaii.com |

# Hawai'i by Land

## Hiking: Take to the Trails

Hiking is the most popular off-beach outdoor activity in Hawai'i, and
for good reason. Conditions are generally fine for meeting the natural
environment face to face, and the natural environment is extraordinary.
The experience is truly rewarding, with few dangers. There's something
Garden-of-Eden–like about walking on a forest trail edged with leaves
bigger than your head and seeing tropical fruit like mountain apple,
guava, wild mango, and avocado, surrounded by jungle greenery and
waterfall streams—especially when it's within minutes of downtown
Honolulu and Waikiki. Waterfall trails lead to waterfall pools, ideal spots
to cool off after a tropical trek. The views are always spectacular. There's

a certain historic continuity to hiking on trails that were carved by ancient trekkers and smoothed by generations of feet long before other means of land travel were available in the islands.

About those few dangers: rainforest means slippery, muddy trails and mosquitoes (take bug repellent). Waterfall valleys are steep and narrow and can flash-flood quickly after cloud-burst deluges upstream, with frightening and sometimes fatal results. Dry hikes on lumpy lava and steep, crumbly dirt trails require paying close attention to your footing and drinking lots of water. No matter what the locals do, avoid hiking in rubber slippers (beach thongs) in favor of supportive footwear (but not your favorite snowy-white sneakers—they won't come home white after a Hawaiian red-dirt trek, muddy forest jaunt, or a rough lava trail). Don't let the views keep you from watching where you put your feet. Yes, it is *Green Mansions* and *Blue Lagoon* and *Castaway* all rolled into one, but stand still while you admire the scenery. Stick to the trails. Rainforested mountains swallow up injured or missing hikers from sight almost instantly. If possible, carry a charged cell phone on remote ventures.

Inviting though the streams may be, don't drink the water or swim with open cuts and risk getting leptospirosis, a wild pig–related bacterial fever. You can get that within minutes of downtown Honolulu, too (at Kapena Falls, a swimming hole wildly popular with kids despite the danger of disease).

Easy-to-reach hiking spots on O'ahu include **Manoa Falls,** a highly traveled trail directly behind Waikiki in upper Manoa Valley. The hike is about 1.5 miles round-trip through a rainforest, with a waterfall. Park near the trailhead off Upper Manoa Road.

The arid, south-shore area around **Makapu'u Head** includes a series of trails with fantastic views of Windward O'ahu and the sea. **Mount Tantalus,** on the Honolulu side of Manoa Valley, has several well-marked trails off Round Top Drive, flourishing with guava, bamboo, liliko'i (passion fruit), and other tropical vegetation. In upper Makiki, the **Hawai'i Nature Center** operates exhibits and guides hikes aimed at helping children discover the outdoors.

For a moderately strenuous O'ahu hike, tackle all or part of **Ko'olaupoko Trail,** a recent, well-maintained option. Park at the hairpin curve on the Windward side of the Pali Highway and walk back behind Mt. Olomana through the mountain rainforest, past waterfalls, down to Waimanolo, eight miles. If the round trip is too much, do it one way and get someone to meet you at the other end. Or hike partway and turn around.

Clubs such as Hawaiian Trail and Mountain and student groups from Chaminade University and other local colleges also post helpful information and maps for O'ahu and Neighbor Island hiking. **Kapalua Nature**

**Center** is Kapalua Resort's ecotourism arm. The resort offers guided hiking tours in its 17,000 acres of Upcountry watershed and pineapple plantation lands. Once a year by lottery, a dozen hikers are dropped off by helicopter with a guide at the top of Pu'u Kukui to walk on a boardwalk through high-country bogs to see rare and endangered species of plants and birds.

Experienced hikers on Kaua'i can retrace the footsteps of early Hawaiians along the **Kalalau Trail** (see state parks) that traverses the stunning Na Pali Coast. An easy hike goes from the Kilauea Point National Wildlife Refuge on the North Shore, where knowledgeable guides recount area history and information on a variety of seabirds that nest in the refuge and other wildlife. If you are not a hiker but want to walk through the lush Kaua'i countryside, go to Limahuli Gardens, a small branch of the National Tropical Botanical Gardens, near the north end of Kuhio Highway. It features native Hawaiian plants and trees along a one-mile hilly loop path through a small scenic valley.

Guided hiking tours can be booked throughout Hawai'i, to bring the countryside to life as only touching and walking through it can. This is the best way for visitors to see otherwise private and inaccessible country; discover shy, indigenous creatures; and understand the context of what you see.

The newest guided hike on Windward O'ahu is a **Kualoa Ranch** trek over a ridge connecting two wild valleys that goes down to the shoreline at Moli'i Fishpond (call (808) 237-7321; or visit www.kualoa.com). Our suggestions for hiking guides include **O'ahu Nature Tours** (phone (808) 924-2473; www.oahunaturetours.com) and, on the Big Island, experts Rob Pacheco and staff of **Hawai'i Forest and Trail** (phone (808) 331-8505; www.hawaii-forest.com) and Hugh Montgomery and staff of **Hawaiian Walkways** (phone (808) 775-0372; www.hawaiianwalkways.com).

Island bookstores and the Internet offer a wealth of information about island hikes. For free trail maps, call the Department of Forestry and Wildlife at (808) 587-0166. Here are a few books of note for those hoping to discover more of Hawai'i on foot:

*Hawaiian Hiking Trails,* by Craig Chisolm, published by Fernglen Press 1999. Detailed look at 50 of the best hiking trails on Hawai'i's six major islands.

*Great Outdoor Adventures of Hawai'i,* by Rick Carroll, published by Foghorn Press, San Francisco 1991. First eco-guide to Hawai'i's best outdoor activities.

*Hawaiian Heritage Plants,* by Angela Kay Kepler, published by Fernglen Press 1998. Thorough presentation of Hawai'i's native plants. Full-color photos.

*Trees of Hawai'i,* by Angela Kay Kepler, published by University of Hawai'i Press 1990. A colorful and informative look at native and introduced trees in the Hawaiian Islands.

*Hawai'i's Birds,* published by the Hawai'i Audubon Society 1993. Full-color guide to native and introduced birds in Hawai'i.

# National and State Parks

Hawai'i's 2 national parks and 52 state parks encompass more than 50,000 acres on O'ahu, Maui, the Big Island, Kaua'i, and Moloka'i. In addition, a number of federal and state historic parks and monuments designate cultural sites worthy of your attention.

**Hawai'i Volcanoes National Park,** home to the world's most active volcano, is one of the nation's oldest and best national parks and a must-see for Big Island visitors. If you're traveling with children, you owe it to yourselves to discover this park together, particularly if Pele, the fire goddess who lives in Halema'uma'u Crater, is producing any spectacular eruptions during your trip (Call for eruption updates: (808) 985-6000, or check the website at http://hvo.wr.usgs.gov.) Your best chance of seeing red lava flows is after sunset at the end of Chain of Craters Road. Park rangers are posted there 2–8 p.m. daily. (See below for details.)

Also on the Big Island, **Pu'uhonua O Honaunau,** the Place of Refuge on the South Kona Coast, is a national historic park on the site of an ancient waterfront sanctuary. A temple has been reconstructed there, within the remaining lava-rock walls built centuries ago. The place has an air of peace you can't miss even on a quick walk-through. It's worth the time to watch local people demonstrate ancient skills and games and help you understand something about old Hawaiian life. There's an annual summer cultural festival in late June or early July.

On the north end of the Kona/Kohala coast, **Pu'ukohola National Historic Site** is an archaeological monument by the sea, the preserved temple from which King Kamehameha I set out to conquer the other islands and unite them into a kingdom in the 1700s. There is an annual cultural pageant here in August.

On Maui, **Haleakala National Park's** 10,023-foot summit is a great place for watching the sun rise, hiking in the vast caldera, and marveling at the claw-footed native Hawaiian nene geese. These birds evolved special feet for life on cinders; they are the state bird of Hawai'i and are endangered. You can also see silversword plants, which are found nowhere else.

Four state parks are especially noteworthy: **Kaka'ako Waterfront Park** along the downtown Honolulu shoreline, on O'ahu; **'Iao Valley State Park** on Maui; and **Koke'e State Park** and **Waimea Canyon State**

**Park** on Kauaʻi. Each provides scenic settings, exceptional views, and activities for young and old. Information on these parks is included below.

For more information on Hawaiʻi's state parks, write to the Division of State Parks, 1151 Punchbowl St., Room 310, Honolulu, HI 96813, or call (808) 587-0300.

## Overall Safety Tips and Park Regulations

- Guard against tropical sunburn.

- Do not drink from streams and ponds or expose an open cut or abrasion to the water. Harmful bacteria may pose a serious health risk.

- Never leave your valuables unattended in a car at a scenic lookout.

- Drinking or possession of alcoholic beverages is prohibited in parks.

- Build fires only in fireplaces and grills. Portable stoves and other warming devices may be used in designated picnicking and camping areas.

- Do not disturb any plants or geological, historical, and archaeological features.

- Skating and skateboards are prohibited where posted.

## National Parks

### *Hawaiʻi Volcanoes National Park*                   *Zone 12 Hilo and Volcano*

**Location** Hwy. 11, about 30 miles from Hilo; follow the road signs and turn left into the park entrance.
**Phone** (808) 985-6000
**Website** As of press time, the National Park website, nps.gov, had been suspended for several months. Until it is reinstated, find information about national parks and historic sites in Hawaiʻi at www.hawaii.com/activities/parks/national.
**Hours** Daily, 7:45 a.m.–5 p.m. Once you are admitted, the park is open all day, every day.
**Admission** $10 per vehicle, good for a week; $5 per person for people hiking or biking in; $20 for a year-long pass; $10 for a seniors lifetime pass
**When to Go** Any time. The best time to see red lava is after sunset.
**How Much Time to Allow** At least half a day, including early evening if the lava is flowing
**Comments** The 377-acre Hawaiʻi Volcanoes National Park was established in 1916, but the mighty spectacle of Kilauea in action has drawn visitors since the 1800s. Then, hardy adventurers were housed in a grass shack on the rim of Halemaʻumaʻu Crater, fire goddess Pele's legendary home. Now Volcano House lodge stands on the rim, an interesting spot for sunset cocktails.

Kilauea Volcano has been erupting in its current phase since 1983. It runs on its own schedule, sometimes fuming quietly, rarely fountaining, more usually spilling fire and liquid rock down its slopes, creating new real estate and black-sand beaches. Live volcanic action is not guaranteed during your visit, but the park features are well worth the trip even when the volcano is quiet. (Call for eruption updates: (808) 985-6000, or check the website at http://hvo.wr.usgs.gov.) A variety of natural "attractions" compete for attention; we suggest that you take in as many as you can, but don't miss the Thomas A. Jaggar Museum, an excellent interpretive center where seismographs and easy-to-understand exhibits help illustrate the scientific theories of volcanic works, and Hawaiian artist Herb Kane's murals illustrate the Hawaiian theory, the legend of Pele.

Just outside the museum is one of several overlooks along the trail to view Halema'uma'u Crater—2.5 miles wide and more than 400 feet deep—within Kilauea Caldera. Halema'uma'u means "House of Ferns," named for greenery that once grew there between eruptions. Now it looks like a cinder pit from hell. That must be the way Pele likes it, and many islanders still believe she lives there, causing eruptions when she is displeased. Her fiery temper is said to be appeased by gifts of gin, a modern embroidery on the legend. Pele is also said to direct her wrath, in the form of really bad luck, on anyone who steals her rocks. The post office and Volcano House are deluged with tons of rocks each year sent back by hapless miscreants. If you want our advice, leave the lava alone.

Start your park tour at the Visitor Center, which houses volcano exhibits and a 200-seat mini-theater showing a terrific 23-minute film about the history of Hawai'i's volcanoes and their significance to the Hawaiian culture. Park rangers can answer questions, suggest itineraries, and conduct an introductory hike from the center. Next door, the Volcano Art Center offers a good selection of works by some of Hawai'i's top artists, including Herb Kane, Peggy Chun, Rocky Jensen, and Dietrich Varez.

Guide map in hand, drive into the park, where you'll soon find the Jaggar Museum and other features. A word of caution: Sulfuric fumes from the craters and steamy fumaroles may be hard on pregnant women, small childen, and people with breathing problems. If this includes you, roll the windows up and head for less fumy features. Otherwise, drive across the caldera floor and stop to look into the yawning fire pit, a ten-minute walk from the parking area. This is the world's only drive-in volcano, predictable enough to observe up close.

The park includes 150 miles of trails of varying difficulty. For an easy walk, Devastation Trail is a good choice that illustrates some of the havoc caused by volcanic action. It is a mile round-trip, paved and wheelchair accessible, through an area that was devastated by the hot fallout from lava fountains from a 1959 Kilauea 'Iki eruption. Look for golden strands in the pahoehoe lava called Pele's hair, as well as "lava tree" molds formed when hot lava surrounded a tree trunk and burned the tree but left the round form of rock cooling on the outside.

For a moderate to challenging hike, try the four-mile loop of Kilauea 'Iki Trail, which descends 400 feet through rainforest, crosses the Kilauea 'Iki crater floor, which might still feel warm under your feet, and returns via the crater rim. Look for birds, insects, steam vents, and cinder cones. Allow two or three hours and bring water. Be prepared for wet weather and steep, rocky terrain. The trail begins at the Lava Tube parking area.

Stop at Thurston Lava Tube on the way out. The 20-minute walk through a forest of lush tree ferns leads into a large, cave-like (and lighted) tube formed by a long-ago lava river.

Chain of Craters Road will take you down to the sea, about half an hour's drive through a moonscape of smooth, ropy pahoehoe lava (one of two kinds of lava—the other is a'a, the rough clumps seen on the Kona coast). The road once traversed the region, but now it dead-ends in more lava. It has been revised many times by recent flows and could be changed again at any time. Watch the coastline for a telltale plume of white smoke—that's where the lava meets the sea.

To get a closer view of the current interaction of lava and ocean, as of summer 2001, drive to the opposite side of the lava flow, near Kalapana, and take advantage of a new access. Kilauea's active flow left the park boundaries to ooze over county jurisdiction areas where former flows buried subdivisions, beaches, graveyards, and the road. Hawai'i County officials rebuilt the end of Highway 130 so that viewers can park and walk a short coastal trail to a viewing area, rather than the former, challenging six-mile hike from the other side of the older flow that trespassed on buried property. Reach the new access by turning off the Hilo-Volcano road, Highway 11, at Kea'au and taking Highway130 through Pahoa.

At the end of the road, park and follow signs to the nearest designated lookout, currently a bluff over the place where molten magma of some 2,000°F drips or rolls into the ocean in a billow of steam, sizzling and spitting and writhing like an agonized creature as fire battles water and eventually loses. The sight is mesmerizing and unforgettable. You are walking on the newest land on Earth. You are watching creation happen.

But do keep your head and stay on the bluff, away from the fragile beach shelf that could crack off and fall in any time. County rescue squads are churlish about saving witless tourists and might charge you for the privilege.

Overnight camping is available at the park via free permit (see Camping).

Overall, be respectful of the park surroundings, which Hawaiians regard as sacred to their culture, and the buried neighborhoods, still people's homes.

## *Haleakala National Park*      *Zone 10 Upcountry Maui*

**Location** The park extends from the top of Haleakala ("House of the Sun") down the southeast flank of the mountain to the sea at Kipahulu near Hana, including scenic waterfall pools at 'Ohe'o Gulch. The summit area is accessible via Roads 37, 377, and 378 up the mountain through Kula, a 3-hour round-trip drive from the Kahului area below. Add more time to get to and from resort areas. Kipahulu, at the east end of the island between Hana and Kaupo, can be reached via Hana Hwy. Driving time is 3 to 4 hours each way between Kahului and Kipahulu.

**Phone** (808) 572-9306

**Website** www.nps.gov/hale (at the time of publication, operation of the National Park Service website was suspended, so until it is reinstated we recommend www.hawaii. com/activities/parks/national for information on national parks and historic sites)

**Hours** Park Ranger headquarters open daily, 7:30 a.m.–4 p.m. The Visitor Center is open daily, sunrise–3 p.m.

**Admission** $10 per vehicle, good for a week; $5 per person not in vehicles

**When to Go** Any time. Haleakala is renowned for dramatic sunsets and sunrises, a mystic experience that draws people from slumber in the middle of the night to be there on time. Be sure to arrive at least 30 minutes early. It's also well worth the 3-hour round-trip drive (from Kahului) at other times of day—including after dark, when it is a fabulous place for stargazing.

**How Much Time to Allow** Up to half a day, depending on whether you take part in park programs. Rangers offer guided hikes on all Haleakala's trails, at the cindery summit, in the cloud forest, or down below in the lush tropical forests of Kipahulu. This is a good option. Take your pick of environments.

**Comments** Haleakala, a dormant volcano, became a separate national park in 1961. The park consists of 29,000 acres, most of it wilderness. At the summit, the park headquarters and Visitor Center house cultural and natural history exhibits.

In the Kipahulu area, all trails begin at the Ranger Station/Visitor Center. The Kuloa Point Trail is an easy half-mile loop toward the ocean that affords a look at the pools and waterfalls, as well as the sea and the Big Island, but go early or late if you want to avoid crowds. Enjoy a picnic on the grass next to the remnants of an ancient fishing shrine and house site.

Check the park bulletin board for a schedule of daily programs and guided hikes. Obey posted warnings. Because the weather at the summit is unpredictable—temperatures range from 40°F to 65°F but with wind chill factored in, can dip below freezing—wear lightweight, layered clothing and comfortable, sturdy shoes. No restaurants or gas stations are available in the park. People with heart or breathing programs should use caution because of the high elevation and thin air.

Limited drive-in and wilderness overnight camping is permitted in the crater and below at Kipahulu. The Hosmer Grove Campground in the summit area is located just inside the park entrance (see Camping section for details on Haleakala camping).

## O'ahu State Parks

### Diamond Head State Monument                    Zone 1 Waikiki

**Location** Diamond Head Rd., between Makapu'u and 18th Avenues
**Comments** Woke up jet-lagged? Go climb Diamond Head! Early in the day when it's cool, you can make the moderate climb to the summit in about 45 minutes to enjoy panoramic views of Waikiki, Honolulu, mountains, and ocean. Ask your hotel concierge for a trail map. You can sign up for a guided walk sponsored by the Clean Air Team of Hawai'i (call (808) 948-3299) on Saturday mornings at 9 a.m.

### He'eia State Park                    Zone 3 Windward O'ahu

**Location** 46-465 Kamehameha Hwy. at Kealohi Point, He'eia
**Comments** Beautiful views of Kane'ohe Bay, Mokoli'i (better known as Chinaman's Hat), and the majestic Ko'olau Mountains. Adjacent to the ancient He'eia fishpond.

### Ka'ena Point State Park                    Zone 5 Leeward O'ahu

**Location** The end of the road, Farrington Hwy., Makua
**Comments** A 778-acre park located at the northwest end of O'ahu. Picnicking and shore-fishing are popular. You can view Kaneana, a large sea cave that is the legendary home of a shark-man. Bring drinking water.

### Kaka'ako Waterfront Park                    Zone 2 Greater Honolulu

**Location** End of Ahui or Ohe Streets off Ala Moana Blvd., Honolulu
**Comments** A little known 35-acre waterfront park located in downtown Honolulu, favored by residents who come here during lunch and pau hana (after work). A waterfront promenade, amphitheater, and picnic areas highlight this scenic park.

## Maui State Parks

### 'Iao Valley State Park                    *Zone 7 Central Maui*

**Location** End of 'Iao Valley Rd. (Hwy. 32) in 'Iao Valley, behind Wailuku

**Comments** The centerpiece is 'Iao Needle, a pinnacle that rises 1,200 feet from the forested valley floor. Be prepared to share it with tour buses that stop for photo ops. Take a look at the multicultural architectural heritage village below. Think about how this placid area was the scene of one of the bloodiest ancient battles. In 1790, King Kamehameha fought to gain control of Maui, and in the aftermath, so many bodies blocked 'Iao stream that they named the site Kepuniwai (damming of the waters).

### Wai'anapanapa State Park           *Zone 10 Upcountry Maui*

**Location** End of Wai'anapanapa Rd., off Hana Hwy., Hana

**Comments** This remote, ocean-view campground features rustic cabins sleeping four to six at $55 per night and free tent camping for up to five days in a grassy open field surrounded by trees. Seek reservations as far in advance as possible, as this is a prized spot. Permits can be obtained at any state parks office. Write to the Maui office at Division of State Parks, P.O. Box 1049, Wailuku, Maui, HI 96793, or call (808) 984-8109.

Restrooms, outdoor showers, picnic tables, grills, and drinking water are available for tent campers. Each cabin has kitchen, living room, bedroom, and bathroom with bedding, linens, and utensils provided. Amenities include good hiking trails, native forest, cave, heiau, a black-sand beach sprinkled with tiny blue shells, and fishing. Ocean conditions seldom are safe for swimming.

## Big Island State Parks

### 'Akaka Falls State Park                 *Zone 12 Hilo and Volcano*

**Location** End of 'Akaka Falls Rd. (Hwy. 220) in Hilo

**Comments** Get off the highway and see some inland wonders now and then, like this sizable waterfall and its jungle valley. It's a short walk through the tropical vegetation to scenic points overlooking the falls; picnic facilities are available.

### Lapakahi State Historical Park         *Zone 11 Kona*

**Location** Akoni Pule Hwy., North Kohala

**Comments** This is an archaeological dig of an ancient Hawaiian fishing village, worth a stop while en route through Kohala District. You can roam through on a self-guided tour and imagine what life was like back then. Interpretive helpers are available to answer questions.

### Kohala Historical Sites State Monument       *Zone 11 Kona*

**Location** On a coastal dirt road to the left off Akoni Pule Hwy., Hawi

**Comments** If you're going to pick one ancient temple site, visit Mo'okini Heiau, believed to be the oldest and largest sacrificial temple, with huge stone walls and a spooky atmosphere. Nearby is the reputed birth site of Kamehameha I, Hawai'i's greatest king.

## Wailuku River State Park  Zone 12 Hilo and Volcano

**Location** Off Waianuenue Ave. in Hilo
**Comments** This 16-acre park is the home of Rainbow Falls, named for the brilliant color bands that form through a misty waterfall. Boiling Pots, a series of pools that appear to "boil" after frequent rains, is nearby. The cave beneath the waterfall is said to be the home of Hina, mother of the demigod Maui.

## Kaua'i State Parks

### Koke'e State Park  Zone 13 Kaua'i

**Location** High up Koke'e Rd., 15 miles from Kekaha. This park and Waimea Canyon State Park adjoin
**Comments** Far from any beach, Koke'e is a special place for its Upcountry atmosphere and native plants and birds. Picnicking, camping, and hiking are the best ways to enjoy this 4,345-acre park, the site of a lookout with an arresting view of Kalalau Valley. Camp cabins are available with woodstoves to ward off the Upcountry chill. Trails of varying difficulty lead off through the woods; pick one that suits your time frame. Even the easy walks take you into native forest. The forest includes California redwoods among the 'ohi'a and koa trees. The 'Alakai Swamp is a boggy treasure for birders intent on seeing or hearing rare native species. The 11-mile Nu'alolo-Awa'awapuhi Loop, with dramatic vistas of the Na Pali Coast, is one of Hawai'i's best hikes. In summer, a very short trout season draws local anglers.

The adjoining 1,866-acre park overlooks spectacular Waimea Canyon, which you can explore on horseback or on foot. It's often likened to the Grand Canyon for its colorful striated geologic layers and steep walls. (See below for camping details.)

Tent camping is free at Koke'e with a five-night limit, but it requires a permit. Permits can be obtained at any state parks office. For more information, write to the Kaua'i office at Division of State Parks, 3060 'Eiwa St., Lihu'e, HI 96766, or call (808) 241-3444. Restrooms, showers, picnic tables, sinks, and drinking water are provided.

Koke'e Lodge has a dozen cabins that sleep up to six people each. The older cabins have a large dormitory-style room, bathroom, and kitchen; newer cabins offer two bedrooms, living room, kitchen, and bathroom. Rates are $45 per night for the two-bedroom cabins, $35 per night for the dorm-style ones. For cabin reservations, write to Koke'e Lodge at P.O. Box 819, Waimea, HI 96796, or call (808) 335-6061.

Other accommodations are available at Koke'e park. For information, call Camp Sloggett (phone (808) 245-5959), Koke'e Methodist Camp (phone (808) 335-3429), or Hongwanji Camp (phone (808) 332-9563). Rates are $40–$96 per night.

A restaurant at the lodge offers Continental breakfast and lunch daily. The Koke'e Museum, located adjacent to the lodge, spotlights Kaua'i's natural history (see Part Seven, Hawai'i's Attractions).

Neighboring Waimea Canyon State Park is located at the bottom of Waimea Canyon, along the Waimea River and Koai'e and Wai'alae streams. Access is via the Kukui Trail, located 7.5 miles north on Waimea Canyon Road.

Free tent camping is available for up to four nights at five campsites on the canyon floor, with a permit. Write the Division of Forestry and Wildlife, 3060 'Eiwa St., Room 306, Lihu'e, HI 96766, or call (808) 241-3433.

The best is Lonomea Camp, located six miles from Kukui trailhead. Lonomea has pit toilets, a picnic table, and roofed shelters. Wiliwili Camp, at the base of the trail, also has those facilities. Hipalau Camp has no toilets but offers a roofed shelter, picnic table, and two refreshing pools fed by waterfalls. Bring your own drinking water.

## Wailua River State Park                                   Zone 13 Kaua'i

**Location**  Along banks of Wailua River off Kuhio Hwy., Wailua
**Comments**  Historic 1,092-acre site within a river valley. Picnicking, boating, and fishing are available, along with paid boat tours to the much-ballyhooed Fern Grotto. Our advice is to skip the touristy grotto ride and, instead, search out the heiau, ancient refuge, and birthstones that are among the historic landmarks in this valley, once reserved for ancient chiefs.

## Moloka'i State Parks

## Pala'au State Park                                        Zone 14 Moloka'i

**Location**  End of Kalae Hwy. in Pala'au
**Comments**  This 230-acre park overlooks historic Kalaupapa, the place where people stricken with Hansen's disease (leprosy) were once banished. Picnicking and camping are available. A short trail leads to aptly named Phallic Rock, a monolith reputed to enhance fertility among women who sleep beside it overnight.

# Camping in the Wilds

Hawai'i has more than 120 campsites and campgrounds on six main islands, with sites ranging from beaches and open mountain terrain to lush green valleys and rainforests. Nearly all fall within the jurisdiction of a county, state, or federal agency and require camping permits. Book as far ahead as possible, and be prepared to take part in a lottery-style competition to get permits, because residents like camping, too. It's an affordable way to vacation in the islands.

For gear, bring a tent with a rain flap or tarp for overnight showers, a ground pad, and lightweight sleeping bags to sleep on (more than in) unless you're headed for cool higher altitudes. You'll need bug repellent and your own drinking water, or you'll need to bring what's necessary to purify any water to drink by boiling it or adding some sort of purifier.

Hawai'i has no animals to encounter in the wilds, except occasional feral pigs and goats. You can scare them away by shouting or making sudden movements. Otherwise, leave them alone and they'll extend the same courtesy. No island plants are poisonous to the touch (except, for some people, mango, which is a relative of poison ivy), but some are poisonous if eaten. Hawai'i does have some creepy bugs of tropical proportions, capable of nasty stings—not the big German brown cockroaches that terrorize visitors but giant centipedes, five inches or longer, scorpions in rocky areas, and black widow or brown recluse spiders under damp wood. Shake out your shoes and bed gear before using them, and wear shoes or use a flashlight to watch your step even in soft grass at night.

If you want to camp without lugging all the gear from home, rent equipment from suppliers such as those listed below, most of which also rent kayaks, mountain bikes, and other outdoor equipment:

---

### CAMPING EQUIPMENT RENTALS

**Oʻahu**
Bike Shop
1143 S. King St.
Honolulu, HI 96814
Phone: (808) 596-0588

Omar the Tent Man
94-158D Leoʻole St.
Waipahu, HI 96797
Phone: (808) 677-8785

**Kauaʻi**
Kayak Kauaʻi
P.O. Box 508
Hanalei, HI 96714
Phone: (808) 826-9844;
(800) 437-3508

**Big Island of Hawaiʻi**
Safari Activities
Gold Coast Center

74-5484 Kauoo St.
Kailua-Kona, HI 96740
Phone: (808) 334-0464

**Maui**
Maui Expeditions
300 Chukai Rd., Bay 15
Kihei, HI 96755
Phone: (808) 875-7470

West Maui Sports
1287 Front St
Lahaina, HI 96761
Phone: (808) 661-6252

**Molokaʻi**
Molokaʻi Rentals and Tours
P.O. Box 28
Kaunakakai, HI 96768
Phone: (800) 553-9071; or
cell, (808) 658-1717

---

## Where to Camp

Here are suggested campsites, in addition to the state parks covered previously. A good resource to learn more is *Camping Hawaiʻi,* a 254-page book by resident camping expert Richard McMahon. More camping information is available on the Hawaiʻi Visitors and Convention Bureau website (www.gohawaii.com).

### Oʻahu

### Bellows Beach Park                          *Zone 3 Windward Oʻahu*

---

**Location**  Located at Bellows Air Force Station, about 2.5 miles northwest of Waimanalo. On Kalanianaʻole Hwy., turn right at the sign marking BAFS and follow the road to the park
**Type of Camping**  Weekend tent camping only, noon Friday to 8 a.m. Monday
**Permits**  Applications accepted no earlier than two Fridays before the requested camping dates. You must apply in person at any satellite city hall on Oʻahu or at the Dept. of Parks and Recreation, 650 South St., Honolulu. Call (808) 523-4525.

**Cost** Free

**Comments** Fifty campsites share an ironwood forest by the beach. Picnic tables, restrooms, drinkable water, and outdoor showers are available. Gentle bodysurfing waves make Bellows a favorite. Swimming and beachcombing are popular year-round.

## Camp Mokule'ia                                     Zone 4 North Shore

**Location** Farrington Hwy. (Hwy. 930), about 4 miles west of Waialua (toward the ocean)

**Type of Camping** Cabins, lodge, and tent sites

**Permits** Write to Camp Mokule'ia at 68-729 Farrington Hwy., Waialua, HI 96791, or call (808) 637-6241, or email moluleia@pixi.com

**Time Limit** None

**Cost** Tent camping: $8 per person per night; cabins: $160 (14 beds) or $200 (22 beds) per night; lodges: $65 (rooms with shared bath), $65–$75 (with private bath), $100 (suites). Optional meal service ranges from $5 to $7 per meal.

**Comments** The best of four campsites on Mokule'ia Beach. Used primarily by groups. The area is peaceful, a sample of the rugged beauty of the North Shore. Swimming and snorkeling are good in summer, but the surf gets rough in winter. The tent area is sparse on facilities, but all campers may use the facilities at the main camp section.

## Kualoa Beach Park                                  Zone 3 Windward O'ahu

**Location** Kamehameha Hwy., country end of Kane'ohe Bay. From Honolulu, head west on the H-1 to the Likelike Hwy. exit. Drive through the tunnel, turn on Kahekili Hwy., and drive about 9 miles to the park entry on the right.

**Type of Camping** Tents only

**Permits** Applications accepted no earlier than two Fridays before the requested camping dates. Group campers must apply for a permit in person at the City Dept. of Parks and Recreation, 650 South St., Honolulu. Call (808) 523-4525; others can also apply at any satellite city hall on O'ahu.

**Time Limit** Five nights, from Friday at 8 a.m. to Wednesday at 8 a.m.

**Cost** Free

**Comments** Facilities include restrooms, showers, picnic tables, sinks, a volleyball court, drinking water, and a public phone. Amenities include scenic views, tranquil atmosphere, the beach, and a commanding photo op: Mokoli'i islet just offshore. Gates to the park close at 8 p.m. and reopen at 7 a.m. Vehicles cannot leave or enter the campgrounds during the night.

# Maui

## Haleakala National Park

Get groceries and gas before you get to the park, at Kula or lower communities. Three camping alternatives are available in the park, listed below.

## Hosmer Grove                                       Zone 10 Upcountry Maui

**Location** 6,800-foot level, just off Haleakala Crater Rd. Watch for the sign indicating Hosmer Grove, which is almost 10 miles from the Crater Rd. turnoff

**Type of Camping** Tent and vehicle camping. Vehicles must stay in the parking lot
**Permits** None. The campground is limited to 25 people, with no more than 12 in a
single group.
**Time Limit** Three nights
**Cost** Free
**Comments** The campsite, a grassy clearing surrounded by trees, has a covered pavilion with two picnic tables and two grills, restrooms, and drinkable water. Hiking is the
activity of choice. A half-mile loop nature trail begins at one end of the parking lot. Pick
up hiking trail information at the park headquarters. Bring extra blankets—it can get
cold at night.

## Wilderness Cabins and Tent
## Campground Inside Crater          Zone 10 Upcountry Maui

**Location** Inside Haleakala Crater, on the Halemau'u Trail
**Type of Camping** Tent and cabin camping
**Permits** Tent permits are issued at the park headquarters on a first-come, first-
served basis on the day of use. The campground is limited to 25 people, with no more
than 12 in a single group. Reservations for Holua, Paliku, and Kapala'oa wilderness cab-
ins must be made 3 months in advance. Be sure to include alternate dates. Write to
Haleakala National Park, P.O. Box 369, Makawao, HI 96768, or call (808) 572-9306.
**Time Limit** Three nights
**Cost** Free for tent campers. The three cabins are $40 (accommodate 1–6 people) and
$80 (7–12 people) per night.
**Comments** Awe-inspiring views of Haleakala Crater, big enough to contain Manhattan
with room to spare, are among the highlights here at the near-7,000-foot elevation. You
are likely to meet the endangered nene goose, Hawai'i's state bird. Facilities for tent
camping are sparse, and the campground is rocky. Cabins contain bunks with mattresses
(but no linens), table, chairs, cooking utensils, and a wood-burning stove with firewood.

## Kipahulu Campground          Zone 10 Upcountry Maui

**Location** Hana Hwy., about 10 miles past Hana
**Type of Camping** Tent and vehicle camping
**Permits** None. Space is limited to 100 people, on first-come, first-served basis. On
busy holiday weekends, arrive early to get your space.
**Time Limit** Three nights
**Cost** Free
**Comments** Camping in this extraordinary spot, a grassy area overlooking the sea
and the 'Ohe'o Gulch pools and waterfalls, is so memorable that even noncampers
ought to get a tent and give it a try. Facilities include restrooms, picnic tables, and grills,
plus the showers and pools provided by nature. Bring drinking water. No food or gas is
available. Swimming and jungle hiking are right at hand.

Exploring the infamous curvy road to Hana and its real-Hawai'i villages, swimmable
waterfall pools, and botanical gardens can be one of Maui's finer nonresort experiences, when you combine the long drive with an overnight stay in the Hana area. Lodging is limited in Hana, and camping at Kipahulu or Wai'anapanapa (see section on State
Parks above) is a great alternative.

## The Big Island of Hawai'i
### Hawai'i Volcanoes National Park Camping

Two drive-in campgrounds (Namakani Paio and Kulanaokuaiki) are located within the national park. These facilities are free, once you pay the entry fee to the park, and are available on a first-come basis, with no reservations, permits, or check-in required. Stays are limited to 7 days in a month, not to exceed 30 days per year. Get groceries and gas before you arrive. Volcano village has two small groceries (look for locally made Lilikoi curd for a tropical treat), and Hilo and Kea'au have supermarkets.

### Namakani Paio Campground        Zone 12 Hilo and Volcano

**Location** Hawai'i Volcanoes National Park, about 5 miles west of the park entrance on Route 11

**Type of Camping** Tent, vehicle, and rustic cabin camping

**Permits** None. For cabin reservations, write Volcano House, P.O. Box 53, Volcano, HI 96718, or call (808) 967-7321. Reservations should be made as far in advance as possible for summer and holiday periods. Cabins are $40 per night for up to four people; $8 for additional people

**Comments** Located at a 4,000-foot elevation, this scenic campground is surrounded by towering eucalyptus and native 'ohi'a trees. Tents are pitched on an open grassy field or under trees. Facilities include a large pavilion with two grills and a fireplace (pack your own firewood; it's not available in these woods), picnic tables, barbecue pits, restrooms, sinks, and potable water. Tent campers can rent showers from Volcano House, which operates ten cabins near the campground. Each cabin has a pair of single bunks and a double bed, picnic table, and outdoor barbecue grill. Toilets, sinks, and showers are provided in a separate building for cabin renters. Expect cool, damp weather. Bring warm clothing, as it tends to get chilly at night—as low as the 30s at this elevation.

### Kulanaokuaiki Campground        Zone 12 Hilo and Volcano

**Location** Hawai'i Volcanoes National Park, about 5 miles down Hilina Pali Rd.

**Type of Camping** Tent and vehicle camping

**Comments** Located at 2,700-foot elevation. No drinking water is available at this new campground. It has three campsites, two of them wheelchair-accessible. Facilities include barbecue grills, a vault-type toilet, and picnic tables.

### Kilauea State Recreation Area        Zone 12 Hilo and Volcano

An additional inexpensive camping cabin for four to six people is located on Kalanikoa Road in Volcano, half a mile from Hawai'i Volcanoes National Park entrance. It's always in high demand. Seek reservations from any state parks office; or write to the Big Island office at Division of State Parks, P.O. Box 936, Hilo, HI 96720. Call (808) 974-6200.

**Cost** $45 per night for one to four people, $5 for each additional person up to six, with a five-night maximum.

**Comments** Count yourself lucky if you're able to stay at this two-bedroom cabin, which is comfortably nestled within a shady grove of trees and ferns, with full kitchen, living/dining room and a bathroom. Blankets and linens are provided.

## Kalopa State Recreation Area      Zone 12 Hilo and Volcano

**Location** Hwy. 19, Hamakua coast, 7 miles from Honoka'a

**Type of Camping** Tent and cabin camping

**Permits** Permits can be obtained at state parks offices in the islands. Write to the Big Island office at Division of State Parks, P.O. Box 936, Hilo, HI 96720, or call (808) 974-6200.

**Time Limit** Five nights

**Cost** Free for tent campers. Cabins are $55 per night for one to four people, $5 per additional person

**Comments** Located in a deep forest of 'ohi'a trees, this well-maintained park houses a campground, picnic area, and two cabins. Facilities in a concrete-block building include restrooms, showers, sinks, and drinking water. The nearby picnic area features a covered pavilion with several tables. The cabins each contain a pair of bunk rooms, toilets, showers, and sinks. Cabin users share a dining hall with a fireplace and kitchen.

## Mauna Loa Summit Cabins      Zone 12 Hilo and Volcano

**Location** Eastern rim of Mauna Loa summit crater. Take Hwy. 11 to Mauna Loa Rd. Drive up the narrow road until it ends at a trailhead and parking lot. Hike the trail 7.5 miles to Red Hill Cabin. Mauna Loa Cabin is located 11.6 miles farther up the trail.

**Type of Camping** High-altitude tent and cabin camping

**Permits** Seek permits first-come, first served at Hawai'i Volcanoes National Park Visitor Center, up to a day before your scheduled stay. Limited to eight people per night per group. For more information, write to the Hawai'i Volcanoes National Park, Volcano, HI 96718, or call (808) 985-6000.

**Time Limit** Three nights

**Cost** Free

**Comments** Used by die-hard hikers able to make the thin-air trek. Located at the 13,250-foot level, Mauna Loa Cabin is near the edge of Moku'aweoweo, Mauna Loa's breathtaking caldera. It offers 12 bunk beds and spare mattresses (so additional people can sleep on the floor). An enclosed pit toilet is behind the cabin. Bring your own stove and drinking water (the water here needs to be treated before use). Tent camping is allowed, but try to get the cabin if at all possible; temperatures can dip below freezing at night. Bring warm clothes. At this elevation, even snow is possible any time. Altitude sickness can pose another problem for lowlanders.

## Spencer Beach Park      Zone 11 Kona

**Location** Hwy. 19, Kohala Coast, south of Kawaihae

**Type of Camping** Tent and vehicle camping

**Permits** Book your reservations early, particularly during the summer. Write to the Dept. of Parks and Recreation, County of Hawai'i, 25 Aupuni St., Hilo, HI 96720, or call (808) 961-8311.

**Time Limit**  One week during the summer, two weeks during the rest of the year
**Cost**  $5 per day for adults; $2 per day for children ages 13–17; $1 per day for children ages 12 and younger
**Comments**  Spencer Beach Park offers some of the best camping on the Big Island, with plenty of picnic tables and a large pavilion, restrooms, sinks, washrooms, changing areas, and showers. The water is drinkable. Swimming and snorkeling are popular here. The campground is located next to Pu'ukohala Heiau National Historical Site.

## Kaua'i

### Kalalau Valley, Na Pali State Park                    Zone 13 Kaua'i

**Location**  End of Kalalau Trail, about 11 miles from Ke'e Beach. Experienced hikers walk in, but this precipitous trail, which has been subjected to 1,000 years of erosion since the ancient Hawaiians first used it, is not for novices. A whitewater tour raft will drop off campers and pick them up in the summer months. The cost is $60 each way. Call (808) 826-9371.
**Type of Camping**  Tents only
**Permits**  Camping in Kalalau is restricted to 60 people per day, so try to obtain a permit as far in advance as possible. For more information, write to the Division of State Parks, 3060 'Eiwa St., Lihu'e, HI 96766, or call (808) 241-3444.
**Time Limit**  Five nights
**Cost**  Free
**Comments**  Kalalau has become too popular to feel alone in the jungle, but is still has appeal as a singular tropical fantasy come to life with its magnificent golden-sand beach, waterfalls, and steep cliffs. The camping area stretches a half-mile behind the beach. The only facilities are toilets and water from nearby Ho'olea Falls. Pack your own drinking water. Safe swimming in summer only. Most of your fellow travelers in this isolated wilderness are likely to have shed their clothes, since the tradition is to go au naturel.

## Moloka'i

### Papohaku Beach Park                    Zone 14 Moloka'i

**Location**  Just off Kaluako'i Rd., western shore. Head west on Hwy. 460 to the turnoff to the Kaluako'i Resort; continue past the hotel along Kaluako'i Rd.
**Type of Camping**  Tent and vehicle camping
**Permits**  Available at the Pau'ole Center Multipurpose Building in Kaunakakai. For advanced reservations and more information, write to the Maui County Parks Dept., P.O. Box 526, Kaunakakai, HI 96748, or call (808) 553-3204.
**Time Limit**  Three nights
**Cost**  $3 per person per night
**Comments**  This site is both easily accessible and fairly isolated. Facilities include restrooms, showers, picnic tables, grills, and drinking water. One drawback is that the beach is unsuitable for swimming.

# Bicycling: Pedal Power

Exploring Hawaiian islands by bike puts you in touch with your surroundings at your own speed. Most of the islands have mountains in the middle, which adds a challenging element.

A few biking tours are available. **Backroads,** the well-known bike vacation agency in Berkeley (call (800) 462-2848 or visit www.backroads.com), has inn-to-inn trips on the Big Island and multisport adventures on Maui and Lanaʻi. **Bicycle Adventures** in Olympia, WA (call (800) 443-6060 or visit www.bicycleadventures.com) has six- and eight-day Big Island trips in winter combining biking and B&B stays.

Bike path systems are still being developed in the place that needs them most: busy, trafficky Oʻahu. Kailua on the Windward side recently added bike lanes through beach park areas and up the Pali Highway. The City and County of Honolulu are developing a master plan for a bikeway system throughout the city. In the meantime, TheBus has free bike carriers on front; bikers can take the bus between biking points.

**Ala Moana Beach Park** in Honolulu and **Kapiʻolani Park** in Waikiki offer scenic, comfortable biking in late afternoon and around sunset. For fitness-minded cyclists, a grueling ride is the winding road up to the 2,013-foot summit of Mount Tantalus.

The roads on Neighbor Islands are more often traffic-free. The Big Island's wide, open spaces, decent roads, and challenging landscape have plenty of bike appeal. Maui has bike-friendly lanes, some with stunning views of neighboring Molokaʻi, Lanaʻi, and Kahoolawe. One candidate is the one-lane road around Maui's northwest end between Kahului and Kapalua. The scenery and the winding road slow everyone down. Stop and get a refreshing shaved ice at Kahakuloa. Or drive up to Kula, on the 3,000-foot shoulder of Haleakala, and cruise along the hilly country road to Ulupalakua and back, through flower farms, jacaranda trees, botanical gardens, and pastures.

One popular cycle adventure is cruising down the steep and scenic slopes of Hawaiʻi's volcanoes—best known on Maui, where several tour companies will outfit you with special bikes and gear, then take you to the top of 10,023-foot Haleakala, and guide you safely down the mountain, 38 miles to the seashore past pasturelands, farms, and forests. Some companies also provide hotel transportation and a snack; others offer unguided tours, letting you set your own pace. Be forewarned—some deceptive grades and curves coming down the mountain have launched even experienced bikers over the side. If you elect to go on your own, take the curves more slowly than you normally would. Dress in layers; the top third of the ride is virtually alpine, while the bottom is tropical. Downhill tours are also available on Oʻahu, the Big Island, and Kauaʻi.

Hawai'i is a terrific place for mountain biking, offering a wide range of terrain, scenic sites, and tracks.

For off-road bike adventures, go to **Moloka'i Ranch** on Moloka'i, where you can stay in a plushy tent cabin, eat communally in camp pavilions, and do your pedaling thing on the 52,000-acre ranch's superb single-track. Mountain biking is one of several activities included in the price of your stay. Here and elsewhere, the rugged trails provide optimal riding conditions, from dusty coastlines to lush forests.

The favorite Maui venue for mountain bikers is **Polipoli State Park,** where you'll find more than ten miles of single-track that winds through thick forests of eucalyptus and redwood trees. On O'ahu, other good trails are found in **Mililani** in central O'ahu, at **Maunawili** in Windward O'ahu, in **Pupukea** on the North Shore, and at **Ka'ena Point** in Leeward O'ahu.

The Big Island offers a wide range of mountain-biking experiences. Experts in the high-altitude sport can ride through a forest at **Mauna Loa,** on the crater rim, cruise the green pastures in **North Kohala,** and more. A mountain-biking trail map is available free of charge at most Big Island bike shops, or call the Big Island Visitors Bureau at (808) 329-7787.

Kaua'i has five single-tracks and nine dirt roads open to mountain bikes. Coastal treks here provide numerous scenic stops and even better views are among the rewards of biking at **Koke'e State Park** and **Waimea Canyon.**

Plenty of dirt roads on Lana'i call to mountain bikers, as well as the challenging climb to the summit of **Lana'ihale,** the island's highest point at 3,370 feet.

Keep in mind these biking safety tips:

- Wear a helmet, comfortable shoes, and close-fitting clothing.
- If possible, carry a first-aid kit and cell phone in case of emergency.
- Familiarize yourself with your rental bike and the tropic heat and humidity before riding off.
- Ride with a partner or a group.
- Bring drinking water, sunscreen, and sunglasses.
- If traveling in a group, keep at least five lengths between riders.
- Don't use headphones while riding or get distracted by views.
- Novice mountain bikers should avoid narrow, single-track trails, which sometimes skirt the edge of dangerous cliffs. Instead, ride on the dirt roads. Be careful on the Big Island, where rough and craggy lava rocks pose a shredding danger to tires and skin.

Hawai'i Bicyling League (call (808) 735-5756) issues a newsletter for local biking enthusiasts. John Alford has written *Mountain Biking the*

*Hawaiian Islands.* The book features maps and photos as well as detailed descriptions of Hawai'i's best biking trails. You can order through www.bikehawaii.com.

Daily rentals run $25–$40 for a mountain bike and $20 for a road bike.

---

**BIKE RENTAL SHOPS**

**O'ahu**
Big Mountain Rentals, (808) 926-1644
Blue Sky Rentals, (808) 947-0101
Paradise Isle Rentals, (808) 926-7777
Raging Isle Surf and Cycle, (808) 637-7707

**Maui**
Extreme Sports Maui, (808) 871-7954
Haleakala Bike Co., (808) 575-9575
Island Bikes, (808) 877-7744
South Maui Bicycles, (808) 874-0068
West Maui Bicycles, (808) 661-9005

**The Big Island**
C&S Cycle and Surf, (808) 885-5005
Da Kine Bike Shop, (808) 934-9861
Hilo Bike Hub, (808) 961-4452
HP Bike Works, (808) 326-2453
Mauna Kea Mountain Bikes, (808) 883-0130

**Kaua'i**
Kaua'i Cycle, (808) 821-2115
Outfitters Kaua'i, (808) 742-9667

**Moloka'i**
Moloka'i Bicycle, (808) 553-3931

---

# Horseback Riding: Back in the Saddle

You may not think of Hawai'i as part of the Wild West, but there's no more western state. Horses were brought to the islands more than a century ago, and a grateful populace, who had either walked or sailed everywhere before that, eagerly took to riding when they got the chance. Horseback riding is a great way to get off the roads and into the countryside of the vast ranches that invite visitors onto their lands for tropical trail rides. In the islands, the wide open spaces lead between volcanoes, along beaches and sea cliffs, and into jungled valleys with waterfalls. The horses are well trained and know their trails, leaving you free to enjoy the views.

Riding adventures are available on all islands, with colorful and personable guides to share local lore. Rates are reasonable, ranging from $55 per person for a one-hour ride to $85–$100 for a two-hour trek. Call for age and weight restrictions if you're concerned: the minimum age for riders is usually eight years old, and the maximum weight ranges to 275 pounds. Book your reservation at least a day in advance, or a week ahead if you have a group. Most rides are limited to 10 to 12 people. You can secure your reservation with a credit card, and most operators also accept traveler's checks or cash. Plan to call on the morning of your ride (or leave a phone number where you can be reached) to check on weather conditions. All riders must sign liability waivers.

A short orientation on horsemanship and safety precautions for island conditions precedes the tour. Previous riding experience is not a requirement; first-time riders are common. Operators will ask your experience level and match you to an appropriate horse. The group will go at the pace of the least experienced rider. Certain ranches offer intermediate- and advanced-level rides. Most island stables use thoroughbreds and quarter horses.

Rides include stops for a picnic lunch or barbecue, a sampling of local fruit, or a cooling swim. Full-cover shoes are mandatory, long pants are suggested, and sun protection is recommended.

---

### HORSEBACK RIDING ADVENTURES

**Oʻahu**

Correa Trails, Waimanolo; (808) 259-9005; nowlin@aloha.net
Happy Trails Hawaiʻi, North Shore; (808) 638-7433; happytrails@hawaii.rr.net
Kualoa Ranch, Windward Coast; (808) 237-7321; www.kualoa.com

**Maui**

Mendes Ranch and Trail Rides, Northwest Maui; (808) 244-7320
Makena Stables, South Maui; (808) 879-0244
Thompson Ranch, Kula; (808) 878-1910

**The Big Island**

Mauna Kea Stables, Parker Ranch; (808) 885-4288
Paniolo Riding Adventures, Honokaʻa; (808) 889-5354
Waipiʻo on Horseback, Waipiʻo Valley; (808) 775-7291

**Kauaʻi**

Esprit de Corps Riding Academy, Kapaʻa; (808) 552-2791; www.kauaihorses.com
Princeville Ranch Stables, North Shore; (808) 826-6777; www.kauai.net/kwc4
CJM Country Stables, Poʻipu Beach; (808) 742-6096; www.cjmstables.com

**Molokaʻi**

Molokaʻi Ranch Outfitters Center; (808) 552-2791; www.molokai-ranch.com

**Lanaʻi**

Lodge at Koʻele Stables; (808) 565-7300; www.lanai-resorts.com

# Hawai'i by Sky

## Hang-Gliding: Free as a Bird

Imagine soaring high above Hawai'i's wilderness mountain ridges, rainforests, azure bays, and jagged sea coasts. Hang-gliding is growing in popularity in the islands, and you can sign up for an instruction course followed by a memorable tandem flight with your instructor, using a traditional glider or a motor-powered glider. **Hang-Gliding Maui** (call (808) 572-6557) offers several adventures using a motorized glider ($95 for a half-hour and $165 for a full hour). As an alternative, try **Proflyght Maui** (call (808) 874-5433)..

## Skydiving: A Leap of Faith

Whether you're searching for the ultimate in aerial views or simply seeking thrills, skydiving may be your choice. **Skydive Hawai'i** provides skydiving experiences for novices and experts alike at Dillingham Air Field in Mokule'ia on O'ahu. The half-day experience includes training and instruction, 15 minutes of flight time to a cruising altitude of 13,000 feet, the jump (in tandem with a professional skydiver), a 5,000-foot free-fall, and 6 or 7 minutes of gliding down to earth via parachute. The cost, $250 per person, includes transportation to and from Waikiki ($180 if you drive yourself). Call (808) 637-9700.

## Biplane Riding: Get Loopy

If the romance of the biplane appeals, you can choose flight-seeing—or with a strong enough stomach, a heart-thumping aerobatic adventure, which includes a dizzying repertoire of loops, spins, rolls, and hammerheads. **Stearman Biplane Rides** (call (808) 637-4461) at Dillingham Air Field on North Shore O'ahu offers single-passenger rides aboard a restored, 1941-vintage, open-cockpit Stearman N2S biplane. A 20-minute North Shore flight is $125; a 40-minute tour over historic Pearl Harbor is $175. Add $35 for an extra ten minutes of aerobatic action.

Also at Dillingham Air Field, **Tsunami Aviation** (call (808) 677-3404) offers an exciting 20-minute ($85) flight with all kinds of topsy-turvy maneuvers—it'll literally turn the island upside-down for you. Tsunami Aviation features the state-of-the-art aerobatic sport biplane PITTS S2B, billed as the "Formula One racer of airplanes."

# Spas: For Your Health

Hawaiians have an ancient word that describes the modern concept of spa treatments for good health: *ho'oponopono,* or making things right. Hawai'i is a healthy place by its very nature and cultural tradition.

Spas devoted to rejuvenation and pampering care are now open on all islands, at moderately priced resorts as well as the luxury spreads, where they are a required amenity. You can find Hawaiian practitioners of ancient healing arts using Hawaiian medicinal plants, massage, and relaxation techniques. Look for spas that use Hawaiian medicinal plants and seaweeds, ocean water, peaceful surroundings, and methods like lomilomi, a vigorous rubbing technique, and hot lava-rock massage to promote good health. All spas offer European, Asian, New Age, and other modern therapeutic techniques.

Spa treatments have become a guy thing, luring men beyond the workout room to the relaxing massages, facials, pedicures, and manicures that women have long enjoyed. Spa treatments are not cheap, but it is easy to treat yourself to some first-class therapeutic pampering on all islands. Several spa programs take advantage of the Hawaiian outdoors—you'll find private outdoor massage cabanas near the sea and open-air facilities within spa buildings. You don't have to be a resort guest for a spa time-out, but be prepared to pay higher fees. Save a little money to take home some spa lotions and potions. Most hotels also offer fitness facilities so you can keep up your workout regimens or start new ones.

Here are some top spa choices.

## O'ahu

### Hilton Hawaiian Village                                    Zone 1 Waikiki

**Phone** (808) 951-6546 (Holistica Hawai'i); (808) 949-4321
**Hours** Daily, 6 a.m.–9 p.m. (fitness) 9 a.m.–9 p.m. (spa)
**Comments** Hilton's new spa opened in fall 2001 in two floors of new Kalia Tower at the state's largest hotel with some very interesting innovations. It is a traditional spa and salon operated by Mandara Spa, which runs luxury spas in Asia and the Caribbean as well as aboard cruise ships and on Maui at the Outrigger Wailea Beach.

The spa is also integrated with a high-tech, medically based wellness center focused on comprehensive health evaluations—the Holistica Hawai'i Health Center, offering diagnostic evaluation by a physician and electron beam tomography screening tests to detect heart problems and other disease (the tests are fast, easy, and noninvasive, using a $2 million ERT scanner). The program, with multilingual staff, also offers personal trainers and nutrition, fitness, and lifestyle workshops. The tests can be used to scan bone density, brain tissue, internal organs, and the colon—a "virtual colonography" alternative to a colonoscopy. Programs range from a half-day executive workup to a seven-day evaluation. Spa treatments are coordinated with the medical program.

After the program is completed, patrons get a complete health summary on their own CD-ROM with all lab and imaging assessments and, later, follow up with their personal doctors. Patrons can volunteer to be part of weight control, anti-aging, and immune enhancement research. For additional details about the wellness center and case histories, visit www.holistica.com.

Mandara Spa incorporates Balinese treatments in the mix of Hawaiian, European, and Asian techniques. It created some new treatments based on Hawaiian ingredients, notably the chocolate macadamia nut scrub and the vanilla-pikake (jasmine) facial. Hawaiian ingredients have been used in a variety of other treatments—ground Kona coffee, fresh coconut, sea salt, limu kala seaweed, ti leaves, and traditional protective plants. Or you could opt for the Kalia tropical pikake-papaya bath. Facilities include 25 private "wet and dry" and massage treatment rooms and some spa suites for couples, friends, and families to share treatments; infinity pool, whirlpool, and sundeck; all the usual showers, lockers, salon services, sauna, and steam rooms, as well as a cafe with spa cuisine and a boutique. Guests can also schedule massages in their rooms between 9 a.m. and midnight.

Spa treatments can be reserved with a credit card; the fee will be forfeited in case of cancellations with less than two hours' notice before the appointment. Children can have spa services but must be accompanied by a parent or guardian for treatments unless they are age 16 or older.

Massages start at $98; packages, $145 for one guest and $290 for two in a suite. The two-and-one-half hour indulgence called "Exploration in Chocolate" is $450 for two sharing a suite.

Service charges of 15% and state taxes are added to the bill; additional tips are at your discretion.

## 'Ihilani Resort and Spa                    Zone 5 Leeward O'ahu

**Phone** (808) 679-0079
**Hours** Daily, 7 a.m.–7 p.m.
**Comments** The 35,000-square-foot 'Ihilani Spa offers some 70 services and treatments, many based on distinctive Hawaiian products and ingredients, including piped-in sea water from the adjoining shore. The spa menu includes a wide range of hydrotherapies, fitness, and relaxation programs, massage treatments, aromatherapies, skin care treatments, and salon services.

Men's and women's lounges are equipped with steam room, sauna, Needle Shower Pavilion, Roman pool, relaxation area, and other amenities. Use fee for hotel guests— $20 during 7–11 a.m. and 2–7 p.m.—is waived if you purchase a spa treatment. The fee for others is $25, plus any treatment fees. The facility also has weight and cardiovascular workout rooms, with classes led by trained staff. Proper athletic footwear is required.

Appointments are scheduled in advance, and patrons who are not hotel guests need a credit card to hold a reservation. Cancel or reschedule any appointment for a treatment at least four hours in advance to avoid being charged half of the treatment fee. No-shows will be charged the full fee. You can request a male or female therapist and alert the spa to any allergies or medical conditions.

Individual treatments range from $25 for a brow or chin wax to $110 for an age-protection facial. Half- and full-day treatment programs are available, ranging from $190 to $390. A 17% service charge is added for each treatment.

The 'Ihilani is one of two places in the U.S. to offer thalassotherapy, an underwater full-body massage using 180 pulsating jet streams of warm sea water. Fresh sea water is pumped directly into the spa for each treatment. The massage lasts 25 minutes and costs $60. Contact the spa for a complete list of services or visit www.ihilani.com.

# Maui

## Grand Wailea Resort Hotel and Spa        Zone 8 South Maui

**Phone** (808) 875-1234
**Hours** Treatments, 10 a.m.–7 p.m.; fitness/workout rooms, 6 a.m.–8 p.m.; beauty salon,
8 a.m.–7 p.m.
**Comments** The Grand Wailea's Spa Grande is Hawai'i's largest at 50,000 square feet,
a favorite with the spa-going world. In 1998, readers of *Condé Nast Traveler* voted the
Grand Wailea as the top spa resort.

The Spa Grande has an "East meets West" philosophy, mixing traditional Hawaiian
healing techniques with European, American, Indian, and Asian spa therapies. Everything's
here: massage treatments, aromatherapy, body treatments, facials, hair care, manicures,
pedicures, waxings, yoga, meditation instruction, racquetball, basketball, and more. Prices
range from $20 for a nail polish change up to $270 for a one-hour "massage-in-stereo"
(two therapists working on you simultaneously). Most soothing is the spa's Termé
Wailea Hydrotherapy Circuit, a refreshing hour-long treatment. You begin with a quick
shower, enjoy some quality time in a Roman bath, and visit the steam room and sauna
before being escorted for a personalized loofah scrub, a cleansing treatment that exfo-
liates surface skin cells and produces healthier-looking skin. The treatment continues
with your choice of specialty baths—Moor mud, limu/seaweed, aromatherapy, tropical
enzyme, and mineral salt—followed by a Swiss jet shower. Sounds invigorating? The cost
is $50 for hotel guests and $75 for non–hotel guests.

Non–hotel guests pay a $30 surcharge added to the first spa treatment (salon and
wellness services not included). The surcharge is waived if you book two or more spa
treatments on the same day. You must be at least 16 years old to use the spa; minors
may receive treatments if accompanied by a parent or guardian. Non–hotel guests need
a major credit card to reserve an appointment. A 50% charge is assessed for no-shows
and cancellations less than two hours prior to your appointment. All spa and salon services are subject to an additional 15% service charge plus tax.

Use of the cardiovascular and weight-training gyms and all fitness classes are complimentary for guests of the hotel. Nonguests are charged $15 a day. Call the resort for
more information or visit www.grandwailea.com.

# The Big Island of Hawai'i

## Four Seasons Resort Hualalai        Zone 11 Kona

**Phone** (808) 325-8440
**Hours** Daily, 6 a.m.–8 p.m.
**Comments** The Hualalai Sports Club and Spa is available only to resident members
and guests of the Four Seasons Resort Hualalai. Here you'll find the full range of facilities, not in smelly closed-up quarters but in the open air as much as possible: 17
indoor/outdoor body treatment rooms, outdoor saunas and steam rooms, private outdoor garden showers, an open-air equipment gym and aerobics gym, a 25-meter outdoor Olympic-style lap pool, half-court basketball arena, Cybex strength machines,

free-weight equipment, treadmills, stationary bikes, tennis courts, and a volleyball court. Lockers and showers are provided, and robes, slippers, shorts, and T-shirts are available on request.

The sports club offers a variety of fitness classes, including high- and low-impact aerobics and aqua aerobics. Spa therapies include several types of massages ($110 for 50 minutes, $140–$160 for 80 minutes), hydrotherapy and body treatments ($65–$125 for 50 minutes), and various combination packages. Fitness die-hards with money to burn can sign up for the multiday Fitness Fantastic package ($700–$1,200), which includes a fitness assessment, three personal training sessions, three 50-minute massages (you'll need them), a hike, and two golf or tennis lessons. For those who prefer to be pampered, the Hualalai Masque package ($400+) includes your choice of the seaweed or Dead Sea mud masque treatment, plus a Vichy shower massage and a 50-minute Swedish or lomilomi massage.

Provide at least four hours' notice if you need to cancel or reschedule your appointment to avoid being charged in full (24 hours' notice is required from December 15 to January 3). Children under the age of 14 are not allowed into the spa. When making an appointment for a spa treatment, you'll be asked to arrive 20 minutes ahead of time to shower and enjoy the sauna, steam bath, whirlpool, and a cold dip. For more information, visit www.fourseasons.com.

# Kaua'i

## Hyatt Regency Kaua'i                                    Zone 13 Kaua'i

**Phone** (808) 742-1234
**Hours** Daily, 6 a.m.–8 p.m.
**Comments** The hotel's ANARA Spa was considered state of the art when it opened in 1991, and it has kept up with the times enough to remain one of Hawai'i's best spa facilities. Here you'll find no fewer than ten massage rooms that overlook private gardens, a 25-meter heated lap pool in the center of the courtyard, a Turkish steam room, a Finnish sauna, and open-air "shower gardens" carved from lava rock. Combine all this with Kaua'i's built-in therapeutic value and you have the makings of a very refreshing and invigorating experience.

Admission into the spa is $5 for hotel guests and $25 for non–hotel guests and includes use of the fitness center. Appointments for treatments should be booked at least a day in advance (especially for treatment packages). Non–hotel guests must reserve their bookings with a major credit card. Cancellation notice must be given at least four hours in advance; otherwise, you'll be charged in full. No one under the age of 16 is allowed in the spa at any time.

Here's a sampling of ANARA Spa services and prices: A half-hour massage is $65, an hour-long massage is $110; one-hour body treatments are $110, herbal wraps are $50; manicures are $40, and pedicures are $65. Treatment packages range from $155 (1.5 hours) to $375 (six hours). Locker rooms are available.

Call the hotel for a full menu of services or log on to their website at www.spa.hyatt.com/kauai/index.html.

---

### HEALTH CLUBS AND FITNESS CENTERS

In addition to health spas, there are health clubs and fitness centers in the islands, if your hotel doesn't offer one. Daily rates are $12–$20, and weekly rates begin at $40.

**O'ahu**
The Gym, (808) 533-7111
Spa Fitness Center, (808) 949-0026
Timmy's Gym, (808) 585-9777
24-Hour Fitness, (808) 971-4653 in Waikiki; (808) 973-4653 in Honolulu

**Maui**
Gold's Gym, (808) 874-2844 in Kihei; (808) 242-6851 in Wailuku;
   (808) 667-7474 in Lahaina
Maui Muscle Fitness, (808) 661-0844
24-Hour Fitness (808) 877-7474

**The Big Island**
The Club in Kona, (808) 326-2582
Gold's Gym, (808) 334-1977

**Kaua'i**
Kaua'i Athletic Club, (808) 245-5381
Kaua'i Gym, (808) 823-8210

---

# Golf: Tee Time

If you look at the Hawaiian Islands as a chain of golf courses in the middle of the Pacific Ocean, you'll begin to see the challenges they pose. Ninety courses on six islands, with exotic names like Hapuna, Ko 'Olina, Ko'olau and Mauna Lani, are set like jewels by the sea, in black lava beds, on turquoise lagoons, near volcanoes, beside lush rainforests, and deep in jungle valleys. Nowhere else on earth can you tee off to whale spouts, putt under rainbows, or play around a live volcano. But be forewarned: many of these courses feature hellish natural hazards —razor-sharp lava, gusty tradewinds, distracting views, an occasional wild pig, and, always, the tropical heat.

There is one major handicap—that big blue ocean between you and the islands poses a time and distance problem. It's impossible to play all of Hawai'i's great courses unless you move here and take up golf full time (which some duffers do).

Ever since a Scotsman opened O'ahu's first golf course in 1898, the game spread across the islands like red-hot lava. Seven 18-hole golf courses blanket the Big Island's Kona/Kohala Coast alone. Golf is now an important attraction in Hawai'i and serious business. Golf employs more people here than do sugar and pineapple—2,870 people in all, including

240 golf pros. Last year, visitors and residents played more than 4.8 million rounds of golf.

## Best and Most Challenging Courses in Hawai'i

### Ko'olau Golf Course, O'ahu

"The toughest golf course in America," according to *Men's Journal,* was originally built as private club for Tokyo high-rollers. But Ko'olau Golf Course on the Windward side opened to the public after the global recession pinched Japan. The 7,310-yard, par 72 course with a slope rating of 155 was designed by Dick Nugent. It offers "demoralizing" hazards like ravines, monster bunkers, a jungle of foliage, and a lone mango tree that blocks the tiny landing approach to the 18th hole, a 474-yard par 4.

### Ko 'Olina Golf Club, O'ahu

The par 72, 18-hole Ted Robinson Ko 'Olina Golf Club course beckons at Ko 'Olina Resort on O'ahu's western shore. This wide open course abounds with lakes, ponds, brooks, and waterfalls. The par 5 fifth hole is rated most difficult. It plays 528 yards to a small narrow neck green guarded by a pond full of black swans.

### Gold Course at Wailea Resort, Maui

Three championship courses distinguish Wailea Resort in South Maui: the newer Gold and Emerald courses, as well as the par 72, 18-hole Blue Course, considered the Grand Lady of Wailea. *Golf for Women Magazine* recently named the Wailea Golf Club one of the three most women-friendly golf facilities in the country. The Gold Course at Wailea gilds the lily on this island already noted for great courses. This Robert Trent Jones Jr. course is a rugged, natural-style 7,070-yard par 72 layout that plays over the foothills of 10,023-foot Mt. Haleakala.

### Kapalua Resort, Maui

Surrounded by a pineapple plantation on Maui's northwest coast, Kapalua Resort's 1,500 tidy acres includes three of the world's most beautiful and challenging 18-hole courses—the Village, Bay, and Plantation courses.

The par 3 fifth hole on the Bay Course gives everyone butterflies; it's a 205-yard long shot across 'Oneloa Bay from the back tees. With the nearly constant wind at your back, you may dodge the surf but hit the bunkers that shield the green's front, back, and right sides.

### The Challenge at Manele and the Experience at Ko'ele, Lana'i

Lana'i may have more deer than people, but it boasts two stunning resort golf courses—the Experience at Ko'ele and the Challenge at Manele. The

Jack Nicklaus–designed Challenge is a target-style course carved from lava cliffs by the sea. The water hazard on the par 3, signature 12th hole at Manele is a wave-lashed coast of jagged lava. This course on the south coast of Lana'i will test your patience and increase your impolite vocabulary. Or face the Experience's signature hole, which plays into a ravine from a knoll 250 feet above the fairway of this Upland course. The layout begins high on the slopes of 3,366-foot Mt. Lana'ihale, complete with Norfolk pine forest and a gallery of deer, pheasant, and wild turkey. Designed by Greg Norman and Ted Robinson, this course features the only bentgrass greens in Hawai'i.

### Hapuna Prince Course, The Big Island

Native grasslands and wild flowers cover old lava flows that rumple the layout of this environmentally aware 18-hole golf course above the Kohala Coast. Designed by Arnold Palmer and Ed Seay, Hapuna is a 6,875 -yard, par 72 course that makes extensive use of the rugged terrain (it stretches from the shore to 700 feet above sea level). One of *Golf* magazine's top 10 new golf courses in the U.S. when it opened, Hapuna was cited for environmental sensitivity and called "the course of the future."

### Hualalai Golf Course, Ka'upulehu, The Big Island

Jack Nicklaus was among the first to tee off on Hualalai, his par 72, 18-hole PGA championship course carved out of black lava on the Kona Coast. He made it look so easy. You can play this course only if you are a guest at the new Four Seasons Resort Hualalai or a resident of Hawai'i's newest, most exclusive golf retreat.

### Mauna Lani, The Big Island

If the Smithsonian Institute ever seeks a golf course for its collection, Mauna Lani is a likely candidate. Set in black lava beside the blue Pacific, this course is, thanks to man and nature, a work of art. Carved from nineteenth-century lava flows, the two 18-hole Francis H. I'i Brown North and South courses feature two striking ocean holes that challenge pros and amateurs who try to beat the records of Arnold Palmer, Lee Trevino, and Raymond Floyd. The signature sixth hole, a 199-yard par 3, is a seascape portrait of lush greens, azure sea, charcoal lava, and gold sand all under a vivid blue sky.

### Princeville Resort, Kaua'i

When designer Robert Trent Jones Jr. first saw the plateau on Kaua'i's North Shore that would become Princeville's golf links, he said he became "truly nervous." It's a reaction most golfers have today when they tee off at Princeville. With its awesome setting above scenic Hanalei Bay and challenging holes (the 205-yard, par 3 seventh tee addresses a wide-mouthed gorge), the Prince Course is rated by some as the most difficult in Hawai'i. The famed 27-hole Makai Course, one of the top 100 courses in the United States, features three separate nines: the Ocean, the Woods, and the Lake; the Ocean/Lake combo is the most popular.

## Golf, Your Way

Hawai'i's famous courses are high on the life-lists of most players who plan their vacations around golf. It's a passion fanned by sunny scenes in televised winter tournaments from resorts like Kapalua, where the water feature might be a humpback in the background, or fabled Mauna Kea and Mauna Lani on the Big Island, with their implausible green-on-lava oases under the volcanoes. When you've got that dream, nothing else will satisfy it. However, golf in Hawai'i isn't necessarily an expensive indulgence. Hawai'i residents who can't afford world-class resort greens fees are equally hooked on the game, and they play golf year-round as often as possible. The islands' resort, municipal, public, military, semiprivate, and private courses, running the gamut of designers, challenges, layouts, and expense, share a measure of distracting natural beauty.

Devoted golfers will no doubt have a course in mind when they choose where to stay. If you just want to play some golf in Hawai'i and not base your vacation around it, be your own concierge and make your own arrangements, so that you can choose the time and place you want to play and the fees you want to pay. Hotels will recommend their neighboring courses to keep their guests close to home. That may be exactly what you had in mind, because fees are lower and tee times often more readily available to resort guests. Plenty of them offer package rates for room, car, and golf with other extras thrown in. If you want to roam, your options include some enticing public and municipal courses—the perennially top-ranked Wailua municipal course on Kaua'i, for instance—where great golf experiences may cost half the fees of resort courses. Think how top-this options, like the Volcano course at 4,000 feet on the edge of Kilauea, or the historic jewel of a plantation course at Ironwood Hills on Moloka'i, will play later at your local clubhouse.

Here are some helpful resources:

- The Aloha Section PGA annual directory of Hawai'i's golf courses. Call (808) 593-2230 to receive the free guide.

- *Island Golf,* a free monthly golf guide with reliable and well-researched information, at www.islandgolfreview.net or call (808) 874-8300.

- *Discover Hawai'i's Best Golf,* an 86-page book by golf writer George Fuller. Issued in 1999 by Island Heritage Publishing, this volume provides vivid descriptions and photos of the state's top courses. Check a bookstore or call (808) 487-7299 to order.

Tee times are usually easy to reserve; the busiest times are weekends and winter tourist season. Oʻahu has the biggest crowd of golfers and the most competition for bookings. Your hopes may be dashed at that course right across the canal from Waikiki: Ala Wai Golf Course is the busiest in the nation. Koʻolau Golf Club, on the other side of the mountains, is considered the most difficult course in the nation, according to *Men's Journal.*

Most courses allow you to request a tee time at least a few days in advance. If you're looking for a last-minute tee time, try **Stand-By Golf,** which gives visitors a discount. The company makes a small margin on each booking, you get discounted rates, and the course managers are happy to fill in empty time slots. Call (888) 645-BOOK.

Shorts are acceptable attire on Hawaiian courses. Collared shirts are often required and a good idea anyway to avoid sunburn on the back of your neck. Soft-spiked shoes are the latest trend.

## Top Picks Among Golf Courses in Hawaiʻi

### GREENS FEES

Based on one 18-hole round, with or without cart:

**Resort Courses** $110–$200
**Semiprivate Courses** $25–$135
**Private Courses** $50–$100
**Public Courses** $14–$135
**Municipal Courses** $42–$54
**Military Courses** $9–$40

## Oʻahu

### Ala Wai Golf Course                                  Zone 1 Waikiki

**Established** 1931
**Location** 404 Kapahulu Ave., Honolulu, HI 96815 (mauka of the Ala Wai Canal. The entrance is on the right off Kapahulu Ave.)
**Phone** (808) 933-7387
**Status** Municipal, 18 holes, par 70
**Tees** Men's: 6,208 yds. Ladies': 5,095 yds.
**Fees** $42 daily. Cart: $14. Accepts tee times a week in advance. Accepts Visa, MC
**Facilities** Driving range lit for night play, pro shop, and restaurant. Club rentals available
**Comments** Busiest municipal course in the United States, averaging more than 500 rounds of golf per day. Hawaiʻi's oldest municipal course and local favorite underwent a facelift in the late 1980s. This is a flat course with some hilly mounds around the greens. The Ala Wai Canal comes into play on three holes. Collared shirts required, no cut-offs.

## Coral Creek Golf Course                    *Zone 5 Leeward O'ahu*

**Established** 1999

**Location** 91-1111 Geiger Rd., 'Ewa Beach, HI 96706 (Head west on H-1 to 'Ewa Beach. Take Fort Weaver Rd. and turn left on Geiger Rd.)

**Phone** (808) 441-4653

**Status** Public, 18 holes, par 72

**Tees** Championship (coral tees): 6,870 yds., (gold tees): 6,480 yds. Men's (blue tees): 6,025 yds. Ladies' (red tees): 5,412 yds.

**Fees** $125. Includes cart. Special $75 twilight rate available after noon. Club rentals: $30. Accepts tee times after the 15th of each month, for the following month. Accepts Visa, MC, AmEx, JCB, and DC

**Facilities** Driving range, putting green, practice area, pro shop, clubhouse, restaurant, beverage carts, and locker room with showers

**Comments** O'ahu's newest course. Water comes into play on 13 holes, and 6 are lined with coral reefs and interconnected by a coral creek. The signature Hole 18 is a short, 381-yard par 4 that demands a precise downhill approach to an island green.

## Hawai'i Kai Golf Course                    *Zone 2 Honolulu*

**Established** 1973

**Location** 8902 Kalaniana'ole Hwy., Honolulu, HI 96825 (from Waikiki, drive east on Kalaniana'ole Hwy. past Hawai'i Kai commerce. The course is on the left side shortly after Sandy Beach Park.)

**Phone** (808) 395-2358

**Status** Public, 18 holes, par 72 (Championship course); 18 holes, par 54 (Executive course)

**Tees** Championship: 6,614 yds. Men's: 6,222 yds. (Championship), 2,116 yds. (Executive). Ladies': 5,591 yds. (Championship), 1,896 yds. (Executive)

**Fees** Championship course: $90 weekdays, $100 weekends. Includes cart. Executive course: $37 weekdays, $42 weekends for 18 holes. $32.75 weekdays, $37.75 weekends for 9 holes. Accepts tee times a week in advance. Accepts Visa, MC, D

**Facilities** Driving range, putting green, pro shop, and restaurant. Club rentals available

**Comments** Championship course at the base of Koko Head Crater includes two hidden lakes and large greens. Breezy tradewinds raise the difficulty level a notch. The Executive course, a long par 3 course designed by Robert Trent Jones Sr., is ideal for beginners. Collared shirts required.

## Hawai'i Prince Golf Club                    *Zone 5 Leeward O'ahu*

**Established** 1992

**Location** 91-1200 Fort Weaver Rd., 'Ewa Beach, HI 96706 (head westbound on H-1, take Exit 5A, and make a left after the sixth traffic light into the club's parking lot.)

**Phone** (808) 944-4567

**Status** Resort, 27 holes, par 36

**Tees** Championship (blue tees): A and B courses: 5,759 yds.; B and C courses: 6,801 yds.; C and A courses: 6,746 yds. Men's (orange tees): A and B courses: 6,237 yds.; B and C courses: 6,175 yds.; C and A courses: 6,274 yds. Ladies' (white tees): A and B courses: 5,275 yds.; B and C courses: 5,205 yds.; C and A courses: 5,300 yds.

**Fees** $135. $90 for Prince Hotel guests. Special $50 twilight rate ($40 for hotel guests) after 2 p.m. on weekdays, 2:30 p.m. on weekends. Includes cart. Club rentals: $35. Accepts tee times 14 days in advance. Accepts Visa, MC, AmEx

**Facilities** Driving range, putting greens, pro shop, locker rooms with showers, tennis courts, clubhouse, and restaurant

**Comments** Three 9-hole courses are played in three 18-hole combinations, providing tremendous replay value. A total of 90 sand bunkers and 10 lakes adorn the 270-acre courses, which were designed by Arnold Palmer and Ed Seay. This course is built on land formerly used for growing sugarcane. It's suitable for novice and above-average players.

## Hickam Golf Course                    Zone 6 Central O'ahu

**Established** 1966

**Location** 900 Hangar Ave., Hickam AFB, HI 96853 (Take the H-1 westbound and follow the signs to Hickam Air Force Base. The sentry will provide directions to the course.)

**Phone** (808) 449-6490

**Status** Military, 18 holes, par 72

**Tees** Championship: 6,868 yds. Men's: 6,412 yds. Ladies': 5,675 yds.

**Fees** Relative or guest of military: $27.50 with cart, $20 without cart. Civilian with military sponsor: $40.50 with cart, $32 without cart. All rates are half-price after 3:30 p.m. Accepts tee times 3 days in advance. Accepts Visa, MC

**Facilities** Driving range, putting green, chipping area, practice bunker, pro shop, clubhouse, restaurant, and locker rooms with showers

**Comments** This is one of the better military courses in the state and one of the busiest in the nation. Lit for night play and surrounded by water. The signature Hole 2 demands a solid tee shot onto a fairway that juts out over water. Collared shirts required; no denim.

## Kapolei Golf Course                    Zone 5 Leeward O'ahu

**Established** 1995

**Location** 91-701 Farrington. Hwy., Kapolei, HI 96707 (head west on H-1, take the Makaha exit, turn left on Makakilo. At the first light, turn left on Farrington Hwy. The course is about a mile ahead on the right.)

**Phone** (808) 674-2227

**Status** Public, 18 holes, par 72

**Tees** Gold: 7,001 yds. Championship: 6,586 yds. Men's: 6,136 yds. Ladies': 5,490 yds.

**Fees** $70 weekdays, $90 weekends and holidays. Includes cart. Special $35 twilight rate available on weekdays after 1:30 p.m. (Monday–Wednesday) and 2:30 p.m. (Thursday–Friday). Club rentals: $30. Accepts tee times 7 days in advance. Accepts Visa, MC, AmEx, D

**Facilities** Driving range, putting green, chipping area, practice bunker, pro shop, and restaurant

**Comments** Built as a centerpiece for O'ahu's ambitious "Second City" development plan. This is a well-contoured, immaculately manicured course, the site of the LPGA's Hawaiian Ladies Open. Water hazards often come into play. The course was designed by noted golf architect Ted Robinson. Collared shirts required.

## Ko 'Olina Golf Club                     Zone 5 Leeward O'ahu

**Established** 1990

**Location** 92-120 Ali'inui Dr., 'Ewa Beach, HI 96707 (head west on H-1; take the Ko 'Olina exit. The exit loops around to the course.)

**Phone** (808) 676-5300

**Status** Resort, 18 holes, par 72

**Tees** Championship: 6,867 yds. Men's: 6,480 yds. Ladies': 5,392 yds.

**Fees** $150. $100 for 'Ihilani Resort guests. Includes cart. Special twilight rate ($75 for 18 holes, $45 for 9 holes) after 2:30 p.m. Club rentals: $30–$40. Accepts tee times a week in advance. Accepts Visa, MC, AmEx, D

**Facilities** Driving range, practice area, pro shop, restaurant, and a locker room with showers, steam rooms, and Jacuzzi

**Comments** Brisk winds make for challenging play. This course is considered to be one of Ted Robinson's best designs. Water hazards pop up throughout the course, including waterfalls, lakes, and ponds. Greens are split-level and multitiered. The course's signature 18th hole—featuring a waterfall to the right of the tee area, spilling into a lake surrounding the green—is a tough finishing hole. Collared shirts required.

## Ko'olau Golf Club                     Zone 3 Windward O'ahu

**Established** 1992

**Location** 45-550 Kiona'ole Rd., Kane'ohe, HI 96744 (Pali Hwy. toward Kailua, turn left on Kamehameha Hwy., and make a left on Kiona'ole Rd. The entrance to the course is on the left.)

**Phone** (808) 236-4653

**Status** Public, 18 holes, par 72

**Tees** Tournament (black tees): 7,310 yds. Championship (gold tees): 6,797 yds. Men's (blue tees): 6,406 yds. Ladies' (white tees): 5,102 yds.

**Fees** $125 daily. Special $75 twilight rate available after 1 p.m. Fees include cart. Club rentals: $35. Accepts tee times up to 30 days in advance. Accepts Visa, MC, and AmEx

**Facilities** Driving range, putting green, chipping range, snack bar, and pro shop

**Comments** This is considered the most difficult course in the United States, even though water comes into play on only one hole. The first hole is a 593-yard par 5. The 18th requires a tee shot over a wide ravine with a precipitous sand trap running the length of the fairway on the right. Exceptionally scenic course, in very high demand. Collared shirts required.

## Luana Hills Country Club                 Zone 3 Windward O'ahu

**Established** 1994

**Location** 770 Auloa Rd., Kailua, HI 96734 (Pali Hwy., toward Kailua. After the third stoplight, turn right onto Auloa and then take an immediate left on the winding road to the course.)

**Phone** (808) 262-2139

**Status** Semiprivate, 18 holes, par 72

**Tees** Championship (black tees): 6,595 yds. Championship (blue tees): 6,164 yds. Men's (white tees): 5,522 yds. Ladies' (yellow tees): 4,654 yds.

**Fees** $95. Special $65 twilight rate available from 2:30 p.m. on weekdays, $85 on weekends. Includes cart. Club rentals: $30. Accepts tee times a week in advance. Accepts Visa, MC

**Facilities** Driving range, putting greens, pro shop, locker rooms with showers and Jacuzzi, restaurant, and cocktail lounge

**Comments** This course is a growing favorite among residents and visitors, so scenic that the city is talking about making it a park. The front nine is carved into the side of Mt. Olomana, and the back nine take you through a tropical rain forest. The par 3 11th hole is a scenic masterpiece dominated by a picturesque pond.

## *The Links at Kuilima*                    *Zone 4 The North Shore*

**Established** 1992

**Location** 57-049 Kuilima Dr., Kahuku, HI 96731 (head west on H-1, exit onto H-2 Fwy., and stay to the right. Take the Wahiawa exit and stay right to Kamehameha Hwy.; the course is about a half hour away.)

**Phone** (808) 293-8574

**Status** Resort, 18 holes, par 72

**Tees** Men's: 7,200 yds. Ladies': 4,851 yds.

**Fees** $125. $75 for guests of the Turtle Bay Hilton at Kuilima or Hilton Hawaiian Village in Waikiki. Includes cart. Special $65 ($45 for Hilton guests) twilight rate on weekdays. Club rentals: $30. Accepts tee times 14 days in advance. Accepts Visa, MC, AmEx, D

**Facilities** Driving range, putting greens, pro shop, and snack bar

**Comments** Designed by golf legends Arnold Palmer and Ed Seay. This is a tough course because of strong tradewinds and plentiful sand traps. Though the course is near the ocean, only one hole (the 17th) provides close views of the surf. Several holes skirt a marine wildlife sanctuary. The back nine are the most scenic. *Golf* magazine ranked the course as one of the top ten new courses in the United States; *Golf Digest* ranked it fourth among the best new resort courses when it opened. No tank tops or cut-offs.

## *Makaha Golf Club*                    *Zone 5 Leeward O'ahu*

**Established** 1974

**Location** 84-626 Makaha Valley Rd., Wai'anae, HI 96792 (head west on Farrington Hwy., turn right at Makaha Valley Rd., and turn left at the fork.)

**Phone** (808) 695-9544

**Status** Resort, 18 holes, par 72

**Tees** Championship: 7,077 yds. Men's: 6,414 yds. Ladies': 5,856 yds.

**Fees** $125. $115 for guests of Waikiki hotels. Includes cart. Special $85 twilight rate after noon. Club rentals: $20. Accepts tee times 14 days in advance. Accepts Visa, MC, AmEx, D

**Facilities** Driving range, putting green, chipping area, clubhouse, and restaurant

**Comments** Formerly the Sheraton Makaha Golf Club. A favorite challenging course offering spectacular views, especially at sunset. Course overlooks the ocean; the back nine play into Makaha Valley. Winds blow down the valley toward the ocean. The par 4 18th hole is one of the most challenging holes on the island, with two bunkers to the left of the fairway, water on the right, and another water hazard fronting the green. Collared shirts required; no denim. Bring a light jacket to be prepared for frequent light rain in the valley.

## Pearl Country Club                 Zone 6 Central O'ahu

**Established** 1967

**Location** 98-535 Kaonohi St., 'Aiea, HI 96701 (West on H-1, take Pearlridge exit, and make a right. Turn right on Ka'onohi St. The entrance is on the right.)

**Phone** (808) 487-3802

**Status** Public, 18 holes, par 72

**Tees** Championship: 6,787 yds. Men's: 6,232 yds. Ladies': 5,836 yds.

**Fees** $65 weekdays, $70 weekends. Includes cart. Twilight rates: $48 2–3 p.m. and $30 after 3 p.m. Nine-hole twilight rate: $20. Club rentals: $30. Accepts tee times 60 days in advance. Accepts Visa, MC, AmEx

**Facilities** Driving range (lit for night play), pro shop, and locker room with showers

**Comments** Older, hilly course that remains popular, especially among residents. Difficult lies provide a good challenge. Overlooks Pearl Harbor and the USS *Arizona* Memorial. No tank tops or cut-offs.

# Maui

## The Dunes at Maui Lani                 Zone 8 South Maui

**Established** 1999

**Location** 1333 Mauilani Pkwy., Kahului, HI 96732 (from the Kahului Airport, head toward Lahaina on Dairy Road until you hit Kuihelani Hwy. [380]. The course is 1.5 miles off to the right. The entrance is marked by green flags.)

**Phone** (808) 873-0422

**Status** Public, 18 holes, par 72

**Tees** Championship: 6,840 yds. Blue: 6,413 yds. White: 5,833 yds. Red: 4,768 yds.

**Fees** $85, includes cart; twilight fees, $39 after 2 p.m. Club rentals, $25. Accepts tee times up to 3 months in advance; check cancellation policy. Accepts Visa, MC, AmEx

**Facilities** Driving range, 15-acre practice facility, putting greens, clubhouse, pro shop, and restaurant

**Comments** Maui's newest and most surprising course is an Irish linksland–style course incorporating natural sand dunes not on the coast, where Maui has none, but inland, where the sea left them a million or so years ago in a valley. Architect Robin Nelson took advantage of ancient dunes up to 80 feet high to provide drama on several holes. His layout requires thought when playing. There is a peek of the sea now and then, but it's mostly rolling terrain with a forest of thorny kiawe trees. Instead, the killer views are of towering Haleakala. The short par 3 third hole is a classic dune hole fashioned after the sixth at Lahinch in Ireland. The course anchors a residential planned development.

## Elleair Maui Golf Course
## (formerly Silversword)                 Zone 8 South Maui

**Established** 1987

**Location** 1345 Pi'ilani Highway, Kihei, HI 96753 (mauka, or uphill, side of Hwy. 31 in Kihei)

**Phone** (808) 874-0777

**Status**  Public, 18 holes, par 71

**Tees**  Championship: 6,801 yds. Men's: 6,404 yds. Ladies': 6,003 yds.

**Fees**  $59; twilight special after 1 p.m., $45. Carts included. Club rentals: $30. Accepts tee times 30 days in advance

**Facilities**  Driving range, night lit, pro shop, and restaurant

**Comments**  Morning and late afternoon tradewinds usually hit the course, and many holes bring the winds into play. Views of the sea are afforded from most of the greens on this public course. The ninth hole is a long par 4 with a pond on the right side.

## Ka'anapali Golf Courses                           Zone 9 West Maui

**Established**  1962 (North), 1997 (South)

**Location**  Ka'anapali Resort, Lahaina, HI 96761 (take Hwy. 30 past Lahaina to Ka'anapali Beach Resort. Turn left at the first entrance of the golf course.)

**Phone**  (808) 661-3691

**Status**  Resort, 18 holes, par 71 (for both courses)

**Tees**  Men's: North: 6,994 yds.; South: 6,555 yds. Ladies': North: 5,417 yds.; South: 5,485 yds.

**Fees**  $130; less for resort guests. Includes cart. Special $80 twilight rate (South course only) noon–2:30 p.m. Twilight rate (both courses) after 2:30 p.m.: $65. Repeat rounds: $42. Club rentals: $30 ($20 twilight rate). Accepts tee times 2 days in advance. Accepts Visa, MC, AmEx

**Facilities**  Driving range, putting green, pro shop, restaurant, and locker room with showers

**Comments**  Two excellent 18-hole courses. The 18th on the North course is one of Hawai'i's toughest finishing holes, with water hazards lined up on the right side and the kidney-shaped green bordered by two treacherous bunkers on the left. The shorter South course, with more forgiving greens and wider fairways, is the likely preference for less experienced golfers. The North hosts the annual Ka'anapali Classic, a Senior PGA Tour event.

## Kapalua Golf Club                                  Zone 9 West Maui

**Established**  1975 (Bay), 1980 (Village), 1991 (Plantation)

**Location**  300 Kapalua Dr., Kapalua, HI 96761 (take Hwy. 30 to past Lahaina and Ka'anapali to Kapalua Resort, turn left at Kapalua Dr.)

**Phone**  Bay course: (808) 669-8804; Plantation course: (808) 669-0507; Village course: (808) 669-7715

**Status**  Resort. Bay course: 54 holes, par 72; Village course: 18 holes, par 71; Plantation course: 18 holes, par 73

**Tees**  Men's: Bay: 6,600 yds.; Village: 6,282 yds.; Plantation: 7,263 yds. Ladies': Bay: 5,124 yds.; Village: 4,876 yds.; Plantation: 5,627 yds.

**Fees**  $180, $125 for resort guests. Includes cart. Twilight special: All rates are half off after 2 p.m. Club rentals: $35–$45. Accepts tee times 4 days in advance. Accepts Visa, MC, AmEx, D

**Facilities**  Driving range, putting green, pro shop, clubhouse, and restaurants

**Comments**  These three courses are among Maui's best, providing gorgeous views at every turn. The Village course features elevated tee shots on many holes, and the 367-yard, par 4 Hole 6 is one of the most scenic in Hawai'i, with stately pines lined up toward the ocean. The Bay course's Hole 5 is one of the world's most dramatic signature holes, requiring a tee shot over 'Oneloa Bay. The links-style Plantation course, highly regarded by many pros, is the home of the PGA Tour's Mercedes Championships. No tank tops or cut-offs.

## Makena Resort Golf Club                    Zone 8 South Maui

**Established** 1983 (split into two separate courses in 1994)
**Location** 5415 Makena Alanui, Makena, HI 96753 (from Kahului Airport, take Dairy Rd. to Pi'ilani Hwy., turn right at the end, then left at the stop sign on Wailua Alanui and go south past Wailea. The entrance is on the left.)
**Phone** (808) 879-3344
**Status** Resort, 18 holes, par 72 (for both courses)
**Tees** Championship: North: 6,500 yds.; South: 6,600 yds. Men's: North: 6,100 yds.; South: 6,200 yds. Ladies': North: 5,300 yds.; South: 5,500 yds.
**Fees** $110. Includes cart. Special $80 twilight rate available from 2 p.m. Club rentals: $35. Accepts tee times 3 days in advance. Accepts Visa, MC, AmEx
**Facilities** Practice range, putting green, pro shop, and locker room with showers
**Comments** Located by the Maui Prince Hotel. Both courses are among the state's best, with views of the ocean, Haleakala, and Mokoka'i, Lana'i, and Kaho'olawe. This course was designed by noted golf architect Robert Trent Jones Jr. Severe slopes and fast greens make for very challenging play. The lack of strong winds at Makena is a big plus. The South Course's 15th and 16th holes are among Hawai'i's most picturesque oceanfront holes. The North Course is generally considered the more difficult of the two courses.

## Sandalwood Golf Course                     Zone 8 South Maui

**Established** 1991
**Location** 2500 Honoapi'ilani Highway, Wailuku, HI 96793 (turn uphill off Hwy. 30, just south of Wailuku)
**Phone** (808) 242-4653
**Status** Resort, 18 holes, par 72
**Tees** Championship, 6,433 yds. Men's: 5,918 yds. Ladies': 5,162 yds.
**Fees** $75, carts included; twilight play after 2 p.m., $70. Golf Program participants, $60. Club rentals, $35
**Facilities** Driving range, pro shop, banquet facility, locker rooms, clubhouse, putting and chipping greens, and restaurant
**Comments** Robin Nelson and Rodney Wright designed this layout among sandalwood trees at Waikapu, nestled into the side of the West Maui Mountains overlooking Maui's isthmus of green cane fields. Sloping fairways and hefty tradewinds can make for a challenging day, along with a lot of elevated greens and par 4s that are long, straight, and into the wind.

## Waiehu Golf Course                    *Zone 7 Central Maui*

**Established** 9-hole course opened in 1933; back 9 added in 1966
**Location** P.O. Box 507, Wailuku, HI 96793 (from Hwy. 340, make a right just past Waiheʻe Park. The entrance is on the right.)
**Phone** (808) 244-5934
**Status** Municipal, 18 holes, par 72 (par 73 for women)
**Tees** Men's: 6,330 yds. Ladies': 5,555 yds.
**Fees** $26 weekdays, $30 weekends and holidays. Cart: $8 per person. Club rentals: $15. Accepts tee times 2 days in advance. Accepts Visa, MC
**Facilities** Driving range, putting green, pro shop, clubhouse, and restaurant
**Comments** Maui's only municipal course. The front nine are relatively flat, whereas the back nine are hilly in spots. This course features one lake and more than 40 sand bunkers. Three holes front the ocean. The signature, par 5 Hole 7 plays along the beach.

## Wailea Golf Club                       *Zone 8 South Maui*

**Established** 1972 (Blue), 1993 (Gold), 1995 (Emerald)
**Location** 100 Wailea Golf Club Dr., Wailea, HI 96753 (from Kahului Airport, take Dairy Rd. to Piʻilani Hwy., drive to southern end of the road and turn right. At the stop sign, turn left on Wailea Alanui.)
**Phone** Gold and Emerald courses: (808) 875-7450; Blue course: (808) 875-5155
**Status** Resort, 18 holes, par 72 (all 3 courses)
**Tees** Championship: Gold: 7,078 yds.; Emerald: 6,825 yds.; Blue: 6,758 yds. Men's: Gold: 6,653 yds..; Emerald: 6,407 yds..; Blue: 6,152 yds. Ladies': Gold: 5,442 yds.; Emerald: 5,268 yds.; Blue: 5,291 yds.
**Fees** Gold and Emerald: $125, $100 for Wailea resort guests. Blue: $115, $85 for resort guests. Includes cart. Twilight $75 rate ($65 for resort guests) available on the Blue course after noon. Club rentals: $30. Accepts tee times 5 days in advance. Accepts Visa, MC, AmEx, D
**Facilities** Driving range, putting greens, pro shop, and restaurant
**Comments** All three courses have breathtaking ocean and mountain views. The Blue course, with wide, open fairways, is the easiest, but it does have 74 bunkers and 4 water hazards. The Gold course, featuring ancient lava rock walls, ranked as one of *Golf* magazine's ten best new courses in 1993. The Emerald course offers stunning views of Haleakala and the Pacific and is considered a friendlier course for high-handicap players. Its signature hole is the 18th, a 553-yard par 5 challenge with a downhill slope. Collared shirts required.

# The Big Island of Hawaiʻi

## Hapuna Golf Course                     *Zone 11 Kona*

**Established** 1992
**Location** 62-100 Kaunaoa Dr., Kohala Coast, HI 96743 (from Kona, drive north along Hwy. 19 past Waikoloa until you see the roads leading to the Hapuna Beach Prince Hotel on the left. Drive a bit farther; the golf course is on the right.)
**Phone** (808) 882-1035
**Status** Resort, 18 holes, par 72

**Tees** Tournament: 6,875 yds. Championship: 6,534 yds. Men's: 6,029 yds. Ladies': 5,067 yds.

**Fees** $135. $85 for resort guests. Includes cart. Special $85 twilight rate ($50 for resort guests) available after 3 p.m. Club rentals: $35. Accepts tee times 2 days in advance. Accepts Visa, MC, AmEx

**Facilities** Driving range, putting green, pro shop, clubhouse, and restaurant

**Comments** This is a sister course to Mauna Kea Golf Course. The demanding links-style course is set amid arid lava flows, natural vegetation, and spectacular scenery. Water hazards come into play on four holes. The front nine play into the winds that blow down from Mauna Kea. The 545-yard, par 5 Hole 3 is regarded as one of the best par 5s in the state, with wide expanses, an imposing ravine, a lake, and a series of bunkers. This is another Arnold Palmer–Ed Seay collaboration. Golfers share the course with several endangered bird species, including the nene goose, Hawai'i's state bird. Unquestionably, this is one of the Big Island's best. Collared shirts required; no denim.

## Hilo Municipal Golf Course  Zone 12 Hilo and Volcano

**Established** 1951

**Location** 340 Haihai St., Hilo, HI 96720 (from Hilo, head south on Hwy. 11, past the Prince Kuhio Plaza. Turn right on Puainako St., left on Kilauea Ave., then right on Haihai St.)

**Phone** (808) 959-7711

**Status** Municipal, 18 holes, par 71

**Tees** Championship: 6,325 yds. Men's: 6,006 yds. Ladies': 5,034 yds.

**Fees** $20 weekdays, $25 weekends. Cart: $14.50 for 18 holes, $8 for 9 holes. Club rentals: $10. Accepts tee times 7 days in advance

**Facilities** Driving range, pro shop, and restaurant

**Comments** The Big Island's municipal course features flat, tree-lined fairways with no sand traps but plenty of water hazards in the form of streams and lakes. This is a good course for average players. Light rains are frequent in Hilo, so pack an umbrella.

## Hualalai Golf Club  Zone 11 Kona

**Established** 1996

**Location** 100 Ka'upulehu Dr., Ka'upulehu, HI 96740 (take Mamalahoa Hwy. Hualalai Resort and the golf course are just 5 minutes north of the airport.)

**Phone** (808) 325-8480

**Status** Private, 18 holes, par 72

**Tees** Championship: 7,117 yds. Men's: 6,632 yds. Ladies': 5,374 yds.

**Fees** $160, cart included. Only Hualalai homeowners or guests staying at the Four Seasons Resort Hualalai may play. Club rentals: $50. Accepts tee times up to 90 days in advance. Accepts Visa, MC, AmEx, DC

**Facilities** Driving range, putting greens, practice area, clubhouse, snack bar, and restaurant

**Comments** Designed by Jack Nicklaus, this beautiful course is the home of the PGA Senior Tour's Tournament of Champions. The 172-yard, par 3 Hole 17 is the signature hole, with an expansive green that demands precise pin placement. The golf club is the first in Hawai'i to be designated an official PGA Tour facility.

## Kona Country Club                          Zone 11 Kona

**Established** 1985 (Kona), 1991 (Ali'i)
**Location** 78-7000 Ali'i Dr., Kailua-Kona, HI 96740 (from the Kona Airport, drive south on Hwy. 11, then turn right down Ali'i Dr. The course is located near the end of the road.)
**Phone** (808) 322-2595
**Status** Resort, 27 holes, par 72 (for both courses)
**Tees** Championship: Ocean course: 6,579 yds.; Mountain course: 6,671 yds. Men's: Ocean course: 6,155 yds.; Mountain course: 5,828 yds. Ladies': Ocean course: 5,499 yds.; Mountain course: 4,906 yds.
**Fees** $125 Ocean, $100 Mountain. Includes cart. Special twilight rate available after 12:30 p.m. Club rentals: $35. Accepts tee times 3 days in advance. Accepts Visa, MC, AmEx
**Facilities** Driving range, putting green, pro shop, restaurant, and lounge
**Comments** The Ocean course is a friendly course for golfers in need of a confidence boost, with wide fairways and easy greens. Much of the course hugs the Pacific, with particularly gorgeous vistas from Holes 11–13. The Mountain course, however, has more hazards and tricky hillside lies. The signature 7th hole is a downhill par 4 (438 yards) that plays straight into the wind and requires a tee shot over a water hazard.

## Mauna Kea Golf Course                      Zone 11 Kona

**Established** 1964
**Location** 62-100 Mauna Kea Beach Dr., Kohala Coast, HI 96743 (from Kona, drive north on Hwy. 19 to the Mauna Kea Resort entrance on the left.)
**Phone** (808) 882-5400
**Status** Resort, 18 holes, par 72
**Tees** Tournament: 7,114 yds. Championship: 6,737 yds. Men's: 6,365 yds. Ladies': 5,277 yds.
**Fees** $195. $110 for resort guests. Includes cart. Special $145 ($110 for resort guests) twilight rate available after 3 p.m. Club rentals: $40 for 18 holes, $20 for 9 holes. Accepts tee times 2 days in advance. Accepts Visa, MC, AmEx
**Facilities** Driving range, putting green, pro shop, and restaurant
**Comments** The first course to be designed using a lava-strewn landscape, this Robert Trent Jones Sr. course is a perennial favorite, although it is quite demanding. The signature hole, the 210-yard, par 3 Hole 3, requires a tee shot over 180 yards of ocean to reach the green. Jones himself rated this hole one of his all-time favorites. The course remains one of Hawai'i's top layouts. Collared shirts required.

## Mauna Lani Resort                          Zone 11 Kona

**Established** 1981 (North), 1991 (split into two courses, adding South)
**Location** 68-1310 Mauna Lani Dr., Kohala Coast, HI 96743 (from Kona, drive north on Hwy. 19 and turn left at Mauna Lani Dr. The golf course is on the left.)
**Phone** (808) 885-6655
**Status** Resort, 18 holes, par 72 (for both courses)
**Tees** Championship: North: 6,913 yds.; South: 6,938 yds. Men's: North: 6,601 yds. (blue tees), 6,086 yds.; South: 6,436 yds. (blue tees), 5,940 yds. Ladies': North: 5,383 yds.; South: 5,028 yds.

**Fees** $185. $95 for resort guests. Includes cart. Special $75 twilight rate available from 2 p.m. Club rentals: $35. Accepts tee times 5 days in advance. Accepts Visa, MC, AmEx, D
**Facilities** Driving range, putting green, pro shop, clubhouse, and restaurant
**Comments** Both courses have spectacular visual appeal and play. The North course, blessed with rolling terrain and thickets of kiawe trees, is the longer course and requires more strategy off the tee. The 140-yard, par 3 Hole 17 is its signature hole, where your tee shot carries from an elevated tee to (hopefully) a green framed by black lava. The South's signature hole, the 196-yard, par 3 Hole 15, requires a bold tee shot over crashing surf. During the winter, the 15th often features another distraction: humpback whales, often spotted in the deep waters. Collared shirts required.

## Sea Mountain Golf Course          Zone 12 Hilo and Volcano

**Established** 1974
**Location** P.O. Box 190, Pahala, HI 96777 (drive south from Hilo on Hwy. 11 to Mile Marker 56. The course is on the left.)
**Phone** (808) 928-6222
**Status** Resort, 18 holes, par 72
**Tees** Championship: 6,492 yds. Men's: 6,106 yds. Ladies': 5,663 yds.
**Fees** $42 weekdays, $45 weekends. Guests of Sea Mountain Golf Course Colony Condominiums receive $10 discount. Includes cart. Club rentals: $25. Accepts tee times 3 days in advance. Accepts Visa, MC
**Facilities** Driving range, putting green, pro shop, and restaurant
**Comments** The front nine here line a picturesque beach, and the back nine are set against a mountain. Beautiful views from everywhere on the course.

## Volcano Golf and Country Club     Zone 12 Hilo and Volcano

**Established** 1922 (as 9-hole course); expanded and redesigned in 1967
**Location** P.O. Box 46, Hawai'i Volcanoes National Park, HI 96718 (drive up from Hilo, past the Hawai'i Volcanoes National Park, and look for Mile Marker 30 on the right. Turn right on Golf Course Rd.; the course is on the right.)
**Phone** (808) 967-7331
**Status** Public, 18 holes, par 72
**Tees** Championship: 6,503 yds. Men's: 6,180 yds. Ladies': 5,514 yds.
**Fees** $62.50. Includes shared cart. Club rentals: $18. Senior discounts available. Accepts tee times 6 months in advance. Accepts Visa, MC, AmEx
**Facilities** Driving range, putting green, pro shop, restaurant, and lounge.
**Comments** Located beside Hawai'i Volcanoes National Park, this course neighbors an active volcano. But the lava flow is a considerable distance away and won't pose a threat. A mostly flat course except for some rolling hills. A pond and three ditches come into play on four holes. Nearly all the tees and some of the greens are elevated. No tank tops or cut-offs.

## Waikoloa Beach Golf Club          Zone 11 Kona

**Established** 1981
**Location** 1020 Keana Pl., Waikoloa, HI 96738 (From the airport, drive north on Hwy. 19. Turn left into Waikoloa Beach Resort, then make a right on Keana Pl. after the third stop sign.)

**Phone** (808) 886-6060

**Status** Resort, 18 holes, par 70

**Tees** Championship: 6,566 yds. Men's: 5,958 yds. Ladies': 5,094 yds.

**Fees** $195. $105 for resort guests. Includes cart. Twilight rate available after 2 p.m. Club rentals: $35. Accepts tee times 4 days in advance. Accepts Visa, MC, AmEx, D

**Facilities** Driving range, putting green, pro shop, and restaurant

**Comments** A challenging course with narrow fairways framed by rugged black lava. An ancient petroglyph field borders the sixth, seventh, and eighth holes, adding a unique sense of place. The 479-yard, par 4 Hole 12, meanwhile, leads to the ocean surf. It features a dogleg fairway and green bordered on the right by the Pacific. Collared shirts required.

## Waikoloa Kings' Course                    Zone 11 Kona

**Established** 1990

**Location** 600 Waikoloa Beach Dr., Waikoloa, HI 96738 (from the airport, drive north on Hwy. 19. Turn left into Waikoloa Beach Resort, then make a right on Keana Pl. after the third stop sign.)

**Phone** (808) 886-7888

**Status** Resort, 18 holes, par 72

**Tees** Championship: 7,094 yds. Men's: 6,594 yds. Ladies': 6,010 yds.

**Fees** $195. Includes cart. Special $110 twilight rate after 2 p.m. Club rentals: $45. Accepts tee times 5 days in advance. Accepts Visa, MC, AmEx, D

**Facilities** Driving range, putting green, practice sand trap, and pro shop

**Comments** Designed by Tom Weiskopf and Jay Morrish, this links-style course was voted among *Golf Digest's* "Best New Resort Course in America" when it opened. A challenging layout characterized by many sand bunkers and lava rock formations with treacherous greens. The signature hole, the 293-yard, par 4 Hole 5, features a long bunker stretching along the left side of the fairway, with two large boulders posing another threat for players trying to reach the green. The course is very playable for resort golfers when played from the regular tees. Collared shirts required.

## Waikoloa Village Golf Club                    Zone 11 Kona

**Established** 1972

**Location** 68-1792 Melia St., Waikoloa, HI 96738 (from the Kona Airport, drive north along Hwy. 19. Turn right onto Waikoloa Rd. and look for the golf course on the left.)

**Phone** (808) 883-9621

**Status** Resort, 18 holes, par 72

**Tees** Championship: 6,687 yds. Men's: 6,142 yds. Ladies': 5,558 yds.

**Fees** $80. Includes cart. Special $55 twilight rate available after 1 p.m. Club rentals: $30. Accepts tee times 3 days in advance. Accepts Visa, MC, AmEx, D

**Facilities** Driving range, putting green, pro shop, and restaurant

**Comments** Oldest of the Waikoloa courses, this scenic layout takes you from ancient lava beds to raging surf. Layout features rolling terrain, dogleg fairways, and two lakes that come into play on three holes. No tank tops or cut-offs.

## Waimea Country Club                                   *Zone 11 Kona*

**Established** 1994
**Location** P.O. Box 2155, Kamuela, HI 96743 (East of Kamuela, aka Waimea, on Mamalahoa Hwy.)
**Phone** (808) 885-8053
**Status** Semiprivate, 18 holes, par 72
**Tees** Championship: 6,661 yds. Men's: 6,210 yds. Ladies': 5,673 yds.
**Fees** $65. Includes cart. Special $50 twilight rate available from 1 p.m. Club rentals: $30 for full round, $25 for 9 holes or twilight play. Senior discounts available. Accepts tee times 2 days in advance. Accepts Visa, MC, AmEx
**Facilities** Driving range, putting green, and snack shop
**Comments** Built on open pasturelands, but features enough tall ironwood trees to keep you honest. There are 28 sand bunkers, and water hazards come into play on five holes. Features large, unrelenting greens. All in all, this is a good course for players of all skill levels. No dress code, but bring a jacket or sweater, as weather conditions here are often cool and misty.

# Kaua'i
## Kaua'i Lagoons Resort                                *Zone 13 Kaua'i*

**Established** 1989
**Location** 3351 Ho'olaulea Wy., Lihu'e, HI 96766 (from Lihu'e Airport, turn left on Ahukini Rd., left again on Hwy. 51, and left again at the stoplight on Kalapaki Beach. The golf course is on the right.)
**Phone** (808) 241-6000
**Status** Resort, 18 holes, par 72 (for both courses)
**Tees** Championship: Ki'ele course: 7,070 yds.; Mokihana course: 6,960 yds. Men's: Ki'ele: 6,674 yds. (blue tees), 6,164 yds.; Mokihana: 6,578 yds. (blue tees), 6,136 yds. Ladies': Ki'ele: 5,417 yds.; Mokihana: 5,607 yds.
**Fees** $130 for Ki'ele, $85 for Mokihana. Includes cart. Special twilight rates ($99 for Ki'ele, $65 for Mokihana) available after 11 a.m. Guests at the Kaua'i Marriott receive $20 off. Club rentals: $30. Accepts tee times 30 days in advance. Accepts Visa, MC, AmEx
**Facilities** Driving range, putting and chipping greens, pro shop, locker rooms with showers, snack bar, and restaurant
**Comments** Both courses here were designed by Jack Nicklaus. The Ki'ele course is the more difficult of the two, with many tee shots needing to carry over ravines. The Ki'ele course is one of Hawai'i's best and offers perhaps the best greens. *Golf Digest* ranked the course as one of the 75 best upscale courses in America. The Mokihana course is more favorable to players with higher handicaps. Collared shirts required; no cut-offs.

## Kiahuna Golf Club                                     *Zone 13 Kaua'i*

**Established** 1983
**Location** 2545 Kiahuna Plantation Dr., Koloa, HI 96756 (in Po'ipu, drive down Po'ipu Rd. and turn left on Kiahuna Plantation Dr. The entrance is on the left.)
**Phone** (808) 742-9595

**Status**  Resort, 18 holes, par 70
**Tees**  Championship: 6,353 yds. Men's: 5,631 yds. Ladies': 4,871 yds.
**Fees**  $75 before 11 a.m., $65 from 11 a.m. to 2:30 p.m. Special $45 twilight rate available after 2:30 p.m. on weekdays only. Includes cart. Club rentals: $30. Guests staying at selected hotels receive discounts. Accepts tee times 30 days in advance. Accepts Visa, MC, AmEx, D
**Facilities**  Driving range, putting green, pro shop, and snack bar
**Comments**  A challenging layout built around historic Hawaiian sites. The course features narrow fairways, water hazards, and plenty of tradewinds. Designed by Robert Trent Jones Jr. Collared shirts required.

## Po'ipu Bay Resort Golf Course        Zone 13 Kaua'i

**Established** 1991
**Location**  2250 Ainako St., Koloa, HI 96756 (in Po'ipu, follow Po'ipu Rd. to Ainako St. and make a right. The course is just past the Hyatt Regency Kaua'i.)
**Phone**  (808) 742-9489
**Status**  Resort, 18 holes, par 72
**Tees**  Championship: 6,959 yds. Men's: 6,499 yds. (blue tees), 6,023 yds. Ladies': 5,241 yds.
**Fees**  $120–$170 before noon, $100–$115 after noon. Includes cart. Special twilight rate available after 3 p.m. Guests staying at selected hotels are eligible for discounts. Club rentals: $40. Accepts tee times 7 days in advance. Accepts Visa, MC, AmEx
**Facilities**  Driving range, putting and chipping greens, practice sand bunkers, pro shop, locker room with showers, clubhouse, and restaurant
**Comments**  Water hazards come into play on 11 holes at this immaculate course; more than 80 bunkers add to the challenge. The 501-yard, par 4 Hole 16 is lined by a lake on one side of the fairway and the ultimate water hazard—the ocean—on the other. The 201-yard, par 3 Hole 17 is another spectacular setting, boasting awesome coastal views from the tee. This is the site of the PGA Grand Slam of Golf, a two-day event featuring the winners of golf's four major championships. Collared shirts required.

## Princeville Resort Golf Courses        Zone 13 Kaua'i

**Established** 1973 (Makai), 1990 (Prince)
**Location**  Makai course: 4080 Leiopapa Rd., Princeville, HI 96722 (from Kuhio Hwy., turn right into the Princeville Resort. The golf course is 1 mile away, on the left.). Prince course: 5-3900 Kuhio Hwy., Princeville, HI 96722 (from Kuhio Hwy., drive past the Princeville Airport. The golf course is on the right.)
**Phone**  Makai course: (808) 826-3580; Prince course: (808) 826-5000
**Status**  Resort. Makai: 27 holes, par 36; Prince: 18 holes, par 72
**Tees**  Championship: Makai: 3,430 yds. (Ocean), 3,456 yds. (Lakes), 3,445 yds. (Woods); Prince: 7,309 yds. Men's: Makai: 3,157 yds. (Ocean), 3,149 yds. (Lakes), 3,204 yds. (Woods); Prince: 6,960 yds. (blue tees), 6,521 yds., 6,005 yds. (gold tees). Ladies': Makai: 2,802 yds. (Ocean), 2,714 yds. (Lakes), 2,809 yds. (Woods); Prince: 5,338 yds.
**Fees**  Makai: $165. Guests staying at Princeville pay $125–$145. Includes cart. Discounted rate of $85 after 1 p.m. $39 twilight rate (for 9 holes) available after 4 p.m. Club rentals: $35 for 18 holes, $17.50 for 9 holes. Prince: $175. $145 for resort guests.

Includes cart and use of driving range. Special $110 rate available after noon. Club rentals: $35–$45. Accepts tee times 14 days in advance. Accepts Visa, MC, AmEx

**Facilities** Makai: Driving range, putting and chipping greens, pro shop, and snack bar; Prince: All of the above plus more putting greens, a full-service spa, and a restaurant

**Comments** The Makai course is actually three separate 9-hole courses that combine to form three different 18-hole layouts. The Ocean course's signature hole, appropriately, requires a tee shot over a stretch of ocean. Lakes come into play on three holes on the Lakes course and one hole on the Woods course. The Scottish links–style Prince course provides a challenge with its rolling hills and multitude of ravines. Views? You can see the ocean from every tee. *Golf Digest* has rated the Prince course as Hawai'i's best. Collared shirts required.

## *Wailua Golf Course*       *Zone 13 Kaua'i*

**Established** 1920 (as 6-hole course); expanded and redesigned in 1962
**Location** 3-5350 Kuhio Hwy., Lihu'e, HI 96746 (from Lihu'e on Kuhio Hwy., drive north to Kapa'a. The golf course is on the right.)
**Phone** (808) 246-2793 or (808) 241-6666
**Status** Municipal, 18 holes, par 72
**Tees** Championship: 6,981 yds. Men's: 6,585 yds. Ladies': 5,974 yds.
**Fees** $25 weekdays, $35 weekends and holidays. 50% discount rates available after 2 p.m. Cart: $14. Club rentals: $15 with $50 deposit. Accepts tee times 7 days in advance. Accepts only traveler's checks or cash
**Facilities** Driving range, putting green, pro shops, and shower rooms
**Comments** One of the best municipal courses in the United States. This is a challenging course with elevated tees. It has served as the site of past Men's Public Links Amateur Championships. No tank tops or cut-offs.

# Moloka'i

Note: At press time, Kaluako'i Golf Course at Kalualo'i Resort was closed pending ownership changes. But golfers vacationing on Moloka'i could be agreeably surprised to discover the following course.

## *Ironwood Hills Golf Course*       *Zone 14 Moloka'i*

**Established** 1928
**Location** Kalae Hwy, Kualapu'u, HI 96757 (just before the Moloka'i Mule Ride barn, 15 minutes from the airport)
**Phone** (808) 567-6000
**Status** Public, 9 holes, par 34
**Tees** Championship: 3,088 yds. Middle: 2,816 yds. Forward, 2,409 yds.
**Fees** $14 for 18 holes; $10 for 9. Rental clubs and carts, $7 each for 9 holes. Tee times reservations advised. Accepts Visa, MC
**Facilities** Driving range, pro shop, and food service. Metal spikes allowed
**Comments** Historic Upcountry course designed for Del Monte Plantation executives. One of the oldest courses in Hawai'i, it has been preserved as a literal link to the past. Its rustic hilly layout, set in the Moloka'i highlands, is a challenging test with brisk tradewinds in the afternoons and fairways of tightly woven Kukuya grass framed by tall

stands of island pine, eucalpytus, and the ironwoods for which it is named. Golfers must drive through narrow shoots of trees, and battle long uphill holes into the wind. After teeing off on the sixth hole, those in the know take only the clubs they need to finish and a driver for the seventh, leaving the rest under a tree for the steep climb to the seventh. Views of this and neighboring islands are breathtaking.

# Lana'i

### The Challenge at Manele                          *Zone 15 Lana'i*

**Established** 1993

**Location**  P.O. Box 310, Lana'i City, HI 96763 (transportation via Lana'i Resorts shuttle)

**Phone**  (808) 565-2222

**Status**  Resort, 18 holes, par 72

**Tees**  Championship: 7,039 yds. Men's: 6,684 yds. Ladies': 5,024 yds.

**Fees**  $200. $145 for guests staying at the Lodge at Ko'ele, Manele Bay Hotel, or Hotel Lana'i. Club rentals: $40 for full round, $25 for 9 holes. Accepts tee times 30 days in advance. Accepts Visa, MC, AmEx

**Facilities**  Driving range, putting and chipping greens, locker rooms, pro shop, and restaurant

**Comments**  Designed by Jack Nicklaus. This is a links-style course that offers great ocean views from every hole. Fairways are open; greens are small and fast. Built on the side of a hill, the course features several changes of elevation and requires several blind tee and approach shots. Winds often come into play. Bring extra balls for Hole 12, a 202-yard par 3 that includes a tee shot across 200 yards of Pacific Ocean. The tee area on a cliff 150 feet above the crashing surf is the picturesque spot where Bill and Melissa Gates were married in 1994. Archaeological sites are among the features. Collared shirts required; no denim.

### The Experience at Ko'ele                          *Zone 15 Lana'i*

**Established** 1991

**Location**  P.O. Box 310, Lana'i City, HI 96763 (transportation via Lana'i Resorts shuttle)

**Phone**  (808) 565-4653

**Status**  Resort, 18 holes, par 72

**Tees**  Championship: 7,014 yds. Men's: 6,217 yds. Ladies': 5,424 yds.

**Fees**  $200. $80 for guests of the Lodge at Ko'ele, Manele Bay Hotel, or Hotel Lana'i. Club rentals: $40 for full round, $25 for 9 holes. Accepts tee times 30 days in advance. Accepts Visa, MC, AmEx

**Facilities**  Driving range, putting and chipping greens, executive putting course, clubhouse, and snack bar

**Comments**  A magnificent course designed by golf greats Greg Norman and Ted Robinson. The front nine were carved from the side of a mountain, and the back nine are more open and flat. Water features are prominent, with seven lakes, streams, and waterfalls. The par 4, 444-yard Hole 8 is the signature, featuring a 250-foot drop from tee to fairway, with a lake bordering one side and thick shrubs and trees lining the other. Even Jack Nicklaus needed seven attempts to get the ball in play here. Hole 17 is surrounded by a lake. Collared shirts required; no denim.

# Spectator Sports

Even without a major professional sports franchise, the islands of Oʻahu, Maui, Hawaiʻi, and Kauaʻi host major sporting events throughout the year. If you're looking to augment your beach time, here's a game plan.

## Football

Hawaiʻi's claim to pro football fame is the game the players all want to play: the **NFL Pro Bowl,** the all-star game that celebrates the end of the season, a week after the Super Bowl, usually in late January. It is held at the 50,000-seat Aloha Stadium on Oʻahu. It's usually sold out weeks in advance, so inquire early for tickets, (808) 486-9300; for credit card orders, call (808) 484-1122. The players and families are in town for pregame festivities and practice for the week preceding the game.

College football all-stars, meanwhile, head for Maui each January for the annual **Hula Bowl.** After being held on Oʻahu for years, this contest has found new life on the Valley Isle, with the 20,000-seat War Memorial Stadium in Wailuku filled to capacity with rabid fans and, not coincidentally, talent scouts from every NFL team. Call (808) 545-7171 for tickets.

## Golf

A handful of major winter professional golf events bring Hawaiʻi's gorgeous links into the snowbound homes of golf fans via television. In early January, the **Mercedes Championships** at Kapalua, Maui, features top players competing for more than $2.5 million in prize money. Call (808) 669-2440.

Formerly the Hawaiian Open, the new **Sony Open** on Oʻahu draws the PGA's best to the Waiʻalae Country Club in Kahala. This January tournament kicks off the official PGA Tour season, with another $2.5 million purse. Call (808) 523-7888.

Also in January is the **MasterCard Championship,** which gathers winners from the previous year's Senior PGA Tour to the Hualalai Golf Club on the Big Island. This tournament, featuring more than $1 million in prize money, kicks off the Senior PGA Tour. Call (808) 325-8480.

In February, the Kapolei Golf Course on Oʻahu hosts the annual **Sunrise Hawaiian Ladies Open,** a 54-hole medal play competition featuring top women's golfers from the United States and Japan. Call (808) 674-2227.

One of the final stops on the Senior PGA Tour is the **EMC Kaʻanapali Classic** on Maui. Held in October, this event annually draws some of the game's greatest legends and old-time favorites. Call (808) 661-3691.

November brings the **MasterCard PGA Grand Slam** to the Poʻipu Bay Course on Kauaʻi. This 36-hole, two-day event features the winners of golf's four major PGA championships (Master's, British Open, U.S. Open, and PGA Championship). Call (808) 742-1234.

## Ocean Sports

A surf meet provides a different kind of experience for sports fans. It's a good chance see Hawai'i's most prized individual sport at its finest while hanging out at the beach, Admission is always free.

Competitors take to the water in four-man heats, each lasting 20–30 minutes. The surfers ride as many waves as they can. A panel of five judges uses a point system to name the winners. Criteria include the size of the waves, length of the rides, board control, and creative maneuvers.

The most prestigious surfing competition is the **Triple Crown** of surfing, held in November and December. The best professional wave riders from around the world gather on O'ahu's North Shore for the **Ocean Pacific Pro** at Ali'i Beach Park in Hale'iwa, **World Cup of Surfing** at Sunset Beach, and **Pipeline Masters** at the famous Banzai Pipeline at 'Ehukai Beach Park. The events occur on the four days of best surf conditions during a period of about two weeks. Recently, a special longboard competition was launched at Ali'i Beach Park. Call (808) 638-7700 or visit www.triplecrownsurfing.com.

The **Morey World Bodyboarding Championships** pits daring ocean athletes against the winter surf each January at the Banzai Pipeline on O'ahu's North Shore. Call (808) 396-2326.

Summer brings the **Outrigger Hotels Oceanfest,** a colorful ocean sports festival headlined by the **Hawaiian International Ocean Challenge,** which features the world's top lifeguards in a variety of ocean-related competitions on O'ahu. Other Oceanfest events include kayak, paddleboarding, and canoe races, as well as the **Wahine Windsurfing Classic.** Call (808) 521-4322.

You won't be able to follow all the action of the annual **Bankoh Na Wahine O Ke Kai** and the **Bankoh Mokoka'i Hoe,** two 41-mile outrigger canoe races from Mokoka'i to Waikiki. (The women's wahine race is held in late September, while the men's race takes place in early October.) But you can watch the colorful finale as the six-member canoe teams paddle to a finish on the beach. Both events draw international outrigger canoe teams from Australia, Canada, and Tahiti, as well as Hawai'i and other states. Call (808) 325-7400.

## Track

Few events are as physically demanding as the zenith of all triathlons, the **Ironman Triathlon World Championship** held each October on the Big Island, where the world's top triathletes plunge into a 2.4-mile ocean swim followed by a 112-mile bike race and a 26.2-mile marathon. Unless it's the annual **Ultraman,** which ups the ante to a 6.2-mile swim, 251.4-mile bike ride and 52.3-mile run. Fair warning: The weekend of the Iron-man is often Kailua-Kona's busiest of the year, and certain visitor necessities, like car rentals, may be hard to come by. Call (808) 329-0063.

## College Basketball

College basketball fanciers focus on Honolulu each year around Christ-mastime for the annual **Outrigger Hotels Rainbow Classic Basketball Tournament,** arguably the nation's best eight-team holiday tournament. A tradition launched in the mid-60s, the Rainbow Classic has a reputa-tion for spotlighting future first-round NBA draft picks. Certainly enough scouts attend the tourney to find them. College teams compete with equal fervor in the annual women's **Asahi Rainbow Wahine Classic** staged in late November, also in Honolulu. Watch for college all-stars in the annual **Aloha Basketball Classic** tournament in Honolulu in mid-April, and you may be previewing more pro standouts of the future.

*Part Nine*

# Dining in Hawai'i

## Experiencing Hawai'i's Multicultural Cuisine

### The New Hawai'i Regional Cuisine

Little more than a decade ago, food gurus planning a trip to Hawai'i might have been advised to "forget the food unless you love cholesterol-laden plate lunches piled with two scoops of rice, potato salad, meat, and gravy." Ironically, today the Islands have become a destination with so many fine dining establishments and cutting-edge chefs that it is impossible to sample all of the best during a single ten-day vacation. Dozens of Island chefs have been guest chefs at the prestigious James Beard House in New York; some, like Sam Choy and Roy Yamaguchi, now have restaurants in several states and foreign countries and have gained international reputation through their own television shows. In less than ten years, Hawai'i Regional Cuisine and its many incarnations—fusion, contemporary, Pacific Rim, Euro-Asian—have captured Island and visitor taste buds, replacing Continental cuisine in hotel dining rooms and restaurants across the state.

### Ethnic Elements

Today's flavorful and sophisticated Hawai'i Regional Cuisine springs from humble beginnings. The earliest Polynesian voyagers brought taro, breadfruit, coconuts, bananas, sugarcane, mountain apples, yams, and Polynesian sweet potatoes among the 27 plants they loaded for survival on their double-hulled outrigger canoes from the Marquesas Islands. Successive waves of immigrants from the 1800s on arrived to work the sugarcane fields, incorporating their own ingredients and styles of cooking. From community kitchens and plantation homes, Chinese, Japanese, Portuguese, Filipinos, and other laborers brought *bento* boxes for lunch in the fields, and at *pau hana* (quitting time), they shared platters

**337**

of ethnic *pupus* (appetizers). Asian flavors—soy sauce, oyster sauce, sesame oil, mirin, homemade tofu—were adopted and combined, incorporating the individual cooking styles of home cooks.

The makings of a cuisine found nowhere else in the world thrived in Island gardens. Backyard plots nurtured exotics like bok choy, daikon, lemongrass, and Kaffir lime leaves, as well as indigenous ingredients—coconuts, bananas, papayas, mangos, star fruit, lychees, breadfruit. When European chefs were eventually imported to create hotel food for Hawai'i's developing tourist business, they tasted what local chefs were doing in Island kitchens and stirred in elements based on their own classical training, and by the early 1990s, Hawai'i Regional Cuisine had taken on intriguing flavors, plus an artistic appearance on the plate.

In 1991, the movement rose faster than a loaf of Portuguese sweet bread set out to proof when a dozen highly trained restaurant chefs formalized the term "Hawai'i Regional Cuisine" by banding together to trade creative cooking secrets and to develop and promote locally-grown produce, meat, and seafood. Today, many Island chefs consult with fishermen, farmers, and fruit growers in order to move exotic and varied homegrown ingredients from ground to gourmet restaurant in the shortest time possible. On the Big Island, fishermen, ranchers, and small specialty farmers who grow taro, hearts of palm, fern shoots, exotic fruit, and herbs are enjoying new popularity with chefs in resort hotels along the Big Island's Kohala Coast. These imaginative chefs delight diners with taro fritters, poi-based sauces, Puna goat cheese appetizers and salads, tropical fruit desserts, and the like. Some chef/owners (like Keo Sananikone of Keo's Thai Restaurants on O'ahu) actually grow their own herbs and greens, or, like Jean Marie Josselin of A Pacific Café on Kaua'i, buy directly from a specific farmer who sets aside plots of produce grown to the chef's specifications.

Frequently, Regional Cuisine menus note the local origin of gourmet items in elaborate descriptions of entrées flavored with ginger and shoyu, cilantro and sesame oil. From the Big Island, for example, you'll find Puna goat cheese (a creamy white cheese produced from goats raised on a particular farm in the Puna district), Waimea strawberries (deliciously sweet and juicy vine-ripened berries grown near the upcountry town of Waimea), and Keahole lobster (a succulent big red or blue lobster raised in aquaculture ponds at Keahole near the Kona International Airport), as well as abalone and crunchy ogo, or seaweed. On Lana'i, island venison is noted as favorite fare on hotel menus.

Gourmet items are available not only in fine dining rooms; they can also be taken home as gifts. In the last decade or so, gourmet coffee cultivation has spread from the island of Hawai'i's Kona district, so now you can buy coffee as a souvenir grown on any island you visit, except Lana'i.

## Fish Facts

One of the most frequently voiced questions about Hawai'i Regional Cuisine concerns a clear-cut definition, including the identity of signature ingredients and dishes. As the genre evolved, certain fresh fish emerged as ingredients unique to the Islands. In the past, mahimahi had always been the fish identified with Hawai'i. Today, mahi, a mild white fish, remains a favorite in the overall scheme of things, but a vast array of other types of fish, which once were caught by fishermen only for their home tables, are now found on restaurant menus.

For the uninitiated, choosing a fish dish can be a challenge, as fish are known by any number of names—local, mainland, and scientific—and often are served in a multitude of preparations listed and described on menus. To allay some of the confusion and encourage the use of fish that are not so well known, the Department of Business, Economic Development, and Tourism promotes a statewide Seafood Festival during the month of July and has published a chart naming and describing various fishes. Following is an abbreviated guide that can help you in choosing a fish dish from an Island menu, though it's always best to ask your waiter for specific descriptions, particularly regarding preparations.

**Aku, Skipjack tuna**    Red, translucent flesh turns to firm ivory-colored meat when cooked. The high fat content makes this fish good sliced raw for sashimi.

**Bigeye 'ahi, Bigeye tuna**    Light red flesh cooks to creamy white. The high fat content makes this fish good sliced raw for sashimi.

**Yellowfin 'ahi, Yellowfin tuna**    Light red flesh cooks to creamy white. The high fat content makes this fish good sliced raw for sashimi.

**Shutome, Broadbill swordfish**    Firm, well-textured, mild-flavored pinkish meat cooks to white.

**Mahimahi, Dolphinfish**    Firm, light flesh cooks to delicate, sweet white meat.

**Ono, Wahoo**    Delicate pink meat changes to flaky and sweet when cooked.

**Opah, Moonfish**    Rich, large-grained flesh ranges from pink to orange to bright red throughout the fish.

**Moi, Threadfish**    Islanders like the moist, mild white meat of this fish steamed, though some chefs prepare it crisp-fried with the edible scales still on.

**Monchong, Bigscale, or Sickle pomfret**    Delicately flavored, smooth, well-textured flesh cooks to moist white meat.

**Onaga, Ruby, or Long-tailed snapper**    The onaga's pale pink flesh, which has a delicate flavor, is considered a good-luck food when served raw. It's also delicious cooked.

**'Opakapaka, Crimson snapper**   A favorite fish in Hawai'i restaurants, with pink flesh that has a mild flavor whether sautéed, grilled, or baked.

If there is a signature dish for Hawai'i Regional Cuisine, it's 'ahi sashimi, served in fine dining rooms and local eateries, sushi bars, and Japanese restaurants—in short, in any number of restaurants of all ethnic persuasions. Sometimes a block of tuna is quickly seared on the outside, then thinly sliced for blackened 'ahi, or sometimes the buttery red fish is simply chilled, sliced, and laid on a bed of shredded cabbage and served with a hot soy-wasabi dipping sauce.

On the cooked scene, a second widely served fish that could symbolize Hawai'i Regional Cuisine is often designated as "local-boy style." One popular restaurant uses ono, a white fish, for the preparation, which is flavored with nori (seaweed)-soy vinaigrette and sizzling hot peanut oil. This fish preparation could be classified as "local-style" regional cuisine, as opposed to "haute" regional cuisine. It's the kind of dish that might pop up at a backyard barbecue or a home lu'au, along with mounds of white rice.

## Lu'au Lore: To Go or Not to Go?

You'll probably hear complaints about commercial lu'aus that range from "Nobody, but nobody, could eat that gray wallpaper paste they call poi" to "The Mai Tai punch was so watered I couldn't even get a buzz on." Nonetheless, if you have never been to a lu'au, it's one of those things you really should experience. Bear in mind, you don't go to a lu'au for fine dining; it's most fun to go with friends; and finally, you've got to mentally put yourself in a "hang-loose mode"—wear your wildest print outfit, tuck a flower behind your ear, and be prepared to go barefoot during dinner.

Visitors can experience leisurely and romantic lu'aus in a garden or on the beach in front of their hotels, or at elaborate, rollicking affairs on a secluded shoreline presented by professional outfits such as Paradise Cove or Germaine's on O'ahu. Some commercial lu'aus include pageantry, with participants dressed like early Hawaiian royalty; all of them include a Polynesian show. Before dinner, guests might have a chance to wade barefoot into the sun-warmed ocean to help pull in the *hukilau* net filled with flopping fish.

In old Hawai'i, the most popular way of preparing food was to *kalua* the meat—chicken, dog, or fish—in an underground oven, and the heart and soul of any lu'au is still the preparation and unearthing of the *imu*. Though dog is no longer part of the menu, current lu'au food is reasonably authentic, except for such items as teriyaki steak, barbecued chicken, and macaroni and potato salads, added to suit all tastes along the buffet line. You'll still find pig roasted to moist tenderness in the *imu,* then shredded; poi, pounded into a pastelike consistency from the cooked taro corm; sweet potatoes; marinated lomi salmon, small pieces of fish with chopped tomatoes and onions; and sometimes 'opihi, a Hawaiian shellfish plucked from wave-washed rocky shorelines and eaten raw as a special delicacy. Chicken or squid lu'au serves as a vegetable dish made of the tender leaves of the taro plant cooked in coconut milk. Many Island feasts ladle out chicken long rice, a tasty dish of chicken cooked with slithery translucent noodles made of rice flour and garnished with green onions, and frequently you'll find laulau, little green bundles of taro leaf, which taste like spinach and contain pork and fish. Lu'au menus are light on vegetables, but usually fresh pineapple, bananas, and other fruits are found on every table. Relishes—Hawaiian salt, 'inamona made of ground kukui nuts, stalks of green onions, and individual bowls of poi— are also placed on every table. Dessert consists of a white cake with layers of haupia, a pudding of sweetened coconut milk thickened with cornstarch, all crowned with a fluffy white frosting and shredded coconut. Additional haupia cut into finger-sized rectangles always tops off a lu'au.

The entertainment at one of these feasts is like a mini-tour of Polynesia. Hawai'i's contribution includes the haunting chants that perpetuate the legends of the past, as well as the graceful hula. And yes, someone in your party is likely to get dragged onto the stage, so take a camera and capture that Kodak moment, or maybe snap Mom digging into the poi bowl with two fingers, the traditional way to enjoy it.

Our final word about poi comes from an expert. Chef Sam Choy, a "local boy" if ever there was one, says, "It is very nutritious and good for you, and if you sample it often enough, you will eventually acquire a taste for it—maybe. If you're not used to it, it's best to eat it when it's very fresh, although some people like it better after it has sat around for a few days and become sour. You must have poi with your lu'au whether you like it or not. It just isn't a lu'au without it."

## Island Dining Scenes

O'ahu, with the largest population and the highest visitor count (about 5 million annually), and as the center of commerce and transportation, naturally has more restaurants than any other island. In general, fine dining is concentrated in the Waikiki area; however, many former hotel chefs have opened freestanding restaurants of their own on the edges of Waikiki or in shopping centers near residential areas. Hotel restaurants tend to be more expensive, but often they enjoy special ocean-side settings and big-name chefs. The cost doesn't keep local residents away; we dine in high-profile restaurants for special celebrations, for business lunches, and with visiting guests.

On the Neighbor Islands, you'll find the best hotel restaurants on Maui at Wailea, Ka'anapali, Makena, and Kapalua Resorts; on the Big Island along the Kohala Coast; on Kaua'i at Po'ipu and Princeville; and on Lana'i in the two major hotels, the Lodge at Ko'ele and Manele Bay Hotel.

Office workers in downtown Honolulu frequent nearby restaurants—perhaps an ethnic gem in Chinatown, an upbeat contemporary getaway in the Aloha Tower Marketplace, or a favorite hangout on Restaurant Row. A multitude of ethnic restaurants with reasonably-priced menus can also be found on the Diamond Head edge of Waikiki along Kapahulu Avenue and a few miles away in Kaimuki.

In the tourist meccas of Lahaina on Maui and Kailua-Kona on the Big Island, many restaurants are of the casual open-air kind. Interestingly, the little upcountry residential town of Waimea on the Big Island has a growing reputation for good food prepared by good chefs in reputable restaurants—Merriman's, Edelweiss, Parker Ranch Grill, Koa House, and Daniel Thiebaut, to mention just a few.

## Trends

When Hawai'i Regional Cuisine became a recognized movement, chefs sometimes went overboard concocting dishes with a combination of flavors that confused the palate. One year, everything came with at least three sauces artistically spread on the plate like an overcomplicated yin-yang design. Another year, stacking was in, so entrées might come piled six inches high in layers that teetered when the plate was set on the table. As with any new movement trying to gain a foothold, sanity eventually returned. Dishes in today's upscale restaurants are still beautiful to behold, but the trend now is toward flavors that are balanced in courses that complement each other.

Most chefs are aiming toward simplicity and freshness, with the true flavor of meat, fish, and poultry enhanced by fresh herbs. Though the vogue continues to lean toward healthier preparations, with lighter sauces made of fruit coulis or puréed vegetables, meat is on the rebound. People do, however, like variety, and fish and seafood continue to be popular, as evidenced by a proliferation of new seafood bars and buffets.

Wine continues to increase in popularity as an important accompaniment. The best restaurants allow experimentation by making available many wines by the glass, so you can match each course to the wine best suited, rather than confine yourself to one bottle for multiple courses. More and more restaurants are listing suggested wines on the menu that have been matched to the entrées by in-house sommeliers or by Hawai'i's only master sommelier, Chuck Furuya.

In addition, micro-breweries have finally come into their own in a number of Island restaurants on all major islands. Some are mainland imports; a few, such as Waimea Brew Pub on Kaua'i and Kona Brewing Company on the Big Island, are local endeavors. In all, you'll find beers made and named for their Island-grown ingredients and flavors, and you'll generally find that the brew pubs offer contemporary food attractively served at reasonable prices.

## The Melting Pot Is Sizzling

On all islands, food festivals with Hawaiian entertainment, arts and crafts booths, and food samples showcase the diversity of Hawai'i's exciting bounty. July is seafood month, featuring public celebrations that include tastings, cooking contests, and demonstrations at markets and restaurants. Spring and summer taro festivals are staged on Maui, O'ahu, and Kaua'i. The Big Island boasts the Try-a-Papaya Festival, a Macadamia Nut Festival, a Kona Coffee Festival, Big Island Bounty, and the Winter Wine Escape. Maui jumps on the food wagon with a wacky Maui Onion Festival, the 'Ulupalakua Thing (agricultural fair), and the Kapalua Wine and Food Symposium. If you're lucky enough to be in the Islands during a food festival, loosen your belt and get set to sample some of the most exciting cuisine around.

# The Restaurants

## Our Favorite Island Restaurants: Explaining the Ratings

We have developed detailed profiles for the best restaurants and for those that offer some special reason to visit, be it decor, ethnic appeal, or bargain prices. Each profile features an easily scanned heading that allows you, in just a second, to check out the restaurant's name, cuisine, overall rating, cost, quality rating, and value rating.

**Cuisine**   In a locale where Hawai'i Regional Cuisine has been seeking to define itself only since 1992, categorizing cuisine becomes a challenging endeavor. Hawai'i Regional Cuisine, itself, is an olio of ethnic foods, so we've ended up with dishes that incorporate Asian flavors, Hawaiian flavors, Cajun flavors, Pacific Rim flavors, Mediterranean flavors, and more. Many chefs prefer not to be categorized at all, as they are afraid this will limit others' perception of their creativity. In most cases, we let restaurant owners or chefs name their own categories. In many cases, fusion cuisines are called simply "contemporary cuisine." Even restaurants that once served classic French cuisine now prepare sauces with a lighter hand and are innovative about using Island-grown ingredients, one of the prerequisites of Hawai'i Regional Cuisine. You can get an idea of the type of food served from the heading, then glean a better understanding by reading the detailed descriptions of specialty items and other recommendations.

**Overall Rating**   The overall rating encompasses the entire dining experience, including style, service, and ambience, in addition to the taste, presentation, and quality of the food. Five stars is the highest rating possible and connotes the best of everything. Four-star restaurants are exceptional, three-star restaurants are well above average, and two-star restaurants are good. One star indicates an average restaurant that demonstrates an unusual capability in some area of specialization—for example, an otherwise unmemorable place that has great saimin (noodle soup).

**Cost**   To the right of the cuisine is an expense description that provides a comparative sense of how much a complete meal will cost. A complete meal for our purposes consists of an entrée with a vegetable or side dish and a choice of soup or salad. Appetizers, desserts, drinks, and tips are excluded. Categories and related prices are listed below:

| Inexpensive | $14 and less per person |
| Moderate | $15–30 |
| Expensive | More than $30 per person |

**Quality Rating**   To the right of the cost appear stars that rate food quality on a scale of ★–★★★★★, where ★★★★★ is the best rating attainable. It is based expressly on the taste, freshness of ingredients, preparation, presentation, and creativity of the food served. There is no consideration of price. If you want the best food available, and cost is not an issue, you need look no further than the quality ratings.

**Value Rating**   If, on the other hand, you are looking for both quality and value, then you should check the value rating. Remember, the perception of value can vary from state to state and country to country. Hawai'i is a tourist destination, so restaurant prices in the state probably compare favorably with prices in New York, San Francisco, and other major tourist destinations, but not so favorably with smaller, residential towns. Because it is a common perception that hotel restaurants are universally overpriced (where else would you pay $4–6 for a glass of orange juice?), we have indicated restaurants of this sort with a ★★ rating rather than a discouraging ★. The ★★ is meant to convey that yes, the restaurant charges perhaps more than you would pay for a similar entrée somewhere else, but because the setting, service, and preparation are exceptional, it's still worth the splurge. We wouldn't want to rate the restaurant a ★, causing a reader to automatically forgo a special dining experience. The value ratings are defined as follows:

| | |
|---|---|
| ★★★★★ | Exceptional value; a real bargain |
| ★★★★ | Good value |
| ★★★ | Fair value; you get exactly what you pay for |
| ★★ | Somewhat overpriced |
| ★ | Significantly overpriced |

**Locating the Restaurant**   On the far right is a designation for geographic zone. This zone description will give you a general idea of where the restaurant described is located. We've divided the six major islands into the following 15 geographic zones.

| | | | | |
|---|---|---|---|---|
| Zone 1 | Waikiki | | Zone 9 | West Maui |
| Zone 2 | Greater Honolulu | | Zone 10 | Upcountry Maui |
| Zone 3 | Windward O'ahu | | Zone 11 | Kona |
| Zone 4 | The North Shore | | Zone 12 | Hilo and Volcano |
| Zone 5 | Leeward O'ahu | | Zone 13 | Kaua'i |
| Zone 6 | Central O'ahu | | Zone 14 | Moloka'i |
| Zone 7 | Central Maui | | Zone 15 | Lana'i |
| Zone 8 | South Maui | | | |

**Payment**   We've listed the type of payment accepted at each restaurant using the following codes:

| | | | | |
|---|---|---|---|---|
| AMEX | American Express | | JCB | Japan Credit Bank |
| CB | Carte Blanche | | MC | MasterCard |
| D | Discover | | VISA | VISA |
| DC | Diners Club | | | |

**Who's Included**   Restaurants open and close frequently in Hawai'i, so most of those we've included have a proven track record. However, some of the newest upscale restaurants owned and operated by chefs who have become local celebrities have been included to keep the guide as complete and up-to-date as possible. Local chains, such as Sam Choy's and Roy's, are included, as are a few franchises that have a distinctly Hawaiian look in food and decor, such as TS Incorporated. Also, the list is highly selective. Our leaving out a particular place does not necessarily indicate that the restaurant is not good, only that it was not ranked among the best in its genre. Detailed profiles of individual restaurants follow in alphabetical order at the end of this chapter. In the section titled "More Recommendations," we've named reputable restaurants that you might want to try for a specific reason—for pizzas, bagels, plate lunches—that don't otherwise merit a full description. These are listed according to their island location, but you might notice that every "best" category may not have a listing on each island. This is not an oversight; an omitted island simply may not have a good restaurant that fits the category.

## THE BEST HAWAIIAN RESTAURANTS

| Type and Name | Overall Rating | Price | Quality Rating | Value Rating | Zone |
|---|---|---|---|---|---|
| **O'AHU** | | | | | |
| ***American*** | | | | | |
| Diamond Head Grill | ★★★ | Mod/Exp | ★★★½ | ★★ | 1 |
| ***Chinese*** | | | | | |
| Double Eight Chinese Restaurant | ★★★★ | Inexp | ★★★★ | ★★★★ | 2 |
| The Golden Dragon | ★★★★ | Mod | ★★★★ | ★★ | 1 |
| ***Contemporary*** | | | | | |
| La Mer | ★★★★★ | Exp | ★★★★★ | ★½ | 1 |
| Hoku's | ★★★★ | Mod/Exp | ★★★★½ | ★★ | 2 |
| 3660 On the Rise | ★★★★ | Mod | ★★★★ | ★★ | 2 |
| The Surf Room | ★★★½ | Mod/Exp | ★★★ | ★★ | 1 |
| Duke's Canoe Club Restaurant | ★★★ | Inexp/Mod | ★★½ | ★★★ | 1 |
| ***Continental/Pacific Rim*** | | | | | |
| Hau Tree Lana'i | ★★★ | Mod | ★★½ | ★★ | 1 |
| ***Euro-Asian*** | | | | | |
| L'uraku | ★★★★★ | Mod | ★★★★★ | ★★★ | 2 |
| Indigo | ★★★★ | Inexp/Mod | ★★★★ | ★★★ | 2 |
| Bali-By-The-Sea | ★★★½ | Mod/Exp | ★★★½ | ★★ | 1 |
| ***French*** | | | | | |
| Michel's at the Colony Surf | ★★★★½ | Exp | ★★★★ | ★ | 1 |
| ***Hawai'i Regional*** | | | | | |
| Alan Wong's Restaurant | ★★★★★ | Mod/Exp | ★★★★★ | ★★★ | 1 |
| Prince Court Restaurant | ★★★★ | Mod | ★★★★ | ★★ | 1 |
| Sam Choy's Breakfast, Lunch and Crab | ★★★★ | Mod | ★★★★ | ★★★ | 2 |
| Sam Choy's Diamond Head | ★★★★ | Mod | ★★★★ | ★★★ | 1 |
| The Pineapple Room | ★★★½ | Mod/Exp | ★★★★ | ★★ | 2 |
| Don Ho's Island Grill | ★★★ | Inexp | ★★★ | ★★★ | 2 |
| ***Hawaiian Fusion*** | | | | | |
| Roy's Restaurant | ★★★★★ | Mod | ★★★★★ | ★★ | 2 |
| ***Hawaiian Traditional*** | | | | | |
| Helena's Hawaiian Foods | ★★★★ | Inexp | ★★★★ | ★★★★ | 2 |

## THE BEST HAWAIIAN RESTAURANTS (continued)

| Type and Name | Overall Rating | Price | Quality Rating | Value Rating | Zone |
|---|---|---|---|---|---|
| **O'AHU** *(continued)* | | | | | |
| ***Italian*** | | | | | |
| Assaggio Ristorante Italiano | ★★★½ | Inexp/Mod | ★★★★ | ★★★★ | 6 |
| ***Japanese*** | | | | | |
| Sansei Seafood Restaurant and Sushi Bar | ★★★★ | Mod/Exp | ★★★★ | ★★★ | 2, 9 |
| ***Mediterranean*** | | | | | |
| Padovani's Restaurant and Wine Bar | ★★★★½ | Mod/Exp | ★★★★½ | ★★ | 1 |
| Cascada | ★★★½ | Mod | ★★★½ | ★★ | 1 |
| ***Pacific Rim*** | | | | | |
| Chef Mavro Restaurant | ★★★★½ | Exp | ★★★★½ | ★★ | 1 |
| ***Seafood*** | | | | | |
| Orchids | ★★★★½ | Mod/Exp | ★★★★ | ★★ | 1 |
| John Dominis | ★★★½ | Mod/Exp | ★★★½ | ★ | 1 |
| ***Steak and Seafood*** | | | | | |
| Hy's Steak House | ★★★ | Mod/Exp | ★★★½ | ★★ | 1 |
| Buzz's Original Steak House | ★★ | Inexp/Mod | ★★★ | ★★ | 3 |
| ***Thai*** | | | | | |
| Keo's in Waikiki | ★★★★ | Inexp/Mod | ★★★★ | ★★★ | 1 |
| **MAUI** | | | | | |
| ***American*** | | | | | |
| David Paul's Lahaina Grill | ★★★★ | Mod/Exp | ★★★★ | ★★ | 9 |
| ***Contemporary*** | | | | | |
| Gerard's | ★★★★ | Mod/Exp | ★★★½ | ★★★ | 9 |
| Plantation House Restaurant | ★★½ | Inexp/Mod | ★★★½ | ★★ | 9 |
| ***Continental*** | | | | | |
| The Bay Club Restaurant | ★★★ | Mod/Exp | ★★½ | ★½ | 9 |
| ***French*** | | | | | |
| Chez Paul's | ★★★★ | Mod/Exp | ★★★½ | ★★ | 7 |

**THE BEST HAWAIIAN RESTAURANTS** (continued)

| Type and Name | Overall Rating | Price | Quality Rating | Value Rating | Zone |
|---|---|---|---|---|---|
| **MAUI** (continued) | | | | | |
| *Hawai'i Regional* | | | | | |
| Seasons | ★★★★½ | Mod/Exp | ★★★★½ | ★½ | 8 |
| Pacific'O | ★★★★½ | Mod | ★★★★ | ★★ | 9 |
| Bamboo Bistro | ★★★★ | Mod | ★★★★ | ★★ | 7 |
| Hali'imaile General Store | ★★★★ | Mod/Exp | ★★★★ | ★★ | 10 |
| Anuenue Room | ★★★½ | Mod/Exp | ★★★½ | ★½ | 9 |
| Hula Grill | ★★★ | Inexp/Mod | ★★★½ | ★★★ | 9 |
| *Hawaiian Fusion* | | | | | |
| Roy's Kahana Bar and Grill | ★★★½ | Mod | ★★★½ | ★★★ | 9 |
| Roy's Nicolina | ★★★½ | Mod | ★★★½ | ★★★ | 9 |
| *Mediterranean* | | | | | |
| Longhi's | ★★★½ | Mod | ★★★½ | ★★★ | 9 |
| *Seafood* | | | | | |
| Mama's Fish House | ★★★½ | Mod/Exp | ★★★★ | ★★ | 9 |
| *Steak and Seafood* | | | | | |
| Kimo's | ★★½ | Inexp/Mod | ★★ | ★★★ | 9 |
| *Vietnamese* | | | | | |
| A Saigon Café | ★★★ | Inexp | ★★★½ | ★★★★ | 7 |
| **THE BIG ISLAND** | | | | | |
| *American* | | | | | |
| Kona Ranch House | ★★½ | Inexp/Mod | ★★ | ★★★ | 11 |
| *Contemporary* | | | | | |
| Café Pesto | ★★★½ | Inexp | ★★★½ | ★★★ | 11, 12 |
| The Grill and Lounge at the Orchid | ★★★½ | Exp | ★★★½ | ★½ | 11 |
| *Continental* | | | | | |
| Kilauea Lodge | ★★★½ | Mod | ★★★½ | ★★ | 12 |
| Edelweiss | ★★★½ | Mod | ★★★ | ★★★ | 11 |
| *French/Asian* | | | | | |
| Daniel Thiebaut Restaurant | ★★★½ | Mod | ★★★★ | ★★★ | 11 |

## THE BEST HAWAIIAN RESTAURANTS (continued)

| Type and Name | Overall Rating | Price | Quality Rating | Value Rating | Zone |
|---|---|---|---|---|---|
| **THE BIG ISLAND** (continued) | | | | | |
| ***Hawai'i Regional*** | | | | | |
| Merriman's | ★★★★½ | Mod/Exp | ★★★★½ | ★★ | 11 |
| Batik Restaurant | ★★★★½ | Exp | ★★★★ | ★½ | 11 |
| Canoehouse | ★★★★½ | Mod/Exp | ★★★★ | ★½ | 11 |
| Coast Grille | ★★★★½ | Mod/Exp | ★★★★ | ★½ | 11 |
| Sam Choy's Restaurant | ★★★ | Mod | ★★★½ | ★★★ | 11 |
| ***Hawai'i Regional/Southwestern*** | | | | | |
| Oodles of Noodles | ★★★½ | Inexp/Mod | ★★★★ | ★★★★ | 11 |
| ***Hawaiian Fusion*** | | | | | |
| Pahu I'a at Four Seasons | ★★★★½ | Exp | ★★★★ | ★½ | 11 |
| Roy's at the King's Shops | ★★★★½ | Mod | ★★★★ | ★★★ | 11 |
| ***Italian*** | | | | | |
| Donatoni's | ★★★★½ | Mod/Exp | ★★★★ | ★½ | 11 |
| ***Pacific Rim*** | | | | | |
| Huggo's | ★★½ | Mod | ★★★ | ★★ | 11 |
| ***Steak and Seafood*** | | | | | |
| Harrington's | ★★ | Mod | ★★½ | ★★★ | 12 |
| ***Thai*** | | | | | |
| Royal Siam Thai | ★★★½ | Inexp | ★★★½ | ★★★★ | 12 |
| **KAUA'I** | | | | | |
| ***American*** | | | | | |
| Shells, at the Sheraton Kaua'i Hotel | ★★★½ | Mod/Exp | ★★★ | ★★ | 13 |
| ***Contemporary*** | | | | | |
| Postcards | ★★★½ | Mod | ★★★½ | ★★★ | 13 |
| Brennecke's Beach Broiler | ★★★ | Mod | ★★★ | ★★★ | 13 |
| ***Continental*** | | | | | |
| Café Hanalei and Terrace | ★★★★ | Exp | ★★★★ | ★★ | 13 |

## THE BEST HAWAIIAN RESTAURANTS (continued)

| Type and Name | Overall Rating | Price | Quality Rating | Value Rating | Zone |
|---|---|---|---|---|---|
| **KAUA'I** (continued) | | | | | |
| ***Hawaiian Fusion*** | | | | | |
| Roy's Po'ipu Bar & Grill | ★★★★ | Mod | ★★★★ | ★★ | 13 |
| ***Island Eclectic*** | | | | | |
| Hamura Saimin | ★ | Inexp | ★★½ | ★★★★ | 13 |
| ***Italian*** | | | | | |
| Plantation Gardens | ★★★½ | Mod | ★★★½ | ★★ | 13 |
| Casa Di Amici | ★★½ | Mod | ★★★ | ★★ | 13 |
| ***Pacific Rim*** | | | | | |
| The Beach House | ★★★ | Mod | ★★★½ | ★★ | 13 |
| Tidepools | ★★★ | Mod/Exp | ★★★ | ★½ | 13 |
| ***Seafood*** | | | | | |
| Duke's Canoe Club | ★★★ | Inexp/Mod | ★★★ | ★★★ | 13 |
| ***Steak and Seafood*** | | | | | |
| Keoki's Paradise | ★★★½ | Mod | ★★★½ | ★★★ | 13 |
| ***Thai/Chinese*** | | | | | |
| Mema Thai Chinese Cuisine | ★★ | Inexp/Mod | ★★★ | ★★★★ | 13 |
| **MOLOKA'I** | | | | | |
| ***Hawai'i Regional*** | | | | | |
| Moanaloa Room | ★★★★ | Mod/Exp | ★★★½ | ★★ | 14 |
| ***Island*** | | | | | |
| The Village Grill | ★★ | Mod | ★★★ | ★★ | 14 |
| Hotel Moloka'i Restaurant | ★★ | Inexp | ★★ | ★★★★ | 14 |
| ***Pizza and Sandwiches*** | | | | | |
| Moloka'i Pizza Café | ★★ | Inexp | ★★½ | ★★★ | 14 |
| **LANA'I** | | | | | |
| ***American*** | | | | | |
| Henry Clay's Rotisserie | ★★★ | Mod | ★★★ | ★★★ | 15 |
| ***Contemporary*** | | | | | |
| The Formal Dining Room, The Lodge at Ko'ele | ★★★★½ | Exp | ★★★★½ | 1½ | 15 |

## THE BEST HAWAIIAN RESTAURANTS (continued)

| Type and Name | Overall Rating | Price | Quality Rating | Value Rating | Zone |
|---|---|---|---|---|---|
| **LANA'I** (continued) | | | | | |
| ***Hawai'i Regional/Mediterranean*** | | | | | |
| 'Ihilani | ★★★★½ | Exp | ★★★★ | ★½ | 15 |
| ***Island Eclectic*** | | | | | |
| Blue Ginger Café | ★ | Inexp | ★★ | ★★★★ | 15 |

## THE BEST HAWAIIAN RESTAURANTS BY ZONE

### O'ahu (Zones 1–6)

3660 On the Rise
Alan Wong's Restaurant
Assaggio Ristorante Italiano
Bali-By-The-Sea
Buzz's Original Steak House
Cascada
Chef Mavro Restaurant
Diamond Head Grill
Don Ho's Island Grill
Double Eight Chinese Restaurant
Duke's Canoe Club Restaurant
The Golden Dragon
Hau Tree Lana'i
Helena's Hawaiian Foods
Hoku's
Hy's Steak House
Indigo

John Dominis
Keo's in Waikiki
L'uraku
La Mer
Michel's at the Colony Surf
Orchids
Padovani's Restaurant and Wine Bar
The Pineapple Room
Prince Court Restaurant
Roy's Restaurant
Sam Choy's Breakfast, Lunch and Crab
Sam Choy's Diamond Head
Sansei Seafood Restaurant and Sushi Bar
The Surf Room

### Maui (Zones 7–10)

A Saigon Café
Anuenue Room
Bamboo Bistro
The Bay Club Restaurant
Chez Paul's
David Paul's Lahaina Grill
Gerard's

Hali'imaile General Store
Hula Grill
Kimo's
Longhi's
Mama's Fish House
Pacific'O
Plantation House Restaurant

**THE BEST HAWAIIAN RESTAURANTS BY ZONE** (continued)

### Maui (Zones 7–10)   (continued)

| | |
|---|---|
| Roy's Kahana Bar and Grill | Sansei Seafood Restaurant |
| Roy's Nicolina | and Sushi Bar |
| | Seasons |

### Big Island (Zones 11–12)

| | |
|---|---|
| Batik Restaurant | Huggo's |
| Café Pesto | Kilauea Lodge |
| Canoehouse | Kona Ranch House |
| Coast Grille | Merriman's |
| Daniel Thiebaut Restaurant | Oodles of Noodles |
| Donatoni's | Pahu I'a at Four Seasons |
| Edelweiss | Roy's at the King's Shops |
| The Grill and Lounge at the Orchid | Sam Choy's Restaurant |
| Harrington's | |

### Kaua'i (Zone 13)

| | |
|---|---|
| Brennecke's Beach Broiler | Plantation Gardens |
| Café Hanalei and Terrace | Postcards |
| Casa Di Amici | Roy's Po'ipu Bar & Grill |
| Duke's Canoe Club | Shells, at the Sheraton Kaua'i Hotel |
| Hamura Saimin | The Beach House |
| Keoki's Paradise | Tidepools |
| Mema Thai Chinese Cuisine | |

### Moloka'i (Zone 14)

| | |
|---|---|
| Hotel Moloka'i Restaurant | Moloka'i Pizza Café |
| Moanaloa Room | The Village Grill |

### Lana'i (Zone 15)

| | |
|---|---|
| Blue Ginger Café | Henry Clay's Rotisserie |
| The Formal Dining Room, The | 'Ihilani |
| Lodge at Ko'ele | |

# More Recommendations

## Best Bagels

*O'ahu*

**Manoa Marketplace**   2764-A Woodlawn Drive, Honolulu (808) 942-2243

## Best Bakeries

*O'ahu*

**Mary Catherine's Bakery**   2820 South King Street, Honolulu (808) 946-4333

**Maui**

**Komoda Store & Bakery**   3674 Baldwin Avenue, Makawao (808) 572-7261. For cream puffs and macadamia nut cookies.

**Kaua'i**

**Kilauea Bakery and Pau Hana Pizza**   Kong Lung Center, Kilauea (808) 828-2020

**Moloka'i**

**Kanemitsu Bakery**   79 Ala Malama Street, Kaunakakai (808) 553-5855. For Moloka'i bread and lavosh.

## Best Breakfasts

*Big Island*

**Pahu I'a**   Four Seasons Hualalai, 100 Ka'upulehu Drive, Ka'upulehu-Kona (808) 325-8000

*Kaua'i*

**Eggberts**   4-484 Kuhio Highway, Coconut Marketplace, Kapa'a (808) 822-3787

## Best Brew Pubs

*O'ahu*

**Brew Moon**   1200 Ala Moana Boulevard, Honolulu (808) 589-1818

*Maui*

**Maui Brews**   900 Front Street, Lahaina (808) 667-7794

*Big Island*

**Kona Brewing Company and Brew Pub**   75-5629 Kuakini Highway, Kailua-Kona (808) 329-2739

*Kaua'i*

**Whaler's Brewpub**   3132 Ninini Point Street, Lihu'e (808) 245-2000

# Best Deli Food
*O'ahu*

**Strawberry Connections**   1931 Kahai Street, Honolulu (808) 842-0278

*Maui*

**Pauwela Café**   375 West Kuiaha Road, Ha'iku (808) 575-9242

*Big Island*

**A Piece of the Apple**   75-5799 Ali'i Drive, Suite 2A, Kailua-Kona (808) 329-4668

*Lana'i*

**Pele's Other Garden**   811 Hausten Street, Lana'i City (808) 565-9628

# Best Down-Home Local Atmosphere
*O'ahu*

**La Mariana Restaurant and Bar**   50 Sand Island Access Road, Honolulu (808) 848-2800

*Big Island*

**Bamboo Restaurant**   'Akone Pule Highway, Hawi (808) 889-5555

*Kaua'i*

**Green Garden**   Highway 50, Hanapepe (808) 335-5422

# Best Fresh Fish
*Maui*

**Mama's Fish House**   799 Poho Place, Ku'au (808) 579-8488

*Big Island*

**Seaside Restaurant**   1790 Kalaniana'ole Avenue, Hilo (808) 935-8825

# Best Golf Course Restaurants
*O'ahu*

**Niblick Restaurant**   Ko Olina Golf Club, 921220 Ali'i Nui Drive, Kapolei (808) 676-6703

*Maui*

**Sea Watch**   100 Wailea Golf Club Drive, Wailea (808) 875-8080

*Big Island*

**The Club Grill**   Hualalai Resort, 100 Ka'upulehu Drive, Ka'upulehu-Kona (808) 325-8525

*Kaua'i*

**Princeville Restaurant and Bar**   Prince Clubhouse, 5-3900 Kuhio Highway, Princeville (808) 826-5050

*Lana'i*

**The Challenge at Manele Bay Clubhouse**   Manele, Lana'i (808) 565-2230

# Best Hamburgers

*O'ahu*

**Kua 'Aina Sandwich**   66-214 Kamehameha Highway, Hale'iwa (808) 637-6067; 1116 'Auahi Street, Honolulu (808) 591-9133

*Maui*

**Cheeseburger in Paradise**   811 Front Street, Lahaina (808) 661-4855

*Kaua'i*

**Bubba's Hawai'i**   4-1421 Kuhio Highway, Kapa'a (808) 823-0069; Hanalei (808) 826-7839, Maui (808) 891-2600

# Best Hawaiian Food

*O'ahu: Local-Style*

**Ono Hawaiian Foods**   726 Kapahulu Avenue, Kapahulu (808) 737-2275

*O'ahu: Upscale*

**Parc Café**   Waikiki Parc Hotel, 2233 Helumoa Road, Waikiki (808) 931-6643. Wednesday and Friday lunch buffet.

*Maui*

**Pukalani Country Club Restaurant**   360 Pukalani, Pukalani (808) 572-1325

*Big Island*

**Kuhio Grille**   111 E. Puainako, Prince Kuhio Plaza, Suite A106, Hilo (808) 959-2336

*Kaua'i*

**Aloha Diner**   971F Kuhio Highway, Waipouli (808) 822-3851

# Best Ice Cream (Locally Made)

Call listed numbers for other outlets.

*O'ahu*

**Bubbie's Homemade Ice Cream and Desserts**   Kahala Mall Shopping Center, Kahala (808) 739-2822; 1010 University Avenue, Honolulu (808) 949-8984

*Big Island*

**Tropical Dreams Ice Cream**   Kress Building, Kamehameha Highway, Hilo (808) 935-9109; Kohala Coffee Mill, 'Akone Puli Highway, Hawi (808) 889-5577

*Kaua'i*

Lappert's Ice Cream   1-3555 Kaumuali'i Highway (808) 335-6121

# Best Italian Cuisine

*O'ahu*

**Matteo's**   364 Seaside Avenue, Waikiki (808) 922-5551

*Big Island*

**Donatoni's**   Hilton Waikoloa Village, 425 Waikoloa Beach Drive, Waikoloa (808) 886-1234

## Best Italian Cuisine *(continued)*
*Kaua'i*

**La Cascata**   Princeville Hotel, Princeville Resort (808) 826-9644

## Best Japanese Tea Houses
*O'ahu*

**Natsunoya Tea House**   1935 Makanani Drive, Honolulu (808) 595-4488. Minimum of ten diners.

*Kaua'i*

**Hanama'ulu Restaurant, Tea House and Sushi Bar**   1-4291 Kuhio Highway, Hanama'ulu (808) 245-2511

## Best Lu'au
*O'ahu*

**Paradise Cove**   92-1089 Ali'inui Drive, Kapolei (808) 842-5911

*Maui*

**Old Lahaina lu'au**   1251 Front Street, Lahaina (808) 667-1998

*Big Island*

**Kona Village Resort**   Queen Ka'ahumanu Highway, Ka'upulehu-Kona (808) 325-5555

*Kaua'i*

**Pa'ina o Hanalei**   Princeville Hotel, Princeville Resort (808) 826-9644

## Best Mexican Cuisine
*O'ahu*

**Rosie's Cantina**   Hale'iwa Shopping Plaza, Hale'iwa (808) 637-3538

*Maui*

**Polli's**   1202 Makawao Avenue, Makawao (808) 572-7808

*Kaua'i*

**La Bamba**   4261 Rice Street, Lihu'e (808) 245-5972

## Best Pizza
*O'ahu*

Pizza Bob's Hale'iwa   Hale'iwa Shopping Plaza, Hale'iwa (808) 637-5095

*Maui*

**Pizza Paradiso Express**   Whalers Village, 2435 Ka'anapali Parkway, Ka'anapali (808) 667-0333

*Big Island*

**Bianelli's Gourmet Pizza and Pasta**   75-240 Nani Kailua Drive, Kailua-Kona (808) 326-4800

*Kaua'i*

**Brick Oven Pizza**   State Highway 50, Kaumualii Highway, Kalaheo (808) 332-8561

*Moloka'i*

**Moloka'i Pizza Café**   Kaunakakai Place on Wharf Road, Kaunakakai (808) 553-5655

## Best Places to Hang Out

*O'ahu*

**The Pier Bar**   Aloha Tower Market Place, 1 Aloha Tower Drive, Honolulu (808) 536-2100

*Maui*

**Hula Grill's Beach Bar**  Whalers Village, 2435 Ka'anapali Parkway, Ka'anapali (808) 667-6636

*Big Island*

**Kona Inn Restaurant**   75-5744 Ali'i Drive, Kailua-Kona (808) 329-4455. Go at sunset.

## Best Plate Lunches

*O'ahu*

**Kaka'ako Kitchen**   1200 Ala Moana Boulevard, Honolulu (808) 594-3663

*Maui*

**Sam Sato's in Wailuku Millyard**   1750 Wili Pa Loop, Wailuku (808) 244-7124

*Big Island*

**Island Grinds**   Hilo Bay Front on the beach near Suisan Fish auction, Hilo (808) 895-0625. Lunch wagon.

*Kaua'i*

**Mixed Plate**   5-5190 Kuhio Highway, 3E4, Ching Young Village, Hanalei (808) 826-7888

## Best Romantic Restaurants

In all cases, ask for a table with an ocean view.

*O'ahu*

**Michel's**   2895 Kalakaua Avenue, Waikiki (808) 923-6552

*Big Island*

**Pahu I'a Restaurant at Four Seasons Hualalai**   100 Ka'upulehu Drive, Ka'upulehu-Kona (808) 325-8000

*Kaua'i*

**Tidepools**   Hyatt Regency Kaua'i, 1571 Po'ipu Road, Po'ipu (808) 742-1234

# Best Seafood Buffets

*O'ahu*

**Orchids at Halekulani**    2199 Kalia Road, Waikiki (808) 923-2311

*Maui*

**The Terrace at the Ritz-Carlton**    1 Ritz-Carlton Drive, Kapalua (808) 669-6200

*Kaua'i*

**Café Hanalei and Terrace**    Princeville Resort, Princeville (808) 826-2760. Friday night only.

# Best Shave Ice

*O'ahu*

**Matsumoto Shave Ice**    66-087 Kamehameha Highway, Hale'iwa (808) 637-4827

*Maui*

**Tobi's Ice Cream and Shave Ice**    1913 South Kihei Road, Kihei (808) 891-2440

*Big Island*

**Oodles of Noodles**    75-1027 Henry, Suite 102, Kailua-Kona (808) 329-9222

# Best Steak Houses

*O'ahu*

**Ruth's Chris Steak House**    Restaurant Row, Honolulu (808) 599-3860

*Maui*

**Outback Steak House**    4405 Honoapi'ilani Highway, Honoapi'ilani (808) 665-1822

*Big Island*

**Big Island Steak House**    King's Shops, Waikoloa Beach Drive, Waikoloa (808) 886-8805

*Kaua'i*

**Kalaheo Steak House**    4444 Papalina Road, Kalaheo (808) 332-9780

# Best Sunday Brunch

*O'ahu*

**Orchids**    Halekulani, 2199 Kalia Road, Waikiki (808) 923-2311

*Maui*

**Grand Wailea Hotel**    3850 Wailea Alanui Drive, Wailea (808) 875-1234

*Big Island*

**The Terrace**    Manua Kea Beach Hotel, 62-100 Mauna Kea Beach Drive (808) 882-7222

*Kaua'i*

**Café Hanalei and Terrace**    Princeville Resort, Princeville (808) 826-2760

# Best Sushi Bars

*O'ahu*

**Kacho**    Waikiki Parc Hotel, 2233 Helumoa Road, Waikiki (808) 924-3535

*East Maui*

**Hakone**    Maui Prince Hotel, 5400 Makena Alanui Road, Makena (808) 874-1111

*West Maui*

**Sansei Restaurant and Sushi Bar**    115 Bay Drive, Unit 115, Kapalua Shops, Kapalua (808) 669-6286

*Big Island*

**Imari at Hilton Waikoloa Village**    425 Waikoloa Beach Drive, Kohala Coast (808) 886-1234

# Best Thai Cuisine

*O'ahu*

**Singha Thai**    1910 Ala Moana Boulevard, Honolulu (808) 941-2898

*Big Island*

**Royal Siam**    70 Malama Street, Hilo (808) 961-6100
**Bangkok Houses**    75-5626 Kuakini Highway, Building 5, Kailua-Kona (808) 329-7764

*Kaua'i*

**Mema Thai Chinese Cuisine**    Wailua Shopping Plaza, 4-361 Kuhio Highway, Kapa'a (808) 823-0899

# Best Theme Restaurants

*O'ahu*

**All Star Café**    King Kalakaua Plaza, 2080 Kalakaua Avenue, Waikiki (808) 955-8326

*Maui*

**Bubba Gump Shrimp Company**    889 Front Street, Lahaina (808) 661-3111

*Big Island*

**Hard Rock Café**    75-5815 Ali'i Drive, Kailua-Kona (808) 326-7655

# Best Vegetarian

*O'ahu*

**Down to Earth Deli**    2525 South King Street, Honolulu (808) 947-7678

*Maui*

**The Vegan**    115 Baldwin Avenue, Pa'ia (808) 579-9144

*Big Island*

**Sibu Café**    75-5695 Ali'i Drive, Kailua-Kona (808) 329-1112. Also serves Asian food.

## Best Vegetarian *(continued)*

*Kaua'i*

**Hanapepe Cafe & Espresso**   3830 Hanapepe Road, Hanapepe (808) 335-5011

*Moloka'i*

**Outpost Natural Foods**   70 Maka'ena Street, Kaunakakai (808) 553-3377

## Best Vietnamese Cuisine

*O'ahu*

**A Little Bit of Saigon**   1160 Maunakea, Honolulu (808) 528-3663

*Maui*

**A Saigon Café**   1792 Main Street, Wailuku (808) 243-9560

## Best Views

*O'ahu*

**John Dominis**   43 'Ahui Street, Honolulu (808) 523-0955

*Maui*

**The Bay Club**   Kapalua Bay Hotel, 1 Bay Drive, Kapalua (808) 669-5656

*Big Island*

**Pavilion**   Mauna Kea Beach Hotel, 62-100 Mauna Kea Beach Drive, Kohala Coast (808) 822-7222

*Kaua'i*

**Café Hanalei and Terrace**   Princeville Resort, Princeville (808) 826-2760

*Lana'i*

**Manele Bay Clubhouse**   Manele Bay Resort, Manele (808) 565-2230

# Restaurant Profiles

## O'ahu

### ALAN WONG'S RESTAURANT ★★★★★

HAWAI'I REGIONAL | MODERATE | QUALITY ★★★★★ | VALUE ★★★★ | ZONE 1

1857 South King Street, 3rd floor, Waikiki/Honolulu; (808) 949-2526;
www.alanwongs.com

**Reservations** Highly recommended **When to go** Anytime, but less crowded 5–6:30
p.m. **Entrée range** $15–30 **Payment** VISA, MC, AMEX, DC, JCB **Service rating**
★★★★★ **Parking** Valet or limited on-street parking **Bar** Full service **Wine selection** Extensive, mostly domestic, good selection by the glass **Dress** Dressy resort
attire **Disabled access** Good, via elevator **Customers** Islanders and visitors.

**Dinner** Every day, 5–10 p.m.

**Setting & atmosphere** Situated a short cab ride out of Waikiki, Alan Wong's is hard to
spot if you're unfamiliar with South King Street, but the third-floor restaurant is worth
the search. Local artwork decorates the walls, and sparkly lights hang overhead. An exhibition kitchen on one side of the comfortable restaurant showcases the action indoors,
while outdoors, lanai diners look across part of the city to the Ko'olau Mountains.

**House specialties** "Da Bag," an appetizer in a billowy foil pillow, is pierced at the
table to yield aromatic kalua pig, steamed clams, spinach, and shiitake mushrooms.
Pacific flavors continue throughout the meal in desserts such as "The Coconut," an
eye-catching ball of Hawaiian Vintage Chocolate filled with haupia sorbet nestled in
tropical fruits and liliko'i sauce.

**Other recommendations** The chef's sense of humor and his seemingly effortless
ability to fuse Asian, Hawaiian, and Continental flavors are evident in such menu
favorites as poke pines ('ahi tartare fried in a crispy, spiky shell), duck nacho (Chinese-style duck on tapioca-scallion chips), and sautéed shrimp and clams (with a spicy
lemongrass/black-bean sauce served with pasta). Even mashed potatoes take on new
meaning when served as roasted garlic smashed potatoes to accompany shellfish.

**Summary & comments** Alan Wong is among Hawai'i's most creative and accomplished chefs, known for his artistry and the hands-on care he continues to provide in
his kitchen despite his many new projects. In recent years other prominent hotel chefs
have opened free-standing restaurants, but Wong's King Street location has withstood
the competition and remains the favorite special-occasion destination. The ultimate way
to sample his style is the always-evolving five-course tasting menu ($65; $90 with wines).

### ASSAGGIO RISTORANTE ITALIANO ★★★½

ITALIAN | INEXPENSIVE/MODERATE | QUALITY ★★★★½ | VALUE ★★★★★ | ZONE 6

Mililani Town Center, 95-1249 Meheula Parkway, Mililani (808)-623-4693

**Reservations** Suggested **When to go** Anytime **Entrée range** Lunch $9–$14, dinner $10–19 **Payment** All major credit cards **Service rating** ★★★ **Parking** Free, in shopping-center lot **Bar** Full service **Wine selection** Average, but featuring a nice selection of Italian wines, 7 by the glass **Dress** Casual **Disabled access** Good **Customers** Mostly locals

**Lunch** Daily, 11:30 a.m.–2:30 p.m.

**Dinner** Sunday–Thursday, 5–9:30 p.m.; Friday and Saturday, 5–10 p.m.

**Setting and atmosphere** A family-friendly atmosphere, but dressy enough to make this a special-occasion spot for the suburbs. Assaggio has a clean, contemporary, open feel—upscale, but not intimidating. The name means "to taste." The restaurant is a distance from town, but consider it for a lunch stop on a trip to see the waves on the North Shore. It's a short hop off the H-2 freeway.

**House specialties** This is fairly simple Italian food, but the menu is large, with choices for everyone, from the spaghetti-and-meatballs kid to the adult with a taste for veal scaloppine with eggplant and mushrooms. Chicken Assaggio is crunchy and flavorful, smothered in garlic, peppers, and mushrooms in wine sauce. The spicy house arrabiata sauce is another no-fail favorite, served with ziti or fresh fish. Sicilian chicken is a hearty comfort meal made with potatoes, peppers, mushrooms, and wine sauce.

**Other recommendations** The Caesar salad for two is excellent; it is tossed and served at the table. Also popular are the ravioli dishes, osso buco, and the many treatments of veal scaloppine (saltimbocca, alla piccata, alla sorrentino, and alla rollatini).

**Summary and comments** Chef/owner Thomas Ky came to this country as a refugee from Vietnam, escaping his homeland alone and destitute as a 14-year-old. He learned English and worked in Chinese restaurants, sometimes several at a time. But once he found work at an Italian restaurant, he identified his calling and within 18 months had saved enough money to go into his first restaurant partnership. Ky does not cultivate celebrity, but he is as successful as any of Hawai'i's restaurateurs if not more so. There are three other Assaggios (Ala Moana Center, Hawai'i Kai, and Kailua). The Ala Moana location may be most convenient for visitors, but the Mililani restaurant is the most consistent in quality, as Ky personally spends most of his time in this kitchen.

## BALI-BY-THE-SEA ★★★½

EURO-ASIAN | MODERATE/EXPENSIVE | QUALITY ★★★★ | VALUE ★★★ | ZONE 1

Hilton Hawaiian Village Hotel, 2005 Kalia Road, Waikiki; (808) 941-BALI (2254), restaurant (808) 949-4321; www.hawaiianvillage.hilton.com

**Reservations** Highly recommended **When to go** Sunsets are most pleasant **Entrée range** $25.50–30.95 **Payment** VISA, MC, AMEX, D, DC, JCB **Service rating** ★★★★★ **Parking** Valet or hotel lot **Bar** Full service **Wine selection** Exceptional; the wine selection has been named "The Best" in 1999 in the local Hale 'Aina Awards— half a dozen wines are available by the glass **Dress** Resort attire, collared shirts and slacks for gentlemen **Disabled access** Good **Customers** Hotel guests and Islanders for special occasions

**Dinner** Monday–Saturday, 6–10 p.m.

**Setting & atmosphere** White linens, candlelight, and fine china and crystal impart an elegance to this romantic, though large, open-air restaurant that overlooks ocean and lagoon vistas. Diamond Head looms beyond the window tables.

**House specialties** The regular menu hints of Chef Jean-Luc Voegele's French background. Escargot in phyllo with warm ratatouille and roasted garlic beurre blanc followed by succulent rack of lamb crusted with macadamia nuts and herbs are two of Voegele's classic presentations. Complete dinners climax with a showy presentation of truffles in a miniature chocolate replica of Diamond Head swirling with dry ice.

**Other recommendations** From half a dozen appetizers you might choose char siu and shiitake pot-stickers with port wine balsamic glaze or shrimp and scallop Provençales. Seafood lovers often go for Island bouillabaisse as a main course.

**Summary & comments** It's not only the open-air dining with soft breezes and lapping waves carrying in from the ocean that make this prize-winning restaurant a favorite of those ready to pop the question, but also the knowledge that they'll receive impeccable service as well as good food to win a sweetheart's heart and hand.

## BUZZ'S ORIGINAL STEAK HOUSE                                       ★★

STEAK AND SEAFOOD | INEXPENSIVE/MODERATE | QUALITY ★★★½ | VALUE ★★★ | ZONE 3

413 Kawailoa Road, Kailua; (808) 261-4661

**Reservations** Highly recommended **When to go** Anytime **Entrée range** $11–30 **Payment** No credit cards **Service rating** ★★★ **Parking** Free in adjacent lot **Bar** Full service **Wine selection** Adequate, many by the glass **Dress** Casual **Disabled access** Good **Customers** Islanders, tourists brought in by Islanders

**Lunch** Every day, 11 a.m.–3 p.m.

**Dinner** Every day, 5–10 p.m.

**Setting & atmosphere** Across the street from Kailua Beach and bordered on one side by Ka'elepulu Stream, Buzz's has the appeal of an old-fashioned beach house. The wait-help wears Polynesian prints and T-shirts to serve customers at wooden-topped tables and booths indoors and on an outdoor deck. Inside, the bar is a local gathering spot for beachgoers and the young people of this family-oriented small windward town a little less than 15 miles from Waikiki.

**House specialties** Salad lovers invariably remember Buzz's bar because avocado is generally among the offerings of tossed greens, sprouts, olives, bacon bits, sesame seeds, and the like. This is a good place to choose fresh fish; thick, juicy steaks; prime rib; and rack of lamb accompanied by a baked potato. If you want good, straightforward food without all the fancy coulis, aïoli, and other sauces of today's trendy cuisine, Buzz's is the place.

**Other recommendations** Share an artichoke surprise, a whole artichoke with a butter, herb, and garlic dipping sauce for an appetizer, before sampling fresh fish prepared Chinese-style. You'll catch whiffs of peanut oil, soy sauce, garlic, ginger, and cilantro when this dish is served.

**Summary & comments** If you sit at the last table on the open-air deck, you'll notice a little plaque commemorating the fact that President and Mrs. Clinton dined at that table during a stopover in the Islands. Lunch at Buzz's is a pleasant way to take a break from a day spent windsurfing or sunning at the nearby beach.

## CASCADA ★★★½

MEDITERRANEAN WITH ISLAND FLAIR | MODERATE | QUALITY ★★★★ | VALUE ★★★ |
ZONE 1

Royal Garden Hotel, 440 'Olohana Street, Waikiki; (808) 945-0270;
www.quisine.com/cascada

**Reservations** Recommended **When to go** Anytime **Entrée range** $18–26 **Payment** VISA, MC, AMEX, D, DC, JCB **Service rating** ★★★★½ **Parking** Complimentary valet or limited on-street **Bar** Full service **Wine selection** Adequate, 10 wines by the glass **Dress** Casual resort attire **Disabled access** Good **Customers** Tourists and Islanders for special occasions

**Breakfast** Every day, 6:30–9:30 a.m.

**Lunch** Every day, 11 a.m.–2 p.m.

**Dinner** Every day, 6–10 p.m.

**Setting & atmosphere** You'll feel as if you made your own special discovery when you wander up a Waikiki side street to this boutique hotel. The restaurant sports a hand-painted trompe l'oeil ceiling that depicts trellises, birds, and flowers. Tables are set inside and out on a marble terrace beside a soothing waterfall that feeds into a swimming pool.

**House specialties** Whatever you do, don't miss sampling the gnocchi with ricotta cheese and spinach, a delicious accompaniment to Mongolian lamb chops or pan-seared pork tenderloin.

**Other recommendations** Salmon tartare, Thai spring rolls, and crab cakes with chipotle sour cream and avocado tomatillo sauces are tried-and-true favorites among the appetizers. Opt for entrées like seafood risotto or fresh Island fish for a lighter meal.

**Summary & comments** *Gourmet* magazine named Cascada one of America's Top Tables. Dining here is like finding a peaceful Mediterranean oasis in the middle of frantic Waikiki. Cascada works equally well for a serious business meeting or a quiet tête-à-tête.

## CHEF MAVRO RESTAURANT ★★★★½

PACIFIC EDGE | EXPENSIVE | QUALITY ★★★★★ | VALUE ★★★ | ZONE 1

1969 South King Street, Waikiki/Honolulu; (808) 944-4714; www.chefmavro.com

**Reservations** Highly recommended **When to go** Anytime **Entrée range** $27–38; prix fixe menus: $48–72 without wines, $66–96 with wines **Payment** VISA, MC, AMEX, DC, JCB **Service rating** ★★★★★ **Parking** Valet only **Bar** Full service **Wine selection** Good **Dress** Dressy resort attire **Disabled access** Good **Customers** Islanders

**Dinner** Tuesday–Sunday, 6–9:30 p.m.

**Setting & atmosphere** Gleaming pink marble at the entry foretells the simple elegance of the interior. A graceful arch divides the upper and lower portions of the dining area, with banquette seating beside two walls of etched glass windows. The intimate 68-seat restaurant is lit with pinpoint lights with tiny shades suspended like stars from the ceiling and decorated with sprays of orchids for a peaceful, refined atmosphere.

**House specialties** Chef/owner George Mavrothalassitis changes his menu every two months, but one dish remains constant. His salt-crusted onaga is elegantly presented at the table, the fish-shaped pastry carefully lifted to reveal a fillet of succulent and steaming longtail snapper. The chef has been preparing the dish the same way for 10 years; he says he is a bit tired of making it, but his customers won't let him remove it from the menu. The essence of Chef Mavro is the pairing of food and wine, and the best way to appreciate his cuisine is through his tasting menus. He offers a choice of three- to six-course dinners, each dish paired with wine, for $67 to $120. Every few weeks, the chef presents his new dishes to the staff and a few guest tasters; they try the dishes with a variety of wines and vote on the best pairings. Majority rules and sets the menu for the next two months.

**Other recommendations** Coriander-crisped beef entrecôte was featured dish in *Wine Spectator* magazine, paired with an Italian Chianti. It is served with artichoke barigoule, slow-roasted tomatoes, angel-hair pasta, and an anchovy–Pinot Noir sauce. A true comfort dish that plays on favorite island flavors is the island chicken and oxtail pot au feu, with its deeply flavored star anise consommé, vegetables, and Yukon Gold potatoes, served with wasabi-flavored rice. The restaurant has recently entered a partnership with the new Hawaiian Vanilla Co., so the pastry chef's new creations with that flavoring, such as Hawaiian Vanilla tapioca, are worth a visit.

**Summary & comments** Chef George Mavrothalassitis is a true culinary artist with a longtime reputation for award-winning food in Hawai'i. He was executive chef of Halekulani when it was first awarded five diamonds by AAA and of Four Seasons Resorts before opening Chef Mavro's Restaurant late in 1998. Dedicated to using fresh Island ingredients, he says his philosophy is not "I have a recipe and I'm going to find an ingredient. I say, I have an ingredient and I'm going to find a recipe." Billed as "affordable fine dining," the tab is still dear, but this is serious gourmet dining for those who appreciate the best.

## DIAMOND HEAD GRILL    ★★★

CONTEMPORARY AMERICAN  |  MODERATE/EXPENSIVE  |  QUALITY ★★★½  |  VALUE ★★  |  ZONE 1

W Hotel, 2885 Kalakaua Avenue, Waikiki; (808) 922-3734; www.whotels.com

**Reservations** Highly recommended, but not required **When to go** Anytime **Entrée range** $22–42 **Payment** VISA, MC, AMEX, DC, D, JCB **Service rating** ★★★★½ **Parking** Valet or on-street meters **Bar** Full service **Wine selection** Extensive, nearly 2 dozen wines by the glass, including Champagne **Dress** Resort attire, no beach wear **Disabled access** Good, via elevator **Customers** Islanders and tourists

**Dinner** Every day, 5:30–10 p.m.; a lighter bistro menu is available Thursday–Saturday, 10–11:30 p.m.

**Setting & atmosphere** The second-floor location of this restaurant, opened in 1998, is a winner, thanks to Los Angeles architect Steve Jones, who incidentally designed Wolfgang Puck's outlets. It's light and airy in atmosphere, with tables nicely spaced, and the view of Diamond Head right outside a huge picture window seems bigger than life. Jan Kasprzycki's vivid mural beside the entry staircase adds a sophisticated touch. The main dining area seats 150, with a serpentine martini and appetizer bar on one side; a separate banquet room holds 125. And a glass-enclosed "Chef's Table" is perfect for ten guests.

**House specialties** A delicately flavored white snapper called 'opakapaka—a longtime island favorite—is crusted with porcini mushrooms, then sautéed and served on a bed of red bliss potato salad and Dungeness crab ragout. For non–fish lovers, two full-flavored specialties are the guava- and mustard-crusted rack of lamb (with goat cheese and roasted garlic gratin) and braised short ribs (with soybean puree and plum wine demi-glace). Chocolate lava cake with coffee ice cream is another memory-maker.

**Other recommendations** It's hard to pass up appetizers like kalua pork lumpia with mango guacamole and spicy mustard sauce and a lighter grilled portobello mushroom with grilled asparagus, Gorgonzola, and polenta. But if you push on to selections from the stone oven, you'll find an even more imaginative rotisserie pork panini with smoky mozzarella, sun-dried tomato aïoli, and arugula on a rustic flat bread.

**Entertainment & amenities** Live music offered Wednesdays and Thursdays, plus late-night entertainment in a club atmosphere on Fridays and Saturdays.

**Summary & comments** This restaurant opened under the helm of the charismatic celebrity chef from Maui, David Paul Johnson. Johnson was replaced less than two years later with David Reardon, a well-respected hotel chef, but Reardon left soon afterward, leaving the kitchen in the hands of one of the sous-chefs, Todd Constantino. The restaurant is still seeking its center amid all this change.

## DON HO'S ISLAND GRILL ★★★

HAWAI'I REGIONAL COMFORT FOOD | INEXPENSIVE | QUALITY ★★★½ | VALUE
★★★½ | ZONE 2

Aloha Tower Marketplace, 1 Aloha Tower Drive, Honolulu; (808) 528-0807;
www.donhp.com

**Reservations** Recommended **When to go** Sunset for best views of a working harbor
**Entrée range** $5.95–16.95 **Payment** VISA, MC, AMEX, DC, JCB **Service rating**
★★★★ **Parking** Valet or in adjacent pay lot **Bar** Full service, good selection of tropical drinks **Wine selection** Adequate **Dress** Casual **Disabled access** Good if using valet **Customers** Islanders and tourists

**Lunch & dinner** Every day, 10 a.m.–9 p.m.

**Setting & atmosphere** This restaurant is a Polynesian nostalgia trip right back to the Hawai'i depicted by Hollywood in the 1940s and 1950s. Walls are covered with surfboards, paddles, rattan, and Don Ho memorabilia and pictures. The salad bar is nestled in an outrigger canoe. The restaurant opens to views of busy Honolulu Harbor on one side, and a thatched roof bar just outside the confines of the restaurant also overlooks the harbor. Pillars decorated like palm trees and a bamboo-lined bar with stools covered in colorful Polynesian prints are all part of the yesteryear atmosphere.

**House specialties** Most fun for sharing is the surfboard pizza with a variety of toppings presented at the table on a miniature surfboard resting on two big pineapple cans. You can get a cheeseburger anytime, but the chop chop salad with rotisserie roast pork and crispy Oriental vegetables is only one of many more interesting choices.

**Other recommendations** Stir-fry dishes—teriyaki beef with broccoli, Phoenix and Dragon with shrimp and chicken, Chinatown noodles, etc.—come in big portions, but the fresh Island fish is better. It comes macadamia-nut-and-pesto crusted, or lu'au-roasted with Hawaiian salt, or local-style with ginger, shoyu, sesame oil, and chives.

**Entertainment & amenities** Seven days a week musicians grace the stage during afternoon happy hour, while bigger-name entertainers often appear on weekends and for special events.

**Summary & comments** People say they haven't seen anything like this place in 30 years, since Don Ho's heyday. The atmosphere receives bigger raves than the food, however. Ho tends to show up several nights a week, generally after 10 p.m.

## *DOUBLE EIGHT CHINESE RESTAURANT* ★★★★

CHINESE | INEXPENSIVE | QUALITY ★★★★½ | VALUE ★★★★★ | ZONE 2

1113 Maunakea St., Chinatown (808) 526-3887

**Reservations** None taken **When to go** Anytime **Entrée range** Lunch or dinner, $8–$9 **Payment** Visa, MC **Service rating** ★★★ **Parking** Metered parking on street or in public lots nearby **Bar** None **Wine selection** None **Dress** Casual **Disabled access** One step up from sidewalk **Customers** Locals, some tourists

**Lunch** Daily, 10:30 a.m.–3 p.m.

**Dinner** Daily, 4:30–10 p.m.

**Setting and atmosphere** Double Eight is a small, bare-bones noodle house, presenting honest Chinese food in Hong Kong style. It's clean and comfortable, right in the middle of Honolulu's bustling Chinatown. Plan a few hours of shopping and browsing in this area, with Double Eight as the perfect spot to rest and replenish.

**House specialties** The hot pot casseroles are savory, satisfying bowls of warm comfort. Try chicken with mushrooms, pig's feet with bean curd, a seafood mix, or tofu and vegetables. The flavors mix wonderfully. One hot pot and some noodles would feed two to three. The cake noodles, thin and crispy, are especially good. They're on the menu with chicken, but pay an extra six bits and you can have them with any of the toppings, such as sour cabbage and pork or beef and broccoli.

**Other recommendations** Double Eight does well by many traditional specialties, particularly ginger chicken (poached and served cold), spicy salt-and-pepper shrimp (quick-fried with heads attached), Kung Pao chicken, and eggplant with garlic sauce.

**Summary and comments** Double Eight is one of those true "finds" for a traveler—an affordable place with character and great food. Best of all, it's a place that locals have come to for years, and these are people with a lot of access to Chinese food. They're good judges.

## DUKE'S CANOE CLUB RESTAURANT   ★★★

CONTEMPORARY  |  INEXPENSIVE/MODERATE  |  QUALITY ★★★½  |  VALUE ★★★★  |
ZONE 1

Outrigger Waikiki Hotel, 2335 Kalakaua Avenue, Waikiki; (808) 922-2268;
www.outrigger.com

**Reservations** Accepted **When to go** Anytime **Entrée range** $7.95–23.95 **Payment** VISA, MC, AMEX, D, DC **Service rating** ★★★ **Parking** Valet or hotel lot **Bar** Full service **Wine selection** Good **Dress** Daytime, off-the-beach casual; at night, it's still casual **Disabled access** Good if using valet **Customers** Islanders, beach boys, tourists

**Breakfast** Every day, 7–11 a.m.

**Lunch** Every day, 11 a.m.–5 p.m.

**Dinner** Every day, 5–10 p.m.—a simpler menu is served in the Barefoot Bar 5 p.m.–midnight

**Setting & atmosphere** *Pau hana* (after work) surfers, paddlers, and tourists hang out at the big wooden bar watching the sunset over Waikiki Beach in this casual, oceanfront eatery. Historic photos, surfboards, and saltwater aquariums bring back memories of the days when Duke Kahanamoku was an Olympic swimmer and surfer extraordinaire.

**House specialties** At dinner try a huge slab of prime rib or awesome fresh fish—'ahi, mahimahi, ono, or 'opakapaka—available in five preparations: baked, firecracker, Parmesan- and herb-crusted, hibachi-style teriyaki, or simply grilled. At lunch this is a convenient spot for anything from a burger to huli huli chicken to Thai-style seafood coconut curry.

**Other recommendations** Breakfast and lunch buffets and a salad bar at dinner boast value "grinds," or if you prefer table service you might order burgers, fries, pasta, and salads.

**Entertainment & amenities** From 4 to 6 p.m. thoroughly modern musicians play Island sounds. On Friday, Saturday, and Sunday, dance bands keep the lower lanai jumping.

**Summary & comments** Duke's is one of the most popular places to hang out after a day on Waikiki Beach for both Islanders and tourists, partly because it opens right onto the sand, but also because local surfers are rightly proud of the great Hawaiian swimmer this restaurant commemorates.

## THE GOLDEN DRAGON   ★★★★

CHINESE  |  MODERATE  |  QUALITY ★★★★½  |  VALUE ★★★  |  ZONE 1

Hilton Hawaiian Village Hotel, 2005 Kalia Road, Waikiki; (808) 946-5336;
www.hawaiianvillage.hilton.com

**Reservations** Highly recommended **When to go** Anytime except Monday **Entrée range** $9–30 **Payment** VISA, MC, AMEX, D, DC, JCB **Service rating** ★★★★½ **Parking** Valet or validated self-park in hotel's garage **Bar** Full service **Wine selection** Good **Dress** Resort attire **Disabled access** Good if using valet **Customers** Hotel guests, Waikiki tourists, Islanders

**Dinner** Tuesday–Sunday, 6–9:30 p.m.

**Setting & atmosphere** Ask to sit on one of the open-air lanais that extends out from the restaurant, for the most romantic views over the Hilton Hawaiian Village lagoon and the little coconut-clad island that rests in its center. The dining room itself has the imperial grandeur of a modern Oriental palace. Golden dragon statues greet you at the entrance, and one wall is lined with lacquer screens decorated with Oriental figures. Tempting aromas float from a circular, glass-enclosed "smoke room" that displays plump juicy roasted ducks. At the back of the restaurant, a private room secluded by a glass partition etched in a lily design is available for groups.

**House specialties** A few signature items on the Cantonese menu are a legacy to Chef Dai Hoy Chang, who opened this first Chinese restaurant in Hawai'i. Imperial beggar's chicken has to be ordered 24 hours in advance, then, when the waiter presents the dish, he shares the legend with you. A beggar who stole a chicken had only lotus leaves to wrap it in. He improvised a pan by covering the leaves with mud from the lily pond and cooking the whole thing in a campfire. At the Golden Dragon, beggar's chicken arrives at the table in its clay encasement, and the diner is given a beribboned "good luck hammer" to crack it, after which the waiter peels away the clay and the lotus leaves and carves the juicy chicken.

You can see the Peking duck, another traditional dish, hanging in the glass house in the restaurant's center before you eat it. It's carved at the table and served with plum sauce rolled in Mandarin pancakes by your waiter, an easy, non-messy way to eat a dish that could otherwise have you licking your fingers all through the meal.

**Other recommendations** Islanders traditionally love the succulent chunks of cold ginger chicken and a tangy lemon chicken dish, but personally, we would opt for the shelled lobster meat with a delicate curry sauce and haupia (coconut pudding). Two chef's signature dinners for $32 and $39 per person feature enough food that you can tuck leftovers in your hotel mini-fridge for dinner the next night.

**Summary & comments** Don't say no when the tea lady offers to tell your fortune (at no extra cost), though you must reveal your birth year so she can determine which animal sign you are in the Chinese zodiac. You'll be amazed at how often the fortune fits your personality. *Gourmet* magazine named the Golden Dragon one of America's Top Tables in 1997 and 1998.

## HAU TREE LANA'I                   ★★★

CONTINENTAL/PACIFIC RIM | MODERATE | QUALITY ★★★½ | VALUE ★★★ | ZONE 1

New Otani Kaimana Beach Hotel, 2863 Kalakaua Avenue, Waikiki; (808) 921-7066; www.koimana.com

**Reservations** Recommended, especially for dinner **When to go** Anytime; at dinner sunset is preferred **Entrée range** Breakfast $9.50–12.95, lunch $7.95–14.95, dinner

**$17.50–35 Payment** VISA, MC, AMEX, DC, D, JCB **Service rating** ★★★★ **Parking** Valet or on-street meters **Bar** Full service **Wine selection** Good, some selections by the glass **Dress** Casual for breakfast and lunch, resort attire at dinner **Disabled access** Good, with ramp to the beach-level terrace **Customers** Waikiki visitors, hotel guests, Islanders

**Breakfast** Monday–Saturday, 7–11 a.m.; Sunday, 7–11:30 a.m.

**Lunch** Monday–Saturday, 11:30 a.m.–2 p.m.; Sunday, noon–2 p.m.

**Dinner** Every day, 5:30–9 p.m.

**Setting & atmosphere** A favorite, unpretentious place for Islanders to take out-of-town guests, the Hau Tree Lana'i's linen-draped tables are snuggled under a spreading hau tree on the beach at the Diamond Head end of Waikiki. If you want a beach-edge table, go early, about 5:30 p.m., and be sure to make reservations noting your request.

**House specialties** Hau Tree Lana'i's signature dish is fresh 'opakapaka (snapper) Oriental style, steamed and garnished with hot peanut oil, soy sauce, cilantro, and green onions. Other favorites among the main courses include filet mignon teamed with the day's fresh catch, seafood penne pasta, shrimp scampi, or, on the wilder side, Thai pesto black tiger prawns and scallops with garlic chili-pepper fried rice. Complete dinners can be made of any entrée item for $6 extra, which adds soup or salad, dessert, and coffee or tea.

**Other recommendations** The manager recommends filet Madagascar, sautéed and served with a creamy green peppercorn sauce, potatoes, and vegetables. Appetizers encompass and combine international flavors ranging from Cajun blackened 'ahi sashimi, to chicken and vegetable lumpia, to hoisin duck quesadilla.

**Summary & comments** Dawdle over dessert at sundown and eventually you'll see someone you know heading home from paddling or surfing. The Hau Tree Lana'i is often named O'ahu's best outdoor dining location in local competitions.

## HELENA'S HAWAIIAN FOODS ★★★★

TRADITIONAL HAWAIIAN | INEXPENSIVE | QUALITY ★★★★½ | VALUE ★★★★★ | ZONE 2

1240 North School Street, Honolulu; (808) 845-8044

**Reservations** None taken **When to go** Anytime **Entrée range** Lunch or dinner, $6–$12 **Payment** No credit cards accepted **Service rating** ★★★ **Parking** A few spots in a small attached lot **Bar** None **Wine selection** None **Dress** Casual **Disabled access** Restaurant would be easily negotiated by wheelchairs, but there are two shallow steps up from the parking lot **Customers** Locals

**Hours** Tuesday–Friday, 11:30 a.m.–7:30 p.m.

**Setting and atmosphere** Helena's is a clean, down-to-earth, no-frills eatery, with the door painted red for good luck. But on the walls you'll find lithographs by Jean Charlot, gifts from the late artist that were personally framed and delivered. Also on the wall: owner Helen Chock's James Beard Foundation Award. In 2000, the restaurant was named a Regional Classic, a special designation for locally owned, neighborhood eateries that best reflect the character of their communities.

**House specialties** The menu is small and entirely devoted to traditional Hawaiian foods. It has remained unchanged for more than 50 years. The pipi kaula short ribs are exceptional—chewy on the outside and pull-apart moist on the inside. The flavoring is one-of-a-kind, drawn from Helena's grill, where they hang to dry slightly before cooking. Butterfish collars, made from the sweet, delicate meat just behind the fish's gills, are served fried or stewed (fried is better, crunchy and flavorful). Salt beef with watercress, soft cubes of brisket in a mellow broth, is perfect comfort food.

**Other recommendations** Lomi salmon, squid lu'au, and kalua pig, all lu'au specialties, are done well at Helena's. Refreshing squares of haupia, or coconut gelatin, are the prefect ending to the meal. You can order à la carte and assemble your own mixed plate. Most items are in the $3 range. Or you can chose one of four preset menus, priced at $6–$12. Whatever you have, don't forget a bowl of poi.

**Summary and comments** Owner Helen Chock ran Helena's almost single-handedly in one location beginning in 1946, winning the hearts (and stomachs) of an extremely devoted clientele. In 2001, after collecting her James Beard Award, she lost her lease and moved to this location, which has all the clean brightness of a new site. Her grandson is now the principal owner, but Chock is still in the kitchen daily, a tiny but unmistakable presence.

## HOKU'S ★★★★

CONTEMPORARY INTERNATIONAL | MODERATE/EXPENSIVE | QUALITY ★★★★½ |
VALUE ★★★ | ZONE 2

Kahala Mandarin Hotel, 500 Kahala Avenue, Honolulu; (808) 739-8777 or (808) 739-8888; www.mandarin-oriental.com

**Reservations** Highly recommended **When to go** Anytime **Entrée range** Lunch $14.95–29.95, dinner $26.50–32.50, vegetarian entrée at $21.95 **Payment** VISA, MC, AMEX, D, DC, JCB **Service rating** ★★★★★ **Parking** Valet or validated in hotel garage **Bar** Full service **Wine selection** Extensive, including half a dozen ports **Dress** Resort attire **Disabled access** Good **Customers** Hotel guests, repeat local diners

**Lunch** Monday–Friday, 11:30 a.m.–2:30 p.m.

**Dinner** Monday–Sunday, 5:30–10 p.m.

**Setting & atmosphere** Hoku's is a stylish restaurant where every table has a panoramic vista of the Pacific, thanks to a multi-level layout. An open kitchen at one end of the dining room showcases a kiawe wood grill, woks, a tandoori oven, and a wood-burning pizza oven. A sushi bar offers additional tidbits.

**House specialties** Hoku's satisfies international appetites in a single appetizer: Indian naan bread with an island-style 'ahi poke dip. Other dishes do justice to the flavors of the world—tandoori chicken salad, herb-crusted onaga (longtail snapper), and wok-fried prawns in garlic, ginger, and chiles. Among the more spectacular dishes is the seafood tower—a chilled mountain of prawns, crab claws, mussels, sashimi, octopus, and lobster, served with six dipping sauces. For the ultimate appetizer (serves four), order it with champagne.

**Other recommendations** The chef's tasting menu, which changes frequently, tops out at $65 for five courses, but it allows you to sample a bit of the best of everything. A similar business lunch special includes a salad, the chef's special entrée of the day, and tiramisu for dessert. The remodeled veranda offers a tasty and generous curry bar during lunch on weekdays, with a sampling of Indian, Japanese, and Thai curries, all the condiments, and three types of rice. Afternoon tea, featuring an exotic selection of loose-leaf teas, beautifully poured, and accented with pastries and mini-sandwiches, is an elegant treat.

**Entertainment & amenities** The restaurant is adjacent to a veranda where live music is featured nightly.

**Summary & comments** Chef Wayne Hirabayashi has come into his own at Hoku's, having taken over from the formidable Oliver Altherr. Under Altherr the restaurant was named top restaurant in *Honolulu Magazine's* Hale Aina Awards, interrupting a streak of wins by the formidable Alan Wong's. They were big shoes to fill, but Hirabayashi, an extremely hard-working and accomplished chef, has definitely made his mark.

## HY'S STEAK HOUSE                                          ★★★

STEAK AND SEAFOOD  |  MODERATE/EXPENSIVE  |  QUALITY ★★★★  |  VALUE ★★★  |
ZONE 1

Waikiki Park Heights Condominium, 2440 Kuhio Avenue; (808) 922-5555;
www.hyshawaii.com

**Reservations** Recommended **When to go** Anytime **Entrée range** $19.95–47.95, market price may be slightly higher **Payment** VISA, MC, AMEX, D, DC, JCB **Service rating** ★★★★½ **Parking** Valet in garage **Bar** Full service **Wine selection** Hy's has a wine list that never ends! **Dress** From dressy attire to resort casual **Disabled access** No ramp for stairs, but staff will help; wheelchair lift available **Customers** Islanders and tourists

**Dinner** Sunday–Thursday, 6–10 p.m.; Friday and Saturday, 6–11 p.m.

**Setting & atmosphere** Meat lovers revel in the traditional formal candle-lit ambience found beyond the massive carved doors to this elegant, Old World club–like room. Rich, warm wooden wall paneling with heavy carved filigree accenting ceiling moldings, gleaming brass chandeliers, and a huge beveled mirror reflect tables dressed in pretty pink cloths.

**House specialties** Start with a grand, garlicky Caesar salad and proceed to your favorite steaks: The Only, a tender New York Strip broiled over kiawe and served with the restaurant's secret sauce; or T-bone, prime rib, or filet of beef Wellington topped with foie gras (in season) and mushroom druxelles, baked in a light pastry and served with Cabernet truffle sauce. Châteaubriand is also a popular choice not always found in other restaurants. Hy's signature dessert is bananas Foster, a French-Creole version of fresh bananas, orange juice, liqueurs, butter, brown sugar, cinnamon, and rum, flambéed table-side and served over ice cream.

**Other recommendations** Seafood combos, lamb, scallops, and scampi can also be ordered with twice-baked potatoes (whipped with sour cream and butter) or with pan-fired O'Brien potatoes, steak fries, steamed rice, or rice pilaf, all accompanied by Hy's famous cheese bread.

**Entertainment & amenities** Audy Kimura, winner of eight Na Hoku Hanohano Awards, strums the guitar and sings Wednesday through Saturday evenings.

**Summary & comments** Even though it's in the heart of Waikiki, Hy's has a loyal *kama'aina* (longtime resident) following.

## INDIGO ★★★★

EURO-ASIAN | INEXPENSIVE/MODERATE | QUALITY ★★★★½ | VALUE ★★★★ | ZONE 2

1121 Nu'uanu Avenue, Honolulu; (808) 521-2900; www.p;aces.com/Indigo

**Reservations** Recommended **When to go** Anytime **Entrée range** $8.25–16.95, vegetarian $7.25 **Payment** VISA, MC, D, DC, JCB **Service rating** ★★★★ **Parking** Valet, street, or nearby Gateway Plaza lot **Bar** Full service **Wine selection** Good, many by the glass **Dress** Casual **Disabled access** Good if using valet **Customers** Islanders and their out-of-town guests, businesspeople at lunch, pre– and post–Hawai'i Theatre attendees

**Lunch** Tuesday–Friday, 11:30 a.m.–2 p.m.

**Dinner** Tuesday–Saturday, 6–9 p.m.

**Setting & atmosphere** Great care has been taken to create a tropical-Eurasian retreat in the heart of old Honolulu by chef/owner Glenn Chu. The indoor part of the restaurant is set in a historic building erected in 1903. With a high ceiling, suspended fans circling lazily overhead, antique carved panels from Indonesia, and big paintings of Chinese goddesses by local artist Pegge Hopper, you get the feeling you've traveled back in time to some exotic foreign locale for lunch. The back of the building opens onto Chinatown Gateway Park. Diners on the lanai are surrounded by lush greenery, with paper lanterns hung overhead and Balinese umbrellas placed here and there. A bar at the edge of the lanai is roofed with ironwood shingles brought from Indonesia.

**House specialties** Appetizers here give diners a chance to taste a variety of textures and flavors, from little steamed, filled dumplings, to spring rolls, to deep-fried wonton and shrimp lumpia served with chipotle aïoli and tangerine sauce. Miso salmon, breast of chicken with peanut sauce, and steamed fish with a soy-oyster-sesame dressing are flavorful entrées.

**Other recommendations** Regulars won't let Chef Chu take the crab-tomato-and-garlic soup off the menu. The pizzettas—duck or chicken—are also good for a light meal, especially if you want to try the signature dessert: Madame Pele's chocolate volcano, a cone-shaped mound of mousse spouting raspberry coulis and crème anglaise, arrives at the table amid a cloud of dry-ice smoke announced by a resonating gong.

**Summary & comments** Located across the park from the historic Hawai'i Theatre, Indigo is a perfect spot for a preperformance dinner. Romantics might like to mention any special occasions when making a reservation, as one table is screened by greenery and set near a bubbling waterfall. Chu has bottled a line of his special sauces, such as raspberry-hoisin sauce, which can be purchased at the restaurant.

## JOHN DOMINIS                                                    ★★★½

SEAFOOD | MODERATE/EXPENSIVE | QUALITY ★★★★ | VALUE ★★ | ZONE 1

43 'Ahui Street, Honolulu; (808) 523-0955; www.johndominishawaii.com

**Reservations** Recommended **When to go** Sunset brings out gorgeous colors over Diamond Head, even though you don't see the setting sun itself **Entrée range** $19.95–68.95 **Payment** VISA, MC, AMEX, DC, JCB **Service rating** ★★★½ **Parking** Valet **Bar** Full service **Wine selection** Good, 8 wines by the glass **Dress** Resort attire **Disabled access** Good **Customers** Tourists and Islanders for special occasions

**Brunch** Sunday seafood buffet, 9 a.m.–1 p.m.

**Dinner** Sunday–Thursday, 6–9:30 p.m.; Friday and Saturday, 5:30–9:30 p.m.

**Setting & atmosphere** On the lower level of this split-level restaurant, a saltwater fishpond is filled with Island fish, stingrays, and lobsters, so you get an effect of water all around, from the ocean outside to the pool inside. A moss-rock wall, koa furnishings, orchids throughout the restaurant, and green pothos vines hanging from the ceiling create the effect of a cool tropical oasis. Near the entry a large, comfortable lounge and 20-seat bar is a fine place to drop by with friends for an appetizer and a glass of wine.

**House specialties** Island fish served in half a dozen different preparations are John Dominis's area of expertise. Everyone loves the 'opakapaka (snapper) en papillote (in a parchment bag), served with freshly made pasta and sautéed vegetables du jour. Mild, moist moi steamed with lemon, shoyu, and ginger delights local diners, though tiger prawns, sautéed scampi-style or stir-fried with black-bean sauce, are also high on the list of favorites. Abalone with white wine and capers, though costly, is another delicacy seldom seen on standard menus. The restaurant is known for live lobster—Hawaiian spinies or live Maine lobste—fresh from the tank.

**Other recommendations** You can order good things to preclude dinner, like stuffed mushrooms with crab and hollandaise, or, for an Island flair, 'ahi poke (made with raw fish). Then, if you haven't gotten your fill of good things, John Dominis's Bailey's mud pie in an Oreo cookie crust filled with ice cream and dressed in Bailey's liqueur sauce is a perfect way to end a meal.

**Entertainment & amenities** A four-piece band, including a vocalist, renders contemporary pop music on Friday and Saturday nights.

**Summary & comments** John Dominis is a five-time 'Ilima winner for fine dining, an award offered annually by *Honolulu Advertiser* and Diamond Head Theater. We hear that service tends to be inconsistent.

## KEO'S IN WAIKIKI ★★★★

THAI/ISLAND | INEXPENSIVE/MODERATE | QUALITY ★★★★½ | VALUE ★★★★ |
ZONE 1

Ambassador Hotel, 2028 Kuhio Avenue, Waikiki; (808) 951-9355;
www.ambassadorhotelofwaikiki.com

**Reservations** Recommended, but not required **When to go** Anytime **Entrée range**
$8.95–16.95 **Payment** VISA, MC, AMEX, D, DC, JCB **Service rating** ★★★★½ **Parking** Valet **Bar** Full service **Wine selection** Adequate **Dress** Resort attire **Disabled access** Good **Customers** Tourists and Islanders

**Breakfast** Every day, 7–11 a.m.

**Lunch** Every day, 11 a.m.–2 p.m.

**Dinner** Every day, 5–10:30 p.m.

**Setting & atmosphere** Creative chef/owner Keo Sananikone designed and decorated this newest of his five Keo's restaurants with teak furnishings, Thai carvings, and Hawaiian artwork. In the heart of Waikiki, the restaurant still has the ambience of a quiet refuge, with indoor and outdoor seating at linen-draped tables surrounded by blooming orchids.

**House specialties** Locally grown filet of catfish, deep-fried with a tapioca crust, and evil jungle prince (a delicious concoction of shrimp, chicken, or beef in a spicy coconut milk sauce) are favorites.

**Other recommendations** You can feel free to try any dishes that sound good, as the chef adapts his Thai recipes to suit Western tastes using coconut milk with no preservatives, prime meat, seafood, poultry, and fresh herbs and produce grown on his own four-acre farm.

**Summary & comments** At the grand opening celebration in January 1999, celebrities, whose pictures line the walls, showed up, just as they used to at the old Keo's on Kapahulu Avenue, now closed. It's fun to try family-style dining here, with each person choosing a different dish and sharing. Keo's has received numerous awards from local and national publications.

## LA MER ★★★★★

NEO-CLASSICAL (CONTEMPORARY) | EXPENSIVE | QUALITY ★★★★★ | VALUE ★★★ |
ZONE 1

Halekulani Hotel, 2199 Kalia Road, Waikiki; (808) 923-2311; www.halekulani.com

**Reservations** Highly recommended **When to go** Sunset for most romantic atmosphere **Entrée range** $36–43 **Payment** VISA, MC, AMEX, DC, JCB **Service rating** ★★★★★ **Parking** Valet **Bar** Full service **Wine selection** Extensive **Dress** Dressy attire **Disabled access** Good, via elevator **Customers** Hotel guests, Islanders for special occasions

**Dinner** Every day, 6–10 p.m.

**Setting & atmosphere** Serene, understated elegance focuses your attention on spectacular views of Diamond Head and glowing sunsets over the ocean, interrupted only by the gracious service of haute cuisine prepared by the French chef. Soft sand colors, reflecting mirrors, waiters in white dinner jackets, and the best of all beachfront views at this second-level fine restaurant can keep you dallying over dinner for more than three hours, despite the fact that the service is the best in the Islands. There's a big bar situated near the restaurant's entry, but it doesn't seem to attract much of a bar crowd.

**House specialties** La Mer's signature fish tartare, a combination of raw hamachi, 'ahi, and salmon, is served with three caviars and three coulis. Two complete dinners of four and six courses are also offered nightly for $85–105. La Mer's soufflé with liliko'i sauce has gained regional fame for dessert.

**Other recommendations** Avoid the most expensive appetizers, such as fois gras of duck for $34, or Beluga caviar for $105, unless, of course, price is no object. Sample medallions of fresh Scottish salmon with golden gnocchi and caviar sauce, or veal chop sautéed with chanterelles. A sip of Port with a selection of French cheeses and walnut bread can be a perfect finish to the meal, though the symphony of La Mer desserts—a selection that includes poached pear with sabayon cream, almond biscuit Napoleon with hazelnut and coffee cream, or candied chestnut nougat in a chocolate tower—is perfect for more than one sweet tooth.

**Entertainment & amenities** Music drifts up from atrium below during dinner hour.

**Summary & comments** This is one of the few restaurants where jackets are suggested but long-sleeve dress shirts are required for men, and on breezy winter nights when the windows are open, women might also want to bring a light wrap. At press time, La Mer was Hawai'i's only AAA Five Diamond Award restaurant.

## *L'URAKU* ★★★★★

EURO-JAPANESE | MODERATE | QUALITY ★★★★★ | VALUE ★★★★ | ZONE 2

1341 Kapi'olani Boulevard, Honolulu; (808) 955-0552; www.luraku.com

**Reservations** Recommended **When to go** Anytime; for value you might try a weekender lunch menu, 4 courses including appetizer, salad entrée, and dessert, for $15–18 **Entrée range** Lunch $8.95–17.50, dinner $15.75–27.50, vegetarian $17.50 **Payment** VISA, MC, AMEX, DC, JCB **Service rating** ★★★★★ **Parking** Complimentary self-parking in garage **Bar** Full service **Wine selection** Good, 20 wines by the glass **Dress** Dressy casual **Disabled access** Good, via elevator from parking building **Customers** Islanders and a few tourists

**Lunch** Every day, 11 a.m.–2 p.m.

**Dinner** Every day, 5:30–10 p.m.

**Setting & atmosphere** L'Uraku has a festive, contemporary setting that comes alive in vibrant colors and multi-colored napkins on snowy white linen-covered tables. Kiyoshi, an artist whose pictures are displayed on the walls, hand-painted table vases, menu covers, and cheerful umbrellas that hang suspended from the ceiling. A big marble-topped black bar near the entrance to the dining room is a good place to relax if you forgot to make reservations.

**House specialties** In the finest dining experiences, each dish should offer up a little surprise in the way the flavors merge. L'Uraku offers many specialties in this vein—veal cheeks, slow-cooked and flavored with soy sauce, so tender they melt like butter; papio filet, pan-seared with a fragrant caper-butter sauce; lobster tomalley, marinated in its own juices, soy sauce, and mirin, then quickly fried with the shell on. The restaurant's approach to miso-yaki butterfish, a Japanese classic, is among the best you'll find in Hawai'i.

**Other recommendations** Assemble your own tasting menu by combining appetizers with downsized portions that the chef calls "Just a Taste," all in the $5–$9 range. Foie gras and pepper-seared 'ahi is touched with a raspberry reduction, yielding a perfect combination of savory and sweet. Sizzling moi carpaccio is flavored with the house-secret ponzu sauce (Japanese soy-citrus) and explodes with flavor. Try also the seared sea scallop served on a ragout made of bacon and salted mustard cabbage with a creamy kabayaki beurre blanc. That same mustard cabbage shows up in the house classic crab cake. L'Uraku regulars would emphasize the baked oyster—plump, succulent, and topped with crab meat and avocado.

**Summary & comments** L'Uraku bills its style as Euro-Japanese, and that is no gimicky pretension. The food here personifies the Japanese respect for clean, balanced flavors and artistry of presentation, fused with all the sophistication and depth of a fine French menu. In the last few years, Chef Hiroshi Fukui has taken his place among the three or four best chefs in the Islands. The dishes here surprise the palate with their complex levels of flavor, yet the chef always respects the freshness of his key ingredients and never covers them up with fussiness, loud spices, or brash sauces. The food here, unlike much traditional Japanese cooking, is extremely wine-friendly, and the staff is well trained in offering suggestions for excellent pairings. For something different, though, L'Uraku carries several premium sakes. Ask for a suggestion.

## MICHEL'S AT THE COLONY SURF ★★★★½

FRENCH/CONTINENTAL | EXPENSIVE | QUALITY ★★★★½ | VALUE ★★ | ZONE I

Colony Surf Condominium, 2895 Kalakaua Avenue, Waikiki; (808) 923-6552

**Reservations** Highly recommended **When to go** Sunset **Entrée range** $26–68.95 **Payment** VISA, MC, AMEX, DC, JCB **Service rating** ★★★★★ **Parking** Valet **Bar** Full service **Wine selection** Extensive, a dozen wines by the glass **Dress** Dressy **Disabled access** Good **Customers** Tourists, hotel guests, Islanders for special occasions

**Dinner** Every day, 5:30–9 p.m.

**Setting & atmosphere** For the romantically inclined, a seat at the ocean's edge, with flickering lights from torches casting shadows on surfers headed home in the setting sun, plus the lights of hotels twinkling all along Waikiki's crescent of white sand, are languid mood setters. This is a fine restaurant and one of the few where table-side service from carts is still the norm.

**House specialties** Michel's food has traditional roots, but it's beautifully presented in updated versions, so you may want to sip a perfectly-iced cocktail while you peruse the menu. Then choose the chef's Hudson Valley foie gras, sautéed and served with a sweet-and-sour poha berry sauce, or steak tartare. Michel's is probably the only restaurant left in Hawai'i that prepares steak tartare table-side, where the waiters mix in crushed capers and onions, Tabasco, ground pepper, and Worcestershire sauce with flair and serve the dish on toast points. Take your time: There's lobster bisque or Caesar salad to come, unless you go straight to an entrée of beef Wellington.

**Other recommendations** Escargot are a good garlicky introduction to Châteaubriand or a lighter crab capellini, sautéed scallops, or 'opakapaka with oyster mushrooms. Don't miss ordering a flambéed dessert to experience the waiter's artistry one last time. Crêpes suzettes, crème brûlée, or strawberries Romanoff (with vanilla cream Grand Marnier and kirsch sauce) are heavenly finales.

**Summary & comments** Plan on an extended dining experience; you may even want to finish dinner with a snifter of Hennessy X.O. Michel's is that kind of place—dreamy, traditional, and lethargy-inducing. And the sunset can't be beat—on a good evening you may even see the infamous green flash as the sun sets on the ocean's horizon.

## ORCHIDS ★★★★½

SEAFOOD/INTERNATIONAL | MODERATE/EXPENSIVE | QUALITY ★★★★½ | VALUE ★★★ | ZONE 1

Halekulani Hotel, 2199 Kalia Road, Waikiki; (808) 923-2311; www.halekulani.com

**Reservations** Highly recommended **When to go** Anytime, but sunset is best, particularly if you sit outside **Entrée range** $27–38 **Payment** VISA, MC, AMEX, DC, JCB **Service rating** ★★★★ **Parking** Valet **Bar** Full service **Wine selection** Extensive **Dress** Resort attire **Disabled access** Good **Customers** Tourists and Islanders

**Breakfast** Every day, 7:30–11 a.m.

**Brunch** Sunday, 9:30 a.m.–2:30 p.m.

**Lunch** Every day, 11:30 a.m.–2 p.m.

**Dinner** Every day, 6–10 p.m.

**Setting & atmosphere** This lovely, light, and airy room is decorated with orchids and has a peaceful feeling even when crowded. Ask to sit outdoors, where the view of Diamond Head seems bigger than life, and Waikiki Beach is just beyond the green lawn.

**House specialties** A well-stocked seafood bar set smack in the middle of the room is only one highlight of Orchids. As a full dinner, it's priced at entrée rates, but as an appetizer course with an entrée it's priced at a remarkable bargain (if you can eat that much), particularly considering that the buffet carries lobster thermidor (rich lobster meat prepared with a brandy cream sauce), as well as 'opakapaka with cucumber slices and wasabi mashed potatoes, garnished with fresh ginger and a citrus-mirin-sake sauce. Oysters on the shell, shrimp, 'ahi poke, smoked ono, seafood salads, and house-cured gravlax are just part of this bountiful buffet.

**Other recommendations** Baked Australian prawns stuffed with king crab and served with freshly made fettuccini, or aromatic five-spice chicken roasted in the tandoori oven, are a few of the interesting treats on a menu that ranges from imaginative to traditional—rack of lamb, filet, and lobster, for example. Lemon curd tart or Halekulani's own tropical sorbets in pineapple, guava, liliko'i, and lychee flavors are light, refreshing desserts.

**Entertainment & amenities** Sunday and Monday, 8:30–10:15 p.m., a pianist plays classical music in the restaurant's atrium; during the rest of the week, it's light jazz and contemporary tunes for diners' listening pleasure.

**Summary & comments** A perfect evening might begin with a cocktail outside at sunset at House without a Key next door, then dinner on the covered patio at Orchids.

## PADOVANI'S RESTAURANT & WINE BAR ★★★★½

MEDITERRANEAN/ISLAND FLAIR | MODERATE/EXPENSIVE | QUALITY ★★★★★ | VALUE ★★★ | ZONE 1

Doubletree Alana Hotel, 1956 Ala Moana Boulevard, Honolulu; (808) 946-3456; www.padovani:-e-gourmet.com

**Reservations** Recommended **When to go** Anytime **Entrée range** Breakfast $9–22, lunch $14–19 (prix fixe, $28), dinner $20–34, multi-course degustation menus $48–75 **Payment** VISA, MC, AMEX, DC, JCB **Service rating** ★★★★★ **Parking** Valet **Bar** Full service **Wine** selection Excellent; several wines by the glass in the restaurant, 24 in the Wine Bar. **Dress** Resort attire **Disabled access** Good **Customers** Hotel guests, tourists, Islanders

**Breakfast** Every day, 6–10 a.m.

**Lunch** Every day, 11:30 a.m.–2 p.m.

**Dinner** Every day, 6–10 p.m.

**Setting & atmosphere** Attention has been paid to every detail to create an elegant, gracious setting that reflects Island-inspired touches used in fine estate homes in Hawai'i. A *maile* lei painted on the wooden floor at the entry leads to the carpeted interior past a polished cherry-wood wine cruvinet. It dispenses several wines by the glass. Nothing but the best—Riedel crystal, Frette linens, Bernardaud china, and Christofle flatware—complements the Old World cart service. Rich golds, jade greens, and cherry-wood furnishings under a low ceiling add a warm, intimate touch. Light fixtures held by geometric chevrons have the look of 1930s Ossipoff-designed homes and were actually taken from a Hawai'i *kama'aina* home.

**House specialties** Philippe Padovani's Mediterranean-inspired dishes rely on herbs and natural seasonings to bring out the peak flavors of ingredients. The menu is divided into "Earth's Bounty" and "Flavors from the Sea," with a full range of appetizers and entrées on each side. The chef's best dishes burst with unique flavors and freshness. Begin the meal, for example, with Hawaiian sweet corn fresh clam chowder or vichyssoise of kiawe-smoked salmon and crab, elegant soups that will amaze you by how creamy and light they can be at the same time. Follow up with bouillabaisse of free-range chicken, crispy confit of duck leg, and pan-fried duck liver or the chef's favorite fish, John Dory, grilled.

The chef and his partner/brother, Pierre, are masters at desserts—more than a dozen are listed on the menu, from a luscious panna cotta of lemongrass and Hawaiian fruits to a créme brulèe with the unexpected pleasure of fresh ginger in the flavoring. The best way to experience them is to order the $15 Symphony of Desserts, with its many mini-portions. The Padovanis are also famed for their fresh sorbets and ice creams.

**Other recommendations** The upstairs Wine Bar offers a less expensive, more casual alternative to the Padovani experience. A generous menu of smaller plates is offered here. Half-portions of dishes such as grilled shrimp fettuccine are available, along with sandwiches, salads, an appetizer cart, carved roast of the day, and a selection of French cheeses.

Padovani has crafted a line of truffles made with Hawaiian Vintage Chocolate and filled with nougat, Amaretto, ginger, fruits, and liqueurs. They are available at his shop in the Royal Hawaiian Shopping Center as well as in gift boxes at the restaurant.

**Summary & comments** Chef/owner Philippe Padovani has a distinguished culinary background in Hawai'i as one of the founding chefs of the Hawai'i Regional Cuisine movement. On his arrival from France, he first served as executive chef of La Mer at the Halekulani Hotel; then he went to the Ritz-Carlton, Mauna Lani, where he launched the Big Island Bounty food festival; and finally he was executive chef at Manele Bay Hotel on Lana'i. Padovani's Bistro & Wine Bar is a family venture with his wife, Pierrette, managing restaurant service, and his brother, Pierre, serving as pastry chef. The Padovani brothers recently bought out their patron and partner and have refocused the menu to reflect more of Philippe Padovani's vision. As a matter of economy, the wine list has been trimmed down, although the Cruvinet system continues to offer an exclusive selection.

## PALOMINO EURO BISTRO ★★★

MEDITERRANEAN | INEXPENSIVE/MODERATE | QUALITY ★★★½ | VALUE ★★★★ | ZONE 2

Harbor Court, 66 Queen Street, Honolulu; (808) 528-2400

**Reservations** Recommended **When to go** Anytime **Entrée range** Lunch $5.95–18.95, dinner $6.95–22.95 **Payment** VISA, MC, AMEX, DC, D **Service rating** ★★★½ **Parking** Valet or self-park in Harbor Court garage **Bar** The full-service bar has one of the largest selections of scotch in town, plus a good selection of Champagnes, a dozen beers on tap, and grappa (Italian brandy) **Wine selection** Good, many by the glass **Dress** Casual **Disabled access** Via an elevator and ramps in the restaurant **Customers** Downtown office workers during lunch, Islanders and some tourists at dinner

**Lunch** Monday–Friday, 11:15 a.m.–2:30 p.m.; lunch is served until 3:30 p.m. in the lounge

**Dinner** Sunday–Thursday, 5–10 p.m.; Friday and Saturday, 5–11 p.m.

**Setting & atmosphere** Palomino seems very cosmopolitan in a glamorous way, with its extraordinary views of Honolulu Harbor through soaring windows and an interior that shines with rose marble–topped tables and counters, highlighted with African woods and art deco hand-blown glass ceiling fixtures.

**House specialties** Palomino's food is rustic Mediterranean-style in approach, well-seasoned with fresh herbs and spices and smoke-infused flavors. A 60-foot exhibition kitchen turns out spit-roasted tenderloins, and cracker-thin crusted pizzas come from a wood-burning oven.

**Other recommendations** Palomino is surprisingly affordable—maybe that's why Islanders can't stay away. The most expensive dinner entrée is whole-roasted Island snapper with Israeli couscous and Moroccan spices for less than $30. Pasta dishes are among the most reasonable, starting at less than $10 and topping out under $20, with spit-roasted seafood ravioli made with prawns, scallops, salmon, and Dungeness crab mascarpone and rosemary-lemon beurre blanc.

**Summary & comments** A curved marble bar that seats 70 is a fun place to meet friends, but be sure to use the valet parking; otherwise you'll get dizzy circling to the top of the parking building past floors of reserved stalls.

## THE PINEAPPLE ROOM ★★★½

HAWAIIA REGIONAL | MODERATE/EXPENSIVE | QUALITY ★★★★ | VALUE ★★★ | ZONE 2

Third floor of Liberty House, Ala Moana Center, Honolulu; (808) 945-8881

**Reservations** Recommended **When to go** Anytime **Entrée range** Lunch $13.50–$16.75, dinner $20–$29 **Payment** All major credit cards **Service rating** ★★★ **Parking** Free in the shopping center lot **Bar** Full service **Wine selection** Extensive **Dress** Casual **Disabled access** Good **Customers** Locals, business crowd, tourists

**Lunch** Daily, 11 a.m.–3 p.m.

**Tea** Monday—Saturday, 3–5 p.m.

**Dinner** Monday—Saturday, 4–9 p.m.

**Setting and atmosphere** The Pineapple Room is located in a department store, but in design and menu it challenges any definition of a shopping-center operation. It has its own entrance but is also accessible through the store, so if you have to wait for a table, you can always distract yourself with some shopping. The decor is warm and elegant, but with contemporary lines that don't intimidate. A large exhibition kitchen fills one corner of the room; consider taking a seat at the counter there if the restaurant's busy.

**House specialties** Chef de Cuisine Steven Ariel trained at the side of the acclaimed Alan Wong and is accomplished in both the Hawai'i Regional Cuisine tradition and in meeting Wong's strict standards. His creativity is displayed in large and small ways—for example, grilled salmon served on a bed of tea-flavored risotto that is rich, unique, and ultimately satisfying; or an Asian slaw that is a fresh, tangy mix of crunchy textures. Wood-fired pizzas are another specialty, topped with lobster, portobello mushrooms, or kalua pig. Pineapple Room crab cakes are generous and flavorful.

Whatever you eat here, leave room for dessert. Pastry chef Mark Okumura's chocolate crunch bars, granitas, tapiocas, and other specialties are all necessary evils.

**Other recommendations** Specials are extensive and change daily; they're always worth a look. The Pineapple Room also offers afternoon tea for $15, including plates of small bites, both savory and sweet. After-work drink specials and finger foods are served at the bar. On many Thursday nights, the restaurant offers five-course menus with wines. Sommelier Mark Shishido is considered among the best in the state for matching foods with wines, so these dinners are sure to offer some eye-opening pairings.

**Summary and comments** The Pineapple Room is the second of Alan Wong's Hawai'i restaurants, but it is different in menu and philosophy from his original King Street site. It is more casual and more accessible, with a bit lower price tag. The restaurant is a good spot to take a break while shopping, but it is also a destination in itself, drawing special-occasion diners attracted by the food, not the shopping.

## PRINCE COURT RESTAURANT ★★★★

HAWAI'I REGIONAL | MODERATE | QUALITY ★★★★½ | VALUE ★★★ | ZONE I

Hawai'i Prince Hotel, 100 Holomoana Street; (808) 944-4494; www.prince-hawaii.com

**Reservations** Highly recommended; required for Chef's Studio **When to go** Anytime, though sunset provides the loveliest view **Entrée range** $19–28 **Payment** VISA, MC, AMEX, DC **Service rating** ★★★★ **Parking** Valet or self-parking in hotel garage ($1 with validation) **Bar** Full service **Wine selection** Extensive, many domestic and imported Bordeaux and Burgundies, 20 wines by the glass **Dress** Resort attire **Disabled access** Good, via elevator **Customers** Islanders, hotel guests, tourists

**Breakfast** Every day, 6–10:30 a.m.

**Brunch** Sunday, 11:15 a.m.–1 p.m.

**Lunch** Every day, 11:30 a.m.–2 p.m.

**Dinner** Monday–Thursday, 6–9:30 p.m.; Friday–Sunday, 5:30–9:30 p.m.

**Setting & atmosphere** Views of boats bobbing lazily at the Ala Wai Yacht Harbor and sometimes a rainbow over nearby Magic Island through floor-to-ceiling windows give this spacious restaurant nearly as much appeal for lunch or Sunday brunch as for an evening repast. Tropical flowers on the tables add a Hawaiian touch.

**House specialties** The most popular item on the menu is a seafood extravaganza that includes Kona lobster, Island shrimp, and sea scallops with coconut saffron sauce, but the lemongrass crab-crusted 'opakapaka (red snapper) on seasoned crab with a Thai curry sauce comes in a close second. All dishes are artistically presented, but the best time to schedule dinner might be on Tuesday or Wednesday, for a Chef's Studio dinner, which includes a "flight" of wines (three matched to four courses). Three courses are prepared in front of guests in the restaurant, and then guests get a mini-tour of the kitchen while the chef completes the dessert course.

**Other recommendations** Monday, Tuesday, and Wednesday evenings, an appetizer shellfish bar featuring poke, sashimi, smoked fish, oysters, California hand rolls, and more, followed by a demi-entrée of the diner's choice, is a great way to sample a variety of Hawai'i's seafood specialties. Friday and Saturday nights, an abundant seafood buffet is a highlight.

The menu at Prince Court changes monthly, but a dessert standby is chocolate soufflé with vanilla ice cream and crème anglaise.

**Summary & comments** Prince Court offers spectacular buffets. Make it easy on yourself and use valet parking, as it's a tiresome drive up many levels to find an empty space in the parking garage.

## ROY'S RESTAURANT   ★★★★★

HAWAIIAN FUSION | MODERATE | QUALITY ★★★★★ | VALUE ★★★ | ZONE 2

Hawai'i Kai Corporate Plaza, 6600 Kalaniana'ole Highway; (808) 396-7697; www.roysrestaurant.com

**Reservations** Highly recommended **When to go** Anytime, though sunsets over Maunalua Bay are especially mood-inducing **Entrée range** $16–33 **Payment** VISA, MC, AMEX, D, DC, JCB **Service rating** ★★★★½ **Parking** Free in adjacent lot **Bar** Full service **Wine selection** Extensive, 10 wines by the glass **Dress** Casual **Disabled access** Good, via elevator **Customers** Islanders and tourists

**Dinner** Monday–Friday, 5:30–9:30 p.m.; Saturday, 5–10 p.m.; Sunday, 5–9:30 p.m.

**Setting & atmosphere** The lounge downstairs is fine in the evening for drinks and pupus, but upstairs is where the dining action is. The best tables, arranged around an exhibition kitchen, are those that are farthest from it and closest to the floor-to-ceiling windows, which look out over Maunalua Bay. This high-ceilinged restaurant is generally a full and vibrant (translate: noisy) place, a sign, says Chef Roy Yamaguchi, that people are having a good time. Soft pink walls decorated with artwork by Island artists, white tablecloths, and fresh flowers on the table complete the picture.

**House specialties** An extensive menu of special items, up to 20, which change every night, is where Roy's Restaurant shines. In addition, eight to ten different fresh fish in a myriad of preparations are available nightly. Tops on the list is steamed fish of the day drizzled with sizzling hot peanut oil and served with rice and Chinese vegetables. Crispy Thai chicken stuffed with Chinese noodles and an exotic mushroom-fungus served with chutney and macadamia nut curry sauce is a poultry favorite.

**Other recommendations** Some dainty eaters like to confine themselves to the appetizers, perhaps a cassoulet of escargot or teriyaki-glazed duck breast in Chinese black bean sauce, so they'll have room for dessert of hot chocolate soufflé or a cobbler made of fresh, seasonal fruit.

**Entertainment & amenities** Various musical entertainers perform in the downstairs lounge on weekends.

**Summary & comments** This is the original of chef Roy Yamaguchi's 20-plus restaurants. The number literally grows by the month as Yamaguchi, in partnership with Outback

Steakhouse, continues to open outlets across the country. The restaurant never feels like a chain operation, however. Yamaguchi has an unerring sense of flavor and has trained his staff well in maintaining his exceptional standards when he is away tending to his empire.

## SAM CHOY'S BREAKFAST, LUNCH, AND CRAB
## AND SAM CHOY'S DIAMOND HEAD                                    ★★★

HAWAI'I REGIONAL | MODERATE | QUALITY ★★★½ | VALUE ★★★ | ZONE 2

580 North Nimitz Highway, Honolulu; (808) 545-7979; www.samchoy.com
449 Kapahulu Avenue, 2nd level, Waikiki; (808) 732-8645

**Reservations** Recommended for dinner **When to go** Anytime **Entrée range** Lunch $6.50 and up, dinner $26.95 **Payment** VISA, MC, AMEX **Service rating** ★★★½ **Parking** Valet or nearby lot **Bar** Full service. A brewmaster at Choy's Big Aloha Brewery within the spacious BLC turns out 8 varieties of beer. His latest is Hibiscus White, infused with Island ingredients like Ka'u orange peel, hibiscus, and coriander. **Wine selection** Good **Dress** Casual **Disabled access** Good **Customers** Islanders, businesspeople at lunch, large family groups and others at dinner

**Brunch** *Sam Choy's Diamond Head:* Sunday, 9 a.m.–noon

**Breakfast** *Breakfast, Lunch, and Crab:* Monday–Friday, 6:30–11:30 a.m.; Saturday and Sunday, 6:30–11 a.m.

**Lunch** *Breakfast, Lunch, and Crab:* Every day, 10:30 a.m.–4 p.m.

**Dinner** *Breakfast, Lunch, and Crab:* Every day, 5–10 p.m.; *Sam Choy's Diamond Head:* Monday–Thursday, 5:30–9:30 p.m.; Friday–Sunday, 5–9 p.m.

**Setting & atmosphere** Breakfast, Lunch, and Crab has a lively atmosphere, with an exhibition kitchen, showcases full of fresh seafood, and table seating in more than one room for true old salts and junior sailors. It's a big restaurant with fun touches, like a fishing sampan with tables in it, and a fountain or two in the middle of the dining room so you can rinse your hands conveniently after ripping into cracked crab legs.

Sam Choy's Diamond Head Restaurant is less casual, with views of Diamond Head through an open window and an exhibition kitchen with counter seating, as well as linen-draped tables. It is no less popular, however.

**House specialties** At Diamond Head entrées such as local-style osso buco with Chinese noodles and shiitake mushrooms, seafood laulau (choice items wrapped in ti leaves and steamed), or the "Choy-sized" salad of the day served in a tortilla shell with local greens shock diners with their sheer sizes. At BLC, the focus is on seafood, with crab and lobster served steamed Chinese-style with black beans, roasted with garlic, or as part of a huge clambake.

**Other recommendations** To truly experience Sam Choy's food, you must try the poke (pronounced po-kay), a traditional Hawaiian appetizer of cubes of raw fish served with onions, soy sauce, seaweed, and various seasonings and oils. The closest Western approximation would be ceviche, but that's really not accurate. Choy is a serious aficionado of poke and offers it in many preparations with international flair. He even offers it fried for those who just can't do raw fish.

**Summary & comments** Chef/owner Sam Choy has chosen to focus lately on his growing star power, primarily television appearances and guest chef stints across the country. When he is in the house he is an unmistakable presence, but he has turned his kitchens over to chefs Elmer Guzman (Diamond Head) and Dave Hamada (BLC). It is these chefs' daily specials that many regulars first turn to on the menus. Both restaurants remain favorites with Islanders because of the large portions and playful treatment given to local standards.

## SANSEI SEAFOOD RESTAURANT AND SUSHI BAR ★★★★

CONTEMPORARY JAPANESE/PACIFIC RIM | MODERATE/EXPENSIVE | QUALITY ★★★★½ | VALUE ★★★★ | ZONE 2

Restaurant Row, 500 Ala Moana Blvd., Honolulu; (808) 536-6286

**Reservations** Recommended for dinner **When to go** Anytime **Entrée range** Lunch $5–8, dinner $16–24 **Payment** All major credit cards **Service rating** ★★★½ **Parking** Validated for Restaurant Row lot **Bar** Full service **Wine selection** Extensive list of wines by the glass and premium sakes **Dress** Casual **Disabled access** Good **Customers** Locals, business crowd, late-night club crowd, some tourists

**Lunch** Weekdays, 11 a.m.–2 p.m.

**Dinner** Daily, 5–10 p.m.; half-price specials after 10 p.m.

**Late-night** 10 p.m.–1 a.m.

**Setting and atmosphere** Owner D. K. Kodama likes his restaurants compact, active, and noisy. When this location debuted, it was more open, with seating spread out; Kodama felt the place seemed lonely at times, so he remodeled to collect the action around an open sushi bar on one side and a crowded bar on the other. Two private dining rooms are available. The decor is heavy on wood and blends Japanese with casual island sensibilities.

**House specialties** Concentrate on the appetizers and sushi rolls here. They're designed for sharing and play into the Sansei philosophy that dining should be fun. Entrées can be an overwhelming mix of competing flavors and are not the restaurant's strong point. Try instead the 'ahi tataki, with its strips of seared tuna in a tangy ponzu (soy-citrus) sauce and tossed with a refreshing mix of sprouts. Calamari salad is a favorite, its sweet, spicy sauce a perfect pairing for a cold beer. Mango salad crab roll, the tempura shrimp roll, and 69 roll (a California roll with strips of eel wrapped around the outside) all take the staid, Japanese sushi tradition and stand it on its head. If you deserve a treat, order the foie gras nigiri sushi, the best dish in the house, but an indulgence at $16.95 for two pieces.

**Other recommendations** Sansei is one of the best deals in town at lunchtime. The plates are generous and actually include fresh vegetable salads that are more than just piles of lettuce. Prices hover around $6 for some very good food. The Chinese chicken salad is a standout, as are the mahimahi or meatloaf sandwiches and the lightly battered and fried mochiko chicken. A small selection of sushi is also offered. Early eaters should note that the menu is half off from 5:30 to 6 p.m. nightly.

**Entertainment and amenities** Karaoke draws a noisy, youthful crowd on Thursdays and Fridays after 10 p.m. Drink specials and half-price sushi are offered after 10 p.m. every night.

**Summary and comments** Kodama is one of Hawai'i's most charismatic and ambitious chefs. His original Maui restaurant perfected his formula of bold, colorful dishes that invite sharing and smiles. On O'ahu, his secret weapon is his mother, Sandy, who works the dining room, offering extremely personal, friendly service. The staff and even the customers call her "Mom."

## SARENTO'S TOP OF THE "I"   ★★★½

ITALIAN | MODERATE/EXPENSIVE | QUALITY ★★★★ | VALUE ★★★ | ZONE 1

'Ilikai Hotel, 1777 Ala Moana Boulevard, Waikiki; (808) 955-5559;
www.ilihakaihotel.com

**Reservations** Recommended **When to go** Sunset is most romantic if sitting at window tables **Entrée range** $15.95–42.95 **Payment** VISA, MC, AMEX, DC, D, JCB **Service rating** ★★★★½ **Parking** Discounted with validation in hotel garage **Bar** Full service **Wine selection** Extensive **Dress** Resort attire **Disabled access** Adequate, via elevator **Customers** Tourists and Islanders

**Dinner** Every day, 5:30–9:30 p.m.

**Setting & atmosphere** The ride in the glass-sided elevator to Sarento's, perched high atop the 'Ilikai Hotel, sets a fantasy mood for this top-notch Italian restaurant. Waiters in dark jackets help adjust your lighting, individually controlled at booths that enjoy panoramic views of the Ala Wai Yacht Harbor, Waikiki's bright lights, and the beach or Diamond Head. The decor in this restaurant is as beautifully Italian (with graceful archways and a green-and-white tiled exhibition pizza and dessert kitchen) as the food. Frescoes on the walls of two cozy private dining rooms and in the main restaurant show scenes typical of the Mediterranean area—a mother cooking, grapes being crushed, gardens. One scene of a large family at the dining table depicts one of the restaurant's three owners, Aaron Placuorakis, his wife, two children, grandfather Sarento, grandmother, uncles, and aunts.

**House specialties** The risotto here has got to be among the best in Honolulu, and at a moment's notice, the chef can stir together any of dozens of variations. Homemade pastas, pizza from a wood-burning oven, osso bucco, filet wrapped with pancetta and topped with fontina cheese, and crisp Jerusalem artichoke chips are superb choices.

**Other recommendations** Lobster ravioli with mushroom cream sauce is a soul-satisfying entrée. Top dinner off with cool tiramisu made of lady fingers, espresso, mascarpone cheese, and liqueurs. *Hint:* One way to keep the dinner cost down here is to go between 5:30 and 6:30 p.m. for an early evening special that includes soup or salad, a choice of several entrées, and dessert. Pizzas are also a value if chosen as an entrée, ranging from $12.95 to $16.95.

**Summary & comments** By request, guests can take a gander at the restaurant's wine cellar and view a bottle of $9,500 Chateau Cheval Blanc stored with some 3,000 other wines.

## SINGHA THAI CUISINE ★★★★

THAI | INEXPENSIVE/MODERATE | QUALITY ★★★★½ | VALUE ★★★★ | ZONE I

Canterbury Place, 1910 Ala Moana Boulevard, Waikiki; (808) 941-2898

**Reservations** Highly recommended for dinner, accepted for lunch **When to go** Anytime **Entrée range** $11.95–31.95 **Payment** VISA, MC, AMEX, DC, JCB **Service rating** ★★★★½ **Parking** Free with validation in Canterbury Place lot **Bar** Full service **Wine selection** Extensive **Dress** Casual **Disabled access** Good **Customers** Tourists

**Dinner** Every day, 4–11 p.m.

**Setting & atmosphere** After dark Singha's exotic magic emerges, though it's not so evident during the lunch hour. During dinner, lights twinkle on the restaurant's mirrors and golden Buddha, and a fountain tinkles in the open-air patio dotted with orchids. Outdoor patio seating at umbrella tables is right next to the street but set at a lower level and surrounded by a wall so it feels like a private garden.

**House specialties** Blackened 'ahi summer rolls with a soy-ginger-sesame dipping sauce and shredded green mango, and boneless breast of duck with Panang curry sauce, successfully combine Hawai'i regional and Thai cuisine. Seafood lovers go for the grilled jumbo black tiger prawns with Thai peanut sauce, or lobster tail with Singha's signature Thai chili, ginger, and light black-bean sauce.

**Other recommendations** If you have qualms about choosing a balanced number of dishes from the à la carte menu, sampling menus for two, three, four, or five people are composed of an appetizer sampler plus an ample variety of entrées and rice, plus dessert, for just under $30 per person.

**Entertainment & amenities** Thai dancers in extravagant headdresses and colorful silk costumes perform on a tiny stage, while rose petals float through the air.

**Summary & comments** Named Honolulu's best Thai restaurant by Gayot's *The Best of Hawai'i Guide*, Zagat Survey, *Honolulu Advertiser*'s 'Ilima Awards, and *Honolulu Magazine*'s Hale 'Aina Awards. Chef/owner Chai Chaowasaree's food is a work of art (melons might be carved into flower shapes, for example) that balances fresh Island ingredients and flavors with Thai spices, fresh herbs, and reduced sauces.

## THE SURF ROOM ★★★½

CONTEMPORARY | MODERATE/EXPENSIVE | QUALITY ★★★½ | VALUE ★★★ | ZONE I

Royal Hawaiian Hotel, 2259 Kalakaua Avenue; (808) 923-7311
www.royal-hawaiian.com

**Reservations** Highly recommended **When to go** Sunset **Entrée range** Breakfast $10–21, lunch $10–20, dinner $25–40 **Payment** VISA, MC, AMEX, DC, D, JCB **Service rating** ★★★★ **Parking** Valet or validated self-parking in hotel garage **Bar** Full service **Wine selection** Good **Dress** Resort attire **Disabled access** Good **Customers** Hotel guests, other tourists, and Islanders for special occasions

**Breakfast** Every day, 6:30–11:30 a.m.

**Lunch** Every day, 11:30 a.m.–2:30 p.m.

**Dinner** Every day, 6–10 p.m.

**Setting & atmosphere** Near the entry to the Surf Room at the Mai Tai Bar, a hula dancer performs old favorites, such as "Lovely Hula Hands" or "The Hawaiian Wedding Song," to live Hawaiian music, while rustling palm trees and lapping ocean waves furnish a dreamy backdrop. The best seating is right beside the sands of Waikiki Beach, where you can watch couples stroll by in the moonlight.

**House specialties** Though Cajun-spiced crab pot-stickers might not sound Hawaiian, the plump little Chinese dumplings with a mustard cream sauce are a great way to dive into this menu, which claims to focus on the flavors of Hawai'i. Pan-fried Pacific salmon in a balsamic vinegar glaze with shiitake-garlic mashed potatoes, or togarashi-peppered 'ahi with Maui onion, Ka'u orange relish, and lime-soy vinaigrette, are two Island favorites.

**Other recommendations** A three-course dinner selection dubbed the Art of Food and Wine includes two glasses of wine for $39.95. Friday seafood buffets and Sunday brunches draw repeat visitors. If you've got a big appetite, the breakfast buffet is lovely to dawdle over.

**Summary & comments** The open-air atmosphere beside Waikiki Beach makes The Surf Room special, so for its fullest impact, request a table as close as possible to the sand. After dining, wander through the elegant old hotel and take a moment to enjoy what is left of the big trees and green lawns at the front entrance. This is the Waikiki from a more gracious era.

## *3660 ON THE RISE* ★★★★

CONTEMPORARY | MODERATE | QUALITY ★★★★½ | VALUE ★★★ | ZONE 2

3660 Wai'alae Avenue, Kaimuki; (808) 737-1177; www.3660.com

**Reservations** Highly recommended **When to go** Anytime **Entrée range** $19–25 **Payment** VISA, AMEX, MC, DC, D, JCB **Service rating** ★★★★½ **Parking** Free in garage **Bar** Full service **Wine selection** Well-rounded; primarily California wines; many great matches for Chef Siu's Euro-Asian-Island flavors **Dress** Resort attire **Disabled access** Good **Customers** Islanders and their visiting guests

**Dinner** Sunday, Tuesday–Thursday, 5:30–9 p.m.; Friday and Saturday, 5:30–10 p.m.; closed Monday

**Setting & atmosphere** Jade green marble floors, a black marble bar, frosted glass panels, and light wood accents are a cool background for this busy restaurant, where repeat clientele are likely to table-hop, saying hello to friends. Indoor tables seat 88, while a street-side lanai surrounded by plants holds another 25.

**House specialties** Appetizers of 'ahi katsu, duck confit ravioli, potato-crusted crab cake; entrées of flaky tempura catfish with ponzu sauce, Chinese steamed 'opakapaka (red snapper), or Angus New York steak 'alaea. Dessert lovers rave about the pastry chef's bread puddings.

**Other recommendations** Desserts are so good that it makes sense to order a sampler of three appetizers to share. Dine lightly on seared scallops with 'ahi taro cake and allow yourself to go crazy on desserts of warm chocolate soufflé cake with mocha sauce and ice cream or mile-high Wai'alae pie, which combines vanilla and coffee ice cream, macadamia brittle, and caramel and chocolate sauces for a sweet treat. For lunch, hale ice tea is a cooling limeade/tea blend, while French-press coffeepots make rich coffee to go with your favorite after-dinner cognacs.

**Summary & comments** Chef Russell Siu's chic restaurant has won countless awards and always places near the top overall in the Hale 'Aina Awards, but for the last two years the restaurant has won first place for its desserts. 3660 has the feel of a favorite neighborhood restaurant because it's outside Waikiki and is not a showy place, but the service and food make it worth the cab fare from your hotel.

# Maui

## *ANUENUE ROOM*

HAWAI'I REGIONAL | MODERATE/EXPENSIVE | QUALITY ★★★★ | VALUE ★★★ | ZONE 9

Ritz-Carlton Hotel, 1 Ritz-Carlton Drive, Kapalua; (808) 669-1665;
www.ritzcarlton.com

**Reservations** Highly recommended **When to go** Anytime except Sunday and Monday **Entrée range** $27–42 **Payment** VISA, MC, AMEX, DC, D, JCB **Service rating** ★★★★★ **Parking** Valet or free self-parking in hotel lot **Bar** Full service **Wine selection** Extensive, 20 wines by the glass **Dress** Dressy resort attire **Disabled access** Good **Customers** Resort guests and Islanders on special occasions

**Dinner** Tuesday–Saturday, 6–9 p.m.

**Lounge:** Every day, 5:30–11 p.m.

**Setting & atmosphere** This elegant room is dressed in rich koa wood, brocade draperies, and chandeliers, giving it an Old World, club-like atmosphere. The walls are decorated with landscapes of the Kapalua area by local artists, and impressive formal arrangements of flowers highlight the entry and the dining areas. A separate dining room with wall sconces carved in the shape of pineapples holds private parties of a dozen.

**House specialties** Start with the seared duck foie gras, a duck confit highlighted with pineapple and vintage port. For an entrée, barbecued rack of lamb with a *paniolo* (cowboy) glaze of poha berry and Zinfandel has a reputation as the best lamb on Maui, though lighter appetites might prefer orange-shoyu caramelized salmon served with gingered jasmine rice and Ka'u lime.

**Other recommendations** For big splurges, grilled Keahole lobsters are fresh from aquaculture tanks on the Big Island, or you can sample the succulent warm lobster in a hearts-of-palm salad dressed with fresh mango and black truffle vinaigrette. To complete what's sure to be a truly special evening, plan ahead and order the rich and light-as-air Grand Marnier or chocolate soufflé when you order your entrée, so it will be ready when you are.

**Entertainment & amenities** The Anuenue Lounge, next to the dining room, features live entertainment Tuesday–Saturday, 8–11 p.m.

**Summary & comments** To make a night of it, you might plan on coffee and cognac in the lounge after dinner. People do get out on the dance floor to cut the light fantastic. *Anuenue,* by the way, is the Hawaiian word for "rainbow"; the restaurant is so designated because rainbows are sometimes visible over the ocean from the Anuenue Room's windows.

## BAMBOO BISTRO

HAWAI'I REGIONAL | MODERATE | QUALITY ★★★★ | VALUE ★★★ | ZONE 7

300 Maalaea Road, Suite 300, Wailuku, Maui; (808) 243-7374

**Reservations** Recommended **When to go** Anytime **Entrée range** Lunch $6–13, dinner $20–30 **Payment** All major credit cards **Service rating** ★★★ **Parking** Complimentary valet **Bar** Full service **Wine selection** Good, 18 wines by the glass **Dress** Resort attire **Disabled access** Good **Customers** Locals, tourists

**Lunch** 11:30 a.m.–3 p.m. daily except Monday

**Dinner** 5:30–9 p.m. daily except Monday

**Setting and atmosphere** High, open ceilings and a sweeping view of Ma'alaea harbor and Maui's south shoreline give the Bamboo Bistro a comfortable, airy feel. You might see green sea turtles or even whales if you're there in the right season. Floors are covered in locally grown eucalyptus, walls in blond bamboo, the bar in black bamboo. The decor is Polynesian, but not the tacky type.

**House specialties** Take your food in small portions here. The chef advocates the Spanish style of tapas dining—although he calls it "tropas," for a tropical touch. Everything on the menu is available in sampling portions, family-style on platters for sharing, or as full-sized entrées. The fresh catch of the day may be ordered four tempting ways—simply grilled, herb-grilled, sesame-crusted, or steamed in banana leaf. Sauces are seamlessly paired with each presentation, from a spicy passion fruit to accompany the sesame-crusted fish to soy-mustard butter for the herb-grilled. Accompaniments include sweet potato Palau, with its surprising mix of coarsely mashed purple Okinawan sweet potato, banana, and taro. Meat dishes include succulent and tender spare ribs braised in black vinegar and star anise, and New York steak with a Szechuan-style salt-and-pepper rub.

**Other recommendations** Don't miss the salad specialties. A bed of baby greens is tossed with sweet strawberries in a Maui onion vinaigrette, then topped with goat cheese baked in phyllo dough. "Pure gastronomic bliss," one reviewer called it. Maui asparagus is served with hearts of palm in a coconut vinaigrette. The house Caesar salad is lightly dressed and includes slabs of 'ahi sashimi.

**Summary and comments** Chef Peter Merriman was the initial driving force behind the Hawai'i Regional Cuisine movement, and his dedication to fresh local produce is legendary. When he opened his first restaurant on the Big Island, Merriman would climb coconut trees, dive for fresh shellfish, and make with farmers deals they couldn't refuse so they'd grow top-quality tomatoes for him. A devotion to freshness is what drives the Bamboo Bistro.

## THE BAY CLUB RESTAURANT                                      ★★★

CONTINENTAL | MODERATE/EXPENSIVE | QUALITY ★★★½ | VALUE ★★★ | ZONE 9

Kapalua Bay Hotel, 1 Bay Drive, Kapalua; (808) 669-5656;
www.kapaluabayhotel.com

**Reservations** Highly recommended **When to go** Sunset **Entrée range** Lunch $9.75–14, dinner $25–38 (vegetarian $21) **Payment** VISA, MC, AMEX, DC, JCB **Service rating** ★★★★ **Parking** In adjacent lot **Bar** Full service **Wine selection** Good **Dress** Resort attire **Disabled access** Good **Customers** Islanders and tourists

**Lunch** Every day, 11:30 a.m.–2 p.m.

**Dinner** Every day, 6–9 p.m.

**Setting & atmosphere** Considered one of the loveliest oceanfront settings on Maui. Tables on the open-air deck fill up quickly, so it's best to make reservations and go early for the full romantic effect of sunset. Inside the restaurant resembles a gracious *kama'aina* beach home, with a fireplace near the entry, a piano surrounded by comfortable linen-draped tables, and low lighting.

**House specialties** From the moment you sit down to dinner, you can munch on crispy lavosh lavished with salmon mousse. At lunch, the Monte Cristo sandwich filled with ham, turkey, and Swiss cheese and sautéed in an egg batter is one of the most reasonable items on the menu. Caesar salad prepared table-side precedes main courses such as scallops and prawns with white truffle risotto and a veal demi-glacé, or a half roasted duck with butternut squash, or a more traditional filet mignon with chanterelles and foie gras sauce.

**Other recommendations** Hawaiian fish are caught fresh daily and can be ordered Mediterranean style (with tomato concasse, lemon, capers, parsley, garlic, and anchovies, in white wine butter sauce) or Oriental style (with shiitake mushrooms, scallions, cilantro, and soy and sesame oil sauce).

**Summary & comments** Shuttles run from Kapalua Bay and the Ritz-Carlton Kapalua, so resort guests do not need a rental car. However, for those staying at Kapalua Bay Hotel, a palm-shaded path along the ocean's edge is pleasant for a pre- or post-dinner stroll. Diners may charge checks to their rooms in either hotel.

## CHEZ PAUL'S ★★★★

FRENCH | MODERATE/EXPENSIVE | QUALITY ★★★★ | VALUE ★★★ | ZONE 7

Highway 30 (4 miles south of Lahaina), Olowalu Village; (808) 661-3843

**Reservations** Highly recommended **When to go** Anytime **Entrée range** $22–36
**Payment** VISA, MC, AMEX, D **Service rating** ★★★★ **Parking** Free in adjacent lot
**Bar** Full service **Wine selection** Good; wine cellar in restaurant **Dress** Resort attire
**Disabled access** Good **Customers** Islanders, a few tourists

**Dinner** Every day, seatings at 6 p.m. and 8:30 p.m.

**Setting & atmosphere** You might smell the garlic wafting in through your open car
window if you drive past this little blink-and-you'll-miss-it roadside restaurant at Olowalu.
Classical French Provençal cuisine is served at 14 linen-covered, candlelit tables. Two mir-
ror-lined walls make the place look bigger, and banquette seating upholstered in green
splashed with pink roses adds an Old World touch. A private dining room seats 22.

**House specialties** Repeat customers often order poisson des iles (fresh fish) with
beurre-blanc sauce, or medallions of veal simmered in chardonnay, lemon, and orange
jus, while the dessert to die for is profiteroles, puff pastry with ice cream in a warm
chocolate sauce.

**Other recommendations** Regulars regard as "très bien" an appetizer of escargot
de Bourgogne presented in their shells in garlic butter. We favored the 'opakapaka
Provençal (snapper with fennel and artichokes). Another recommended entrée is the
Tahitian, duck à l'orange presented with a variety of tangy fruits.

**Summary & comments** It's a nice surprise to learn that here, unlike on many contemporary French menus, soup or salad and vegetables are included with entrée items.
Chez Paul is owned by Belgium-born Lucien Charbounier, who joined with chef Patric
Callares in 1999 to update the menu. Chez Paul was named Maui's best French restaurant by the readers of *Maui News* in 1998 and has been recommended in *Travel/Holiday*
magazine.

## DAVID PAUL'S LAHAINA GRILL ★★★★

CONTEMPORARY AMERICAN | MODERATE/EXPENSIVE | QUALITY ★★★★½ | VALUE
★★★ | ZONE 9

127 Lahainaluna Road, Lahaina; (808) 667-5117; www.lahainagrill.com

**Reservations** Highly recommended **When to go** Early or late to avoid the 7 p.m.
crowd **Entrée range** $24–37 **Payment** VISA, MC, AMEX, DC **Service rating**
★★★★★ **Parking** On street or in adjacent lot **Bar** Full service **Wine selection**
Extensive, many by the glass **Dress** Resort wear **Disabled access** Good, separate
wheelchair access **Customers** Islanders and tourists

**Dinner** Every day, 6–10 p.m.

**Setting & atmosphere** This lively bistro, composed of two dining rooms plus the
Chef's Table (which provides an exceptional, personalized dining experience for up to

eight guests), is located next door to the old restored Lahaina Inn. The restaurant has a Victorian ceiling of pressed-tin panels embossed with an abstract design. Soft peach, blue, and sand tones in the decor are set off by simple black chairs at candlelit tables set with white linens, Mikasa china, and fresh flowers. In addition, the full menu is available for those seated at the bar.

**House specialties**  David Paul's signature dish of tequila shrimp with firecracker rice competes with the kalua duck with reduced plum wine sauce, seasonal vegetables, and Lundberg rice for first place on the dinner menu. Kona coffee–roasted rack of lamb boasts a full-flavored Kona coffee Cabernet demi-glaze served with garlic mashed potatoes.

**Other recommendations**  The vegetarian eggplant Napoleon and the Maui onion-crusted seared 'ahi (tuna) with vanilla bean rice and an apple cider soy-butter vinaigrette are light enough to reserve room for dessert—a luscious triple berry pie of raspberries, blueberries, and black currants topped with crème fraîche, or the Hawaiian Vintage Chocolate decadence, a flourless torte served with chantilly cream and raspberry port sauce. "Flights" of wine are offered nightly. Generally these consist of a tasting of three wines, either whites or reds.

**Entertainment & amenities**  Thursday through Saturday evenings, a jazz pianist plays and sings.

**Summary & comments**  If you'd like a quiet little table in the corner for a romantic dinner, ask for Table #28, #29, or #34. These tables for two are tucked into an out-of-the-way corner of the restaurant, where you can check out the action in the dining room, but the action can't check you out! A few of David Paul's most recent awards include *Honolulu Magazine*'s Hale 'Aina Award, received six years in a row for Best Maui Restaurant, as well as the 1998 Legendary Service Award, as voted by the readers of *Maui News*.

## GERARD'S

CONTEMPORARY ISLAND/FRENCH  |  MODERATE/EXPENSIVE  |  QUALITY ★★★★  |
VALUE ★★★★  |  ZONE 9

Plantation Inn, 174 Lahainaluna Road, Lahaina; (808) 661-8939;
www.gerardsmaui.com

**Reservations** Recommended **When to go** Anytime **Entrée range** $26.50–32.50
**Payment** VISA, MC, AMEX, DC, D, JCB **Service rating** ★★★★★ **Parking** In nearby
lot **Bar** Full service **Wine selection** Excellent, 10 wines by the glass **Dress** Casual
resort attire **Disabled access** Good for garden-level dining, adequate via a back entry
for in-house dining **Customers** Tourists and Islanders for special occasions

**Dinner**  Every day, 6–8:30 p.m.

**Setting & atmosphere**  Seated in this plantation-style inn, diners in Gerard's might feel as if they are eating in someone's gracious old-fashioned home dining room. Walls are papered in a pink-and-beige floral design, windows are stained glass, and tables are lit with candle lamps. You can also sit outside on a porch screened with plantings.

**House specialties** Starting with the appetizers, people rave about the calamari sautéed with lime and ginger and the shiitake and oyster mushrooms in puff pastry. Though the menu changes annually, chef/owner Gerard Reversade's confit of duck and his roasted Hawaiian snapper, served with vegetables and potato purée or rice pilaf, are a constant.

**Other recommendations** Islanders go for 'ahi tartare with taro chips; mainlanders love the fresh Kona lobster and avocado salad. Rack of lamb with mint crust is filling, but most people find room to share spoons over crème brûlée or flourless chocolate cake.

**Summary & comments** Reversade opened this special restaurant in 1982, and over the years his traditional French cuisine has been adapted to Island tastes, so sauces are lighter and hints of Island flavors and ingredients show up. He has been featured on PBS's *Country Cooking* and the Discovery Channel's *Great Chefs of America*. The wine list repeatedly receives *Wine Spectator*'s award of excellence.

## HALI'IMAILE GENERAL STORE ★★★★

HAWAI'I REGIONAL | MODERATE/EXPENSIVE | QUALITY ★★★★½ | VALUE ★★★ | ZONE 10

900 Hali'imaile Road, Hali'imaile; (808) 572-2666;
www.haliimailegeneralstore.com

**Reservations** Highly recommended for dinner **When to go** Anytime Monday–Friday **Entrée range** $17–32 **Payment** VISA, MC, DC, D, JCB **Service rating** ★★★★½ **Parking** In adjacent lot **Bar** Full service **Wine selection** Good, many by the glass **Dress** Casual **Disabled access** Adequate, via ramp **Customers** Islanders and tourists

**Lunch** Monday–Friday, 11 a.m.–2:30 p.m.

**Dinner** Monday–Friday, 5:30–9:30 p.m.

**Setting & atmosphere** Chef/owner Bev Gannon's Hawai'i Regional Cuisine is famous throughout the Islands, but you'll still feel as if you've made a discovery when you search out the restaurant, located in a restored 1920s plantation store in the middle of nowhere, surrounded by sugarcane and pineapple fields. The only drawback is that the noise level inside can be irritating if you like peace while dining.

**House specialties** The crab boboli is legendary for lunch, while for dinner it's a good idea to check the fish preparations, as they vary every night. As an appetizer, sashimi Napoleon, a crispy wonton layered with smoked salmon, 'ahi tartare, and sashimi and served with a spicy wasabi vinaigrette, is always in demand. Rack of lamb Hunan-style keeps Islanders coming back for more.

**Other recommendations** *Paniolo* ribs done with a secret lime barbecue sauce and coconut seafood curry also have local enthusiasts. As pastry chef, Gannon's daughter Theresa whips up chocolate macadamia nut caramel pies, liliko'i cheese torte (a sweet tart), gingerbread with caramelized pears, a variety of crème brûlées, and piña colada cheesecake.

**Summary & comments**  Chef Bev Gannon was one of the founding members of the Hawai'i Regional Cuisine movement and has been featured many times in national publications such as *Bon Appetit*. Locally the restaurant has won the Best Maui Restaurant title and is a favorite stomping ground for upcountry residents. *Hint:* It's a treat to see the store after dark during the Christmas season, when it's dressed in full holiday regalia.

## *HULA GRILL*

HAWAI'I REGIONAL  |  INEXPENSIVE/MODERATE  |  QUALITY ★★★★  |  VALUE ★★★★  |
ZONE 9

Whalers Village, 2435 Ka'anapali Parkway, Ka'anapali; (808) 667-6636;
www.hulapie.com

**Reservations** Recommended for dinner **When to go** Anytime, but it's best to sit on the open lanai at sunset **Entrée range** Lunch $6.95–10.95, dinner $14.95–24 **Payment** VISA, MC, AMEX, D, DC **Service rating** ★★★★ **Parking** Validated, in shopping center garage **Bar** Full service **Wine selection** Good, 10 wines by the glass **Dress** Casual **Disabled access** Good **Customers** Tourists and Islanders

**Lunch** Every day, 11 a.m.–10:30 p.m. (pizzas, salads, sandwiches served through the dinner hour in the casual Barefoot Bar area)

**Dinner** Every day, 5–9:30 p.m.

**Setting & atmosphere**  Hula Grill is set in a re-created Hawaiian plantation home, with the main dining room an open-air lanai at the ocean's edge. During the day you'll see beachgoers sunning and walking along Ka'anapali's golden sands; at night flickering torches light the path along the beach. Near the entry, koa walls and shelves in a library area are decorated with Hawaiian collectibles, while an exhibition kitchen allows you to watch the chefs if there's a wait for a table. Smokers can relax in a stepped-down waterfall room or a designated section of the Barefoot Bar.

**House specialties**  Even the appetizers are special at Hula Grill. As a starter you can order Asian-style dim sum, such as scallop and lobster pot-stickers served in bamboo baskets, or Hawaiian-style *pupus*, like wok-charred 'ahi seared on the outside, sashimi-style on the inside, and served with a dipping sauce of wasabi and shoyu.

Hula Grill's signature entrée is macadamia nut roasted fresh Island 'opakapaka, garnished with a sauce made of Hana rum and mango and served with bamboo rice. Some diners swear by the Hawaiian seafood gumbo, a linguini dish with fresh shrimp, fish, clams, and scallops that can be ordered from mild to spicy hot.

**Other recommendations**  At lunch this is a great place to pop by for a casual bite to eat, maybe a warm focaccia chicken sandwich with Monterey Jack cheese, roasted poblano pepper, avocado, and tomato–chili pepper aïoli. Pizzas topped with Puna goat cheese, fresh spinach, tomato, and mushrooms come crispy hot from the kiawe wood–fired oven. You might want to share Hula Grill's famous dessert—a homemade ice-cream sandwich, made with two chocolate macadamia-nut brownies, vanilla ice cream, and raspberry purée and whipped cream.

**Entertainment & amenities** It's easy to slip off the beach for a Lava Flow, a piña colada–like drink made with fresh coconut, pineapple juice, and rum and topped with a strawberry "eruption," during happy hour, when a guitarist and vocalist entertain from 3 to 5 p.m. Hawaiian musicians return during dinner hours from 6:30 to 9 p.m., and hula dancers sway at table-side around 7 p.m. every night.

**Summary & comments** Chef Peter Merriman is the same Big Island chef who was instrumental in officially founding the Hawai'i Regional Cuisine movement. Merriman's other restaurant on the Big Island offers a completely different dining experience than Hula Grill, though both are true to fresh Island ingredients. Hula Grill has won the Restaurant of Distinction Award and been named as the Maui restaurant with the best ambience for three years in a row by the readers of *Maui News*.

## KIMO'S                                                          ★★½

STEAK AND SEAFOOD | INEXPENSIVE/MODERATE | QUALITY ★★★ | VALUE ★★★★ | ZONE 9

845 Front Street, Lahaina; (808) 661-4811; www.hulapie.com

**Reservations** Recommended for dinner **When to go** Anytime; to sit outside in the upstairs dining room, go early—it's first-come, first-seated **Entrée range** Lunch $6.95–10.95, dinner $6.95–23.95 **Payment** VISA, MC, AMEX, DC, D, JCB **Service rating** ★★★½ **Parking** Limited on-street or use Lahaina Center lot and walk a couple of blocks **Bar** Full service **Wine selection** Good, 8 wines by the glass **Dress** Casual **Disabled access** Access to the main dining room upstairs is inadequate for wheelchairs, but seating is available downstairs in a secondary dining area near the bar **Customers** Tourists, some Islanders

**Lunch** Every day, 11 a.m.–3 p.m.

**Pupus** Every day, 3–5 p.m.

**Dinner** Every day, 5–10:30 p.m.

**Bar** Every day, open until 1:30 a.m.

**Setting & atmosphere** This two-level restaurant is a casual place where it's easy to drop by for lunch or a cocktail downstairs at sunset, then find your way upstairs for dinner. Kimo's takes full advantage of its ocean's-edge setting, with an open lanai perched one story above the rocks and lapping waves. Signal flags promote the sailing motif, and tropical foliage adds an Island touch. At night, flaming torches cast flickering shadows on the spreading limbs of a rustling monkeypod tree. You can order from the full menu or a lighter menu at the bar, which seats 22 downstairs.

**House specialties** Kimo's fresh fish might be ono, 'ahi, onaga, a'u, mahi, opah, 'opaka-paka, or lehi, depending on what comes in on any given day. Of four preparations, Kimo's Style, baked in garlic, lemon, and sweet basil glaze, has widespread approval.

**Other recommendations** Meat eaters swear by the prime rib, but fencesitters are likely to choose the top sirloin and Tahitian shrimp (touched up with a bit of garlic and cheese) combination. Try a lighter, healthier lunch, such as the veggie sandwich that boasts Maui onions, fresh tomatoes, sprouts, cheese, and avocado, and then you can afford to top it off with the dessert that sailors swim to shore for—the original hula pie, a wedge of vanilla macadamia-nut ice cream nestled in an Oreo cookie crust.

**Entertainment & amenities** Kimo's is the place to be Friday and Saturday nights from 10 p.m. to midnight, when live rock-and-roll music livens the night. Monday–Friday, 7–8 p.m., there's live Hawaiian music.

**Summary & comments** Interestingly, local people voted Kimo's, in the heart of touristy Lahaina, Maui's best restaurant in the *Honolulu Advertiser*'s 'Ilima Awards. The restaurant has neither a "big-name" chef nor a nationwide reputation, but Kimo's entrées come with Caesar salad, carrot muffins, sour cream rolls, and steamed herb rice, so you don't go broke ordering à la carte. Generous portions and fairly priced food of a consistent quality probably had a lot to do with the vote, too. It's one of the nicest Lahaina bars to sit in and have a drink at sunset.

## LONGHI'S                                              ★★★½

MEDITERRANEAN/ITALIAN | MODERATE | QUALITY ★★★★ | VALUE ★★★★ | ZONE 9

888 Front Street, Lahaina; (808) 667-2288; www.longhi-maui.com

**Reservations** Recommended for dinner **When to go** Anytime **Entrée range** Breakfast $2.50–12.50, lunch $8–16, dinner $17–27, except for lobster at $55 **Payment** AMEX, VISA, MC, DC, D, JCB **Service rating** ★★★ **Parking** Free valet at dinner, free self-parking in adjacent lot **Bar** Full service **Wine selection** Extensive, many Italian wines and 3 house wines, 20 by the glass **Dress** Casual **Disabled access** Good for downstairs dining **Customers** Tourists and Islanders

**Breakfast** Every day, 7:30–11:30 a.m.

**Lunch** Every day, 11:45 a.m.–4:45 p.m.

**Dinner** Every day, 5–10 p.m.

**Setting & atmosphere** This sleek, cosmopolitan, open-air restaurant has a fun and casual ambience. Big black-and-white tiles cover the floor downstairs, interrupted only by a wide staircase that leads upstairs to additional koa-topped tables open to the trade winds.

**House specialties** Here, nobody wants to stop at just one appetizer, even if it's as good as the grilled portobello mushrooms with goat-cheese pesto. Follow it with shrimp Longhi, a classic first, served on opening night more than 20 years ago. Plump white shrimp are sautéed in butter, lemon juice, and white wine, then fresh Maui basil and tomatoes are simmered before it's all served on garlic toast. Fresh white fish, often onaga, prepared with white wine and garnished with grapes, is another longtime specialty.

**Other recommendations** The in-house bakery prepares oven-fresh cinnamon buns, macadamia-nut rolls, coffee cakes, quiches, and cheesy jalapeño and pizza bread. Pastas, freshly made on the premises, and salads, all composed of fresh vegetables, are available both at lunch and dinner. Desserts are presented on a tray and served to you even as you point your finger at macadamia-nut pie, cheesecake, or strawberry mousse cake, though you may want to order a special chocolate or Grand Marnier soufflé in advance.

**Entertainment & amenities** Longhi's is the place to be on Friday nights from 9:30 p.m. to closing, when various live bands play music to swing to on the upstairs dance floor.

**Summary & comments** Created in 1976 by "a man who loves to eat," Bob Longhi, the restaurant has remained a family affair, with son Peter the general manager and daughter Carol O'Leary an executive chef. It's a winning combination, as the restaurant won best overall restaurant in the *Maui News* readers poll in 1998 and has repeatedly received *Wine Spectator*'s Best Award of Excellence since 1988. Longhi's has an all-verbal menu, which can prove irritating or exciting, depending on your mood. On the plus side, it gets diners to interact with the waiter, new menu items can be introduced easily, and you can get a true description of the food that you order. On the other hand, it can be difficult to remember all the choices (especially if you've had a libation or two), and it's easy to lose track of what you're spending.

## MA'ALAEA WATERFRONT RESTAURANT ★★★½

SEAFOOD/CONTINENTAL | MODERATE | QUALITY ★★★★½ | VALUE ★★★ | ZONE 7

50 Haouli Street, Ma'alaea; (808) 244-9028; www.waterfrontrestaurant.com

**Reservations** Highly recommended **When to go** Sunset for outside **Entrée range** $17.95–54 **Payment** VISA, MC, AMEX, DC, D, JCB **Service rating** ★★★½ **Parking** Free in upper level of adjacent condominium garage **Bar** Full service **Wine selection** Extensive, 30 by the glass **Dress** Resort attire **Disabled access** Adequate, via elevator **Customers** Islanders and tourists

**Dinner** Every day, 8:30 p.m.–closing

**Setting & atmosphere** Remodeled in 1998, this elegant oceanfront restaurant has pretty textured pale green walls, white tablecloths decorated with candles and tropical flowers, and scenic Island paintings on the walls. Outdoor dining on the deck is lovely on a balmy night, but bring a sweater if the trade winds are up.

**House specialties** Depending on what the fishermen bring in, seven or eight different kinds of Island fish are served daily in your choice of nine preparation styles. This means there are always 50 or more choices to make while you nibble on homemade bread slathered with the house's special beer-cheese spread or watch the table-side preparation of your Caesar salad.

**Other recommendations** Besides the rack of lamb, Ma'alaea Waterfront specializes in game meats, so you might find venison, red deer, pheasant, or ostrich, on a rotating basis. For dessert, the white chocolate blueberry cheesecake will satisfy every cheesecake aficionado.

**Summary & comments** Ma'alaea Waterfront Restaurant is a family endeavor, opened in 1990 by the Smiths: Bob, the chef; Gary, the manager; and Rick, the detail man. Their success is evidenced by the fact that the restaurant has repeatedly been named by the readership of *Maui News* as the restaurant with the best seafood and best service. Local voters repeatedly mention the warmth of the proprietors and the intimate ambience of the room.

## MAMA'S FISH HOUSE ★★★½

SEAFOOD | MODERATE/EXPENSIVE | QUALITY ★★★★½ | VALUE ★★★ | ZONE 9

799 Poho Place, Ku'au; (808) 579-8488; www.mamasfishhouse.com

**Reservations** Highly recommended **When to go** Anytime, but sunset is most romantic **Entrée range** Lunch $14–28, dinner $27–36 **Payment** VISA, MC, AMEX, DC, D, JCB **Service rating** ★★★★ **Parking** Valet or adjacent lot **Bar** Full service **Wine selection** Excellent, half a dozen by the glass **Dress** Casual resort wear **Disabled access** Good, but it's some distance from the lot **Customers** Tourists and Islanders

**Lunch** Every day, 11 a.m.–3 p.m.

**Pupus** Every day, 2:30–3 p.m.

**Dinner** Every day, 5–9:30 p.m.; closed Christmas Day

**Setting & atmosphere** You'll find Mama's reminiscent of a rambling, open-air beach house, at the end of a gecko-patterned walkway beside the ocean, with cool green lawns and shady coconut palms out front. A wooden bar and wooden paneling inside are made of tropical almond, monkeypod, and mango wood. It's a perfect place to while away an afternoon over a Mai Tai Roa Ae—the same kind of fresh fruit and rum concoction originated by Trader Vic's years ago—or to sample other retro drinks: Singapore Slings of Raffles hotel fame, Zombies, and Scorpions.

**House specialties** Fishermen get written credit for catching the fresh fish on this menu, so the fish is always top-notch, whether you have ono, 'ahi, uku, or opah. Preparations include sautéed with garlic butter, white wine, and capers; grilled with Thai red curry; fried with Maui onion, chili pepper, and avocado; or served with honey-roasted macadamia-nut-lemon sauce. A signature dish, Pua me hua Hana, features sautéed fish with fresh coconut milk and lime juice served surrounded by fresh tropical fruit and accompanied by Moloka'i sweet potatoes.

**Other recommendations** To sample Island-style cooking, try a laulau, a bundle of mahimahi baked in ti leaves and served with tender, moist kalua pig. Another imaginative entrée with local flair is crispy kalua duck with mango-mui glaze served with baby bok choy and wild rice. Traditionalists can always get Black Angus New York steak or veal shank roasted with Asian spices served with portobello mushrooms, wasabi mashed potatoes, and Kula vegetables.

**Summary & comments** In 1999, the Fish House added rattan tables and chairs and decorated an open-air area near the entrance to look like old Hawai'i—they dubbed it "Grandma's Living Room." The room has become a popular spot for locals, who come to hang out, listen to the strains of vintage music, and nibble on *pupus* rather than order a full-blown meal from a menu that most Islanders consider "higher end." In contrast to the windsurfers who show up from nearby Ho'okipa Beach, there are occasional celebs—Jason Alexander for one—who have discovered the charms of Mama's Fish House and Grandma's Living Room. For five consecutive years, Mama's has won a five-diamond award from *Hospitality Sciences*. Locally, *Maui News* readers have named it as serving the best seafood, and it has been named a restaurant of distinction in *Honolulu Magazine*'s Hale 'Aina Awards.

## PACIFIC'O ★★★★½

HAWAI'I REGIONAL | MODERATE | QUALITY ★★★★½ | VALUE ★★★ | ZONE 9

505 Front Street, Lahaina; (808) 667-4341; www.pacificomaui.com

**Reservations** Recommended **When to go** Sunset for best ocean views **Entrée range** Lunch $8.50–14.50, dinner $19–25 **Payment** VISA, MC, AMEX, DC, JCB **Service rating** ★★★★ **Parking** Free in lot across the street **Bar** Full service **Wine selection** Excellent **Dress** Casual **Disabled access** Adequate, but it's a long way from the parking lot **Customers** Tourists and Islanders

**Lunch** Every day, 11 a.m.–4 p.m.

**Dinner** Every day, 5:30–9 p.m.

**Setting & atmosphere** This is a pleasant spot for indoor or outdoor dining at tables shaded by umbrellas and set right at the edge of the ocean. Inside, ceiling fans suspended above the checked marble floor lazily stir the air. A long bar is bordered by tables beside windows wide open to the ocean breezes and to views of three islands.

**House specialties** You'll see why Chef James McDonald has won Taste of Lahaina competitions ever since 1993 when you try his appetizer of prawns and basil wontons served with a spicy sweet-and-sour sauce and Hawaiian salsa. Another Taste of Lahaina winner is Asian Gravlax, slices of house-cured salmon on a warm sweet-potato applejack with wasabi chive sour cream, radish sprouts, and caviar.

**Other recommendations** Artistic presentations include fresh fish, prepared seared in sesame with Kula lettuce and wasabi, or tandoori-flavored with Indonesian spices and caramelized Maui pineapple, or crispy deep-fried in a seaweed wrapper, or steamed in shiitake-sake bouillon in an old-fashioned Chinese bamboo steamer. A melt-in-your-mouth dessert of pineapple lumpia and macadamia nut ice cream is a beautiful blend of texture and taste.

**Entertainment & amenities** Thursday–Saturday nights 9 p.m.–midnight, the indoor/outdoor restaurant at ocean's edge attracts jazz aficionados with live jazz performances.

**Summary & comments** The same chef/owner, James McDonald, also owns I'o, a black-and-white metallic modern restaurant next door.

## PLANTATION HOUSE RESTAURANT ★★½

CONTEMPORARY | INEXPENSIVE/MODERATE | QUALITY ★★★★ | VALUE ★★★ | ZONE 9

Plantation Course Clubhouse, 2000 Plantation Club Drive, Kapalua Resort; (808) 669-6299; www.theplantationhouse.com

**Reservations** Recommended for dinner **When to go** Anytime **Entrée range** Lunch $6.50–13, dinner $21–25 **Payment** VISA, AMEX, MC, DC **Service rating** ★★★ **Parking** In adjacent lot **Bar** Full service **Wine selection** Extensive **Dress** Casual **Disabled access** Good, drop off at front door **Customers** Golfers, tourists, and Islanders

**Breakfast & lunch**  Every day, 8 a.m.–3 p.m.; light menu 3–5 p.m.

**Dinner**  Every day, 5:30–9 p.m.

**Setting & atmosphere**  Cool mountain breezes and views of velvety-green fairways and distant blue ocean are a calming backdrop seen through paned windows that open to catch the breeze. Natural light woods, comfortable rattan chairs, and lazy overhead fans add to the relaxing atmosphere. A double-sided fireplace creates a warm glow in the evening, and by the bar, a big mural of workers in the pineapple fields depicts Kapalua's plantation past.

**House specialties**  Plantation House is known for Australian double-cut lamb chops with rosemary-bordelaise sauce and for fresh Island fish—try the Taste of the Rich Forest preparation, done with a mushroom crust on a bed of tot soi (Chinese spinach) with garlic mashed potatoes. Mediterranean-inspired fresh fish specials are seasonal and change monthly.

**Other recommendations**  A wide variety of appealing choices exists: smoked salmon Benedict dotted with capers for breakfast; chicken Caesar salad, burgers, or pasta at lunch; and desserts that range from old-fashioned Moloka'i sweet bread pudding to flashy bananas Foster, or da kine brownie with vanilla ice cream, chocolate sauce, whipped cream, and macadamia nuts.

**Summary & comments**  Chef Alex Stanislaw is coaxing this restaurant away from typical golf-course food to provide a more elevated dining experience in the Pacific Rim style. Specials incorporate the flavors of Italy and southern France, showcasing fresh local produce. The aim now is more fish and salads, less meat and starch. Plantation House is a work in progress, but it is a good alternative to the pricier restaurants of the Kapalua Resort hotels. Guests of both hotels may charge meals to their rooms and ride a free shuttle to the restaurant.

## ROY'S KAHANA BAR & GRILL
## AND ROY'S NICOLINA                       ★★★½

HAWAIIAN FUSION | MODERATE | QUALITY ★★★★ | VALUE ★★★★ | ZONE 9

Kahana Gateway Shopping Center, 4405 Honoapi'ilani Highway, Kahana; (808) 669-6999; www.roysrestaurant.com

**Reservations**  Highly recommended **When to go** Anytime **Entrée range** $13–26 **Payment** VISA, MC, AMEX, DC, D, JCB **Service rating** ★★★★½ **Parking** Free in shopping center lot **Bar** Full service **Wine selection** Excellent, 10–15 by the glass **Dress** Casual **Disabled access** Good, via elevator to upstairs restaurants **Customers** Tourists and Islanders

**Dinner**  Nicolina: every day, 5:30–9:30 p.m.; Roy's Kahana Bar & Grill: every day, 5:30–10 p.m.

**Setting & atmosphere**  Even owner Roy Yamaguchi admits there's not a lot of difference between these two restaurants that sit side by side on an upstairs level of a West Maui shopping center. Originally, he opened them with differing concepts in mind, but found that people liked his original ideas, so both restaurants are guided by the same corporate chef, and both offer 20 to 25 specials nightly. Roy's Kahana has a long bar near the entry and a centrally located open kitchen, so the high noise level seems to make it more suited to a lively, younger crowd, while Nicolina has a quieter appeal. Nicolina's kitchen is enclosed, but diners can enjoy lanai seating. Both have wooden-topped tables and local artwork that changes every six weeks; the art is available for sale.

**House specialties** Since items change so rapidly, you never know what you'll find, but everything is made with the freshest local ingredients and has Euro-Asian and international flavorings. Appetizers like Szechuan baby-back ribs or Roy's shrimp and pork spring rolls with hot sweet mustard and black bean sauce set a spicy scene for perhaps a lighter entrée. Lemongrass-crusted shutome (swordfish) reflects a touch of Thailand, with sticky rice and basil peanut sauce. Hibachi-style salmon and blackened 'ahi entrées are signature items in both restaurants.

**Other recommendations** The left side of the menu is made up of Roy's signature dishes, prepared the same throughout the chain, down to the garnishes. The right side reflects the in-house chef's daily inspirations, which lean more toward Hawaiian than Asian flavors. For a standard dish worth a taste, try the dim sum "canoe" for two, a sampling of the traditional Chinese treats done up with more Hawaiian ingredients.

**Summary & comments** Roy Yamaguchi has won so many awards that it's difficult to credit them to his specific restaurants. *Gourmet* magazine's Top Tables, *Honolulu* magazine's top 20, *Maui News*'s best overall Maui restaurant, the James Beard Foundation, and many others applaud this imaginative and energetic chef, whose name was attached to more than 20 Roy's restaurants (with plans for more) throughout the country in 2002.

## A SAIGON CAFÉ

VIETNAMESE | INEXPENSIVE | QUALITY ★★★★ | VALUE ★★★★★ | ZONE 7

1792 Main Street, Wailuku; (808) 243-9560

**Reservations** Recommended, especially for dinner **When to go** Anytime **Entrée range** $6.75–17.95 **Payment** VISA, MC, AMEX, DC, D, JCB **Service rating** ★★★★ **Parking** In adjacent lot **Bar** Full service **Wine selection** Limited **Dress** Casual **Disabled access** Good **Customers** Islanders and a few tourists

**Lunch & dinner** Every day, 10 a.m.–8:30 p.m.

**Setting & atmosphere** Sit at the low wooden bar with roll-around chairs, or choose a Formica-topped table or booth for lunch and dinner in this basic, white-walled restaurant minimally decorated with Vietnamese carved and lacquered art. A gold statue of Buddha greets guests at the door, ceiling fans whir overhead, and the TV might be on at the bar. It's a low-key place that can be difficult to find because there is no sign.

**House specialties** It's almost de rigueur to start with cha gio (fried spring rolls)—little deep-fried bundles of ground pork, long rice, carrot, and onion wrapped in rice paper; the waiter will show you how to roll them in romaine lettuce with mint leaves and vermicelli noodles, then dip them in sweet-sour garlic sauce before enjoying them.

Among any number of in-demand Vietnamese entrées, garden party shrimp dipped in a light batter, deep-fried, and served with sautéed ginger and green onions on bean sprouts and lettuce (with rice on the side) is one of the most delicious.

**Other recommendations** With 92 items on the menu, it's hard to make a choice, let alone describe the best. Green papaya salad is a much-loved starter. For lunch, any of the noodle soups—with seafood and chicken, calamari and shrimp, or wonton, and others—provide a big bowl of steaming goodness. There are several rice-in-a-clay-pot variations done with chicken, catfish, shrimp, or pork.

**Summary & comments** Everybody loves A Saigon Café, and regulars love the proprietor, Jennifer Nguyen, as well. Nguyen opened the restaurant in January 1996, but the identifying sign is still stored in a box somewhere. The sprightly, hard-working proprietor says, "We've been so busy, we've never gotten around to putting it up!"

## SANSEI SEAFOOD RESTAURANT
## AND SUSHI BAR ★★★★

JAPANESE/PACIFIC RIM | MODERATE/EXPENSIVE | QUALITY ★★★★½ | VALUE ★★★★ | ZONE 9

The Shops at Kapalua, 115 Bay Drive, Kapalua; (808) 669-6286; www.sanseihawaiian.com

**Reservations** Highly recommended **When to go** Anytime **Entrée range** $12.95–37.95 **Payment** VISA, MC, AMEX, D, JCB **Service rating** ★★★★ **Parking** In shopping-village lot **Bar** Full service **Wine selection** Extensive **Dress** Resort attire **Disabled access** Adequate **Customers** Islanders and tourists

**Dinner** Every day, 5:30–10 p.m.; karaoke Thursday and Friday from 10 p.m.

**Late night:** Tuesday–Saturday, 10 p.m.–2 a.m.

**Setting & atmosphere** Booths and tables fill up fast in the intimate 120-seat restaurant, which includes a sushi bar and cocktail lounge area, so reservations are wise. Restaurant decor blends a bit of Japan with a Maui plantation look. The glass panel of the entry door is etched with a pineapple, and a window beyond the bar showcases a garden of tropical plants. There are samurai pictures on the walls, and the sushi bar, with its scalloped awning, could have come straight from Tokyo (as some of the sushi chefs did).

**House specialties** The idea here is to try a lot of dishes and share. With sushi this is a no-brainer, and Sansei offers up delicious tidbits from crab and mango salad hand roll to spider rolls with soft-shell crab to bagel rolls with smoked salmon, Maui onion, and cream cheese. The family-style concept applies to the entrées as well. Pass around the house special Peking duck breast with shiitake potato risotto. Other favorites: Asian rock shrimp cake and nori ravioli of shrimp and lobster.

**Other recommendations** Pay attention when the waiter describes nightly specials like asparagus tempura and fresh fish preparations, or try shrimp tempura deep-fried in a light-as-air batter, or a healthy preparation of grilled fresh mahimahi on Kula greens. Granny Smith baked apple tart is a pure American finish to any meal.

**Entertainment & amenities** Sansei's karaoke after 10 p.m. on Thursday and Friday draws a happy crowd.

**Summary & comments** Even big-name Maui chefs gather at this casual restaurant set unobtrusively in the Kapalua Shops center. Chef/owner D. K. Kodama says his menu reflects the way he likes to eat, with playful flavors and bits of this and that. In 1999, Sansei was named Best Maui Restaurant by *Honolulu Magazine*'s Hale 'Aina Awards, and in 1998 *Maui News* readers called it the best sushi bar on Maui.

## SEASONS ★★★★½

HAWAI'I REGIONAL | MODERATE/EXPENSIVE | QUALITY ★★★★½ | VALUE ★★★ |
ZONE 8

Four Seasons Resort, 3900 Wailea Alanui, Wailea; (808) 874-8000;
www.fourseasons.com

**Reservations** Highly recommended **When to go** Sunset is spectacular from the panoramic seating on the lower level **Entrée range** $36–42; multi-course tasting menus, $78–145 **Payment** AMEX, VISA, MC, DC, D, JCB **Service rating** ★★★★★ **Parking** Complimentary valet or self-parking in covered hotel lot **Bar** Full service **Wine selection** Extensive; tops on the list is a 1994 Silver Oak Alexander Valley for $160; a dozen wines by the glass **Dress** Resort attire, jackets optional **Disabled access** Good, via elevator **Customers** Hotel guests and Islanders for special occasions

**Dinner** Tuesday–Saturday, 6–9:30 p.m.

**Setting & atmosphere** Seasons enjoys a spectacular setting, with sweeping ocean vistas the entire length of Wailea's coastline offering glimpses of the island of Kahoolawe through the tops of swaying coconut palms. Superbly executed service complements the understated decor of crisp white linen tablecloths, oversized hurricane lamps, and unassuming French china. Natural materials accent the decor with caramel-colored marble side tables, slate tile floors on the lower lanai, and heavy rattan and leather chairs throughout.

**House specialties** One of Hawai'i's most popular fish, onaga, is seared crispy on top with julienned endives and puréed snow peas, or you might want to try an updated version of an old favorite, roasted rack of lamb in a Cabernet sauce paired with Camembert potato soufflé and confit tomato.

**Other recommendations** Salad of charbroiled Keahole (Big Island) lobster and Moloka'i sweet-potato purée; for dessert, the Hawaiian Vintage Chocolate Surprise is made of chocolate over Tahitian vanilla ice cream.

**Entertainment & amenities** A Hawaiian trio serenades diners with traditional sounds of Hawai'i from 7 to 10 p.m. nightly, and a dance floor beckons romantics. In the adjacent lobby lounge, a guitarist strums contemporary tunes from 8:30 to 11 p.m.

**Summary & comments** This is the only restaurant on Maui with a master sommelier. Repeat diners say Seasons is what a hotel restaurant should be. It has a gracious elegance that makes an Absolut martini straight up with a twist, stirred not shaken, just right as a predinner cocktail. Free shuttles operate between all Wailea hotels, so if a postdinner snifter of Remy Martin XO also seems just right, you need not worry about driving your car.

## The Big Island

### BATIK RESTAURANT ★★★★½

HAWAI'I REGIONAL  |  EXPENSIVE  |  QUALITY ★★★★½  |  VALUE ★★★  |  ZONE 11

62-100 Mauna Kea Beach Drive, Mauna Kea Beach Hotel; Kohala Coast; (808) 882-7222; www.maunkebeachhotel.com

**Reservations** Highly recommended **When to go** Anytime **Entrée range** $29–48, vegetarian $24, prix fixe menus $65–85 **Payment** VISA, MC, AMEX, DC, JCB **Service rating** ★★★★★ **Parking** Valet or hotel parking lot **Bar** Full service **Wine selection** Extensive **Dress** Evening resort wear **Disabled access** Adequate, via elevator **Customers** Tourists and Islanders celebrating special occasions

**Dinner** Monday, Wednesday–Friday, and Sunday, 6:30–9 p.m.; closed Tuesday and Saturday for house lu'au and clambake/seafood buffet

**Setting & atmosphere** This is Mauna Kea Beach Hotel's premier restaurant, and care has been taken to do everything right. Batik panels decorating one wall are authentic, there are candles and tropical flowers on the tables, and a bronze charger rests under fine china plates for a look of burnished elegance. Patio tables overlooking Kauna'oa Bay were added in 1999 for those who prefer outdoor dining.

**House specialties** Thai-style curries are the house specialty and the most often ordered entrée on the menu, though some people prefer to choose traditional items like beef Wellington, crispy salmon with saffron pepper jus, or lobster tail with saffron risotto. Meals are accompanied by tandoori oven–baked naan bread. Starters, such as langostinos sautéed in garlic and served with angel-hair pasta with lobster sauce, or scallop ravioli with ginger-lime sauce, are as satisfying as the entrées.

**Other recommendations** The number-one choice from the decadent dessert menu is a Grand Marnier soufflé, but the warm Valrhona chocolate cake comes a close second.

**Entertainment & amenities** A classical solo guitarist strums tunes every evening. After dinner in the Batik Lounge, a jazz duo performs from 9 to 11 p.m. nightly.

**Summary & comments** This place was once on the stuffy side, but today jackets are only recommended, and the food and decor have been finely honed to provide a high-quality dining experience.

### CAFÉ PESTO ★★★½

CONTEMPORARY  |  INEXPENSIVE  |  QUALITY ★★★★  |  VALUE ★★★★  |  ZONES 11, 12

Wharf Road and Mahukona Highway, Kawaihae Center, Kawaihae; (808) 882-1071; www.caefpesto.com
308 Kamehameha Avenue, Hilo; (808) 969-6640

**Reservations** Accepted **When to go** Anytime **Entrée range** $13–28 **Payment** VISA, MC, AMEX, D, DC, JCB **Service rating** ★★★ **Parking** Adjacent parking lot **Bar** Full service **Wine selection** Limited, some by glass **Dress** Casual **Disabled access** Good **Customers** Islanders and tourists

**Lunch** Every day, 11 a.m.–4:30 p.m.

**Dinner** Sunday–Thursday, 4:30–9 p.m.; Friday and Saturday, 4:30–10 p.m.

**Setting & atmosphere** Café Pesto in Hilo and at Kawaihae Harbor both have a bright, cheerful outlook, with black-and-white flooring and big windows reflecting a contemporary art deco theme. Kawaihae has a more intimate feeling, with a low ceiling, while the Hilo restaurant is in the historic S. Hata Building, which retained the high ceiling of turn-of-the-century architecture when it was restored.

**House specialties** Café Pesto is known for its use of fresh Island ingredients and simple healthy preparations, particularly its Island fish, served sautéed or grilled. A wood-burning pizza oven fired on kiawe or 'ohi'a produces ten different pizzas, including one where you compile as many ingredients as you like. The Marguerite cheese pizza is most popular, but the Oriental al pesto pizza is a top vegetarian choice, with eggplant, sun-dried tomatoes, and roasted garlic.

**Other recommendations** Pastas are great; risottos are creamy and good, particularly the seafood risotto made with Keahole lobster, prawns, scallops, and grilled local fish. A beef tenderloin of Kamuela Pride beef comes with lobster tempura and garlic prawns served with mozzarella mashed potatoes. The macadamia-crusted apple pie and the chocolate ganache torte are desserts to diet for.

**Summary & comments** Café Pesto won the local Hale 'Aina Award for Best Big Island Restaurant in 1999. Diners pen comments such as "Move the restaurant to where we live," or "You cook better than my wife, but don't tell her." Both restaurants have a smoke-free policy.

## CANOEHOUSE ★★★★½

HAWAI'I REGIONAL | MODERATE/EXPENSIVE | QUALITY ★★★★½ | VALUE ★★★ |
ZONE 11

68-1400 Mauna Lani Drive, Mauna Lani Bay Hotel & Bungalows; Kohala Coast; (808) 885-6622; www.maunalani.com

**Reservations** Highly recommended **When to go** Sunset **Entrée range** $23–50 **Payment** VISA, MC, AMEX, D, DC, JCB **Service rating** ★★★★ **Parking** Valet or hotel lot **Bar** Full service **Wine selection** Good **Dress** Resort attire **Disabled access** Adequate, but it's some distance from the parking **Customers** Resort and hotel guests and Islanders

**Dinner** Sunday–Thursday, 6–9 p.m.; seafood buffet only on Friday & Saturday

**Setting & atmosphere** A torchlit path with a little bridge over a koi-filled stream and the ocean waves lapping on the beach a few steps away set the scene for a romantic evening. Inside, a huge koa canoe is the focal point. You can choose semi-privacy by sitting in a raised booth, choose to be in the middle of things at a table, or join the conviviality at a central bar.

**House specialties** Imaginative entrées include miso-sake marinated mahimahi with stir-fried soba noodles, and grilled lemon-pepper scallops with wild mushroom mashed potatoes.

**Other recommendations** It's tempting to try two appetizers, perhaps kalua pork spring rolls or baby-back ribs grilled with guava hoisin sauce, instead of an entrée, just so you can try the intriguing preparations. If you still have room for a decadent dessert, try the CanoeHouse Chocolate Pillar, a rich torte with vanilla sauce and fresh berries.

**Summary & comments** The food is innovative, the setting lovely, and wines suggested for each entrée are available by the glass. It almost makes paying the hefty bill worth it.

## COAST GRILLE  ★★★★½

CONTEMPORARY/HAWAI'I REGIONAL | MODERATE/EXPENSIVE | QUALITY ★★★★½ | VALUE ★★★ | ZONE 11

62-100 Kauna'oa Drive, Hapuna Beach Prince Hotel, Kohala Coast; (808) 880-1111; www.hapunabeachprincehotel.com

**Reservations** Recommended **When to go** Sunset under the stars if you sit outside overlooking the ocean **Entrée range** $20–50 **Payment** VISA, MC, AMEX, DC, JCB **Service rating** ★★★★ **Parking** Valet or hotel lot **Bar** Full service **Wine selection** Extensive **Dress** Resort wear **Disabled access** Adequate, via elevator and curving ramp walkway **Customers** Hotel and resort guests and Islanders for special occasions

**Dinner** Every day, 6–9:30 p.m.

**Setting & atmosphere** This is a big, spacious restaurant where you can sit at interior tables (which is a waste of an exhilarating view), out on the deck, or at banquettes that face the ocean when the breeze is a little too nippy for comfort. Tables inside the multi-level, circular building seem dwarfed under a high ceiling but give you a nice feeling of privacy from neighboring diners. Natural woods and soft lighting tone down the empty effect.

**House specialties** The oyster bar is a rare find in Island restaurants, while Kona lobster, raised just down the coast, comes in a steamer basket with shrimp, Manila clams, and Waipi'o taro ravioli. The hotel is the home of the Sam Choy Poke Contest, a blessing for seafood lovers, as many types of poke, generally made of raw fish, seaweed, and spices, are available.

**Other recommendations** For non–seafood lovers, there's peppercorn-crusted lamb rack with star anise sauce, or grilled smoked veal chop. The dessert sampler eases the pain of making a decision, but you might want to order the warm chocolate pudding with fresh nutmeg ice cream in advance so this creamy rich treat will be ready when you are.

**Summary & comments** Sit outside at sunset on warm summer and fall evenings to fully appreciate the inspiring view of turquoise ocean and white sand.

## DANIEL THIEBAUT RESTAURANT                    ★★★½

FRENCH ASIAN  |  MODERATE  |  QUALITY ★★★★  |  VALUE ★★★★  |  ZONE 11

65-1259 Kawaihae Road, Kamuela; (808) 887-2200

**Reservations** Suggested **When to go** Anytime **Entrée range** Lunch $8.50–$15, dinner $20–$26.50 **Payment** All major credit cards **Service rating** ★★★★ **Parking** Free, on site **Bar** Full service **Wine selection** Extensive, with 35 selections by the glass **Dress** Casual **Disabled access** Good **Customers** Locals, tourists

**Lunch** Weekdays, 11:30 a.m.–1:30 p.m.

**Dinner** Daily, 5:30–9:30 p.m.

**Setting and atmosphere** Daniel Thiebaut is set in the former Chock In Store and Family Home, which has been part of this ranching community since the turn of the century. The character of the cheerful yellow structure has been preserved, with five dining rooms that reflect the rooms' original uses: a dress shop, for instance, plus the general store and the family's dining parlor. Warm wood floors and period furnishings reflect the plantation times. Vintage Hawaiiana is a large part of the decor.

**House specialties** Local produce is at its freshest in this cool, mountain farming community, and Thiebaut's takes advantage of the bounty. French techniques are applied in combination with Asian flavors. The chef's signature Hunan-style rack of lamb comes with an eggplant compote and goat cheese made in nearby Mauna Ke'a. Salmon is served with ravioli filled with spicy wasabi and topped with kaffir lime sauce. A corn cake flavored with a lemongrass-coconut-lobster sauce is also a house favorite.

**Other recommendations** Lunch is quite affordable here, and it's an eclectic mix of dishes—from two eggs any style (with roasted tomato) to a mixed grill of lamb chop, beef tenderloin, and chicken sausage. Several vegetarian entrées are on the menu, including avocado spring roll with smoked tomato coulis, pad thai noodles with tofu and wild mushrooms, and macadamia-crusted tofu with cilantro-tahini sauce.

**Summary and comments** Chef Daniel Thiebaut came to the Kohala Coast from his native France by way of such diverse assignments as the Manila Hotel, Gleneagles Hotel in Scotland, and Switzerland's Winter Resort. As you would expect from a chef with that résumé, he came to Hawai'i as a hotel resort chef, but he has chosen a more intimate expression for his own restaurant, opened in 1998. Daniel Thiebaut was recognized in *Condé Nast* in 2001 as one of the 100 hottest new restaurants in the world.

## DONATONI'S                    ★★★★½

ITALIAN  |  MODERATE/EXPENSIVE  |  QUALITY ★★★★½  |  VALUE ★★★  |  ZONE 11

Hilton Waikoloa Village, 425 Waikoloa Beach Drive, Waikoloa; (808) 886-1234; www.hilton.com

**Reservations** Highly recommended **When to go** Anytime **Entrée range** $19.25–45 **Payment** VISA, MC, AMEX, D, DC, JCB **Service rating** ★★★★½ **Parking** Valet or complimentary hotel parking lot **Bar** Full service **Wine selection** Extensive wine and champagne list **Dress** Resort attire **Disabled access** Adequate, at some distance from the parking lot **Customers** Hotel and resort guests, some Islanders

**Dinner** Every day, 6–10 p.m.

**Setting & atmosphere** This is an intimate, romantic restaurant reminiscent of old Italy, and it seems even more dreamy if you have the chance to sit outdoors next to a saltwater canal where boats drift by in the moonlight—almost like being in Venice.

**House specialties** With a name like Sascia Marchesi, is it any wonder the Milanese-born chef is an expert in preparing the northern Italian cuisine served at Donatoni's? Among his best dishes are Torre Di Granseola e Vitello (king crab and veal scaloppini with lemon sauce) and a daily fresh catch of fish served with risotto and fresh asparagus.

**Other recommendations** Delectable pastas may be ordered as appetizers or entrées. Traditional tiramisu and exquisite crème brûlée take top dessert honors at this restaurant.

**Entertainment & amenities** A violinist strolls from table to table in the evenings.

**Summary & comments** More than one publication has lauded Donatoni's for its Italian food and romantic atmosphere. Oddly, the romantic ambience is nearly as heady inside (with opulent chandeliers and pretty upholstered booths and chairs) as it is outside beside the waterway.

## *EDELWEISS*

CONTINENTAL | MODERATE | QUALITY ★★★★ | VALUE ★★★★ | ZONE 11

Highway 19, Waimea; (808) 885-6800

**Reservations** Recommended **When to go** Anytime for dinner except Sunday and Monday; go early on weekends to avoid waiting **Entrée range** $18.50–24.50 **Payment** VISA, MC, AMEX **Service rating** ★★★★ **Parking** In adjacent lot **Bar** Full service **Wine selection** Average **Dress** Casual **Disabled access** Good **Customers** Islanders and some tourists

**Lunch** Tuesday–Saturday, 11:30 a.m.–1:30 p.m.

**Dinner** Tuesday–Saturday, 5–8:30 p.m.

**Setting & atmosphere** You feel as if you're back in Bavaria in this charming chalet-restaurant with rustic redwood furnishings, traditional blue-and-white curtains, and rich aromas of robust food wafting from the kitchen over the room's 15 tables.

**House specialties** You'll always find a delicious rack of lamb on the menu. Complete dinners include everything but dessert, for which you can choose the three-layer raspberry, vanilla, and chocolate Edelweiss torte, or rice pudding.

**Other recommendations** More than a dozen specials might be served nightly—Texas wild boar, venison ragout, Black Forest chicken, veal chalet Emily—so you never get tired of the menu. A word of warning: Sometimes the chef gets a little heavy on the salt.

**Summary & comments** Edelweiss has been a Big Island favorite for years, steadily withstanding competition from new, trendy restaurants that have come and, in many cases, gone from the Big Island dining scene.

## THE GRILL AND LOUNGE AT THE ORCHID ★★★½

CONTEMPORARY | EXPENSIVE | QUALITY ★★★★ | VALUE ★★★ | ZONE 11

1 North Kaniku Drive, The Orchid Hotel, Kohala Coast; (808) 885-2000;
www.orchid-maunalani.com

**Reservations** Highly recommended **When to go** Anytime **Entrée range** $28–50
**Payment** VISA, MC, AMEX, D, DC, JCB **Service rating** ★★★★½ **Parking** Valet or
free self-parking in hotel lot **Bar** Full service **Wine selection** Extensive **Dress** Dressy
resort attire **Disabled access** Good, via elevator **Customers** Hotel and resort
guests, Islanders for special occasions**Dinner:** Every day, 6:30–9:30 p.m.

**Setting & atmosphere** Comfortable club-like atmosphere, with richly polished koa
wood bar and wall paneling, enhances relaxed dining. Tables are covered in beige Frette
linens and softly lit with candle lamps. Chairs are upholstered in rich tapestry, while the
walls are hung with scenes by local artists.

**House specialties** The Grill and Lounge is especially good for the grilled meat items
on the menu. Rack of lamb is crusted with pesto accompanied by apple-smoked bacon,
sweet potato, and wild mushrooms, and garnished with tropical fruit chutney. Veal chops
are similarly crusted with Parmesan and served with a sweet corn risotto and Waimea
tomato fondue. To start, Maui onion soup topped with imported Gruyère and Reggiano
cheeses, or warm baby-spinach salad garnished with fresh buffalo mozzarella, sets the
taste buds tingling.

**Other recommendations** The oven-roasted breast of organic chicken (mainlanders might call it "free-range") oozes melted Puna goat cheese and is served with baby
bok choy and roasted garlic potatoes. Dessert lovers have to ask which selections of
soufflés are available nightly, though for a lighter conclusion, you might opt for the apple
Florentine served in a crust of crisp macadamia nut butter snaps.

**Entertainment & amenities** Classical guitarist Charles Brotman, whose instrumental CDs can be found in Island music outlets, strums contemporary tunes most
evenings. Couples often linger a while to take advantage of the restaurant's dance floor.

**Summary & comments** The Grill and Lounge has been recognized by *Gayot's The
Best of Hawai'i* for fine dining.

## HARRINGTON'S ★★

STEAK AND SEAFOOD | MODERATE | QUALITY ★★★½ | VALUE ★★★★ | ZONE 12

135 Kalaniana'ole Street, Hilo; (808) 961-4966

**Reservations** Recommended **When to go** Anytime for dinner except Wednesday
**Entrée range** $14.75–27.95 **Payment** VISA, MC **Service rating** ★★★★ **Parking**
In adjacent lot **Bar** Full service **Wine selection** Adequate, about 30 wines **Dress**
Casual dress, no tank tops, no swimwear for women **Disabled access** Good **Cus-
tomers** Tourists and Islanders

**Lunch** Monday–Friday, 11 a.m.–2 p.m.

**Dinner** Monday–Saturday, 5–9:30 p.m.; Sunday, 5–9 p.m.

**Setting & atmosphere** Harrington's is in an old brown freestanding building on the edge of the Ice Pond in Hilo; it's best viewed in kinder lighting after dark. Inside, hanging plants and other greenery, blue tablecloths, and tropical flowers on the tables create an intimate atmosphere.

**House specialties** Among reliable choices like prime rib, New York steak, and teriyaki steak offerings, the Slavic steak is a tasty chilled mainland sirloin sliced thin and topped with a savory garlic butter sauce.

**Other recommendations** Dinners, including seafood selections—fresh fish, lobster, prawns, calamari, scallops—come with a choice of starch and salad. If you're a vegetarian in a world of steak eaters, opt for the eggplant parmigiana. Waiters tempt you by presenting desserts on a tray. If you can't say no, try the house cheesecake with strawberries or liliko'i.

**Entertainment & amenities** On Thursday, Friday, and Saturday nights a musician livens up the lounge with contemporary Hawaiian music.

**Summary & comments** The menu in this old standby may have been updated by new ownership several years ago, but basically if you liked steak and seafood restaurants 20 years ago, you'll find this pleasant restaurant comforting in a world of nouvelle cuisine.

## *HUGGO'S*                                                         ★★½

PACIFIC RIM/MEDITERRANEAN  |  MODERATE  |  QUALITY ★★★½  |  VALUE ★★★  |
ZONE 11

75-5828 Kahakai Road, Kailua-Kona; (808) 329-1493; www.huggos.com

**Reservations** Recommended **When to go** Sunset for most romantic lighting **Entrée range** $16.95–37 **Payment** VISA, MC, D, DC, JCB **Service rating** ★★★ **Parking** Adjacent lot **Bar** Full service **Wine selection** Adequate, a dozen by the glass **Dress** Casual **Disabled access** Good **Customers** Islanders and tourists

**Lunch** Every day, 11:30 a.m.–2:30 p.m.

**Dinner** Every day, 5:30–10 p.m.

**Setting & atmosphere** With tables in an open-air restaurant set just above water's edge, Huggo's proved such a popular place for sunset watchers that the owners opened an adjacent waterfront lounge with a similar view next door called Huggo's on the Rocks. The new bar, which serves lunch and *pupus* at dinner, is also a popular hangout for longtime Huggo's loyalists. The established restaurant is decorated with marine memorabilia, big anchors, lamps that must have come from some oceangoing vessel at one time, rope lines, and natural wood. One open-to-the-elements deck has half a dozen tables shaded by big umbrellas.

**House specialties** The fresh local seafood is the reason Huggo's has earned a dedicated following. Try sesame-crusted mahimahi or coconut-kiwi ono, both delicately flavored white fish adeptly seasoned.

**Other recommendations** A number of vegetarian choices and a juicy cut of certi-fied Angus prime rib gives non–seafood lovers a chance to enjoy Huggo's casual atmos-phere and fine food.

**Entertainment & amenities** Performers render live contemporary music nightly at the adjacent bar, for diners who want to hang out before or after the meal.

**Summary & comments** Ask for a table by the window to fully appreciate Huggo's oceanfront appeal.

## KILAUEA LODGE                                                      ★★★½

CONTINENTAL | MODERATE | QUALITY ★★★★ | VALUE ★★★ | ZONE 12

19-4055 Old Volcano Road, Volcano Village; (808) 967-7366;
www.kilauealodge.com

**Reservations** Highly recommended **When to go** Anytime, but post-nighttime lava viewing is always fun **Entrée range** $15.50–33 **Payment** VISA, MC **Service rating** ★★★½ **Parking** Adjacent lot **Bar** Full service **Wine selection** Good, some wines by the glass **Dress** Casual. Bring a sweater; Volcano nights can be cool **Disabled access** Adequate, via lift **Customers** Islanders and tourists

**Dinner** Every day, 5:30–9 p.m.

**Setting & atmosphere** This mountain lodge, surrounded by tree ferns in the cool, secluded Volcano area, dates from 1938, when the property was a scouting retreat. A stone fireplace glows in the dining room, which has a vaulted cedar ceiling, hardwood floors, local artwork, and a rustic, remote appeal.

**House specialties** The cool climate is great for duck l'orange with red cabbage and potatoes du jour or a rich seafood Mauna Kea, pasta made with bay shrimp, prawns, fresh 'ahi, scallops, mushrooms, capers, and basil-wine sauce. Lighter appetites go for the fresh Island fish. The Lodge's signature dessert is Portuguese sweet bread pudding gar-nished with a variety of fruit sauces.

**Other recommendations** This is a cozy place to sip a full-bodied red wine and nib-ble away on an appetizer, such as Brie cheese deep-fried in coconut batter and served with brandied apples and bread.

**Summary & comments** Kilauea Lodge has long been considered *the* place to eat in Volcano, and people from Hilo often drive the half hour from town to enjoy the "getting-away-from-it-all" feeling the lodge provides.

## KONA RANCH HOUSE                                                   ★★½

AMERICAN | INEXPENSIVE/MODERATE | QUALITY ★★★ | VALUE ★★★★ | ZONE 11

75-5653 Ololi Street; (808) 329-7061

**Reservations** Recommended **When to go** Anytime **Entrée range** Breakfast $4.75–11, lunch $5.95–12, dinner $10.95–37.95 **Payment** VISA, MC, AMEX, DC, D, JCB **Service rating** ★★★ **Parking** In adjacent lot **Bar** Full service **Wine selection**

Limited, all by glass **Dress** Casual **Disabled access** Good **Customers** Islanders and tourists

**Breakfast** Every day, 6:30 a.m.–2 p.m.

**Lunch** Every day, 10 a.m.–4 p.m.

**Dinner** Every day, 4–9 p.m.

**Setting & atmosphere** This family-style restaurant is divided into two sections. The Paniolo Room has booths handy for a quick lunch; the Plantation Lana'i is nicer for dinner or Sunday brunch, with white wicker chairs, flowers, and candles in the evening.

**House specialties** Known for good breakfasts of omelets, eggs Benedict, and pancakes, this place is especially busy on Sunday mornings. At dinner, big barbecue platters are the draw, but the menu is so varied you'll find Tex-Mex and vegetarian items as well.

**Other recommendations** You can choose fresh local fish—'ahi, mahimahi, and ono—prepared broiled, Cajun, sautéed, and fried. Meals come with salad, vegetables, and starch.

**Summary & comments** Ample food, reasonable prices, and pleasant surroundings are the reason this family restaurant has been an Island favorite since 1981.

## MERRIMAN'S                                               ★★★★½

HAWAI'I REGIONAL  |  MODERATE/EXPENSIVE  |  QUALITY ★★★★½  |  VALUE ★★★  |
ZONE 11

'Opelo Plaza II, Highway 19 and 'Opelo Road, Waimea; (808) 885-6822; www.goodfood@lv.net

**Reservations** Highly recommended **When to go** Anytime for dinner **Entrée range** $12.95–25.95 **Payment** VISA, MC, AMEX, JCB **Service rating** ★★★★★ **Parking** In adjacent lot **Bar** Full service **Wine selection** Extensive **Dress** Casual **Disabled access** Good **Customers** Tourists and Islanders

**Lunch** Monday–Friday, 11:30 a.m.–1:30 p.m.

**Dinner** Every day, 5:30–9 p.m.

**Setting & atmosphere** Set in the heart of Big Island cowboy country, Merriman's is a classy, understated restaurant with an exhibition kitchen. Artwork by local artists is ever-changing and available for purchase. Light colors and potted palm plants add to the pleasant contemporary ranch country feel.

**House specialties** Chef/owner Peter Merriman serves fresh, locally raised meat and produce, available in dishes that reflect the cooking styles of Hawai'i's various cultures. The restaurant's signature dish is original wok-charred 'ahi, seared on the outside, sashimi-rare on the inside, available as an appetizer or an entrée. New York steaks are from nearby Parker Ranch, while the lamb, raised at Kahua Ranch, is prepared differently each day. You might find herb-roasted leg of lamb served with mango port wine jus, or a rack of lamb. Lokelani Farms grows special tomatoes just for Merriman's, while Honopua Farms raises an organic spinach that turns up on plates tossed with hot balsamic vinegar and garnished with pipi kaula (spicy dried beef) and crumbled bacon.

**Other recommendations** Fresh Island fish is served sautéed with shellfish and vegetable nabemono, herb-grilled on mango chutney, or sesame-crusted with spicy liliko'i sauce and tomato papaya relish. Vegetarians will appreciate pan-fried Asian cake noodle served with a medley of vegetables: broccoli, snow peas, cauliflower, and carrots, with a spicy black-bean sauce. Dessert lovers say the coconut crème brûlée is the best they've had, though some prefer the liliko'i passion-fruit mousse.

**Summary & comments** This is probably the Big Island's favorite restaurant. The chef/owner's reputation for the best food on the island is so widely known that visitors (including celebrities like Robert Redford and Kevin Costner) drive from miles away to Merriman's for special occasions. *Hint:* Take a sweater, as the restaurant can get cool in the chilly Waimea night.

## OODLES OF NOODLES

HAWAIIA REGIONAL/SOUTHWESTERN FUSION | INEXPENSIVE/MODERATE | QUALITY
★★★★½ | VALUE ★★★★★ | ZONE 11

75-1027 Henry Street, Suite 102, Kailua-Kona; (808)-329-9222

**Reservations** Not necessary **When to go** Anytime **Entrée range** Lunch or dinner $8–$17 **Payment** All major credit cards **Service rating** ★★★★ **Parking** Free in the adjoining shopping center lot **Bar** Full service **Wine selection** Good, 17 wines by the glass **Dress** Casual **Disabled access** Good **Customers** Locals, tourists

**Hours** Daily, 11 a.m.–9 p.m.

**Setting and atmosphere** Chic and contemporary, Oodles of Noodles shows off clean lines in its slate floors, warm wood furnishings, and brightly painted walls. Original art by Dietrich Varez, Shelly Maudsley White, and Debra Thompson provide even more personality.

**House specialties** Noodles obviously rule here, and it's a cross-cultural menu, pasta being an international language. You'll find Japanese udon, Italian linguine, Chinese chow mein, Thai rice noodles, all in seemingly endless presentations. Go simple with a steaming bowl of Vietnamese pho or a local favorite, saimin, made especially savory with duck broth and lup cheong (Chinese sausage). Or sample one of the Signature Noodles, such as wok-spiced 'ahi in a casserole with orecchiette pasta, or Southwestern-style fettuccine with grilled chicken and ancho-chipotle chili cream.

**Other recommendations** The restaurant also offers an extensive selection of salads and vegetarian entrées that, again, tour the world. Visit Asia through sweet-sour Thai salads topped with grilled fish or chicken and crispy noodles. You can go Mediterranean with linguine in a traditional presentation with kalamata olives, tomatoes, and roasted garlic.

**Summary and comments** Chef Amy Ferguson Ota is the former executive chef at the Ritz-Carlton Mauna Lani, among the first women to attain that level with a U.S. luxury hotel group, but she gave that up to run this intimate, freestanding restaurant dedicated to noodles. Ota began her career in Texas and was influential in the development of a regional cuisine in the Southwest, then in Hawai'i became a founding member of the Hawai'i Regional Cuisine chefs. Her specialty is blending the two styles with a solid foundation in classic French cooking. In 1995 she was nominated for a James Beard Award for the Pacific Northwest region, which includes Hawai'i.

## PAHU I'A AT FOUR SEASONS                                    ★★★★½

HAWAI'I FUSION | EXPENSIVE | QUALITY ★★★★½ | VALUE ★★★ | ZONE 11

Four Seasons Resort Hualalai, 100 Ka'upulehu Drive, Ka'upulehu-Kona; (808) 325-8000; www.fourseasons.com

**Reservations** Recommended **When to go** Sunset is most romantic **Entrée range** $25–43; 4-course chef's tasting menu plus dessert, $65; with wine pairings, add $20 **Payment** VISA, MC, AMEX, D, JCB **Service rating** ★★★★★ **Parking** Complimentary valet or hotel lot **Bar** Full service **Wine selection** Extensive **Dress** Resort wear **Disabled access** Adequate, via paved pathways **Customers** Hotel and resort guests and Islanders celebrating special occasions

**Breakfast** Every day, 6–11:30 a.m.

**Dinner** Every day, 5:30–10 p.m.

**Setting & atmosphere** Outdoor deck seating features candlelit tables, with spotlights illuminating the rhythmic surf, and is romantic even for hand-holding at breakfast. Cross a wooden bridge suspended across a natural fishpond to reach the polished mahogany-and-teak interior, where a four-foot rectangular aquarium that stands nine feet tall holds colorful reef fish. Candles in black sand in hurricane lamps light individual tables. Check out three original hand-colored woodcuts by Charles Bartlett (circa 1921–1922)—"Duke Kahanamoku," "Surfing at Waikiki," and "Hawaiian Fisherman"— displayed on restaurant walls.

**House specialties** There's a mind-boggling daily breakfast buffet that's even more extensive on Sundays for brunch. At dinner, an 'Ahi, 'Ahi, 'Ahi appetizer features the popular tuna in a trio of preparations: sashimi, seared, and poke. Steamed 'opakapaka Oriental style with shiitake mushrooms, Chinese parsley, and ginger-shoyu is both good and good for you.

**Other recommendations** As with most top-notch hotel restaurants, you'll find a plethora of fresh Island fish on the menu, which may save enough on calories that you'll feel no guilt at plunging into the kope pukolu (coffee trio), a tower of classic tiramisu and cappuccino crème brûlée on a cinnamon sugar puff pastry, and homemade espresso ice cream wrapped in a coconut wave cookie. On the other hand, Vintage Chocolate soufflé, a melt-in-your-mouth warm delight, is also a pretty spectacular finish to a meal.

**Entertainment & amenities** Island entertainers torch dance nightly from 6:30 to 9:30 p.m.

**Summary & comments** This is the closest to the beach you could possibly sit without spreading a towel in the sand for a picnic, but the price may reduce you to opting for a real picnic next time.

## ROYAL SIAM THAI ★★★½

THAI | INEXPENSIVE | QUALITY ★★★★ | VALUE ★★★★★ | ZONE 12

70 Mamo Street, Hilo; (808) 961-6100

**Reservations** Accepted **When to go** Anytime except Sunday **Entrée range** $7.95–12.95, vegetarian dishes start at $4.95 **Payment** VISA, MC, AMEX, DC, D **Service rating** ★★★ **Parking** On street **Bar** Full service **Wine selection** Very limited **Dress** Casual **Disabled access** Adequate **Customers** Islanders and some tourists

**Lunch** Monday–Saturday, 11 a.m.–2 p.m.

**Dinner** Every day, 5–8:30 p.m.

**Setting & atmosphere** This small restaurant seats about 50 at booths that line the walls and central tables covered with pink-and-white striped tablecloths. Pictures of the Thai king and queen, Buddha, and Thai dancers hang on the walls. Sprays of orchids and potted trees add a colorful touch.

**House specialties** Diners always love the deep-fried spring rolls made with either vegetables only or pork and vegetables and served in the traditional way, with mint and lettuce leaves to roll them in and a sweet-sour sauce for dipping. The most popular entrée on the menu is Buddrama, chicken prepared with spinach and peanut sauce, though curries, which can be ordered mild, medium, or hot, are also favored. Choose yellow or green curry with chicken, beef, or shrimp, or a healthy vegetarian curry with basil, green peas, and eggplant.

**Other recommendations** The chef's favorites are Thai garlic shrimp and cashew chicken with orders of sticky rice. Thai jasmine rice and brown rice are other starchy choices.

**Entertainment & amenities** The sound system plays subdued Thai music to set the mood.

**Summary & comments** Quality- and value-wise, though it's certainly not fancy, this is sometimes called the best food in Hilo. In 1999 the restaurant expanded, adding a second room that can seat about 25 people. It can be booked for private parties, though it's normally used for dinner seating.

## ROY'S AT THE KING'S SHOPS ★★★★½

HAWAIIAN FUSION | MODERATE | QUALITY ★★★★½ | VALUE ★★★★ | ZONE 11

King's Shops, 250 Waikoloa Beach Drive, Waikoloa; (808) 886-4321; www.roysrestaurant.com

**Reservations** Highly recommended **When to go** Early to avoid crowds **Entrée range** $14–27 **Payment** VISA, MC, AMEX, D, DC, JCB **Service rating** ★★★★ **Parking** Shopping-center lot **Bar** Full bar **Wine selection** Very good, some by the glass **Dress** Casual, no tank tops for men, no swimwear **Disabled access** Good **Customers** Islanders and tourists

**Lunch** Every day, 11:30 a.m.–2 p.m.

**Dinner** Every day, 5:30–9:30 p.m.

**Setting & atmosphere** This Roy's, with green carpets, a green marble bar, an exhibition kitchen, and window tables that overlook a golf course lake, is the nicest yet of Roy Yamaguchi's popular restaurants in Hawai'i.

**House specialties** Sample grilled Szechuan-style baby-back ribs or Thai noodle peanut chicken salad at dinner, or choose among entrées like imu-roasted pork laulau, pizza, or sweet sake-glazed shrimp. Blackened Island 'ahi, served in spicy hot soy mustard butter sauce, is a Roy's standby. More than half a dozen fish and their preparations change nightly, as do appetizers, pizzas, pastas, salads, and soups.

**Other recommendations** Salads and sandwiches at lunch are complete meals, such as the teriyaki Big Island beef sandwich or fresh Island fish of the day with ponzu sprout salad, as are the pastas, like penne pasta with Neopolitan sauce and chicken, shrimp, or beef.

**Summary & comments** It's no problem matching a wine to any of the Euro-Asian flavors, given the extensive wine list. Youngsters are welcome; Roy's offers a children's menu and crayons. According to the chef's mood and the ingredients available, often more than 30 menu items change nightly, so you will never get bored with the food no matter how many times you return.

## SAM CHOY'S RESTAURANT ★★★

HAWAI'I REGIONAL | MODERATE | QUALITY ★★★★ | VALUE ★★★★ | ZONE 11

73-5576 Kauhola Street, Bay 1, Kaloko Light Industrial Park; (808) 326-1545; www.samchoys.com

**Reservations** Highly recommended for dinner **When to go** Anytime **Entrée range** $16.95–24.95, daily specials can top out at $31.95 **Payment** VISA, MC, D **Service rating** ★★★★ **Parking** In adjacent lot **Bar** None **Wine selection** Bring your own **Dress** Casual **Disabled access** Good **Customers** Islanders and tourists

**Breakfast and Lunch** Every day, 6 a.m.–2 p.m.

**Dinner** Tuesday–Saturday, 5–9 p.m.

**Setting & atmosphere** During the day, Sam Choy's is a casual, local-style restaurant frequented not only by workers from the surrounding area but also by visitors looking for real local food. In the evening, the room undergoes a transformation with white cloths and colored napkins added to the tables, but you can still watch the cooks zip around the open kitchen.

**House specialties** Islanders love the seafood laulau, an assortment of fresh fish, vegetables, and spinach steamed in a lu'au leaf. Equally famous is Sam's seafood trio, three types of local fresh fish, one served seared, one ogo-crusted in crispy tempura, and one macadamia-nut crusted. All meals come with soup or salad and a choice of rice or potato.

**Other recommendations** Duck, lamb chops, macadamia-nut-crusted pork loin, and teriyaki steak round out a dinner menu that's sure to round out an average person's body. Big hearty breakfasts of stew omelets or fried poke (barely seared seafood and seaweed) are filling, and omelets come with rice, home fries, or hash browns, and toast and jelly. At lunch, specials change daily, but a big steaming bowl of saimin (Island-style noodle soup) is always on the menu.

**Summary & comments** Sam Choy is Hawai'i's most famous, and his restaurants are known almost as much for their *big* portions as for the high-quality food with a real local touch and robust flavors. Expect to take home enough food for the next day's lunch.

## Kaua'i

### THE BEACH HOUSE ★★★

PACIFIC RIM | MODERATE | QUALITY ★★★★ | VALUE ★★★ | ZONE 13

5022 Lawa'i Road, Po'ipu; (808) 742-1424; www.the_beach_house.com

**Reservations** Highly recommended **When to go** Sunset **Entrée range** $18.95–32.50 **Payment** VISA, MC, AMEX, DC, JCB **Service rating** ★★★★ **Parking** Valet or street **Bar** Full service **Wine selection** Extensive **Dress** Resort wear **Disabled access** Good; valet parking is free for disabled **Customers** Tourists and Islanders

**Dinner** *May 2–October 1:* every day, 6–9:30 p.m.; *October 2–May 1:* every day, 5:30–9:30 p.m.

**Setting & atmosphere** Artwork by local artists can be purchased right off the walls, if you have time to tear your eyes away from floor-to-ceiling windows that showcase Po'ipu's best ocean view. It's most romantic at sunset, when surfers and frolicking whales might still be spotted.

**House specialties** A kiawe wood–burning grill adds a flavorful touch to kal-bi-style lamb rack or Jawaiian pork tenderloin with jerk spices.

**Other recommendations** The on-property chef, under the guiding wing of Kaua'i's well-known chef Linda Yamada, prepares such delicacies as wok-charred mahimahi in a ginger-sesame crust and lime-ginger sauce, or seared sea scallops with a polenta herb crust and papaya-avocado guacamole. Save calories on a stack of portobello mushrooms with spring vegetables, then splurge on Toasted Hawaiian, a white-chocolate cake layered with haupia (coconut pudding), white-chocolate mousse, macadamia nuts, and caramel sauce.

**Summary & comments** Make reservations early and request a seat by the window for the full effect of this beach area's stunning views. In 1998, The Beach House won honors as the top restaurant on Kaua'i in the local Hale 'Aina Awards.

### BRENNECKE'S BEACH BROILER ★★★

CONTEMPORARY | MODERATE | QUALITY ★★★½ | VALUE ★★★★ | ZONE 12

2100 Ho'one Road, Po æipu Beach; (808) 742-7588; www.brenneckes.com

**Reservations** Recommended **When to go** Sunset **Entrée range** $9–35 **Payment** VISA, MC, AMEX, D, DC, JCB **Service rating** ★★★ **Parking** In 2 adjacent lots **Bar** Full service **Wine selection** Limited **Dress** Casual **Disabled access** Poor, but staff will carry wheelchairs up the stairs **Customers** Tourists and Islanders

**Lunch** Every day, 11 a.m.–4 p.m.

**Dinner** Every day, 4–10 p.m.

**Setting & atmosphere** Climb the stairs to this restaurant situated across from Poʻipu Beach Park in a freestanding blue building. Then sit by an open window so you can see surfers, palms, blue ocean, and golden sands just beyond the petunia-filled window boxes.

**House specialties** After a trip to the salad bar, specialties called *makai* (from the ocean) and *mauka* (from the land) arrive sizzling from the kiawe charcoal broiler. Fresh Island fish, Hawaiian spiny lobster, or Brennecke's signature scampi with choice of barbecue, teriyaki, or garlic sauce will satisfy most diners.

**Other recommendations** Sea breezes through the open windows and a varied menu of Kauaʻi *pupus,* including fresh sashimi caught by local fishermen, New York steak and mushrooms, and nachos with peppers, make this a great spot for a glass of wine or one of Brennecke's world-famous Mai Tais.

**Entertainment & amenities** The restaurant sound system usually carries either 1960s or Hawaiian tunes.

**Summary & comments** Brennecke's is handy if you've had enough sun and sand but still want a peaceful beach-side ambience while you eat a big burger for lunch. The open-air view makes this place an old favorite. For quick and casual snacks, Brennecke's Deli downstairs serves cool shave ice and sandwiches with your choice of fillings.

## CAFÉ HANALEI AND TERRACE    ★★★★

CONTINENTAL (WITH ISLAND INGREDIENTS)  |  EXPENSIVE  |  QUALITY ★★★★½  |  VALUE ★★★  |  ZONE 13

Princeville Hotel, Princeville; (808) 826-2760; www.princeville.com

**Reservations** Recommended **When to go** Anytime, though sunsets are best **Entrée range** $26.95–31.95, (vegetarian dish $21.95); 3-course dinner $43.95 **Payment** VISA, MC, AMEX, D, DC, JCB **Service rating** ★★★★★ **Parking** Valet or hotel lot **Bar** Full service **Wine selection** Good **Dress** Resort wear **Disabled access** Good, via elevator **Customers** Resort and hotel guests, Islanders for special events

**Breakfast** Every day, 6:30–11 a.m. includes buffet

**Lunch** Every day, 11 a.m.–2:30 p.m.

**Dinner** Every day, 5:30–9:30 p.m.

**Setting & atmosphere** Café Hanalei and Terrace enjoys the most stunning view of any restaurant on Kauaʻi; it overlooks Hanalei Bay and Makana Peak (the jutting spire of land that gained fame as Bali Hai in the movie *South Pacific*). A placid reflecting pool is on one side of the covered terrace seating, and when rain sprinkles over the bay, it becomes an artist's extravagant scene; sometimes a vivid rainbow arches across the misty sun-streaked sky. Inside, you have a feeling of soaring space, as the restaurant is surrounded by towering windows and the ceiling is two floors above the lobby level.

**House specialties**　The restaurant's Sunday brunch buffet is both a gourmand's and a glutton's dream-come-true, with made-to-order omelets, seafood, salads, and a dessert spread that requires at least two trips. Breakfast buffets the rest of the week are well stocked with Island fruit. At dinner the most popular entrée is steamed Hawaiian snap-per, a sweet, white fish prepared with fresh ginger, cilantro, and shiitake mushrooms. Such a low-calorie meal calls for a decadent dessert—chocolate macadamia-nut pie or Kona coffee crème brûlée.

**Other recommendations**　Sushi addicts are lucky if they come by on Saturday, Sun-day, Tuesday, or Wednesday: On those nights, sushi chefs handcraft these little balls of rice and seafood to order in the restaurant.

**Entertainment & amenities**　The lilting music of a pianist and a vocalist filters down from an upstairs lobby bar to diners who eat inside.

**Summary & comments**　The view is what people remember, but the food and ser-vice also make dining a pleasure.

## CASA DI AMICI

ITALIAN/CONTEMPORARY | MODERATE | QUALITY ★★★★ | VALUE ★★★ | ZONE 13

2301 Nalo Road, Po'ipu; (808) 742-1555; www.casadiamica.com

**Reservations** Requested **When to go** Thursday–Saturday if you like piano music **Entrée range** $13–27 **Payment** VISA, AMEX **Service rating** ★★★★ **Parking** In adjacent lot **Bar** Full service **Wine selection** Excellent **Dress** Casual **Disabled access** Good **Customers** Islanders and tourists

**Lunch** Tuesday–Friday, 11:30 a.m.–2:30 p.m.

**Dinner** Every day, 6–9 p.m.

**Setting & atmosphere**　Windows open to the balmy air around this comfortable Po'ipu restaurant. Casa di Amici means "house of friends," and with rattan furnishings under ceiling fans inside and sweeping views to the ocean on the deck outside, it feels like the kama'aina home the building once was. If you must wait for a table, a small open-air bar is near the entry, where a big fish tank is filled with colorful reef fish for your diversion.

**House specialties**　The Italian menu is translated into English, so you can figure out what you're getting when you mix and match your favorite pasta with perhaps a salsa arrabiatta—spicy tomato with sautéed pancetta and chilis. The most popular item on the menu is a porcini-crusted chicken breast in a sun-dried cherry, port wine, and mushroom sauce.

If you like bold flavors, try Japanese mahogany-glazed salmon served on frijole chorittos and black beans, or salmon steak painted with heavy soy sauce, sprinkled with furukake, baked and garnished with jalapeño-tequila aïole, and served on a corn husk.

**Other recommendations**  Picatta (as in veal picatta) and marsala sauces are particularly flavorful and rich. The chef loves Mexican/southwestern food, so he's proud of his chili verde risotto. He has fun with risotto, creating classic four-cheese risotto, Indian curried lamb, kalua (usually pork), and other variations. Besides the bananas Foster, a dessert with a tropical appeal is Sugarloaf—upside-down cake topped with liliko'i cream.

**Summary & comments**  Some entrées are available in light portions, but once you taste the house scampi with a good red wine, you may want more. Because of the variety of ethnic flavors in his preparations, the French-trained chef/owner describes his restaurant as "the most un-Italian Italian restaurant you'll ever be in." It has been given high marks by *Zagat*, the *Los Angeles Times*, *Gourmet*, the *Chicago Tribune*, and other food writers.

## DUKE'S CANOE CLUB

SEAFOOD  |  INEXPENSIVE/MODERATE  |  QUALITY ★★★★  |  VALUE ★★★★  |  ZONE 13

Kaua'i Marriott Resort and Beach Club, Kalapaki Beach, Lihu'e; (808) 246-9599; www.marriotthotels.com/lihhi

**Reservations** Recommended **When to go** Anytime; for cocktails at the Barefoot Bar, show up 4–6 p.m. for reasonable prices and live entertainment **Entrée range** $10.99–24.99, market price for lobster **Payment** VISA, MC, AMEX, D **Service rating** ★★★½ **Parking** In adjacent lot **Bar** Full service **Wine selection** Adequate **Dress** Casual **Disabled access** Adequate **Customers** Tourists and Islanders **Lunch** Every day, 11:30 a.m.–11:30 p.m. downstairs

**Dinner** Every day, 5–10 p.m.

**Setting & atmosphere**  At this Polynesian-style restaurant with open-air views onto Kalapaki Beach, diners can sit downstairs at the Barefoot Bar for lunch, snacks, afternoon cocktails, and people-watching, or amble upstairs for dinner. A tinkling stream and waterfall, edged by lush plantings, creates an outdoor garden effect even in the building's cool, shady interior.

**House specialties**  Fresh fish is the name of the game after a trip to Duke's "all-you-care-to-eat" salad bar. Entrées come with salad, herbed rice, muffins, and sourdough bread. Best of the five preparations for fish is "Duke's Style," baked in garlic, lemon, and sweet basil glaze, although if you want to spice things up a bit, you might go for the "Firecracker Fresh Fish" preparation with tomato-chili-cumin aïoli, served with black bean, Maui onion, and avocado relish.

**Other recommendations**  Macadamia-nut-and-crab wontons are such delicious little deep-fried pockets of Dungeness crab, cream cheese, and macadamia nuts served with a mustard plum sauce, you might be tempted to limit dinner to these appetizers and a trip to the salad bar.

**Entertainment & amenities**  A strolling trio of guitar and ukulele players presents Hawaiian-style dinner music in the restaurant upstairs. Downstairs on Thursday and "Tropical Friday" afternoons, a band entertains, and tropical drinks are a special happy hour price.

**Summary & comments** This is an easy, casual place to grab a hamburger as you come off Kalapaki Beach for lunch or enjoy a Mai Tai at sunset, and then climb the stairs for a pleasant dinner. Unfortunately, service isn't always as attentive as it should be. *Keiki* (children's) dinner items, which also include the salad bar, make this a reasonably "nice" place to take kids, a welcome change from fast-food dinners.

## HAMURA SAIMIN

ISLAND ECLECTIC | INEXPENSIVE | QUALITY ★★★½ | VALUE ★★★★★ | ZONE 13

2956 Kress Street, Lihu'e; (808) 245-3271

**Reservations** Not accepted **When to go** This little café is always busy, especially on rainy days, but right after opening there might be a lull **Entrée range** $5–15 **Payment** Cash or traveler's checks **Service rating** ★★ **Parking** Limited in lot and on street **Bar** None, diners can bring libations **Wine selection** None **Dress** Casual **Disabled access** Accessible, but there is no ramp over an entry step **Customers** Islanders and adventuresome tourists

**Lunch & dinner** Monday–Saturday, 10 a.m.–midnight; Sunday, 10 a.m.–9 p.m.

**Setting & atmosphere** This is down-home Hawai'i on a dusty side street in Lihu'e. The restaurant is in a single-board, plantation-style building, with louvered windows that let in a breath of air that is never enough on a muggy summer day. Counter space fills the center of the restaurant, there are a few tables, and you'll note good-luck porcelain cat statues and other Island touches.

**House specialties** Everybody ends up at Hamura's at one time or another for a big steaming bowl of saimin that's especially good on a wet, windy, Kaua'i winter day. The saimin special bowl has a little bit of everything: noodles garnished with vegetables, won-ton, fish cake, chopped boiled egg, sliced pork, green onion, and sliced luncheon meat.

**Other recommendations** Soup is the ticket at Hamura's, but carnivores will love the grilled chicken skewers and beef sticks. Manapua, big bread-like buns with a savory filling, are also favored, while liliko'i chiffon pie is a don't-miss dessert.

**Summary & comments** Hamura Saimin has been a Lihu'e standby for so long it's an institution. Go for a steaming bowl of soup, but don't expect to be blown away by fancy food or service; just enjoy the fun of having a unique local experience.

## KEOKI'S PARADISE  ★★★½

SEAFOOD AND STEAK | MODERATE | QUALITY ★★★★ | VALUE ★★★★ | ZONE 13

Po'ipu Shopping Village, Po'ipu; (808) 742-7535; www.hulapie.com

**Reservations** Recommended **When to go** Anytime **Entrée range** $8.95–23.95, or market price **Payment** VISA, MC, AMEX **Service rating** ★★★ **Parking** In adjacent lot **Bar** Full service **Wine selection** Good **Dress** Casual **Disabled access** Good **Customers** Tourists and Islanders

**Lunch** Every day, 11 a.m.–11:30 p.m.

**Dinner**  Every day, 5:30–10 p.m.

**Setting & atmosphere**  From outside in the generally crowded parking lot of this centrally located resort shopping center, you wouldn't expect to find a pleasant, cool boathouse-style restaurant set on a peaceful lagoon with tropical foliage and a thatched-roof bar. It takes you back to the Hawai'i depicted on movie screens in the 1950s.

**House specialties**  Fresh seafood, from starters of sashimi or chowder to a fresh-catch entrée served in your choice of five preparations and sauces, is most popular. Types of fish served depend on what is delivered that day and could range from 'ahi (tuna) to ulua (pompano) to opah (Hawaiian moonfish). For dessert, the hula pie with an Oreo cookie crust filled with ice cream is made for sharing.

**Other recommendations**  For a taste of local flavor, order Koloa pork ribs glazed with plum sauce or Balinese chicken marinated in lemongrass and served with a lemon shoyu sauce, or try both in a combination plate. A variety of steaks are served with garlic mashed potatoes.

**Summary & comments**  You can get just about any down-to-earth food you're in the mood for. You feel as if you are getting your money's worth, as healthy-sized entrées all include Keoki's Caesar-style salad, fresh-baked bread, and herbed rice, all served in a pleasant Polynesian setting.

## *MEMA THAI CHINESE CUISINE*  ★★

THAI/CHINESE  |  INEXPENSIVE/MODERATE  |  QUALITY ★★★★  |  VALUE ★★★★★  |
ZONE 13

4-361 Kuhio Highway, Wailua Shopping Center, Kapa'a; (808) 823-0899

**Reservations** Accepted **When to go** Anytime **Entrée range** $7.95–16.95 **Payment** VISA, MC, AMEX, D, DC **Service rating** ★★★ **Parking** In adjacent lot **Bar** Full bar **Wine selection** Limited **Dress** Casual **Disabled access** Good **Customers** Islanders and tourists

**Lunch**  Monday–Friday, 11 a.m.–2:30 p.m.

**Dinner**  Every day, 5–9:30 p.m.

**Setting & atmosphere**  Set in a tiresome little strip mall, Mema Thai Chinese is surprisingly attractive, with pretty pink linen tablecloths and lovely Oriental rosewood chairs. Orchid sprays add to the gracious atmosphere.

**House specialties**  Curries come in colors of the rainbow—red, green, and yellow—made with your choice of vegetables, chicken, pork or beef, shrimp, or fish, and other seafood. A local dish named evil jungle prince, a savory blending of coconut milk, basil, and red chili, can also be ordered with seafood (including calamari), poultry, or meat.

**Other recommendations**  There's plenty to satisfy vegetarians here; many dishes can be ordered with tofu instead of meat, such as rice noodles with cabbage, mushrooms, and carrots, or stir-fried broccoli with oyster sauce.

**Summary & comments**  *Thai Scene* magazine once named Mema "one of the ten best Thai restaurants outside Thailand." You may want to sit toward the back of the semi-divided room, away from the bar and the entrance to the kitchen, for the most peaceful dining experience.

## A PACIFIC CAFÉ                                        ★★★★½

PACIFIC RIM | MODERATE | QUALITY ★★★★½ | VALUE ★★★ | ZONE 13

4-831 Kuhio Highway, Suite 220, Kaua'i Village Shopping Center, Kapa'a; (808) 822-0013

**Reservations** Highly recommended **When to go** Anytime, but it's less crowded 5:30–6:30 p.m. **Entrée range** $22–26 **Payment** VISA, MC, AMEX, D, DC **Service rating** ★★★★★ **Parking** Shopping center lot **Bar** Full service **Wine selection** Extensive, several by the glass **Dress** Casual **Disabled access** Good **Customers** Islanders and tourists

**Dinner** Every day, 5:30–10 p.m.

**Setting & atmosphere** The pretty-in-pastel restaurant has light-colored wooden tables, a few colorful tropical floral arrangements, and paintings from nearby Wyland Art Galleries decorating the walls.

**House specialties** The wok-charred mahimahi served with julienned vegetables and lime-ginger sauce is an award winner that never fails to please. Another popular standby on what is otherwise a most inventive menu is the certified Black Angus New York steak.

Two desserts have a loyal following: Crème brûlée is pure ambrosia enveloped in a crispy pastry crust. Or you can order a hot Vintage Chocolate tart. Prepared individually, the chocolate tart takes 15 minutes, so order while you're still eating, or be prepared to relax over coffee while you wait.

**Other recommendations** Almost too pretty to eat, the tiger eye sushi is sliced into thin, melt-in-the mouth slices that resemble tiger eyes, because the 'ahi (tuna) that it's made of encases green asparagus and tobiko roe. The 'ahi is dipped in tempura, then flash-fried on the outside, so the inside slices remain sushi rare.

**Summary & comments** For years this classy Kapa'a community restaurant has been *the* place to go for beautifully presented dishes with complex flavors made with homegrown ingredients. Chef/owner Jean Marie Josselin works with an Island farmer who grows herbs, lettuces, fruit, and vegetables to meet the restaurant's specific requirements.

## PLANTATION GARDENS                                    ★★★½

ITALIAN | MODERATE | QUALITY ★★★★ | VALUE ★★★ | ZONE 13

2253 Po'ipu Road, Kiahuna Plantation; (808) 742-2216; www.outrigger.com

**Reservations** Recommended **When to go** Anytime after 5:30 p.m. for dinner; for cocktails and pizza, drop by between 4 and 5:30 p.m. **Entrée range** $13.95–27.95 **Payment** VISA, MC, AMEX, DC **Service rating** ★★★★ **Parking** In adjacent lots

**Bar** Full service **Wine selection** Excellent **Dress** Kaua'i casual **Disabled access** Good **Customers** Tourists and Islanders

**Dinner** Every day, 5:30–10 p.m.

**Setting & atmosphere** Gardens with torchlit paths, rock work, a rich wood interior, and veranda dining offer a lovely setting for Italian food served in a historic Polynesian home, which once belonged to an early sugar baron.

**House specialties** Many items on the menu change monthly, but Plantation Gardens is known for its fresh fish and house-made pastas. The signature pasta dish, pappardelle fantasia, is a wide saffron pasta sautéed in white wine, herbs, and spices and tossed with fresh garden vegetables and shrimp. Fish of the day varies depending on what the fishermen bring to the door. If you hang out around the display kitchen, you can watch your pizza with portobello mushrooms, pancetta, and fontina cheese emerge sizzling from the wood-burning oven. A kiawe broiler gives steaks and fish that special smoky flavor.

**Other recommendations** Currently on the menu, manzo brasato is slow-roasted pot roast served with mascarpone mashed potatoes (whipped with sweet Italian cream cheese), served with gravy and fresh veggies of day, which might be bok choy and Koloa asparagus when in season.

The restaurant is famous for a classic tiramisu, but the banana liliko'i cream cheesecake with cream cheese frosting is equally decadent.

**Entertainment & amenities** If you're lucky, you may hit a weekend summer night when a rising Kaua'i group might drop by to play.

**Summary & comments** Fresh herbs are plucked from the garden out back, and Island fish might have been picked or caught only hours before reaching your table.

## POSTCARDS                                                    ★★★½

CONTEMPORARY | MODERATE | QUALITY ★★★★ | VALUE ★★★★ | ZONE 13

5-5075 A Kuhio Highway, Hanalei; (808) 826-1191

**Reservations** Highly recommended **When to go** Anytime for dinner **Entrée range** $14–22, fish are market price **Payment** VISA, MC, AMEX **Service rating** ★★ **Parking** In adjacent lot **Bar** None **Wine selection** Bring your own **Dress** Casual **Disabled access** Adequate **Customers** Islanders and tourists

**Brunch** Sunday, 8 a.m.–noon

**Breakfast** Every day, 8–11 a.m.

**Dinner** Every day, 5–9 p.m.

**Setting & atmosphere** Set in a small restored single-board plantation-style house with a front porch, the restaurant has the charm of an earlier era.

**House specialties** Gourmet vegetarian cuisine and savory seafood dishes draw repeat visitors. Start with an organic salad, or Thai summer rolls with spicy peanut sauce, then plunge into fresh fish or shrimp tacos or sample the taj triangles, crusty phyllo pastry filled with potatoes, peas, carrots, and Indian spices served with tropical chutney. Youngsters love the fresh fruit smoothies and cheese quesadillas.

**Other recommendations** If you're tired of hotel food, this is possibly Hanalei's next best bet for breakfast. Sunrise Scramble features sautéed tofu with onions, garlic, and herbs mixed into the eggs. Other highlights include a full espresso bar, Irish red-roasted potatoes, homemade muffins, fresh orange juice, and Hanalei hotcakes.

**Summary & comments** Guests sign the guest book with notes like "We ate here three nights in a row" and "The best seafood in the Islands."

## ROY'S PO'IPU BAR & GRILL                    ★★★★

HAWAIIAN FUSION  |  MODERATE  |  QUALITY ★★★★½  |  VALUE ★★★  |  ZONE 13

Po'ipu Shopping Village, 2360 Kiahuna Plantation Drive, Po'ipu Beach; (808) 742-5000; www.roysrestaurant.com

**Reservations** Highly recommended **When to go** Early for a quieter dinner, later for a livelier crowd **Entrée range** $17–32 **Payment** VISA, MC, AMEX, DC, D **Service rating** ★★★★ **Parking** In shopping center lot **Bar** Full bar **Wine selection** Excellent, many wines by the glass **Dress** Casual **Disabled access** Good **Customers** Tourists and Islanders

**Dinner** Every day, 5:30–9 p.m.

**Setting & atmosphere** Chef/owner Roy Yamaguchi's sleek shopping center restaurant is a mecca for fans of what he dubs Euro-Asian Pacific cuisine—Asian seasonings mixed with French techniques. The restaurant has a very airy feeling, with windows that let in the night air. The exhibition kitchen is enclosed by glass, so the noise level is kept down. A newer expansion and lounge area across a public walkway brings shoppers seemingly through the middle of the restaurant.

**House specialties** Hibachi-style salmon and oven-roasted pot roast have emerged from a long list of specials as steady favorites. Seafood lovers might choose fresh seared 'opakapaka (snapper) with orange shrimp butter and Chinese black-bean sauce. Dark-chocolate soufflé and volcanic puffed pastry filled with caramelized apple are dessert winners.

**Other recommendations** It's fun to go for dim sum and appetizers followed by a pizza from the wood-fired oven, so you have a chance to sample a number the culinary creations available. Or, couples might share appetizers like lemongrass shrimp sticks with Thai chili cocktail sauce, or pot-stickers with spicy peanut satay sauce, or escargot cassoulet with caramelized onions and creamy polenta.

**Summary & comments** Diners return again and again to this most popular restaurant in Po'ipu, so Roy's chefs make sure they will never get bored with the menu by offering 25 or more specials nightly.

## SHELLS, AT THE SHERATON KAUA'I HOTEL          ★★★½

AMERICAN  |  MODERATE/EXPENSIVE  |  QUALITY ★★★★  |  VALUE ★★★  |  ZONE 13

Sheraton Kaua'i Hotel, 2440 Ho'onani Road, Po'ipu Beach; (808) 742-1661; www.sheraton-kauai.com

**Reservations** Recommended **When to go** 6–7 p.m. for sunset ocean view **Entrée range** $15.50–36 **Payment** VISA, MC, AMEX, DC, D, JCB **Service rating** ★★★★ **Parking** Valet or hotel lot **Bar** Full service **Wine selection** Good **Dress** Resort wear **Disabled access** Good **Customers** Tourists

**Breakfast** Every day, 6:30–11 a.m.

**Dinner** Every day, 5:30–9:30 p.m.

**Setting & atmosphere** Floor-to-ceiling windows let the trade winds and the sound of the waves drift off the ocean to diners on the lanai and inside this high-ceilinged restaurant. The airy, tropical room has rattan furnishings set under elaborate shell chandeliers that remained intact through Hurricane 'Iniki, which destroyed the hotel in 1992.

**House specialties** Baby rack of lamb prepared with herb and hoisin sauce is *'ono* (delicious), though non–meat lovers might prefer the fresh fish and prawns served with spicy pineapple, baked sweet potato, Kaua'i slaw, and steamed rice, for a touch of Island flavor.

**Other recommendations** Appetizer crab cakes are a perennial favorite, but the restaurant is really known for a dessert called Mount Wai'ale'ale, which is a mountain of chocolate-mousse cake piled with sorbet and fresh Island fruit.

**Summary & comments** This big, pretty hotel dining room is located adjacent to The Point, a great spot for predinner cocktails indoors or out-, where the ocean view is even more encompassing. Note that children ages 12 and under eat free (maximum two children per table).

## *TIDEPOOLS*

PACIFIC RIM | MODERATE/EXPENSIVE | QUALITY ★★★½ | VALUE ★★★ | ZONE 13

1571 Po'ipu Road, Hyatt Regency Kaua'i, Po'ipu Beach; (808) 742-6260

**Reservations** Highly recommended **When to go** Anytime **Entrée range** $22–40 **Payment** VISA, MC, AMEX **Service rating** ★★★★ **Parking** Valet or hotel lot **Bar** Full service **Wine selection** Adequate **Dress** Resort attire **Disabled access** Make prearrangements; it's quite a distance from the parking lot via an elevator and a service tunnel **Customers** Tourists, hotel guests, a few Islanders for special events

**Dinner** Every day, 6–10 p.m.

**Setting & atmosphere** Romantic tropical atmosphere makes this restaurant special for honeymooners and longtime lovers. Torchlit paths lead to the restaurant, which floats on a fish-filled lagoon; some thatched dining huts hold single candlelit tables for total privacy under Kaua'i's starry skies.

**House specialties** Tidepools serves interesting grilled entrées seasoned with Hawaiian 'alaea sea salt, such as chicken breast filled with Puna goat cheese and a lemongrass butter sauce, or pork chops topped with Asian pear marmalade, but fish and seafood are truly most appropriate for this watery restaurant. Macadamia-nut-crusted Island fish with Kahlua, lime-ginger butter sauce, and jasmine fried rice is the signature dish. A selection from ten kinds of Island fish is offered nightly, and the server can describe each fish in detail. You can order four different preparations: sautéed with liliko'i butter, grilled with papaya and mango relish, steamed with sweet chili and lime sauce, or blackened with Hana Bay rum pineapple sauce.

**Other recommendations** Combination plates are the most expensive, but by ordering from a menu of ten combination items you can sample meat *and* seafood. Don't miss banana chocolate silk, a heavenly combination of bittersweet chocolate silk with bananas and cream, crème anglaise, and caramelized macadamia nuts.

**Summary & comments** You don't need to be afraid to take the kids to eat at Tidepools, as the restaurant actually offers a children's menu, with most items from $5 to $11—pasta, hamburger, chicken nuggets—and they will be enchanted by the lagoons all around.

## Moloka'i

### HOTEL MOLOKA'I RESTAURANT ★★

ISLAND ECLECTIC  |  INEXPENSIVE  |  QUALITY ★★★  |  VALUE ★★★★★  |  ZONE 14

Box 1020 Kamehameha Highway; (808) 553-5347; www.hotelmoloki.com

**Reservations** Accepted **When to go** Anytime **Entrée range** $10–19 **Payment** VISA, MC **Service rating** ★★★ **Parking** Free in hotel lot **Bar** Full service **Wine selection** Adequate **Dress** Casual **Disabled access** Good **Customers** Tourists and Islanders are split about 50-50

**Lunch** Every day, 11:30 a.m.–2 p.m.

**Dinner** Every day, 6–9 p.m.

**Setting & atmosphere** Being right on the beach in this open-air restaurant enhances the feeling of old Polynesia imparted by decorative tiki carved pillars and outrigger canoes pulled up on the nearby shore. You can sit under the roof at candlelit tables, or at plastic tables arranged on the adjacent pool deck.

**House specialties** Cockeyed Moloka'i coconut shrimp, dipped in batter, rolled in coconut, and deep-fried may not be good *for* you, but it's good. Soups and specialties change daily, so one night the theme might be Oriental, with Chinese food, another it might be country-and-western, featuring barbecued back ribs and chicken, while Friday and Saturday, prime rib is the featured dinner.

**Other recommendations** This is truly a menu with something for everyone. There's Chinese chicken salad or taco salad, and mahimahi comes with your choice of caper sauce, papaya-pineapple relish, or pepper sauce. If you've been hanging loose at the bar, down a big bowl of mana'uele (taro) boy chili or Moloka'i stew before heading out into the night.

**Entertainment & amenities** Island-style musicians make this one of the few places to hang out after dark on Moloka'i on Friday and Saturday nights.

**Summary & comments** For a hotel restaurant, prices are surprisingly reasonable, and the management's goal is to keep them low in hopes of building a clientele of loyal Moloka'i residents.

# MAUNALOA ROOM ★★★★

MOLOKAʻI REGIONAL | MODERATE/EXPENSIVE | QUALITY ★★★★½ | VALUE ★★★ |
ZONE 14

The Lodge at Molokaʻi Ranch, #8, Maunaloa; (808) 660-2725;
www.molokaʻi-ranch.com

**Reservations** Recommended **When to go** Anytime **Entrée range** $19–39 **Payment** AMEX, MC, VISA **Service rating** ★★★★ **Parking** Free in hotel lot **Bar** Full service **Wine selection** Good **Dress** Resort wear **Disabled access** Excellent **Customers** Tourists, Islanders for a very special occasion

**Breakfast** Monday–Saturday, 7–10 a.m.

**Brunch** Sunday, 11 a.m.–1 p.m.

**Lunch** Sunday–Monday, 10 a.m.–4 p.m.

**Dinner** Sunday–Monday, 6–9 p.m.; Wednesday, prime rib buffet.

**Setting & atmosphere** Inside the decor follows a ranch theme with wooden tables, chairs with pineapple print seats, and chandeliers with electric candles in a wagon wheel shape. Views from an open-air deck stretch three miles to the ocean. Deck chairs are metal with woven lau hala seats and backs that sport the Molokaʻi Ranch logo, the profile of a cow.

**House specialties** The chef describes his menu as Molokaʻi Regional because he buys as many ingredients locally as possible and blends flavors originating with the various ethnic groups that populate Molokaʻi. He also mixes his own spices and grows many of his herbs just outside the Lodge. This is one of the few menus that feature Molokaʻi opihi (a crunchy limpet that is an island delicacy) as an appetizer or pan-seared venison as an entrée. Corn and crab bisque, followed by macadamia nut–crusted catch of the day on spinach surrounded by lobster-coconut curry sauce and garnished with pineapple-ginger relish are two of the menu's stars.

**Other recommendations** Big, tender, crispy coconut shrimp come with an orange-ginger sauce for a tasty appetizer. A truly island-style entrée is panko-crusted ʻahi (tuna) wrapped around a fern shoot, packaged in nori (seaweed), and seared crisp on the outside and rare on the inside. Cut into slices, it's served with rice and a fern shoot salad. A carving station at Sunday brunch might feature prime rib, lamb, or other succulent meats. Brunch will run you $22.95, or $27.95 with champagne.

**Summary & comments** Bar none, the Moanaloa Room serves the finest haute cuisine on the island. It's also the priciest restaurant on Molokaʻi, but dining here is a splurge you should enjoy at least once during an island visit. After dinner, it's a pleasure to relax in the Great Room with its enormous stone fireplace and listen to acoustic Hawaiian music strummed and sung by a ranch *paniolo* (cowboy). Often, a hula dancer joins him—either a pretty Molokaʻi wahine (lady) or, when the bar next door is slow, the bartender might render a dance or two.

## MOLOKA'I PIZZA CAFÉ                                      ★★

PIZZA AND SANDWICHES  |  INEXPENSIVE  |  QUALITY ★★★½  |  VALUE ★★★★  |
ZONE 14

15 Kaunakakai Place, on Wharf Road; (808) 553-3288

**Reservations** Not accepted **When to go** Anytime **Entrée range** $4.50–12.99 **Payment** Cash only **Service rating** ★★ **Parking** Adjacent lot **Bar** None **Wine selection** None **Dress** Casual **Disabled access** Good **Customers** Locals and tourists

**Breakfast** Available all day

**Lunch & dinner** Monday–Thursday, Sunday, 11 a.m.–10 p.m.; Friday and Saturday, 11 a.m.–11 p.m.

**Setting & atmosphere** This is a clean, air-conditioned cafe with booths and tables in a spacious room. It's a Moloka'i family kind of place, often decorated with artwork and thank-you cards by schoolkids. Some of the Formica-topped tables are set in a smaller, quieter area at the front of the restaurant away from kids, and there is also outside lanai dining, where guests are welcome to bring their own wine or beer to enjoy with dinner.

**House specialties** Fresh fish is served at market price whenever available. Wednesday nights a Mexican menu featuring burritos, fajitas, tacos, and nachos is added for variety, and Sunday nights prime rib is the big draw.

**Other recommendations** You can order pizza by the piece, or a Molokini pizza for a single person, or get a big one to go or to eat in. Chicken dinners come with rice or french fries and hot veggies. Sandwiches, pasta, salads, and frozen yogurt are also on the menu.

**Entertainment & amenities** Strolling musicians are hired for big private parties and sometimes for special holidays.

**Summary & comments** Eventually everyone stops by the Pizza Café. Kids hang out here after school, and tourists stop by for a slice of pizza, as it's one of the few places that serves until 10 p.m. nightly.

## THE VILLAGE GRILL                                      ★★

ISLAND ECLECTIC  |  MODERATE  |  QUALITY ★★★½  |  VALUE ★★★  |  ZONE 14

Maunaloa Highway, Maunaloa Town; (808) 552-0012

**Reservations** Recommended **When to go** Anytime; 5–6 p.m. for the early-bird special; it gets busier later **Entrée range** $17–24.50 **Payment** VISA, MC, AMEX, DC **Service rating** ★★★ **Parking** Adjacent lot **Bar** Full service **Wine selection** Adequate, with several wines in a reasonable price range **Dress** Casual **Disabled access** Good **Customers** More tourists than Islanders, but a good mix

**Dinner** Every day, 6–9 p.m.

**Setting & atmosphere** Remodeled in 1998 by Moloka'i Ranch, the former Jojo's Cafe still sports a historic bar that once graced O'ahu's Pearl City Tavern, but it now has a bronze countertop with a lariat design. The restaurant has a Western feeling, with light fixtures sporting Western-designed shades, and saddles and cowboy pictures on the wall, but most people prefer to sit outside on the screened deck to enjoy the stars above this quiet little town.

**House specialties**  Good, filling entrées, like prime rib, New York steak, and pizza are flavored with locally grown herbs. There's always a fresh catch of the day that can be ordered sautéed, broiled, or Cajun style, plus lobster and king crab. Try a "sky high pie" for dessert, a mound of vanilla, macadamia, and coffee-flavored ice cream in a graham cracker crust with custard, strawberry, and chocolate sauces.

**Other recommendations**  Wok-seared Asian stir-fry, with veggies, shrimp, and scallops, and baby-back ribs impart a Moloka'i flavor. A local favorite for dessert is liliko'i-coconut cream pie, a coconut–passion fruit cream pie on a macadamia cookie crust made with a layer of haupia (coconut pudding), glazed with passion fruit, and topped with whipped cream and toasted coconut flakes.

**Summary & comments**  Much of the fun here comes from cooking your own entrée on a stone grill brought to your table. Dinner in this small-town restaurant makes you feel as if you're rubbing elbows with the local folks, even though tourists are likely to be sitting at the next table.

# Lana'i

## BLUE GINGER CAFÉ

ISLAND ECLECTIC | INEXPENSIVE | QUALITY ★★★ | VALUE ★★★★★ | ZONE 15

409 7th Avenue, Lana'i City; (808) 565-6363

**Reservations** Accepted, but requested only for large parties **When to go** Anytime **Entrée range** $5.50–13.95 **Payment** VISA, MC **Service rating** ★★★ **Parking** Street **Bar** Full service **Wine selection** Limited **Dress** Casual **Disabled access** Good **Customers** Islanders, *kama'aina* travelers

**Breakfast**  Every day, 6–11 a.m.

**Lunch & dinner**  Every day, 11 a.m.–9 p.m.

**Setting & atmosphere**  Set in a little single-board plantation building in Lana'i City's main square. Diners order and pick up food at the counter and eat at tables draped with plastic cloths in this old, somewhat grubby-looking restaurant. An inexpensive alternative to Lana'i's costly hotel dining rooms.

**House specialties**  Try the tasty vegetarian breakfast omelet that comes with rice, or order fresh-baked apple turnovers or cinnamon rolls to carry back to your hotel, as this is Lana'i's only bakery outside the hotel bake shops. For lunch, the bacon-cheddar cheeseburgers are better than Big Macs, but you might want to try the local soup called saimin, a generous steaming bowl of noodle soup garnished with sliced fish cake, green onions, and shredded egg. At dinner, sautéed mahimahi with capers, onions, and mushrooms is the signature dish. Top it off with an ice cream dessert. Blue Ginger serves Dave's ice cream, made in the Islands with local ingredients.

**Other recommendations** Banana or blueberry pancakes accompanied by cappuccino for breakfast. For dinner, if an Island-style plate with a choice of teriyaki beef, katsu chicken, hamburger steak with gravy, plus rice and macaroni salad, sounds like too much cholesterol for one meal, there's also New York steak with a baked potato or shrimp scampi.

**Summary & comments** This has been a Lana'i hangout owned by the same family for years. Blue Ginger and the little deli called Pele's Other Garden, located across the park, are the best independent restaurants around the square in central Lana'i City.

## THE FORMAL DINING ROOM, THE LODGE AT KO'ELE

CONTEMPORARY | EXPENSIVE | QUALITY ★★★★½ | VALUE ★★★ | ZONE 15

Lodge at Ko'ele, Keomuku Drive, Lana'i City; (808) 565-7300;
www.lanai-resorts.com

**Reservations** Highly recommended **When to go** Anytime, but sunset is generally more peaceful; the restaurant can get crowded by 7 p.m. **Entrée range** $34–42 **Payment** VISA, MC, AMEX, DC, JCB **Service rating** ★★★★★ **Parking** Valet, hotel lot **Bar** Full service **Wine selection** Excellent **Dress** Jacket required **Disabled access** Adequate **Customers** Hotel guests, other tourists, and visiting Neighbor Islanders

**Dinner** Every day, 6–9:30 p.m.

**Setting & atmosphere** Relaxed elegance sums up the ambience of this refined restaurant overlooking the fountain, a man-made lake, and the croquet lawn of Ko'ele Lodge. With fine silver and sparkling crystal, twinkling lights in the chandelier, and a fire in the dining room's own fireplace, this is a peaceful place for a romantic dinner.

**House specialties** The chef makes flavorful soups with Lana'i-grown herbs and produce and creates dishes that fit the cool lodge atmosphere: onaga with garlic butter, corn, and spinach; roasted Lana'i venison loin rolled in pancetta; and foie gras served with a balsamic reduction.

**Other recommendations** Rack of lamb with English mint cake. A lighter option is seared Hawaiian 'ahi with foie gras, cauliflower/parsnip puree, and veal reduction.

**Entertainment & amenities** Dinner music, often traditional Hawaiian melodies, piano, or classical musical scores, drifts in from the adjoining lobby. You can extend what is sure to be an expensive evening by relaxing in the Lodge's lobby after dinner with a snifter of brandy in front of a crackling fire in either of two massive fireplaces.

**Summary & comments** This could be the perfect place to pop the question, as lovers enjoy an intimate feeling of isolation in this quiet dining room. Tables are far enough apart to whisper sweet nothings, and the food is delicious. No wonder The Formal Dining Room keeps winning awards.

## HENRY CLAY'S ROTISSERIE ★★★

AMERICAN COUNTRY | MODERATE | QUALITY ★★★½ | VALUE ★★★★ | ZONE 15

Hotel Lana'i 828 Lana'i Avenue, Lana'i City; (808) 565-7211; www.hotellani.com

**Reservations** Highly recommended **When to go** Anytime **Entrée range** $12–28 **Payment** VISA, MC; guests of all 3 island hotels have signing privileges to their rooms **Service rating** ★★★ **Parking** Hotel lot; many people ride a shuttle from Lana'i's other 2 hotels **Bar** Full service **Wine selection** Good, especially California wines, many of which are available by the glass **Dress** Casual **Disabled access** Adequate **Customers** Tourists and Islanders

**Dinner** Every day, 5:30–9 p.m.

**Setting & atmosphere** Two fireplaces create a warm glow on knotty pine walls, oak floors, and a granite-topped bar. Rich floral tapestries in mauve, green, and gold, Island scenes by Lana'i artists, and outdoor lanai seating add to the old Hawai'i country charm. Diners can watch the chefs and rotisserie action through a display window into the kitchen.

**House specialties** The chef/owner, Henry Clay Richardson, has ties to the South, so his ragin' Cajun shrimp is only one example of some of the Louisiana-style menu items. The restaurant is recognized for rotisserie chicken and wild game, including venison, quail, rabbit, and duckling, as well as fresh-caught Hawaiian fish. Salads—Caesar or Hawaiian greens with Roma tomatoes, feta cheese, and Maui onions—are à la carte, but meals come with fresh vegetables, rice or potatoes, and French bread.

**Other recommendations** For a bit more of the southern flavor, try seafood jalapeño pasta or eggplant Creole. Everything is made from scratch, so you can't miss by sampling the pâté, clam chowder, or pecan pie.

**Summary & comments** Lana'i visitors often say this is the best dinner value on the island, considering the cost in comparison with the major hotel restaurants.

## 'IHILANI ★★★★½

HAWAI'I REGIONAL/MEDITERRANEAN | EXPENSIVE | QUALITY ★★★★½ | VALUE ★★★ | ZONE 15

Manele Bay Hotel, 1 Manele Road; (808) 565-7700; www.lanai-resorts.com

**Reservations** Highly recommended **When to go** Anytime **Entrée range** $32–40; vegetarian menu, $28–32 **Payment** VISA, MC, AMEX, DC, JCB **Service rating** ★★★★★ **Parking** Valet **Bar** Full service **Wine selection** Extensive **Dress** Jacket required **Disabled access** Good **Customers** Tourists and visiting Neighbor Islanders

**Dinner** Every day, 6–9:30 p.m.

**Setting & atmosphere** Fine china, silver, and lace-bedecked tables under hand-blown Italian crystal chandeliers are a lovely backdrop for dining in this formal dining room, which boasts a soothing view of pool and ocean from tables on an upper and lower bank.

**House specialties** The chef presents picture-perfect food in entrées such as roasted pheasant breast with foie gras and Madeira truffle sauce, pan-fried veal loin, or sautéed 'opakapaka (snapper) served with ragout of white beans, pancetta, and fresh thyme. Many of the more than a dozen desserts include sweets and truffles made of Hawaiian Vintage Chocolate. Diners can order an extensive selection of gourmet cheeses from the à la carte menu.

**Other recommendations** A nightly degustation menu of six or seven courses can be ordered paired with wines for $95 or sans wines for $65 per person. Prices may change according to what is featured. You might begin with oysters, then sample Maine lobster with shiitake mushrooms, proceed to pan-fried 'ahi, and savor a main course of roasted muscovy duck breast in red wine port sauce with Moloka'i sweet-potato purée and sautéed endive. Next, a selection of cheeses and walnut bread is served, plus a dessert selection followed by Hawaiian Vintage Chocolates and mignardises.

**Entertainment & amenities** Classical background music is set at a pleasant listening level.

**Summary & comments** This is the kind of dining experience that is more than just grabbing a bite to eat. Expect to take several leisurely hours to do all the courses justice.

# Part Ten

# Shopping

In Hawai'i, when the sun gets too hot, the sunburned go shopping. And what a bazaar they'll find—everything from funky T-shirts to worldly imports and a growing selection of made-in-Hawai'i clothing, art, sports gear, and jewelry.

Because the islands have attracted an increasingly international crowd—particularly free-spending young Japanese for whom Hawai'i has become a cheap ticket to European designer boutiques—shopping prospects have soared from dismal to extraordinary in recent years.

Smart-shopping Americans found they could bargain for the best selection this side of Hong Kong in Asian pearls, jewelry, antiques, and other imports. The trickle-down effect also lured American discount stores, that in turn brought everyday prices down in other island stores. When sugar plantations shut down, the company-owned stores, where so many workers shopped exclusively, soon followed. That left a lot of young people with better jobs and bigger dreams and more money to spend than their immigrant field-worker parents ever had. Obviously, retail makes up a large share of the Hawaiian economy.

The Aloha State is known for high costs, understandable because most of the goods—and every piece of glass, nail, and board in the buildings that contain them—are imported. But the low sales tax of 4%, charged at 4.176%, makes purchases more palatable, and some items just can't be found anywhere else. Besides, there's no going home empty-handed after an enviable trip to Hawai'i, so bring an extra suitcase and get ready to shop! Here are suggestions to maximize the experience.

## Buy Hawaiian

Local arts and crafts are flourishing. Finding them is often as much fun as giving them for gifts. Local wares sold by their makers dominate the frequent arts and crafts fairs held throughout the islands. Particularly fine are the **Pacific Handcrafters Guild** fairs held periodically on O'ahu.

Hawaiian product stores have sprung up everywhere (see some listed below). Occasionally you'll find local things among the cheap imports in tourist-zone kiosks and souvenir stores. You can find local books, music, aloha wear, and other goods at favorable prices in the national chain stores, such as **Costco, Longs, Sears,** and **Borders** and in the local chain, **ABC** stores.

Hawai'i's indigenous products range from inexpensive to very dear. They include foods—macadamia nuts, coffees, teas, wines, tropical jams, syrups, honeys, candies, and real Maui potato chips—soaps and cosmetics with tropical ingredients and fragrances; fiber arts made of coconut leaf, lauhala, or pandanus and other natural materials; aloha print fabrics made into shirts, baby clothes, totes, dresses, glasses cases, and even golf bags; Hawaiian books and music; warm-weather designer clothing; hand-painted clothing; windsurfing and surf boards and equipment; furniture and boxes handmade from tropical woods; one-of-a-kind Hawaiian appliquéd quilts, sewn only with permission of the family that created the design; and gold heirloom jewelry, Ni'ihau shell jewelry, and all kinds of artwork.

One solution to the nice-but-not-too-nice gift dilemma is packaging. Buy some affordable soaps or foods and bed them in an aloha fabric or natural fiber inside a lidded lauhala box, tie it with fiber ribbon, and decorate it with a shell. Gifts are sold prepackaged this way, too.

Hawaiian heirloom gold jewelry, monogrammed Victorian-style pieces in an arcane style created for nineteenth-century royals, is the precious gift of choice for special occasions in the islands. *Insider tip:* Most women in Hawai'i wear at least one solid oval gold bracelet ornately patterned and bearing their name in Hawaiian in black enameled script. Mothers may wear their daughters' bracelets until the girls are older. Many bracelets never come off. Many women wear them by the armload in Hawai'i, where it is safe enough and the local style. Admiring them is an effective way to start a conversation and get some hints on designs.

Heirloom jewelry has branched out to include medallions, pendants, watchbands, link bracelets, rings, and earrings for men as well as women. It is sold at jewelry shops throughout the islands and at jewelry counters in other stores, including the Japanese chain **Daiei.** In Waikiki, you can visit the factory and showroom at **Royal Hawaiian Shopping Center** to watch jewelry being made and buy some, if you wish.

Jewelry prices vary by gold weight and creative design. A bracelet might cost anywhere from $250 for a simple pattern on a thin band to $1,200 or more for a complex design on a larger band. This is a subjective purchase based on design, but do shop around enough to satisfy yourself that the price is fair for what you want. Shop for a bracelet early in your trip, to allow time for sizing and name engraving. The case samples are inscribed *"Kuuipo"* or "my sweetheart."

Ni'ihau shells are exquisite and extraordinarily expensive if you view them as just another shell necklace. After all, a strand of dyed "coral" costs $10, and a strand of the least expensive Ni'ihau shells costs more than $100 and fancy museum-quality ones can run up to thousands of dollars. Consider that each nearly microscopic Ni'ihau shell is picked off the beach on the private ranch island of Ni'ihau by one of its few inhabitants and then sorted, pierced, and strung into a traditional design. Visitors to Kaua'i, Ni'ihau's neighbor island, are most likely to learn to appreciate the beauty of these treasures and to see a variety displayed in shops and museums. You may even find some shells on a West Kaua'i beach.

## Specialty Shopping

It's hard to avoid places to shop, beginning with lobby stores in hotels, where stylish, good-quality resort clothing and swimsuits can often be found. In Waikiki, you can run the full gamut by strolling through shops at a luxury hotel like **Halekulani** or **Royal Hawaiian Hotel** and then walking to the varied boutiques of **Royal Hawaiian Shopping Center** and on across the street to **Liberty House** and the colorful jumble of kiosks surrounding the **International Market Place.** Walk out the back to Kuhio Avenue, jump on TheBus and get off at **Ala Moana Center,** which reinvented itself to cater to high-end shoppers on its new upper floors with a Nieman's and plentiful designer boutiques, in addition to its usual wild assortment of department stores, island stores, and restaurants.

On up Ala Moana Boulevard, **Ward Centre** and **Ward Warehouse** are smaller boutique collections of island style clothes, gifts, and restaurants. On up the street on the left, find **Aloha Tower Marketplace, a** harborfront complex of shops, food, and entertainment with the added amusement of container ships bringing more goods to the active harbor. Shoppers can prowl while mates down a freshly brewed beer at Gordon Biersch and watch the ships go by. If you're looking for national-brand outlet shops, drive out to **Waikele Centre,** west of the airport on H1, and find familiar names.

We know you can find all the malls and local branches of national chain stores you know and love, so we won't waste your time except to say: expect slightly higher prices on some items, even at Wal-Mart. **Hilo Hattie's** matching aloha wear and Hawaiian goods are everywhere, and they will find you if you don't find them. But that's not all there is. Here are our recommendations for some places to find local arts and crafts and Hawaiian goods. Hours of operation are subject to change.

# O'ahu

## Ali'i Antiques of Kailua
**Location**  21 Malunui Ave., Kailua; Zone 3, Windward Coast
**Phone**  (808) 261-1705
**Hours**  Monday–Saturday, 10:30 a.m.–4:30 p.m.
**Description**  Ali'i has a separate building filled with Hawaiian kitsch and all kinds of treasures, including jewelry. Great place to prowl the island past.

## Crazy Shirts
**Location**  International Market Place, Waikiki (more than 20 locations throughout the state); Zone 1, Waikiki
**Phone**  (808) 922-4791
**Hours**  Daily, 8 a.m.–11:30 p.m.
**Description**  Hawai'i's homegrown T-shirt shop, featuring hundreds of colorful, local-themed designs, is ubiquitous, but the International Market Place location is the biggest of the line.

## Harry's Music Store
**Location**  3457 Wai'alae Ave., Honolulu; Zone 2, Greater Honolulu
**Phone**  (808) 735-2866
**Hours**  Monday–Friday, 9:30 a.m.–5:30 p.m.; Saturday, 9 a.m.–5 p.m.
**Description**  Old Hawaiian records, sheet music, and 'ukulele are among the vintage items offered at this small but famous stop for Hawaiian music aficionados.

## Hawaiian 'Ukulele Company
**Location**  Aloha Tower Marketplace, Honolulu; Zone 2, Greater Honolulu
**Phone**  (808) 536-3228
**Hours**  Monday–Saturday, 9 a.m.–9 p.m.; Sunday, 9 a.m.–6 p.m.
**Description**  Specializes in hand-crafted Hawaiian 'ukulele and other instruments, plus accessories, songbooks, and instruction booklets.

## Irene's Hawaiian Gifts
**Location**  Ala Moana Center, Honolulu; Zone 2, Greater Honolulu
**Phone**  (808) 946-6818
**Hours**  Monday–Saturday, 9:30 p.m.–9 p.m.; Sunday, 10 a.m.–7 p.m.
**Description**  Hawaiian gifts and souvenirs, including koa boxes, porcelain dolls, soaps, perfumes, note cards, dish towels, and Hawaiian quilt kits.

## Island Treasures
**Location**  629 Kailua Rd., Kailua; Zone 3, Windward Coast
**Phone**  (808) 261-8131
**Hours**  Monday–Saturday, 10 a.m.–6 p.m.; Sunday, 10 a.m.–4 p.m.
**Description**  Artworks and Hawaiian-style crafts, gifts with flair created locally.

## The Islands Best
**Location**  Ala Moana Center, Honolulu; Zone 2, Greater Honolulu
**Phone**  (808) 949-5345

**Hours**  Monday–Saturday, 9:30 a.m.–9 p.m.; Sunday, 10 a.m.–7 p.m.

**Description**  Wide range of Hawaiian gifts and souvenirs, including soaps, crafts, stationery, and arts.

### Montsuki

**Location**  1148 Koko Head Ave., Honolulu; Zone 2, Greater Honolulu

**Phone**  (808) 734-3457

**Hours**  Monday–Saturday, 9:30 a.m.–4 p.m.

**Description**  Stylish apparel fashioned from vintage silk kimonos.

### Native Books & Beautiful Things

**Location**  Ward Warehouse and 222 Merchant St., Downtown, Honolulu; Zone 2, Greater Honolulu

**Phone**  Ward (808) 596-8885; downtown (808) 599-5511

**Hours**  Ward: Monday–Saturday, 10 a.m.–9 p.m.; Sunday, 10 a.m.–5 p.m. Downtown: Monday–Friday, 8 a.m.–5 p.m.; Saturday, 10 a.m.–3 p.m.

**Description**  Fine collection of Hawaiian books, crafts, artworks, apparel, and gifts.

### Nohea Gallery

**Location**  Ward Warehouse, Honolulu; Zone 2, Greater Honolulu (also at Sheraton Moana Surfrider in Waikiki and Kahala Mandarin Oriental in Kahala)

**Phone**  (808) 596-0074

**Website**  www.noheagallery.com

**Hours**  Monday–Saturday, 10 a.m.–9 p.m.; Sunday, 10 a.m.–5 p.m.

**Description**  One of the best galleries for island arts and fine crafts in all media.

## Maui

### Hasegawa General Store

**Location**  Hana; Zone 10, Upcountry Maui and Beyond

**Phone**  (808) 248-8231

**Hours**  Monday–Saturday, 7 a.m.–7 p.m.; Sunday, 8 a.m.–6 p.m.

**Description**  An old-fashioned general merchandise store, so beloved that a song was written about it. Founded in 1910, this family-run store sells the necessities and some frills for residents and visitors to faraway Hana.

### Hawaiiana Arts & Crafts

**Location**  Cinema Wharf Center, Lahaina; Zone 9, West Maui

**Phone**  (808) 661-9077

**Hours**  Daily, 10 a.m.–8 p.m.

**Description**  Handmade arts and crafts by some of Maui's best artisans, including raku pottery, woodcrafts, and woven baskets.

### Honolua Store

**Location**  Office Rd., Kapalua Resort; Zone 9, West Maui

**Phone**  (808) 669-6128

**Hours**  Daily, 6 a.m.–8 p.m.

**Description** Historic plantation grocery store features books, gifts, and clothing, along with groceries and beverages.

# The Big Island of Hawai'i

## Alapaki's
**Location** Keauhou Shopping Center, Kailua-Kona; Zone 11, Kona
**Phone** (808) 322-2007
**Hours** Monday–Saturday, 9 a.m.–6 p.m.; Sunday, 10 a.m.–5 p.m.
**Description** A lava rock archway welcomes you into a shop full of made-in-Hawai'i ceramics, koa, woven lauhala goods, 'ukulele and other instruments, pillows, wall hangings, stationery, and more.

## Big Island Candies
**Location** 585 Hinano St., Hilo; Zone 12, Hilo and Volcano
**Phone** (808) 935-8890
**Hours** Daily, 8:30 a.m.–5 p.m.
**Description** Locally made chocolates and candies. Large windows let you watch confections being made in the adjoining factory.

## Cook's Discoveries
**Location** Waimea Center, Waimea (on Hwy. 19); Zone 11, Kona
**Phone** (808) 885-3633
**Hours** Monday–Saturday, 9 a.m.–6 p.m.; Sunday, 10 a.m.–5 p.m.
**Description** This well-chosen array of somewhat pricey Hawaiian goods includes aloha wear, books, art, music, language tapes, hats, stationery, Kona coffee, confections, and other gifts. This is one of the best shops to browse for Big Island arts.

## Hula Heaven
**Location** Kona Inn Shopping Village, Kailua-Kona; Zone 11, Kona
**Phone** (808) 329-7885
**Hours** Daily, 9 a.m.–9 p.m.
**Description** Vintage collectibles—old aloha shirts in mint condition, antique hula dolls, original menu art.

## Harbor Gallery
**Location** Kawaihae Shopping Center, Kawaihae; Zone 11, Kona
**Phone** (808) 882-1510
**Hours** Daily, 11:30 a.m.–8:30 p.m.
**Description** Diverse collection of island art, including koa wood, sculptures, paintings, ceramics, and jewelry.

## Sig Zane Designs
**Location** 122 Kamehameha Ave., Hilo; Zone 12, Hilo and Volcano
**Phone** (808) 935-7077
**Hours** Monday–Friday, 9 a.m.–5:30 p.m.; Saturday, 9 a.m.–3 p.m.
**Description** Zane's striking Hawaiian prints in fabric, dresses, shirts, and sarong-like pareos.

## Kaua'i

### Kong Lung Co.
**Location**  Keneke Rd., Kilauea; Zone 13, Kaua'i
**Phone**  (808) 828-1822
**Hours**  Monday–Saturday, 9 a.m.–9 p.m.; Sunday, 10 a.m.–9 p.m.
**Description**  Set in a historic stone building, this is one of Kaua'i's most famous shops. Collectibles, housewares, jewelry, apparel, and fine gifts make it a worthwhile stop on your way to the North Shore.

### Ola's
**Location**  Hanalei Trader Building, Hanalei; Zone 13, Kaua'i
**Phone**  (808) 826-6937
**Hours**  Daily, 10 a.m.–9:30 p.m.
**Description**  Jewelry, glassware, woodcrafts, soaps and other handcrafted goods are for sale at this fun-to-browse shop.

### Yellowfish Trading Company
**Location**  New Hanalei School Center, Hanalei; Zone 13, Kaua'i
**Phone**  (808) 826-1227
**Hours**  Daily, 10 a.m.–9 p.m.
**Description**  Antiques and knickknacks, vintage aloha shirts, photographs and posters, Hawaiian furniture, and kitchenwares.

## Moloka'i

### Big Wind Kite Factory
**Location**  120 Maunaloa Hwy., Maunaloa; Zone 14, Moloka'i
**Phone**  (808) 552-2364
**Hours**  Monday–Saturday, 8:30 a.m.–5 p.m.; Sunday, 10 a.m.–2 p.m.
**Description**  Kites of all shapes, sizes, and designs, some made on site; imported gifts. The friendly owner provides free kite-flying lessons (at an adjacent open field) with "no strings attached."

## Lana'i

### Akamai Trading
**Location**  408 Eighth St., Lana'i City; Zone 15, Lana'i
**Phone**  (808) 565-6587
**Hours**  Monday–Saturday, 9 a.m.–6 p.m.; Sunday, 9 a.m.–5 p.m.
**Description**  General store with an interesting selection of island necessities, souvenirs, gifts, and locally made jams and jellies.

### Gifts with Aloha
**Location**  Seventh St., Lana'i City; Zone 15, Lana'i
**Phone**  (808) 565-6589
**Hours**  Monday–Saturday, 9:30 a.m.–5:30 p.m.
**Description**  Made-in-Hawai'i gifts, including resort wear, koa wood products, scented candles, books, and hand-quilted pillow covers.

# Shopping Centers

## O'ahu

### Ala Moana Center
**Location**  Ala Moana Blvd., next to Waikiki; Zone 2, Greater Honolulu
**Phone**  (808) 955-9517
**Website**  www.alamoana.com
**Hours**  Monday–Saturday, 9:30 a.m.–9 p.m.; Sunday, 10 a.m.–7 p.m.
**Number of Stores and Restaurants**  More than 200
**Description**  Department stores, upscale European and American boutiques, jewelry, gifts, outdoor gifts and gear, drugstore, supermarket, shoes, cartoon art, candy, software, sandals and slippers, swim and beachwear, toys, sports gear, Tahitian and Hawaiian fabrics. This one of the largest shopping centers in the United States and is certainly one of the most pleasant with its open-air tropical gardens and ponds. Free entertainment daily on the stage at in the middle of the Center, usually music and/or dance.

### Aloha Tower Marketplace
**Location**  1 Aloha Tower Dr., foot of Bishop St. downtown; Zone 2, Greater Honolulu
**Phone**  (808) 528-5700
**Website**  www.alohatower.com
**Hours**  Monday–Saturday, 9 a.m.–9 p.m.; Sunday, 9 a.m.–6 p.m.
**Number of Stores and Restaurants**  About 75
**Description**  Hawaiian woodcrafts, furniture, gifts, swimwear, coffee, candies, cartoon art, tropical apparel, cigar shop, shoes, magnets, and perfumes; plus changing goods, imports, and clothing in numerous kiosks. Stores are arrayed at the foot of historic ten-story Aloha Tower, where you can take the elevator to the top, enjoy panoramic views, and imagine the scene when this was the tallest building in town.

### International Market Place
**Location**  2330 Kalakaua Ave.; Zone 1, Waikiki
**Phone**  (808) 926-2205 or (808) 923-0833
**Hours**  Daily, 9 a.m.–11 p.m.
**Number of Vendors and Eateries**  About 150
**Description**  Outdoor maze of kiosks features jewelry, T-shirts, pareo, handbags, touristy souvenirs, and imported knickknacks. Bargain like crazy to improve the prices—everybody here wants to sell.

### Pearlridge Shopping Center
**Location**  231 Pearlridge Center, 'Aiea; Zone 6, Central O'ahu
**Phone**  (808) 488-0981
**Hours**  Monday–Saturday, 10 a.m.–9 p.m.; Sunday, 10 a.m.–6 p.m.
**Number of Stores and Restaurants**  More than 170
**Description**  Department stores, electronics, outdoor goods, toys, books, drugstores, apparel, candy, lingerie, men's wear, videos, stationers, shoes, glasses, and movies. The most interesting thing about this suburban center is the monorail

linking two complexes, which was built so that development would not imperil the prized Sumida watercress farm below. (Better yet, skip the shopping and get some of the superlative watercress, sold in huge bunches at island markets and eaten stems and all.)

### Royal Hawaiian Shopping Center
**Location** 2201 Kalakaua Ave.; Zone 1, Waikiki
**Phone** (808) 922-0588
**Hours** Daily, 9 a.m.–11 p.m.
**Number of Stores and Restaurants** About 160
**Description** Upscale designer boutiques, biker logos, jewelry factory, sports apparel, collectibles, and island wear. Frequent free entertainment, usually Hawaiian music and dance, by the waterfall at the central Kalakaua entrance.

### Ward Centre/Ward Warehouse
**Location** 1050–1200 Ala Moana Blvd.; Zone 2, Greater Honolulu
**Phone** (808) 591-8411
**Hours** Monday–Saturday, 10 a.m.–9 p.m.; Sunday, 10 a.m.–5 p.m.
**Number of Stores and Restaurants** 100 (restaurants mostly at Ward Centre; mostly shops at Warehouse)
**Description** Books and music, gifts, gadgets, stationery, island ceramics, University of Hawai'i gear, chocolates, tropical wear, tropical home furnishings, art galleries, bath shop, shoes, crafts, holiday ornaments, sandals and shoes, apparel, toys, and perfumes. Free band concerts, shows, and exhibits throughout the year.

## Maui

### 505 Front Street
**Location** Front St., Lahaina; Zone 9, West Maui
**Phone** (808) 667-2514
**Hours** Monday–Saturday, 10 a.m.–9 p.m.; Sunday, 10 a.m.–6 p.m.
**Number of Stores and Restaurants** More than 25
**Description** Oceanfront boutique mall at the quiet southern end of Lahaina. Unusual shops include Hawaiian products, spa goods, clothing, souvenirs, gifts. Live jazz outdoors at Pacific 'O restaurant on Thursday, Friday, and Saturday nights.

### Ka'ahumanu Center
**Location** Ka'ahumanu Ave., Kahului; Zone 7, Central Maui
**Phone** (808) 877-3369
**Hours** Monday–Friday, 9:30 a.m.–9 p.m.; Saturday, 9:30 a.m.–7 p.m.; Sunday, 10 a.m.–5 p.m.
**Number of Stores and Restaurants** About 75
**Description** Department stores, books, gifts, toys, cards, jewelry, cartoon logos, dime store, coffee, shoes, apparel, photo processing, movies, and community events.

### The Shops at Wailea
**Location** 3750 Wailea Alanui Dr., Wailea Resort; Zone 8, South Maui
**Phone** (808) 879-4474

**Number of Stores and Restaurants** More than 25
**Description** Resort wear, upscale designer boutiques, gifts, galleries, woodcrafts and furniture, toys, camera shops, sundries, ice cream, and swim and beachwear. Frequent events and food festivals.

## Lahaina Center
**Location** 900 Front St.; Zone 9, West Maui
**Phone** (808) 667-9216
**Hours** Generally, Monday–Saturday, 9 a.m.–10 p.m., Sunday, 9 a.m.–6 p.m.
**Number of Stores and Restaurants** 30
**Description** Aloha wear, gifts, sundries, apparel, T-shirts, swimwear, jewelry, children's shop, microbrewery. Free hula shows Wednesday and Friday, 2 and 6 p.m.

## Whalers Village
**Location** 2435 Ka'anapali Pkwy., Ka'anapali Beach Resort; Zone 9, West Maui
**Phone** (808) 661-4567
**Website** www.whalersvillage.com
**Hours** Daily, 9:30 a.m.–10 p.m.
**Number of Stores and Restaurants** 60
**Description** Upscale boutiques, jewelry, scrimshaw, Hawaiian koa furniture, gifts, art galleries, island apparel, and general goods. Free hula performances 7 p.m. nightly except Tuesday and Thursday.

# The Big Island of Hawai'i

## Keauhou Shopping Center
**Location** 78-6831 Ali'i Dr., Keauhou; Zone 11, Kona
**Phone** (808) 332-3000
**Hours** Monday–Saturday, 9:30 a.m.–6 p.m.; Sunday, 10 a.m.–5 p.m.
**Number of Stores and Restaurants** 40
**Description** Supermarket, drugstore, dime store, hardware, coffee, art gallery, and movies. Craft demonstrations and talk story sessions are held Fridays, 10 a.m.–2 p.m.

## Kings' Shops
**Location** Waikoloa Beach Resort; Zone 11, Kona
**Phone** (808) 886-8811
**Hours** Daily, 9:30 a.m.–9:30 p.m.
**Number of Stores and Restaurants** About 40
**Description** Souvenirs, jewelry, art gallery, T-shirts, gifts, and sunglasses. Free entertainment Tuesday and Thursday evenings.

## Prince Kuhio Plaza
**Location** 111 Puainako St. (off Hwy. 11, near Hilo airport); Zone 12, Hilo and Volcano
**Phone** (808) 959-3555
**Hours** Monday–Friday, 9:30 a.m.–9 p.m.; Saturday, 9:30 a.m.–7 p.m.; Sunday, 10 a.m.–6 p.m.

**Number of Stores and Restaurants** Over 75
**Description** Department stores, books, videos, drugstore, gifts, apparel, swimwear, and movies.

## Kaua'i

### Coconut Marketplace

**Location** 484 Kuhio Hwy., Wailua; Zone 13, Kaua'i
**Phone** (808) 822-3641
**Hours** Monday–Saturday, 9 a.m.–9 p.m.; Sunday, 10 a.m.–6 p.m.
**Number of Stores and Restaurants** Over 70
**Description** Gifts, music, jewelry, clothing, Hawaiian products, swimwear, movies. Free entertainment (including hula) daily at 5 p.m.

### Kukui Grove Center

**Location** 3-2600 Kaumuali'i Hwy., Lihu'e; Zone 13, Kaua'i
**Phone** (808) 245-7784
**Hours** Monday–Thursday and Saturday, 9:30 a.m.–5:30 p.m.; Friday, 9:30 a.m.–9 p.m.; Sunday, 10 a.m.–5 p.m.
**Number of Stores and Restaurants** About 50
**Description** Department store, Kaua'i products, jeans, shoes, and swim and beachwear.

### Po'ipu Shopping Village

**Location** 2360 Kiahuna Plantation Dr., Po'ipu Beach Resort; Zone 13, Kaua'i
**Phone** (808) 742-2831
**Hours** Monday–Saturday, 10 a.m.–9 p.m.; Sunday, 10 a.m.–6 p.m.
**Number of Stores and Restaurants** About 20
**Description** T-shirts, art galleries, swimwear, gifts, sandals, sunglasses, cosmetics, and clothing. Free Polynesian shows Tuesdays and Thursdays at 5 p.m.

# Swap Meets and Flea Markets

Bargain hunters on O'ahu should check out the major swap meet, the **Aloha Stadium Swap Meet** held in the parking lot surrounding Aloha Stadium on Wednesday, Saturday, and Sunday (and some holidays) from 6 a.m. to 3 p.m. You'll find an astounding variety of new and used merchandise, treasures and trash, eel-skin leathers, imports, baskets, fresh produce, plants, and even fresh fish. Feel free to bargain, it's part of the fun. Admission is 50 cents a head for people over age 12. The sun can be relentless, so go early and dress casually for shopping with the local folks. Call (808) 486-6704 for more information.

# Part Eleven

# Entertainment and Nightlife

## Hawai'i Nightlife

In Hawai'i you can experience Hawaiian music, song, and dance. Or you can see of the kind of things that you have back home. But you must at least once go to a lu'au (**Paradise Cove** or **Germaine's** on O'ahu, **Old Lahaina Lu'au** on Maui, **Kona Village Resort lu'au** on the Big Island are top choices for commercial lu'au), see the *Don Ho Show* in Waikiki, and, above all, experience *'Ulalena* in Lahaina on Maui. Many other shows are entertaining, and some are hokey, but if you want a good evening out, by all means see the top shows mentioned here. A lu'au is the traditional cultural event. Don Ho is, well, Don Ho. *'Ulalena,* most exciting of all, is simply excellent entertainment, a new but authentic version of the Hawai'i story, told in a *Cirque du Soleil*–type production.

Hawaiian music is alive and well, not just at Don Ho's but **Duke's Canoe Club** in Waikiki or **Chai's Island Bistro** and **Henry Kapono's** new club at Aloha Tower Marketplace. You can see Jerry Santos and Olomana at the **Paradise Lounge at Hilton Hawaiian Village.** After a long dry period, popular contemporary Hawaiian musicians are back playing in Waikiki.

The islands are full of gifted musicians and singers, such as Keali'i Reichel, Ho'okena, Willie K., Amy Hanaiali'i Gilliom, Makaha Sons of Ni'ihau, the Peter Moon Band, Robbie Kahakalau, and Na Leo Pumehana, to name a few. They appear on all islands, so check the local papers' entertainment sections.

O'ahu is Hawai'i's night life center with nightclubs, cocktail lounges, local bars, karaoke clubs, adult entertainment clubs, and hostess bars. The nightclub scene revolves around the **Ocean Club, Rumours,** and **Wave Waikiki.**

If you're staying on an outer island, bring a good book. Folks may well draw their shades early. Only a few spots, like Kihei and Lahaina on

Maui, stay open after dark with clubs drawing crowds that linger past midnight. Otherwise, night life may be limited to hotel lounge acts (some of which are quite good). You came to the islands to relax, remember?

# Performing Arts

Sooner or later, everyone plays Honolulu. The beach city attracts worldly entertainers who regularly perform at Neal Blaisdell Center, Waikiki Shell, and elsewhere. If your timing's good, you may see the Bolshoi Ballet, the Beach Boys, or even the Rolling Stones (who played Aloha Stadium) and for a lot less than on the mainland. Jazz singer Diana Krall and Sir Elton John appeared one night in adjoining concert halls.

## MAJOR CONCERT AND PERFORMING ARTS VENUES

Check *Honolulu Weekly* or the local dailies for appearances and dates. Here are some contact numbers and general locations for many of the concert venues in Hawai'i.

### O'ahu

| | | |
|---|---|---|
| Aloha Stadium | Zone 6 | (808) 486-9300 |
| Hawai'i Theatre Center | Zone 2 | (808) 528-0506 |
| Neal Blaisdell Center Arena | Zone 2 | (808) 591-2211 |
| Neal Blaisdell Concert Hall | Zone 2 | (808) 591-2211 |
| Waikiki Shell | Zone 1 | (808) 527-5400 |

### Maui

| | | |
|---|---|---|
| Maui Arts and Cultural Center | Zone 7 | (808) 242-7469 |

# Dinner Shows

Waikiki isn't Las Vegas, nor does it want to be, so don't expect extravaganzas. Your choices are limited to a few entertaining dinner shows—something of an oxymoron. People who enjoy good food don't usually go to dinner shows. Food is often mediocre, tickets are expensive ($129 for a magic show), seating is clumsy, and, with few exceptions, the shows are forgettable. But here are six shows worth a look because they can only be seen in the Islands, dinner entrees are of sufficient variety to satisfy even picky eaters, and, in most cases, the price of admission won't cause sticker shock.

## O'ahu

### Creation—A Polynesian Odyssey

**Location** 120 Ka'iulani Ave., 'Ainahau Showroom, Sheraton Princess Ka'iulani Hotel, Waikiki

**Phone** (808) 931-4660

**Show Times** 2 shows Tuesday, Thursday, and Saturday, 5:45 and 8:30 p.m. Dinner seatings at 5:15 and 8 p.m.; cocktail seatings at 6 and 8:30 p.m.

**Length** 90 minutes

**Cost** $105 per adult ($72 per child age 7–12) for the premium dinner; $62 per adult ($34.50 per child) for the standard dinner, first show; $55 per adult ($30.75 per child) for the second show; and $32 per adult ($21 per child) for the cocktail show.

**Discounts** Discount coupons available inside "Best of O'ahu" booklets. Hotel guests receive a two-for-one coupon.

**Type of Seating** Long tables facing the stage. First come, first served.

**Menu** All-you-can-eat buffet. Prime rib, shoyu chicken, chow mein noodles with vegetables and char siu, beef curry stew, mahimahi, fresh salad, fruits, cakes, and ice cream. The premium dinner is a sit-down meal of lobster tail, tenderloin steak, salad, rice or potato, dessert, and two drinks.

**Vegetarian Alternative** Salads at buffet.

**Beverages** Mai tai, draft beer, soft drinks, juice, coffee.

**Description and Comments** High-tech stage show follows Polynesian voyagers with vivid sound and light effects. Good choice for young families.

## Don Ho Show

**Location** 2300 Kalakaua Ave., Hoku Hale Showroom, Waikiki Beachcomber Hotel, Waikiki

**Phone** (808) 923-3981

**Website** www.donho.com

**Show Time** Sunday–Thursday, 7 p.m.

**Length** 90 minutes

**Cost** $52 per adult ($26 per child ages 6–20) for the dinner show; $32 per adult ($16 per child) for the cocktail show; for the show only (no dinner), adults are $20, children are $10.

**Discounts** None.

**Type of Seating** Table seating.

**Menu** A sit-down dinner of chicken, prime rib, mashed potatoes, salad, and dessert.

**Vegetarian Alternative** Varies nightly.

**Beverages** Tropical drinks, wine, beer, soft drinks, juice, tea, coffee.

**Description and Comments** Over age 70 now, Don Ho is still the king of Waikiki, attracting full house audiences five nights a week. He also attracts bright young talent in Hawai'i and offers them a chance to shine in his show.

## Magic of Polynesia

**Location** 2300 Kalakaua Ave., Waikiki Beachcomber Hotel, Waikiki

**Phone** (808) 971-4321

**Show Times** 2 shows nightly, 6:30 and 8:45 p.m. Dinner seating at 5 p.m.; cocktail seating at 6 and 8 p.m.

**Length** 75 minutes

**Cost** $129 per adult ($89 per child age 4–12) for deluxe dinner; $64 per adult ($42.50 per child) for the standard dinner; $35 per adult ($25 per child) for the cocktail show.

**Discounts** Entertainment Book coupons offer 20% off for the cocktail show.

**Type of Seating** Table seating. Smaller tables seat 10; larger tables in rows seat 40. First come, first served. A seat toward the back gives better overall view.

**Menu** Sit-down dinner of roast beef, chicken, rice, steamed vegetables, cake.

**Vegetarian Alternative** Steamed noodles with vegetables. Request in advance.

**Beverages** Tropical drinks, wine, beer, soft drinks, juice, coffee.

**Description and Comments** John Hirokawa, a local boy taught by David Copperfield, delivers superb illusionist skills with Polynesian themes in family-oriented magic show.

## Society of Seven

**Location** 2335 Kalakaua Ave., Main Outrigger Showroom, Outrigger Waikiki Hotel, Waikiki

**Phone** (808) 922-6408

**Website** www.angelfire.com/hi/societyofseven

**Show Times** 2 shows Tuesday–Saturday, 5 and 6:30 p.m.

**Length** 80 minutes

**Cost** $62 per adult ($45 per student age 13–20; $37 per child age 12 and under) for the Sunset Dinner package; $57 per adult ($39 per student, $25 per child) for the Ali'i Buffet (6:30 p.m. show only); $65 per adult ($50 per student, $40 per child) for the Pikake Buffet (8:30 p.m. show only); and $35 per adult ($20 per student, $18 per child) for the cocktail package.

**Discounts** None.

**Type of Seating** Cabaret-style table seating.

**Menu** Buffet includes meats, fish, chicken, rice, salad bar, and dessert. Sit-down dinner includes choice of prime rib, chicken or fish, and starch, vegetables, and dessert.

**Vegetarian Alternative** Pasta.

**Beverages** Tropical drinks, beer, wine, mixed drinks, soft drinks, juice, coffee.

**Description and Comments** Hawai'i's longest running show (30 years and counting), for one reason: it's good fun. Comedy, Broadway tunes, musical skits, impressions, oldies, contemporary hits, and audience participation make for a fun evening.

## YES! International Revue

**Location** Polynesian Palace Showroom, 227 Lewers St., Outrigger Reef Towers Hotel, Waikiki

**Phone** (808) 923-7469

**Show Times** Tuesday–Sunday, 6 and 8:30 p.m. Dinner seating at 5 p.m.; cocktail seating at 6 and 8 p.m.

**Length** 85 minutes

**Cost** $59 per person for the dinner show; $35.50 per person for the cocktail shows.

**Discounts** None.

**Type of Seating** Table seating. Tables are too close together.

**Menu** Filet mignon, mahimahi, mashed potatoes, steamed vegetables, salad, roll, dessert.

**Vegetarian Alternative** Pasta or salad.

**Beverages** Tropical drinks, mixed drinks, beer, wine, soft drinks, juice, coffee.

**Description and Comments** Variety show with Los Mayas living body "sculptures" in silent slow motion. DisGuyz sings Beach Boys hits. Mime comic Joe Monti provides laughs. This is a good family show.

# Maui

## 'Ulalena

**Location** Maui Myth and Magic Theater, 878 Front St., Lahaina
**Phone** Toll-free (877) 688-4800, (808) 661-9913
**Website** www.ulalena.com
**Show Times** Tuesday–Saturday, 6 p.m.; 8:30 p.m. additional shows Tuesdays.
**Length** 90 minutes
**Cost** $45 adults, $35 children, $25 under age 12.
**Discounts** None.
**Type of Seating** $10 million, state-of-art-theater with stadium seating, features live Hawaiian chant and music with 8-channel surround sound.
**Food** Snack bar in lobby.
**Beverages** Beer, wine, soft drinks, juice, coffee.

**Description and Comments** Best original, creative show in Hawai'i. A *Cirque du Soleil* production by the Montreal troupe blends island myth and fact in culturally keen theatrical performance. If you go to Maui, you must see *'Ulalena.*

## Warren & Annabelle's

**Location** 900 Front Street, Lahaina
**Phone** (808) 667-6244
**Show Times** 2 shows, Monday–Saturday, 6:45 and 8:15 p.m.
**Length** 60 minutes
**Cost** $36. Guests must be age 21 or older. Special pupu (hors d'oeuvres) packages are available: $64.50 includes show, dessert, coffee, and 2 drinks; $74 includes show, appetizer platter, 2 drinks; and $90 includes show, appetizer platter, dessert, 2 drinks, and coffee. Prices include tax and tip.
**Discounts** Coupons offering a 20% discount available in hotel lobbies.
**Type of Seating** Table seating for pupus and cocktails. Intimate 78-seat theater (stadium seating). First come, first served.
**Menu** Unless you order pupu, everything is à la carte. Pupu menu includes spicy crab cakes, coconut-battered shrimp, chicken satay, and crab-stuffed mushrooms. Desserts include chocolate truffle cake, crème brûlée, deep-dish apple pie, and New York–style cheesecake.
**Vegetarian Alternative** Request in advance.
**Beverages** Tropical drinks, specialty drinks, beer, wine, soft drinks, juice, coffee.

**Description and Comments** "Close-up" magician Warren Gibson performs sleight-of-hand tricks in the cozy theater with Annabelle, a piano-playing ghost who takes requests.

# Before- and After-Dinner Lounges

Major resort hotels on all the islands offer good Hawaiian music, jazz, and a place to dance or relax with an after-dinner drink and enjoy the evening. Here are some of the best.

## O'ahu

**Duke's Canoe Club, Outrigger Waikiki** (808) 922-2268

Open-air beach club full of young couples full of beer and mai tais boogeying to Hawaiian music.

**House Without a Key, Halekulani** (808) 923-2311

Sophisticated, elegant open-air setting ideal for sunset cocktails.

**Lewers Lounge, Halekulani** (808) 923-2311

When you want the most romantic hideaway, come and hear late-night jazz in the finest hotel.

**Mai Tai Bar, Royal Hawaiian Hotel** (808) 923-7311

Beach bar non-pareil. Here you can sip a cool one in your swimsuit and watch babes and hunks go by.

**Paradise Lounge, Hilton Hawaiian Village** (808) 949-4321

The living room setting is cozy venue for Olomana, one of Hawai'i's best-loved Hawaiian-music groups.

## Maui

**Anuenue Lounge, Ritz-Carlton-Kapalua** (808) 669-6200

Dark koa-wood lounge for sophisticated couples who want dancing after dark to grand piano tunes.

**Hula Moons, Outrigger Wailea Beach Resort** (808) 879-1922

Nostalgic bar filled with old photos and vintage art with live Hawaiian music on weekends.

**Tsunami, Grand Wailea Resort** (808) 875-1234

High-tech disco with dressy couples dancing to DJ'd Top 40 tunes. Loud, noisy, and fun.

## Big Island of Hawai'i

**Billfish Bar, King Kamehameha's Kona Beach Hotel** (808) 329-3111

Big fish on the wall, big fish tales at the bar, and big drinks, too. Hawaiian music, weekends only.

**Honu Bar, Mauna Lani Bay Hotel and Bungalows** (808) 885-6622

A favorite Kohala Coast night spot, this chic wine bar full of couples offers jazz, dancing, and late-night dinners.

**Shipwreck Bar, Kona Village Resort**

Lift a mai tai toast to Johnno Jackson, who hit the reef in 1959 aboard his 42-foot schooner (the hull forms the bar) and founded Kona Village. No music, just ocean breezes and strong drink.

## Kaua'i

**Duke's Canoe Club, Kaua'i Marriott Resort and Beach Club** (808) 245-5050
Beachside shrine to Duke Kahanamoku, Hawaiian music on weekends.

**Stevenson's Library Hyatt Regency Kaua'i Resort and Spa** (808) 742-1234
Koa wood–lined old boy's club (ladies welcome) lined with books, vintage art. Jazz in the evening.

# Dance Clubs and Nightspots

Anyone who wants to whoop it up in the tropic night should make plans to do all their boogeying on O'ahu, although Maui shows some signs of a burgeoning night life. You can find late-night amusement on Lahaina's Front Street on Maui, but don't expect a scene elsewhere. The legal drinking age is 21. Clubs come and go; schedules and formats change often. Check with your hotel concierge for up-to-the minute details.

## NIGHTCLUBS BY ZONE

### Zone 1: Waikiki

| | |
|---|---|
| The Cellar | No frills bar and dance venue |
| Esprit Lounge | Live music nightclub and hotel lounge |
| Fusion Waikiki | Alternative club |
| Hard Rock Café | Internationally known music-theme restaurant |
| Nashville Waikiki | Authentic Waikiki watering hole |
| Scruples Beach Club | Waikiki beach bar that's not on a beach |
| Wave Waikiki | Alternative nightclub and rare alternative live music venue |

### Zone 2: Greater Honolulu

| | |
|---|---|
| Brew Moon | Hip Island dining spot; beer brewed on site |
| Don Ho's Grill | Nostalgic, casual, pier-side hangout |
| Kapono's | Local Hawaiian music on Honolulu waterfront |
| Ocean Club | Chic downtown nightclub and discotheque |
| Rumours | Oldies disco and nightclub |

### Zone 8: South Maui

| | |
|---|---|
| Hapa's Brew Haus | Locals-meet-tourists Neighbor Island hangout |

### Zone 9: West Maui

| | |
|---|---|
| Maui Brews | 10,000-square-foot eatery and club in Lahaina |

# O'ahu

## BREW MOON

HIP ISLAND DINING SPOT FEATURING ECLECTIC DECOR AND BEER BREWED ON SITE

**Who Goes There**  20–45 crowd; office workers, college kids, and professionals

1200 Ala Moana Blvd., Honolulu (at Ward Centre); (808) 593-0088
Zone 2    Greater Honolulu

**Cover** None **Minimum** None **Mixed drinks** $4–$5 **Wine** $4.50 and up **Beer** $3.25–$5.50 **Dress** Anything from aloha shirts to casual business attire **Specials** "Zero Gravity Hour" offers $3–$5 beers, $4–$6 wine, and half-price appetizers, including their addictive Beer Crackers, tasty Fire-Roasted Ribs, and hefty Heavy Metal Nacho platter; 4–7 p.m. daily **Food available** Jambalaya, chicken curry, herb-crusted sirloin, burgers, shakes, and daily fish specials

**Hours** Monday–Wednesday, 11 a.m.–1 p.m.; Thursday–Saturday, 11 a.m.–2 a.m.; Sunday, 2 p.m.–midnight

**What goes on** One of Honolulu's newest venues where customers can people-watch, mingle, and listen to music ranging from Top 40 hits to reggae beats to blues to jazz. Occasionally, live contemporary Hawaiian and jazz are performed Wednesday (9 p.m.–midnight) or Sunday (5–8 p.m.) nights.

**Setting & atmosphere** Brew pub with a view of Waikiki and Honolulu. Dining room features art deco furniture and eclectic menu. Check on their beers online at www.brewmoon.com.

**If you go** Try going at "Zero Gravity Hour" to catch half-priced Lunar Sampler—five four-ounce servings of Brew Moon beer—or other award-winning beers.

## THE CELLAR

NO-FRILLS BAR AND DANCE VENUE

**Who Goes There**  18–30; 20-somethings, people-watchers, visitors, and curfew-breakers

205 Lewers St., Waikiki Imperial Hotel; (808) 923-9952    Zone 1    Waikiki

**Cover** $5 **Minimum** None **Mixed drinks** $3.75 and up **Wine** $3.50 **Beer** $3.50 **Dress** Casual **Specials** $1.50 drink specials are offered throughout the night **Food available** None

**Hours** Wednesday, Friday, and Saturday, 8 p.m.–4 a.m.; Tuesday, Thursday, and Sunday, 9 p.m.–4 a.m.; closed Mondays

**What goes on** A variety of entertainment and dance themes, including Top 40 hits, hip hop, R&B music, and a male dance revue every Wednesday, Friday, and Saturday, 8–10 p.m. Dancing nightly.

**Setting & atmosphere** Dark and smoke-filled, always packed with two bars. Nightly drink specials and a come-as-you-are attitude.

**If you go** Call ahead to find out what the evening's theme is. If the all-male revue isn't for you, check out Ladies' Night on Wednesdays.

## DON HO'S GRILL

NOSTALGIC, CASUAL PIER-SIDE HANGOUT

**Who Goes There** 21–55; visiting families, beach boys, and music lovers

I Aloha Tower Dr. (Aloha Tower Marketplace), Honolulu; (808) 528-0807

Zone 2    Greater Honolulu

**Cover** Varies **Minimum** None **Mixed drinks** $4.25–$5.50 **Wine** $4 and up **Beer** $2 and up **Dress** Board shorts, sandals, khakis, and the obligatory aloha shirt **Specials** Happy hour daily, 4:30–6:30 p.m.; half-priced appetizers and $2 draft beers **Food available** Seared 'ahi, calamari, pizzas, sandwiches, and salads

**Hours** Monday–Wednesday, Sunday, 10:30 a.m.–11 p.m.; Thursday–Saturday, 10:30 a.m.–2 a.m.

**What goes on** Live Hawaiian entertainment daily. Sunday–Wednesday, 6–8:30 p.m.; Thursday–Saturday, 9 p.m.–closing.

**Setting & atmosphere** Open-air Polynesian-style retro shrine to the man who made "Tiny Bubbles" an anthem. Rattan chairs and bamboo furniture fill this harborfront restaurant decorated with photographs and memorabilia from Ho's heyday. Sometimes he even appears here.

**If you go** Explore the waterfront and go up Aloha Tower to the observation deck.

## ESPRIT LOUNGE

LIVE MUSIC NIGHTCLUB AND HOTEL LOUNGE

**Who Goes There** 18–45; locals, hotel guests, professionals, and live music fans

2255 Kalakaua Ave. (Sheraton Waikiki Hotel), Waikiki; (808) 922-4422

Zone I    Waikiki

**Cover** None **Minimum** 2 drinks **Mixed drinks** $5.25–$5.50 **Wine** $5.25 **Beer** $3.50–$3.75 **Dress** Casual **Specials** None **Food available** Pizzas, sandwiches, hot wings, and nachos

**Hours** Sunday–Thursday, 4 p.m.–12:30 a.m.; Friday–Saturday, 4 p.m.–1:30 a.m.

**What goes on** This is a popular and stylish nightspot where the entertainment ranges from energetic live shows with local bands to dancing (R&B, Top 40). Entertainment is featured 8:30 p.m.–12:30 a.m. Tuesday–Thursday and 8:30 p.m.–1:30 a.m. Friday and Saturday.

**Setting & atmosphere** A dark, candle-lit room connected to the hotel's beach bar/lounge. On the left, cocktail tables and shimmering lights hang over a small dance floor next to the main stage. On the right, a relaxed, open-air beach bar lounge area.

**If you go** Go early for live music acts.

## FUSION WAIKIKI

AN ALTERNATIVE CLUB

**Who Goes There** 21–28; night owls, retro geeks, and cool-kid wannabes.

2260 Kuhio Ave., 2nd floor, Waikiki; (808) 924-2422    Zone I    Waikiki

**Cover** $5 Friday and Saturday, free the rest of the week **Minimum** None **Mixed drinks** $3 and up **Wine** $3 and up **Beer** $3 and up **Dress** Come with what you have on, as long as it isn't ragged, tattered, or torn **Specials** DJs and drink specials nightly; karaoke on Mondays; well-drink specials on Thursdays; Kids Club on 1st and 3rd Sundays (on the lower level) drops the minimum age for entry to 18. **Food available** None

**Hours** Monday–Thursday, 9 p.m.–4 a.m.; Friday–Saturday, 8 p.m.–4 a.m.; Sunday, 10 p.m.–4 a.m.

**What goes on** Dancing nightly. Occasional live entertainment and club circuit parties. Friday and Saturday nights are reserved for the club's weekly male revue show.

**Setting & atmosphere** Up a narrow staircase, a small, dark alternative club full of couples. Energy, spunk, and character—from patrons who don't care where you come from, what you do, or where you have to be. A discreet banner outside the stairway points the way to the stars.

**If you go** Be prepared to stay late, because the serious action starts after midnight.

## HARD ROCK CAFE

INTERNATIONALLY KNOWN MUSIC-THEMED RESTAURANT

**Who Goes There** 18–50; tourists, music lovers, T-shirt collectors

1837 Kapi'olani Blvd., Waikiki; (808) 955-7383   Zone 1   Waikiki

**Cover** None **Minimum** None **Mixed drinks** $4 and up **Wine** $3.50 and up **Beer** $3.50–$4 **Dress** Casual **Specials** None **Food available** Hard Rock Cafe's pig sandwiches, pot roast, grilled fajitas, burgers, barbecue chicken

**Hours** Dining: every day, 11:30 a.m.–11 p.m.; bar: Saturday–Thursday, 11:30 a.m.–12:30 a.m.; Friday, 11:30 a.m.–1:30 a.m.

**What goes on** Live entertainment Friday and Saturday, 10 p.m.–1 a.m.

**Setting & atmosphere** Same place, different artifacts. Honolulu has Eddie Van Halen's guitar, a bust of Mick Jagger, and an outfit worn by No Doubt's Gwen Stefani.

**If you go** Long wait—sometimes up to an hour—to eat. Get a table outside to avoid conversation-killing decibel levels in main room.

## KAPONO'S

LOCAL HAWAIIAN MUSIC ON HONOLULU WATERFRONT

**Who Goes There** Locals, tourists, and Hawaiian music lovers (age 21 and over)

1 Aloha Tower Dr. (Aloha Tower Marketplace), Honolulu; (808) 536 2161
Zone 2   Greater Honolulu

**Cover** Call Entertainment Hotline for schedule and cover, (808) 537-9611 **Minimum** None **Mixed drinks** $4.25–$5.50 **Wine** $4 and up **Beer** $2 and up **Dress** Aloha attire, shorts, sandals, casual wear **Specials** Happy hour 4–8 p.m. $2 draft beer, 25% off drinks, wine. **Food available** Open for lunch, pupus, and dinner featuring chef Russell Siu's local cuisine.

**Hours** Every day, 11 a.m.–2 a.m.

**What goes on** Hawaiian music every night. Singer and guitar player Henry Kapono, one of Hawai'i's top performers, appears and hosts Willie K., Kapena, John Cruz, and Fiji.

**Setting & atmosphere** Indoor/outdoor bistro and club on Honolulu waterfront.

**If you go** Go early on weekends to see big-name Hawaiian entertainers.

## NASHVILLE WAIKIKI
AUTHENTIC WAIKIKI WATERING HOLE

**Who Goes There** 21–30; college cowpokes, country bumpkins, and the occasional curious visitor

2330 Kuhio Ave., Waikiki; (808) 926-7911    Zone 1    Waikiki

**Cover** None **Minimum** None **Mixed drinks** $3–$5.75 **Wine** $3.50 **Beer** $3 and up **Dress** From blue jeans to shorts, from boots to sandals; shirts and footwear are required; 10-gallon hats are optional **Specials** Nightly line-dancing lessons offered 7–9 p.m. **Food available** Chips and popcorn.

**Hours** Every day, 4 p.m.–4 a.m.

**What goes on** Music provided by Hawai'i's top country DJs nightly. Pool tournaments Sundays and Tuesdays; dart tournaments Wednesdays.

**Setting & atmosphere** Two-step in hula-land at Waikiki's only country-and-western bar. This joint has bullhorns, saddles, copper paneling, drink specials, and a posse-sized dance floor.

**If you go** If line dancing doesn't do it for you, try Vegas Night, on Wednesdays.

## OCEAN CLUB
CHIC DOWNTOWN NIGHTCLUB AND DISCO

**Who Goes There** 23–35 (no one under 23 admitted); urbanites, locals, tourists, and singles

500 Ala Moana Blvd. (Restaurant Row); (808) 526-9888
Zone 2    Greater Honolulu

**Cover** Tuesday–Thursday, $4 after 8 p.m.; Friday, $5 after 8 p.m.; Saturday, $5 after 9 p.m. **Minimum** None **Mixed drinks** $1.75 and up **Wine** $3.75 and up **Beer** $3.50–$3.75 **Dress** Gap and Banana Republic; men must wear collared shirts; hats and athletic wear prohibited **Specials** $2 for most drinks Tuesdays and Paddlers' Night on Thursdays; Thursdays, win cap for wearing aloha shirt, free cover **Food available** Calamari, spring rolls, crab dip, teriyaki steak, chicken wings, and nachos

**Hours** Tuesday–Thursday, 4:30 p.m.–2 a.m.; Friday, 4:30 p.m.–3 a.m.; Saturday, 6 p.m.–3 a.m.; closed Sundays and Mondays; available for private parties

**What goes on** Live local musicians perform on a sporadic basis. Dancing Tuesday–Thursday nights to Top 40 hits, R&B, hip hop, and urban beat.

**Setting & atmosphere** Trendy spot features two bars, a kitchen that pumps out high-end pupus, and an open-air lounge. Expect loud music, cheap drinks, and a young crowd.

**If you go** Sooner or later everyone shows up here, but don't go here to celebrate your 21st birthday. Only those age 23 and over are allowed.

## RUMOURS
OLDIES DISCO AND NIGHTCLUB

**Who Goes There** 18–45; tourists and locals

410 Atkinson Dr. (Ala Moana Hotel), Honolulu; (808) 955-4811
Zone 2    Greater Honolulu

**Cover** $5 on Sunday, Tuesday, Friday, and Saturday, $10 after 9 p.m.; free before 9 p.m. daily and on Wednesday **Minimum** 2 drinks **Mixed drinks** $3.75 and up **Wine** $3.75 and up **Beer** $3.75 and up **Dress** Anything goes except beach wear, tank tops, and slippers **Specials** Free pupus daily 5–9 p.m.; dance to the music of the 1960s and 1970s during Big Chill Night on Fridays **Food available** Nachos, potato wedges, steak strips, veggie platters, pizzas, burgers, wontons, and cheesecake slices

**Hours** Tuesday–Friday, 5 p.m.–3 a.m.; Saturday, 9 p.m.–3 a.m.; Sunday, 5–9 p.m.; closed Monday, but available for private parties

**What goes on** Different theme every night, from ballroom dancing and country music to Top 40 mixes and Latin dancing.

**Setting & atmosphere** Waiters/waitresses decked out in formal black-and-white attire. Rust-colored, old-style lounge chairs, two-story club. Huge TV screen flanks dance floor.

**If you go** Bring your dancing shoes and be prepared to strut your stuff. People will be watching.

## SCRUPLES BEACH CLUB
WAIKIKI BEACH BAR THAT'S NOT ON A BEACH

**Who Goes There** 18–25; tourists, people-watchers, and celebrities

2310 Kuhio Ave., Waikiki; (808) 923-9530    Zone 1    Waikiki

**Cover** $5 for those age 21 and over, $15 for those age 18–20 **Minimum** 2 drinks **Mixed drinks** $4.75 and up **Wine** $4.75 and up **Beer** $4.75 and up **Dress** Jeans, skirts, trousers, and shorts; no athletic wear **Food available** None

**Hours** Every day, 8 p.m.–4 a.m.

**What goes on** Dancing to Top 40, alternative, and reggae beats.

**Setting & atmosphere** This club is so tacky it's cool—from the bamboo-paneled walls to plastic palm leaves hanging from the pillars. There isn't anything in the way of food or views—unusual for a beach bar—but what you get is a dance floor open to 4 a.m. and a bikini contest every Thursday night at midnight.

**If you go** Check out Wall of Fame to see who got here before you—Robert De Niro, Jim Carrey, and Jean-Claude Van Damme, to name a few.

## WAVE WAIKIKI

ALTERNATIVE NIGHTCLUB AND RARE ALTERNATIVE LIVE MUSIC VENUE

**Who Goes There**  18–28; college kids, eccentric folk, jocks, and alterna-lovers

1877 Kalakaua Ave., Waikiki; (808) 941-0424   Zone 1   Waikiki

**Cover** $5 after 10 p.m. daily, none before 10 p.m. **Minimum** 2 drinks **Mixed drinks** $5 **Wine** $4–$5 **Beer** $4–$5 **Dress** Slacker garb and Gen-X gear is the norm **Specials** Each week boasts a different drink special; happy hour 9–10 p.m. and 1–4 a.m.; 18 and up on Mondays **Food available** None

**Hours** Every day, 9 p.m.–4 a.m.

**What goes on** Live entertainment (various themes, including classic and alternative rock) and DJs nightly 9 p.m.–4 a.m. Live bands are featured Wednesday–Friday, and Thursday is Ladies' Night.

**Setting & atmosphere** Two-story hot spot hosts live alternative bands. Large, wooden dance floor fronts the Wave's big-screen TV and performance stage.

**If you go** Take a cab, parking is scarce and pricey. Kick back in air-conditioned, second-floor lounge, with full-service bar and a people-watching perch.

# Maui

## HAPA'S BREW HAUS

LOCALS-MEET-TOURISTS, NEIGHBOR ISLAND HANGOUT

**Who Goes There**  21–35; celebrities, locals, and visitors

41 E. Lipoa St., Suite 4A, Kihei; (808) 879-9001   Zone 8   South Maui

**Cover** Varies **Minimum** None **Mixed drinks** $4–$6 **Wine** $5–$7 **Beer** $4 **Dress** Come as you are **Specials** Ladies Night every Thursday **Food available** Pizzas, burgers, and sandwiches

**Hours** Every day, 4 p.m.–2 a.m.

**What goes on** Nightly entertainment featuring a variety of live bands, dancing, bikini contests, and comedy acts.

**Setting & atmosphere** The hot spot on the Valley Isle.

**If you go** Go before 8:30 p.m. to enter free.

## MAUI BREWS

10,000-square-foot eatery and club in Lahaina

**Who Goes There**  18–35; postgrads, whale-watchers, beach boys and girls

900 Front St., Lahaina; (808) 667-7794   Zone 9   West Maui

**Cover** None **Minimum** None **Mixed drinks** $3.50–$6 **Wine** $3.50–$6 **Beer** $3.25 and up **Dress** Casual, no swimwear or tank tops **Food available** Pizza, pasta, steak, and sandwiches

**Hours** Every day, 11:30 a.m.–2 a.m.

**What goes on** Hip hop on Tuesday; salsa on Wednesday; local entertainment on Thursday; disco on Friday and Saturday; and an open-mike night on Sunday. Maui Brews Night Club is open 9 p.m.–2 a.m. The restaurant is open 11:30 a.m.–2 a.m. daily.

**Setting & atmosphere** Dining and dancing in an island bistro setting. Thatched-roof bar features full bar and more than 30 beers.

**If you go** Dinner reservations are suggested.

## Adult Entertainment

Since World War II, when prostitution was legal and soldiers and sailors queued up for Hotel Street hookers in Chinatown, Hawai'i's night life has been X-rated. Not a whole lot has changed since then. Street walkers work Waikiki after dark and strippers dance "totally naked" in clubs near the convention center. So-called adult clubs and services are advertised in the sports pages of the *Honolulu Advertiser* and the *Honolulu Star-Bulletin* as well as the Yellow Pages of Honolulu's phone book. O'ahu's most popular establishments, like **Rock-za** and **Femme Nu,** are on Kapi'olani Boulevard near the Hawai'i Convention Center and on Ke'eaumoku Street, near Ala Moana Center.

*Tip:* Avoid clubs on Hotel Street in Chinatown, where transsexual hookers work street corners, and drugs (mostly crack) are readily available despite police presence.

# Index

# Hotel Index

# Restaurant Index